TEACHERS ON THE EDGE

For over 25 years, the journal *Writing on the Edge* has published interviews with influential writers, teachers, and scholars. Now, *Teachers on the Edge: The WOE Interviews, 1989–2017* collects the voices of 39 significant figures in writing studies, forming an accessible survey of the modern history of rhetoric and composition. In a conversational style, *Teachers on the Edge* encourages a remarkable group of teachers and scholars to tell the stories of their influences and interests, tracing the progress of their contributions. This engaging volume is invaluable to graduate students, writing teachers, and scholars of writing studies.

John Boe taught writing at the University of California, Davis for over thirty years. He has published more than a hundred articles and essays, including his essay collection *Life Itself* (1994). He was an editor of *Writing on the Edge* from 1989 to 2012. He performs as a professional storyteller and is currently completing a book of interviews, *Living the Shakespearean Life*.

David Masiel teaches writing at the University of California, Davis, where he has served as editor of *Writing on the Edge* since 2012. His essays, articles, and reviews have appeared in *The New York Times Magazine, Outside Magazine*, and *The Washington Post*. He is the author of two novels: *2182 Kilohertz* (2003), a *New York Times* Notable Book in 2002 and *The Western Limit of the World* (2007).

Eric Schroeder taught writing at the University of California, Davis for thirty years. He co-founded *Writing on the Edge*, serving for many years as senior editor, with primary responsibility for editing the WOE interviews. His book, *Vietnam, We've All Been There: Interviews with American Writers*, was published in 1992.

Lisa Sperber teaches a range of writing classes at the University of California, Davis. In addition, she is a consultant in the University Writing Program's robust Writing Across the Curriculum program. Her other teaching and research interests include transfer and threshold concepts.

TEACHERS ON THE EDGE

The WOE Interviews, 1989–2017

Edited by
JOHN BOE, DAVID MASIEL,
ERIC SCHROEDER, LISA SPERBER

Routledge
Taylor & Francis Group
NEW YORK AND LONDON

First published 2017
by Routledge
711 Third Avenue, New York, NY 10017

and by Routledge
2 Park Square, Milton Park, Abingdon, Oxon, OX14 4RN

Routledge is an imprint of the Taylor & Francis Group, an informa business

© 2017 Taylor & Francis

The right of the editors to be identified as the authors of the editorial material, and of the authors for their individual chapters, has been asserted in accordance with sections 77 and 78 of the Copyright, Designs and Patents Act 1988.

All rights reserved. No part of this book may be reprinted or reproduced or utilised in any form or by any electronic, mechanical, or other means, now known or hereafter invented, including photocopying and recording, or in any information storage or retrieval system, without permission in writing from the publishers.

Trademark notice: Product or corporate names may be trademarks or registered trademarks, and are used only for identification and explanation without intent to infringe.

Library of Congress Cataloging-in-Publication Data
A catalog record for this book has been requested

ISBN: 978-1-138-28848-5 (hbk)
ISBN: 978-1-138-28849-2 (pbk)
ISBN: 978-1-315-26785-2 (ebk)

Typeset in Bembo
by Apex CoVantage, LLC

CONTENTS

Preface ix
DAVID MASIEL
Project Notes and Acknowledgments xi
LISA SPERBER
Foreword xiii
JOHN BOE AND ERIC SCHROEDER

Toby Fulwiler 1
"The Mechanism Is Writing"
Eric Schroeder

Mike Rose 10
"Imagine a Writing Program"
Susan Palo

Richard Lanham 26
"Learning by Going Along"
Carolyn Handa and Gretchen Flesher

Andrea Lunsford and Lisa Ede 43
"Collaboration as a Subversive Activity"
Alice Heim Calderonello, Donna Beth Nelson, and Sue Carter Simmons

Linda Flower 54
"Helping Writers Build Mansions with More Rooms"
Jill Wilson

James Berlin 66
"Dialectical Notions"
Brian A. Connery and Van E. Hillard

Peter Elbow 81
"Going in Two Directions at Once"
John Boe and Eric Schroeder

Cynthia L. Selfe 102
"Nomadic Feminist Cyborg Guerilla"
Carolyn Handa

Donald Murray 116
"Mucking about in Language I Save My Soul"
Driek Zirinsky

Joseph Williams and Gregory Colomb 128
"The Takeaway"
Donald Johns

Patricia Bizzell 145
"Radical Pedagogy"
Sidney I. Dobrin and Todd Taylor

James J. Murphy 157
"Setting Minds in Motion"
Mardena Creek

James Moffett 171
"Individualize"
Eric Schroeder and John Boe

Charles Bazerman 181
"Writing Is Motivated Participation"
Margaret Eldred

Joseph Harris 194
"Changing Habits of Thinking"
Thomas West

Ira Shor 204
"Every Difference Will Be Used Against Us"
Andrea Greenbaum

Walter Nash "Incertitude's Her Element" *David Stacey*	218
David Bartholomae "Stop Being So Coherent" *John Boe and Eric Schroeder*	234
Walker Gibson "A Nest of Singing Rhetorical Birds" *Margaret M. Strain*	252
Charles Moran "A Sense of Professional Well Being" *Margaret M. Strain*	261
Nancy Welch "Imagining Stories" *Fred Santiago Arroyo and Alice Gillam*	273
Lynn Z. Bloom "Once More to the Essay" *Jenny Spinner*	290
William E. Coles, Jr. "Failure Is the Way We Learn" *John Boe and Eric Schroeder*	298
Keith Gilyard "I Have Fun Playing with Language" *Sharon James McGee*	313
Ken Macrorie "Arrangements for Truthtelling" *Eric Schroeder and John Boe*	328
Wayne Booth "Covering Almost All of Life" *John Boe*	341
Pat Hoy "I Want to Rip Your Heart Out" *Mel Livatino*	350

Claude Hurlbert 368
"Where Meaning and Being Gathers"
Krystia Nora, Roseanne Gatto, Dawn Fels, and Elizabeth Campbell

Sondra Perl 387
"There's Humor and There's Tears"
John Boe

Deirdre McCloskey 399
"Humanomics"
John Boe and Ed Kahn

Doug Hesse 414
"Cultivating Writerly Sensibilities"
Eric Leake

Victor Villanueva 423
"Some of It Is Serendipity"
Donna Evans

Quintilian 434
"Data Don't Breathe"
James J. Murphy

Nancy Sommers 444
"Enter the Process in Uncertainty"
Eric Leake and David Masiel

Kathleen Blake Yancey 453
"It's Their Story That Turns Your Head"
David Masiel, William Sewell, and Hogan Hayes

Carolyn Miller 462
"A Set of Shared Expectations"
Brenda Rinard and David Masiel

Linda Adler-Kassner 472
"Everything Gets to Writing"
Lisa Sperber and Carl Whithaus

Appendix: Composition Flow Chart *484*
HOGAN HAYES

Index *486*

PREFACE

When I took over from John Boe as editor of *Writing on the Edge*, I did so with scant knowledge of composition theory. My experience was practical: I had been writing and teaching for 20 years—working in a range of writing genres and teaching everything from high school English to college composition, literature, and creative writing. The extent of my reading in the field rested on articles here and there, and textbooks, of course. Somewhere in there I discovered Joseph Williams on style, which served as a vital bridge between my twin realities: a fiction writer teaching composition.

Yet as editor of an academic journal—however unorthodox that journal may be—I faced the practical need to judge submissions based on currency, originality, and academic relevance. Our contributors referenced a swirl of theories and pedagogies, using terms like *current-traditional, expressivism, cognitive theory, social-epistemic pedagogies*—to say nothing of a host of articles grounded in cultural studies, genre theory, visual rhetoric, multimodality, and transfer pedagogies. I could judge good writing, but as a professional writer, I found composition theory unfamiliar, the terms sometimes inconsistent, and the concepts often abstract and confusing.

I turned to mentors, colleagues who had done it longer and understood it more deeply—among them John Boe, Eric Schroeder, Marlene Clarke, Chris Thaiss, Carl Whithaus, Sarah Perrault, and Jerry Murphy. Their perspective, knowledge, advice, and encouragement made the editing of WOE not only possible but challenging and enjoyable—my own kind of advanced education.

WOE too was a source. As a journal known for favoring readability and creativity mixed with new perspectives on teaching writing, the back issues of WOE were a valuable primer, and of all the writings in WOE, the interviews stood out, partly for the range and influence of the writers and scholars interviewed and partly because of the interview genre itself. The appeal of this form comes from its inherent informality, from the sense of voice and personal connection. With the interview we can engage with or at least overhear a conversation with someone whose perspectives we value. The academic interview goes a step further: like learning itself, the interview is dialogic, an attempt to satisfy our impulse to ask questions as a means of understanding.

Teachers on the Edge reflects the best of those interviews, with 37 influential teachers and scholars whose teaching and writing span from the mid-20th century to the present, displaying a range of research interests over time. Most of our subjects were interviewed at the height of their research productivity, but many were interviewed early in their careers and still others after their retirement from active teaching and research. In all cases, they are interviews of teachers, by teachers, and for teachers, but as such, they represent a unique resource for students in writing studies. Individually they are a delight, but collected all in one place, they reveal a staggering breadth of coverage.

In deciding how to present these interviews, we faced several choices: in what order to present, to edit or not to edit, to update or to leave in their original form. After much discussion and debate, we elected to present them in the order of their original publication. As readers may note, they reflect not only the work of each interviewer but also the moment in time when they were interviewed, and in total create complex, multiple, even competing narratives.

As we see in Hogan Hayes's refreshingly lucid "Composition Flow Chart," the map of the discipline is a matter of fluid dynamics—a river of ideas. Yet no diagram can chart all the branches and confluences, to say nothing of the back eddies that sometimes strand us in one spot for a bit too long. In their way, the WOE interviews help to chart those varied movements, providing a fascinating glimpse into the field and the people who have helped form it. Above all, they engage human stories that hold scholarship as the climax of an intellectual journey.

As editors of WOE, operating in the spirit of the journal's original mission, we hope all readers—teachers and students alike—will find these interviews enjoyable and useful, as engaging for their humanity as for their ideas.

David Masiel
Editor, *Writing on the Edge*

PROJECT NOTES AND ACKNOWLEDGMENTS

Between the teacher-scholars we interviewed, the interviewers, and the introduction writers and reviewers, over a hundred people were involved in composing this anthology. The interview introductions, a key feature of this collection, were all written by members of the UC Davis Writing Program: lecturers with a range of backgrounds, writing studies teacher-scholars, and graduate students in our designated emphasis in writing studies. Many of us, perhaps like you, are relatively new to the field of writing studies, and this project has been part of our acculturation, part of the process by which we are gaining discourse community knowledge. While the interviews help us to grasp the exigence of a scholar's work, the introductions provide an overview of the scholar's main contributions to the field. Rather than take up debates, we've tried to discuss each scholar's work from their perspective.

I am grateful to the following people for their contributions to this project, on top of busy teaching schedules, graduate studies, and family obligations: Katie Arosteguy, Sophia Bamert, Jane Beal, Alison Bright, Pamela Demory, Grant Eckstein, Sarah Faye, Greg Glazner, Hogan Hayes, Sarah Klotz, Aaron Lanser, Eric Leake, David Masiel, Kenya Mitchell, Matthew Oliver, Beth Pearsall, Sarah Perrault, Sarah Powers, Mandy Proctor, Michal Reznizki, William Sewall, Agnes Stark, Carl Whithaus, and Nathanial Williams. I am particularly grateful to our esteemed reviewers for responding to our work: Lisa Ede, Hogan Hayes, Andrea Lunsford, Jerry Murphy, Sondra Perl, Sarah Perrault, and Christopher Thaiss. The collaborative nature of this volume would not have been possible without David Masiel's vision and radically democratic tactics. Working with my colleagues has reminded me in a very concrete and heartening way that writing is a social activity.

Teachers on the Edge was originally conceived by Eric Schroeder nearly 15 years ago. The current incarnation is the work of a small group of UWP faculty and graduate students who gathered in 2012: David Masiel, Lisa Sperber, Pamela Demory, Grant Eckstein, Hogan Hayes, and Katie Arosteguy (who also managed reprint permissions). Pamela Demory, our production editor, was a one-woman stage crew, quietly reformatting endless files from the original desktop publication. Eric Leake supported the project from a distance; in addition to conducting several interviews, he volunteered to write introductions when we needed help. Thanks to the final-hour volunteers who finished reformatting files: Sophia Bamert, Sarah Faye, Greg Glazner, William Sewall, and Agnes Stark. Thanks to our department chair, Carl Whithaus, for his support, especially in the form of funds to hire an indexer. Special thanks to Amy Clarke, who first suggested the usefulness of this volume for pedagogy courses, and to Jerry Murphy for his sage advice throughout.

It was impossible to work on this project without thinking of John Boe and Eric Schroeder, our editorial emeriti, who edited and published these interviews for 23 years, and themselves wrote—together and apart—19 interviews, 9 of which are included in this anthology. Eric held interviewers to a high standard, requiring they immerse themselves in the interview subject's work. Thank you for your tireless commitment and for giving us the opportunity to keep learning.

Most of all, thank you to the many interviewers whose engagement forms the backbone of this book and, of course, to the teacher-scholars who continue to engage us.

Lisa Sperber
Managing Editor
Teachers on the Edge

FOREWORD

John Boe and Eric Schroeder

When we started WOE, we didn't know what it would be or might become. But there were certain things that were important to us. The biggest of these was readability—we wanted to produce a journal that people who taught writing would actually read. We found we never got around to most of the articles in *College English* and *College Composition and Communication*. Some people thought we were joking when we said we wanted WOE to be equal parts *Rolling Stone* and *College English*, with the more equal part being *Rolling Stone*. We wanted articles that sounded more like E.B. White than like Jacques Derrida. We wanted *voice*.

So it was natural for us to want to include interviews in each issue. As writing teachers, we were attracted to the idea of talking to writers about writing. But because we proposed to be a publication about writing and the teaching of writing, we decided it would be good if, in addition to including these interviews with well-known writers, we included interviews with people in composition studies. Serendipity played a role, as it would do subsequently. We were putting on a conference for writing teachers at UC Davis, and our keynote speaker was to be Toby Fulwiler, who had recently published *The Journal Book* and was gaining a name for himself as a spokesperson for the Writing Across the Curriculum movement. Fulwiler agreed to be the writing teacher interviewed for our first issue.

We were fortunate that at the time, one of us had been working on a collection of interviews for about eight years at that point (Eric's *Vietnam, We've All Been There: Interviews with American Writers*). So using Eric's experience as a template, a bunch of us set about to interview writers and writing teachers. The process included the query letter, setting up the interview (which often involved travel), trying to read everything the subject had ever written (for this reason, we never tried to interview Updike or Oates), preparing a list of questions, recording and transcribing the interview, and (perhaps most challenging of all) editing the interview. It was obvious to us that no one would want to read an unedited transcript. So we freely cut false starts, repetitions, long-winded questions, unclear remarks, and so on. The subject always had final take on what went in or out, although most of our subjects asked for very few changes.

All six of the original editors—John Boe, Eric Schroeder, Brian Connery, Margaret Eldred, Susan Palo, and Carolyn Handa—agreed that the interviews in our first issue were a success (Oliver Sachs, Michael Herr, and Toby Fulwiler) and that we should try to replicate the pattern of an interview with a writer and another with a teacher of writing in subsequent issues. This turned out to be easier said than done. There would be periods of feast in which WOE editors would be out doing interviews and we'd be getting submissions and queries for more. But the inevitable famine would come. Having two interviews for each issue became an enormous source of stress in our lives. But almost all of our editors and editorial board did some interviews. And even in times of plenty, the interviews could be stressful, particularly when done by someone new to the genre. More and more we learned that editing interviews was an art in itself.

It was a privilege to talk with so many writing teachers (aka composition theorists) about their work. In doing these interviews and in reading and editing them, we learned from some of the best people in the business about how to do a better job teaching writing. Our thanks go to everyone who we interviewed for this book and to everyone who did these interviews.

TOBY FULWILER

Toby Fulwiler's first two books (which were co-edited with Art Young), Language Connections: Writing and Reading Across the Curriculum *(1982) and* Writing Across the Disciplines: Research into Practice *(1987), established Fulwiler as a leading voice for Writing Across the Curriculum (WAC), which was then expanding nationally. In 1987 he edited what was perhaps his most influential work,* The Journal Book. *In it, Fulwiler argued that teachers should write with their students and devote a set amount of each class period to directed writing as a way of furthering students' understanding of a subject—whether English literature or physics.*

As early as 1978, Fulwiler saw that although many educators were interested in critical thinking, they did not recognize the link between critical thinking and writing. He pioneered the faculty workshop model—now common to WAC programs—to help his colleagues in other disciplines understand that "writing makes the classroom focused, intellectually challenging, on-target, activity-oriented" and student-centered in ways that lecture alone cannot. To accomplish this, he made extensive use of journal writing, not only in the classroom but also in faculty workshops, to foster "writing to learn" as a means of learning to write.

Fulwiler published four additional scholarly books and authored and co-edited nine textbooks, along with dozens of articles and chapters in books. He was a professor of English and the Director of Composition at the University of Vermont, where he taught a wide variety of courses in composition and English literature. He retired in 2002 and now works as a woodturner making bowls from Northeastern hardwoods. He keeps two journals—a personal one and another devoted to his woodturning.

—*Matthew Oliver*

"The Mechanism Is Writing"

Eric Schroeder

Fall 1989

WOE: What got you interested in composition theory? Had it been something you studied in graduate school and then intended to pursue in your professional career?

FULWILER: I was appointed to be the director of freshman comp at Michigan Tech in 1976, and my PhD is in American literature from Madison, so I really had to stop and figure out what is it you do if you're going to direct a freshman writing program. I went to a summer seminar at Rutgers in 1977—really a lucky chance—my chairman suggested that I do that. It was a three-week summer seminar deliberately aimed at introducing the ideas of James Britton into this country. So James Britton had been there, Nancy Martin was there, Janet Emig, Lee Odell, and Dixie Goswami, a bunch of people who were working on theories of writing and learning, and for me that was new stuff. It was at that point in the summer of 1977 that I was introduced to a whole bunch of new people and names—Macrorie, Emig, Elbow, Kinneavy, Britton—people I had no knowledge of. I was a very traditional American literature teacher. That virtually changed my professional life because I realized how I thought I could use those ideas.

WOE: When you went to Michigan Tech was part of your purpose, as they saw it, to set up a writing across the curriculum program?

FULWILER: Writing across the curriculum was a language I learned that summer at Rutgers, but it coincided with complaints by the engineering faculty, and administrators, and alumni that engineers didn't communicate well. We thought about some options; as Director of Freshman English, I worked with my chair, Art Young, to figure out how to respond to that need. Our response was not to set up an entry or exit test or a proficiency test; it was not to add one more junior-level writing course. It was to say, "Well, if we had our druthers, we'd have all the faculty members at Michigan Tech doing a little bit more with writing." Our argument became that really the only way that people become better with language is by using it a lot. And so we wanted to have more active reading, writing, speaking—everything—going on in all classes. That's how we started the program that we called writing across the curriculum; that's just about the time that Elaine Maimon was starting a parallel program at Beaver College. And some other programs were starting up in that same vein at that time.

So we were in that '76–'77 period when schools were starting such programs. We invented our own model, the intensive faculty retreat, for doing it. That's how I got started. Those terms just weren't widely known at that time.

WOE: What do you do at the faculty retreats? Presumably their purpose is to get faculty members at the institution to see the value of writing in their own classroom.

FULWILER: The ultimate purpose of the faculty retreat as we saw it was to change the faculty's ideas about the way language works. Our experience told us very quickly that faculty who have not carefully examined language use—whether they're engineers or historians—generally saw written language as language by which to measure students. We wanted to expand the options for which written language could be used. Like oral language. Everybody uses oral language for all kinds of things—for small talk, discovery, questioning, statements. We simply wanted to make the case that written language could and should be used in the same variety of ways. Thus Britton's theory of expressive, transactional, and poetic language was very useful to us. So when we would invite the faculty to these workshops they would come in and sit down and we'd give everybody a journal. The participants would be 15–30 faculty from all disciplines: engineering, history, biology. We'd mumble a few words of introduction and then we'd ask them to write something. Throughout the first day of the workshop, for example, we would continually throw out prompts to have the participants write about. We would ask them to begin with what makes writing hard. Think about yourself as a writer; write for five minutes. And then we would talk about that. One of us would make a running list on the overhead while we talked about it. And people would say real predictable stuff: "Writing's hard"; "I don't have time for it"; "It's hard because people judge me by it." And then we would spring another question on them: "When does it get easier?" They would write for a few minutes about that, saying things like, "Well, it's easier when you're writing a letter to a friend or writing for yourself" or "It's easier when I have time" or "It's easier when I have a word-processor" or "when I have a fountain pen" or whatever. But a whole bunch of idiosyncratic reasons. I would point out that what we had now in the first hour of the workshop is people talking about their own writing. We've also already got them using the journal to think with. But we don't point that out yet.

Many of the faculty members who came there thought they were going to start complaining about student writing. Or else they think that they're going to have a workshop on spelling for two days. All of a sudden in the beginning hour the tables have been subtly turned; they are now talking about how frustrating it is, how difficult it is, to write. And sometimes how joyful. So now we've also generated a couple of lists: Here's what makes writing easier for faculty—friendly audiences, feedback, etc.; here's what makes it more difficult—a highly judgmental writing situation. We then simply put both of these lists up and ask: "Do you think your students have any of the same troubles?" Well, it's glaringly obvious that their problems are exactly the same. Then we ask them to write again: "What's one insight you've got now?" After that we'll have people break in groups of three and talk about those insights. Next I'll ask, "Does anybody want to share what they've been talking about?" Either my partner or I would be writing on the overhead, so we're getting a wide list of ideas, all kinds of stuff that they're throwing out.

They begin to generate empathy for student writers because they begin to see that it's a much more complicated business. They quickly see that what's hard about writing is organizing, focusing, thinking—call it conceptual stuff. As soon as they compare that to the litany of their own difficulties, we have them. Because as soon as they tie writing to conceptualization, that's the bridge to their own discipline. Every single college teacher will tell you that he or she is interested in critical thinking. Every single one. As soon as they see that writing is another way of expressing the flaws in your thinking they begin to realize that the more that you write the more you begin to patch up those flaws. So we give them a break and then have them do another piece of writing and then do more with the response groups. The next day we have them come back and revise a piece of writing. All of those kinds of activities in the workshop are meant to generate empathy for the students who they put in the same situations. And they're meant to get them to explore with the students the way that language works. It is not always evaluative. We want professors to get the notion that it's not always evaluative, that it's discovery oriented and process oriented.

I do a talk in the afternoon of the first day about the different functions of language for the writer's self, for the speaker's self, especially as a tool to think with. I always argue that that's the primary function. That it's probably more important than the communicative function. Thus on the first day of a workshop I'm trying to get the faculty to change their view of language. I actually don't care so much that they learn the trick of journal writing at the start of their class—I'm much less concerned about that. If I can get them instead to change their notion of language, then any good teacher can figure out her own translations.

WOE: So what typically happens when they have this new-found empathy and they go back to their classrooms? Do things change?

FULWILER: Let me begin by saying that the workshop ends the first day with us showing samples of student writing from different disciplines. The two things that make an enormous difference in the workshop's success are 1) if, for instance, they can see samples of actual student writing in math if they're math teachers, and 2) if they can do some of the writing themselves. These two things. When they come back the second day of the workshop, their attitudes are entirely changed. They're really excited now. The second day they want to explore more what they can actually do in class. The first day they're somewhat skeptical. But I think that by the end of the second day we generally sell the whole group on these ideas.

WOE: You also seem to be setting them up for something else. In your books you talk about the continuum from the didactic teaching style to the guided style to the open style. Thus perhaps subconsciously you also seem to be introducing the notion that teachers have options available, that they don't always have to stand up for 50 minutes and go through their traditional routine.

FULWILER: By the end of the first day the faculty realize they've just had a pedagogy workshop, something that they did not expect. And what we've just done (if we're any good at it) is we've just modeled every single principle and activity that we're trying to suggest for their classes: they've done the writing, they've done the small-group talk, they've watched how it works, and they've had an alternate pedagogy offered to them which is highly student centered. A totally different model than most of them are used to.

When they get back to their classrooms, a large range of things happen: from nothing—being overwhelmed by their curriculum, by their research, they don't have any time, they mean to do some of these things but they don't (that's usually the case)—to faculty who have actually changed the entire nature of their instruction. They absolutely begin to understand that they can teach most of their material inductively. The people who go that far would have already been on this wavelength initially, and we serve to give them legitimization. And of course there are a whole bunch of responses in between. It's very hard, actually, to keep track of what they're all doing. I'm sure that half of them are not doing as much as we wish.

WOE: At Michigan Tech there are now still lots of people, though, doing these types of things in the classroom.

FULWILER: All across the curriculum. And certainly now at Vermont writing is a common activity; it's not something that's unusual.

WOE: What about the traditional holdouts, like, for instance, math and engineering?

FULWILER: The sciences generally have the most difficult time with it because they teach other languages. They don't have a difficult time with it if they go to the workshop. The difficult part is getting them to go to the workshop because they think that anything to do with writing doesn't concern them. The savvy science and math people who come, who realize that language is a broader issue, really are incredibly interesting people. One of my co-leaders now is a chemist. Another is a historian. It's almost impossible to predict areas of interest. At Vermont, none of the philosophers, the most language-centered people, come; on the other hand, the whole geology department—all seven people—have come.

WOE: In our own writing workshop program here at UC Davis, we get lots of requests for writing workshops from geology, from the wildlife and fisheries program, from biology.

FULWILER: I continually get such input from similar departments at other colleges. Departments in colleges of letters and sciences tend to think that they already know all that stuff, that there's not much in it for them. The trick is getting faculty members to attend a two- or three-day workshop; if they do, we can usually provide them with an interesting experience.

WOE: Aren't there some natural, built-in obstacles to this type of teaching? It seems to me that the ideal situation where these kinds of activities work best, no matter what the discipline, is the small class. But what happens when you get, say, over 100 people in your course?

FULWILER: It's just harder. You can do less, it's true. But you can do things. We had one follow-up workshop where we invited people who had been to the initial workshop to come for the day, and we simply brainstormed techniques for writing in large classes. I didn't even run that workshop; I was just a participant. Dave Barrington, who's a botanist, was chairing it. We ended up with an overhead transparency filled with about 25 ideas for using more writing in large section classes. (We defined large classes as classes with 80 students and up; there are different kinds of large—there's large and megalarge.) But just by getting those people who teach large classes together (I don't teach large classes) and brainstorming, we came up with a whole bunch of options. That's the kind of thing that we will typically do. It wouldn't do any good at all for me to go there and tell them, "Here are twelve techniques that you can use."

WOE: In other words the whole notion of learning as discovery works equally well for students and faculty.

FULWILER: Because they take ownership. That list generated by the group is owned by the group and they're more likely to try something out. So that's the model that we keep working with.

At the same time we're doing this, we're trying to interest people more in their teaching. We have really good success with many faculty members who see a whole new route to their teaching. At Vermont the standards for publication keep going up and up, the standards for promotion and tenure get tighter and tighter, and neither is weighted in favor of teaching. Not only at both schools at which I've taught, but at most schools I've visited there's a similar tension. How can you run a program that says invest a little more time and thought in your teaching when the criteria for promotion are more and more skewed towards research?

One of our strategies to combat that trend has been workshops stressing people's *own* writing. These publication workshops sometimes get people really interested. A number of people have said that they've written books or articles because the workshops have given them the courage to do so. Of the faculty members who come to workshops, many of them have gotten low grades in freshman English themselves. Even though you're a world-class geologist, you may be nervous about your writing. And you've certainly not shared it in the kind of small groups we're talking about. So one of the things I think we do is help people to be a little bit more confident about their own writing. We also really disabuse them of the notion that we English teachers are the experts on all writing.

WOE: It's true that so many people have the "corrective" view of us—that our chief purpose (and joy) is to correct other people's language. We're always fighting to overcome that stereotype. I think that a lot of people in composition, people who see themselves as composition professionals, would be familiar with many of these techniques and use them in composition classes. I'm very interested, however, in how these techniques might be used in other classes. For instance, you teach American literature; how do you use them in your own classes, in a more traditional setting, what you've termed the "didactic" model?

FULWILER: Savvy composition instructors know everything we've been talking about regarding the workshops. The trick is: what would be appropriate translations of process-writing activities into, say, a history class? My writing class—and probably yours—is really a rewriting class; we spend much of our time rewriting. If you're a history teacher you cannot do that; you cannot turn your class into a rewriting class in any major way. We suggest, though, if you knew that that was going on in freshman English, you could build on that; you could depend on your students knowing something about group critiquing; you could make assignments which depended upon those things. Personally, I would *rather* use journals in a literature class than in a writing class. In a writing class the multiple drafts take so much of the time, journals get put in the background.

But when I'm teaching American literature there are an infinite number of things to ask students to write and think about. So I keep trying to figure out in my own teaching all those different kinds of process-writing activities. For instance, I use short papers, peer groups. The trick here is that if you have students writing a paper for your literature or your history class, and the students arrive in class with their drafts, the traditional custom is to collect them. But supposing when your students arrive with their papers, you had them break into small groups and read them to each other, making suggestions for change; then they take them home, work on them, and turn them in the following week. Now that ends up being a radical pedagogical move with implications far beyond writing. What you're saying is that it would be worth class time, time you would normally be lecturing, presenting your ideas, for students to share their own ideas and be critiquing them. Furthermore, you could not possibly look in on all the groups, so you're turning over control of class time to your students. That's another radical idea that some professors don't want any part of. But other professors will recognize that the notion of filling students up with knowledge is a pretty medieval notion. If you've got other modes of delivering information, class time can be used for other things. So we make the case that it's legitimate to write in class, to talk in small groups—for the teacher not always to be in control of the class.

This is a radical pedagogy as opposed to the traditional one that puts the teacher always in control. So I would say that probably any technique that we invent in a comp class has a translation to other classes. If professors who have a difficult time talking for 80 minutes (lecturing for 80 minutes is a pretty deadly activity anyway) added some writing and small-group talk, the 80 minutes would just be gone; they'd never have enough time. And their students wouldn't be bored sitting there. An entirely different kind of learning operation would go into effect.

WOE: Let me give you a hypothetical situation. If it's week five in your American literature course and you're reading *Moby Dick*, what would happen in class that week? What kinds of activities are you doing in class and how much time is used for different activities?

FULWILER: The standing assignment in that class is that everybody keeps a journal. Before they even come to class they've been writing reactions to whatever they read. So presumably on Monday night if they've been reading some *Moby Dick*, they've written at least a response to it. It could be a "I like it" or "I don't like it" response or it could be something more profound than that. When they come in for the first class I'll write a question on the board that will draw them in in some way. I've had them break up into small groups and ask them to see what they could find in the first page: take the first page, go back and read it more slowly, and see what you notice. I've asked them, "What are your first responses to *Moby Dick*?" We find out what they are, write them on the board, and go from there. At some point I may pose a problem to the class; it could be from a quote that's problematic in some way. Or I could give each of the six groups in the class a particular quote and ask them what its significance is. With five minutes left in the class I would probably—if there's time—ask them to write about the most important thing that they've learned in that class.

For the next class I may give them a particular journal assignment, a question or problem to write about: "Look at this for the next class and read so far in the book." Again, I'll probably start the next class off with a little bit of writing and then we'll do some small-group work. That class is divided into six groups of five students each, and they always sit with their groups in class, so for me to move to group activities happens very quickly. We keep going at the book in that way. Sometimes, though, I'll say, "Let me read you something and see how you react." I'll take four or five problematic or challenging lines in a chapter, and I'll read them—just those lines—and I'll give people three minutes to write a response. Just to see where those lines take them. I'm usually operating somewhere between the new critical idea—formalist criticism—and reader response criticism. As a teacher I'm training myself in those methods. I go back and forth between careful attention to the text and careful attention to the text inside your head.

WOE: You haven't mentioned lecture at all.

FULWILER: Most of the time I end up doing mini-lectures. If it's a good class, these are in response to questions. In other words, if I can get the right question I'll find myself giving some background on something I know about Melville. It just fits in. Lecturing's entirely different if it's in response to a question. I don't ever start a class with a lecture. When they happen, they're mini-presentations.

WOE: The sort of radical teaching practices that you've been describing seem to be gaining more and more acceptance—indeed they're beginning to be commonplace—in composition programs. But what about teaching and pedagogy in general? Do you see any effects of writing across the curriculum when you look at the state of higher education in America? What's it going to take to change higher education in America?

FULWILER: That's an interesting question. I think that by now something like 40% of American colleges and universities have a program that they call writing across the curriculum. Five years ago that would not have been the case and 10 years ago the term was hardly heard of. Many schools in both the secondary and higher education systems are interested in what they call critical thinking (which is what writing across the curriculum is) but often those programs are divorced from language. I see writing across the curriculum taking hold at lots of places, but I see the follow-up work to make those programs become part of the curriculum as very difficult. My own school included. But pressures of growing classes, of publication, continually conflict with the need to do more with writing. And I don't see those pressures or that conflict as going away. I would say that concerned faculty who care about their teaching and their research (which I think you have to care about) are in a continual state of dissatisfaction. And the way the curriculum operates, it's not easy to resolve that: the larger the class the more difficult the writing problems become. I don't have any Pollyanna views on that score.

Writing across the curriculum is essentially an undergraduate reform movement, and a lot of college administrators are recognizing that fact. But we're not just talking about writing as writing; we're talking about modes of establishing more community among faculty and students alike. All this talk about student-centered learning was going on back in the '60s when I was in graduate school. We used to talk about Jonathan Kozol versus Paulo Freire: "student-centered learning." But at that point we didn't know about writing. We just hadn't put that quite into the picture. The writing is what makes student-centered learning happen. It's the writing that makes the classroom focused, intellectually challenging, on target, activity oriented, in a way that strictly talky classes never were. So I think that what we have now is the mechanism to do what we imagined doing in 1967 when we talked about giving students more control over their education. The mechanism is writing. When people write they give power to their own voice and ideas.

MIKE ROSE

Mike Rose's contributions to writing studies encompass a wide scope, but his overall message has been clear: American democracy demands equality in education. In his famous multigenre book, Lives on the Boundary: A Moving Account of the Struggles and Achievements of America's Educationally Underprepared *(1989), Rose draws on personal narrative to demonstrate that those often labeled "remedial" do not lack innate ability but lack the environmental conditions and socialization for college preparation that others take for granted. Rose shows that these students bring diverse knowledge and intelligence that is usually subdued in "developmental" courses. In "Language of Exclusion: Writing Instruction at the University," Rose employs historical deconstruction to demonstrate how institutions use labels such as "remedial" and "illiterate" to keep students in "scholastic quarantine," when in fact literacy levels in America have risen dramatically over time. Rose offers us a reminder that the classroom can be a place of rich dialectical opportunity and that diverse students can truly enrich intellectual endeavor within the academy.*

Rose has published multiple books on the politics of education from the individual to the sociopolitical level, and has contributed substantial work on cognition in writing. His other works include Back to School: Why Everyone Deserves a Second Chance at Education *(2012),* The Mind at Work: Valuing the Intelligence of the American Worker *(2004),* Possible Lives: The Promise of Education *(1996), and* Writer's Block: The Cognitive Dimension *(1984). His career in education spans from kindergarten teaching to adult literacy, including early work teaching at-risk populations in the Los Angeles area. Since 1994, he has been a research professor at the UCLA Graduate School of Education and Information Studies. He currently writes Mike Rose's Blog, where he reports on current legislation, promotes reform, and offers social commentary on education at all levels.*

—Agnes Stark

"Imagine a Writing Program"

Susan Palo

Spring 1990

WOE: I'm particularly interested in what you call the cognitive dimension of writing. I wondered if you could define that and explain the source of your interest.

ROSE: I can probably work better from the latter part of your question than from the former. In the late '70s, I was in a graduate program in the UCLA School of Education in counseling psychology. The teacher of a course in counseling was very interested in cognitive psychology, so he expanded the traditional readings to include the emerging work in cognitive psychology. At the same time, I was teaching Introduction to Literature. So I started looking at my students' writing problems through the lens of cognitive psychology and saw some interesting things. As I talked to students and looked at their papers, an idea emerged that I developed later in the work on writer's block: some of the students seemed to be laboring with rules and strategies that were very rigid and one dimensional, without multiple paths, multiple options. And that seemed to me to be profoundly out of synch with the nature of writing. Rhetoric, the whole world of discourse, is so multi-operational—there're so many possible ways to achieve a good end—that no rule or strategy will be fully functional if it's narrowly conceived and stripped of discourse contexts. Yet these students were operating with rules and strategies that were algorithmic and isolated, like simple mathematical formulas. That was where my interest started: my reading was overlapping in a very interesting way with my teaching, enabling me to understand some things I hadn't quite understood before. Then Ruth Mitchell and Mary Taylor of UCLA's Writing Research Project introduced me to the early work of Flower and Hayes, and that helped me feel more comfortable about applying cognitive psychology to student writing.

WOE: Did your readings help you see the students' problems or see something else?

ROSE: Certainly I had seen the problems before. We all as teachers see students who get stuck, who get stymied, who give us very stunted products. Cognitive psychology was giving me an understanding of causality that I didn't have before.

WOE: An understanding that the causality was not behavioral and that it was not emotional?

ROSE: Right. We have a bit of folk wisdom to explain what happens when people who should be able to write can't write; we tend to rely on emotional, psychodynamic explanations: she's afraid of revealing herself, or he has a very strong superego or a strong inner critic. That's a legitimate way to look at things, and it certainly holds true for many of us, but cognitive psychology was opening up another way to understand writing problems, a way that had more to do with the instruction that the students might have had that wasn't as good as it could be or maybe misunderstandings that they themselves had developed as they sat in classes and tried to make sense of writing.

WOE: Did your work in cognitive psychology affect your teaching?

ROSE: Any reading that strikes us in a powerful way must influence our teaching. But I think cognitive psychology got me to look in a close, systematic way at the processes behind the production of a text. And it gave me a set of terms, a framework.

WOE: What is that framework?

ROSE: The framework of rules and strategies and higher-order assumptions that can drive the way we, as writers, do what we do when we compose. As is the case with any discipline, cognitive psychology gives you a vocabulary, some lenses, and that was helpful to me.

WOE: How does this framework show up in teaching?

ROSE: It leads you to look beyond the written product, to look beyond an error on a page, beyond an assignment that goes awry. You're always asking yourself the question, "Why is this person doing this? What rules, or strategies, or approaches, or assumptions is he or she operating with that might be leading to these errors, these problems, these kinds of texts?" In cognitive educational psychology, particularly in research on math and science, there's a nice history of people investigating what they call "buggy rules," the off-kilter rules you find when you probe kids' errors in mathematics problems. I took that whole way of looking at things and brought it to bear on writing.

Mina Shaughnessy's *Errors and Expectations* came out right around that time, and she was saying a very similar thing: when she talks about the "intelligence" of a mistake, she is telling us we have to look beyond the surface of an error to see the logic of it. Working in a different domain, the cognitive psychologists in education had been saying that, too. There's a lot that's valuable to us in that math-science work. I know it influenced me and others, Glynda Hull, for example.

WOE: So far these ideas seem to apply particularly to one-to-one teaching or tutoring. But how is classroom teaching informed by such things as a knowledge of the cognitive dimensions of writing?

ROSE: In classroom instruction you become sensitive to the way that people can misinterpret what you're saying or—when it comes to writing—how they can take a statement about an assignment and convert it into a one-dimensional rule because there's something satisfying in doing that. It reduces anxiety; it gives a way to operate in a world that's very confusing. And the world of discourse is very confusing; there are no simple answers.

As a teacher, you become much more conscious of context. If you talk about stylistic rules or organizational patterns, you're also mindful that your explanation might be rigidified, interpreted narrowly. You might even talk to the class about that. You might return to those rules and patterns later and try to sketch out possible contexts for their use. Let me give you an example. A while back it was popular to get students to improve their style by getting them to find and eliminate all or most all of the *to be* verbs in their writing, so they would avoid certain stylistic patterns that could be dull or clumsy. But if you stop there, you run into the danger of some students thinking the best style is one in which all *to be* verbs are removed. By returning to this notion about *to be* verbs two or three or more times as the class progresses and pointing out contexts in which the suggestion about *to be* verbs holds and contexts in which it doesn't, you would show students that discourse contexts often determine the degree to which stylistic advice applies. That's the general awareness that I see developing from some of the work I've used.

The second thing to say about the cognitive perspective in terms of the classroom—and this does not stem from the writer's block work—is that cognitive literature on the development of competency gives you an appreciation of how complicated writing tasks can be and, therefore, helps you to think more systematically about how you can sequence assignments to help develop competence. But we have to be careful here, because the behaviorist tradition gives us a very rigid notion of sequencing in the curriculum. Generally, the behaviorists' notion was, you take a task and you break it down into as many subtasks as you can. That's the idea behind programmed instruction. Now there's something sensible about that. Human beings can learn complicated tasks by breaking them down into do-able tasks. Unfortunately, when that's applied to discourse in a narrow way, you end up with skills-and-drills instruction, a kind of atomizing of discourse, a kind of mechanical segmenting of language work into all these mini-components that rarely add up to something rich.

I'm suggesting that an alternative to the behaviorist perspective is to think of what you want students to be able to do—to be fairly explicit about that; in fact, you *should* be explicit so that the task is not mysterious; and then think about what assignments, in-class exercises, mini-writing tasks, readings, and class discussions you can use to build toward your goal. If for example you want students to be able to write critically about passages in economics, you might begin with posing a problem. You'd pose an economics problem familiar to them, one that is part of their world—a problem that cognitive psychologists would say is part of their background knowledge. You would get discussion going, maybe one having to do with their work or the financing of their schooling. Cognitive psychologists would say that discussion activates schema, that is, their own background knowledge, and brings it to bear on this academic task before them. Then you move on and give them a small, accessible reading about a particular economic theory. You'd discuss that. You'd do all the things that good teachers know how to do: you'd get everybody to talk, you'd refer to one student's answer to another student's question, and you'd then begin to apply this theory to the discussion you'd had the day before. Then you'd have them write; maybe they would write a synopsis or summary, or maybe they would write a critique of this little theoretical passage based on their own experience that they had brought forth the day before. Maybe that writing would lead to the reading of some more complicated, longer passage, or maybe several economics passages taking different points of view. And you'd develop a further, fuller and richer, writing assignment from that.

That's the way to think about sequencing. It's not a breaking down of a complex task into a jillion little atomized subtasks. Rather, it's a consideration of ways to build competence, ways to build on what students already know and move them towards what they don't know, taking on new material and assisting them to stretch. This takes you into what Vygotsky calls the "zone of proximal development," moving students constantly just beyond what they're capable of doing on their own.

Jerome Bruner's notion of scaffolding is similar: as you move students ever outward from what they can do comfortably to what they can just barely do, you must provide all sorts of scaffolding, as the metaphor goes, or assistance. In classroom discussion, for example, as you're watching a student struggling to articulate a notion, with your good teacher's instincts, you wait for the right moment and then you move in and assist, provide a word, a framework, trying to help the student better conceptualize and express an idea.

WOE: Do you think that this approach is particularly appropriate to writing instruction?

ROSE: I sure do. I think that the best writing classes are ones in which there is a hell of a lot going on, and the teacher becomes a kind of conductor, leading, prompting, guiding—but the work is being done by the students, and it involves all the communication modes. Students are talking: they're talking to the teacher, they're talking to each other, and all of that talk is in some way building from reading they've done or problems that have been posed or writing that they've produced themselves. And it's leading toward something else; it's leading toward another piece of reading or another writing task, always just beyond what they can readily do, helping them grow as writers.

WOE: What sort of content in a writing class works best with this? How important is the content of the course compared to how the course is taught?

ROSE: In composition studies—although here composition studies has been influenced by bigger debates in education in general—we've fallen into the trap of entrenching ourselves into two camps. First there's the process camp that sees the important thing as being *how* we do things: what sort of classroom we conduct, what kind of discourse we encourage in the classroom, how we respond to what students say and write, and the content often takes a back seat. On the other hand are the content people, and they tend to be identified with the more traditional, sometimes even neo-conservative line. And those folks say, "No, no; what's important is the content, the *what*. We've overemphasized the *how* since Dewey." This is essentially E.D. Hirsch's complaint. In literature, of course, these are the people who are more canonical in their orientation. They maintain that it's the body of knowledge that you're teaching that's important and, in fact, go further and say that there are certain bodies of knowledge that you have to teach and that those bodies of knowledge in themselves will convey what is central to education: clear thinking, moral vision, and discriminating taste. The problem with this way of representing teaching is that, like any dichotomy, it simplifies the complex nature of language learning and language use. Both "process" and "content" work together in a profound way. A focus on process without a concern for content can degenerate quickly into a formulaic, often superficial set of routines. A focus on content without a concern for the process becomes at its worst a narrow focus on a revered body of knowledge. Both of these concerns have to be part of a teacher's thinking when he or she prepares a curriculum.

WOE: What kind of content is best suited for a writing class?

ROSE: That completely depends on context, as any discourse issue depends on context. My own bias is that in a freshman writing course in a traditional college or university, we need to spend a significant amount of time on the kinds of reading and writing that our students need to do to succeed in college. That doesn't mean we convert this into a mindless service course; rather, we take as the field of discourse the context in which we are working. That field of discourse is academic discourse, what we have come to call critical reading and writing: analyzing texts, probing an argument, posing alternative hypotheses, trying to understand the assumptions behind a claim, and being able to criticize them. And the discourse structures that students are often asked to use as they do these things are, among others, comparing, classifying, summarizing, and analyzing. And it's my belief that in a traditional college or university we should be getting at all this through the use of representative academic texts. These form the "content" of the class, but in line with what I was saying earlier, the challenge is how to use this content in a truly "process-oriented" way. The focus of instruction may be a poem, the content may be a piece of literature, but it's extremely important that the students are engaged very actively in thinking, writing, and talking about that piece: that's how all the process insights come into such valuable play. How do you encourage students to talk to you and each other? What classroom conditions do you set up so that students are free to be critical, to speak their minds? Or what conditions can you set up to help them stretch what they're trying to articulate—and here that notion of scaffolding comes in. How do you help them better articulate the insight that they're working with?

But let me also say that there are many other settings where I could imagine very different kinds of content being necessary. Take, as a different example, a community college course in a program leading to a terminal technical degree, say refrigeration repair or automotive repair. To drag the traditional canon in here is a big mistake, and most people realize that, except for some of the people writing best-selling books about what's wrong with education in our country. But imagine the instruction where students are doing things like the following: they have to troubleshoot what might be wrong with a carburetor and they have to do that in writing, even if their writing is very flawed. They use writing as a tool to learn and to probe and to help them better articulate their thoughts. They have to present their analysis to the class; they have to explain and discuss their line of reasoning as they are trying to figure out what might be wrong with this carburetor. Some of the reading they do will be focused on issues that are pertinent to automotive repair—all kinds of content related to electricity, mechanics, combustion, all of that. And some of the reading and the discussion would have to do with the broader political and social contexts in which they do their work. In fact, in some of the best and most exciting vocational programs that's what really inspired teachers are doing.

WOE: I'm interested in your word "inspired" teachers. Looking at some of the examples in *Lives on the Boundary*, where you describe your own teaching—say with the veterans—some of the things you've done are so specific and focused and so appropriate that it makes someone else wonder: well, is this ability to teach this way a gift, an inspiration? How do other people learn to help students with this cognitive sequence?

ROSE: Even though I use the word "inspired," Susan, I don't fully buy the Romantic model of teaching expertise. I think we can help lots of people become better teachers by—I'm going to say this in a simple way, but the process leading to this could be very rich and complex—getting them to ask, for example, questions like, "What do I really want these students to be able to do and what should I do? What conditions should I establish, what assignments should I provide that will help them reach my goal?"

Another question that we could get teachers to ask, when they see a failed performance or a problematic performance, would be, "My goodness, this is interesting. What's going on here? And how can I find out what's going on here? What questions should I ask the student in conference that would help me understand better how he came to write this in this way?" And yet another question—truly the fundamental question—is "What do they know already, and what about my own background and training might be keeping me from seeing it?"

Those questions would enable people to become more effective teachers. But the "training program" that would lead them to pose those questions might take a long time, might be very rich, might put them through a whole series of different experiences both in the community and the classroom, would expose them to certain kinds of readings, would, in many cases, involve them in very deep examinations of their own assumptions, assumptions that are a part of our culture, about intelligence, about literacy, about language, about the way learning occurs. So, although I've said the questions in a simple way, it would be naive to suggest that it's an easy process to lead teachers to ask those questions. But things are being done. Cyndy Greenleaf in Berkeley's School of Education, for example, is trying to develop computer-based instructional materials to lead student teachers to more readily ask such questions.

WOE: We're beginning to get to your last book, *Lives on the Boundary*. It seems that while we're talking about attentiveness on the part of the teacher to the cognitive aspects of learning, really, we are moving well beyond cognition. Your earlier work focused on cognitive dimensions of, say, writer's block, but in the recent book you have a line where you refer to the "effect of despair on cognition." The phrase suggests to me not only that you have widened your focus from writing to education but that your analysis of causality is extending beyond cognitive and even emotional factors to social and political dimensions. Let's back off and talk about you for a minute. How did you make this move?

ROSE: I'm glad the move is evident. When I was doing the writer's block work—that's about 10–12 years ago, almost the first stuff I published—I was looking at one relatively unexamined dimension of a complex problem. But even in *Writer's Block: The Cognitive Dimension*, I make it fairly clear, I hope, that I am not debunking the play of psychodynamic variables or situational variables, but I am trying to look as clearly as I can at this one dimension: cognition.

But, if I were writing that book today, I would probably do it very differently. And I think that the shift, to answer your question, the widening of my conceptual lens came with a 1985 essay that I wrote as a chapter in *When a Writer Can't Write* ["Complexity, Rigor, Evolving Method, and the Puzzle of Writer's Block: Thoughts on Composing-Process Research"]. There I call for a complex methodology that takes into consideration the situational and affective or emotional aspects of composing as well as the cognitive. It was with that essay that my work started to shift. The next thing that I wrote, if I remember correctly, is "The Language of Exclusion." That essay is very much a social, cultural examination of the language that we use in universities to talk about writing instruction. With the "Complexity, Rigor" essay I tried to consciously set out a research framework, and with the "Language of Exclusion" essay I engaged for the first time in what some folks would call cultural criticism—I don't want to put a high falutin' label on it because I'm not schooled as a cultural critic, but I've been told that there's a cultural critical cast to the essay. That flatters me.

WOE: You talk about boundaries, about crossing boundaries; to what extent do you see the writing instruction at a university as presenting a boundary or as, perhaps, helping people cross boundaries?

ROSE: For a long time I've seen the writing class as a central place where you really can look at the reading and writing of university work in a way that is enabling and critical, that encourages students to build their critical awareness of both the writing act and the contexts in which they deploy it. A writing class is also a place where you work very hard to enable students to master the various conventions, strategies, and structures that are simply part and parcel of that kind of intellectual reading and writing. When writing courses are done right, they are powerful courses that enable students to cross from being outside the academy into being inside. Unfortunately, every one of us knows stories that form a legacy of freshman composition courses as gatekeeper courses, courses that do not invite in but regulate entrance.

WOE: Given your focus on culture in *Lives on the Boundary*, particularly on matters of ethnicity, race, and gender, to what extent do you think it's productive to have those matters explicitly a part of composition instruction?

ROSE: I think that is a very complex question. Some of my colleagues at the UCLA Writing Program have developed curricula that have at their center issues of ethnicity. They're the freshman composition courses, by and large, not electives. Now sometimes these courses have been wildly successful, powerful courses.

WOE: What has allowed that, do you think?

ROSE: Both the skill of the teacher in handling material that can be very difficult, very painful, very explosive and, as well, a happy mix, a good chemistry in the students. Sometimes those courses have not been very successful, and sometimes the teachers, most of whom are white, find themselves confronting their own assumptions that need to be brought out and discussed, for example, that African-American students are necessarily going to like to read Alice Walker rather than an author who isn't African-American. It's a very complicated issue because, in developing such a curriculum we teachers have to examine very carefully our own assumptions and our motives . . . and, let's face it, our own fears. It also calls for us, through conversations with friends and colleagues who are people of color, to examine our backgrounds and the ways we have been socialized to think about difference, to think about color, to think about class.

WOE: How does this content present problems to the students?

ROSE: Well, for starters, some students of color have very complicated reactions to a curriculum so focused on their own and other people's ethnicity. They ask questions like, "Why are we being given this? Is this what you would give to everybody? What is it that you think, teacher, that makes you assume that I'm automatically going to like to read African-American authors rather than what I suspect everybody else is reading?" That's one reaction. Other reactions are that some ethnic minority students feel very strange and uncomfortable seeing or reading representations of themselves where people are, for example, speaking in dialect or with accents, or are using slang. Again, I have heard students of color say, "I don't talk this way and nobody in my family talks this way. Doesn't this give a representation of my people that in some way fits white people's stereotypes?" These are just two examples of the concerns and questions that students raise, and sometimes they catch teachers off guard.

But, please understand, I'm not raising these concerns as an argument against developing richer curricula. Absolutely not. I think we all have to work hard to figure out what is going to enrich the curriculum, to make the curriculum be representative of class and cultural differences and gender issues. We have to be thinking about this, but we also have to realize what a profoundly complex issue it is, because we're doing this work from within a society that has a long history of racism, class prejudice, and sexism—and this history plays out in ways that we can't predict and sometimes offends our students and surprises the hell out of us.

WOE: Often in *Lives on the Boundary* I sense that your model for teaching is the model of the best teaching that you had at Loyola, teaching which we often associate with the small liberal arts college. In some ways it's fairly traditional there's a great deal of interaction between the instructor and students and between the students, and often the instructor models or leads the students through material, developing the examination of a text or ideas. How does that sort of vision inform your idea of the university classroom?

ROSE: Well, good point. I wouldn't want to deny that I was profoundly influenced by certain people in my own past, and those people did rely on more "traditional" models of instruction.

WOE: And, as you've pointed out, these may be traditional models of a more elite education than at, say, UCLA or the other UC schools.

ROSE: That's interesting. The class is assumed to have something to say and students are engaged; there's lots of interaction. Somewhere I say about one teacher, Jack MacFarland, that he brought a prep school curriculum to my working-class high school. The notion that some of my models of really good teaching were determined by fairly traditional teachers is worth thinking about. I never had the experience of group work or any of the kinds of things that are so central to a lot of pedagogy today. And I think that what's happened to me as I've taught over the last twenty years is that some of these techniques and approaches have woven their way into my own notions of what really good instruction is and how I run my own class, although, still, I think I run my class in what some teachers would probably call a relatively traditional way. But I'm convinced that such instruction has value.

WOE: Actually, I'm asking a rather simplistic question. I'm thinking about the extent to which teachers, particularly teachers of writing, work with and develop what we sometimes call the student's own voice versus the extent to which we model and engineer sequences of assignments that will introduce students to using the voices of the academy. And that the latter is something the old, traditional model did very well for the few.

ROSE: That traditional model did that very well; the problem—the tragedy—was that it did it for such a small number of people.

WOE: And people who actually spoke quite alike, too. So tell us more about whose voices we're working with in the writing classroom and which voices we're bringing out.

ROSE: One thing I wanted to show to a broad reading audience in *Lives on the Boundary* was that folks who had been assumed to not be capable of entering these conversations, and talking that talk of the academy, and doing that work, and engaging in those tasks—that when you set the right conditions, they in fact can do it. They can do it just fine.

That's one of my agendas: to dispel the notion held by both an elitist educational system and by a sometimes well-intentioned but problematic developmental educational system (people who teach developmental students, developmental studies programs, remedial courses) that these students can't do this work, and therefore they substitute a remedial curriculum that, for example, is built on narrow reading and writing tasks or is focused on the student's personal experience alone. I wanted to show both those audiences that, again and again in my experience, students who have been assumed to be incapable of engaging in a traditional, elitist curriculum can in fact engage in it just fine when the conditions are right.

Implied in your question is a further interesting question. In working within a traditional curricular model aren't there some dangers: while you may be successful in enabling these students to talk the talk of the academy, in so doing you may, as well, remove, squelch, get them to be ashamed of their own voices, their own backgrounds, their own languages? Or students may sound hollow, may sound like they're mimicking academic language. That certainly happens, too, and I think you could read Richard Rodriguez's *Hunger of Memory* as an account of these things happening. But the real danger here is that we, once again, think in too dichotomous a way about these issues. Susan, we are so locked in this culture into a binary way of thinking. What ever happened to dialectic, to complex transaction?

WOE: I know—all my questions are very binary.

ROSE: But that's understandable because it reflects the way that our profession talks about these issues, so that on the one hand you have the "voice" people and on the other hand you have the "academic discourse" people. But we have to realize that each of these positions is both legitimate and problematic. We have to figure out ways to bring them into a kind of dialectic, into a kind of dynamic tension. To introduce students to academic language does not necessarily mean that you have to degrade and distance them from their own experience, their own voice, their own language.

One of the most powerful writing classrooms would be one in which the agenda of the curriculum was to bring these two voices consciously into focus and allow the students to discuss the nature of each, the way one can dominate the other, how it feels to use each one, and so on. I was talking to Ira Shor about this issue, and in the book he's working on now—I want to be careful about not misrepresenting a fleeting conversation—he is saying something that strikes me as just right. He says that what emerges in the classroom should be a third language, a kind of wonderful language that is a mix of both personal and academic, as students both come to reflect on and appreciate their own voice as well as attempt to engage this other kind of voice that is more distant from them. I could imagine that that translates into the kind of classroom where, in talking about an academic text, students are free to engage it at any point they want to and with any language they want to. The key thing here is to get them to think critically in any mode of discourse that feels right to them, that helps them engage that text. Shor says, I think, that an exciting third language develops, a kind of interlanguage—tentative, fresh, reflective and exploratory.

WOE: In *Lives on the Boundary*, which addresses issues of pluralism, you have combined so many genres in your own writing: autobiography, case studies, even new journalism in some of the vignettes, where you sometimes assume the point of view of someone other than yourself. How did you evolve as a writer toward this mixing of genres?

ROSE: Long before I started to write about writing and about education, I wrote poems. I wasn't a very good poet. I finally got to the place where I was sort of OK. But I loved doing it. There's just something about that kind of close, careful, crafting attention to language that was blissful for me. It sounds stupid, it sounds corny to say it, but I can't tell you how many hours were passed engaged, lost in writing poetry. Lawrence has a remark, something about "I disappeared into the canvas"; I disappeared into that language. So I guess that that facility has been rattling around, inside of me, the ability to work closely with language. That was there.

The way that the form of this book developed was interesting. I had been writing poems and had been fortunate in publishing a lot of them, but I had never had any luck breaking out of the world of the tiny, tiny, small magazine. And I finally just got real frustrated with that. So one day I sat down and tried to write something that I had never written before, which was a prose sketch, almost a prose poem but not quite that refined or precious. It was a sketch of a drive down through central California to Calexico. And I really enjoyed doing that. And, honest to God, Susan, I don't think that I had ever before that time written what people would call nonfiction prose; I mean I had certainly written a million school papers and I had been lucky enough to publish some articles and books, but I had never written the kinds of things you'd find in *Atlantic* or *Harper's*, until I did that, and clearly it was influenced by the poetry. It was more poetry than an essay. I liked doing that little sketch about the drive to Calexico, so I started to fool around with some sketches of where I grew up, my neighborhood, my high school. And it hit me: wouldn't it be fun to see if I could write something that combined these kinds of sketches with the scholarly work I had been doing—you know, a few lines from, say, Harold Rosen's "The Nature of Narrative" combined with a few lines of a narrative of my own making. And make no mistake about it, writing "The Language of Exclusion"—where I did some historical research and tried to understand the way a different era would think about language problems—that also helped move me toward writing the non-fiction essay. So the poetry, and the historical orientation of "The Language of Exclusion," plus this serendipitous idea to see if I could combine these different kinds of writing, is where it started.

WOE: What enabled you to use your self and your family so much in the book? How were you able to do that? I would think it would be hard.

ROSE: I'm sure the willingness to write about the family came from the poetry. In the early eighties I got real intrigued with our family history and the possibility of writing poems about it. So, when I would go back and visit them, back in Ohio and Pennsylvania, I would spend hours talking to my uncles and aunts and getting all these wonderful, old stories. These people were all skillful tale tellers, with that Mediterranean touch with a story. And they told all these stories—great ones filled with accents and gestures—and I just loved them. I would write them out in a little journal and play with them. They turned into lots and lots of poems. So I think that the willingness to write autobiography came from the fact that for about three or four years before that I had been writing so many poems about the family. It also enabled me to write about the family with a certain distance. A lot of people have said to me, "Jeez, it must have been so painful writing about the family?" or, conversely, "Don't you feel tremendously vulnerable and revealed—all these people now read about your family?" But I swear to you, I have not had those feelings, perhaps because of two things. One is the distance that comes from crafting the stories, and the second is that I have the sense that I'm using the family portraits and my own life in service of a larger point. It somehow makes the personal stuff less, well, confessional and self-referenced to use it as part of an argument about our misperceptions of the intellectual capacity of poor people.

WOE: How self-conscious was your mixing of genres, given your topic? You talk about the pluralism of America, the pluralism of Los Angeles, of UCLA, of students. At the very end of *Lives on the Boundary* you say we need a "revised store of images of educational excellence, ones closer to egalitarian ideals—ones that embody the reward and turmoil of education in a democracy. . . ." And then you say, "At heart, we'll need a guiding set of principles that do not encourage us to retreat from, but move us closer to, an understanding of the rich mix of speech and ritual and story that is America." And your book is just such a mix.

ROSE: Thank you. I would love to think that the book does some of that. How self-conscious was that? Again, I think it evolved. I hate to rely on the cliché that I've seen so many times in print, but I realize it's true: the purpose and the shape of the book emerged as I worked on it. I didn't have a clear plan in the beginning. It was almost playful in the beginning, as you can see from what I've said. But by the time I'd gotten two or three chapters together, I began to see some of the ways this was going to work. And then I began to draw threads together and create resonances. About that time, Bloom's and Hirsch's books became prominent. The presence of those books certainly shaped the way the last chapters developed. I don't see my book as a response to them, but I do think that parts of it were shaped by the way they had defined the discussion of education in America.

WOE: We are getting back, I think, to education, to teaching. I wanted to ask you earlier about how your model of teaching fits into a research university.

ROSE: We in America have simply got to be more creative about the way we envision what the research university can become. I've been troubled that so many of the speeches I hear and the things I read about the future of the university are simply recycling the same old shibboleths and the same old visions. We haven't moved at all, it seems, beyond the nineteenth-century German seminar room. Things have gotten much more corporatized—absolutely; research in most universities is driven by government funds—absolutely. Of course, there are many differences. But when people begin to rhapsodize about what the university might become, it's a slightly snazzier version of what it already is. We need to think of how the university can begin to be more pluralistic in its response to research and learning.

WOE: Could that happen in writing programs?

ROSE: Where better? Writing programs would be a wonderful and natural place for it to happen, but they would have to be given a much more solid place within the institution than they currently have. People's jobs would have to be redefined in a significant way, given the status structure. But imagine a writing program that was truly central to a university's mission: within the institution, the teaching of writing would be seen as not only an extremely important educational task but also as a very rich source of inquiry, a rich source of the production of knowledge; in that program all kinds of courses would be taught, but also learning and teaching would be studied and you'd have a variety of ways that faculty could fulfill the research function: from theoretical work to curriculum development. This writing program would also extend into the schools and the community. Faculty would work with teachers, with students in the schools, and perhaps with various members of the community and various adult education programs. All of this could also be a focus of research.

In fact, a writing program might provide a very nice model, a kind of pressure point if you will, for a university to begin to re-examine itself and the way it defines the pursuit of knowledge, the way it defines itself in relation to the society. It would raise questions about its very traditional split between research and application and about its valorizing of so-called "pure" research—the purer the research the better—over application. Such a program would be a chance for the university to begin to examine some of the fundamental contradictions in its structure and its history.

A writing program would be an ideal place to consider how we can truly combine research and practice. Right now universities constantly talk about how important it is that their professors do research and how research enriches teaching, but everybody knows that few university people think in a deep way about the connection between research and teaching; they don't think in wide-ranging structural or organizational ways about how to bring the two together. A writing program is a good place to think about that mix because rhetoric is an applied art; the very work you do involves practice; it involves pedagogy. It would be a chance to raise pedagogy—as Mariolina Salvatori at Pitt is trying to do—from the netherworld it so often inhabits. Such a writing program would also provide a chance for the university to rethink the rather narrow set of roles that it currently provides. We have professors who teach, increasingly, upper-division and graduate courses and who do research, and then we've got all these lecturers and TAs who are trotted out to do all the other work that nobody has the time or desire to do. What a silly, reductive separation of roles that is.

So, yes, the answer to your question is that a writing program could be a place—in an enlightened university, with the right kind of support—where not only new and better teaching could be done and new and better research could be done, but also a place, in the true spirit of inquiry and self-reflection, that would allow the university to raise some fundamental and very interesting questions about itself as it moves into the last decade of the twentieth century. What should a research university be in a pluralistic democracy? The models we have pretty much come from societies other than the kind of society we have.

WOE: A writing program could be a place where there would be an exciting mix of the different stories and different voices; in a writing program—with writers, researchers, teachers—people could write, teach, and reflect on writing and teaching in ways that helped each other's efforts.

ROSE: Isn't that true. And wouldn't it be a way to fulfill one of the agendas that the research university claims as its own: the deep and respectful examination of the whole range of languages, and voices, and stories that comprise American discourse. It would be a wonderful place where writing researchers, sociologists, linguists, historians, and literary people could meet and do both applied and theoretical work.

RICHARD LANHAM

Richard Lanham's scholarly career has ranged widely, as even a selective glance at his bibliography reveals. He has written books on all matters rhetorical: on the human impulse for style (The Motives of Eloquence, 1976) and the pedagogies that variously exploit and discourage that impulse (Style: An Anti-Textbook, 1974), on literacy (Literacy and the Survival of Humanism, 1983), on emergency self-help for writers (Revising Prose, 1979, Revising Business Prose, 1993), and on a method for recognizing and describing prose styles (Analyzing Prose 2003).

Lanham earned his PhD from Yale University, after which he began his teaching career at Dartmouth College before joining the faculty at UCLA. He founded the UCLA Writing Program in 1979 and served as its first director. From the outset, Lanham's work has been grounded in classical rhetoric and history, specifically the application of classical principles to changing technologies and circumstances. Known for his acidic critiques of prolix style in academic, business, and government writings, his work since this interview has focused predominantly on analyzing the evolution of rhetoric in the context of digital media. The Electronic Word: Democracy, Technology, and the Arts (1993) focuses on the sea-change brought on by the personal computer and the inherent interactivity of electronic media. His most recent work, The Economics of Attention (2006), explores the influence of the Internet, providing in part a practical manual for managing information overload. Long a champion of clarity and readability, Lanham has never shied from the practical and the contemporary in communications and media. Since his retirement from teaching in 1994, he has continued his work as a media and editorial consultant. This interview was conducted by former graduate students of Lanham's.

—David Masiel

"Learning by Going Along"

Carolyn Handa and Gretchen Flesher

Fall 1990

WOE: How did you learn to write and get your ideas about writing? Who influenced you and what influenced you?

LANHAM: I guess I learned by going along. I never had a writing course. The closest I ever came was a graduate seminar in rhetorical figuration in Renaissance literature given by Helge Kökeritz, and that's where I started getting interested in style. I honestly don't know how I learned. I very, very soon came to sweat a lot of blood over the prose I wrote and to work on it a lot, but I don't know where that came from. I wrote a lot of papers when I was an undergraduate at Yale. I have them all, and I look back at them and I was not given much stylistic advice, though the commentary on the papers was copious. Now that I know how much such commentary costs to write on a paper, I'm amazed at the level of it. But no one ever said anything about how I wrote, though my prose was full of prepositional phrases and other elements of the official style.

I've never asked myself this question. I first noticed the official style when I was in the military. I worked in the army cryptography center at the Pentagon. One of the things that I did was to break long cables from various parts of the world that were going to the White House or other places. And this meant spending four or five hours reading and enciphering or deciphering government prose. And that's where I first started noticing it as a particular artifact. There wasn't much to do about it then; you were just transferring it. But I guess that's when I began. Then I worked for the federal government when I got out of the military, for the Smithsonian, and I started noticing government prose a little bit more. But I didn't write much. Then I went to graduate school.

I remember that some of my papers in graduate school were reproved for being too argumentative, or too pointed, or too lively. At one point somebody said, "Do you really want to write like F.R. Leavis?" And I thought, well, he's gotten a lot of attention! But I guess I was thought to be too argumentative or contentious and not polite enough, and I suppose that attribute has endured. But beyond that, I don't know. I just learned as I went along.

When I was writing *The Motives of Eloquence* I had a whole file drawer full of the drafts of that book—[*gestures*]—that long, and when students would ask me, "Do you do to your prose what you're making me do to mine?" I had a wonderful stage prop. I would take a copy of the book and I would say "See this?" And then I would pull out this file drawer with a dramatic gesture and say, "Those are the drafts!" But finally I needed the file space so I had to throw them away.

WOE: You did an early version of portfolio assessment on our writing. I remember all those multiple drafts that you made us turn in. And if I think about it, I learned to write in your Renaissance Nonfiction Prose seminar. It was the only class I had in graduate school that asked me to revise papers, to do a lot of papers, more than one. I remember doing five or six papers, always having to turn in a paper, and turning in a portfolio at the end. When I think about it now, you were doing writing as process, you were doing portfolios, things that are in now, but you did them a long time ago, more than ten years ago. How did you come to have us do that?

LANHAM: I haven't thought about that. I started doing that when I started teaching at Dartmouth. I was asked to teach a creative writing course. And I said, "I can't. I don't know how. I'm not a creative writer. But Barkus is willing! I want to show that I'm an adaptable young person. Why don't you give me a section of the remedial course? Nobody wants to teach that. And you're embarrassed that you have it. Let me teach that." And I had such fun that that became one of my regular courses.

WOE: You're kidding!

LANHAM: It was clear then that the people in the class were either slothful—in a couple of cases—or simply extremely mathematically or quantitatively inclined and had never had much writing experience. I said, "Well, let's just do a lot of writing and then at the end try to give you some reasonable grade. It's silly to give you a letter grade on the basis of one paper. Why don't you do a bunch of papers and put 'em in an envelope at the end of the course, and I'll go over all of them and see whether you've made something like reasonable progress." They thought that was a spiffing idea, and I thought that was a reasonable way to do it. So that's how we did it.

The Dartmouth class was a wonderful class. The kids were so neat! And when they found out what was going on, some of them turned out to be terrific writers. I didn't care what they did! They did parodies and novels. It seemed to me they needed to be loosened up. So they could do anything. Jokes! We did a session on—it was all men in those days—dirty limericks and things like that.

I must say I don't do portfolios in classes with 75 students. I have a triage system of saying that if you write the paper early, I will read it and comment on it by the sixth or seventh week. If you turn it in in the eighth week—first option—I will read it, comment on it, we will have a conference on it, and you can revise it. Second option, I will read it and comment on it, but no revision. And third, if you turn it in the last day I'll just give it a grade. That way at least I can read them all myself, and I get somewhere between a third and a half of the class which voluntarily asks for some other version, either for comments or, in many cases, for revision. But you can only do one revision, and as you know, that's pretty late in the game to catch your students, but you can teach them a lot. Nobody has asked them to look at a verbal surface; they've always been asked to look through it. And it really is like riding a bicycle. Once you learn that you can do that, then you learn you can do it yourself. And I pass out a lot of recommendations for *Revising Prose*. I tell them to go buy it, soak it in some milk and eat it like a communion wafer—make it part of themselves! And they often do so.

WOE: What got you interested in composition theory? Was it just a logical move from your study of rhetoric and from the book that began as your dissertation work on Sidney's *Arcadia*?

LANHAM: Well, I really just lurched from crisis to crisis. I don't want to make it a more organized proceeding than it was. When I came to UCLA they had a course called Writing for High School Teachers. And nobody wanted to teach that, because teaching high school teachers was a very low-rent thing, which well-bred research universities shouldn't do at all—it was thought to be a penalty box kind of experience. But it seemed like a pretty good idea to teach high school teachers how to teach and how to write. So I volunteered to teach that course and taught it for a while.

Some time or the other I started getting interested in it theoretically because at the same time I was doing my *Handlist of Rhetorical Terms*, which came right out of Kökeritz's course. When I was looking up all those terms in the back of Sister Miriam Joseph's *Shakespeare's Use of the Arts of Language*, I thought there's gotta be a list somewhere that's easier to use than this! It turned out there was. It was Heinrich Lausberg's *Handbuch der Literarischen Rhetorik* in two volumes in German! Well, that seemed not quite the right thing so I made a list. When I came to UCLA I started using some of these terms in the Shakespeare course, and the students kept asking me what they meant. I had compiled a list of a couple of pages' worth at Dartmouth, so I made that ten pages' worth, and then I said, what the hell, I'll do the handlist. So I got myself interested in the history of rhetoric that way.

I never had any courses in it. The closest I got was Wimsatt's seminar when I was an undergraduate. He gave a graduate seminar in the history of criticism which included, of course, lots of classical rhetoric, but presented as the history of criticism. He also gave an undergraduate version of it, which you had to get into by special application with recommendation letters. It was a VERY tough course. Wimsatt paid attention to your stuff. My favorite comment, "wordy wordy wordy," is just a rip-off of what he used to write on my papers: 'Wordy, wordy, wordy!" He was very contemptuous of low-level stylistic errors, or indeed low-level errors of any sort. But you were sitting at the foot of a great man. If he took out the lash, you despised not the rod of instruction! Anyway, I never took a course in rhetoric; there wasn't any such thing at Yale: there wasn't any composition program. There wasn't anything like that at Dartmouth. I just sort of came to it a piece at a time, I guess.

WOE: It's not unusual for people to have come to be in composition and rhetoric without much formal training in composition and rhetoric, but I can't think of anyone else who comes at it from the verbal surface. Everybody else has looked at it as a problem to solve by improving the writer's planning strategies. You still have a very different approach.

LANHAM: From the very beginning what made me looked upon at UCLA as a kind of licensed lunatic amongst my colleagues was a sense that writing papers was the most important thing students did. And that paying attention to those papers was very important. I covered papers with comments in ways that composition teachers would now find horrible. I was thought of as a brute because I did this.

I can remember after I'd been there a year or two, a student came in and sat down and said "Professor Lanham, what is this thing you have about papers?" And it occurred to me then that I really was a product of an Ivy League education that emphasized them. There was always that tradition that this was an important thing. If you can get into heaven by grading papers, I've got a guinea seat. I just did it forever. I did it to the point of exhaustion. Those years when we taught the gigantic classes that I was just saying are now returning, I tried to grade all my own papers and it ended up in stupefaction. That was part of the Dartmouth training. We read about 20,000 words a week of freshman prose when I was at Dartmouth. Every student wrote a five-page paper every week. And every paper was revised and sent back to the student and revised by the student and resubmitted. So there was a gigantic amount of paper writing there. And I think that expectation I carried to UCLA, where such paper writing was by no means the tradition.

It was out of that exasperation, I suppose, that I did the *Revising Prose* books. I thought surely with so much repeatable error we can just isolate that and have a book about it and then we can get on with other things. I can say, "You do all the things that *Revising Prose* teaches you not to do. Here, take this book, go away, learn these lessons, come back, and then we can talk about other things." And to the extent that that book has been used the way I wanted it to, as a supplementary text for situations like that, I think it's worked. But I didn't have any formal training in rhetoric; I never had a composition course; I never had any training in composition courses, and of course the *Anti-Textbook* started out by rejecting the whole technique! I was asked by a big publisher if I wanted to do a freshman text. And the amount of money that they were talking about was so great that I thought, "Shucks! I don't know what my price is, but it's much lower than that!" So I went down the hall to Ron Freeman's office. Ron, God rest his soul, was our composition director. And I said give me the ten bestselling products on the market. I took 'em back and looked through them and said, "I can't do it!" It wasn't conscience. It was stylistic misfit. Somehow I just said, "I just can't do this, that's all." My voice would expire. You can't make jokes in this genre, and I'm always making jokes. You know that rhyme:

They gave him a job that couldn't be done,
And he said by God he would do it,
And he took on that job that couldn't be done,
And by God he just couldn't do it!

Well, that's what that was. So I wrote a letter to the guy who asked me if I'd be interested, saying "No," but at length. And he wrote back and said, "Well the letter has been circulating in our office. The letter is so funny. Why don't you write a book like that letter?" So I did. I had some time that summer and I sat down and I wrote the *Anti-Textbook*. And I sent it to him. And he wrote back, "Well, not THAT kind of book! We couldn't really publish that." So I had a pal, Whitney Blake, again God rest his soul, director of Yale Press. And I said "Well, Whitney, the commercials aren't going to touch this stuff. I don't know whether you're interested in this. Maybe I could sell it to you as a satire or something." And he looked at it, and then the Yale people who were there liked it a lot. So they said fine! That's how it came to be.

Then I guess I was fixed in the role of the madman of composition in my department. And that's what caused me to do other things, do the graduate course. Try to train the TAs. I just sat in a lot of TA sections where I thought the TAs didn't know how to analyze a piece of prose. That's where the *Analyzing Prose* book came from and that's where the course came from. I thought, well, shucks, there's gotta be a book that does it. There doesn't seem to be one; so I wrote one, and tried to get that course going. Anyway, I just fell into these things one after the other. Just the way I somehow seem to have fallen into the electronic text thing. It just seemed like the logical extension of it. I had Renaissance rhetoric on one side and composition on the other. And they both seemed to me to be part of the same world: they were worlds that I cared about, so I didn't feel, as everyone else felt, that suddenly I had compromised my proper research career in order to do this comp work.

WOE: People still feel that if you're in comp, you have compromised yourself.

LANHAM: There's still a lot of violent, astonishing pressure. Certainly I've felt it all my life. It's a good thing I have the kind of temperament I do because otherwise I would have been downcast. And it's amazing that that persists—prejudice against rhetoric—when the whole world of theory is nothing but the revival of rhetoric. It seems quite bizarre. But I don't understand that any more than I understand why, with the whole of Kenneth Burke's work before them, a lot of these ideas waited to emerge until Derrida came along. But that's what happened.

So, OK, an unorthodox, inexplicable background that should have let me be the Washington lawyer that I would have been if I hadn't jumped off the train. How did a nice guy like me get into a job like this? I don't know. The same way I did the expert witness stuff. Somebody called up one day and said, "Would you like this job?" and sure, why not?

WOE: Your talk, "Confessions of an Expert Witness," was so interesting. I guess Gretchen knew about your being an expert witness, but I never knew you did that.

LANHAM: Well, I did decide to come out of the closet. Because I had deliberately not talked about it. It makes people wonder whether you are compromising your scholarship. But I seem to be doing enough writing. In fact, I often spent what normally would be vacation time testifying. The *Shampoo* case was a solid month. That was my vacation. But it was also a lot of fun.

WOE: What's interesting to me, too, is—as you said at the end of your talk—that it makes you value coming back to the university and being able to push truth as far as you can without having these tight restrictions.

LANHAM: Well, I feel that strongly. I wasn't aware of it until I saw how lawyers have to think. The ones I've worked for are mostly very smart. They work phenomenally hard. They make a lot of dough. But they're always working to task. If something comes and they say, "Gee, isn't that an interesting idea," there's never any time to reflect on it because there's this brief, it's got to be filed tomorrow at ten o'clock, and it's focused on this case. So their thinking, though fierce and tough, is always in harness. And you see what an extraordinary luxury it is for us when somebody says, "Go away and be smart. About something." In effect, that's our brief as research scholars. And if it's the pleonastic *do* in the *Pardoner's Tale*, well, that's good, that's terrific. If you want to write about Renaissance shorthand systems the way Helge Kökeritz did, terrific. It's not a wonder that we don't get paid very well for doing it, because it is so free a thing to do that you can fit it into the pressures of society where prices have to be paid. So when somebody does it, it's a pretty neat thing to be commissioned to do in life. Of course, when you have whatever epiphany any of us has, it's really the best thing. It's like whiskey and sex put together! When I fancied I figured out what was really going on with *Tristram Shandy* and with Uncle Toby, I was lying on my couch and it was a real *eureka* experience. I said, "By God, I know what makes this work!" It really is just about the best, the most exciting thing you can know about. And when they win a case, I'm sure the lawyers feel very great excitement, and, when they bill out for those phenomenal sums, they feel extremely excited. But that sense of just finding the answers is the real luxury in our business.

WOE: Is there any particular research in composition that's going on today that really interests or excites you? Where do you think composition research should be going?

LANHAM: Well, I guess I've now become a disciple of chaos theory and no longer believe in central planning. And therefore I'm uncomfortable with the idea of saying it should go in one direction or another. I think smart people should go on being smart. I think the whole explosion of thinking about this world, about composition—I don't mean to sound like a Pollyanna—is really pretty marvelous. I'm much more interested in it than I was in those ten books that I took back from Ron Freeman's office. I was just talking to David Kaufer last night at a party about the work he's doing trying to model information distribution in a new and complex way. I just think that's phenomenal. But so are a lot of other things. I remember when I was being considered for a job at Carnegie Mellon—Linda Flower and I had a long discussion and she seemed to think I was an opponent of the kind of stuff she did. *Tout au contraire!* I've always thought that it was extraordinarily interesting. I thought Mike Rose's *Writer's Block* book was wonderful, and I think his new book, which everybody likes, is just marvelous. I think bringing together, as he did, his own experiences and some sense of the "remedial student" from the inside is an order-of-magnitude step ahead. I think all the work that is trying to make remediation into something less stigmatized and more understandable and part of the normal course of events is really wonderful.

The kinds of analyses that are being made of professional language I suppose are some of the things that impress me the most. A book that's just knocked my socks off is by Don McCloskey, an economist at Iowa. It's about the rhetoric of economics. It's a funny book. He's just blindingly smart. And he comes at it from the point of view of a rhetorician and a Hellenist and an econometrician. A marvelous book. He started a whole unit at Iowa that's talking about the rhetoric of professional languages, and the proceedings of his first conference have been published as a book called *The Rhetoric of the Human Sciences*, which is full of excellent essays. Bazerman's essay on scientific writing. That whole area of professional language is part of the growing self-consciousness of inquiry itself in this country. But that's not the only kind of thing that's going on.

In the computerized part of the woods, I'm more interested in the renegotiation of the ratio between alphabetic and iconographic information, which is one of the themes I'm trying to think about now and one of the primary ways that the economics of information is being revolutionized right now. I'm more interested in that than I am in the quantitative studies which have been part of computing and the humanities for a number of years—the gigantic concordance on one hand, statistical studies that try to move either toward some kind of grammatical study or parsing or whatever, interest me less than this whole field of renegotiating the visual image. So those are some of the things going on that interest me. I think electronic text is going to be the major kind of change that people earning their living the way we do will have to come to terms with. But I'm preaching to the choir here.

WOE: Can you talk about the ideas that you're working on for your book on electronic text?

LANHAM: The electronic word essay that I did for *New Literary History* opens out some of the ideas. The idea that animates the book is that there is a convergence between technology and the pressures of the democratization of higher education and the development of literary and other kinds of theory and that these three are all moving in one direction. And an essay talking about that came out in the *South Atlantic Quarterly*. So that is the backbone of the book.

I'm also very interested in the way the development of the visual arts from Italian futurism and Dada onward foreshadowed and really worked out first the aesthetics of electronic information display. I have a lecture I've been giving in various forms here and there about this, a slide lecture, and that's going to be part of the book. I'm more and more convinced that the fundamental thinking or much of it about the aesthetics of electronic text comes from the writings of John Cage. So I've been trying to bumble my way around the strange world of experimental music. That's going to be a section in the book, somehow, though if I had world enough and time—and maybe even if I don't—I would just sit down and take six weeks and write a little monograph about that, because it's altogether a remarkable convergence and extremely interesting.

The book is going to talk about how I think electronic text affects both pedagogy and the structure of the curriculum. I've been trying to write about the curriculum for all my career and never with any great success. It's a subject that for some reason touches everything, colors everything it touches, with boredom and tedium. And I don't know why. I wrote a long study of it some years ago which I had the courage and the good sense to throw away. I didn't do it all at once; it took me about five years of throwing it away a chapter at a time before I realized that the whole book was worthless.

But I didn't, unhappily, get it out of my system, so I'm going to talk a little bit about that kind of thing as electronic text affects it, the implications of electronic—I don't have a word for it—delivery systems. For example, Robert Winter, my colleague in the music department, wrote a Hypercard program on the *Ninth Symphony* that changes how the curriculum will progress—what progression would mean—in as profound a way as electronic text changes the whole nature of the university departmental structure. It's going to have a chapter or some part of a chapter on the implications of electronic text for the university administrative structures. And that is a subject that as far as I know no one else is thinking about.

It's also going to reflect a little bit on an area that I've been poking my nose into during the last couple of years, and that is libraries and library schools and what libraries are about and what library schools should teach. How all those things are going to get together in that book, I don't know. I wrote a draft of it on my Guggenheim year but it wasn't really any good. I know when things are no good or when I'm not ready to write something, because the life just goes out of my prose. It just gets dull and sticky. So I think I'm going to throw that away, too, and start all over again and try to just write it out then. I have to revise the two *Revising Prose* books before September and I have to finish the second edition of my *Handlist of Rhetorical Terms*. We have to get the computer version of the rhetorical terms book at least ready for beta test. It's going to be a Hypercard program to run on the Macintosh.

WOE: How would I work the *Handlist* if I got it now, because I'm used to the old *Handlist*?

LANHAM: It's a set of Hypercard stacks that follows the book, roughly speaking, but a lot of differences will come from the medium. I thought I would do this because I'd learn a lot and this book would be valuable to people in a digital form. The nature of the book, which is elaborate interreferentiality, is a natural for a hypertextual environment. So with those proud premises in hand, we bashed on. I got a little dough and hired a research assistant.

We've been trying to figure out what to do. All kinds of things change. For example, what do you do for an introduction? Well . . . I mean you've got an introduction, but in a book it's easy. I always think second editions ought to keep the preface of the first edition and then amend it. That's my view. So we write second editions saying, "Well, I predicted this and I was full of . . . stuff." Or, "It worked out." And I want to do that in some way, but you can't just keep the old introduction: it doesn't make sense to do that and have it scrolling down into view—that's stupid. How do you do that? How do you organize it? What buttons do you have? And when do people press 'em?

There's an alphabetical list which you start out with, pressing an index button, and you get an icon which is a card file going from "a" to "z." You press "c" and you get a long list of terms; if you're looking for *chiasmus*, you press *chiasmus* and up comes the term with, in this case, not only an example but an animation.

We're going to have at the end a list of about 50 basic terms which is going to replace the terms especially useful for literary criticism. These are all, if we can manage it, going to have animations and they're going to have pronunciations. We're also trying to put in a little button so that if it says, "Cicero says this," it will say who Cicero is. And we're beginning to do a table of authorities in which you say, "OK. What does Cicero say about chiasmus? What does Quintilian say?" And you can get at least some of those. Now we can't do very many of those because there's not enough room.

But what it amounts to is extending the audience both up and down. Down toward beginning people in rhetoric. I want people to be able to jump into this who don't know who Cicero is and be able to get, in effect, an education in style.

WOE: This would be so good! Students really get turned on when you show them just a few little rhetorical structures. They have so much fun. Not to mention their instructors.

LANHAM: Well, we're going to design it with a completely open architecture. Nothing is going to be locked or closed. And it's very clear that people will start customizing this in radical ways and that they will make unauthorized copies. I guess I'm saying that this will all be ripped off. But in a way it's designed to be. That is, I really want these terms and the stylistic edifice that you can build with them to get back into the bloodstream of the scholarly world. And I think it certainly will this way.

Suppose you had this to play around with and you could do anything you wanted with it. You could add terms, subtract terms, play with it, and put it on your network, take the 50 basic terms and put it on your server. I say, "We're going to have an exercise in these basic five figures" and take you right back to the exercises of a Tudor schoolboy—no bad thing to do! So I think that when I come to your lab a year after you started using it, it will be unrecognizable. You will have completely changed it and moved it around. We talked about the pains of authorship there—that your baby is being genetically rearranged after you've given birth to it. You know, you're not so damned pleased by it, but in a way, you have to be. That's the logic of that form.

If I wanted to get rich, that wasn't a very smart way to do it. If I wanted to see whether these things, this form, could be more readily assimilated into all kinds of pedagogies, it's a very good thing because it's not as sexy a product as Robert Winter's *Ninth Symphony*. I mean 897 rhetorical figures are not what you call easy and forthcoming. If you can sell this, you can sell anything. But it stands for a whole tradition, and of course, always has. I think it is something that's going to be very important for people and maybe using it might get some people interested in classical rhetoric as a whole.

WOE: Is this the first time you've really produced—if you call it producing—a book that isn't a book anymore? The *Handlist* can be printed as a book, but it's an entirely different thing from the *Handlist* on disk. Have you done that before?

LANHAM: No. I did some television programs, but that's different and not interactive. This is the first time that I've come up against the stylistic, the rhetorical, the emotional changes that non-linear, open-architectured texts make on you, and it's very interesting.

It's of course a copyright nightmare. Part of the *Handlist* has already been computerized in an IBM environment by somebody who just wanted to use it. There is a place in Europe that's putting on line all of the rhetorical terms.

The question is not that, though, but to construct agile and imaginative pathways and an imaginative visual design. I happened to share a taxi with a woman from Apple to whom we demonstrated this product last week, and she liked it a lot but said we really need the services of a visual designer who's used to designing computer interfaces. Marry, well bethought. We're going to avail ourselves of one.

It just is so interesting to wonder how to do these things—the question of how you visually structure intellectual relationships: if you're constructing pathways, what kind of logos do you use? And you try to have a "logology" consistent across the document, across the program, the system, whatever it is. These are things I'm sure visual designers know about and study, but it's a new kind of ballgame.

To try to teach myself this, I'm teaching a course next quarter on the visual element in prose. We're going to talk about this changing icon/alphabet relationship and talk about typography and traditional type design and electronic type design. I'm going to try—I have no idea whether it'll work or not—using a desktop publishing system, Quark Express, as a pedagogical system—to teach the basic kinds of issues that are involved in designing text. I'm scared to death about this course because I don't know how to run Quark Express. I'm just learning and it's hard to teach a lab course.

WOE: Who is going to be in this course?

LANHAM: It's limited to fifteen undergraduates, but all kinds of different departments; there are only a couple of English majors, who are interested in the visual element in writing. Apple has a student representative and he's taking the course. So he knows how to run things. And they were kind enough to allow me to hire a consultant. She's a student, and she knows the system. So I have a backstop for my own ignorance. But it's going to be fun and that's what I think I need to know if I'm going to keep on—as I'm hoping to do—designing things like this.

Robert Winter has got to be the best schoolteacher I've ever seen in action. His programs—his Beethoven and Mozart courses—were taped and sold and broadcast over KUSC. He's a National Merit lecturer. He's done this phenomenal *Ninth Symphony* course, it's just super, and he and I are going to try a new undergraduate core curriculum course in the digital arts—the relationship of art, music, and literature and how they come together in digital expression. It really would take some doing.

WOE: Where do you get your ideas? Why Dada? How come John Cage's music? What is the mechanism that gets you to read and to study these things that later turn out to make sense? What do they have in common as objects of attention?

LANHAM: Well, I'll say something that may seem egotistical but I don't mean it to be. I somehow seem to have a kind of natural intellectual beam or center of things that I'm interested in (and I come across a lot of things), and when they're in my field, I understand them right away. When I read the Gleick book on chaos, I said, "OK, this is very clear: rhetoric is a theory of chaotic systems. Verbal systems. Piece of cake." I find this and recognize that it's grist to my mill right away.

And I just read a lot of different stuff. I've been interested in art history since I was an undergraduate. I could have been a major if I'd chosen to declare it that way. I was training to become an architect. So I read Venturi's book about Las Vegas because I just wanted to read it, and then I thought, "Well, this is the only sensible theory of the curriculum that's been produced in the twentieth century." Venturi didn't know it because he didn't write about the curriculum and the curriculum people didn't because they never read Robert Venturi.

I guess what it comes from finally is that I've never been a happy disciplinarian. My career would have been much more tranquil and I suspect I would have risen to such wealth and honor as academics get in a more precise and accomplished trajectory if I had stayed within a single field. I never thought that way. I know when I get outside my beam. It's just like one of those bombing beams—you go on either side of it and the noise stops.

My mind seems to have a logic of its own and I follow it. When I don't follow it, it tells me by being bored and shutting down. And I don't really have any control over it. It's interested in what it wants to be interested in and I can say, "Don't do that! They'll think you're crazy! Don't do that. Write another book on Sidney. Write a third book. Christ, you'll know more about Sidney than anyone." The second book you write is boring and you don't write it.

All the things that I think about and write about seem to me to make sense within some larger vision of things. And I've spent my life trying to decide what that is.

As I say, it seems to me that much of the most interesting writing about rhetoric is really writing about architecture. Well, the architects aren't interested in that, though a couple—Charles Jencks—use rhetorical terms like *chiasmus* or *gradatio* or things like that. I've always been this way, and when I read books about cryptography or electronic satellite surveillance or all these loony things I read about: I just have some sense that it's something I want to know.

I had a funny instance of that. I wrote an article during my Guggenheim year called "The Q Question." It turned out to be an essay review of a dozen books. I didn't set out to write that review; I was just reading those books because I wanted to read them. One of them was about the Anthony Blunt case, one of them was John Scully's autobiography, one of them was a book about Renaissance education, and one of them was the occasion I was asked to review Arthur Kinney's book on Renaissance rhetoric.

When I sat down to write it—I wrote that essay in one day—out it came, verbally, virtually unchanged. I took out a couple of books on legal theory because I either had to spend a lot more time with them or no time at all.

Suddenly I woke up in the middle of the night and said, "All these books belong together. They're all part of it. I'm reading them"—(though I didn't know it)—"to answer the same question." I just sat down one morning and wrote the whole thing.

Now, it's nothing I really have any control over. But I'm convinced I'm not a lunatic and I'm convinced that these things do belong together. And that they are part of a coherent story. So I've been willing to just go ahead and put them in. I wrote a long essay that's coming out in a Canadian journal called *Texte*, which started out as the introduction to the second edition of the *Handlist*. I reflected on what had happened to rhetorical figures in the twenty years since this book first appeared—and it's been in print for twenty years. That's kind of scary. I ended up writing this gigantic essay—the kind I never write, with 110 footnotes—but it's about all these things: sociobiology, chaos theory, role theory. In every one of those cases, in fact, formal or informal thinking about rhetoric is occurring.

But it is a wild collection of things and much too long to publish in the *Handlist*, so it was completely useless. I had to get it published and go write another one. That wasn't what I had in mind. I've been trying to pull it all together.

My colleagues don't understand this at all; I wouldn't try to begin to explain it to them. When they asked me what I was doing in my Guggenheim year, I used to say, "I'm writing this book." They said, "What is it about?" and I said, "I don't know." "What do you mean you don't know?" "I just don't know yet." But that was quite true. I knew somewhere what it was going to end up being, but it didn't come out to be that until I finally (I hope, knock on wood) got it straight. But I knew these things were going to come together somewhere and I was going to be able to see the pattern I wanted to see.

It's a catastrophic pattern which I absolutely disrecommend. It's the worst thing in the world to be or to do in the Academy because the Academy comes divided into subjects and departments. And if you don't observe those you get yourself in the marmalade over and over. I wrote a book on *Tristram Shandy*. Well, the people who read *Tristram Shandy* and the eighteenth century know that book, but they never read the *Motives of Eloquence* because that's about the sixteenth century and you don't ever read books in the sixteenth century if you're in the eighteenth century. And somebody else who's done both of these is also interested in composition? Well, that's ridiculous! People live in these water-tight compartments, and to move from one to the other is suspect. To move outside of literary study puts you way, way out in right field. It's the worst kind of pattern, I think, for an academic. But I couldn't have done it any other way.

And—I talk as if my career's over now; I hope not—I've really done whatever I wanted to do, whatever seemed like fun, the most fun then. Including doing the Writing Programs. That was the right time to do that. To try to start a writing program and run it and see what it was like to run an organization, to make sure that everybody had a chair and a desk and a job and was doing what they should.

I think that for most people—certainly for me—one of the great pleasures of a research career is that you do evolve some kind of coherent view of the world that belongs to you. It's much smarter, though, if you do your three books on Sterne or you become the Sterne person and you write nothing but Sterne. I really feel very, very lucky that somehow things have come together in the way they have in my own life.

So that's how I also blundered into multimedia, because it seemed the computer was the most interesting thing in rhetoric that could possibly have occurred. It was occurring and it was going to change the arts, and I don't know why I immediately then thought of Lichtenstein's comic book paintings, but I did. Because it obviously has to do with scale change, which is a fundamental thing in computer information, and it obviously has to do with this vibration of looking at things and looking through them. The whole idea of cartoon painting is big and small and taking what is a medium—making a picture out of teeny little dots—and blowing it up so that you see the dots and look at them rather than through them. It seemed like an isomorph, just a dead map of the same kind of thing occurring a different way. But I just always, hey, you know, follow these things.

I don't know why I got interested in Cage. I guess because he seemed so outrageous and such a smartass. I thought, "He's got to be my kind of guy. I'm sure I'm going to like him when I get to know him." And it turned out that I did. That he made so many people so mad is just wonderful. He can't be all bad! It would be a book by itself, I think, talking about Cage. Then I started listening to some of the music. And some of it's hard to hear both in the sense that it sometimes offends your ears and the sense that it's hard to track the records down and listen to it. But I had a stroke of luck there because of the coming of the CD and the fact that lots of people—record companies and private persons—are selling their collections of vinyl records to go CD. So I just go to the contemporary and electronic music bins at Record Surplus and buy all these records for a dollar apiece and listen to them.

WOE: They've probably scarcely been played.

LANHAM: Well, no, they haven't been played much. They're not worn out like recordings of the Beethoven *G-major Piano Concerto*. They haven't been worn out by use. Some of them are as strange as birds in the garden. But some of them, it's just fun to see what the hell is going on.

I even got the very hard-to-get records of a guy, a lunatic named Harry Partch who created not only his own set of instruments, reinvented all the instruments, but created a new system of tonality instead of the well-tempered system. I got his records and they're wonderful—they're terrific.

The sound is phenomenal. I am, as you know, a hi-fi freak, and they're incredibly well recorded and the sounds themselves, the instruments, are phenomenal. So I managed to do that. I haven't made any use of Harry Partch yet, but—nothing is wasted! Harry's gonna come in there. I've got a use for Harry. I don't know what it is yet. Maybe it's gonna be a background for some television program or something I do. But Harry's in the pipeline.

It's hard to know what to teach, though, because I'd like to teach a lot of multidisciplinary courses, and the UCLA environment is about the worst in the world for that. In a small college it would be much easier to do, but one where learning is so compartmentalized makes it very, very, very hard. Each graduate student is involved in a *cursus honorum* within that department, and if you wander outside it people wonder if you're a little flaky or soft.

I'm sure this is going to change, though, and I'm sure that the undergraduate curriculum in the arts and letters is absolutely going to be metamorphosed by electronic text. It can't be any other way. And that's going to be just extraordinary fun. All these contracts are, in fact, being renegotiated. But they're all being renegotiated off campus. The university doesn't know anything about them, all these revolutions that are happening, over and over, in computer graphics companies, in the multimedia work being done by the big movie studios, by Disney for Epcot in Orlando, by MCA for their new Orlando park. I have a dear friend who lives up the road from me who is supervising this whole new—they hate to call them attractions; they've got a more eulogistic epithet—theme park in Orlando that MCA is doing. He just comes back and makes me envious. I wish I had that job. So all kinds of interesting things are happening. They're not happening very much in the universities and that's a great pity. But they'll have to.

WOE: Is there something we should have asked you but didn't?

LANHAM: I don't think so. I guess I've talked about what I'm doing, as well as figured out some things that I used to be doing that I hadn't thought about for ten years, like getting interested in writing. You witnessed something new in my career just now before we came up here. That talk on copyright was the first scholarly talk I've given about that part of my life, which has after all been fairly appreciable and has gone on for twenty years. I've worked on nearly fifty cases of one kind or another. I've gotten a fairish education in certain aspects of copyright law. I've gotten a fairish education in certain aspects of the entertainment business—in deal making if not filmmaking. I've gotten a fairish kind of education in the actual pressures of two-sided argument in a courtroom. I've gotten a very interesting perspective on the fragility of the copyright umbrella. The whole history of Anglo-American copyright law is based on print. And that envelope is now going to be changed absolutely. It's very fragile. I've gotten an idea about how that works that I didn't have before.

So I guess I've had what amounts to a second career. It took a lot of time: sometimes it's brutally hard work. That's the only part of me that we haven't covered. And I'm now talking about it a little bit more theoretically. I guess the copyright work will be a part of my intellectual environment from now on. That part of my life has been subversive: I never talked about it in a formal way or appended it to my bio-bibliography, which I now do. This is a part of my life I guess I'll start talking about.

ANDREA LUNSFORD AND LISA EDE

Friends since graduate school, Andrea Lunsford and Lisa Ede are leading theorists of collaborative writing and feminist rhetoric. From their first co-authored article in Rhetoric Review *in 1983 to their edited collection* Writing Together: Collaboration in Theory and Practice *(2012), these scholars have challenged the field of rhetoric and composition to move beyond Enlightenment individualism and recognize "how much of the world's writing is done collaboratively, how much knowledge is cocreated and coproduced."[1] In the era of Wikipedia, their turn to collaborative authorship has never been more relevant. Lunsford and Ede have also published prolifically on issues of audience, new media, and the history of rhetoric.*

Andrea Lunsford completed her PhD in English at the Ohio State University in 1977. She has written or coauthored 14 books, including the composition handbook The Everyday Writer *(2005). Lunsford and Ede's* Singular Texts/Plural Authors: Perspectives on Collaborative Writing *(1990) was the impetus for the following interview. This text argues that singular authorship remains the academic ideal but fails to address the collective nature of on-the-job writing, the poststructuralist critique of the founding subject, or the voices of women historically silenced by the ideal of the independent male author.[2] Lunsford returns to issues of women's rhetoric in* Reclaiming Rhetorica: Women in the History of Rhetoric *(1995) and takes up new-media composing in* Writing Matters: Rhetoric in Public and Private Lives *(2007). Lunsford received the 1994 CCCC Exemplar Award for outstanding contributions to the field. Retired since 2013, she served as director of the program in Writing and Rhetoric at Stanford University from 2000–2012.*

Lisa Ede also attended the Ohio State University for her doctorate, graduating in 1975. Now retired from active teaching, Ede taught rhetoric and writing at Oregon State University from 1980–2013. Ede has authored, co-authored, edited, and co-edited eight books including Work in Progress: A Guide to Academic Writing and Revising *(1989),* Situating Composition: Composition Studies and the Politics of Location *(2004), and* The Academic Writer: A Brief Guide for Students *(2008).*

—Sarah Klotz

---

1 Lunsford, Andrea and Lisa Ede, ed. *Writing Together: Collaboration in Theory and Practice*. Boston: Bedford/St. Martin's, 2012: (4). Print.
2 Lunsford, Andrea. "Rhetoric, Feminism, and the Politics of Textual Ownership." *Feminism and Composition: A Critical Source Book*. Ed. Gesa E. Kirsch et al. Boston: Bedford/St. Martin's, 2003: (180–93). Print.

"Collaboration as a Subversive Activity"

Alice Heim Calderonello, Donna Beth Nelson, and Sue Carter Simmons

Spring 1991

WOE: When did the two of you first begin to collaborate?

EDE: We first decided to collaborate when we both lived in the Northwest. We were driving along the coast in Oregon, just having fun, and we began talking about the book we wanted to do with Bob Connors in honor of Ed Corbett (*Essays on Classical Rhetoric and Modern Discourse*). So it must have been about 1983. Anyway, we were riding along and one of us said that Ed was such a wonderful person that surely he'd be very pleased to see his students were friends and that they were working with one another. Then we got to talking about what we might do for the book; each of us had thought of writing an essay as well as editing the collection. Suddenly one of us said, "Why don't we collaborate on something together?"

LUNSFORD: I don't think we even said "collaborate," though. I don't think that verb was in our vocabulary. We just said "do it together."

EDE: After we made the decision to write together, we told Ed and got an astonished response. He said that he couldn't figure out how we'd do it, that our writing together was the most extraordinary thing! We got a lot of remarkable reactions. People would take us aside and give us advice, or treat us like we were Martians or as if we had some kind of weird game going. Colleagues seemed astounded or worried.

LUNSFORD: Or suspicious.

WOE: What were they suspicious of?

LUNSFORD: How we could write together. Who was doing what writing? Who was the author? Where did the authority lie?

EDE: People also asked very specific questions. They would say, "All right, you are co-authoring this, but really Andrea wrote the first part and you wrote the second, right?" Or they'd ask, "One of you had final control over the style, didn't you?" And when we would say "no," they treated us like we were people who had just been to the New World. Or like we were incapable of doing something by ourselves—so feebleminded alone that we had banded together. Two women with ONE BRAIN!

WOE: Were some of the people who were "warning you off" colleagues in your respective departments?

LUNSFORD: Yes. They just couldn't understand.

EDE: One colleague even called me up and said, "Lisa, you've got to stop doing this. You're not going to get tenure."

WOE: Did anyone say what a wonderful idea your collaboration was, that it was so exciting?

LUNSFORD and EDE: Nope.

WOE: Not one?

EDE: Not to me.

LUNSFORD: Never.

WOE: But you'd known each other for a long time; you were good friends, and that helped you with all of this. Right?

LUNSFORD: Yes, we got to know each other in graduate school. Lisa graduated ahead of me in '75, and I graduated in '77. After we finished we went on to other places, but we kept in touch. We have always been friends.

EDE: During the years when I was in Brockport and you were in Columbus and then in Vancouver, though, we were not as close as when I moved to the West Coast. Our physical proximity was an absolute precondition for working together in those early years, don't you think?

LUNSFORD: Yes. It would have been impossible otherwise.

EDE: But also, we already knew that since we had similar work habits and styles we would not have radical problems, although our writing styles have changed somewhat.

WOE: Have your styles changed in the same direction?

LUNSFORD: A little; my style has gotten more complex and Lisa's has gotten a bit more simple syntactically.

EDE: I like dashes.

LUNSFORD: And I like things sort of stark. Lisa left-branches and embeds and I tend to move relentlessly from subject to verb.

WOE: Sounds like an effective collaboration.

LUNSFORD: Well, it took us a while to realize that. I'd go through and remove dashes; Lisa would put them back.

WOE: What about your collaborative styles; have they changed?

LUNSFORD: We have done a number of different kinds of collaboration. In fact, today, for the very first time, we sat and composed together at the computer, with me moaning every moment because I hate composing at the computer. In the past, we have divided things up, drafted separate parts and then traded them, or we've worked on the same text longhand. We've even written things over the phone.

WOE: How do you do that?

EDE: It's not hard, actually, except you have to be very explicit about what you're referring to.

LUNSFORD: The very last part of our most recent book was written that way. We talked for probably an hour and a half and then I wrote it down. I was the one who put the words down on paper; Lisa was in Rhode Island, or somewhere.

EDE: Massachusetts.

LUNSFORD: Massachusetts, and she didn't have any equipment or anything. In essence, we wrote it on the long-distance telephone call, and then I just marked it down.

WOE: You sound like remarkable friends and collaborators. Have you ever had tugs-of-war or disagreements over your writing?

LUNSFORD: Sure. We've had some squabbles.

EDE: But we usually negotiate things. Although I remember a very difficult time in Seattle when Andrea and I were meeting at a motel to write.

LUNSFORD: We would arrive with our typewriters.

EDE: And they would extend check-out time for us. We were doing an article for *Written Communication*; it was Andrea's 40th birthday. We worked until midnight that night. We really had trouble with that article and had already gotten an extension on the deadline. We got up the next morning and worked on it, but it still wasn't finished, and we had to leave. Since Andrea can write anywhere, she said, "Let's just go finish this in our car," which was in an incredibly horrible parking lot. I said, "Andrea, I can't. I just cannot." And Andrea was saying, "Yes you can; you can do it." Finally, I just had to put my foot down and we ended up going to a noisy restaurant.

WOE: Did you take your typewriters in with you?

EDE: No. We were exhausted.

LUNSFORD: I think if we hadn't been friends, really committed friends, we would have had a big fight, because that was also the time when Lisa kept changing the opening sentence. Everything depended on the opening, and Lisa would say, "No, I think I have to take Rosenfeld and move him up here." And I would say, "Okay," and rewrite that part and then she would change her mind and tell me to put it back the other way. This went on and on and on.

EDE: It was a complicated article.

LUNSFORD: It was; it was very hard for us. But I was peeved—although there was nothing Lisa could do about it in trying to make it right. I was irritated, and here I was staying up all night on my 40th birthday—supposedly a "big" one.

WOE: Wait a minute. Andrea, you wanted to write in a grungy parking lot on your birthday?

EDE: No. No. Her birthday was actually the night before, and *then* we'd written until late in a grungy motel room with plaster-of-paris flamingos hanging on the wall. We were dead. Right before midnight, Andrea took a shower and said, "What's for dinner? Let's have a party."

But seriously, I don't think we have ever had really big disagreements, certainly not about content. We just work our way through, and if one of us says something doesn't feel right, then we talk about it.

LUNSFORD: I think, too, that because we have been friends a long time, we have been through some periods of real adversity together, the kind of experience that you most often have with family members. Those struggles tie you to someone and make you want to stretch yourself around difficulties. Lisa and I have that history, which makes it pretty unlikely that we'd fall out over something like a pair of dashes.

WOE: Given your own experiences and problems with collaboration and the skepticism of your colleagues, is collaboration something you'd recommend to other faculty—especially to those just starting out?

EDE: My immediate response is that you need a supportive relationship. And whether you are working with someone who is more established than you are or whether you are working with a peer and are both first-year people, collaboration can be very efficient. There are things that you can do together that you might not be able to do alone, and often that allows you to have a kind of scope and significance that you're simply unable to have by yourself. When Andrea and I started writing together, she knew more about classical rhetoric, and I was more immersed in contemporary rhetoric. Working together, we could teach each other.

LUNSFORD: I enjoy my collaboration with Lisa so much that I prefer doing projects together over writing alone. However, I would never suggest that a young faculty member do all scholarship collaboratively and simply hope that everything will be all right. I think that new faculty members should discuss collaborative writing with their chairs or with those who will be evaluating their scholarship. If possible, a beginning faculty member should choose a department with a senior person in rhetoric and composition who could make a strong case for the value of the junior member's collaboratively produced work. Fortunately, our professional organization is starting to support faculty members as they begin to challenge traditional modes of scholarship. In today's mail I got a copy of the CCCC's statement for chairs, deans, and provosts on how to evaluate work in rhetoric and composition; included is a strong statement about collaboration.

EDE: Andrea's cautionary statements are really important: people at the start of their careers have to be careful. And if they choose to collaborate, they have to be careful about whom they collaborate with.

WOE: What advice about selecting a good partner would you offer to people who have never collaborated?

LUNSFORD: A collaborative writing dating service. You get matched up.

EDE: But assuming you couldn't rely on *that*, there are a few suggestions I could make. First of all, I think the selection of one or more collaborators should depend in part on your needs. I could imagine, for example, a situation where I would choose to work with someone primarily because of what she knew or because that person and I have been investigating the same subject. Under these circumstances we might or might not be friends, but for pragmatic reasons a collaboration makes sense. On the other hand, I don't think anyone would embark on the kind of sustained collaboration that Andrea and I have had over the years without there being other reasons to work together.

LUNSFORD: For instance, if a job is too big for one person. I think that is one of the reasons that graduate students or faculty with heavy teaching loads can collaborate successfully and productively: they want to do big projects and there's not enough time to do them alone.

EDE: I think there are some other requirements also. Successful collaborators probably share certain work habits and ways of thinking. A couple of years ago, Andrea and I began to realize that we approached work somewhat similarly. For instance, if we make commitments, we tend to keep them, we can meet deadlines within reason, and we are both fairly linear thinkers. Then too, we tend to behave similarly as writers: one of us doesn't prewrite pages and pages to discover one nugget while the other outlines everything. As a result of our collaboration with one another and with others, we have also discovered that interpersonal skills are very important. The ability to articulate how you're feeling, to stop and comment, or to be aware that someone is demonstrating discomfort and to respond to that before she goes crazy is absolutely essential.

LUNSFORD: One of the most interesting things about collaborative writing is that you become less invested in your writing. Lisa and I have talked for many years about our perception that we have less ego involvement in the things that we write together than we used to have in things that we wrote alone. The quality of a collaborative experience is strongly related to each collaborator's ability to be receptive, to let everything show—the stupidities, the backsliding and illogicalities, and everything else that goes into writing a text—as well as to be open to those things in the other person, and to the other person's strengths. Something necessary within our own collaboration is our willingness to lead or to follow or to do both in a particular project. That is largely unstated between us, but important, I think.

WOE: Collaboration certainly creates special challenges for all of us in our roles as scholars. Does it also present problems for us in our roles as teachers?

LUNSFORD: Yes. In my opinion it does, especially with respect to assigning grades. In a recent graduate class that I taught, I saw that I was going to have trouble grading the students' performance, since much of the work was to have been done collaboratively. I brought my dilemma to the class, explaining that grading could discourage people from taking risks and might undercut the trust we were trying to establish. The students' reactions were extraordinarily varied: some felt a need for a grade; others didn't want any grades. We finally agreed they would write analyses of their contributions to and performance in class and that grades would be individually negotiated in conference with me. The evaluation process required a great deal of time, although the class had only 13 people in it. I could not undertake this kind of process with an undergraduate class of 45 students.

WOE: Was it difficult to discuss pedagogical problems associated with collaboration in your book?

EDE: We struggled with our fourth chapter, "The Pedagogy of Collaboration," all the way to the very end.

LUNSFORD: I had a goal, something driving me, to make that chapter as pragmatic as possible. I wanted to instruct teachers how to use collaboration in their classes, to provide them with a little blueprint of what to do on Monday, and so on. When Lisa started to resist that idea, we changed the pedagogy section of the book significantly. Through a series of discussions with Lisa, I came to see the potential problem of teachers' reading our chapter and going into their traditional, institutionally constrained, patriarchal classrooms, attempting to introduce collaboration without any introspection or any changes in the way that power is distributed in the class or the academy.

WOE: What did you finally decide to do with that chapter as a result of your discussions?

EDE: We made our difficulties part of the chapter itself. At the start of Chapter 4, we discussed our initial vision of the chapter and explained why we couldn't write it that way, *why* it wasn't right to do that. The crunch comes when you try to take theoretical ideas and apply them. I still have a kind of uneasiness about the chapter.

LUNSFORD: And I'm just not completely satisfied with what we came up with. It is going to be very interesting to me to see the reaction to that chapter.

WOE: I certainly can see that writing Chapter 4 presented you with many difficulties to work out. Were there any other parts of the book that presented particular challenges?

LUNSFORD: Oh, yes—how to list our names. For instance, when we started writing together, we decided we would list our names alphabetically, but someone said to us—

EDE: Ed Corbett. He asked us how we were going to list our names. We told him we were going to list them alphabetically, a decision that we thought would be perfectly clear to people. But he said, "No way!" Then we started alternating our names.

WOE: When you publish together, you alternate whose name is listed first?

EDE: Yes. We have tried to do so, though we have not always been able to keep in sequence.

LUNSFORD: I have completely lost track of whose turn it is to go first.

EDE: Me too. Still, we definitely have made the effort to alternate.

LUNSFORD: In this book, we wanted very much to subvert the tradition of first and second author. We played around with a lot of different things. In the preface of the book, we say we thought about taking a new name, like Analisa Lunsede, or Edesford.

WOE: Oh, I like that!

LUNSFORD: But we decided that taking a new name would put people to so much trouble that it didn't seem like a good idea in the long run. Next we tried my favorite idea, having our names in a Mobius-strip design. We tried to do that on the computer, but we just couldn't get the three-dimensional perspective right. Then the editor thought of what we finally used. The verso and recto of the title page have a border at the top, starting in the middle of one of our names and running them together. The border reads, "drealunsfordlisaedeandrealunsfordlisaedean..." and trails off. The border begins again on the bottom of the pages. Lisa's name will actually be listed first in the card catalog because the names will be cataloged alphabetically. But still, we wanted some typographical representation of our attempt to subvert the tradition of first author, something that would say to our readers, "We know you will look for the first author, and we have tried to keep you from being able to find her."

WOE: Aside from Ed Corbett's initial concern with how your names would be listed when you first began to write together, were there other people or experiences that made you become so concerned with how the authorship of this book would be attributed?

EDE: I think it came out, in part, from my tenure experience. My department has been very supportive of our co-authoring, but even so they have treated it as a difficult problem that they had to solve. First, my chair asked Andrea to write a letter talking about our collaboration. Later, the college committee also wrote and asked Andrea for comments. We took these requests very seriously because we knew of individuals who were denied promotion because their co-authored and co-edited works were not considered.

WOE: At all?

EDE: At all. As though they didn't exist. In addition, I had been party to many discussions at my university about how co-authored or co-edited books are evaluated. There is a very strong belief throughout our field and others that there is a first or "primary" author who must be identified. My chair and I argued about this with other university administrators, who were fairly unrelenting. Andrea's and my desire to subvert the tradition of who is the first author in our book grew out of our personal experience, but also out of all the anomalies we were finding in our research. While we were doing our research, and talking about our own problems with the tradition of first author, we would get these bits of material from people who had found out about our research.

LUNSFORD: We had big files, slips of this, little notes of that, pieces cut from newspapers. We didn't know what to do with all these materials, so we just kept stuffing them into our files. One day while Lisa was here in my house—we were sitting out in the sun room—we decided to put them in the book. We decided that preceding each chapter, there would be some pages set in different type where we would put all of these little bits of things. We decided to call them intertexts. Our practical goal was to get as many of these intertexts into the book as possible, but our theoretical goal was to demonstrate the ways in which our book was written by many people besides ourselves. Many voices, many names appear in between the chapters.

EDE: With the intertexts, we tried to make a pastiche that would have these voices talk with each other; they are just presented with no comment. We have, for example, a piece about a computer program that writes poetry; a statement by John Gardner about how much his wife helped him write his book and how had the world been different, he might have called her coauthor; and a clipping from the Hershorn Museum catalog about collaboration in the arts a friend of mine from Brockport had sent me. Next to that, we have a wonderful statement by the one surviving member of the two Irish coauthors, Sommerville and Ross. After one of them had died, the survivor said that just as an established legal firm does not change its name when one of the partners dies, she will not, either.

WOE: From these examples, it seems you found that when people write together, the concept of authorship, of "who the author is," becomes very complicated.

LUNSFORD: Yes, especially in fields like the sciences where credit and power are toted up based on who is listed as the first author.

WOE: Do you mean that even if the authors are listed alphabetically, the assumption is that the first author listed gets all or most of the credit as the "primary" author?

LUNSFORD: Yes, the first author is *the* author. In some fields, there are huge fights over who gets credit for authorship. You might have heard in the news recently about the AIDS research which was delayed in publication for 10 years because some of the people were fighting over who would be listed as first author.

EDE: Occasionally, we found that one journal within a discipline might encourage authors to be listed alphabetically, but that is very rare. The prevailing practice is still that the first author is the primary author. Not only that: the practice of cataloging and indexing compounds the already-complicated ethical questions about how authorship is attributed when there are multiple authors. For example, some indexes that routinely deal with material by scientists who are working as professors require that a first author and any other authors be listed. But other indexes that deal with research done on a contract basis will not mention authors, even if they are listed on the title page. As a result of these arbitrary practices, some indexing services are taking authorship away from people who want it and giving authorship to people who don't.

WOE: In the humanities, or at least in literary studies, the concept of authorship has been problematic for theorists for some time now. Did you come across similar concerns in other fields?

EDE: Yes, we came across research in several fields about the practical, procedural, and logistical questions of co-authorship as it is being practiced today. If you read articles about how computers are making authorship obsolete, you can see that we are actually in a state where the material conditions of authorship have changed. All of a sudden Foucault in "What Is an Author?" doesn't seem to be looking ahead—

LUNSFORD: —but seems, instead, almost old fashioned.

EDE: Yes, Foucault was discussing, on a theoretical level, practices those of us in the humanities have been completely oblivious to, even though they are happening all around us.

LUNSFORD: And meanwhile, those people in other fields are completely unaware of the attacks on the construct of the author and the subject in literary theory. One of the most surprising items on this topic was a book by a librarian, a cataloger, called *Corporate Authorship: Its Role in Library Cataloging*.

EDE: Addressed to other catalogers, his book is a practical guide, completely isolated from the theoretical concerns of our field. Yet the author does a deconstruction—although he would not call it that—of authorship, describing writing as writing in, writing out, writing down, writing up, and writing over. All these *functions* for writing. The consequence of his deconstruction is that library catalogers have to abandon any concept of authorship as originary, as "intellectual property."

WOE: What does he propose to replace it with?

LUNSFORD: Author function, as Foucault would say.

WOE: You have said on other occasions that you think collaboration is potentially a subversive activity. Why is that?

LUNSFORD: We obviously think it is subversive; in fact, Lisa and I were writing about that today. But potentially only.

EDE: Collaboration, as it is predominately practiced in the United States today, seems to us not to be subversive but just a very efficient means towards achieving a goal. As such, the subversive potential can easily be co-opted, and all kinds of complicated issues having to do with ownership can be raised. One of the people we interviewed, for example, was an engineer. After five hours of interviewing him and his team members we found out, at the very end, that his secretary played a substantial role in the production of their texts, not just coordinating various aspects of the process, but in actually doing a lot of the writing, gathering together boilerplate materials, and so forth.

LUNSFORD: But the engineer was so dominant—his voice and stance were so powerful—that he erased everybody else. Another potential problem with collaboration is that it can create a set of circumstances where responsibility is totally absent; authority isn't situated *anywhere*, and so it exists nowhere You think of the *Challenger* disaster as sort of the perfect example of collaboration gone berserk, where nobody is willing to take responsibility and things fall apart. Or collaboration can be a masquerade for the same old patriarchal, hierarchical structures—the patriarchal wolf in collaborative sheep's clothing.

EDE: Still, collaboration can be subversive even if it is hierarchical. A group of people can get together in many different ways that could be characterized as subversive. Collaborative writing is a culturally situated activity; we could do an ethnographic study of two teams that seem to be hierarchically organized and find that one is functioning radically differently from the other. So we need to resist any kind of categorical statements about the relationship between how a group is structured and its potential for subversive activity.

WOE: Do you think that collaborative writing is subversive within the academy?

LUNSFORD: Yes, within the institution, to some extent, and within the classroom collaboration is subversive because it challenges notions of individual authorship and responsibility for an autonomous text. We know also that it challenges our whole system of testing, measurement, and evaluation and that it questions the way we, as teachers, respond to and assess our students. Collaborative practices are often at odds with traditional classroom structure, which locates the authority for assigning a grade solely with the teacher. Our whole system of evaluation is shot through with the notion that a "creator" resides somewhere in the head of each person, and that this creator can be isolated, defined, tested, measured, and compared; everything that Lisa and I discovered in the course of our project challenges that notion and makes us uncomfortable as teachers and evaluators.

WOE: What future studies in collaboration would you suggest?

LUNSFORD: Certainly there is a lot of room for pedagogical research. No one knows enough about how collaborative groups really work.

EDE: We need to do ethnographic and longitudinal studies.

LUNSFORD: We also need to think more about the concept of "The Author"—and how it may differ from "writer."

EDE: Yes. One of the wonderful things that we discovered in our research was a statement about authorship from an 18th-century German dictionary, which basically said that the dictionary was a means of expressing God's truth and that many people worked on it. The writer was listed along with many others—the papermaker, the book binder, gilder, scholar—as contributing to this work.

LUNSFORD: One of our intertexts is from a woman who is writing interactive fiction for a computer program. She is writing the story—the plot, the dialogue, everything—but she is "just" the writer. The programmer is The Author.

WOE: But what do you call a person who buys the program and writes a story?

LUNSFORD: Good question.

LINDA FLOWER

Linda Flower has published extensively on the composing process, and remains one of the most frequently cited authors in the field of composition and rhetoric. Her initial research focused on monitoring the cognitive processes of writers as they composed. Working with cognitive psychologist John R. Hayes, a colleague at Carnegie-Mellon University, Flower taped sessions during which writers thought aloud as they composed. Analysis of these sessions revealed information about the behavior of writers that was previously difficult to observe and collect. Because of her work, protocol analysis became an important research tool for the study of the composing process, leading to improved instruction by providing writing teachers a more complete understanding of cognitive processes in the production of text.

In Reading to Write: Exploring a Cognitive and Social Process (1990), *Flower and her colleagues explore how students approach reading assignments, concluding that the reading process, like the writing process, involves a complex mix of cognitive and social factors. When students are asked to read, they consider the context of the assignment, reading based on what they think or know about the subsequent writing assignment. In* The Construction of Negotiated Meaning: A Social Cognitive Theory of Writing (1994), *Flower examines how writers negotiate meaning when faced with conflicting ideas and tension between forces like contexts, expectations, rhetorical situations, and personal goals. Her more recent work explores rhetoric in the public sphere, looking at ways in which marginalized voices and communities can establish rhetorical agency. In 2009 Flower received the Rhetorical Society of America Book Award for* Community Literacy and the Rhetoric of Public Engagement (2008), *in which she argues that community literacy allows for intercultural dialogue, which calls for people from different cultural groups to interact with ideas that differ from their own. In addition to encouraging groups to learn from each other's experiences, these conversations can empower members of marginalized groups who do not often have a public voice. Due to the collaborative nature of community literacy, differences can spark discovery and change. Cultural imbalances and differences are addressed rather than ignored, allowing groups to work together to negotiate what it means to be in a community together.*

Linda Flower is a professor of English at Carnegie-Mellon University where she has served as co-director of the National Center for the Study of Writing and Literacy, and Director of the CMU Center for University Outreach.

—Mandy Proctor

"Helping Writers Build Mansions with More Rooms"

Jill Wilson

Fall 1991

WOE: How did you first get interested in composition research?

FLOWER: Like many other graduate students, I was thrust into teaching a writing class where I realized that the explanations I gave to students had to be explanations I would be willing to hear about my own writing. I felt the burden of having to tell students something substantive about how to improve their writing. The information available at the time didn't speak to me at an adult level and certainly didn't speak to me as a graduate student who was struggling to write a dissertation. The need to say something substantive motivated me to talk to people in psychology. When I began, I was trying to find out more about how readers understand texts because that seemed to be something that we might know something about.

I was reading psycholinguistics and linguistics, trying to understand what to do to speak to a reader. Unfortunately, that reading didn't bring me any closer to that kind of thinking. But about the same time I met Dick Hayes, a psychologist, who was interested in problem solving. I was interested in writing as an instance of problem solving. Working together, we had an opportunity to investigate thinking processes in ways that have departed from other work in problem-solving research because writing takes you off in new directions. Writing is a much more complicated process than many other topics studied in cognitive psychology. My research has taken a right turn from there, or maybe a left turn.

WOE: And taken a turn also from the typical kind of research that would be done in composition. So it was, in fact, a wedding of the two fields?

FLOWER: Yes. And for me it was a way to try to get at the thinking because that was problematic in my own writing—trying to figure out how I was going to do this. The problem wasn't prose style. It was writing an article that would find its way in the competitive discourse community of literature studies. At the time, my work was in literature and I wanted to find a way to say something new about 19th-century literature. Yet I had the sense that one ideally should be white-haired, 50, and male to have the ethos and voice to write in that field. How did someone who didn't fit this profile become a publishable, publishing writer?

WOE: So you developed a method of using protocols to learn what a writer is thinking while composing. Has what you have learned about protocols changed your own writing habits? Do you approach the task differently now?

FLOWER: When I began the research, I was trying to find something out during the day that I could consider myself during the night and then tell my students about the next day. What the cognitive psychology tradition of research offered in particular was not only the problem-solving paradigm but also the expert/novice method as a way of teasing out what's important in the data—the differences in how more and less experienced writers approach the task.

At the beginning, the goal was to find out what expert writers were doing and at the same time identify what caused problems for other writers. Novice writers have other strategies. College students, for example, have strategies that may have worked very well in high school. In my reading-to-write study I learned that students have a logic in their writing, that they bring an approach based on the culture of recitation from high school to their college writing tasks, even though some of their assumptions are not a good fit with what their instructors may be assuming without making articulate. Part of the research is designed to help us understand the logic that kids are bringing to the writing task.

WOE: It seems important to help students understand what approach works for them. When I used your text in my class, we discussed the strategies described as weak and strong. I tried not to make moral judgments but to encourage students to consider what worked best for them.

FLOWER: Yes. I think there's a real tension in this research—in the expert/novice paradigm that wants to describe expert strategies, that wants to say there is a better way to build this mousetrap, that wants to say here are some things experienced writers do and here are some typical garden paths inexperienced writers go down.

The work I'm doing now with collaborative planning grew out of earlier work which looked at expert/novice differences in planning and suggested that the experienced writers spend a lot of time thinking about things like their purpose and its relationship to the reader. Expert writers consider how the reader will react and figure out a text strategy that will guide the reader "here" rather than "there." These writers sit back and say, "Okay, now where am I? How can I put this all together?" This kind of consolidation is not characteristic of novice writers.

When experienced writers hit a conflict, they handle it by rising above the immediate problem and thinking about the whole plan. Novice writers will not do this. If their task is to write about their job, for example, they might say "I'll try to write about my job for these girls." But when they try to talk about engineering in girl talk, they run into problems. So they abandon that and just talk about the job, and then they'll move into easy talk. Finally, they realize that this approach isn't going to work for those girls and they'll stop. They're hopping back and forth off of trains that aren't going to get them to the same place.

WOE: And they're unable to conceptualize?

FLOWER: Yes. They can't jump back up to a plan that might handle both these things. When you see this happen, you want to tell writers that there are real differences in what novice and expert writers are doing and that consolidation helps to solve some problems. So that's one thrust of my research—to share good techniques.

But there's a real problem with that. You mentioned one. Sometimes what looks like a good strategy may not work. But that's the least problem. Actually, much more important is that students often don't understand what you're talking about. When you describe a strategy, some students will say, "Oh, that's what that is. Yeah." They're ready to learn; they're ripe to have a name and metacognitive control over something. When this happens, you feel good and you're home free. But there's also another group in the class who don't do this, who can't do this.

WOE: Yes, and they don't perceive the problem at all. They don't understand what you're talking about.

FLOWER: So you name the strategy or you describe it, and it's still not going to make any difference. You can't teach thinking by simply—well, you can teach some aspects of thinking by simply describing and opening up possibilities. That's really important. You can give people a tremendous leg up sometimes just by helping them see things. But at the same time, that's clearly not enough for many other students. I think that's become the next problem for me. It's one thing to see some things that are worth teaching. But it's something else to help students experience the process of using a strategy and eventually mastering it. That's where collaborative planning is taking me. In collaborative planning, students sit down with each other and talk about the process as it is happening.

WOE: Because the writer is not doing the planning for herself, the situation provides the writer with a guide who acts in a metacognitive way; the other student, the guide, is there to prompt the writer to think about *how* she's thinking.

FLOWER: It's really a student simply asking, "Have you thought about it? Tell me what you've thought." And this back-and-forth discussion helps the writer to think on the spot.

WOE: Yes. Children often talk to themselves aloud as they learn something new. They tell themselves what to do next. Some research in child development has suggested that children with certain learning disabilities don't talk to themselves while they do things. The metacognitive process of telling yourself what you are doing and what to do next is crucial for learning. In the case of collaborative learning, the partner serves the metacognitive function of talker. If someone outside can serve that purpose for you, then maybe you'll internalize it and start to do it for yourself.

FLOWER: Yes, and of course, the big question is, what is the "it" that you are doing? One of the most powerful metaphors to come out of cognitive research says that in thinking things through, people are actually "constructing" meaning; they are constructing a network of ideas. Now if you have a very limited representation of your task or of what your reader needs, you may construct a relatively limited meaning. Whereas a writer who has a complex representation, who has set a lot of goals for him or herself, who keeps imagining a reader talking back, and so on, keeps building on this mental network in response to all these goals, constraints, prompts, and possibilities. The writer literally constructs a different, expanded meaning. And the process of writing itself helps you build these webs of meaning—the very words you use call up not only other words, but like Bakhtin describes, they call up other voices, stances, contexts. Or the need to write a topic sentence or transition forces you to draw an inference, build a connection that wasn't there in your thinking before.

What happens in joint planning sessions is similar. Students are encouraged to generate a richer representation of how their ideas are linked to other people's ideas, to other people as readers, to their own experience. It's providing a time and a space and helping writers build mansions with more rooms.

WOE: When you talk and write about research, you almost always do so in the context of an educational situation. Your work is directed toward helping people learn to write, which is one of the things I like most about your research. But so often research in composition has no secure home in the university. The composition program is often a stepchild of the English department. Many times the faculty who teach composition are not tenure-track faculty, so they seldom have the time or funds to do research. What could or should be done about the place of research in composition departments around the country?

FLOWER: The kinds of scholarship and research you can do in composition represent some of the most exciting possibilities in English studies today because I think they're a way to get at the process of making meaning and of thinking. Not just isolated people thinking, but the kind of thinking that is related to social perspectives, to values, to issues of equity and diversity. The kinds of questions that you ask in rhetoric and composition are not rarified questions posed by a group of professional elite talking to itself.

WOE: And asking esoteric questions?

FLOWER: Yes, that's a very good word. The research I'm interested in poses fundamental questions about the nature of literacy and about the ways people construct meaning for themselves and others. I think this kind of work is at the heart of what English studies can and should be doing for both intellectual and social reasons. For one thing, that kind of study, compared to studying the canon (which has its value too), enfranchises the abilities of all kinds of people with all kinds of languages, cultural and ethnic backgrounds, and roles in life. I think it can play an important part in broadening our idea of English departments as places to study the literate powers of everybody, not just people who possess one kind of literacy, one particular literate practice, like writing the freshman theme as a particular literate practice.

I am very lucky because I am able to get support for the work I do. I can get somebody to transcribe my tapes and I have the opportunity to work with some brilliant, motivated graduate students. I'm in a wonderful research environment. But I don't see research as having to go on only in that kind of environment. I guess I see myself as doing two kinds of research. One I think of as classroom inquiry. I don't think I've ever taught a course without somehow trying to learn something about my students and at the same time find a way for them to be researchers about themselves, as writers. Some of the efforts have bombed. But I've learned a lot. The classroom has been the starting point and locus of research for me, especially in the past few years. The reading-to-write book I'm doing is really a classroom inquiry, starting with the students doing dorm-room protocols and then coming back to the classroom to discuss their experience. I was using the technique because I thought it would make students learn something. But it just knocked me over when they came back and started talking about what they learned about their own writing. Everybody in that room had a different conception of what the task was. And it was a miniature task—I'd made it open ended like a lot of college writing tasks. Suddenly, I realized that this is the most important thing that I may have to teach in this class. In the next few years that discovery led to a more and more formal study where those kinds of observations could be tracked, could be tested more carefully, could be balanced by converging evidence and provide a bigger picture of both the social dimensions and the cognitive dimensions of that representation.

The history of collaborative planning, however, has a funny twist. We were in the middle of an exploratory study of planning [to appear in *A Rhetoric of Doing*, Sage], and we began experimenting with using the computer as a collaborative partner to prompt more rhetorical thinking. We had a hunch that some of the differences you see between experts and novices are a case of "don't" not "can't," and we wanted to see more of what freshmen could do if they thought to. We were developing a better research tool, but our subjects were coming back saying, "This would have really helped me on my last paper; can my roommate come in to be a subject?" If a dialogue with a computer could do this, think how much more you could accomplish with a person.

I began to see how collaborative planning could help me translate our research on planning strategies into my teaching. It got students working in a supportive social setting, thinking about rhetorical decisions, not in the classrooms, but in the dorm room, in the midst of writing. Although students often talk informally about papers, they hadn't worked with each other in such a systematic, supported way. They hadn't worked with a partner who was dedicated to helping them develop their own plan, or who kept asking them to think about the hard things such as, what is your purpose, how will your reader respond to that? And because these collaborative sessions set some goals for building a good plan, they encourage students to come back to reflect on their own planning and thinking.

So it seems to me that research works in a number of ways. It leads to new hypotheses about teaching and learning that you translate into how you conduct a class. And the classroom itself is a place to conduct inquiry, provided that you are also using that inquiry to teach something useful. But I would go beyond that. I don't think that you can teach well if you aren't—in some way—engaging students themselves in an examination of their own writing. The Making Thinking Visible Project is just an extension of this idea. This year around 25 of us are teaching collaborative planning in western Pennsylvania high schools, community colleges, colleges, and universities. We're all doing it as a way to look at our students. We meet every month and share discovery memos with each other about what we're learning. We're trying to use this experience to learn something about our students in a very low-cost way. Research done in this way gets teaching out of the classroom and into the dorm room and also gets learning working both ways.

WOE: So many people who teach composition at the college level are isolated; for example, there may not be anybody else on their campus who even knows about protocol analysis or other kinds of research approaches. If they want to try doing some research, they don't have a network of researchers nearby. It might be valuable to have some kind of clearinghouse for beginners to find a mentor. I think many faculty are afraid to try research because they don't think of themselves as researchers. They don't think of themselves as knowing how to design a study or how to make sure they go about it in the most efficient and effective way. So they may abandon the whole idea because they don't have a mentor or a network of people who can respond to their ideas.

FLOWER: Yes. I admire people who conduct inquiry without a support group because it's so critical to have other people who care about what you are doing when you're just beginning. I think it's been wonderful the way the CCCC Research Network has grown and the classroom research groups too. These groups are crucial. I also think it is important to change our model of what it means to do research. There are different ways to conduct research. Some are more formal, and those have certain things they do well. But I think there's another kind of research which is incredibly valuable. It's the kind we're calling classroom inquiry. Our model is not the model of educational psychology, which focuses on an intervention, usually by the teacher, and a control group, and asks, "Did this work better than the other thing that was done?" That's one model of research and it does certain things well. It's not the model I use. Most of my published work is more formal versions of a process of tracing, but that still takes support, a network of people, other people working with you, and funds for transcription. And I think there's another kind of inquiry that I do in my own classes that I don't publish unless I keep doing it for three years and develop it into a study like the reading-to-write study, but that's more . . . more . . .

WOE: More exploratory?

FLOWER: Yes, more exploratory. The goal is not just for you to learn something, but for the students to learn something. And so the inquiry becomes a way you actually spend part of the class time. For instance, I use collaborative planning as a way for students to look at their own planning but also just to look at their own writing. That means that I have to take time not only to teach whatever it is I want to teach, but also I have to take time for students to spend a class session talking about what they have discovered and provide time for them to do an assignment, which allows them to reflect on what they have learned. It seems to me that the model differs from some kinds of classroom inquiry in that it's critical for students and teachers to have actual observational data. Simply introspecting about your own writing process allows people to see what they already understand and that can also be very useful, but it's not enough. If you want people to come to genuine new insights that often counter what they may have already thought, they need to have some data that's independent of what they remembered as they were doing it. That seems to me to be a kind of model which makes inquiry a central part of effective learning. It's different from designing a study. In fact, what often happens is that you begin with the first kind of inquiry and you learn something which helps you design a study.

WOE: Yes. And that's when you need help, I think. At least I felt that way doing my research. I felt that I really needed to be in an environment where I could develop more confidence that I was approaching the study in a sound manner, that I wasn't overlooking something that other researchers already knew because they had been through it before. I think that's when it began to dawn on me that it would be nice to have some kind of a clearinghouse for novice researchers, or perhaps a NEH mini-grant which would allow me to visit a research center, maybe just for a few weeks. This would provide an opportunity to observe other researchers in action and would also help establish a network of professionals for those of us who are struggling on our own. I think the lack of this kind of professional connection causes a large gap between those faculty who work in the research-oriented institutions and those faculty who would like to engage in some research effort but who are outside that elite community.

FLOWER: There are several reasons for that gap. First, the model of research that we have had in education for the last 20 or 30 years is restrictive—and that model doesn't necessarily represent what's being done in much of the really interesting educational psychology work even now. Another model, one you see in English journals now, which tries to describe the nature of scientific research using historical documents, also contributes to the gap. You hear people talking about positivism and Descartes without a very clear grasp of the methods that are really being used in rhetoric and composition. There's a very simple-minded notion that if it's research, it's positivistic.

    I think that a lot of the writing in English is making that gap even wider by painting very simple caricatures of research that are essentially based on what English professors like to do best, and that is read other people's theoretical work (preferably the older the better) and then build nice self-consistent arguments on the basis of that. The alternative to that would be to actually understand the research that's going on now and its methods. And that's entering a whole different discourse. It's probably easier to read Descartes than it is to understand contemporary rhetorical research.

WOE: Exactly. Because it's difficult. It's thorny. Current research is looking at complicated procedures and processes and actions—human behavior.

FLOWER: I guess what I want to argue is that classroom inquiry is really a very doable kind of inquiry that still has the power of using observation as a springboard. Not that you're simply amassing truth from evidence. It's not a positivistic move. You do have to make great leaps and inferences, but you're supporting them and you're looking for rival hypotheses in your own data. That's an important starting point. For me, it's important just to be doing classroom inquiry as a teacher, even if I never did the other kind of research.

WOE: I think the difficulty is that many faculty who are now teaching composition were students of literature and were not introduced to the kind of research now done in composition. Many of us feel removed from empirical research techniques. I felt uncertain when I first approached classroom inquiry. My graduate education provided a library research class, not an empirical methods class. I had to go back and learn new techniques. I found the Lauer/Asher book *Composition Research* to be very helpful in outlining different kinds of approaches to research, most of which are applicable to rhetoric and composition. It delineates the characteristics of each approach, some of which do not rely on statistical analysis or control and experimental groups. The book gives you a sense that you can engage in research without being a statistical wizard.

FLOWER: Yes, and at the same time even the process studies differ from ethnography in that they're not based on the observer taking lots of notes and building themes. They involve more control from the beginning because you're trying to track some specific thing, because you've got a question, or you're using the comparison. I think a lot of people gravitate toward ethnography because they feel, "Well, if I can simply take lots of notes about what I observe and collect all the papers, that will do it." This simplified image would probably make an ethnographer turn over in her grave because ethnography is terrifically difficult.

The process-tracing studies share some of that concern for collectively developed grounded theories, but they tend to have more of a focus because you're actually after some process you're interested in, and you can set up the study to look at differences and how students handle the process. The goal for me now is to do process tracing that doesn't simply look at what people are doing, at the behaviors or activities, particularly something like collaborative planning. One way to do that is to teach something and observe whether people did what you asked them to do. That's important. It's useful to see if the teaching took in any way.

The concept I'm working with is strategic knowledge. I want to get at my students' strategic knowledge. I want to know not just the strategies or the things they do, but I want to know the goals they're setting. In the reading-to-write study what really mattered was not just what writers were doing, but what they *thought* was the purpose of the whole endeavor. Teachers usually never have access to that. The study made it clear that we don't talk very much about something as simple as representation of the task.

WOE: Except to the extent that we say, "You didn't follow the assignment and therefore your grade is lower." I think many teachers suspect that the reason students don't follow an assignment is that they deliberately interpret it in a way that makes it easier for them to do. But actually, because they *don't* really understand what the teacher has in mind, they reconstruct the assignment in a way that they can do it.

FLOWER: Yes. And the teacher then can come along and say they took the lazy way out. Yet if you hear the students trying to figure out what they're supposed to do and hear their confusion and guesswork, you realize they're trying to figure it out as best they can. They're using their past experience with school, and they're using the things they can do well, which is what we all do. But no one is speaking to the dilemmas they're having in the middle. We don't introduce them to more strategies or maybe indicate what their text should look like. We never speak to the goals that are driving that process. I'm referring to strategic knowledge as a trio of things. As you'd expect, it includes strategies in the middle, and the goals people have on the one end, and on the other end—an awareness. Everybody has some awareness and some people have a lot more of it than others. An important part of understanding a writer's strategic knowledge is knowing whether when she does something, she does it by choice. We need to know if the student was aware of having a choice. Did she have control over the process? Or is it something she has always done? If we create a highly motivating situation and offer a lot of support, writers can do wonderful things. Then we think they have learned how to do that. We feel wonderful because they write these beautiful papers. But in fact—and this is a hard thing for us to face as teachers—when students move into a less motivating situation with less support, they may not continue to write as well.

WOE: Yes. I have always been leery of the research I've done on my own classroom teaching because it's so hard to separate what indeed the students learned as a result of a strategy that I used and how much was a result of other factors. Sometimes students worked hard because they wanted to please me; sometimes they felt a genuine need to do it themselves. I guess that's a criticism always leveled at classroom research.

FLOWER: So it seems to me that one of the things we need to better understand is students' strategic knowledge. One of the best sources we have is their insight into their own strategic knowledge. It not only will help us increase their awareness of what they're doing, but it will help us get a bigger picture of why they think they're doing what they're doing. We need to learn how big their sense of options is and what the field of possibility looks like to them.

WOE: One of the consistent themes in your writing is that researchers need to pool their information or should see themselves as colleagues working collectively to better understand that big picture. Yet there are those in leadership positions who view the field of rhetoric and composition as being separated into camps, each in competition with the others and sometimes mutually exclusive. In your writing, however, you repeatedly stress the importance of tapping all the sources of information we have to build a theory we can all share. Why is it that the acceptable professional approach is to fragment, to be divisive and competitive, rather than to seek knowledge cooperatively and share it?

FLOWER: One way to understand these phenomena is to consider them as discourse practices. I think somebody interested in the history of academic work, especially in English, would say it has something to do with the highly individual private nature, the whole romantic paradigm of the writer as the poet/genius. The English professor becomes a parallel to that. For example, the idea of doing collaborative research has been problematic for people trying to get tenure in English departments. The very fact that you've collaborated is viewed with some suspicion in some places.

The history of sciences, however, has roots in collaborative work. There are different philosophical underpinnings, I think, for both those positions, but whatever their sources, they clearly lead to different discourse practices. In English, the way to support your own position is to engage in conflict with another position and defeat the straw man that you've set up. It's just a standard technique in English study. Another method is the discourse practice of critique. Because in critique there is no responsibility to suggest a better world. Rather it's to layout clearly with your Socratic powers the failure of the current one. In fact, when you listen to people doing critiques and ask them what they would do in response, you may hear some very disappointing responses, especially from people who practice the art of critique exclusively.

The difficulty is that when you come up with a positive response, you're certain to make mistakes, you're certain to be wrong, there's certain to be flaws in whatever you do. And the discourse practice of educational research assumes that. What you're doing in research is trying to do a better job than you have done before or than somebody else has done. You recognize that what works for education is going to change from time to time too. You know there aren't final answers.

WOE: Do you think that the people who are genuinely engaged in research in composition are much more collaborative among themselves than those people who are more engaged in the old-style theoretical research?

FLOWER: Oh, I think so.

WOE: And I see that as a new kind of paradigm that's developing in the field. One which I find very comforting. There's a positive, constructive approach to building some kind of foundation of knowledge, of examining what we know about composition and testing it and maybe discarding some of it later.

FLOWER: That's another feature of that paradigm. Not only do you build, you try to construct a positive image of what could be possible, but you also recognize that your theorizing and your intuitions are not always right and that your guesses about how students are going to use something or do something are often wrong. That's why the kind of purely theoretical claims for what we should teach leave me cold, because I know that there are lots of things that sound wonderful in theory and on paper, but we still need to test our own beliefs.

WOE: The approach you take is a much riskier one because you can find out that some premise you have doesn't test out to be accurate. But that risk is what accounts for the excitement in the field. It's much more alive than simply standing back from a distance and theorizing. I see those two approaches as co-existing in the field right now.

FLOWER: Well, there is also a kind of assumption, I guess, of living with your own limitations. You can't do educational research without knowing that something like the reading-to-write book is the best you could have done at the time or almost the best, but, boy, you could sure do it better now. Last year's work always leaves you feeling a little, you know, rueful—is that the word I want? Yes. You know that's going to happen, but you also have to take a very positive, optimistic position. You have to believe that given what we know now, this research is going to help us better understand what's happening when students write.

JAMES BERLIN

James Berlin was a leading figure in the field of rhetoric and composition, and in the cultural studies movement within composition. He believed passionately in social justice and considered his work—both as a teacher and a theorist—to be part of a larger social mission toward creating a true American democracy, where every citizen could participate fully and share power equally. The composition classroom, he believed, was the logical site for working toward that goal. He taught composition at Wichita State University starting in 1975, directed the Freshman English program at the University of Cincinnati from 1981–1985, and served as English professor at Purdue University from 1987–1994. He published three influential books: Writing Instruction in Nineteenth-Century American Colleges *(1984)*, Rhetoric and Reality: Writing Instruction in American Colleges 1900–1985 *(1987), and* Rhetoric, Poetics, and Cultures: Refiguring English Studies *(1996; 2003), co-edited the major collection* Cultural Studies in the English Classroom *(1993), and published numerous articles in* College English, Pre/Text, *and other composition journals. Early in his career, he developed what would become an influential analysis of the "rhetorics" at work in composition pedagogy. These include the current-traditionalist approach—evident in the majority of available textbooks—the individually centered expressivist approach, and the cognitive process movement. Berlin argues that a social rhetoric—what he defines as the "social epistemic" approach—offers the most effective means for teaching composition because it acknowledges the contingent nature of knowledge. Rhetoric, as Berlin writes in his 1988 "Rhetoric and Ideology in the Writing Class,"[1] is "a political act involving a dialectical interaction engaging the material, the social, and the individual writer, with language as the agency of mediation" (488). In his final book, published posthumously in 1996 with a second edition issued in 2003,[2] Berlin argues for a thoroughgoing revision of English studies based in social epistemic rhetoric, a revision that would erase the boundary between poetics and rhetoric. The book situates Berlin's work amid the ongoing debates about rhetoric and composition, illustrating continuing influence in the field.*

—Pamela Demory

---

1 Berlin, James A. "Rhetoric and Ideology in the Writing Class." *College English* 50 (1988): (477–494).
2 Berlin, James A. *Rhetorics, Poetics, and Cultures: Refiguring English Studies*. West Lafayette, IN: Parlor Press, 2003.

"Dialectical Notions"

Brian A. Connery and Van E. Hillard

Spring 1992

WOE: I want to ask a little about you personally. Your work suggests that we are, as a profession, a product of who we once were. To what extent are you as a researcher and theorist a product of who you once were?

BERLIN: Well, I started out in Victorian literature, and I realized just recently that I was attracted to that field because it encouraged an approach to literary texts that was closely allied with intellectual history. As Patrick Brantlinger explains in *Crusoe's Footprints*, his recent book on cultural studies, Victorian studies was early on organized as a kind of cultural studies. In other words, the literary texts were not the center of attention in the way they were in formalist criticism. The literary texts were instead always situated in concrete historical conditions. And, of course, this is why cultural studies now seems such a natural turn for me.

So anyhow, I was in Victorian literature and had absolutely no luck in finding a job teaching it. (In fact, I've never taught one course in Victorian literature, and if ever I'm asked to, I will refuse because I like having a perfect record.) Instead I got a job teaching composition at Wichita State. There I found myself researching Victorian literature and teaching composition, and I couldn't live with that fragmentation. It was conceivable that I could have done that juggling act for a long time: teach composition, publish in Victorian literature, and get tenure. But I had a hard time not wanting to know more about what I was doing in the classroom.

In my third year, I got a postdoctoral fellowship to Carnegie Mellon, working with Richard Young. And that's when I was really awakened to the world of rhetoric. I decided that since I had a degree in nineteenth-century literature, I would try to do a history of rhetoric in nineteenth-century England. I went back to Wichita State, however, to discover that the library just wouldn't support that kind of project. The books weren't a problem, because of interlibrary loan, but the periodicals were: you just have to have them physically present. So I started working with American rhetoric in the nineteenth century.

Then I got the job as director of freshman composition at Cincinnati, and that transformed me radically. I was treated with such disdain by a significant number of my fellow faculty members. Now, I don't want to overgeneralize. There were people who were very generous, but there were also people who made it a policy to be unpleasant to me for no other reason than my being in composition.

I started questioning my profession. I entered English studies because I thought it was a counterculture. I thought it represented a viable political alternative. I was a staunch liberal who believed in the inherent political progressiveness of knowledge and schooling, and I had my whole faith shaken. I started moving more and more left, until finally Marxian explanations of what was going on struck me with a new resonance. I began to see the way knowledge served as cultural capital in reinforcing dominant class relations rather than challenging them.

Another thing that was happening was that in my classes I was moving in the direction of epistemic rhetoric. I had been introduced to the paradigm during the Young seminar. Also, Victor Vitanza, who was another participant in it, had begun a reading group in poststructuralist thought—particularly Derrida and Foucault. In discussing these new ideas with my graduate students, I wanted them to challenge me. (It wasn't as agonistic on my part as it sounds since they were often challenging me whether I asked them to or not.) In these dialogues, my epistemic notions that language constructs reality were constantly shaken by their materialist arguments. They were offering Marxist positions; they would get led into that position of a kind of dialectical materialism against the idealism of my radical social constructionism. And so I finally realized that Marx was a solution to our conflict.

So there was no steady progress, but I was responding to my conditions, which, obviously, were creating changes in my perspective.

WOE: When you began writing your history, what were your expectations and hunches about what you might find?

BERLIN: Through reading Foucault, I got the notion of looking for differences. From the start, my hunch was that "rhetoric" is a plural noun. In other words, I didn't expect to find, as in some histories of rhetoric, a single conception of rhetoric, some bedrock, essential concept that undergirds all these rhetorics. I started seeing rhetorics as capable of generating radical differences. And that's what I was looking for when I began writing these histories.

This probably sounds surprising to some people since John Schilb, who called me the "great taxonomizer," has accused me of ignoring differences in the interest of finding commonalities. However, while I'm looking for differences, I don't think that anything goes. In any historical moment, you will find radical divergences in rhetorics, but the ones that survive have to appeal somehow to certain conceptions that are part of the historical moment. In other words, it's true that superstructure is not a simple mechanical reflex of the mode of production, the economic base. There is, instead, this interaction between the two so that on the superstructural level, the level of rhetoric, great diversity is possible. On the other hand, the rhetorical notions that gain currency and survive are the ones that are compatible with the dominant form of base–superstructure interaction, what I would call after Foucault (used very liberally) a larger epistemic regime.

And that is what I was looking for: rhetorics that represented dominant epistemic regimes. In turning to Marx, I realized that in the twentieth century what we're getting in rhetorics was a conflict among the ruling class, or at least its official representatives, the professional middle class. This class does not agree on certain questions of epistemology, certain questions of ethics, and certain questions of politics. So these different rhetorics then are in effect arguments among the people who have the right to speak.

In the book on the twentieth century, I then moved from a focus on epistemology found in my nineteenth-century history to a concern with ideology. I began to see that even epistemology is based on political conceptions, so that we embrace the epistemology that best supports our utopic ideal of what we want the world to be.

WOE: At the end of *Rhetoric and Reality*, you review the last ten years, examining what and where rhetoric is today, and you suggest a movement toward the social epistemic rhetoric. Is that what you continue to see?

BERLIN: Yes. Part of the result of the exchange between Linda Flower and me in *College English* has been that Linda is now actively trying to find space for social structures. She could not resist examining what she was bracketing, what she admitted she was bracketing, and she was bracketing the social.

On the other hand, I should say that I don't think that the expressionists will ever do this, because for most of them the social is simply always suspect. The communal, for them, by its very nature, distorts the individual, and prevents the individual from realizing his or her innate and inherent character. So I don't think that they will ever move in this direction. On the other hand, you know, Peter Elbow has been reading people like Polanyi, and when he writes an essay like the recent one in *College English*, in which he talks about turning off the audience and ignoring it, at least he is taking into consideration that the social dimension is there, although he is still presenting it as suspect. Of course, the thing that I find bizarre about that essay is that I don't know, given the poststructuralist subject, how you turn off the audience, how you suddenly bracket out the very elements that construct you. The private voice is always a dialogue, I think.

WOE: You've spoken of a movement in your own work from interests in epistemology and philosophy and in the whole-language event and how meanings get constructed to an interest in ideology. And you spoke about Linda Flower, who purveyed a kind of positivist or cognitivist epistemology and is trying to pack the social realm into that system. It seems to me that there might be dangers in moving toward ideology at the expense of truly reforming the ways that people understand the crucial differences between information and idea. In other words, it seems like there's a leap that's been made here, but we're still left with Jakobsonian models, even in the face of what looked to be contexts that wouldn't allow for this. Anne Berthoff talks about this in terms of poststructuralism, in that it still employs the positivist model and just attempts to place it in a new context.

BERLIN: I think that the problem we have in the U.S. is that we have been deprived of Marx. For intellectuals in Europe, Marx is part of the air that they breathe. One would no more consider omitting Marx from one's education as an intellectual than one would think of omitting Freud. On the other hand, in the U.S. it's commonplace for people to know Freud quite well and know nothing about Marx. As a result, even when we do talk about Marx, we get a positivistic model. We don't understand the notion of the dialectic. So even when we talk about language constructing reality, we omit this dialectic between the subject and the object, in other words between the concept and the percept (to use the Kantian terms) in which the conceptions we bring to our experience are constantly being challenged by that experience, and the experience by the conceptions. The result is that conceptions change and that in turn makes for a different experience as we see other things that we didn't see with the old concepts. This constant dialectical operation doesn't enter the equation in our understanding of language and experience. That's why we get this instrumental, atomistic, billiard-ball notion of causation instead of this complicated interaction in which causes can be effects but effects can also be causes in these elaborate interlocking structures that don't move in a simple linear way.

One of the things that I was criticized for by Sharon Crowley, who reviewed my book and didn't like anything about it, was that I presented the formation of expressionistic rhetoric and showed how three different groups of people who did not agree with each other nonetheless all sponsored this notion, supported this notion of expressionistic rhetoric. This development in structuralism is called overdetermination. It is possible for people who disagree about most things to yet come together at one particular point of this larger cultural structure.

That kind of thinking is simply not encouraged in this country. It's because Locke is our philosopher, because of our belief that truth is always in the individual percept and never to be considered in some larger context; on the contrary, the faith is that if we can get rid of Bacon's idols, the idols of our mind and the idols of our culture, then we can get in touch with the thing itself, with the truth.

WOE: We're so tempted to commodify knowledge. That's fostered in the system as well.

BERLIN: Absolutely. That's part of the notion of cultural capital I mentioned earlier. I was talking to an assistant professor we just hired who sent his dissertation to a publisher immediately after its completion. He just got it back, and he's revising it. I said, "You know, if you publish that, then you'll have tenure." He said, "That's all there is to it?" I said, "Yeah, but eventually the ante will go up so that we'll probably not only expect an assistant professor to publish the dissertation but we'll expect it to be well reviewed." I've been in this business for fifteen years and I've never seen anybody squeeze people like humanists do. In order to keep a job in any department you have to do more and more for less and less. Some community colleges now (not many but a few), are actually expecting people to teach three or four classes a semester and to publish too in order to keep their jobs. As the supply of potential professors went up, the ante went up too. I had the horrifying experience of seeing people squeezed by having the rules change on them in mid-career. For three years they were expected to be outstanding teachers and so they were and they won awards, but then in the fourth year the university committees decided that a certain number of articles was needed for tenure. The idea is that you change quality into quantity. This is, of course, part of our educational heritage. Edward Thorndike and G Stanley Hall long ago argued that anything that exists at all exists in some quantity and can be measured. And you would think people would say, "That's baloney," but in fact that idea proved so compelling that when you look at composition programs in the '20s and '30s you find all this number-crunching going on. And it's difficult for me to look upon this with any degree of an air of superiority, since I did the same thing as director of freshman English in order to justify myself and my program to my superiors. That's what they understand. My job was to interpret the numbers in a way that supported what I thought to be a good freshman English program. I began to appreciate Mark Twain's quip that there are lies, damn lies, and statistics. In fact, realizing that these numbers were texts that were then open to multiple interpretations helped me with my own thinking about rhetoric.

WOE: Your work addresses the issue of the professionalization, in the sociological sense, of the profession of rhetoric. I wonder what you see as the positive and the deleterious effects of professionalization.

BERLIN: I think we in composition have arrived. I think we now have a subject of study, we have methods for the study, we have graduate programs that certify bona fide members of our academic discipline. I think the battle for respectability within the university community is won. Now what we're going to face is a kind of fragmentation that is inevitable whenever dealing with the human sciences. I've been at conferences where people have said, "Why do we have so many paradigms? Why don't we have the kind of monolithic paradigm that biology does, for instance?" Well, what these people don't understand is that even biology has more than one paradigm. It's just that they don't dwell on their differences the way we do or discuss them as openly (and I won't go into the reasons for this here). We in composition have these competing paradigms and we're going to have to learn to live with them. We are going to be engaged in constant disagreement. What's useful now is that at least most of the time we're talking with one another. I do have arguments with Linda Flower and Peter Elbow in *College English*. I think that's good and that's healthy. The alternative is to have empires in which they go off and do their paradigm and I go off and do mine, and we just don't bother each other. Our careers would all be safe and settled, but the discipline would suffer.

Another thing that I frequently hear is "Why do you call it 'composition?' Why don't you just call it 'rhetoric?'" Well, the terms are never innocent. What's currently going on is that the term "rhetoric" is an arena of struggle for ownership. It has become respectable and people want to claim it for their particular subjects. When you look at books on literary theory or books on historiography, you will find "rhetoric" in the index. People are talking about "rhetoric." In the past, the term was a kind of placeholder. People in literary studies would use it for whatever language they didn't want to talk—as in, "That's mere rhetoric." They could dismiss any language act simply by labeling it "rhetoric." Now, however, the term has designations that cannot so easily be dismissed.

What's happened in rhetorical studies is that we're now getting different and competing conceptions of rhetoric and its study. We get the International Society for the History of Rhetoric—the *Rhetorica* crowd. They want, from my perspective, to divorce rhetoric from practice, to aestheticize it. Even when they deal with the history of rhetoric, it's difficult to understand that they're talking about people who taught rhetoric. Aristotle was a teacher of rhetoric. He did not think it demeaning that he had to correct freshman themes. Plato did this. Later, Quintilian did this, for crying out loud. In fact, most of the major figures in the history of rhetoric have been teachers. But the *Rhetorica* crowd doesn't want to talk about this. They want to consider rhetoric in these grand intellectual terms. Rhetoric then becomes this lofty aspiration to the realm of pure thought. What bothers me about this is that it divorces rhetoric not only from the classroom but from the concrete historical conditions.

Then you get the people who go to the opposite extreme. They don't want to call what we study "rhetoric." They want, like me, to call it "composition." But they want to divorce it from any kind of theory, any kind of historical sense at all, and just talk about the classroom today.

I think the healthiest response is to have the dialectical notion that the classroom is the center of what we do in the sense it is the point at which we test both theories and practices as they unfold before us. Our work is involved in the shaping of our students' subjectivities, their very consciousnesses. English teachers as keepers of the language are one of the most important elements in producing a certain kind of subject at the end of a college education, and we have to realize our responsibility in doing this in the rhetoric classroom as well as in the literature classroom. This is where we have this marriage between theory and practice.

I'm often surprised by how anti-intellectual some people in rhetoric are. I'm publicly criticized in print—Maxine Hairston and Peter Elbow are not the only ones—for being too theoretical. Those people never seem to notice that I never ever present an essay without talking about its relation to practice. One thing I've liked about composition ever since I got into it is that the classroom is always situated at the center of it so that even when we're doing theory we have to bring it back to the classroom. So that, yes, the question of what the hell to do on Monday morning is always important to me. When I forget that, then I'm in trouble.

Overall, I think we've arrived with some measure of security in the establishment. I am encouraged. We have 60 graduate students in rhetoric at Purdue and I am constantly impressed by the kinds of projects that they devise. For example, students often use ethnographic studies to study signifying practices, rhetoric in concrete, lived situations. One student, Jennie Dauterman, went into a hospital and looked at nurses writing a training manual. She didn't plan to be drawn into considering power and knowledge relationships but she couldn't help it. It was there. These nurses were writing the manual for themselves, but the real power was in the hands of the doctors. And so the nurses had to keep responding to these different audiences. Another student, Myrna Harrienger, studied signifying practices of ill, elderly women in a nursing home, examining what happens to their discourse in the institutional setting from a Foucaultian perspective. Still another student, Gary Heba, is examining the semiotic codes of youth cultures after the manner of Dick Hebdige's *Subculture: The Meaning of Style*. I think these are the kinds of studies we will see more of, studies that explore the worlds of work and culture as well as the classroom.

WOE: Your comments on rhetoric and literature and graduate students seem to have taken us into a discussion of the English studies program of tomorrow. How do you envision English studies under the new assumptions which you and others seem to have? How will these new assumptions be realized institutionally?

BERLIN: I think there's a decentering that's going on now. I think in terms of the power networks in the academy, English departments are prepared now to look to places other than those on the east and west coasts for models of what they're supposed to be. It's interesting to realize just how limited our conceptions of what we've been doing have been until just recently. For instance, at the end of World War II, 80% of the Ph.D.s in English were produced by 20 schools. Not 20% of all schools, but 20 schools. New Ph.D. programs didn't appear in any great number until the '60s and '70s. They're a post–World War II phenomenon. (Purdue's English department, for example, has only had a Ph.D. program since the '60s. In fact we know where all of our graduates are—I think we've only lost track of two out of over 250. It's wonderful—that's one of the features that encouraged me to teach there: they actually care about what happens to their people after they get degrees.)

I think that the potential here is that schools will follow the example of Carnegie Mellon and Pittsburgh and SUNY Albany and Syracuse—that is, they will devise their own models of English studies rather than relying on traditional patterns and traditional schools. They'll say, "We can't do Yale or Hopkins or Duke—we'll never have the resources." I've been at places where the English department was dying to be in the top 20. Unfortunately, as soon as they've got a number of people who've published in a way that would put them in the upper ranks, one of the top 20 schools would hire these people away, at better salaries, with better working conditions, simply because they have the resources to do so. And so the department returned to its outsider status. Again, there's this hierarchy and a positioning in it. How do we know we're worthwhile if we're not in the top 20?

So I think most schools have to say, "Look, we can't compete with those people, and we shouldn't be competing with them. We have different kinds of students. Our students want different things from us. We want different things for our students. Or we ought to want different things for them since their conditions are not the same as those of the students from the schools that we're trying to emulate."

My hope and faith is that these schools are going to start creating programs that respond to their actual conditions. I think this does happen now, but almost no one talks about it. In other words, what seems to be the unofficial curriculum—the undergraduate writing courses and film courses and popular culture courses and special-topics literature courses (war novels or sports fiction, for example)—are not talked about in official versions of what a department does. This kind of curriculum is already in place at most institutions where undergraduates are taken seriously, and teaching receives high priority—by the faculty if not by administrators. The other model of the profession, however, continues to be the official ideal. The example of the research scholar whose business is not teaching but publishing continues to be given credence, even at places where people are teaching three and four courses a semester. In the official curriculum, the "coverage" principle is constantly forwarded—the official periods (especially years ending in two zeroes), the official canon, the official scholarship. At some schools this leads to doctoral programs so difficult that it becomes all but impossible to finish a Ph.D. I've seen schools that require students to take five preliminary examinations. After that, you're not ready to write a dissertation—you're ready to retire! That's not fair.

As I already mentioned, a number of schools are designing new versions of English studies and new programs of graduate study. Southern Cal, for instance, has now introduced a graduate program in which every program is individually devised. I asked Ross Winterowd recently, "How many people do you have in rhetoric?" He said, "I don't know. They're not arranged that way. They're not organized that way. That's not the taxonomy we use anymore. We simply don't know who's in eighteenth-century, who's in Victorian." That's a wonderful idea to create graduate programs that don't rely on these old coverage models and these fixed periods, but instead recognize that we are dealing with reading and writing practices broadly conceived, in relation to people in a concrete historical moment; and this concern for signifying practices, consciousness, and history applies to the present as well as the past.

So I'm hopeful. I think that even if the cultural studies programs are not reproduced at other institutions, they're going to have an effect on what we do in undergraduate programs as well as in graduate programs. They are going to force us to think in new ways about what we're doing. But it will not be easy. One of the things that Thomas Kuhn says about paradigms is that they don't shift because of rational debate alone. They shift because the old guard dies. It leaves, for a better world, or it retires. So it may be that the ideas that are coming into play may not have their full effect until 20 years from now.

WOE: This may be a pessimistic view, but since the English department has been traditionally a very powerful department, is there any way to forestall English departments from spreading what they see as the good word: "You're doing signifying practices, though you didn't know that. We have a whole conceptual scheme ready for you to get reformed within"? It's very liberating for anyone doing any kind of research across the academy to realize, "OK, as a biologist I have been working on symbolic forms" or "As a painter, I am participating in some kind of signifying practice." Is there anything to forestall us acting as the progenitors of this vision? And are there any dangers in us doing so?

BERLIN: There are dangers. In fact, Christine Farris has discussed some of them in an essay that's appearing in *Cultural Studies in the English Classroom*, a collection that Michael Vivion and I are editing for Boynton/Cook. In studying the writing across the curriculum program at Indiana University, Christine discovered that our notion of the constructedness of knowledge is not the notion that's found in other disciplines. She talks about resisting the tendency to colonize or imperialize, to impose our notions on professors in journalism, art history, and science classes. She pays special attention to an introductory journalism class, in which there is a strong positivist bias: the conviction that there is something out there waiting to be recorded, and if we ask the right questions we're going to find out exactly what it is.

WOE: So journalists are, in some sense, enemies. Their whole notion of how language works is so different. I don't know how to accommodate that.

BERLIN: Well, it seems to me like the old marginal man or marginal woman concept. The marginal figures—in other words, people who had a foot in two different cultures or groups—were once thought to be those people who made changes. Further study by sociologists revealed that wasn't true. It was the person who was firmly a part of the community who created change. In short, we're not going to create change in journalism. If journalism is going to change, it has to be people within the journalism community who do it. And all we can do is to create dialogues and hope for the best.

The thing to keep in mind is that this linguistic turn—this move toward epistemic rhetoric—is apparent across the academy. There's virtually no discipline now that doesn't have members who are talking about rhetoric. Even in empirical psychology, Kenneth Gergen, for example, has a social constructionist model of cognitive psychology. We also have the study of Greg Myers on the social construction of biology and Donald McCloskey on the social construction of economics. There's the *Rhetoric of the Human Sciences* series published by the University of Wisconsin Press. I'm not pessimistic. Changes are going to take place, or at least the potential for them exists.

But we have to remember—and here we are back to ideology—that there's a lot at stake in these discussions. The journalist's commitment to this positivist notion of truth is an important part of a larger ideological notion of the way that decisions are made in a democracy. Richard Ohmann has pointed out repeatedly that we keep looking at the concrete specific detail and never notice the larger concept that's determining what in any given situation the relevant concrete specific detail is. And this practice of course serves the interest of certain powerful groups, as the close attention to the concrete details keeps us from seeing larger patterns of power and privilege.

WOE: So what are you doing on Monday morning? How does your understanding of theory and your understanding of our history translate into practice?

BERLIN: I've devised a course in composition studies and cultural studies, an English 101 course, that looks from the outside like expressionist writing. It's not, of course, but it does focus on student experience. Cultural studies here converges with rhetoric in that cultural studies deals with signifying practices and their formations of subjectivities within concrete conditions. We look at some of the very obvious ways that language shapes our consciousness. Students do talk about their experiences, but the point of doing so is to locate in their experience the semiotic codes that they are enacting. I teach them some simple structuralist and poststructuralist tools of analysis. First they look for key terms of any text or experience they are considering and identify the binary oppositions that make up the structure of these key terms. Any key term has meaning only in relation to some opposite term, although this term is often not articulated in the text or experience being examined. We then look at these structures to see how they form race, class, and gender codes. This is Roland Barthes's first level of mythology. (I don't call it that since I have enough trouble convincing my students that this is worth studying, and if I called it "myth" it would be impossible.) We look carefully at these first-level narratives. Then—and this is the hardest part of what we do—we try to fit the race, class, and gender patterns that they discover in their everyday experiences into larger narratives having to do with economic and political conditions.

We begin with a unit focusing on advertising and how advertising affects them, and this sets up all the language that we use. Then we go on to education, recreation, work, and gender (for special treatment), and finish with a unit on individuality.

Students read texts that not only demonstrate these codes at work but also problematize these codes. For instance, we read Aileen Pace Nilsen's "Sexism in English: A Feminist View" on the ways in which terms that are gender specific are always pejorative in the case of women. Students see that when this binary structure is created, and, for example, there's a "master" in opposition to a "mistress," the feminine invariably carries negative connotations. This kind of essay actually contributes to the methodology. Most of the essays we read, however, are there for analysis. Students are finally asked to look at their own experience, in school for instance, to see how they have been coded. And the center of the course is to locate conflicts in the codes that they're enacting.

For instance, they'll look at the social class structure in the schools they attended. There are almost no freshman students that I've encountered that don't know what groups there were in their high school and who was in those groups and where they themselves stood in this hierarchy. They talk about what they learned in observing these groups. This is a part of their unofficial curriculum. We are organized into groups. So how are these groups coded? How do they dress? How do they act? What are their future prospects?

The biggest obstacle in the course is that students will acknowledge the codes and acknowledge the conflicts, but the dominant narrative by which they live is that all conflicts are resolved by individual decision making and individual choice. Everybody in the end resolves conflict in her or his own particular private way and lives happily ever after. And students argue this even though they know that the group that used drugs is on a path toward self-destruction. In fact, the most important part of their education has been the denial of conflict. And when they recognize conflict, they dismiss it as not being very important, or they leave it up to the individual to resolve. There are no societal problems, only private and personal problems.

The teachers who use this approach have encountered resistance. At first we were very concerned about this, because, as you know, we have this notion that our students should be happy, should enjoy learning. After a while, we decided that the resistance is probably a good thing. This is the first time that many of our students have ever complained about anything to the people who are causing their discomfort. They have been, by and large, "yes people." They have been expected to take orders and do what they're told, and they've been rewarded for doing so. Here they're rewarded for doing just the opposite. We realized that once we get this critique going, everything gets critiqued including the assignments and the entire course.

We came to that conclusion when we discovered that the evaluations that the teachers get here are as high as, or higher than in other sections. So even though they're complaining, at some level the students recognize that the experience is worthwhile.

WOE: You're a master teacher too. You're training graduate students. How do you go about that?

BERLIN: I supervise eight graduate students. I write their syllabus for the first year, and I tell them what to do. And of course this is counter to the notions of participatory democracy, but at certain points in our education it is often necessary for us to be guided in quite specific directions. Would you want a brain surgeon who wasn't guided carefully by a mentor, a master surgeon? Would you want a brain surgeon who says, "Well, I saw a movie on this procedure once, and I think I'm going to try it"? Mentoring is a part of the training to be a teacher. And then during the second year, when the students are through with me, they are free to go on and try other methods.

What we should have is a course that graduate students would be required to take, so that they could simultaneously look at other paradigms. We did that at Cincinnati. Teaching assistants were required to take a course in the theory and practice of composition during their first term in the classroom. So while I was forcing them to teach according to my paradigm, I was constantly making them aware of other paradigms. They knew right off what the alternatives were. At Purdue, we have 200 graduate students and it's difficult to provide a course for so many people.

WOE: So in theory, you would agree with Gerald Graff that it's important to teach the controversy.

BERLIN: Exactly. The problem with Graff is that Graff's conflicts are narrow, academic conflicts; they're professional disputes. I find that he doesn't situate them within a larger politics. In the same way *Literature against Itself* treats the theoretical issues in an English department as if they're local and parochial. English departments are responding to the larger curriculum which in turn is responding to economic, social, and political conditions. We don't get that in Graff's books. Not only does he omit composition (which is a way of saying, "I'm going to give you a story of this English department marriage but I'm only going to talk about the husband"), but then the larger political context is ignored. I think that's the problem with his notion of teaching the conflicts.

What we're trying to do is to situate these conflicts within students' lives, to see that they have consequences for their experiences on a day-to-day basis.

WOE: It seems that there is power in the rhetoric of giving witness to individual experiences. This has something to do with the making of empathy, with creating toleration of difference, and the welcoming of conflict. This is something that hasn't been fostered in the past.

BERLIN: We want to disabuse the students of the notion that they are the kind of completely autonomous individuals that they think they are—not because we're engaging in an academic dispute, but because we think it's dangerous for them constantly to make decisions that have been determined for them and then to attribute these decisions to personal choice. For instance, I'll ask students, "What do you want in a job? Create an idea circle. Just put 'Job' in the middle, and then put spokes out from that word, and write what you want in a job." They do this for ten minutes, and then I have ten students go to the board to record their responses. We find that of the ten terms that each came up with, eight or nine of them are identical. I say, "Is this an individual choice? Did you all look into your own heart of hearts and decide what you want in your work? Or is this an idea of work that has been given to you as part of your culture, that you've been asked to subscribe to?"

I don't want to deny their individuality. I think that a certain amount of individuality, as well as agency, is possible. But you can't be an individual until you find out what's not individual. And their notion is that everything, as well as every person, is a totally unique case.

WOE: That's the heart of Freirean methods, that students make this important discovery that you share ideas, that you're not alone in your ideas. That's the point of the culture circle, in terms of how language works in the first place.

BERLIN: Freire has been very helpful to me. There's been a lot of criticism of Freire because, after all, his methods were developed among third-world peasants who were illiterate, while we're dealing with first-world college students. And it's true that there are differences that are important. But there are some features that are very consoling. For instance, when the peasants resisted Freire too. Hegemonic discourse is so powerful that even though they've been victimized by it, it was comforting. It was what they had come to know and live as the truth. And to abandon it was painful.

That's similar to what happens with my students. There are all these certainties that are suddenly being problematized. But that's the notion of liberal arts education that I grew up with; it's supposed to question your ordinary way of thinking about things so that you begin to think about things in better ways, and then it's possible to improve the conditions of your experience.

The teachers I always liked best were the ones who asked me to look at the world from a perspective I had never considered. And having done so, I didn't always find the new view worth hanging onto. But the process helped me make better sense of my life and my society. This is what I'm trying to do for my students. I don't expect them to agree with the perspectives I ask them to entertain. (And this is a good thing since so few do.) But I insist that they cannot simply ignore other perspectives and points of view. The world is too complicated and changes too fast to be interpreted and understood forever with a set of ideas that we bring to college with us at age eighteen. My hope is that my students leave my classroom better prepared to see the problems they have been taught to ignore or deny—the problems of the poor and the ill and the victimized—and more able to imagine solutions to them. The aim of education in a democracy, I think, is not simply to earn a safe refuge from the ills of the world, but to make the world a better place for all of us.

PETER ELBOW

Peter Elbow came to prominence, indeed became something of a composition cult figure, with the publication of his first book, Writing Without Teachers *(1973). This book and its sequel,* Writing With Power *(1981), reflect his longstanding concern with the process of writing, a concern that grew out of his personal experience and frustrations with academic writing and writer's block. His ideas have not only gained widespread critical and popular acceptance, but they have also shaped the field of modern composition practice. Since his interview with* WOE *in 1992, Elbow has written an additional 19 articles and four books, continuing to attract writing teachers with his accessible prose about the importance of messiness and the individual voice. In the updated 1998 editions of* Writing Without Teachers *and* Writing With Power, *Elbow defends the important role he believes chaos, intangibility, and mystery play in the composing process and advocates again for teacherless groups meant not to critique but to listen to one's writing. In his 1999 collection of essays entitled* Everyone Can Write, *Elbow argues for the inherent ability he believes everyone has for expression. His most recent book,* Vernacular Eloquence: What Speech Can Bring to Writing *(2012), argues that features of everyday speech, or vernacular literacy—defined as the native language used in the home, in one's culture, or in technological settings—can inform good writing practices. He acknowledges and complicates the divide between "correct," Standard English and versions of English that are often viewed as less prestigious and "bad." He has received numerous prestigious awards, including the 2007 Exemplar Award by CCCC for his outstanding contributions to the profession. Elbow is Professor Emeritus at the University of Massachusetts Amherst.*

—Katie Arosteguy

"Going in Two Directions at Once"

John Boe and Eric Schroeder

Fall 1992

WOE: Let's start biographically, with a high school teacher you mention in your writing, Bob Fisher.

ELBOW: I went to a boarding school in New Hampshire, Proctor Academy, because my older brother and sister had gone away to college and I felt left alone, like an only child. Furthermore, growing up in New Jersey I had gone skiing a few times and I wanted to ski. Bob Fisher was a very young guy who was excited about literature, excited about writing. He made writing and reading books part of your life. We'd read Dostoyevsky. He would ask us to write about deep things. I also remember writing a fairy tale. He loved ideas and he took us seriously, inviting us to love ideas and to take deep dives into profundity. I loved that.

He was a good teacher, funny and full of energy. I loved writing with him. And he was a skier. He made me think I'd like to be like him, so I said to myself, "I'd like to be a boarding school English teacher."

WOE: And then you went to Williams. Did the teachers there make your writing better or worse?

ELBOW: I want to say worse. I'm sure I learned a lot and became much more sophisticated, but . . . [*pause*]

I partly went to Williams because Bob Fisher had gone to Williams. I had been very successful at Proctor Academy, which was not a very good school. It wasn't Exeter or Andover. One of the things that I liked about it was that they had what they called a "liberal" course, for kids who were not planning to go to college. The science courses I took had a lot about electricity and plugging things into the wall. It wasn't just College Board LSAT science.

Anyway, I didn't have a very fancy education, so when I got to Williams I had to struggle. Because I had loved math best in school, I thought, "I'll be a math major, it's so beautiful." Then I took freshman calculus. By the end of the year I may have got a B, but it was pretty much a gift. I was struggling. I was an earnest good boy, but I didn't get it. In English I got an F on my first freshman writing paper, then a D. These things you don't forget. I think on the third paper I got some pretty low grade, some form of D, and the comment was "Mr. Elbow, you continue your steady but far from headlong rise upward."

WOE: I remember those kinds of comments in freshman comp at Amherst.

ELBOW: The ethos was the same, the snottiness and the notion that you have to knock these freshmen down to zero in order to build them up right. I hate that.

I don't like to think of my whole career as reacting to something, but in a sense everything I do is reacting to that. The idea that you have to beat people down in order to educate them right makes me mad. I was enormously eager and diligent. I was a boy who wanted approval very very badly, so I said, "I'll do whatever you want." Just like many of our own students. I worked hard and was successful by the end of freshman year. By the end of my college career I had very good grades. That's why I got the scholarship to go to England.

WOE: It sounds as if you not only did well but enjoyed academic life after your difficult freshman year.

ELBOW: I learned to be sophisticated. I admired my teachers, so that by the time I was a junior or senior at Williams, I thought, "Well, it was nice wanting to be a boarding school teacher, but now I want to be a college professor. I want to be like these guys." The main attraction was the sophistication, learning to "pass." I think that is a quality of mind, like the believing game. I feel a little sheepish about this, but in the summers I used to sometimes sneak into yacht club dances. I would dress up in madras or something. I wanted to be like those people. I wasn't, but I could do both things. The naive side of myself sort of went underground: that's one angle I think back on a lot.

I grew up Catholic (although my father was Jewish, and I'm only beginning to realize I'm a Jew). Somehow Catholicism stuck. I went to church every Sunday and believed everything. (And I remain religious in a nontrivial way.) But at Williams College in the fifties, my teachers didn't think it was smart to be a Catholic. There was a sneer towards serious religion, so I learned to keep it under wraps. (I wanted to be friends with some of my teachers and I was. I would hang out with some of these impressive teachers—in a way wonderful men—who scorned people who went to church.) I have this image of being at Williams: I'd go off to church every Sunday and I'd even go to confession.

Also my religion gave me a serious internal life in the sense that you couldn't live at a boy's school without masturbating, and you couldn't be a Catholic in the fifties without being constantly taught that you shouldn't masturbate. The amount of psychic energy you spent with the issue is sad, but it did give you an internal life. Odd, isn't it, that the repeated experience of trying to be good and feeling you are bad gives you such a strong sense of self. And a mental life. You are really *somebody* if you continually do what they say you mustn't do—and feel bad about it.

The different parts of my life are, in a sense, not well connected to each other. I metaphorically relate this to my eyes sometimes. My eyes were crossed when I was born. When I was five years old I had an operation to pull them apart, but they never learned to work together. They drifted more and more apart. My brain is always getting two different messages, which it can't put together, which most people can put together in some way. My brain is used to contradictory messages.

WOE: Why did you want to study in England?

ELBOW: I spent the summer of my junior year wandering in Europe and I wanted to go back, so I just tried for every scholarship I could. Actually I wanted to go to Italy; it was so alive and romantic. But the only scholarship I got, after trying for tons and tons, was a two-year scholarship that Williams gave for Exeter College in Oxford. The tutor for years and years at Exeter College was Neville Coghill, whom I met later—a wonderful sweet man—but he left the year I came. The guy who took over for him was Jonathan Wordsworth, the grandnephew of the poet. It was his first year as a don, and he was practicing to be a sardonic, ironic, Oxford don. The style in England was quite tough. Just in repartee people said things I thought were insulting but they sort of took for granted. I don't know whether this is more characteristic of Oxford or of English academics in general. But this was pre-Beatles, when I think of England as a little more uptight.

Wordsworth didn't think he was being mean, but I thought he was. He would make fun of my writing. He would give the assignment, and you would come in each week with a paper. One week he said go home and read Marvell's "On a Drop of Dew" and write something interesting. So I wrote this paper about the poem and began to read it to him: "On a drop of dew—" [*flat American accent*]. And he interrupted me: "On a drop of dew" [*clipped Oxford accent*]. Then he said, "Elbow, maybe that's why you don't understand poetry. You don't know what it sounds like!" He was just having fun, but I was a tender youth and for me a part of schooling was to get patted on the head. I wanted praise, and he wouldn't praise me. And there was no grading. At one tutorial he was cleaning his rifle as I was reading the essay!

He was just having fun, but I got to the point that I couldn't write essays for him, because I was so scared of being ridiculed. But I was so earnest that I would spend the whole week trying to write a paper, starting paragraph after paragraph, but not succeeding. Week after week, I'd come in and say "I haven't got a paper." So I owe my interest in writing to him.

I tried to quit. I came home the summer between the two years and asked Williams College if I could postpone the second year and finish it a year later. They said no, so I went back. I eventually changed tutors, survived, took those exams, and got a second. I didn't have to be ashamed. I was enormously grateful. The exams are awful—nine three-hour exams. But once you were in the examining room you had to write.

At Oxford the British tradition of articulateness is so strong. One reason British academics write so well is that everyone values the turned phrase, the elegant phrase, and I (as you can tell) stumble and jumble around in my talk. I'm not naturally articulate. That's another reason I'm interested in writing. I've so often had the experience of having some wonderful idea, trying to tell it to people, and having them say, "That's stupid." And I can't convince them. So I'm always going home and saying to myself, "Dammit, I'm going to make this idea work." So writing has become a way to try to push my ideas into the world because I can't push them very well in speaking. Writing is like closing your eyes, like getting away from the audience for a while. I've always had the experience that people who disagree with me always argue better than I can. I can never think of a reasonable response.

WOE: What happened when you returned from England?

ELBOW: My plan was still to become an English professor. (I had a classmate who wanted to become a professor who had the sense to study a *different* subject at Oxford. To have done something different would have been really smart. But I was too earnest. I took the subject I cared about.)

When I came home, I knew I was having trouble being a student. But people said to "just get the Ph.D. out of the way." I ran around New England trying to get a last-minute job at a private school. But I couldn't get one and I had my place at Harvard, so I went.

I was having trouble with my life. I was in love with an English girl and she wouldn't come over and marry me. I was taking graduate courses, and I wasn't sure I loved literature enough. But the main thing was my writing. It was a horrible struggle and my papers weren't very good. They were mostly B minuses, which is like failing in graduate school. I remember Alfred Harbage, the Shakespeare guy, who must've been the chair of graduate studies, saying to me, "You have to do better than this or you can't stay." I was in trouble, and some time near the end of fall semester I wanted to quit. But I was always a prudent, pragmatic person, so I said, "I'll give myself six weeks or so to make up my mind." So I came back the second term. Somewhere in February or March I quit.

It wasn't just that I couldn't write the papers; I was unhappy. I was in therapy, shrinking my head. Being a prudent child, I didn't just quit, I took a medical leave of absence. I always felt this was perhaps a terribly cowardly thing to do, although I did feel that I was losing my mind because I was crying all the time. I experienced crying all the time as losing my mind. I was a very controlled person, and I was losing control.

So I quit, continued to shrink my head, and experienced myself as a total failure. With one part of my mind I said, "This is a medical leave of absence," which meant I could come back somehow, but with the other part of my mind, I said, "I am never going to have anything to do with the world of books."

I got a job taking census, bicycling around Cambridge and Somerville, knocking on doors. This was in 1960. Then I got a job at a school holding a stopwatch for kids who were practicing college boards. I tried to get a job teaching kindergarten, but no one would hire me. I think I looked a little crazed, and there weren't many men teaching in the early grades then.

In the middle of the summer through an old teacher of mine I got a job at MIT: there'd been a fight and a purge and they needed bodies. I wasn't sure I would be able to do it, but it was a job. I was just an instructor—it only paid $5000 and I never could have stayed—but it was a nice job. That was a big turning point. I was trying to put my life and my emotional life together. Although I was very scared about my teaching, I discovered that it was fun to teach. What I loved about it were the things that were different from graduate school. It wasn't English, it was mostly great books: the Greeks and Romans, the Bible and the Middle Ages. So I wasn't trying to do English lit anymore. And the wonderful thing about the Greeks—Socrates, Aeschylus, and Homer—is that in a sense they are about life. Because I was teaching MIT freshman, the agenda was not "Is this good literature?" or "What do we think about it?"; the agenda was "How can we find something useful in these books for our lives?" That was a wonderful question. I didn't have to love the books or the field, I just had to find something that could connect to our lives. In a sense, to ask how can books connect to our lives is the best introduction into books, to the intellectual life. I taught there three years. This course was meant to teach writing, but your eye was on the *Odyssey* or Thucydides. I wasn't thinking about writing so much. I was just trying to get people to write essays as well as they could. After those two years a chance came along to be at Franconia College, which a friend of a friend was starting. There were only five faculty members, so it was exciting.

I was at Franconia from 1963 to 1965. Again it wasn't teaching writing. We had a two-year interdisciplinary course. But I must have been thinking about writing, because while I was at Franconia I wrote a little pamphlet for my students called something like "Thoughts on Writing." I remember saying, "Think of a sentence as a line of force. Don't think of a sentence as a bunch of correct things, but as a piece of force, and how to keep the energy in it," or something like that. At a certain point I sent it to Ken Macrorie. And he said very nice things about it and encouraged me. So that I guess was the first thing I ever wrote about writing, in a way the first thing I ever wrote.

We were all teaching this interdisciplinary course together, and nobody was an authority. I theoretically knew more about Socrates, and someone else knew more about Darwin, so we were always picking each other's brains. I remember writing memos about Socrates, getting very excited and printing them out on purple ditto to my five colleagues, just writing to give my thoughts about Socrates. That was the first time I began to feel that writing had a real function, was something you did for a real reason as opposed to an assignment at school.

I was gradually learning to write, but Franconia, being a shoestring place, looked like it was going to fold. Because all the students had failed in school, over and over—no one else would come to this odd new college—they were the opposite of the MIT students—it was really interesting. And it was an interesting faculty. We discovered that if you were really supportive with these students and if you had fun in your teaching, they turned out to be smart (even though they had started out looking dumb). That experience made me feel something was the matter with education, that things needed to be changed, and that I would love to change things. But I knew that if I didn't have a Ph.D., people would never listen to me. They'd say, "Well you don't like it because you couldn't do it." So I said, "I better get myself a Ph.D." I looked into getting one in education or in psychology—those were my interests then—but I discovered it would take me a long time to get a Ph.D. in those fields. Even though I felt a certain annoyance about literature, I could get a Ph.D. there much quicker.

WOE: So your decision to pursue a Ph.D. in English was utility!

ELBOW: It was very much a utility degree. I said to myself, "I don't care about literature; I want a Ph.D.—fast!" I knew I didn't want to go to Harvard. I looked at Brandeis. I kept things carefully at an arm's distance there. I didn't want to get involved. I worked at home like I was going to work at a job. I didn't get to know any of my teachers, just did my duty. I wanted to get this thing done. I didn't want to get caught.

I did OK, although I was very scared of writing. I made myself a rule: every time a paper was due, I had to have a draft (of the same length as the paper) done a week before the paper was due. So then I knew I had a week to play with it. And I was sufficiently scared that I actually made myself keep up that discipline. I was very self-conscious about writing, scared I wouldn't be able to do it. I've sometimes said that I kept a kind of "journal," but it's not quite true; I would simply write notes to myself as I was writing these papers. If something happened that struck me, I would write a note—sometimes just on a little scrap of paper—and would slip these pieces of paper into a folder. Especially if I got stuck, I would take another piece of paper and say, "You're stuck on this damn paper, so write about why you got stuck." I thought if

I learned what had happened, maybe it wouldn't happen next time. And then when I got unstuck, I would try to remember to take a moment to write about how I got unstuck. So these notes to myself piled up in this folder. That went on for the three years I was at Brandeis and another year after I left. That folder full of notes turned into *Writing Without Teachers*. I made myself (again being diligent) finish my dissertation. I even made myself revise it to see if I could publish it—before I took out that folder of notes and said, "I'd like to do something with this."

There was an interesting character at Franconia, Bob Greenway, a psychologist, from Brandeis actually, who was interested in metaphor and thinking. He got me interested in that, so when I was at Brandeis I tried to write a long paper about metaphor, which was a mess. Then I tried to write a dissertation on it. I spent a whole year actually trying to write a dissertation about metaphor, but it was just too much of a swamp, so I fell back onto a Chaucer paper, saying, "I guess I can do a dissertation on Chaucer." Which in a way made sense, because it was safe, circumscribed. I did succeed in making a nice short dissertation.

The work in Chaucer was about a subject that has turned into an important theme for me: opposites. I love the Chaucerian saying, "the tongue returns to the aching tooth." The book ended up being called *Oppositions in Chaucer*. I started from *Troilus and Criseyde*, saying, "It's about freedom and necessity, so let's look at the poem. Does the poem affirm freedom or necessity?" And it seemed to me that when I looked very carefully, the poem proved that everything was free and the poem proved that everything was determined. The notion that things that are logically opposite can both be true must have been running in my mind, but I feel grateful that I picked it up in Chaucer. Having done this work on opposition in Chaucer makes me feel more [*pause*] dignified in my continuing interest in opposites.

The thing that's happening to me now is that I am so often seen as a naive, romantic expressionist person—

WOE: [*interrupting and quoting*] "—hopelessly romantic bourgeois late capitalist naïf" as you described this characterization somewhere.

ELBOW: Completely one sided, just one end of the spectrum. James Berlin's picture of the field and its history has become so definitive that his terms are sort of cast into stone. But I feel like I'm complicated (I feel like a sophomore saying this). I'm always being portrayed as simple. If you are enthusiastic for feeling, it is taken for granted that you must be against thinking. I *love* thinking. I love cognition. Sometimes I get in trouble with my teaching because I'm too cognitive, too theoretical. In a certain sense I'm guilty of believing in the body but forgetting it exists, believing in feelings but leaving them out. I'm very much the academic. I don't get credit enough for being complicated because at some level, somewhere along the line, I became temperamentally a person who is going two directions at once. It sounds a little grandiose, but

I want to define it as one of my life's works to work out an intellectual justification for going in two directions at once, for maintaining things that look irreconcilable to be—if not reconcilable, at least both true, both deserving one hundred percent affirmation.

WOE: What did you do after you finished your dissertation?

ELBOW: I taught again at MIT for four years, beginning in 1968. This was the sixties, when we were giving As to all students. We were thinking about the war and the draft. I applied to be a conscientious objector but my draft board refused. I went down for an interview and then wrote an extensive appeal. Unsuccessful rhetoric. I was very scared—sitting looking at a I-A. I didn't feel I could go to Canada. I hoped I would have the courage to go to jail. But in the end I wasn't called. This experience has made me feel really strongly that if there is to be any army at all, everyone has to be eligible for the draft. I never thought seriously about wars and killing till I was looking at I-A. My first piece of published writing was trying to explain the conscientious objection regulation for the *Christian Century*.

My own children like to say "Daddy was a hippy" as a way to ridicule me, and I do have a strand of beads. While I didn't wear them much, I did wear them occasionally. My wife now wears them.

I'm very fond of MIT, especially compared to Harvard. MIT's so wonderfully nonsnob. It's a more human place. They pretend less. I think they're smarter than the Harvard people. And MIT structurally and educationally is more adventuresome. If somebody has an idea for a good program and makes a good argument for it, they'll say OK. For example, all MIT freshman courses are pass/fail.

Then the chance came to go to Evergreen in 1972. It was a question of being a gadfly at MIT or being in the mainstream at Evergreen, an experimental place. Even though students made fun of me the first year ("an uptight Easterner"), it was a wild, wonderful place. But it was a hard place to teach. You had to teach with your character, because there wasn't the flywheel of standard, academic structures and rituals. No grades, no departments, no standard courses, everything interdisciplinary. And we insisted on never teaching any course or program more than once—at least in the early days. In a regular school the flywheel of custom keeps everything going. When everything is up for grabs you have to teach hard and well. I wasn't so good at it, but I was all right.

I finished *Writing Without Teachers* just as we were moving out to Evergreen in 1972. So I wrote it at MIT. I mailed in final revisions from Chicago. Over the nine years at Evergreen I wrote *Writing With Power*, and just as that was coming out I was leaving. By that time I knew I was interested in composition. I wrote *Writing Without Teachers* really not knowing about the composition community. I knew Ken Macrorie existed, but I was guilty of trying to write in a field and not even knowing the field existed. By the time

I got to *Writing With Power*, I knew there was such a thing as composition, and I wanted to be involved in the game. This was hard to do at Evergreen because it was on the west coast and was such a busy teaching placing.

WOE: Not only do people who criticize you misread you, but so too do some of your supporters. When *Writing Without Teachers* came out, those of us who were solidly in the counterculture saw you as one of us, saw it as a counterculture book. Did you see it this way?

ELBOW: My wife makes fun of me sometimes, saying, "The style of that book invites the reader in bed with you." Sometimes people get enthusiastically in favor of what I say, then I hear what they're doing, and it makes me nervous. They're going too far, being too naive. They're not willing to give credit to the opposite. Sometimes when teachers get excited with freewriting they throw over the traces and say, "Let's just have nothing but chaos." I love chaos, but I love order too.

WOE: In talking about freewriting you seem at times to almost view it as mystical.

ELBOW: The freewriting principle is the principle of juice, of letting go, of garbage, of finding diamonds among the garbage: all the metaphors you can make about free writing! It's very authoritarian—"You must not stop writing for ten minutes"—but it does feel like it's the source of everything.

When we were doing the book on freewriting I spent a couple of years feeling guilty because people would send me questionnaires asking things like "How often do you freewrite?" and "When do you freewrite?" In one sense I don't freewrite, except in my teaching. But teaching gives me lots of occasions to freewrite. In another sense I freewrite all the time. I've developed a "freewriting gear" and I don't set the clock. If I get stuck I can get myself going. At first freewriting is a totally artificial activity; but it's a question of whether with practice you can internalize it a little bit. *Writing Without Teachers* represented my figuring out the principle of freewriting—that you should let loose and be generative and then be critical later. But I really couldn't quite practice what I preached. When the book was finally out, I would get students in my classes to do it, but I had to gradually learn to practice what I preached. I am finally pretty good at it.

Writing Without Teachers is in a way about two things: it's about freewriting and it's about teacherless groups. I guess I did freewriting at MIT, but I did teacherless groups when doing volunteer teaching in the sixties in Roxbury. It's like I was testing a new drug on a minority population. I didn't dare do teacherless groups with my MIT students. I did dare when teaching for free, with deprived minority adult students. I guess that's shameful and perhaps backwards. But the question in teaching is always where to find an occasion to try something out, because it always feels [like] you can't try it out in your regular teaching. We need arenas to do these things.

WOE: Do you find it ironic that the ideas in *Writing Without Teachers* have become widespread academic practices, that something which was formerly so countercultural is now institutionalized, seen as standard?

ELBOW: I'm now sometimes seen in the composition scholarly community as rearguard, old fashioned! I don't feel like I've ever had a chance to be in the center. But in the community of teachers I feel I am in the center. It's a community I feel so grateful to. It's nice to be old and treated with respect. But among the vanguard of scholarship I am sort of regarded as retro. And freewriting stands for everything bad. That irks me and I'm always wasting too much energy trying to prove that I'm an intellectual, a scholar, a theorist, that I'm not right wing or something. I wish I didn't do that, but I always hate for people to think bad about me. I guess I'm still the naive kid. It's the same in my teaching. I'd be a better teacher if I didn't so much want my students to like me.

WOE: It is hard in teaching to break out and try something that's different, that's weird. How do you give yourself liberty to do that?

ELBOW: I think that's a very serious issue. Where do we find the opportunities to try things out? In my present life I get invited to give workshops. I get to try things out when I'm 200 or 2000 miles away from home. And I figure "I'm outta here. I'm never going to see these people again in my life." It's wonderful. I can do things I wouldn't dare do at home. And because I was invited they have to be pleasant to me, and since they decided ahead of time that I was smart or nice, they're predisposed to play the believing game with me. On the other hand, in my own class—especially my own freshman class—my students would just think I was a nut and not very clear.

Seriously, I'm lucky that I can do this. I think for most teachers it's hard. I wish we had more structures like some colleges have—a January term, for instance. Little teeny arenas for trying things out, for experimental courses. There's not enough of that. It's true that these rules are self-imposed and all you need is courage, but it's hard in your regular teaching to do something wild. Everything always seems high stakes.

WOE: Especially if you're teaching the same course over and over. And you have your sense of what the course is, in terms of your institution, in terms of your curriculum. When you do something different you think, "Oh my God, it's not 103A anymore. What am I doing?"

ELBOW: I think we could be more structurally clever. For instance I've been thinking recently that I could "jump start" a course, taking the first few weeks of it and defining that time as a different space. I've been doing this a little bit with my freshman course. For two weeks we have all writing: no revising, no feedback, lots of sharing. So because the students don't have to work hard at revising—nothing's graded, there's no feedback, and a lot of the writing's even private—I can ask for an enormous amount of writing. I say to them, "This is a peculiar two weeks. It's like decompression and having an orgy of writing, and then we'll start the regular course." I like that because then we can experiment: it's only a short time and soon it will be over. This strategy isn't perfect, because it seems to set an odd model and some students think I'm crazy. I have a hard time with freshmen, getting them to work hard enough. I believe in revising too! And I want everything beautiful.

WOE: It's so easy just to spend time doing one half of the writing process and not bring in the other one.

ELBOW: Both with my colleagues and also with my students, I sometimes use the metaphor of schizophrenia. I say to my students, "Try to be schizophrenic." I'm trying to do these two opposite things at once.

WOE: You did a five-year stint as a writing program director. Were the teachers under your rule made more free? Did you institute changes?

ELBOW: Again it was sort of accidental. We wanted to come east and there were two possible jobs, one at Albany and one at Stony Brook. I wanted the one at Albany because the Stony Brook one involved administration. But they didn't offer me the Albany job. I ended up glad because people have so often said to me, "These are interesting kooky ideas, but they would never work in the mainstream." So I had a chance to try to institute some of them in the mainstream. As you know, it's difficult and scary to administer something. The best thing was that in my second year Pat Belanoff came.

The first year I taught the practicum I tried to tell them about composition. That was hard on these first-year teachers. They kept saying, "Tell us what to do, don't tell us how you *could* do this or you *could* do that." One of my problems is that I buy into the myth about myself that I'm a wild one-sided person, so I have to keep from overdoing the Peter Elbow. For this reason I limit my effectiveness. I'm always finding teachers who do a better job with my stuff than I do because they're not always stopping to say, "Well, this may be crazy, but...."

It took me a year to realize that what I wanted to say to them was, "I'm going to make you teach my way, my curriculum, but I'm going to try to make you feel not too oppressed because I promise you when this semester is over you can teach however you want. But for this semester you've got to do it this way." They didn't mind, because at least they got an answer as to what to do tomorrow and the next day and the next day. So I stopped holding back.

I used our course to enact the kind of course I wanted for freshmen, for all writers. I laid out a syllabus, assignments, and topics, and some constraints for the students to work with that forced them to teach in the way I wanted them to. Mainly I made them write and do peer feedback. I tried to make them be writers, to feel what that feels like. So your question about freedom interests me. I ended up restricting their freedom. But I liked the bluntness: "I'm going to spend a semester of brainwashing, but then you can do whatever you want." I was able to make a big dent on how many of them wrote and taught. After a few years there was a community that most graduate students really appreciated (although some fought it, which is obviously understandable).

If you're running a writing program and you have an agenda or a program, you are the enemy. I wasn't used to that. I pictured myself as the friend of the underdog, and they thought of me as the dirty authoritarian bastard. I had to learn to deal with that. In a way that was good for me: I learned to be the bad guy. I don't like being the bad guy, but I learned to do it. People got pissed off at me; students would come in and complain.

I felt like I was the ally of the teacher, but I also felt like I was the ally of the freshman, so that if some teacher was abusive I had to stick up for the freshman against the teacher. We didn't have a very formal system, but there were times when a student would complain about something and we would actually stick up for the student.

Here's a classic education story. In the old days at Stony Brook, Freshman English was taught mostly by faculty members, then it got bigger and got taught by graduate students; it used to be a two-semester course, then it became a one-semester course. Then faculty members would call up and say, "I've got this kid in my class who can't write, and he got an A in Freshman English. What are you guys doing down there?" You've heard all this.

WOE: Recently.

ELBOW: In effect the faculty was doing to graduate students what the public is now doing to schoolteachers: giving them worse conditions, and then complaining about their teaching. They wouldn't have been able to do that to their colleagues. Then the faculty instituted a proficiency exam which undermined the teachers. No matter what grade you got in your Freshman English course, you had to pass a proficiency test (this has happened in a number of schools). What's horrible is that the teacher is tempted to teach to the proficiency test. And the best way to teach to a proficiency test is to teach the five-paragraph essay: play it safe, don't get too interested in your topic or you might write a crummy exam. Pat Belanoff and I wanted to change that.

It's not as if no one else had used portfolios. But I don't think anyone used them quite the way we did. We couldn't just get rid of the proficiency exam because the faculty said in effect, "We insist on quality control. We don't trust the workers on the factory line." We needed an alternative form of quality control. So the portfolio was a way to say to the university, "We will make sure an incompetent teacher of Freshman English won't pass a rotten apple."

At the end of the semester students produce a portfolio. For a student to pass the course he or she has to get a grade of C, but in order to get that C her portfolio has to be judged acceptable not only by her own teacher, but by another teacher. The three of us here could be in a small group and we'd shuffle up the portfolios. You'd read mine, and give it a pass or fail, above or below C. You don't have to spend long with the portfolio: If it is very good, you can skim it; if it is very bad, you can skim it; if it is in the middle, you have to read and think. So if I think the portfolio passes and you think the portfolio passes, I can then give whatever grade is needed, even an F if the guy cut too many classes. But if neither of you will give it a passing grade, I can't give it a passing grade. As a collaborative reading of portfolios, it's a wonderful compromise. It doesn't take all the power away from the teacher, just a significant piece of the power, and it forces us to collaborate a little bit. It's not horribly hard, but it is more trouble. And it helps teaching.

I'm excited to see people exploring portfolios in so many ways. I feel proud to have helped start that. But portfolios have become a fad, sort of like freewriting. I sometimes hear people say, "Yeah, I use freewriting. I love it. I collect it and grade it!"

WOE: How do you feel about "academic discourse" and "writing in the disciplines"? Especially about English teachers teaching writing in the disciplines in a formal sort of way?

ELBOW: I wrestle with that. I tried to put my thoughts together in that *College English* essay [January 1991]. I guess I felt vulnerable because my instincts in teaching have tended to neglect academic discourse and to stress informal writing and freewriting. All these smart people, who I respect so much, say that is irresponsible: "What are we going to do for our students to help them survive in other courses?" I finally concluded that we can't teach academic discourse except the discourse of our own disciplines, and even in our own disciplines, there are different academic discourses. I think it's a mistake in a freshman course to set our sights on teaching academic discourse. We just can't do it. Plus, most of our students are not going to be academics. They are going to have to write papers, but they're not going to be academics. I think there's a useful distinction, which David Bartholomae doesn't make, between "school writing" and "academic discourse." Our students have to do school writing, but there's no one kind of school writing.

I want to say to these people, "We should be more self-conscious in our teaching, and we should help make our students more self-conscious about discourse, try to help them adjust to different discourses." It's not as if they aren't savvy about different teachers wanting different things. But we can be a little better about it, make that a subject of our talk.

I want to teach students to connect writing to their lives. My goal in a writing course is that students should write by choice after the course is over. That's my highest goal: that people will make writing part of their lives, will keep writing. I figure that academic writing will be taught to them by teachers in their major, but if I can make them love writing, if I can make them fluent, if I can make them able to think on paper, if I can make them able to develop a train of thought, to start with feelings, impulses, contrary feelings, and blurts, and develop that into a coherent piece, then they're in great shape. I wish I could say I do that. It's really hard.

I constantly struggle with my teaching of freshmen. Because I try to do freewriting, try to make them like writing, to grade so that they're not wrestling for grades (I use a kind of a contract), they write comfortably. If I wanted to make fun of myself, I'd say I teach my freshmen how to write an acceptable paper with an incredibly little investment of energy. And they are very grateful for that: "You taught me how to toss off a paper in half an hour!" But they feel writing as a much more comfortable, natural activity.

The writing I see from my freshmen sometimes seems too naive. I compare student papers with my colleagues and with the graduate students I teach with; I look at some of their students' papers, and I say, "My freshmen aren't writing such wonderful papers." I'm not sure what to do about that. I'm getting them to be themselves on paper—and when they are themselves, guess what? They are naive. I guess people like Bartholomae would say, "Of course! You've just laid out the problem beautifully, and suggested the solution. Your job is to help them develop *different* selves." I see the logic, but that's just what I don't want to do. It feels to me that that's just what my own college teachers did, and I'm still mad. They made me feel that sounding like me or being me was unacceptable, was awful. I didn't realize I was mad at the time. I just swallowed their values and put all my energy and intelligence into a push to distance myself from that naive kid I was. Oh, dear, I hope I'm not wrong about all this, but I just feel so strongly—I yearn so strongly—that it's got to be possible to be yourself and sound like yourself and *still* be very smart and sophisticated. But I certainly haven't learned how to make it happen in 14 weeks in a required freshman writing course.

WOE: Do you think the use of computers has changed anything?

ELBOW: It used to be when I'd talk to people about making a mess first and then going and cleaning it up, the scientists always thought that was the craziest thing. After all, humanists have a certain ideological interest in the mess, in chaos. But scientists were the first people to get comfortable with writing on computers—more comfortable in writing a messy first draft, because it's only electrons on a screen, or whatever they are. I began to notice a lot of scientists and engineers who said, "I've learned how to just pour everything into a first draft, into a file, and then clean it up." My humanist friends took a bit longer to do that. So to generalize, I think computers have made people more comfortable with making a mess. And I love that. Two things that computers are good at are making a mess (because it's just a file) and making it neat, cleaning it up. You press the print button and it's beautiful. It may be a horrible piece of writing but it's beautiful. Those are the two essential things in writing: making a mess and cleaning it up.

Here's a fruitful idea. What's on my computer screen before I print it out is somewhere between a mental event and a piece of text. It's sort of half in my mind and half on paper. It's neither fully inside nor fully outside. It's mediated. It's what Winnicott calls "transitional space."

WOE: So much of your work seems to me very psychological, seems to me even Jungian: your interest in the reconciliation of opposites, for example. And you often seem to be talking about getting in touch with the unconscious, but actually wanting to heighten consciousness, not just allowing the ego to sink into the unconscious. Yet you rarely refer to Jung, much less Freud. Is that a conscious decision?

ELBOW: I have tended to soft pedal the sense in which my writing grows out of my own personal psychological struggles. One whole angle comes out in the freewriting essay, "Toward a Phenomenology of Freewriting" [*Journal of Basic Writing*, Fall 1989], in which I talk about where I learned. In a way I think my primary relationship to freewriting—and probably my relationship to written language—comes from two periods in my life: one was when I quit graduate school and felt like I was falling apart, and the other was when I got a divorce and felt like I was falling apart. Both times I was doing therapy and shrinking my head for all I was worth and wasn't quite sure if I was going to make it. Especially the second time. As I said in the article, I couldn't tell people how it was inside me. I could type fast, so I just blurted all my feelings on the paper, my feelings of desperation and fear and pain and of being at my wits' end. There were really times when I thought, "I don't know how I can deal with this." It became a way of surviving. If I wrote about my problems, I could get through the day. One day at a time. So that became my primary relationship to writing, where I learned to think and feel on the paper. Maybe that's why metaphors come into my prose. I don't know that I have more metaphors than most people. Everyone's mind is the same, everyone has dreams at night, but I think because I've done so much writing, I've learned to let them get into my prose.

I've always been nervous about talking about the psychological side very overtly, partly because it's personal and partly because among academics it's a no-no. When *Writing Without Teachers* came out, a lot of people said, "Well, this is too therapeutic. This is too much about feelings." So in a way I was always trying to prove it was all academic, not too psychological.

A lot of my writing is psychological in the sense of trying to figure out how my life works. And I have given a lot of my money to psychiatrists. I did all this therapy, which didn't really help me stop acting in a self-destructive way. The primary therapeutic experience in my life was with a guy who did groups, from 1969 to 1972, when I was at MIT the second time. Frankly I have to hand it to him and to the group setting. It was partly the group process and partly that he was very skillful and powerful. (I didn't always like it. It was difficult and painful. I spent some time hating him; I guess transference was happening.) It really changed me. I began to learn to live better. I began to learn to connect to other people a little more. I guess my fear and my instinct to run away from life began to turn around. I'd always been a loner, but learning to connect with the group over three years was the most successful therapeutic time in my life. I was trying out groups in my teaching, but in fact the main group in my life was a psychotherapy group. It was not without teachers but had a very powerful, conventional, orthodox Freudian. He did lay very low, didn't say very much, but his presence was heavy.

WOE: Classical Freudians basically offer Therapy Without Analysts.

ELBOW: He forced people to use the group. I tried to fight this for a while, but he forced us to use each other. So that was my most powerful experience with a group. It's too corny to say it, but in brief it saved my life. I began to learn to live in a way that was not self-destructive or dead-endish—to learn to be a not-totally-lonely, unable-to-connect-toother-people person.

A little light bulb went off three years ago: "This is why I'm so pissed off at people who think I'm unsocial." The primary experience of my life was learning to be social, and the primary event behind *Writing Without Teachers* is social, is the lifesaving necessity of connecting with other people. And I think the effect it had on the profession was to get people interested in groups. When I give in to my anger, I am furious with people for not recognizing that in my work I am profoundly social; it's the most important aspect of my work, although I'm profoundly interested in all this individual stuff too. But I have not talked much about the fact that a psychotherapy group was the primary experience behind that angle of *Writing Without Teachers*. (In that essay of mine that's in *Pretext* [Spring/Summer 1990], I talk a little bit about that.) I've failed to be as brave as I should be at simply talking turkey about these things. Again it's this tendency not to take chances, to be a respectable academic. As you can tell from this interview I'm interested in my life. One finds one's own life interesting.

At the end of the essay about Paulo Freire, "The Pedagogy of the Bamboozled" [in *Embracing Contraries*], I discuss the hunger to merge with other people, a subject I don't talk about very much in my writing, yet it is a deep hunger for me. It even connects to freewriting. Humans need that merging. Obviously that's what produces Nazism: the hunger to belong. One of the accusations I have about the composition world is that everybody has to be in on the latest thing. The field of English seems prey to groupthink. There's this hunger to belong. Someone at lunch the other day was eloquent, saying how in our devotion to diversity we sometimes have this horrible unwillingness to accept a diverse point of view. In the whole field of literature and composition, it's dangerous to say something that's not in fashion. And that comes from the hunger to merge.

WOE: In *Writing With Power* and *Writing Without Teachers*, one of your metaphors is the cooking metaphor. In some ways those seem like elaborate recipe books, full of these little things that will help you.

ELBOW: I got a letter from a clever woman who said, "I read *Writing Without Teachers* and you're not really a cook." Cooking is a very powerful word for me, but it's a metaphor, like the way chemists use the word. It means alchemy. In a way it's naughty for me to use that word.

WOE: You do provide tricks. In different circumstances or with different psychological types, do all the tricks work? Do they work better for certain kinds of people? You mentioned that you don't do some of these things any more, perhaps because your psyche has changed.

ELBOW: Actually a big problem for me is that, on the one hand, I instinctively try to honor the notion that different people need different things. I try not to be too universalizing. On the other hand, I feel deeply that everybody is just like me. I think somewhere in *Writing Without Teachers* I say, "It's all research based on a sample of one." It's naughty to say, "It's universal; everybody's the same." I try to respect difference, but I am guilty of a kind of belief that people are deeply alike.

So my strategic problem is to try to get all these things in there and yet not try to make everybody do them. We had the same problem in our textbook: how to get the stuff in there and not be too dictatorial to the reader: to say, "Take whatever you want, sample here and there." I want to get my hands on the readers and make them do everything, but I know I can't. So I have to be nice and say, "Take what you can use." But in my megalomaniac heart I think if I am clever enough, I can get them to do it. And I am seductive, I am strategic. I try to be nice, because I try to get my way. My wife gets on me that I'm the youngest child and youngest children do that; they get their way by being nice or charming. So I try to be nonpushy and all that, but I want to get them to do it. That's rhetoric! How do you get people to believe you when you can't hit them over the head? Sometimes I think I get in trouble from being too strategic. I think I'm now at a stage in my life where I should learn to be a little more direct and overt. You see the same thing in my voice struggles—I continue to work on voice.

There are a couple of themes that have been running straight through my work. The believing game and the doubting game is one touchstone because it's right there from *Writing Without Teachers* on. And voice. My latest published piece about voice is "The Pleasures of the Voice" [Chris Anderson, ed. *Literary Nonfiction*], four or five years ago. What I said about voice in *Writing With Power* is so critically naive: I talked about "real" voice. I guess it's kind of Jungian, but it's about people having a real self. I get in trouble with it anyway, so that the more recent essay is an attempt to be critically sophisticated about it.

I'm seeing the cycle over and over again, from being a naive person to learning to be sophisticated, and then trying to do justice to one's naiveté again. Like going from Proctor Academy to Williams College. I still think the train of thought and the careful distinctions I worked out about voice in that essay are right. In fact I'm still trying to use them in a new essay, but I want to stop and say, "Come on. Let's say it in a naive way." I want to talk about voice as magic. My favorite chapter in *Writing With Power* is the "Magic" chapter at the end.

I want to say about voice that we know, all rational people know, that language is a series of random semiotic signs, where there's no real relationship between the sign and the thing. Only children and Socrates in his weak moments thought there was a relationship between "C-AT" and the cat. It's a failure of critical thinking when we mistake the symbol for the thing. But now I want to say that, yes, that's true; however, the most economical, interesting, and fun way to describe success in writing is to make writing function *as though* it were magic. To write right is to make the word "C-A-T" cause someone to have a hay fever reaction to cats. If you do it right, words function magically. And that's a definition of voice.

Maybe it's a shortcut to skip the rational. In other words, I can't explain rationally how a set of random symbols can actually trick a person into thinking it's the real thing, but if we get people to try to be magical, they can do it. A better example is voice in another sense. If I tell people, "Don't use such a heavily nominalized style, don't use so many passives, don't use so many adjectives, blah blah blah, and your writing will be crisper," that's hard, that's a lot of work. If I tell them, "Don't sound like such a pompous ass," they get it immediately and they don't have to know anything about nominalization. They change their syntax. So we can shortcut theoretic knowledge by using the metaphor in that way. We shortcut theoretic knowledge by using magic. Let's take pieces of writing and figure out which ones have magic, and then let's try to do magic. I think that's a nice angle into voice.

I want to read more and study more about the human voice itself. It took me a long time to realize that if I'm interested in voice then covertly or implicitly I am interested in importing the body into the realm of writing. The body is where the voice comes from. I'm going to teach a graduate seminar this fall about performance in language or language as a performance. At a totally intuitive level, I'm sure our writing will improve if we perform voice, if we move our bodies.

WOE: I understand what a useful shortcut it can be to tell students not to be such pompous asses, to get them to use a more natural voice, but how can we tell the profession as a whole not to be such a pompous ass?

ELBOW: It's become clear to me recently what my vocation is. I'm not so sure I'm a good teacher of adolescents, but what I would really love to do is to change the academic world. It's taken me awhile to realize that I am deeply an academic person because sometimes I feel I'm not. Sometimes I feel the profession won't accept me because I write too funny, blah blah blah, but dammit I am an academic. I've finally written enough books that there's no doubt about it. *Writing Without Teachers* would have been an interesting, funny book, and that's it; but somehow I've persisted One of my fears has been that I will disappear off the face of the earth and my work will never be heard of again. As I began to be attacked, that fear got triggered. It's taken me a while to realize this (and it's sort of hard to say this), but I think it's too late to wipe me off the face of the earth because I've written enough and enough people have heard of my writing and used it.

I am an academic, and what I hate about academics is this business of pomposity and condescension. Other academic things are in my own life: fear of other people, fear of feelings, fear of the unconscious, fear of naiveté. But

I would like to change these academic attitudes; I'm pissed off having experienced them myself: 1) in my own education when people condescended to me and ridiculed me and thought I was stupid when I wasn't stupid; and 2) from colleagues who think I'm stupid when I'm not stupid. The root of this behavior is condescension; many people in the profession think there's only one way to be an academic, to be fancy in some way. But how do you change these attitudes?

Writing is one way. This is a funny way to say it, but I have something *they* need. There's this one problem that academics face: they'll perish if they don't publish. And I can help them in their writing. I mean, scratch an academic and you'll find someone who's in trouble with writing. All academics have suffered with their writing. I've begun to be encouraged by doing workshops away from home. For the first time last year I worked up the courage to do a workshop on my own campus, where I didn't couch it as "How can we help our students' writing?" I was just out front: "Let's have a workshop about our own writing." I was scared to do this at my own college, but it was successful.

WOE: Did any English professors come?

ELBOW: No. But that didn't surprise me. They are the last. But people were appreciative. They really wanted to work on their writing. What's wonderful about writing is that it is a leveler. You get people to be honest about what happens to them when they write, to talk about the pain and the mess and the struggle, then you give them the lollipop, the relief of getting into a supportive group. And that's a leg into humanizing teaching.

WOE: I wish we could get people not to be pompous asses when they write about literature. The irony is that literature is almost by definition not pompous ass writing.

ELBOW: Yes. These are the most unforgivable sins in Chaucer and Shakespeare—the only sins they are really *mad* at. It's interesting what's happened with reader response criticism. It was fashionable for a while, then it was dropped like a hot potato. My hypothesis is that English departments dropped it because it looked as though there was some danger of actually having to talk honestly. And English professors didn't want to do that, especially the theorists.

A funny thing here is that I've always admired literature. I love C.S. Lewis. I can be accused of being an elitist. In a way I am. I certainly had an elite education. I'm so troubling to some people because it seems as if I'm only interested in bad writing and low standards, but I love excellence, I love the amateur tradition, C.S. Lewis and such, which is tainted with elitism. It's the old-boy thing. It's hard to rehabilitate all that from the elitism it comes wrapped in, but scholars like Lewis did know how to talk about literature in a humane way. I'd love to save that, to get that back.

Our University of Massachusetts writing program has sort of kept literature out of the freshman writing course. They've made students' own writing the center and that's wonderful. But I would like to have some poems and stories as readings. There's a simple reason: poems and stories talk about feelings. The customary thing in most writing courses is to bring in editorials and essays, but I love poems and stories because they are about feelings.

The profession of literature is sort of stuck. If it is to be a highpowered profession with a high-powered scholarship, people can't just write books and articles at a naive level. The fancy talk gives you fancy stuff to publish. When I was in graduate school going through the hardest time of my life, I was reading Shakespeare and developed this train of thought about freedom and necessity in Shakespeare; it was about freedom, and necessity, and me, and getting a divorce. I've always wanted to write a book about Shakespeare's plays from a totally personal point of view but I haven't figured out how to do that.

CYNTHIA L. SELFE

Throughout her distinguished career, Cynthia Selfe has set the standard of excellence in digital rhetoric, work she continues as the OSU Humanities Distinguished Professor at the Ohio State University. In graduate school at the University of Texas in the 1970s, Selfe learned to do word processing on a mainframe, and in 1986, while many campuses were still debating the usefulness of personal computers, Selfe published her first book, Computer-Assisted Instruction in Composition: Create Your Own. *Since then she has written, co-authored, and edited dozens of articles, journal special issues, and books, including (with Patrick W. Berry and Gail E. Hawisher)* Transnational Literate Lives in Digital Times *(2012). Selfe co-directs the 11-day Digital Media and Composition Institute held at Michigan Tech, and with Gail Hawisher she founded the highly influential* Computers and Composition: An International Journal; *this and other work led to their being awarded the Technology Innovator Award from the CCCC Committee on Computers in Composition and Communication in 2000. She also received the CCCC Exemplar Award for outstanding contributions to the field in 2014.*

Such community recognition is fitting given that Selfe's work is characterized by community building—whether within the classroom or among scholars—as much as by technology use. In keeping with this community focus, even those who have not seen Selfe receive one of her many awards might recognize her from the Digital Archives of Literacy Narratives table at CCCC (daln.osu.edu), where she, Dickie Selfe, and her team collect participants' audio and video stories. As of 2014, the Digital Archive has collected more than 5,000 narratives, enriching the discipline and adding to her many contributions to computers and writing, and to the field of rhetoric and composition more broadly.

—Sarah Perrault

"Nomadic Feminist Cyborg Guerilla"

Carolyn Handa

Fall 1992

WOE: How did you end up as a writing teacher and a computers and writing expert?

SELFE: When I graduated from the University of Wisconsin in 1973, I really wanted to go into the Peace Corps. I was dedicated to that idea. At Wisconsin in those days there was quite a bit of political unrest; I was inspired by the sixties and wanted to go. It was the only job where I ever got turned down flat. They didn't want me. I didn't know whether it was because I was on a black list because of political activity or because they didn't need English teachers. Anyhow, they saw right through me. So instead I went to Scotland on an exchange program. I taught English for about six months in a small coal-mining town west of Glasgow called Auchinleck, and I did some hitchhiking around Europe. Then I came home late in August just before school started. The only job I was able to get was in a small all-Black school district right outside of Houston, Texas.

WOE: Was that where you were raised?

SELFE: That's where I went to high school and where I met my husband Dickie. Dickie and I went to high school together. I swear to God! After we graduated, Dickie went to college in Lubbock at Texas Tech University, while I went to the University of Wisconsin, to Scotland, and then back to Houston to teach at this all-Black school district outside of the city. It was the poorest school district within a 200-mile radius, the only school district that had no air conditioning in Houston in the summer.

WOE: And you took this assignment because you came on board at the last minute?

SELFE: At the last minute. Well, I just couldn't find any other job. (I wondered why it was so easy to get a job there. I was so slow!) But the work at that junior high school taught me just how rough our educational system was for students and teachers. As a young teacher I was astounded at the depth of ignorance I saw in *teachers* who were unequal to the task of educating students in this place and making any kind of a substantive difference, the way I thought I was going to make a difference when I was a young teacher.

One day a young woman walked down the aisle in my classroom to ask me a question. This guy stuck his foot out and tripped her. I got really angry and wrote a note to the principal, Mr. Lundy: "Mr. Lundy, please discipline George because he tripped Sally while she was walking down the aisle." I had the kid take the note to the office. Two minutes later he comes back. He's holding the note and he's pointing to this word. He says, "Mr. Lundy wants to know what an 'aesell' is. It was the word "aisle," and our own Principal didn't know how to spell. This district, *because* it was poor and Black, got the worst of everything: the worst and most ineffective principals, the shoddiest physical plant, the leftover teachers. For these kids, education was separate and *not* equal! I thought: "now I can make *some* change, but this is ridiculous!" By that time Dickie had graduated from Texas Tech and was getting his Master's degree at the University of Texas, Austin. We had been seeing each other, so I decided to go to the University of Texas at Austin to get a Master's degree and maybe figure out how I could do the job of teaching a little bit better than I was doing it at the time. I went to Texas by mistake.

I just happened to bumble on Texas in the golden age when Jim Kinneavy, John Ruszkiewicz, Lester Faigley, Maxine Hairston, Steve Witte, Ed Farrell, and Julie Jensen were there—all the people who had made and continue to make a real difference in composition studies and in English education. I was fortunate enough to get into the English ed. program during the time when Kinneavy held a joint appointment with English and English ed. I was *exceedingly* lacking in promise. During the first two years I was assigned to supervise student teachers as they went out to the schools and did their student teaching.

This was ironic. They thought I knew something. I thought I knew nothing. It was really sort of funny, sort of pathetic. I did my best, and I tried with the students. But who knows how much damage I did! Then Ed Farrell left the Headquarters of the National Council of the Teachers of English and came to teach at Texas, and for some reason he was able to see things that nobody else saw. He paid attention to my writing, for instance. He made me understand that *how* I said things, *how* I wrote them, was important. He made me understand that how I wrote about something was important because it reflected some underlying content or logic that was important to other people, that could make a difference to other people. Wow, writing as social action! He was the first teacher that paid attention to my writing.

WOE: Who do you feel influenced your educational development and teaching attitudes the most?

SELFE: Ed Farrell for teaching me how to write and for teaching me the truth of what Mike Rose said in *Lives on the Boundary*—that sometimes you have to pay attention to the person's own language at the surface level of prose, at the level of the sentence, at the level of the word. You have to be able to suggest alternative diction as that writer learns how to make meaning in the language that you're asking her to make meaning in. I was impressed with Ed. I still am. He just retired this year. He has influenced my teaching a lot. He taught me how important it was to read students, too. He taught me how to look at a person—I can't always see things as clearly as he did because I'm not a good judge of character—and find promise. I was always impressed that he was able to do that. I thought, "Well, gosh, what do you see? What do you see when you look at a student?" I wish I could look at people and have those bionic eyes where you could look at them in infrared or some other wavelength and see where that promise is. With some people I can see promise right away. But with others it escapes me and I don't realize it until later.

Jim Kinneavy was a hero of mine, too, and a mentor. He taught me how to be kind. I'm still not great at that, but he taught me what a wonderful thing kindness is. He was just a nice person to everybody. He was as nice to the graduate students he worked with as he was to the chair of the department or to the dean. Probably nicer, in a genuine sort of way. Jim taught me intellectually what a delight it could be to study and to learn—and how to dress!

Art Young was also a mentor. Art taught me a couple of things, exceedingly important things. First, how to be delighted and gratified with the work of the people around you, your colleagues and the students with whom you work. And second, how to obtain professional gratification just by looking at how wonderful these people are. He taught me in an intellectual way how to make your values as a teacher of composition and writing influence or shape the values that you use to structure a program, to administer a program, to do your scholarship, to start a computer-supported writing facility—that all of these grow organically from what you know to be true as a teacher, or from what you know as a teacher or want to achieve as a teacher, and how important it was to integrate those things, rather than have your scholarly life separate from your administrative life or your teaching life.

WOE: Yes, those are usually separate, the administrative life especially.

SELFE: Some people separate their scholarship from their teaching, too. Art was wonderful in showing how your scholarship could grow out of your teaching, that in fact the connection might be really good. There wasn't a lot of time at Michigan Tech in those early days to be geeking around. You *had* to make fruitful connections to get the job done.

WOE: What kinds of things do you do in a computer classroom during the first week of classes? What do you want your students to understand and think about as they go into this kind of learning space?

SELFE: Well, maybe not in a week, but I want students to become critical readers and writers of their own experiences and the experiences of others, their own texts and the texts of others. And I want them to understand that social exchanges, or collaborative exchanges, can help them become critical readers and writers. These notions really form the center, the focus for what I want them to achieve when they go into the computer-supported writing environment. I try to talk to them about how computers and computer technology can support the processes involved in their becoming these critical readers and writers of their own and others' experiences, and in that context, we discuss the political nature of language within these environments. So I try to introduce them to these writing environments by telling them what goals I have for them as students in writing classes, and then I try to show them how the environment we've created is actually shaped by these goals and how they can use the environment to their advantage in achieving the goals. That's what I want them to learn.

WOE: So you show them that the focus is on them and not the machines.

SELFE: Yes, we really work hard on that. We try to make gentle fun of the machines so that the hardware and the software don't assume a greater importance than the students and the goals that we have as writing teachers. That's hard to do because computers are physical objects that immediately commend themselves to your attention. But we talk about the philosophical and the educational goals that we have as a center or a lab or a space—the writer's environment—and try and focus on that first.

WOE: In the decade or so that you've been working in a computer classroom, have you noticed any change in the kind of student you get? Do students now seem to take more easily to the computer environment or did they always take pretty easily to it?

SELFE: I honestly can't tell you that with any kind of certainty. I think students have gotten much smarter, but it's probably only me that's seeing them as smarter because when I first started teaching I was too stupid to know that they were smart. So the older I get the more I'm able to see just how smart they are and how much they bring to the computer-supported spaces in which they work. When I work with graduate students like Johndan Johnson-Eilola, Stuart Selber, Karla Kitalong, and Kate Latterell at Michigan Tech—especially those in computers and composition, but others, too—I realize just how smart students are, and how they learn despite *us*. One of the things I wish I had known and brought to teaching earlier in my career is some sense of humility. And I didn't. I just didn't recognize how smart they were when I started.

WOE: We never do.

SELFE: Now I'm getting smarter, I hope, about that. Not smart enough, though, to realize how earnest and forthright and intelligent they are when they come to school.

WOE: Your work seems to have undergone such a major and maybe radical shift from 1986 when you published *Computer-Assisted Instruction in Composition: Create Your Own* with NCTE, to the keynote speech you're giving this year at the Eighth Computers and Writing Conference. Do you perceive this shift? And if so, can you identify how and why it happened?

SELFE: In the work we do, one of the benefits of not being intellectual giants ourselves is that we're able to feed very much off the ideas of others. One of the most wonderful things about my career as it's unfolded is that I've gotten to work with generous and wonderful colleagues and learn so much. Their intellectual influence leaks into my work in ways that are productive for me. So, for instance, when I began writing that first book, *Computer-Assisted Instruction. Create Your Own*, I had just come to Michigan Tech. I started working with Art Young and that book was very much influenced by his work on writing across the curriculum. His work gave me enough confidence to say "Start with what you know about teaching writing, the teaching of writing, and your own work as a writer and use that to shape computer-assisted instruction." But then the more I worked with Art and Toby Fulwiler and Bruce Petersen, the more I realized the social implications and dimensions of their work, the more composition studies as a field was acknowledging social constructivism. So the next book, *Creating a Computer-Assisted Language Facility*, incorporated much more of that kind of work.

Meanwhile, of course, Marilyn Cooper came to Michigan Tech, and her work on critical theory has strongly influenced my more recent work—the article we did in *College English* ["Computer Conferences and Learning: Authority, Resistance, and Internally Persuasive Discourse," 52:8 (December 1990), 847–869]—the Baktinian perspective, her work on the ecology of writing, systemic implications that influence our work as teachers. Jennifer Slack is at Michigan Tech. She has introduced me to the field of cultural studies, as has Johndan Johnson-Eilola. Gail Hawisher has helped me enormously with educational theory and with research methodology. Billie Wahlstrom has taught me about communication theory. So every person I've had the fortune to work with has influenced my own work in productive ways. The best work I think I do in computers brings in theory from outside of computers.

WOE: You talk about us composition teachers as "reform-minded educators committed to social change and political action within larger social, ideological, economic landscapes," and you emphasize the importance of our learning to understand our travels through electronic spaces, both local and wide-area networks, in global as well as local terms—and, it seems to me, you emphasize the global. Can you explain why you feel the global terms are so important?

SELFE: I became convinced that if we created these small local spaces in computer networks, we could effect change by letting people learn in ways that were different from the regular classroom. And because these spaces were invisible to administrators and because they were designed by us, we could effect change in those spaces. Then the students who are learning in them would take the values from those small spaces and effect their own changes in different ways that might affect the systems within which we work.

But the more I read in postmodernism, the more I started to realize how ideology works at many levels, simultaneously and in articulation with other social forces. Because such forces are so dispersed, there is a grid of control that influences almost everything we do, even in these minute spaces. I realize how optimistic it was to think that our actions and our students' actions in those spaces would be more influenced by our own values than they would be influenced by the other cultural forces exerted through ideology. It occurred to me, after reading Terry Eagleton, after reading Mark Poster and Catherine Belsey and some of the other critical and social theorists, that if I didn't consider this in a larger context—a political context, an ideological context—I'd be in danger of suggesting that local change is separate and can occur without being influenced by the context of global change. I need to understand more about how ideology is articulated with cultural forces, how change is articulated with tradition.

I'm slowly trying to expand my frame of study: right now I tend to think of the State in terms of George Bush and the American sort of government, the military/industrial complex. But I'm beginning to see that we have to think in terms of other countries, too, and the fact that the military/industrial complex does not stop at state borders. In fact cultural hegemony deterritorializes state borders and exerts control on a global basis. If we don't understand global systems and global constraints, I don't think we're going to be able to act effectively or understand our actions within local spaces. The more we think globally the more exciting our work can be, because we think of people like Anne Villems in Estonia and Bernie Susser in Japan and the influence that their work is going to have on ours. We can also recognize the web of constraints that ties us together and the web of possibilities that can provide us with ways, as teachers, of extending the radical, democratic project that I think many of us are committed to. This is the project of changing oppressive situations so that groups or individuals who are oppressed gain more equal access to opportunities than they now have. If I see that set of possibilities at a global level, it gives me hope. We can work to effect changes in small ways within this larger context, but nonetheless in meaningful and effective ways. Computers can be a way of extending that discursive territory for the radical democratic project.

WOE: Now about virtual space and official highways, both electronic and otherwise: how did you come to see these highways as official? How did you begin to realize that we need to move on unmapped and unmarked paths that avoid the destinations of what you call state-authorized transportation vectors: roadways, airwaves, railways, computer networks, and how did you come to see so clearly that the State has assumed control of these spaces through legislation and regulation? I think a lot of us don't see the official highways. We're just driving on them, sending our electronic mail over them. So when you point out to us that they're there, they're official, then we can try to get off.

SELFE: Paul Virilio's book *Speed and Politics: An Essay on Dromology* was pretty influential to me there because Virilio pointed out that the state opens up these spaces for settlement by discontented populations, like opening up these computer spaces as sort of a social pressure valve.

WOE: I can see the West opening up.

SELFE: Yes! That's exactly what that was! The highway system, the West, the open seas, all of those spaces.

WOE: Are we like those weird renegade people?

SELFE: Exactly! Exactly! The State (which includes us, incidentally), opens up the space of the nets and then it exerts that increasing control, through legislation, through regulation, to control movement within these official vectors, or routes, that it gets people to construct. They're in the process right now—the State, we, they, we—are in the process of enacting increasing amounts of control over this space. We're in a transition stage where that control has not solidified yet or become totally legislated or regulated, and there are still spaces to maneuver to enact tactics in ways that are unofficially sanctioned. The joy that the Megabunnies [members of Megabyte University, an electronic list] have, for instance, in finding electronic ways into libraries that they're not officially sanctioned to use, those ways will become regulated at some point. Packet-switching technology is now making it possible for the corporate owners of phone lines to think about how they will regulate and charge for the amount of information that goes over the lines. But right now we still have the possibility of following the lead of hackers, who go in through the backdoors of these systems. They use the official channels, but in unofficial ways.

Our students at Michigan Tech, who have a great love of learning but limited financial resources, have discovered a great system to get into our campus mainframe for free. Normally, they are charged if they use over a certain amount of CPU time on our local backbone. So they call out through Telnet and go through four or five different countries and come back into the campus mainframe from outside the university where they're not charged by time. They're able to use the nets to subvert the official security system on our own computer despite attempts to commoditize education. These tactics only last as long as it takes for the official groups to recognize them and then stop or legislate or regulate or secure those channels. Michel deCerteau describes such resistant actions as "tactics." Guerillas who enact such tactics, he says, must be "quick as a fox and twice as sly." We have to be able to enact tactics, those almost invisible small gestures, in ways that are quick and clever enough to change continually so that the official powers don't recognize them as important. If we can continue looking to the Megabunnies or to the students we work with to discover ways of subverting official channels (which they naturally do, just by the force of coping with their daily lives), we can extend the virtual landscape or the electronic landscape for the democratic project. We can extend the democratic landscape as fast as the State closes off or regulates or legislates it. We can commit ourselves to discussions of democracy, control, and freedom in these expanded territories.

WOE: Another concept that interests you is the computer network as war-machine. Can you explain this concept briefly?

SELFE: The computer as war machine is a concept that Johndan Johnson-Eilola introduced to me in a paper that he wrote based on Virilio's *Speed and Politics*: Donna Haraway, Gilles Deleuze, Felix Guattari, and others also allude to the notion or address it directly. Virilio argues that the State and the Military (and sometimes combinations of both) use computer technology to exert power, control, and violence on various populations. For Virilio, computer networks, electronic landscapes, are "war machines" that reconfigure the speed and violence enacted by the State and by its citizens. He notes that the computer's first task was solving some very complex equations aimed at determining the trajectory of anti-aircraft projectiles and airplanes. Virilio also claims that these computer networks serve State violence by de-territorializing existing landscapes, erasing current territorial boundaries separating countries and their peoples. Localities, places, and elements that used to be distinct and separated by a buffer of distances are now juxtaposed in official time and space, he says. When territorial space disappears and time contracts within electronic landscapes, the State can wage war with increased speed. Speed multiplied by computers and computer networks, Virilio notes, virtually eliminates the time available for a citizenry to reflect.

This characterization of the State and its tendency toward violence isn't all that farfetched or exaggerated. We can see that it's at least partially accurate. The Cuban missile crisis, Virilio says, became a crisis because the placement of Soviet missiles in Cuba threatened to reduce the Americans' defensive warning time to thirty seconds. Our government has continued to see computer-supported systems both as threats and as powerful weapons.

Virilio adds that a final characteristic of war machine technologies is their ability to support the State in its occupation of intellectual and spiritual territories as well as geographical territories. Workers are devalued not only by the State's continuing co-opting, but by technology itself; workers' bodies are transformed into technological "prostheses," into bodies without souls, domesticated robots that serve the State's appetite for additional speed and violence. Those who doubt this merging of humans and machines can refer to any of the current descriptions of projects to develop neural networks, "living brain machines," computer viruses, or biological memory. Our government is a mainstay of funding in such projects, often through its military agencies. Of course, we *are* our government, so we are implicated, too. Virilio's ideas apply to our own situation. If the landscape of electronic networks seems to offer a promising space for some localized and limited educational reform, then, according to teachers of English, the possibility of systemic change and progress on a more extensive political level seems less likely within these spaces. If Virilio's vision is accurate, we are seeing a kind of double-action containment, an opening up of free spaces (an act that provides a social pressure valve for official State systems) and, at the same time, the increasing regulation and containment of these spaces. Within electronic terrains in the growth of the Internet [a network of networks], the development of NREN [the National Research and Education Network], the computerization of industry, we could be seeing the ways in which resources (speed and expertise, in particular) are developed and used to support other purposes (education, the delivery of State services, research) until they're needed to enact war. Really, if electronic landscapes are so broadly controlled by the State and in the service of the State and, further, if we are part of the State, can reform-minded teachers hope to use these discursive spaces for political action that leads, by an imperfectly traced path, toward an expanded democratic project? I think so, but we're going to have to go into this thing with our eyes wide open and our powers of critical thinking on high!

WOE: What you're saying calls to mind your idea of the nomadic feminist cyborg guerilla. Would you talk about that idea?

SELFE: The nomadic feminist cyborg guerilla is a kind of English teacher-activist who uses computer technology, a politically active being who employs the available technology as a medium for effecting political and educational change to support the expanded project of radical democracy. This kind of being uses technology not as a war machine, but as a discursive territory for extending democracy.

The notion of a feminist cyborg always reminds me of my own contradictions in the current complex system of cultural relations, my own complicity as a teacher, as a taxpayer, as a general citizen wienie. Like me, cyborgs, even feminist cyborgs, are part war machine, part humanist. As Haraway notes, they are partial, faithless, cynical, and therefore unpredictable. But contradiction and plurality can be comforting, too. The concept of a feminist cyborg embodies the realization that no discursively constituted political structure—not even the State—is totalizing; thus, the concept of cyborgs acknowledges that we could be involved in encouraging some hope for the day after the apocalypse. Now if we understand that cyborgs are the illegitimate offspring, in Haraway's terms—of militarism, patriarchal capitalism, and state socialism—we can also recognize that illegitimate offspring often betray their origins. In fact, cyborgs can teach us how much power the margins have and what tremendous things we can gain by ignoring and changing traditional boundaries.

This last statement begins to get at a final reason that the role of nomadic feminist cyborg guerilla appeals to me. Starting with caution and contradiction, I recognize that I'm part of the regularly dispersed, complexly constituted social formation I have called "the State" and that I am thus implicated in all of its oppressive and violent actions. I can also see that I'm partly implicated in those actions the State designs to support democratic participation: the State's support of civil rights (as partial and gap ridden as that political fabric is); the State's support of equal employment opportunities for women (as unsystematically and inconsistently applied as that support has proven itself); the State's commitment to universal education (as problematic and inequitable as that commitment has been). So really, the term "feminist cyborg" reminds me that the State itself and the virtual spaces it designs and maintains are potential sites where democratic antagonisms can emerge. As a feminist cyborg, I can see what Laclau and Mouffe call lithe possibility" of extending the social project of "radical democracy" into new, expanded social territories, especially through the political action undertaken in virtual spaces.

If nomadic feminist cyborg guerillas commit themselves to supporting discourse about radical democracy within computer nets, the unstable, partial, temporary discursive formations that individuals construct could serve as forces that extend and transform the existing intellectual and political terrain; these formations could have, in Ernesto Laclau and Chantel Mouffe's words, the "profound subversive power" characteristic of radical democratic discourse. This would be especially true if the discourse that nomadic feminist cyborg guerillas sponsor in these on-line conversations among friends and co-workers, colleagues and students, on bulletin boards and in virtual classrooms had as a common goal the complex articulations of possibilities and gaps, of connections and contradictions in current democratic political action. This discourse would become discussions of how we have succeeded and how we have failed to enact democracy within the United States, how we have succeeded and how we have failed to support democratic action around the world. I know English teachers are already working in these directions; Shirley Haley-James, ex-president of the NCTE, is using the Internet to support her efforts toward an International Consortium of English Teachers through the NCTE. Gail Ha wisher and the NCTE Instructional Technology Committee are continuing to work on NCTE Net, a web of English teachers connected by technology, which could provide a forum for radical, reform-based teaching and learning.

With such discursive projects (as contradictory and partial as they're bound to be), we could help construct what Laclau and Mouffe call those complex "chains of equivalence" that exist among various forms of oppression in our culture, and, thus, collectively wield political power. We could, for instance, help articulate the connections between the general cultural oppression of women and the oppression of groups under-represented within our educational system, between the economic inequities manifested in our classrooms and the violence in our city streets, between the increasing inability of schools to address the needs of students and the waging of war in the Persian Gulf, between larger classes and apathetic voters who can't decide between Bill Clinton and George Bush. Nomadic feminist cyborg guerillas would have to recognize these discussions as necessarily contradictory and gap ridden. But we might also learn where our current educational conversations succeed, where they constitute new social and logical formations, where they create different political spaces for the expansion of radical democratic struggles. We'll also learn where our efforts fail. With such discourse focusing on the democratic antagonisms that arise from existing hegemonic structures, we can extend the project of radical democracy, even as we participate in the system we critique.

WOE: Do you have any thoughts about the future of hypertext?

SELFE: Yeah, I do. I think eventually there won't be computers without hypertext. Every application will be hypertextual. We're moving toward hypertextual environments in everything. But hypertext might become increasingly less visible because it will become more ubiquitous. So the Internet, for example, will have a hypertext base soon, instead of the kind of base it has now. I don't see why anybody would stay with a non-hypertextual structure when they have hypertext. But for users, it's got to become much more accessible through a variety of different products and projects. As John Slatin said, we've got to work on rhetorical approaches to hypertext. We've got to create conventions and strategies for negotiation and navigation through hypertext.

WOE: Have we learned something from teaching in computer classrooms that we can take to non-computer classrooms?

SELFE: Some of the more interesting things I've learned about computers I've learned by studying work outside of computers: in critical theory, or cultural theory, or rhetorical theory, or communication theory, or any one of the other theories that feeds our discipline. It's a generative or dynamic sort of hermeneutic. That is, I work in a classroom (whether it's in the computer lab or outside of the computer lab) and that changes my thinking about theoretical work, and then I read more theoretical work and that changes my practices in classrooms, and then that in turn changes the way I read theory, which in turn reinforms what I do in classrooms. Computers serve, for me, as an entry point, a catalyst for thinking about how to enact classroom change.

There are points of antagonism—ruptures, I think Laclau and Mouffe call them—sites of disruption that make you pay attention to what's happening in computers and networks. So the computer allows me to see the antagonisms or the articulations among certain sets of problems or challenges. They point out to me singularities or disruptive knots in the fabric of my life and the lives of others. Then I try to use theory and practice to worry those knots.

WOE: You seem to be saying that since computers aren't the main focus, it doesn't bother you when you don't have them for a while.

SELFE: That's right; in fact, I only occasionally teach in computer classrooms.

WOE: How did you get the idea to start up *Computers and Composition*?

SELFE: Well, it wasn't my idea; it was Kate Keifer's idea. Back in '83 or '84 Kate Keifer and I were involved in what we called the fifth C, or something like that (the 4Cs committee on computers—5th, 6th C—I don't know how many Cs!). It was a special-interest group on computers that met at the 4Cs. And one year when we were there we both said maybe we ought to put out a newsletter about what's happening in this field. Kate said, "My husband works for a company and he has access to a computer," and I said, "Well, I'll help you. I think that'd be fun! Let's do a newsletter." And so we started with that. Hugh Burns was in one of the early issues, Helen Schwartz too. They wrote these columns and Kate typed them on her husband's computer and had it printed out. And we sent out the first issue of *Computers and Composition*. It was really great.

Again, what made it great was the colleagues and the students who worked on it. Kate, of course, was the visionary, but from the beginning students at Michigan Tech were involved with the editorial work. They would read the pieces and think about ways in which we could change the journal. And it developed and evolved. With each year students would suggest something new: "What a marvelous idea! We'll try binding it like this!" Johndan Johnson-Eilola, for example, was influential with his work on the journal, and Kelley Johnson-Eilola was involved with some of the early issues. Other students have worked on designing it, being business editor and manager, setting up the editorial procedure. Gail Hawisher does the lion's share of work in *Computers and Composition* now. She does all the work sending manuscripts out to readers. She does all the work in looking at reviews and suggesting to authors how to handle manuscripts and getting the manuscripts back and deciding what goes in each issue. At Michigan Tech we do the close editorial work, with teams of students who work on each article. They also do the production work. They handle almost every aspect of it. There's always an associate editor or editors; right now they're Bill Williamson and Amy Ait-Bella. They arrange the editing teams and the schedule of production. It's wonderful work for them because they learn every aspect of publication.

WOE: You're preparing your graduate students to go out and begin the difficult job of teaching writing and using computers to do it. Are there certain attitudes you try to encourage or instill in them? What would you like brand-new teachers in this discipline to be aware of?

SELFE: I want them to feel a humanistic, philosophical obligation to recognize where our educational and cultural systems are unjust or problematic and to work to change those systems to make life better for people. I would love the students I work with to feel that obligation. At the same time, if they only felt that terrible weight of responsibility, I would be failing them. So I also want them to know the joys of teaching students who are so bright and the joys of working with colleagues who are so good and generous in their intellectual gifts, and the absurdities and the humor of working within systems that are sometimes ludicrous. On the best days, these systems are funny, on the worst days they are bleak indeed. But frankly, students teach me more about those two things than I do them. Students bring that sense of humor with them to almost everything they do. They also teach me about my obligation to change unjust systems. So it's not as much what I want to pass along to them as recognizing what they're telling me that I ought to be teaching them and taking it seriously. And when I pay attention, I know that they're right. I don't always pay attention. Sometimes it escapes me. But when I pay attention, they teach me the right things.

WOE: What are you most proud of in your work with computers and composition?

SELFE: In a strange way, I'm proud of the people I've had the opportunity to work with, the colleagues that I've had the opportunity to work with. It makes me feel good to see other people be so good. But I'm proudest of the students I work with because they are so bright, so wonderful, and they're going to do the kind of work in education that needs to be done, that is going to change the educational system in which they work in ways that will extend the democratic project. Students like Johndan Johnson-Eilola and Stuart Selber and Karla Kitalong and Kate Latterell, they're such good teachers. They teach me so much in everything I do. Their work is so good, their reading is so wide, their thinking is so different from ours that every day I learn something from them. And in a strange way all of this gives me a pride in teaching—not that I have taught them that—but the fact that they're so good, so wonderful and so smart. That gives me great joy, great delight.

DONALD MURRAY

A Pulitzer-prize winning journalist, Donald Murray (1924–2006) came to composition as a successful writer and became a key figure in establishing process pedagogies. His work focused on the relationships between writing and the teaching of writing. In his seminal A Writer Teaches Writing, *first published in 1968, Murray argues that students are most effectively taught using a pedagogy based on the experiences of professional writers, outlining a process theory that has become standard writing instruction in schools and universities. His* Write to Learn *and* The Craft of Revision, *both published in 1998, influenced a generation of teachers, the latter work providing a framework for students to see how revision influences their improvement as writers and thinkers.*

Murray taught successful writers of every type: academics, journalists, and novelists. He told his students that talent was common but hard work rare, and he lived by the maxim "never a day without a line." He started almost every morning by writing, and ended almost every night with a note on what he would write the next day. The author of more than a dozen books, Murray might be best remembered to readers outside of composition for the hundreds of columns he wrote over twenty years for The Boston Globe *as well as his two memoirs,* My Twice-Lived Life: A Memoir (2001) *and* The Lively Shadow: Living with the Death of a Child (2003), *in which he reflects on grief and healing after the loss of his 20-year-old daughter in 1974.*

In this, his first of two interviews with WOE, Murray reflects upon the field that he helped create, and which he worries could be losing touch with the act of writing and the experiences of writers. He is present here as a writer who revels in the discoveries of writing and as one who continued to learn to write every time he sat down to it.

Murray taught for many years at the University of New Hampshire, where he directed the first-year composition program, chaired the English department, and helped establish both an undergraduate journalism program and a graduate program in composition studies. After twice dropping out of high school, Murray served as a paratrooper in World War II, earned a college degree in 1948, and worked his way from newspaper copy boy to winner of the 1954 Pulitzer Prize for Editorial Writing. The annual Donald Murray Prize, sponsored by the Creative Nonfiction Standing Group at CCCC, is named in his honor. Many of Murray's pedagogical practices—emphasizing prewriting, examining one's own writing process, and engaging in staged, multiple revisions—have become composition mainstays. A posthumous collection of his writing, The Essential Don Murray (2009), *is subtitled simply:* "Lessons from America's Greatest Writing Teacher."

—Eric Leake and David Masiel

"Mucking about in Language I Save My Soul"

Driek Zirinsky

Spring 1993

WOE: You've described yourself as a veteran of surprise. What's surprising you in the writing you've been doing recently?

MURRAY: The next word, the next phrase. What I am saying now that I didn't know I was going to say a millisecond ago. I live within the evolving text. That is my homeland where I am most happy, between intent and realization.

WOE: Of all the things that you've written, what's your personal favorite?

MURRAY: Whatever I'm doing: next week's *Boston Globe* column, the novel, the poetry that will be published in a book by Nightshade Press in 1993, the new book I'm doing for Boynton Cook Heinemann, the next revisions of my HBJ college texts, the whole smorgasbord on my writing table. All of it. I love writing. I'm lost in my work. I pay little attention to what I have done.

WOE: This morning you were drawing instead of writing. What are you learning from drawing?

MURRAY: The same thing as writing but even more because I am not an artist. I have the disadvantage of knowing how to write, I make fewer accidents. I do not know how to draw, so the experience of the drawing is more intense, more unexpected. I am lost in the drawing. I see a different Proposal Rock on paper than I see with my eye, and, as I switch from pen to brush, or a combination of both, I see the rock with my eyes and with the lines on the page—and the memory of the lines in the drawing that went before. That is very exciting to me: it is my scholarship. I become a scholar of the rock.

For me, the drawing is an artistic experience and that is enough. It doesn't need to be understood, explained, not even shared any more than we need to share a thought, an image, a feeling. As Archibald MacLeish said in "Ars Poetica": A poem should not mean but be." And yet drawing illuminates the act of writing. What I think and feel is changed as I write it. I understand those natives who feel their soul is stolen if they are photographed. I am stealing that rock from nature. There is the rock in reality, then there is the Murray Rock, a represented rock.

I am also a student as I draw or write. I have to understand these trees and these rocks and these shadows, and the drawing of the line. I was working with a brush yesterday, and the brush has its own dynamic, and it instructs me the same way a sentence instructs me. This instructive line is never what I see in my head. It's different and each drawing is different. It's the experience of celebrating the world. To real scholars and researchers this sounds pretty gooey—and goofy, of course. I was celebrating the world. I was seeing that rock more clearly than I would see it in any other way.

WOE: Do you plan to explore this relationship between art and writing?

MURRAY: Sure I do. I have proposed papers on the subject—to CCCC, for example—but have been turned down. I even have a fantasy of giving up writing and doing nothing but art, escaping from my own competence, I suppose.

My love affair with writing hasn't yet run its course. I am still learning to write, but if that stops happening, I'll switch to painting and drawing. I'm a writer. I write to save my life, to live. Recently I've been having some emotional problems that seem to be side effects of drugs I'm taking for physical problems—typical of old people—and now I often write not to extend the scholarship in our discipline but as therapy. Mucking about in language I save my soul.

WOE: Do you think writing should be taught as therapy?

MURRAY: Of course. Writing is thinking. It's thinking about what we know and need to know, what we read and overhear and think and connect and study and try out and believe and disbelieve. Writing is central to education, even in a computer age as the world becomes more complex because the world is shrinking. We have to speak to each other in words and images and sounds and actions. We have to write and listen to the writing of others.

WOE: In some ways, you're looked at as a founding father of the modern composition field, yet, from other conversations we've had, I sense you feel disappointed in the direction this profession has taken.

MURRAY: I feel uncomfortable talking about this. I have been well treated: promoted, tenured, published, invited to speak. But lately I've had some strange rejections. In one recent rejection my work was described as "quaint," and another piece was turned down because it was "too Murrayesque." And I have been disappointed that professional organizations haven't seen the value of discussing the relationship of writing with another craft such as drawing. Of course it bothers me, but not for long. I have my writing to do, and I lose myself in the page at hand.

The changes that have taken place in our discipline are inevitable. I knew what was going to happen, and I helped them happen. When you professionalize inquiry, produce and hire professionals, you get professionals. I could not have been hired to replace myself when I retired. I didn't have the education, the degree. Pat Sullivan, who replaced me when I retired, is much better educated than I am. We're very different people. I think it's wonderful. She's a colleague and a friend, and I greatly admire her. I couldn't do her theoretical studies. She's also a very good painter and writer (maybe she could do my work).

We've developed a hierarchy in our discipline, a kind of papal organization that likes certain kinds of theology. I was at one university as a visiting professor. Someone was using my material in a seminar on teaching writing, but I wasn't invited to speak because I wasn't a theorist. I wasn't intellectual. It's a bizarre world. Even if I were hireable today, my books would not be scholarly enough. They wouldn't be respected. Well, that isn't quite true. Scholars put me in a funny pigeon hole where I feel uncomfortable, though it's a very nice velvet-lined pigeon hole. It's also very patronizing and insulting. People say I don't manipulate theory, which is a crazed notion. We all have theories. I'm very theoretical, but my theory doesn't start in the sky imposed by Jehovah. My theory starts with the grains of sand: the daily writing. This illuminates and creates theory. The academic world too often applies an idea to a subject matter, rather than discovering it from evidence. That's all I'm doing. I'm discovering the writing process from the specifics. And that's very controversial with my colleagues. They think that writing is craft, and it can't be theoretical.

To me, writing is an intellectual activity, not something you do with your big toe when you're dead drunk. I'm not seen as an intellectual by intellectuals because I tend to use short sentences and short words. I think a lot of my work connects to people who take writing seriously and who are working with students and working with their own writing, and that's very gratifying. I talk with writers and teachers. Not only is what I say driven by theory, I imagine myself as a philosopher of composition. However, I'm seen as a practitioner, a dirty word. I'll accept that. I practiced teaching and learned from my students; I practice writing and learn from my drafts.

WOE: You mentioned that changes in the discipline are inevitable. You also seem to feel that the way you're currently regarded by the academy is inevitable.

MURRAY: It *is* inevitable, so I don't let myself get upset about it. Most of us who helped create the discipline didn't know we were doing that. I didn't know there was a discipline. The people at the University of New Hampshire who made the difference in composition were Tom Carnicelli, who was a medievalist; Lester Fisher, an Americanist; I taught journalism. Later Don Graves came to the Education Department as a specialist in early childhood education who also taught the philosophy of education. Nobody *wanted* any of us to work in the teaching of writing. In fact, the work in composition at first was held against us—and perhaps still is—for not being academically serious.

I certainly was criticized by the other writers in my department for working with English teachers, as well as by the literature people. Our academic colleagues didn't respect those of us doing this until we published. Not many of them respected us afterwards, but they had to pay attention to the volume of publication: mass equals status.

I did sometimes feel that perhaps I had failed to be the writer I might have been. Perhaps they were right; perhaps it was not the work I should have been doing. On the whole these thoughts made me work harder. I understood what would happen if we became academically respectable. And yet I fought for our becoming a discipline. I wanted people to do research in the teaching of writing and the writing act itself, in how effective writing is made. I'm disappointed in what's happened, but I'm not the least bit surprised.

WOE: What are some of the other results?

MURRAY: You know, Driek, I can't understand most of the articles in *CCC* and *College English*. People think I'm kidding when I say that. I'm not. One of my books was reviewed recently, and I don't know whether the reviewer was for or against it. Friends have translated the professional language she used, and they couldn't agree on what she said. I just can't read most articles in our discipline. Literally. I'm not saying I don't want to read it. That's another issue, but I try to read it. I don't understand the language; I don't understand what they're saying. I'm not bright enough.

Of course there is some work I can read. Much of it is interesting or is political (and I agree with the politics), but none of it has anything to do with writing or teaching writing. At least I can't see the connection.

WOE: How would you characterize our discipline today?

MURRAY: As a black hole. There's interesting work going on but only a vast emptiness when it comes to looking at how writers write.

WOE: If you are not reading the scholarship in our profession, what are you reading to understand more about writing?

MURRAY: There's a whole secret scholarship written by writers. I read all the interviews that come out—*The Paris Review* interviews, in *Writing on the Edge*—a journal that is a wonderful exception in the discipline. Writers' interviews fascinate me. All writers. I'm just fascinated with the great spectrum of writers. There are many anthologies now, often collected together for political reasons—Latino writers, Native American writers, certainly women writers—but I read them for the craft. No art is dumb. The academic world sees the act of making as unintellectual and stupid. As if writers are let out of the swamp, and they're all covered with hair, and they do this thing but don't know what it is.

Writers do know what they do. They can write about it, and we can learn from it and pass our learning on to students. Recently I've learned a great deal from David Huddle's *The Writing Habit: Essays* [Gibbs-Smith Publisher, Peregrine Smith Books, Salt Lake City, 1991], John Jerome's *The Writing Trade: A Year in the Life* [Viking, New York, 1992], Robert L. Root

Jr.'s *Working at Writing: Columnists and Critics Composing*. I can't keep up with this secret literature. I just measured the books, mostly writers talking about writing, stacked *in front of* the bookcases in my office: fourteen feet, six inches. There's a vast amount of resource material about what writers have said about writing. It's just not used.

I read writing to be instructed by my masters and mistresses. Yet writers themselves often believe the myth that writing is a magical art, that they don't know what they're doing. Many writers who have become teachers in the university are terrible teachers because they believe the magical myth, and they don't take their job seriously. They say it can't be explained, but if you talk to them, they know what they're doing. I have never met an inarticulate writer, although I've met a lot of writers who would not want to talk in public about what they do.

When I meet a writer, we immediately talk in the same way as a teacher talks to a teacher, a cop to a cop, a judge to a judge, a mechanic to a mechanic. We all know our territories and our crafts, and we can immediately talk in shorthand. But writers, taking on a romantic pose with outsiders (their students are often outsiders), often deny being intellectual and knowing what they're doing.

WOE: What do you think should be the relationship between writers and our discipline?

MURRAY: Writers play several roles in the academy. They visit and are a campus adornment, read, sign books, take bows. Or they join the faculty and teach "creative writing": fiction or poetry to advanced undergraduates or students in graduate writing programs. They visit schools and enrich a few classrooms for an hour, a week, or more. Those roles are all fine, but they do not help our understanding of how good writing is made.

I imagined in the sixties that I would lead an army of writers into the academy, that they would take composition research and teaching seriously and that they would be taken seriously. Together we would begin to understand how effective writing is made, and our new knowledge would change what we teach and how we teach it. But I looked over my shoulder, and I was alone—or almost alone. The result is that people have taken me much more seriously than I've taken myself. They have allowed me—in a terrible way—to become the speaker for writers. I don't speak for writers; I speak for *a* writer. I'd hoped many better writers would enter the discipline.

WOE: Will there be a place for writers in composition in the future?

MURRAY: Nope. It's harder now that there is a body of scholarship, a canon guarded by high priests. The profession has no place for writers, and writers have no interest in the discipline that does not seem to relate to them or what they do. Writers are not taken seriously. Writing researchers do not think writers have anything to contribute. They seem to believe writers are dumbly inspired. I see virtually no work on writing. *Writing on the Edge* is the only journal I've seen in years that consistently publishes articles that take writers seriously, that listens to writers, asks writers questions. I know of virtually no studies going on now on how people write. This is a personal disappointment to me. I'm very self-centered. I wanted research in writing to teach *me* how to write better.

WOE: Where does your own work fit into this?

MURRAY: I study my writing and share what I am learning. I am compelled to do this. Perhaps it was toilet training. And what I write to myself has been published, much to my surprise. I would do what I am doing if it wasn't published because I need to do it. I've gone on my lonely way, and it's been very satisfying because since childhood I've been fascinated with writing. You've got to realize I began the research for my book *Shoptalk: Learning to Write with Writers* [Boynton Cook Heinemann, Portsmouth, NH, 1990] when I was in the 9th grade (and I was a student who was going to drop out in the 10th and 11th grades, flunk out in the 12th). I'm glad to be published, but I realize what a limited and idiosyncratic contribution my work is.

WOE: Are you saying that there's no place for a writer in the field of composition?

MURRAY: I've seen no evidence that writers are being invited to join it. Writers are not seen as having anything to contribute to the study of writing. What do writers know? At universities, practitioners are generally suspect, more so in literature departments than in drama or art. There you have an overwhelming number of people who are critics and a very few practitioners. And there's a real snobbery about the practitioners. They're not seen as central.

On the other hand, while I wouldn't want to study piano with someone who doesn't play, I must say that the record of writers who teach isn't very good. Few writers, I have to admit, have taken teaching seriously even when they are only asked to teach small numbers of selected upper-class or graduate students. There are some—Mekeel McBride on our campus, for example—who take teaching seriously, but she's in a minority, and her concern with teaching is *not* considered appropriate or respectable by most of her writer colleagues.

WOE: Many believe that the freshman writing course should be an entree into academic discourse. Do you reject that point of view?

MURRAY: Yeah, I reject that. In my own experience as a university director of freshman English and initiator and frequent director of a sophomore composition course, I know these courses are expected to do this. But at most colleges our students don't write during the first two years of college. They don't write papers or essays because the teachers say they're overworked, and they may be. So the students go through whole courses with short-answer exams or other kinds of projects. I know people in history departments that never require writing. In fact, many students graduate in many departments without ever writing a paper. And to be honest, most academic writing is unreadable, even by specialists. We don't want our students to write like their teachers, do we?

Outside of freshman English, students have no academic discourse community for at least the first two years of college. I went around my own department and around every department at the university to find what writing was required. My own department members have high standards for writing, but that doesn't mean they agree on what good writing is. Our psychology department had three distinct genres they wanted students to learn in freshman English, genres that had contradictory demands.

WOE: So instead, what might the freshman writing course be?

MURRAY: Thinking. Writing is thinking. When you write, you discover what you know about your world and what you need to know. Writing instructs. Teach writing and we teach thinking. It is essential to an education. Freshman English should provide an entree into life. First of all, it's an opportunity to look at your life and articulate your life. To say what's important to you, what your world is like, and what you need in your world. This last question, which is a very individual matter, is the most significant question to face. Is it a practical question for college writing? I think it is. Writing about your life, about a personal experience, forces you to impose distance and objectivity. Later when a teacher assigns a paper on another topic, you have some confidence in your own writing process or method. You have a way of taking confused ideas and putting them together in a rational way so somebody else can understand them.

When I first taught freshman English my idea of teaching it was very clear. I thought I'd ask the history students to write history and the psychology students to write psychology and the physicists to write physics. Except I forgot what it was like in school. The psychology majors hadn't yet taken a course in psychology and the historians hadn't studied history, so they had no material yet to write about in those subjects. The writing in my course came back to being autobiographical by default. I'm very comfortable with that. But the academic world wants to intellectualize everything and wants everything to come from the head rather than the heart, wants to demand a kind of false distancing, wants people to adopt languages that are not yet their own. This may not be natural to you. The outcome is that you're taught to have the right traditional opinions. To be successful in the freshman English program in the way that the university thinks you should be, you have to satisfy other masters.

WOE: This view of freshman writing has caused you to be called a romantic, or an expressionist. How do you respond to that?

MURRAY: I hear that. "Expressivist" is the term that seems to be used around here a lot. And I don't know what "expressivist" is, but I suppose the "v" in there is somehow insulting. Now if I was called "exhibitionist" I could agree. I've been obscenely compelled to show my own writing methods. I feel as distant from many of the people I've been grouped with as I do from my enemies. Many of these people are not writers (this opinion is my snobbery); they express a philosophical point of view that I may or may not share.

The craft of writing is a demanding, intellectual craft. I've dedicated my life to it. It has high standards; it is demanding. It is satisfying. It is fun. It is my salvation and my joy. I'm a writer. I had never dared call myself that when I came to the academic community at the age of 39. I found myself categorized in an English department as a "writer." That is a high calling. I'll accept it.

When I taught I was demanding. I expected you to take your strengths and improve them, exploring your own subjects in your own way. You'd meet with the class and share your writing. You'd meet with me in an individual conference every week and demonstrate you were teaching yourself whatever worked, whatever needed to work. That's demanding. I expected you to write better than you had ever written before.

WOE: At a certain point New Hampshire was looked at as a significant center of interest in writing and the writing process. What was it like being part of that group?

MURRAY: First of all, there was much less collaboration than people think. Much less agreement and much less sharing. And much more respect than most people could imagine. Respect for diversity. And companionship as each of us went our own way. We created an environment where people could function on their own. I certainly never had any sense of a movement or community in some vast political sense.

WOE: You didn't have a shared understanding about writing, or a common agenda?

MURRAY: Only in a very broad sense. We had respect for each other, we gave each other support, we encouraged difference in our students (who were treated as colleagues) and in ourselves. But we would disagree on an enormous number of issues.

Very early during my time here I set about hiring other people. When I retired there were three people in journalism who were tenure track, and three people in composition in the English Department. Now there are four in composition, and next year there will be four in journalism. We hired people that were very diverse. Tom Newkirk, Bob Connors, Pat Sullivan, and John Lofty—all very different people. It was really funny when we hired Newkirk, the one person who has stimulated my own learning more than any other and who has never feared to criticize my work. When we were interviewing him, his mild Ohio manner fooled some of my colleagues. To them he seemed too obsequious to my work. I howled. The people in the department who were saying this didn't know my work. Tom had been attacking it vigorously—and effectively—but in a polite way. I was in favor of hiring him because of his distance from where I was. I don't think any of us have tried to reproduce each other. There's a great deal of diversity with the people that teach here.

Since I was Freshman English Director, the course has been supervised by Tom Carnicelli, by Lester Fisher, by Gary Lindberg, by Andy Merton—very different people. With some of these people, I would totally disagree on almost anything, but we would still respect each other and like each other. Diversity. I don't find any need to have consistency between one edition of a book of mine and another. I'm trying to explore and trying to learn. I'm not trying to advocate something. I never felt an evangelist, never felt part of a movement.

WOE: How would you reinvent the composition profession?

MURRAY: A friend of mine ran for PTA president and then never called a meeting. I'm not sure we need a profession. But if you want to teach writing you might do what Ron Fanning, a writing teacher at Mesa Community College in Arizona, did when he wanted to become an artist. He went to the artist in the area that he admired the most and said, "I want to be a painter." The artist said, "Well, if you will provide canvas and paint and come by when I'm working, I'll let you work beside me." If we wanted to teach writing, we ought to find people who are writing well and study beside them.

WOE: What kind of research would you like to see?

MURRAY: I would like to see close, precise examinations of the writing act. How do people write? How do the best students write? In any class, whether you're teaching in a prison or a remedial class in the inner city or rural schools, there are students in the class who write better than others. Where do they get their ideas? How do they revise? How much do they do in their head and on the paper?

WOE: The important research of the writing processes seems to have stopped. Does the profession think that those questions have been answered? Or did it get frustrated with the difficulty of answering them?

MURRAY: The questions just don't interest the people training young scholars. Practitioners—student and professional—are not respected. The profession today is not interested in writing, it is interested in grand ideas around writing, in political issues, in ethnographic issues—all valuable—not what happens when one word collides with another on the page and unexpected meaning is born.

I don't think the profession tried to answer the questions enough to get frustrated. I think the questions were seen as insignificant, questions of skills, not intellectual inquiry, not political issues. The work being done is often impressive, but it has no center. The center should be what happens in an individual sentence. That's my center.

WOE: I find it problematic to talk about writers and use that term in such a way that it excludes people who are writing in the academic world.

MURRAY: I think it is a matter of snobbery, and I'm uncomfortable with it. But in the academy I would want to have good writers of history, good writers of science, good writers in criticism. Most academic writers do not do enough writing to get up to speed, and they do it from some very different traditions. The trouble with academic writing is that in a career people produce one book or two or a few articles. My colleagues who do publish a lot are saying, "I'm going to do an article this year." I understand this: with their teaching loads and other interests, they're not writing. But when you're riding a bicycle, you have to get some velocity and put some miles on each day. Academic people write dissertations and ten years later publish them. They go whole years without writing, weeks and months and days. They do a very good job despite this, but they don't know the craft. And then they're writing for an audience that is prepaid. As a general rule, nobody writes books who is not already in the club. And they're not read except by people who are already interested in the subject. Once the book is finished, there's a finite audience for it.

To be called a writer, you have to write every day. It has to be your way of life, your way of learning. Students need to learn from the best people, the people who are good in the craft. You want to hear from those people and learn from the masters in the field. And then you want to learn from the best students, the best people studying what they do. I learned from my students all through my teaching. My best students taught me all the time. We should pay attention to the people that are doing it. It is a craft, but the academic world doesn't see it as such.

I don't really mean to put down academic writing. But those of us who write for people who don't want to read our stuff, who have no interest in it, are totally in a different game. We're writing for people who we have to attract and hold. We have to communicate to people who don't know the subject. We're authorities communicating to people who are more intelligent, perhaps, but are not interested in what we're writing about. If you can do that, you can take that craft and apply it to other writing. It would be possible for academics to learn to write more clearly except for the fact that most professions say the less clearly you write, the more profound you are. That doesn't worry me so much when the field is sociology or history. But when you have a field called composition and rhetoric, and an organization with Communication in its name, you've got a real problem.

WOE: Is there no place in composition for a theoretical conversation?

MURRAY: There is a place for such conversations. I'd just like to see more conversations that include writers, not exclude them. I don't want to put down the work that people are doing. But *I* feel outside that particular conversation. Academics in composition need to understand that most writing is intended for somebody who is not willing, who is not paid to read. Many teachers are, for some reason, willing to put up with bad writing to get the content. I think bad writing reflects bad thinking.

When I interviewed scientists and medical people as a reporter, I found that the beginning people, the assistant professors, were terrible sources. When I got to the Nobel Prize winners, they could always describe what they were doing in words that I could understand. They are the leaders of their profession because they see simplicities. Now, in our own field, certain writing is inexplicable. Sometimes I think people don't know what they're saying, so they use jargon, they use terminology in idiosyncratic ways. It creates very little communication. People will respect academics who come from a certain school, or have published a certain thing. But if you ask them, "What in the world did that guy say?" they'll say, "Well, I guess the usual thing," or something like that.

This demonstrates bad thinking. Some academics write laboriously because they have no real interest in it. Let's face it—most of the people writing academic writing are not writing because they have something to say that they're burning to explore, but because they've got to get promotion. It isn't internally driven, although I think there are strategies internally driven writers can hand to those people so that they can do their externally driven writing.

WOE: That's really the dilemma of freshman composition: on the one hand, you want to help people get to the point where they have internally driven writing to do; on the other hand, there's an expectation that you'll help people get ready to do better externally driven writing. And these are in conflict with each other.

MURRAY: It's totally dishonest. Because it wants bodies and money, it wants to support its graduate students or whatever, the English department says to the university, "We'll teach your students how to write well for you." In fact, it doesn't do that. It teaches the traditional course: literature and occasional writing. And it teaches writing English papers that have no relation to what most students will ever do in their lives.

I want to teach a composition course that teaches good critical thinking. I don't see that happening now. I don't think you can have good critical thinking unless you know something about the subject, so that means, yes, most of the writing in freshman English is going to be autobiographical, because people don't have a profession yet, they have a life. The palette they have to work from is a voice which is their own. They can learn to adapt that. They have a mind; they have a view of the world. They adapt that. Each of these is unique. Your background is different from my background. Your gender is different; your generation is different. We all bring to bear on the world our own individual vision. In my case that's expressed largely through language, written language.

The excitement for me every morning is not to write ideas I have had but to write and find that I have ideas. Writing to me is an exploration. We don't ever learn to write, because we don't ever learn to think. But I do believe in process, we are constantly learning to write, to draw, to survive.

WOE: And that's what we should teach our students?
MURRAY: And ourselves.

JOSEPH WILLIAMS AND GREGORY COLOMB

Joseph M. Williams (1933–2008) and Gregory G. Colomb (1951–2011) played a prominent role in developing the Little Red Schoolhouse writing curriculum at the University of Chicago, a program for advanced undergraduate, graduate, and professional students that emphasized clarity and audience awareness in both academic and professional writing. The development of that curriculum resulted in a series of influential writing handbooks designed to be pragmatic and straightforward, beginning with Williams's original Style: Lessons in Clarity and Grace (1981), and leading through numerous collaborations on revised editions, including the widely used 4th Edition, Style: The Basics of Clarity and Grace (published after Williams's death, with introduction by Colomb). Now in its 12th edition (co-authored by Joseph Bizup), Style is distinct in its thorough treatment of writerly choice and audience awareness, avoiding easy platitudes of "right" v. "wrong" while eschewing "the irresistible lure of obscurity" that they found throughout the professional and academic disciplines.

Williams and Colomb also co-authored (with Wayne Booth) The Craft of Research (1995) a Critics' Choice Award-winning book that guides students through the process of drafting and compiling an accessible report, essay, or dissertation. They later co-authored The Craft of Argument (2002), wherein they detail the ways that argument and persuasion bind communities both public and professional. As in all their collaborative efforts, they emphasize clear methods for achieving sound structure and style.

Williams was Professor of English at the University of Chicago until his retirement in 1999, serving as Director of University Writing Programs from 1987–1990. In 2006, he won the Legal Writing Institute's Golden Pen Award. As exemplified in his incisive and well-known article, The Phenomenology of Error (1981), Williams was also remarkable as a scholar of written language, puncturing simplistic pronouncements about "correct style" by observing the pundits' violations of their own rules.

Colomb taught for nine years at the University of Chicago, later serving as the Director of Programs in Professional Writing at the University of Illinois at Urbana-Champaign; he was Professor of English language and literature at the University of Virginia until his death in 2011.

—Nathanial Williams and David Masiel

"The Takeaway"

Donald Johns

Fall 1993

WOE: Who and what were the influences that caused you both to pursue writing as an academic subject?

WILLIAMS: The first was my journalism teacher in high school, Mr. Skinner. I was a sports columnist for the high school newspaper. I loved writing, and he loved writing. We would sit and talk about what worked, what didn't. I can't remember a thing he said, but he took my writing seriously, I think because it was going to appear in print. As a result, I felt that a story *had* to be right.

The biggest influence on me was Gordon Wilson, who died about a couple of years ago. He directed the writing program at Miami University of Ohio for 20 years, was a former president of 4Cs, an extraordinary man. When I got out of the Army, I went back to Miami to get an M.A. and became a teaching assistant—two sections of freshman composition. But unlike teaching assistants at a lot of other schools, we weren't just thrown into a classroom with a book and told to teach. Gordon put us through a training program that I now realize was revolutionary for its time. Because of his intense dedication to quality and to students, I felt like it was a great privilege to teach comp; I wasn't being asked to perform a service. That feeling has stayed with me, because twenty-five years later I still feel teaching freshmen is important work, and I still do it. I have a hard time understanding people who complain about it being just service.

Then when I went to the University of Wisconsin to get my Ph.D., I had the good fortune to fall in with Fred Cassidy, the director of the *Dictionary of American Regional English*. First day in class he impressed me as someone else who was utterly dedicated to his work, Old English, so I decided that to keep working with Fred I had to become a linguist. In fact, halfway through my Ph.D. in literature, I stopped to do all the coursework necessary to get a Ph.D. in linguistics, then finished the Ph.D. in literature.

My dissertation was called "Trans-Sentential Grammatical Constraint." It was, I think, the first dissertation in discourse analysis written in this country. Strange stuff, but Fred supported it. I never published it because I couldn't imagine anybody would be interested in it. But it got me interested in discourse as opposed to sentences. I got a job at Chicago, where again I lucked out and fell in with a group of people who looked upon teaching freshman comp and the humanities course that replaced it as important work. Again, they saw it not just as service but as a significant part of a student's education.

Then in 1968 I got a phone call from the American Medical Association: could I give a seminar for editors of the *Journal of the AMA*? Being a poor assistant professor, I said, "Sure, I can do that." When I hung up I said, "Oh God, how do I do that?" First I read a lot of medical writing, which turned out to be absolutely baffling. But since I had been interested in machine translation, I thought I would treat it like that. Imagine medical writing is a foreign language and I have to translate it into something I can understand. What would be the rules of translation? That moved me permanently out of linguistics as a formal theory of sentences into discourse and style. Out of that came a lot of the stuff on style that I've been mining now for these many years.

To sum up, I got interested in writing through a bunch of happy accidents. I've been in the right place at the right time all my life.

COLOMB: Actually, my story and Joe's are similar, though there's a generational difference. I had one of those rare educations where you spent most of your time writing. When I think back to high school, I can't remember a time that I didn't have a paper due in a week or two. A lot of my teachers made writing a primary value. The one who stands out was Paul Farkas, who was a Holy Cross brother when he began teaching me but was married by the end of the year. It was an interesting and exciting year, in more ways than one. I was in the happy situation of being in a small group of students who, because we worked on the school newspaper, weren't able to take the regular English course. We had a special class Paul taught after school with a group of ten sitting around a table. That senior English class felt like a graduate seminar. Clearly we weren't doing that level of work, but what I learned from Paul got me through the first years of college English without trying very hard.

I did my undergraduate work at Rice University, where I studied linguistics and anthropology because I was fascinated by language, and English because I loved literature courses. When it came time to go to graduate school, I had to decide between English and linguistics. Stephen Tyler, my anthropology advisor, told me, "You don't want to go to graduate school in linguistics. You're interested in texts, not sentences. If you do graduate work in linguistics these days, you'll have to do transformational grammar"—which means, sentence grammar. His line—which I'll never forget—was, "Go to an English department; so long as you talk about literature, they'll let you do anything." Which was only partially true.

I went to the University of Virginia in the early heyday of theory. One of my dissertation directors was Ralph Cohen, who had recently founded *New Literary History*, the first theory journal in the States. I wrote my dissertation on eighteenth-century poetry, but I spent most of my time studying language-based theory and semiotics. I ended up teaching at the University of Chicago—thanks in large part to Joe. A year or two later, at a poker game, Joe, Frank Kinahan, and I cooked up the idea to give some advanced lectures in writing. The name "Little Red Schoolhouse" was born that night. We created a series of lectures, and I found a way to do the work I had been waiting to do all along: my work in literary analysis, in literary theory, in linguistics, in text studies all made sense in the context of these lectures. Like Joe, I feel lucky to have gotten into the profession at a time when there were big questions to be asked, and it was possible to come up with some good answers.

Joe had already done the work that showed up in the first edition of *Style*, so we had a good story to tell about sentences. But we had very little to say about things larger than sentences. That challenge was what led Joe and me to begin working together. The work we have done on text structure emerged the next year when the Little Red Schoolhouse became a course and the two of us were obliged to come up with something for graduate students to teach. Joe and I sat in a room week after week with those graduate students and began to formulate a theory of what a text would look like.

WILLIAMS: We were writing the book one week at a time.

COLOMB: The graduate students tell a story—I don't know how true it is—that the high point of the sessions was the day when I was writing on the blackboard, and Joe was walking behind me erasing and replacing the words I was writing, and I was erasing his behind him. True or not, the story captures a sense of what was happening. That was a very creative time for us. We needed to offer those grad students something to teach, and we didn't much like what was available in the literature. Nobody seemed to have good answers about how texts got put together and what mattered to readers, which are the crucial questions.

Within a year of the Little Red Schoolhouse—this would be 1982 or '83—one of our neighbors said, "Can you do this for lawyers?" Having done it with the medical profession for years, Joe had some experience. We tried it with lawyers, and it was successful. Consulting gave us a much wider experience of what writing is like up close. It's one thing to study texts; it's another to be close to those who produce them. I think we learned as much from being inside the world of professionals who write as we did from teaching students and looking at what students write.

WILLIAMS: And since they were paying a lot of money, if they said, "I don't understand," we didn't have the luxury of saying, "Well, read the book." If we didn't make them understand, we didn't get another consulting job with that firm. So we were always under the gun to be as clear, as useful, as transparent, as pragmatic as we could without losing the theory behind it. And we couldn't talk theory. When you're teaching freshmen, you can get away with almost anything. But when someone who's as old as you are and making a lot more money says, "Wait a minute, explain that," you don't brush them off. You explain it, and if you don't get it right the first time, they'll say, "I don't understand. Try it again."

WOE: Besides being forced to clarify your own approach and presentation, what other things did you learn from that experience?

COLOMB: With the consulting we learned right off the value of what our clients called "the takeaway": "How does what you told me today bear on tomorrow?" That became more important to us in our teaching. We didn't see others around us worrying how students were going to do three years from now. Instead of asking how students were doing in class today or on the paper tomorrow, we asked, "Will they still be able to say the words and perform the tasks that they've learned in our classes a year from now, two years from now?"

WILLIAMS: As we worked with different groups—investment bankers, lawyers, judges, managers—we also discovered that although we do a lot of talking about different universes of discourse and different conventions, there are *universals* of discourse that cut across all fields. There are differences within fields, and we honor the differences, but we also have to honor the universal principles.

WOE: What are some of the important universals?

WILLIAMS: Oh, I think all the stuff in *Style*. We've been able to sell that to doctors, lawyers, Indian chiefs across the board.

COLOMB: That includes the new material we've been doing on text structure, which shows up in the Chicago edition of *Style*, and even the business we're working on now with problem formulation. We don't know how universal that is, but it seems to cut across a lot of academic situations. You can find the answers to these questions if you do the research, if you study what writers do, how readers react, and how writers can relate to readers in different ways.

WILLIAMS: We began by trying to answer questions not from the writer's point of view, "Do good writers do this?" but rather from the reader's point of view—"How do readers read it?" I think because both of us come out of backgrounds in which we responded to literature. We first wondered why doctors or lawyers respond to different kinds of writing as they do. Why do they say one text is good, another bad? We figured that if we could understand why people responded the way they did, then in our simpleminded, pragmatic way we could tell writers, "When you write like this, you will get this kind of response." Rather than starting with the way writers write, we've started with the way readers read.

WOE: How does that work when, say, you give college students an essay by a writer like Stephen Jay Gould and find that a fairly large percentage of them can't understand it?

WILLIAMS: Well, I think that most of them understand more than they say. I would start by taking a little snippet from Gould that presumably a lot of people could understand, and then change it so it's less readable but says the same thing. Sometimes people don't see the difference between the styles of passages because they're just not very good readers. But more times than not people will say, "Oh, I don't like this one at all, but I think I could get through this one if I had to."

Another useful exercise is to take a relatively clear passage from Gould and say, "Now change it to make it *less* readable—nominalize the verbs, get rid of the agents. But don't create something that's just stupid; come up with plausible sentences. Now look at those two passages, one written in the changed style and the other in the original. Which would you choose to go on reading?" Is it a neutral choice: flip a coin, I'll read one rather than the other? Usually, even if they say they don't see the difference, they'll intuitively pick the more readable one. And then we can raise the next, equally important question: "For this passage in this particular situation, which is better, the more or less readable version?"

We've realized that simply holding out a single passage as a good or bad model is a mistake because it requires an act of imagination to see that good passage as worse or that bad passage as better. More than that, it's virtually impossible for students to go beyond their first response. They'll say, "Yeah, I think I like this passage." But when you ask, "What is it on the page that's making you respond that way?" they are stumped. The passage is just a lot of words. It's not until you can give them a vocabulary for seeing what's going on behind the words that they can explain their own responses.

COLOMB: Stephen Jay Gould may be exactly the wrong way to get students to see a relatively simple feature of style, if his work poses a challenge in understanding, as opposed to a challenge at the level of style. At some point we want students to deal with texts like Gould's, but Gould may not be the way to help them grasp the principles.

For example, we have found that undergraduate business students do not respond well to examples taken from academic business writing. Show them two passages from business journals—one abstract and difficult and another relatively simple—and they say, "I can't see the difference because I don't understand either one. They're both unintelligible." That's OK, since I don't want to teach them to write journal articles but to understand the difference between abstract and clear style. We just avoid the journals and give them passages that they can understand, where they can see the difference.

WOE: What are the differences between the Chicago edition of *Style* and the HarperCollins edition?

COLOMB: The HarperCollins edition of *Style* stops at sentences and what we call topic strings. (Even the topic string material emerged only through the second and third editions.) But writers also need to control the structures above the sentence level, what we call text structure. That structure, too, is easy to teach: it has recognizable patterns, it affects readers' responses in predictable ways, it reveals some parts of the text as especially important to readers—and so to writers. We've written up that work in the two chapters that were added to the University of Chicago edition of *Style*. We've been working on those questions since 1982, and that work represents about half of what's in the Little Red Schoolhouse materials.

WOE: In the second edition of *Style* you explain the roles of agents and actions within a sentence by saying, "State who's doing what in the subject . . . and state what that 'who' is doing in your verb." But in later editions you change to the metaphor of characters acting out a story. It's a more complex explanation, and I believe my students found the earlier version easier to follow.

WILLIAMS: What's at stake is a prototypical definition of what counts as a clear, direct sentence. The problem with the first definition is that it would rule out a lot of passive constructions which are perfectly appropriate. So I had a choice between being simple and memorable, or being faithful to the facts of the matter. It became a little more complicated to be faithful to the facts of the matter.

COLOMB: That's a fallout, really, of more sophisticated questions we had been developing. The reason for the shift to character is that when you start looking at how focus at the beginning of sentences creates point of view, you begin to recognize that each discipline has its own set of preferred characters. And while it's true that in many contexts the default character is a human agent, in professional writing of all sorts, human agents are not the preferred character but all kinds of other characters, some conceptual, some nonhuman.

WOE: Some students have noticed that in one chapter, "A Touch of Elegance," the examples were all by men.

WILLIAMS: There will be examples from women in the fourth edition, coming out this year. If you want to trace a more interesting evolution in *Style*, take a look at the first edition in regard to gender-neutral language, and then look at each successive edition—you'll see a steady progression. I have Susan Miller to thank for making me think about this. The position regarding gender-neutral language that now exists in *Style* was hers when she first read the manuscript of the first edition. I wasn't ready to come around to that position then, but I've come around to it now.

WOE: Do the two chapters in *Style* on larger structures involve your work on problem solving?

WILLIAMS: No, but we're going to include it in the new edition of Turabian's guide to term papers that Greg and I are working on with Wayne Booth.

COLOMB: It's the latest wrinkle in our story about how writers put together texts, and how readers understand them. It is based on the work that appears in the Chicago edition of *Style*.

WILLIAMS: The fundamental principle is that all of the linguistic structure we talk about consists of two levels. If you're familiar with *Style*, you're familiar with these pairings: subject–verb, character–action, topic–comment, old–new. The work that Greg is talking about at the paragraph level and higher has exactly the same structure. There's a fixed geography of units of discourse. Certain positional units are always there and never change their order—like the order of subject–verb and topic–comment. There's also a second level of semantic content that you can move around. And just as there's a privileged co-occurrence between fixed subjects and variable characters, fixed verbs and variable actions, so we claim that there's a privileged co-occurrence in this geography of paragraphs and higher-level structures.

Our most recent work with problem formulation follows the same pattern, particularly as problems are articulated in introductions. There is, apparently, a predictable pattern to the geography of introductions. It's a dramatistic model, with two variations. The pattern might begin with what I'm calling "stasis." Consider, for instance, a fairy tale analogy: "Once upon a time on a sunny day in April, Little Red Riding Hood was skipping through the woods on her way to her grandmother's house." In this opening everything is fine. The equivalent of that in academic and professional writing is something like, "The literature on problem solving is rich indeed." The next move in a fairy tale, of course, is a disruption: "Behind a tree, the wolf lay waiting to spring out at Little Red Riding Hood." Something has dramatically disrupted the stasis, creating anxiety. The equivalent of that in the academic world is, "But the literature on problem formulation is thin to the point of nonexistence." In other words, we open by invoking something stable that we can agree on and then disrupt it with a "but."

Now the fairy tale could have opened: "Once upon a time, the wolf was lurking behind a tree just waiting for Little Red Riding Hood to come skipping down the path." That's a fairy tale that opens with disruption rather than stasis. The equivalent in academic writing is, "The problem of the viability of tungsten in ion replication studies has long eluded the best efforts to solve it." Just open with disruption. The job of the rest of the introduction is to return you to stasis, or to promise it. The job of the rest of the fairy tale is to return you to "once upon a time, Little Red Riding Hood was skipping through the woods"—everything's fine again. The equivalent in the academic paper is, "In this essay I will explain how problem formulation works, and here it is." Stasis, disruption, promise of a return of stasis.

Now the disruption is the problem, but, in fact, problems are more than just disruptions. For our purposes, a problem has to consist of two elements: (1) a destabilizing condition—"The literature on problem posing is thin to the point of nonexistence"—and (2) the cost of leaving that condition unstable or the benefit of stabilizing it—"As a consequence, we have no way to explain to our students how to articulate an interesting problem, much less find one in the first place." In other words, you don't have a problem unless you have both something that destabilizes the world or our experience of it and the cost to some community of interest of leaving their world or experience destabilized. So the sequence of an introduction is really the sequence of a story: Stasis–Disruption–Resolution. Through that fixed sequence, we can move different kinds of elements in different combinations.

So we're pursuing a model of introductions and a grammar of problem formulation that builds on a bi-level structure. Underlying all this is our attempt to explain why teachers can look at the introduction of one essay and say: "This is not a promising start. It is one more of those papers that I'm going to have to slog through," then look at another essay, and say: "I think I'm going to enjoy reading this." How do we account for those responses? Well, you can say one is just more interesting than the other. But what *makes* it interesting? It's the structure of what makes it interesting that we're studying.

If you want an example of problem formulation, Stephen Jay Gould, whom we were talking about before, has got this pattern down cold. All of his columns in *Natural History* follow a particular form: "Here's something that seems not important (stasis), but, in fact, there is a puzzle in it, and if we don't solve this puzzle, look at all the consequences that will follow (disruption with a problem)." Then he resolves the disruption by solving the puzzle for us. He has mastered a prototype introduction.

WOE: Are there then some consistent psychological structures running through both fairy tales and academic essays?

COLOMB: It has to be true that fairy tales have the structure they have at least in part because we have the psychology we have. It also has to be true that academic papers have the structure they have partly because we have the psychology we have. That relationship is complicated and hard to specify. But it would be very surprising if it wasn't relevant that these two kinds of texts are the products of the same brains.

WOE: How has your experience outside the academy affected your attitude toward academic writing?

COLOMB: Because we've spent a lot of our time over the years working with and attending to professionals who write, I think our attitude toward academic writing has changed substantially. Academic writing now seems much more peculiar than it ever did. We understand much more the degree to which it's a special case that has in some instances little relation to writing that's grounded in my needs as a person who's living a life and conducting a business or a career. When it comes to writing, the transition from the academy to the world of work is by no means seamless.

WILLIAMS: I've had a similar experience, but because Greg is more into literary theory than I am and maybe because I did as much work in linguistics as in literature, I stand outside of literary criticism and say: "Lit crit is a truly aberrant and marginal kind of writing." When I look upon the writing of my colleagues in the English Department and they look upon mine, there's a curious inversion of judgment. I say: "What a peculiar thing you're doing. But you enjoy it. Go ahead and do it. You should understand, though, that in the great scheme of things our society gives you a privileged place where nobody asks you to account for what you're doing." They, of course, look at the writing program and marginalize it by saying: "We're going to humor you and give you this privileged position where you can do what you want to do, but you should understand that in our scheme of things, we are giving you a privilege." So we have this nice balance. What a peculiar and privileged position we're both in. It's an odd relationship that has worked out quite well for me.

WOE: How has your practice in teaching writing changed?

COLOMB: It's important to remember that there's no freshman composition at Chicago, but a humanities common core course that includes a focus on writing instruction. That course is taught by most of the humanities faculty. So our first efforts toward a writing program focused on the advanced level. The first course was intended not for people beginning to learn what the academy is like but for people who know the academy and need to consolidate that knowledge in a way that's useful for the rest of their lives. That's a very different perspective on teaching writing. It has shaped much of what we do and accounts for many of the differences between the things we do and what we see our colleagues at other institutions doing.

WILLIAMS: Our colleagues spend immense amounts of time on invention and prewriting: "Let's think of something to write about. What anthology will we use? Are we going to teach gender, race, and class? What content can we give these students to write about, and how are they going to think about it? How are they going to plan? Where are they going to get their ideas? Maybe we should have them talk about personal experience because that's what they know." When dealing with juniors and seniors, our assumption has been that they've already been doing prewriting in those years and years of anthropology, music, and sociology. So we say: "You know a lot, and you've been reading a lot. Now you're going to use all that knowledge to solve some problems." If you looked at a Schoolhouse syllabus, you would not see a word about invention. For us the serious part of process begins with a draft. People look at the Schoolhouse materials and say: "This is all product oriented."

There's a sense in which that's true, but for us the process begins the moment you've got a product to work on, and to interrogate and revise.

WOE: Have some people criticized your approach for being too knowledge based as opposed to process based?

WILLIAMS: It's easy to caricature different positions. I've heard people argue the position that to tell students, "Here is what you should know," is coercive, that it is a form of indoctrination that does not allow students their own voices. These teachers think it is better to have collaborative learning groups where students work on a problem and discover for themselves knowledge that they will then possess rather than simply having been told.

What I'm about to say in no way rejects collaborative learning. The Schoolhouse crucially depends on weekly collaborative learning groups where everybody shares papers, shares responses and analysis, and shares ideas for making them better. But collaborative learning has one fundamental problem. If there is no shared language to begin with, you are unlikely to develop a useful one. My analogy is this: if you're an engineer and you have to know calculus to do your job, you can sit around in collaborative learning groups for the rest of your life and not invent calculus. How do you get students to know calculus? I guess you stand up in front of a room and show them, "This is how calculus works." Students have to have the analytical language to begin with. You say, "Do you get it now?" If they say, "No, I don't get it," you say, "Well, I'll teach you some more." When they have calculus, then they can go off to find and solve problems that are really important, and at that point, when they work in groups, they have the common language of calculus—or any of a dozen other analytical languages that they would not develop on their own.

Writing is similar: you can have students sitting around in collaborative groups until hell freezes over, and they will not learn to see the structures of discourse. They'll not see how sentences work. They won't understand that all subjects are not characters, that all verbs do not express actions. They won't see any of the elements at these multiple levels of discourse that Greg and I have been talking about. So my response is, "All right, I'll stand up and I'll tell you how it works. This is not espousing values that you should live by. This is simply how it works: the sun comes up in the east, and it goes down in the west." A lot of people find that to be coercive and offensive, even indoctrination.

But it beats the hell out of me why teachers think that collaborative groups can or should discover on their own knowledge that already exists for the taking. Somebody could say, "Williams and Colomb, what you're teaching is false"—that's an empirical question. We'll say, "OK, let's figure out a way to test these things." We might be wrong. Our *knowledge* might be wrong—in which case we would change to teach what is right.

We're very careful about keeping empirical knowledge separate from "should." "Is" is not "ought." We don't tell anybody, "You ought to write in this way." What we say is, "If you write in this way, readers are likely to respond by thinking you write clearly. If you write in another way, readers are likely to respond by thinking you don't. Write however you want, so long as you understand what the consequences are. I am not your father. I'm simply telling you cause-and-effect relationships." As I said, we might be empirically wrong about our predictions, but our experience for the past ten years makes me think that we're right.

COLOMB: When you put it that way, though, you can seem to sell both the Schoolhouse and calculus short. Calculus is in fact not taught very well by people standing up in front of a room saying how calculus is done. Recent work has shown that the very best calculus teaching comes when you put students in groups, then structure their experience so that they begin to develop the principles of calculus through that experience—after, that is, you have articulated the principles for them. And if you think about the Schoolhouse, that's exactly the way we work. We don't get up and say, "This is right, now do it." We'll show students two examples and say, "Which one do you like better?" They'll say, "We like this one better." "Well, let's look at two more. Which of these do you like better?" We're never in the position of saying, "Forget what you say. Here's the way it works." What we say is, "Now that you have decided that these passages cause you to have a certain response, and these other passages have a different effect, let me explain to you an easy way to characterize that difference."

We're helping students to get a self-conscious command over their knowledge and abilities in the same way that the best calculus teaching does. We want students to know enough to be able to control their language rather than to be controlled by it.

WILLIAMS: I agree with that one hundred percent, but somewhere they have to start with the terms of calculus. How do you get the terms of calculus? Well, you have to read them or somebody has to tell them to you. You're not going to invent them on your own. Where do you start with the terms of discourse and style? You can either read them, or somebody can tell you.

WOE: It puzzles me how people can teach a writing course without a handbook or style guide, at least as a reference.

WILLIAMS: In my judgment, they aren't teaching writing; they're warehousing students.

WOE: What are the differences you see between writing across the curriculum and writing in the disciplines?

WILLIAMS: There are matters of discourse, sentence structure, and the formulation of problems that cut across all disciplines—academic writing and business writing, medical writing, government writing—and those are the universals that cut across the curriculum. These days we assume all of our students are going to move through a number of different professional worlds. And they ought to understand those things that cut across disciplines. Those are brute facts that they just need to know. At the same time, they have to understand the kinds of discourse found in different fields. Philosophers don't sound like chemists, don't sound like lit-crit types, don't sound like biologists. Those are different worlds, different languages, different universes of discourse. The Schoolhouse tries to avoid (but doesn't always succeed) being painted white or black with the brush of either "Writing ought to be taught only in the disciplines" or "Everything is the same, and there are no disciplinary differences." I don't believe in either one of those absolutes, but rather a kind of judicious balance: "Here's what's universal, but within that universality there are local conventions, and you have to understand how to maneuver among those as well."

COLOMB: We have to work hard to keep that balance and avoid being pushed toward one pole or the other. For ten years now we've been making the case—chiefly through these Chicago Institutes—that not only writing but critical thinking varies across disciplines. And we've tried to show how some of those disciplinary differences—what I've called "disciplinary secrets"—might be explained as variations on more universal structures and how others seem to be entirely local. But just as it's hard to avoid being forced into the polarized camps of process and product, so we find it hard to get people to hear both sides of our story about disciplinary differences.

WOE: Can writing teachers effectively teach the local knowledge within these disciplines?

COLOMB: If they learn it. We have. We both teach writing in law, and lawyers regularly ask us where we got our law degrees—because we know the conventions about as well as they do. I'm pretty good at teaching writing in chemical engineering because I spent two years learning what it means to think and write like a chemical engineer. You can't expect composition teachers to say: "I'm ready for anything. Tell me the discipline and I'll start teaching it tomorrow." No one can know all the disciplines, but it's certainly possible to learn some of them. The most useful way to look at it is that there are things that seem to be true about writing, and things that seem to be true only about *this kind* of writing; together these make the teaching of writing a shared responsibility between the writing teacher and those in the disciplines. This recognition can result in a very productive relationship for both parties.

Toby Fulwiler has raised another aspect of the writing across the curriculum/writing in the disciplines issue: the political relationship between the activity of teaching writing and the disciplines themselves. We have found that when students and professors are put in possession of good, self-conscious accounts of the way their discipline behaves on paper, of the nature of the conventions, of the force of the conventions, the experience is perceived by all as liberating—not in the sense that we tell them what to think, but that we help them to make choices about things which had previously seemed natural to them and therefore beyond any choice. When I work with another department, I don't walk in with an agenda to undermine their way of thinking about what they do. I do have the agenda of giving them a way to think well and hard about what they do and the language they use to do it.

WOE: Do you see any prospect of writing breaking out of its identity as a service and becoming a discipline in its own right?

COLOMB: Because writing is part of the social fabric of all the disciplines, there's a sense in which writing needs to have the marginal position it has with respect to the overall intellectual enterprise of the university. It's a terrible shame that this position also turns into social marginalization, that a horizontal difference becomes a vertical difference of power and prestige.

There are many things worth studying about writing as such, but for most students what is most worth studying is writing as it bears on the lives they are going to lead. You would hardly listen if the anthropology department argued, "Look, we think anthropology is really important and you ought to require it of every first-year student; there ought to be 'freshman anthropology' because anthropology is really what students ought to know." Everyone needs to study writing because writing figures in all the disciplines. Since students must write in the disciplines, we are always in a partnership role, which is always going to be a marginal role, and I think an appropriate role.

Is there a discipline? That's a harder question. Ask me in ten years. But I will say this. In order to learn what we believe is important about how people write, we spend a lot of our time reading things from all over the map. I can't imagine we're alone in this. If you ask me what a graduate curriculum in writing ought to be, I'd say it ought to involve a lot of disciplines. And it's that variety of questions and points of view that brings the knowledge you need to be a writing teacher.

WOE: Marginalization seems to take place at the university because of intellectual differences as well as social differences. Students are especially at risk of marginalization since they don't always understand the kinds of differences that exist. Isn't part of our responsibility to recognize these differences and try to act on that recognition?

WILLIAMS: There's a particular social difference in our students that interests me. When we academics find a problem, we think of it as a good thing. When most students encounter a problem, they think of it as a bad thing. They think we all try to avoid problems. But we academics are attracted to problems. The problems we're attracted to are purely conceptual, problems of ignorance, missing information, unknown causes, misunderstanding, confusion, contradiction. The problems that most students are willing to take seriously exist out there in the world. They are the tangible problems of AIDS and homelessness, how do I buy a car, my girlfriend doesn't love me anymore, and so on. There's a big social difference between us and those students who, when they face the kinds of problems that we love—how many prime numbers are there? What happened to the Anasazi Indians after 1275?—say to themselves, if not to us directly: "Who the hell cares?" They can't understand, literally cannot understand, why anybody would be interested in these things. So what if Falstaff is different between *Henry IV Part One* and *Part Two*? It doesn't help much to tell them: "We care. This is our life. This is what we do here."

Now there are some students who are immediately attracted to our kind of conceptual problems. I don't think it's a matter of economic class, though there's probably a correlation. I don't think it has anything to do with race, gender, sexual preference, whatever. But it's a big social difference. It is too easy for teachers to look down upon those students who simply stare blankly when we try to get them to think seriously about conceptual problems. And the student who really responds—"Gee, why is Falstaff so much less interesting and attractive in *Part Two*? Oh, gosh, I want to figure that out"—that's our kind of student. That's the kind of student we're immediately drawn to and we are most willing to reward. Well, that's a difference that people don't talk about very much, but it's a profound social difference.

WOE: And if you took seriously the idea that you're incorporating awareness of social difference into your teaching methods, you wouldn't be satisfied with that? You'd see it as your responsibility to reach and somehow engage both types of student?

WILLIAMS: You've got three choices. Too many of our colleagues say in effect: "You're not cut out for this community. Get out." More constructively, we can expand the range of problems we are willing to let students tackle. Or we can try to explain to them why conceptual problems are interesting and bring them into the community of those who care about our problems. The best solution is probably a combination of the last two. I think I was attracted to conceptual problems simply by teachers who were excited about them. At first I thought: "Why are you excited about the pronunciation of vowels in London in 1400? Whew, boy, that's kind of dumb to spend your life thinking about that." But if some teacher was just so excited about an idea—no tangible consequences, not going to earn any money, not going to change the world—the excitement became contagious.

COLOMB: One of the more important benefits of the writing in the disciplines/writing across the curriculum movement has been to make teachers more conscious of those students who are and will remain outsiders to their disciplines. It has helped them to see that they have a greater responsibility than merely to invite students in: "If you want to be like me, come be like me; otherwise you'll get your 'C' or 'D' and go away with your ticket punched." In coming to understand how much of learning is being socialized into a discipline, teachers have become much more aware, not only of the seductive appeal of those students who nod and whose eyes brighten every time you get to the good parts, but also of their responsibility to all those students who have no good reason to "come on in" but nevertheless need what we have to teach them. This too is part of the diversity that teachers need to learn to accept and even to embrace.

WOE: Do you practice what you preach with your own writing?

COLOMB: Well, Joe and I write pretty differently. Joe is one of those writers who likes to keep everything in his head as long as he can before he starts writing. I just write. I dump. I throw away three quarters of what I start with. In fact, my process is relatively cyclical: I'll write for a while, take stock, maybe outline what I've done so far, then write some more. I often treat early drafts as a warm-up, tossing them out and starting from scratch. I routinely use my own advice as a way of dealing with the not-very-elegant and not-very-controlled product of that kind of writing. I try to force myself to write as fast as I can type, and if I could dictate to my word processor I would do that. As I tell my students, if you know you are a good editor, you can save all of those worries until after you've got something down and you know what you think.

WILLIAMS: We do a lot of editing of each other's writing and have achieved a relationship where if I write something and I give it to him, it is no longer mine. It's his. He can do anything he wants to it, and I'm not going to feel bad about it. And if I get something back, well, now it's mine, and I can do what I have to do. The person who gets the last cut, of course, is the person who speaks for both of us.

COLOMB: I think that if we looked at the things we did together, we wouldn't be able to identify features that belong to one or the other.

WILLIAMS: That's right. When I read something that all makes sense to me and then later discover that he cut out some big chunk that I originally thought was really hot stuff, I assume we didn't need that chunk. If I didn't notice it was gone, neither will the reader.

WOE: Do you use the strategies you've developed in your own work?

WILLIAMS: Oh, sure. I'll write stuff, look at it, and say, "This is all summary." Then I'll try to locate the problem I've raised. For instance, I just finished an article on language and Elizabethan social history for an Oxford Press collection called *English in Its Social Contexts*, edited by Tim Machan and Charley Scott. It's a collection of essays on historical sociolinguistics. After I'd thought I'd finished it, I can remember feeling very uncomfortable. Somehow something was wrong with it. So I said, "Well, why don't I follow my own advice here and look at the problem I've posed?" When I looked, there wasn't any problem. I knew what the problem was, but I had not articulated it. The moment I was able to articulate that problem at the beginning, I was able to revise it and the rest of the article fell into place.

WOE: What *was* the problem?

WILLIAMS: The problem was most people think our attitudes toward the social use of language and notions about linguistic corruption and the social degeneration that will follow "bad" language were developed in the eighteenth century by prescriptive grammarians and their concern with rationalizing English usage. That is not true. The prescriptive grammarians did a lot in that direction, but the idea that orderly language and social order are intimately connected developed in the late sixteenth century, between 1560 and 1600. In the late sixteenth century, attitudes toward language changed. Earlier, social attitudes toward orderly and disorderly language reflected country vs. city differences. But later in the century, the established social hierarchies began to be threatened. The result was that the language of the lower classes was seen not just as crude, but because they were socially threatening, their language was socially threatening. They even corrupted language, making it somehow degenerate, foul, impure. So the idea of "pure" vs. "impure" language and the idea that "bad" grammar can corrupt the social order didn't develop in the eighteenth century, and it wasn't based on the idea that language should be rationalized.

Our own attitudes toward language, which make language somehow connected to an orderly society, seem to have their origins in social change in late-sixteenth-century London. The cost to us of not understanding any of this is that we don't see how our own attitudes toward language and society reflect our own anxiety about social order. The changes in language and in social structure in Elizabethan England surprisingly illuminate a great deal about our contemporary attitudes toward language.

It helped me to deliberately go through this problem-solving formula in my own mind. I've always relied on these sorts of explicit strategies. I think you have to have a vocabulary, a structure, before you can make sense of the buzz of experience, ideally a bunch of structures that you can try out. I'm reminded of an experience I had as a graduate student. A couple of friends and I were taking a course in phonology, and the professor was talking about the glottis and we had to read about muscles and cartilage and so on. My friends and I decided to be hot shots, so we talked a medical student into taking us over to the autopsy room so we could look at the glottis. We walked into this room full of zinc tubs, and he ripped off a sheet over one of the tubs. Inside is a headless cadaver. Off in the corner of this zinc tub is this massive *thing*—it looked like road kill, just a formless heap that didn't make any sense to me. He reached in and grabbed it, and he started slapping the parts together, whop, whop, whop, and all of a sudden it was a head. If you know what the parts are and where they go, you can do the most amazing things. Well, I looked at my essay, and I went whop, whop, whop, and it was an essay.

PATRICIA BIZZELL

While the 1960s open-access movement led to increasingly diverse universities, Patricia Bizzell came to believe that academic discourse was still controlled by the dominant culture and was therefore antagonistic to other forms of discourse and their practitioners. In her influential article "Cognition, Convention and Certainty" (1982), she challenges the belief that academic discourse is inherently superior and urges teachers to empower students, particularly basic writers, by teaching them academic discourse as a set of conventions that comprise one kind of discourse rather than treating such conventions "as if they simply mirrored reality."[1]

Twenty years later, in Alt Dis: Alternative Discourses and the Academy *(2002; co-edited with Christopher Schroeder and Helen Fox), Bizzell argues that writers draw on traits from home discourse communities to form "alternative discourses" that "make possible new forms of intellectual work."*[2] *Bizzell has produced a large body of work and received numerous awards, including the CCCC Exemplar Award for outstanding contributions to the profession (2008). She has also served as the president of the Rhetorical Society of America (2004–2006). Her current work focuses on the intersection of religion and rhetoric, particularly women's rhetoric in 19th-century American and Jewish rhetoric. She received a master's degree in Jewish liberal studies from Hebrew College in 2010.*

—Lisa Sperber and Beth Pearsall

---

1 Ibid (99).
2 Patricia Bizzell. "The Intellectual Work of 'Mixed' Forms of Academic Discourses." *Alt Dis: Alternative Discourse and the Academy.* Ed. Christopher Schroeder, Helen Fox, and Patricia Bizzell. Portsmouth, NH: Boynton/Cook, 2002: (5). Print.

"Radical Pedagogy"

Sidney I. Dobrin and Todd Taylor

Spring 1994

WOE: You've been a dedicated writing teacher as well as a prolific writer for quite a few years. Would you tell us about your writing process?

BIZZELL: I should say first that I love to write. I've been writing ever since I was a little kid; I always wanted to be writer, and I love having a job where I get to do a lot of writing. It's not always easy for me to write, but I really like it.

My writing process has changed over the years. My habit used to be that when I wanted to write something I would sit and write it all at once. In fact, I wrote the first draft of an undergraduate senior thesis in a twenty-four-hour period; I just sat at my desk and wrote and wrote and wrote and wrote until it was done—a hundred-page paper or something like that. I continued to write that way; if I knew I had to write a paper for a conference or something, I'd have to set aside a two- or three-day period when I didn't have anything else to do and write it. But once I had kids, I couldn't continue that kind of writing process because I wasn't allowed. I couldn't send the kids away for two or three days while I wrote a paper. So I had to learn to use much smaller blocks of time to do my writing and to break the process down into more discrete stages. It seems to have worked out all right for me.

WOE: You mentioned the role your children play when you're writing. Several scholars, such as Jane Tompkins, are calling for recognition of the personal in scholarly writing. And in the introduction to your latest book you identify the significant impact that becoming a mother has had on your work. Yet outside of that introduction we see few personal references in your writing. Do you believe that the personal has a role in scholarly writing?

BIZZELL: Well, the short answer to the question is "Yes, absolutely." But my feelings are very complicated. When I see the personal coming into scholarly writing, I want it to be there for a reason. I think sometimes it comes in because the author wants to dramatize himself or herself or claim sympathy or show off, and I don't think that's appropriate. But when the person clearly has personal information we need to understand the argument, then the personal is really appropriate. I would give as models of combining personal and academic writing Patricia Williams's book, *The Alchemy of Race and Rights*, and everything bell hooks has ever written.

You're right in your perception that there hasn't been much of the personal in my writing. I found that introduction very difficult to write because I don't like to talk about myself. I would have found it even more difficult to write if I hadn't tried to imagine Dave Bartholomae as my audience. Since I've known him for a long time, I just pretended that I was talking to him. I find it very hard to talk about myself and to bring in the personal. (This is a feeling and not a principled position!) My writing style is very linear and logical, somewhat devoid of personal references. I see the personal in my writing in the kinds of allusions that I make, like bringing *Blade Runner* into the paper I read today or Isocrates into another. I'm also discomforted in using my students as examples. Again, I did that in the paper today, but I almost never do that.

WOE: Few of your works, with the notable exception of *The Rhetorical Tradition*, are collaborative. Do you resist collaboration in your scholarly writing?

BIZZELL: I don't think it's accurate to describe me as a person who resists collaboration. It's true that the only person I have collaborated with is Bruce Herzberg, my husband. So you might say that's not a fair case, or you might say that's the worst case—if I can collaborate with my husband, I ought to be able to collaborate with anybody! We've published a number of articles together; we've done *The Rhetorical Tradition*, three editions of *The Bedford Bibliography*, and we're now working on another book together; so we've published quite a few articles collaboratively. Also, I think if you look at the references in my publications, you'll see that I have often acknowledged help that I have received from informal readers of manuscripts or from people I have corresponded with; even if they haven't published anything I could cite as an influence, I'll put in a footnote saying "private correspondence with so-and-so." I've made a conscious effort to indicate the part that other people play in the generation of ideas in my essays.

WOE: It sounds as if you see the role of collaboration as going beyond "let's sit down and write a piece together" to "would you discuss a piece with me?"

BIZZELL: If you understand the concept of intertextuality, you have to say that all writing is collaborative. I'm influenced by my teachers and by the people that I've read, and it doesn't make sense to me to say that I have somehow produced my writing all by myself. That's absurd. There are lots of forms of collaboration in addition to actual coauthorship, and I've employed many of them. I also think co-authorship is a great thing. There ought to be a lot more of it. English studies, particularly literary studies, is behind the rest of the world in acknowledging the importance of collaboration and co-authored pieces. Composition studies is better than literary studies in that regard.

WOE: Should writing teachers themselves be proficient writers?

BIZZELL: That's a politically loaded question. You learn a lot about writing by writing; I think it's a good thing to write. I know that there are professional development movements for writing teachers modeled on the Bay Area Writing Project where teachers are encouraged to write. I'm in favor of all that, and I think that it is in general a good idea for writing teachers to be writers.

Even going that far, I'm uncomfortable with saying "proficient" as if, somehow, if you're not a good enough writer, you're not allowed to be a writing teacher. I also would want to be very careful about making dedicated teachers who don't do a lot of writing feel their contribution isn't valuable. I think it's possible to be a good writing coach without doing a lot of writing yourself. I have had teachers who I thought were great writing coaches who I don't think did much writing themselves. I also think it's possible to be a very proficient writer and be a lousy writing teacher. So I would be hesitant to make any kind of simple equation and say you have to be this in order to be that. It sounds too exclusionary to me.

WOE: You suggest that "writing could not be seen as a skill or set of skills, analogous to the set of skills one must master in order to ride a bicycle." You continue by proposing a model that suggests writing is an ongoing process, that it is a "lifelong process": "A person could be said never to finish learning to write." You also claim that in order for students to survive in the academic setting they must comply with certain conventions. Thus, you seem to be suggesting that writing is both a "closed-capacity" and an "open-capacity" skill.

BIZZELL: I think I would want to emphasize the "open-capacity" side. Maybe the thing to say is that as you are writing and learning to write, you master conventions at a certain point, and then they become part of what you use to accomplish certain tasks you're working on. Once you've mastered these conventions, you're done mastering them; it's "closed" in that sense—you're now just using them. But some of my earlier writing on the mastery of academic discourse conventions probably didn't emphasize that once you've learned enough about academic discourse conventions to use them comfortably, to survive in the academy, you should also feel empowered to manipulate them, to alter them, to change them, and to push the academy to change. In that sense, the learning of conventions might not be a finished or a closed skill, but would be one that opened out into new kinds of conventions and new kinds of writing strategies—one that offered you a position in which you were not simply conforming to something that was being demanded of you, but exercising persuasion to change the institution that had previously asked you to conform.

WOE: You write in the introduction of *Academic Discourse and Critical Consciousness* that you "hoped to develop a writing program that would be college-wide, diverse and voluntary." What is your rationale in offering a voluntary program if, as you also argue, students need to learn academic discourse in order to be successful college writers?

BIZZELL: It's a contradiction, but I have no problem with contradictions. I developed a distaste for requirement-driven writing programs while I was working in one at Rutgers. I wanted to try a different model when I went to Holy Cross and was fortunate enough to be in a position where I could do that. I think a case can still be made for the damage that requirement-driven programs do; however, that doesn't mean that a voluntary program is an adequate replacement either. It has its disadvantages. The most obvious is the one you pointed out: students can opt out of it, and, thereby, opt out of getting the help they really need. I just don't know what to do about that contradiction. Frankly, there's something troublesome to me about taking up the sort of colonialist position of saying to the students, "Well, this is for your own good. So even though you think you don't need this, I think you need it, and I'm going to make you have it." That seems disrespectful to the students and doesn't really work. As you well know, students who are dragged into a writing class don't cooperate very well.

WOE: I wonder if by making the program voluntary, the students come to realize that they need those skills: that it becomes their responsibility to be able to survive in the academic world?

BIZZELL: I'd like to make that argument, to say that it's the beginning of empowerment to choose to take the writing course and to take an active stance toward what you're learning and how you're going to use it. I'd like to say that the requirement-driven courses do seem by their very structure to be imposing conformity. All the time I've been at Holy Cross, I've promoted a voluntary program and never pushed for a writing requirement.

However, I'm just about to change my mind on that. In fact, I just started bugging people a little about having a writing requirement at Holy Cross. But I'm interested in a compromise, having a writing requirement that can be met in a variety of ways. For instance, you could take a first-year writing elective, an upper-class writing elective in the English Department, or a writing-intensive course outside the English Department. In the writing-across-the-curriculum program we have anywhere between fifteen and thirty writing-intensive courses offered outside the English Department every year. I'd like to say, "Okay, students do have to take a writing course, but we're not going to take everybody in their first year and force them into a specific course. Students meet that need when and in the way they're ready to meet it."

WOE: You claim that in order for writing programs to be good, "they must be indigenous." Does this mean that there can be no general writing program characteristics that transcend local contexts?

BIZZELL: No. If you're trained—in graduate school, for example—you learn some components that good writing programs generally have. When you go out to develop a writing program someplace, instead of saying, "Well, I know what good writing programs are/should be, and here's what we're going to have," you should first talk to the people who are there—do the kinds of things that Paulo Freire's literacy instructors do in terms of generating themes for their students. They have general ideas about how to teach literacy, but they just don't present words to people. Instead, they do a lot of research to find out what's going to resonate for people in that particular community. I think that's what writing program administrators should do too. That's what I mean by it being an indigenous program: it might be guided by general principles, but the specifics of how the program is built up should be derived from its context.

WOE: At one time you embraced the utopian promise in Freire's pedagogy of liberation through literacy and critical consciousness. Recently, however, you wrote that you "reject the idea that any form of literacy in and of itself can provide critical distance on the world or, one may as well say, critical consciousness." Though you implicitly reject Freirian pedagogy, do you nonetheless believe that radical pedagogy should play a role in composition teaching?

BIZZELL: My problem with Freire is really a philosophical problem. Specifically, it seems to me that he believes that a simple study of reality will reveal structures of oppression, and that all you have to do is clear away the debris that prevented people from seeing them and point to them, and people will say, "Oh yes, I'm being oppressed, and this is what I have to do to get out of my oppression." He actually uses a lot of scientific and academic language and metaphors to describe how people's vision will penetrate through to the truth. In the title essay of *Academic Discourse and Critical Consciousness*, I naively catalogued all of these similarities between Freire's language and academic language of argument. I now think they share this language because they're making a similar philosophical mistake, which is to assume that study can somehow reveal the true nature of reality. Furthermore, once this true nature is revealed, it will be revealed to be oppressive; once it's revealed to be oppressive, people will automatically be inspired to resist it. I no longer believe that process takes place. I'm still deeply committed to radical pedagogy, but I would now say that this pedagogy is a persuasive ideological project from start to finish. I have to offer my values and techniques and fight against the ones that are in opposition to me and just try to persuade people to go my way. I can't rely on pointing to reality to make them go along with me.

WOE: In your more recent works, you argue that academic discourse is not a means to critical consciousness, but you call for a unified academic discourse "including the greatest possible diversity of participants and remaining open to change in response to the cultural literacies of new groups who want to join in our projects." You add, "We may wish to do away with an oppressive academic discourse, but we cannot do without any academic discourse at all." How should we balance this tension?

BIZZELL: Beats me. Damned if I know. I'm rejecting the possibility that academic discourse can give us a window on reality, and, as a result, reality will become transparent to us. But I think that academic work performs useful social functions. The academy as a social project does things that aren't done well elsewhere. Anybody who wants to have access to those projects, to participate in them, should be able to do that. On the one hand, we need some kind of unified academic discourse so that those projects can continue to go forward, but, on the other hand, we need to have within that academic discourse more tolerance for diverse voices so that as the projects go forward the participation will be more democratic. It's hard to think of an example. One might be the democratization of the literary canon; as a project it would be very difficult to accomplish outside the academy. You need the resources of the academy to do that—to find the material that's been ignored and to bring it into American literature courses. But, obviously, you need maximum participation in that project for it really to do what it's intending to do in terms of diversifying the canon. You need to make it possible for scholars of color to participate—for all kinds of scholars to participate—for students coming into the academy from diverse backgrounds to get a purchase on that project.

I'm increasingly testy with career-oriented academics who put their career priorities ahead of fostering the ethos of academic discourse, whether they're in literature or composition studies. I thought that there were a lot of people taking politically correct positions in bashing E.D. Hirsch because they didn't want to take politically incorrect positions, but they shouldn't even be thinking about political correctness. They should be thinking about what's going to be best for everybody—what's going to be best for the students. I really believe that. I really don't care if somebody thinks I'm politically incorrect. My goal in life is not to make sure that I never say anything that is politically incorrect. My goal in life is to try to make the best schools for everybody to teach in and to learn in and do whatever is necessary to bring that about. I get annoyed when I see people who are afraid to take a chance on recommending something because they think it might sound politically incorrect.

I know that people don't want to start the cycle of oppression and exclusion all over again. I certainly sympathize with those concerns. I don't want to do that either, but my feeling is that we have to do something. It's not enough to just sit there and say, "Well, since I don't want to risk imposing anything on my students that might be oppressive, I won't set any agenda for them at all. They can read whatever they want." I don't think we'll get anywhere that way.

WOE: How might we in English studies become more useful to society at large? Or do you believe, with Noam Chomsky, that we should not be concerned with trying to be socially useful?

BIZZELL: I would say that we can be socially useful in ways that people traditionally thought that English studies was socially useful. For the sake of argument, I can imagine some past time, which probably never existed (but let's pretend that it did) when people had an uncomplicated notion that what English studies did was good for society: it taught people to be effective communicators, and it also informed them about their cultural heritage through literature that was spiritually satisfying and spiritually nourishing. People thought in a rather uncomplicated way that's what English studies does and that it was worth doing. Then we discovered that there was a big problem with that idea, which was that only certain people were learning how to be effective communicators and only certain people were being spiritually nourished by the literatures being taught. It turned out to be a project with a lot of built-in exclusions.

I somewhat naively say it wasn't that those were bad ideas, they were just exclusive. We should just make sure that we empower all our students to learn what they want to learn about being effective communicators; we should try to inform *all* of them about literature that will be spiritually nourishing to them, and we should learn from them about what that literature is. That requires this massive multiple education project—everybody learning about everybody else. But I have an old-fashioned view of those goals suitably being revised as appropriate goals. It's only a tiny thing that we do for society by taking these goals for everybody, but we shouldn't be greedy and say, "Well, since I'm not saving the universe, then what I'm doing is totally worthless." Maybe we should be a little more realistic about what good is enough good without feeling too down on ourselves.

WOE: In "Cognition, Convention, and Certainty," you call for a powerful theory in composition studies to help us "retaliate against literary critics who dominate English studies." What kinds of things would this theory attempt to account for? Do you see Stanley Fish pushing us toward such a theory?

BIZZELL: That's an interesting question. That article, which was published about eleven years ago, assumes an opposition between composition studies and literary studies. I don't think I would set up the terms of the problem that way anymore. I think that composition and literature are really converging, even more dramatically than they seemed to be ten years ago under the rubric of rhetoric. Their concerns are becoming more and more common, and what they're both doing is, to an increasing degree, rhetoric. So the theory would be some kind of theory of rhetoric—a means of persuasion. What are the cultural archives? How do you establish an ethos? How do you construct persuasive discourse? How do you respond to it and negotiate it and engage in dialogue? A lot of things that were the concerns of classical rhetorical instruction can be the concerns of a contemporary rhetorical theory for a unified English studies.

Fish is one of the people who sees this potential power of rhetoric, and certainly his work has influenced me. However, I don't think he's got it yet.

I always wonder what Fish thinks about this sort of moral agenda that I like to talk about. Does he think that it is important or not important or silly or deeply important but deeply personal and not to be spoken of in public? I think it's hard to say where he's coming from on that. He gets a lot of flak for just being a glib arguer with no values and no moral commitments at all, and he always takes the position that's hardest to defend because he'll look even more brilliant when it turns out he can defend it—his role being that of the troublemaker. I don't think that flack is fair either to the person that I know (not that I know him well) or to undercurrents of something else going on that I catch in his work. If you asked him in an interview whether English studies should be socially useful, he'd put you off; he definitely wouldn't answer the question.

WOE: In "Kuhn, Scientism, and English Studies," you argued that compositionists must not fall into scientism. In an interview in *WOE*, Linda Flower—someone often considered the representative of cognitive, if not scientistic, composition studies—admits to becoming more aware of the social aspects of writing. Do you think this is evidence that we are, in fact, moving away from scientism?

BIZZELL: "Kuhn, Scientism, and English Studies" was written to try to head off a specific kind of work I saw people beginning to do in composition studies which was scientistic in that it seemed to be taking empirical research on writing processes and leaping from limited empirical study to a kind of procrustean pedagogy where students were being stretched and cut to fit the results of those studies prematurely. I have that worry about any kind of social science research. I ultimately just don't believe in it. I always want more examples, but this type of research is going to say, "Okay, well now we have enough examples, so now we know what we should do to all students is X, and let's make sure we do it thoroughly to them." That worries me, and I saw that beginning to happen in writing instruction. I was trying to caution people against doing that.

I was fearful Linda Flower was doing that in her early work. You could find her saying things like the writing process is hierarchical and recursive and that the trouble with bad writers was they don't recurse enough or something. She doesn't do that anymore. It may be partly as a result of the influence of my work, but then, of course, her work has had a profound influence on me because if I started out by arguing against what she was doing, then obviously I had to find myself as her other.

We may be moving away from the scientism I thought I saw happening twelve years ago partly because we're more secure as a discipline: people are no longer frantically looking for any method they can call composition research. But there's always a danger of taking some test result and saying that all of a sudden this tells us how to treat every student. We should always be on guard against this danger.

WOE: Until the publication of *The Rhetorical Tradition*, most compositionists would not have associated you with scholarship in the history of rhetoric. What contributions from ancient rhetoric are most useful to compositionists today, or do you believe along with Brannon and Knoblauch that such contributions are extremely limited if not nonexistent?

BIZZELL: I want to rephrase the question. I certainly disagree with the position taken in Brannon and Knoblauch's book *Rhetorical Traditions in the Teaching of Writing*, that the effect of the premodern rhetorical tradition on modern writing instruction is only pernicious and, therefore, that premodern rhetoric should all be thrown out and we should try to wipe out its influence on us as quickly as possible. I don't think they even agree with this position anymore, to tell you the truth. What we should be doing is looking at premodern rhetoric to see how we can use it and what we find interesting there, not with the sense that it's some sacred tradition. There's a tremendous archive of material that we can use—perhaps in a revisionist way. I like Susan Jarratt's work with ancient rhetoric, for example. The kind of appropriation and revision that she's doing on that work is exciting to me—or Jan Swearingen's work, which is very scholarly, very knowledgeable, but also motivated by contemporary concerns in composition and rhetoric and not by service to a classical text. It's not that we have to have classical rhetoric in order to be legitimate; it's just so interesting. I was fascinated by what I discovered in doing the research for *The Rhetorical Tradition*. I came away with all these ideas for more things that I wanted to study and write about.

WOE: In what ways can we balance our commitment to ethics with our understanding that we are always already entangled in ideology?

BIZZELL: I wouldn't deny for a moment that my ethical commitments are induced in me by the effects of ideology. I don't claim to have received an epiphany. I'm fully a product of my education and my times, and I'm deeply swayed by ideologies that cause me to have these ethical commitments. But for me that's not a problem—even if I have to say that there is no transcendent source of my ethical commitments, that they are purely historically generated. I'm just locating myself in a historical tradition and affirming it, trying to be part of it, fostering it, and not being a passive recipient of it.

WOE: Lately, you've been interested in the work of Fredric Jameson. What do you believe is his contribution to composition studies?

BIZZELL: I found two things most provocative in Jameson: first of all, his characterization of postmodern culture, which seemed to clarify a lot of things for me about what I was struggling with in terms of an unease or spiritual malaise—a discomfort that I felt in my own life and that I have discerned in my students' lives. He was describing a sense of why we felt it: because we were living in this postmodern culture.

Second, his general notion of cognitive mapping, and the specific example of it that he gives of storytelling, are strategies that can be adapted for rhetoric. They are, in fact, deeply rhetorical strategies. I found them provocative indicators for a certain kind of pedagogy. I think I depict him as being much more negative about postmodern culture and much more eager to resist it than he would depict himself. I don't think he wants to be seen as an attacker of postmodern culture. But I think he is because the logic of his ethical commitment to social justice means that he has to resist postmodern culture by encouraging a restoration of a sense of history which will show people how to get together to effect social change and that they need to get together to effect social change.

WOE: In "A Postmodern Critique of the Modern Projects of Fredric Jameson and Patricia Bizzell," Nancy McKoski writes, "Like Jameson, in believing that only a totalizing, universalizing, rationalistic (masculinist, Western) politics is 'genuine,' Bizzell refuses to regard the historical significance of a postmodern politics, which she writes off as the quietistic liberal or antifoundational belief in pluralism and difference. That is, like Jameson, she does not want to acknowledge the politics of the postmodern, a politics that seriously challenges traditional political and academic modes of operation." Is this a fair criticism?

BIZZELL: Yes, I'd say she's right on the money. Actually, I think she's right to see me as critical of postmodern politics, although I'm not entirely sure what she means by postmodern politics. Let's suppose that postmodern politics means highly local politics, politics of very particular groups each working for its own agenda and speaking its own story and putting forward its own priorities. If that's what postmodern politics means, then I'm not satisfied with that; that's not enough for me. I want to find some way to get those groups together to make a common cause among them. That doesn't mean that they all have to become one group or that everything they do has to be done together. I don't see myself as universalizing their concerns. I would say that the common ground has to be built on very specific material circumstances or historical circumstances that they might share or a legacy of oppression from the same source. But, yes, indeed, I do want to move beyond the local and try to get these groups together to make common cause against a common oppressor; I don't think that's universalizing. It may be totalizing in some sense. If it is, I stand convicted.

I don't fully understand why I get accused of being rationalistic in the sense of masculinist, Western. It's true that in hoping that these groups will get together for concerted action, I base that hope on the possibility that they can persuade each other, that they can engage in discourse that's mutually comprehensible. I never said anywhere that would be discourse where I, by my logic, compel you to agree with me in some legalistic notion of linear argument. If you read what I say about persuasion, you can see that I'm talking about sharing experience and sharing cultural archives and trying to acknowledge the reality of each other's experience as much as that's possible. It will never be completely possible. The idea of joining together that I'm imagining is a utopian idea that hasn't been achieved, and it may not be achievable.

But it seems to me that we'd get better results if we acted like we were working towards it rather than if we said it was impossible and everyone should just paddle their own canoe. I don't like this version of postmodern politics because I don't see it getting us anywhere. I think everyone's just paddling their own canoe over Niagara Falls, and it's fostering more hatred and strife and hatred of difference and violence and all things I abhor.

The biggest criticism of my scholarship that a lot of people have mounted, Joe Harris among others, is that in advocating teaching students academic discourse I was advocating all students to conform to a monolithic, unitary set of academic conventions. I wasn't doing that. I can go back and look at "Cognition, Convention, and Certainty," for example, and find where I say that I hope students will change the academy. Even at the very beginning I never depicted a one-way street of forcing students to conform to some monolithic discourse. I think I was placing a heavy emphasis on the social contexts of learning to write because I saw a view in ascendancy that ignored the social context. I wanted to emphasize that the social context was there so it wouldn't get ignored, so we wouldn't just talk in terms of individual writers and their cognitive processes—we needed to bring the social back in.

JAMES J. MURPHY

James J. Murphy is a distinguished teacher, scholar, and publisher. A prominent scholar in the field of rhetoric, Murphy has published extensively on the history of rhetoric in the ancient, medieval, and Renaissance periods, as well as the history of language and writing pedagogies. Though his primary focus has been on classical rhetoric, Murphy also writes and lectures on the relation of rhetoric to composition and composition pedagogy. In Quintilian on the Teaching of Speaking and Writing (1987, 2015), Murphy demonstrates the ways that "the master teacher of Rome" employed methods that echo and support modern theory. As editor of A Short History of Writing Instruction from Ancient Greece to Modern America (1995, 2013), Murphy contributes cogent and insightful essays on the ways that rhetorical tradition has shaped and influenced current pedagogy and scholarship.

Murphy has authored or edited twenty-four books, including A Synoptic History of Classical Rhetoric (1972), The Rhetorical Tradition and Modern Writing (1982), and Rhetoric in the Middle Ages: A History of Rhetorical Theory from St. Augustine to the Renaissance (1981), which won both a Winans-Wichelns and an SCA Book Award and was translated into Italian and Spanish. He was the founding editor of Rhetorica: A Journal of the History of Rhetoric, and is a Distinguished Scholar in the National Communication Association. In 1983 he founded Hermagoras Press.

Since his retirement from University of California, Davis, in 1991, Murphy has remained active in the field, publishing two new editions of his books in recent years, as well as serving as series editor (with Krista Radcliffe) of Landmark Essays (Routledge). Murphy remains a frequent lecturer and contributor to colloquia at the Davis campus as well as his alma mater, St. Mary's College of California—class of 1947. He has served on the editorial board of Writing on the Edge since the journal's founding in 1989, and continues to serve as editorial advisor and mentor. He is a Fellow of the Medieval Academy of America, and a Fellow of the Rhetoric Society of America. As Professor Emeritus at UC Davis, he serves on the steering committee for Rhetoric@Davis, an active research cluster for UC Davis graduate students and faculty, founded in 2012.

—Michal Reznizki and David Masiel

"Setting Minds in Motion"

Mardena Creek

Spring 1994

WOE: You describe yourself as a rhetorician. What do you mean by rhetoric?

MURPHY: Rhetoric is about future discourse—the study of how to prepare for writing or speaking in the future. So it deals with how to find ideas, how to arrange them, how to put words to them for the sake of an audience. If it's speaking, it also has to include remembering your ideas and expressing them well to the audience. It's about preparing now for the future.

WOE: Did your interest in rhetoric grow out of the way you were educated?

MURPHY: It came in a rhetorical way. I went to Catholic grammar school in San Francisco, the Christian Brothers' High School. In my sophomore year, I was sitting in my English class when the principal walked in and tapped me on the shoulder. He took me out in the hall and said, "You're going to be on the debate team." Not "Would you like to be?" but "You are *going* to be." This was in the days when if the teacher told you to do something, you did it. So I got started in interschool debate in high school. That got me interested in rhetoric. Years later, in 1961, I wrote *The Debater's Guide* with Jon Ericson.

WOE: Did this debate experience affect your writing?

MURPHY: Yes, undoubtedly it did. The key to successful debating, as the *Debater's Guide* makes clear, is the ability to think in outline terms so when you hear a thousand words from your opponent, you don't remember a thousand words; you remember three ideas you can respond to. Debate teaches you how to listen and select. And, of course, it teaches you how to think on your feet.

Of course I was also in a Christian Brothers' school where writing was frequent and assumed. I don't think they had any writing course; instead there was writing in every class. And this writing was meticulously graded and corrected and watched, so you just got used to having your writing critiqued.

WOE: What about college? What kind of writing did you do there?

MURPHY: I attended St. Mary's. It was the first Great Books school on the West Coast. One of the instructors, Brother Robert, had been at St. John's of Annapolis and brought the whole Mortimer Adler Great Books system back with him to St. Mary's.

So when I started there in 1941, there was a required four-year, eight-semester Great Books course. It started with Sophocles and ended with Freud, and we had to write papers every quarter about these great readings.

WOE: Was the goal of the Great Books curriculum rhetorical, to create what the Roman's called *facilitas*—"the capacity to produce appropriate and effective language in any given situation"? Did you, for instance, do imitations and explications?

MURPHY: We had to write commentaries on texts and to paraphrase texts. One of the early Great Books assignments was to take something like one of Sophocles' works and write an abstract of it. But writing was just assumptive; it was "across the curriculum" well before that was a term. It was very European. European schools still don't have separate writing classes. They just write all of the time.

WOE: So you learned to write by writing frequently?

MURPHY: Constant practice was the key. My first job after college—with United Press—got me going as a semi-professional writer. I had to write five or six thousand words a day. Of course, that kind of writing is highly mechanical. There are only five ways to describe a head-on collision and three ways to describe what a speaker has said. You find that out after about a month. That kind of writing may be formulaic but it is fast, so you get used to doing things fast.

WOE: What do you think of the "Writing Across the Curriculum" movement? Is it just a way to do what we should be doing in other ways?

MURPHY: I think so. It's just a stopgap in a desperate situation. Everything today is so fragmented.

WOE: Given the fragmented nature of the American school curriculum, is the goal of creating *facilitas* achievable even to a small degree?

MURPHY: There are two imperfect answers to that question. The first is to realize that raising the consciousness of students is the best thing you can do under the circumstances. If you are talking about juniors or seniors in college, for instance, maybe the most efficient thing to do is to increase their level of awareness about what they need to do. It's too late for you to do it. If you've got them in K to 12 where you've got the time, then those mechanisms, those processes, those progymnasmatic exercises can be used incrementally and the student doesn't need to know what's happening to him. I didn't know. But when you're working with adults, I think that sense of awareness is what you can give them. You see so many people out in business for a few years who become aware of what they should have been aware of as university students. And they go back to school and pay $1500 for a weekend seminar.

WOE: What are those students looking for when they come back?

MURPHY: The things sophomores should know. They finally see the need for it. I've taught English composition courses, public speaking courses, and group discussion courses, and in all three of those sectors that sense of awareness, that sense of need, is critical. I've often thought that if you spend ten weeks with somebody and he comes out thinking, "Gee, I need to do this," it doesn't matter what you've done in between. The mechanics aren't the question. And if they don't have that sense of need, they come out thinking what so many students do: "I did English. I'm finished. I don't need that anymore." The current fragmented educational system creates that kind of thinking.

Which brings me to my second imperfect answer: we could reassemble the disassembled university—but that's an institutional problem.

WOE: Could you explain what you mean by the disassembled university?

MURPHY: Let me give an example. At Princeton I taught a class called composition, a mixed speech/writing class offered by the English Department. It was modeled on the nineteenth-century Cornell system where speaking and writing were taught at the same time as interrelated activities. As you may know, for a while Ivy League schools pursued that plan rather than having separate courses. Around the turn of the century, schools like Cornell, Dartmouth, Brown, Princeton—not Harvard—had these courses where every aspect of language use was taught. The different aspects weren't regarded as separate activities. We'd call such classes communication courses today.

WOE: Did they call these classes Rhetoric?

MURPHY: Frequently. Cornell did. If you look at the long, long history of the subject of "language use"—and I prefer that term to the word "rhetoric"—you see how in ancient times there were four different traditions: the Sophistic, the Platonic, the Aristotelian, the Isocratean. The Sophistic tradition had no influence. The Platonic had no later influence. The Aristotelian had some influence on the Romans, but it was Isocrates' system that most influenced the Romans. The Romans really set the pattern for language-use study in the Middle Ages and the Renaissance right up into the early part of this century. Quintilian's plan was the backbone of English education in the Elizabethan and Tudor periods. When transplanted to America, it dominated the studies of language use into the early part of this century.

My aunt graduated from Watsonville High in 1907. She left me one of her notebooks, and it was practically right out of Quintilian. It was filled with progymnasmatic exercises they had to write out. This was in Watsonville, California—a little farm town!

WOE: Why did this tradition end if it had worked so successfully for so long?

MURPHY: In the 1880s Harvard's English Department began to redefine the nature of English studies to emphasize literary-critical scholarship at the expense of rhetoric. They threw rhetoric out of the department and reduced composition to a second-class status. This is when the classical curriculum began to crumble. Then in 1917, the oral teachers walked out of the NCTE and formed what is now called the Speech Communication Association Later linguistics split off from the English Department. One hundred fifty years ago what we call philosophy would have been taught in the same classroom as what we call rhetoric. Ironically, Harvard's now got a "writing program" again!

WOE: Do you see any hope for reintegration?

MURPHY: Not in the immediate future. Especially when you keep importing administrators at the various levels who not only want to perpetuate this fragmentation but also want to increase it. When Cicero was nineteen he falsely blamed Socrates for setting up a system in which one set of teachers teaches us to think and another set teaches us to speak. Well, here it is two thousand years later, and we have one set of teachers who deal with reading and another set who deals with writing: it's the same problem! The Humanist system had much less fragmentation than there is now.

To get back to your earlier question about whether writing centers are a good thing. I think in the long run they will defeat themselves. You've already got two separate buildings for reading and for speaking. Now we've got a third one for writing. In the short term, I think writing centers are useful especially in one political sense where they can encourage writing across the curriculum in ways a department cannot. I think the adjunct writing classes are a grand idea, but look how rare they are. I don't think they can solve the problem.

WOE: Do you see any remedies for this fragmentation?

MURPHY: In a way the whole composition/literature movement is an attempt to do this. And there are moves afoot at some schools to reintegrate language-use curriculum. Ohio State has a separate composition unit with thousands and thousands of students enrolled. And the composition people have been holding monthly meetings with three rhetoricians in the Speech Communications Department. At Illinois, the English Department and the Speech/Communication Department are working toward a joint program.

How many places are there, however, where composition/writing-center faculty are holding joint meetings with the literary faculty in the same department? I think what's happening nationally is that rhetorically minded people of various kinds are coming together in an interdisciplinary sort of way, but not directly within the English department. If, on this wide scale, something new emerges, it won't be something that calls itself rhetoric. It would be fatal to use the older term.

WOE: Why does the term "rhetoric" bother people so much?

MURPHY: Part of it is historical The second Sophistic period, the late antique period, gave rhetoric a very bad name. When Harvard threw rhetoric out of its English Department in the 1880s, this action reinforced the negative connotations. And when the oral/written split occurred in 1917, it caused a lot of animosity, with a lot of residual bad feeling and appropriation of names. And then, of course, politicians use the term "rhetoric" in a pejorative way all of the time. If you look in a dictionary, the first definition of rhetoric is usually style—often in a pejorative tone.

WOE: I'd like to go back to your earlier remark that one "imperfect solution" is to raise students' consciousness about what they need to know. You are a widely published scholar, but you are also a teacher who has won a Distinguished Teaching Award. How have you gone about raising your students' consciousness?

MURPHY: When I was a sophomore in college I read Thomas Aquinas' little book on teaching called *De Magistro* in which he says, "The learner learns; the teacher does not teach." I think that is an absolutely critical point. If you want people to get some data, you can have a data collection in a book, which is like a pot of stew. If you want them to have some stew, have them get a spoon and go to the pot. But if you want them to take something away other than the data, they've got to have some feeling that they've got to learn themselves. And if they don't learn how to learn themselves, then anything you do is hopeless. Worse than that, it's probably damaging.

Obsession with data killed grammar in this country and also killed classical studies. "Learn these 38 rules by Tuesday, or I'll rap your knuckles!" And so people remember them until Tuesday, and then it's just as though you've poured water in the Mojave Desert. There's nothing left over. If, however, you learn how words fit together, how it's *fun* to fit them together, and to make transitions—this learning might go on to real life; it might stick.

WOE: I once heard you say, "It's possible for students to spend four years here and not do any thinking." You suggested then that this wasn't so much the fault of the students as of the system and its data-obsessed teachers. But how do teachers help students learn for themselves, help them make the connections?

MURPHY: Asking questions, certainly. For about the last ten years that I taught, I started the first class of every quarter by walking in and asking the students, "Why did you sit down?" I began with that line because it raised the question of our relationship. Why was I standing while they were sitting in rows? Why were they sitting in rows? And they didn't know. They'd never thought about it. They'd been sitting and listening passively for years, and they never questioned the procedure. Students march through the university like sausages on a conveyer belt. At the end of the process they come off the production line—they're commenced.

WOE: Your classes are very interactive. The class I attended had over 200 students sitting in desks screwed to the floor, but you didn't let that stop you. You had students solving problems in small groups, reading aloud, standing up front explaining and debating. During the last class session, you put a rope down the middle of the room and asked the Ciceronians to sit on one side and the Aristotelians on the other. Students came to the front to defend their choices and to try to persuade others to come over to their side. As the hour progressed, there was a lot of movement from side to side. I saw one student change sides three times. You seemed willing to try anything.

MURPHY: *Audax* or audacity is one of the hallmarks of the orator, as Cicero points out. He means that the person who wants to get something across to another person has got to be willing to take chances, be willing to do things even if he doesn't know how they're going to work or whether they're going to work. So in practical terms a teacher has to be willing to take a lot of chances. A lot of things just don't work! You try to get a discussion going and nothing happens—it's terrible. Therefore, a lot of people shrink back and just don't try anything. There's a kind of a Newtonian law: a mind set in motion tends to stay in motion. Therefore—this is another rhetorical principle—it almost doesn't matter what you say if it gets that mind moving. It can be a question; it can be a diagram; it can be something someone else in the class has said, or something the reading says.

A lot of teachers make the mistake of saying, "Here's the reading. We're going to make sure you understand it. We're going to go through it and pick it apart." That's merely one technique, the French explication of the text. You go through and look at every word. That's part of the exercise of explication, which goes back to ancient times. You've probably heard me talk about the grammarian Priscian's commentary on the first twelve lines of the *Aeneid*. He wrote seventy-four pages on the first twelve lines, not only word by word, but sense by sense, tense by tense. I think some teachers when they have a textbook want to make sure the students are marched through that textbook. That may not always be the best thing to do because it's the subject that matters, not the book about the subject.

We're very fortunate in that whatever we do using language is about language. If we were physicists we might have a different problem. There's the buzzword—*engage* the students—but it's more than engaging them; it's getting them to do the work themselves. One of the things that really sets my teeth on edge is when someone in the coffee room says, "I'm going to teach Shakespeare." Granted they're speaking ungrammatically to start with, but what they mean is that they are going to promulgate something. They never say, "I've got an opportunity to see if I can get sixty-five people thinking about Shakespeare." They never say that.

WOE: In your class, you didn't allow students to take notes, although they were all sitting there, pens poised, waiting to hear Murphy's take on classical rhetoric.

MURPHY: At the end of the term, some of them had even started to do this in their other classes.

WOE: Could they do it?

MURPHY: Yes, because they had begun to take responsibility for their own memory—not only their own memory but their own selective process. If you take notes, there's a tendency to put everything down because you don't know what's important. If you eliminate the notes, you are immediately engaging them in a critical activity—figuring out what's important and what's not important.

WOE: You also had them do a lot of group work, got them interacting with one another. Do you attribute this method to your rhetorical background?

MURPHY: Dialectical confrontation is critical. If you put together the principle of confrontation and the rhetorical idea that it almost doesn't matter how you start the process, then teaching is a matter of momentary ingenuity. Frequently in that class I would go in not knowing exactly which tack to take.

Sometimes it would depend on what somebody said, on the mood. A medieval example of this phenomenon is that language is like a wheel with meaning in the center, so it doesn't matter what spoke you pursue to get to the center; it will take you there. The worst thing that can happen if you've got the nerve, the audacity, to pursue this approach, is that it fails utterly. If this happens you can always say, "OK, *why* did that fail utterly?" and move that very disaster into a discussion point.

WOE: You mentioned the word "engage" as being a buzzword. You often point out that a lot of the current buzzwords and techniques are really old ideas in new dress. Have you seen anything truly innovative going on in the teaching of composition in the last fifteen years?

MURPHY: Well, one new thing—and I don't know what to think about this—is empirical research.

WOE: The "process hunters and model makers," as you say in one of your articles, "have begun to replace teachers."

MURPHY: Did I say that? I told Linda Flower that I think it would be fun for the two of us to get together and write a piece about Quintilian and the Flower-Hays model. I think that would be fun because the Flower-Hays model could be seen as a version of Book X of the *Institutio Oratorio*, where Quintilian talks about adult writers who are revising and editing their own materials, going through drafts and relying on their memories.

I think one of the problems placed on our Western culture by Science with a capital S is the difficulty caused when you have something that you've not seen before and it's got a name you haven't seen before. Is it a new *thing* or a new *name*? If a scientist discovers a new species of insect or a new species of flowers and gives it a new name, that's fine. When some twenty-three-year-old assistant professor writes an article for *College English* and gives something a new name, is it a new thing or a new name for an old thing? And that's a constant question for people who haven't seen enough flowers to know that this species is a common one. The other part of that topos is that every generation, in a sense, has to write its own rhetoric in its own language.

It can be fatal to use an old pejorative name: you couldn't go to the state board of education and sell Quintilian. But you might be able to go to the state board and sell them an incremental process model.

I don't think anybody who studies rhetoric seriously would say that you can simply pick up Aristotle or Cicero and teach them in Coalinga. Nobody is really saying that, but a lot of people are increasingly saying that we can take ancient rhetoric (and call it that) and bring it into the twentieth century. Look at what Sharon Crowley has done for Macmillan, for instance: she's written a book distilling the best of ancient rhetoric into what she calls "a unique textbook on composition"—*Ancient Rhetoric for Contemporary Students*. When major commercial publishers like Macmillan get involved, you can be sure they count on having a lot of interested readers.

WOE: Winifred Homer's book *Rhetoric in the Classical Tradition* came out in the late 1980s. And, of course, Corbett's *Classical Rhetoric for the Modern Student* has been around since the mid-sixties. To what do you attribute this growing interest in classical rhetoric?

MURPHY: Ed Corbett was probably the groundbreaker in the composition field, but there has been a growing scholarly interest in rhetoric since World War II. There have been more histories of rhetoric written in the last decade than I suppose there have been in the whole history of Western culture. I added it up the other day. There are about fifteen histories of rhetoric—not all classical rhetoric—such as Winnie Horner on Scotland or Nan Johnson on nineteenth-century America. But at the same time, rhetoric has come under some pretty vicious attacks.

WOE: Knoblauch and Brannon have certainly taken exception to the assumptions and approaches they associate with the classical tradition.

MURPHY: They really take a swipe at rhetoric. And in the speech communication field, the empiricists are completely separating themselves from the rhetorical tradition. They're following the Baconian/Cartesian "doing" to its ultimate. In a department meeting debating whether to continue the classical rhetoric course as one of the four core courses in the program, one of my colleagues, a pure empiricist, argued that classical rhetoric had nothing to do with the work he did. We outvoted him, but we didn't convince him. His argument was that he has to be free to investigate empirically anything that he sees interesting without an obligation to see its connection with anything else. This approach is Cartesian. But since he doesn't have any history, he doesn't know it's Cartesian. Since he regards history as antithetical to what he does, he will not know history. By his light he cannot know history. It would be a fault for him to try to see historical antecedents of ideas. This makes conversation difficult. It's interesting to speculate whether this same resistance will occur in empirical studies of composition.

WOE: There seems to be a real push for writing teachers to do research in the classroom. Is this kind of research legitimate?

MURPHY: I would think it is. My caution would be that not every effusion is worth the recording. When *College English*—which only comes out four times a year—devotes twelve of its precious pages to someone's personal experience, the experience better be pretty good to warrant that space.

WOE: What people writing about rhetoric interest you?

MURPHY: There are, of course, a number of revisionist histories—self-professed revisionist histories. Bill Covino's, for instance. The gender-related revisionists are interesting. Andrea Lunsford has a magnificent book coming out called *Reclaiming Rhetorica*. It contains fifteen essays about women orators and writers, people like Sojourner Truth, Marjorie Kemp, Aspasia. Not all the writers are women, but it's a fascinating book because rather than being a history it's an enthymeme. It's a whole set of examples, of essays about people showing that it can be done, case studies about women who have made it as writers or speakers.

WOE: So it makes a case that rhetoric hasn't been exclusively a white male province?

MURPHY: One of the biggest objections to classical rhetoric is, of course, the cultural one. This was a hierarchical, slave society, male—not male-dominated—entirely male. Men were beyond being "dominant"; they ran things. But the entire ancient world was like that. For example, it wasn't until 1852 that women could own property in England. *Reclaiming Rhetorica* is an enthymeme that suggests we ought to look more to the historical background to see what women have been doing. And that's important. On the other hand, it's an absolute fact that men were dominant. And to suggest otherwise is to be historically inaccurate. One can deplore the fact; one cannot change it.

WOE: A lot of composition teachers don't really know enough about classical rhetoric to be able to judge its limitations or its merits. What would you advise teachers to read if they wanted to get a good sense of this approach to teaching communication skills?

MURPHY: If you were on a desert island and could take only one book, what would you take? The reason that I did that Southern Illinois Press publication *Quintilian on the Teaching of Speaking and Writing* was precisely to try to point out that rhetoric isn't just antique; it's a system. Little fragments of that system show up in every textbook.

WOE: Yes, I certainly see it in most of the texts I've used over the years—no matter how much they try to sell themselves as innovative!

MURPHY: In terms of primary sources, if the person is educated enough, he or she should read Aristotle's *Rhetoric*. The problem with the *Rhetoric*, though, is that it is a part of a system itself. You can't read the *Rhetoric* by itself and get out of it what's really in it. You have to precede it with Aristotle's ethics, politics, and psychology.

Our Western educational system has been basically Ciceronian ever since the Middle Ages. All through the Middle Ages the lower schools were

Ciceronian/Quintilian without knowing it. These processes carried on and were revitalized in the Renaissance, then shipped over to Cambridge, Mass. If people know that it is a system they can decide (a) whether they want the system, or (b) whether they want parts of it, or (c) whether they want none of it. One of the reasons that I wrote "The Modern Value of Ancient Roman Methods of Teaching Writing, with Answers to Twelve Current Fallacies" for the first issue of *WOE* was to try to answer some of the modern objections to this ancient approach.

WOE: What do you think of E.D. Hirsch and his call for cultural literacy? You and Hirsch have similar backgrounds and interests, but you seem to have arrived at different conclusions.

MURPHY: Hirsch's argument is that as a nation we are ignoring important facets of the political humanistic environment that made us what we are. If we forget this environment, we are going to wander off in all directions. I agree absolutely. His attempt to make a canon is what drew all of the criticism. However, he's making an argument; he's not making a taxonomic list. So he's going to say these thirty-one things—or however many there are—are essential. As a rhetorician, I would encourage him to pick some specific numbers to make the point in order to have an apparent specificity about it, to show what the issues are. But what's the point of having a cultural artifact if no one can get near it? If nobody can read it, if nobody can write about it, if nobody can think about it? So both sides of the content/form amalgam are necessary. You and I happen to be more on the form side in the classroom. A literary faculty, or a philosophical faculty, is almost entirely on the content side, hoping that the people will come to them with some ability. In the ideal world, of course, both form and content are necessary.

WOE: Is it possible to integrate them in one classroom?

MURPHY: I know there are literature faculty who base their classes on the idea that if we are going to write about something, we might as well write about their subject. The same argument applies to physics, biology, sports—any subject. This structure was followed for 2000 years and it can be followed by any resolute person today.

The question is whether it is worthwhile to try to get everybody to change the structure. I would say so. But how would you do this? Would you get yourself elected head of NCTE and then lobby the NEH and the Department of Education? Do you want to lead by example as Hirsch tried to do? That's another model. My personal way is to try to sow seeds of Quintilianism with a small *q* everywhere.

WOE: What do you think about computer-aided instruction, the whole idea of the interactive classroom achieved through networks and the consequent decentering of the teacher and his/her authority?

MURPHY: I think it has limited uses. Again, no one thing is going to work every hour of every class. The studies are already beginning to appear in the K–12 segment that computer use basically doesn't change anything. I say beginning because there are just a few studies out. That result is very reasonable. I can remember when the wire recorder—the predecessor of the tape recorder—was going to revolutionize education. Everybody and every school went out and bought half a dozen wire recorders, which a couple of years later were replaced by tape recorders, and a couple of years later by TV sets. Temporarily valuable.

WOE: Proponents of CAI often point out that the network erases gender, race, those qualities that may create communication barriers among students. But do you see the lack of orality in such a classroom as a problem?

MURPHY: It's not inherently a problem. This is only one of many things that occur. There are some advantages to doing it—more flexibility, the immediate response. The enormous popularity of E-mail proves that. It's probably better to play E-mail than to watch *Cheers*.

WOE: Could you talk a little bit about the relationship between your teaching and your research? I have heard you argue and seen you demonstrate the fact that it's quite possible for someone to be an excellent teacher and also manage to do his writing or her research.

MURPHY: Well, the standard answer is that a research sense is necessary in order to identify what is important enough to try to bring to the attention of the students. I think that from the psychological point of view it's all one thing. I've had a lot of ideas for research directions come to me from student remarks or student questions. The "why" in their questions often gets me thinking.

I'm sure a scientist who needs a $200,000 piece of equipment to pursue a quark is not going to be able to turn off the machine and go to his eleven o'clock class and utilize his research that very hour. It would be difficult—perhaps impossible—to fill in the knowledge gap. But for people dealing with language, I don't see how there can be a gap. The wheel-and-the-spoke analogy comes to mind again. It all resonates—which brings us to the so-called publish or perish dilemma at a research university. I don't think there is a dilemma at all. If you don't want to live that way, then why are you there? If you can't think they are interrelated, what business do you have pretending?

WOE: You are a publisher as well as a scholar and a teacher. How does having a press fit with your other interests?

MURPHY: Hermagoras Press got started in 1983 because the tax laws changed in 1982. The government placed an inventory tax on books, so thousands and thousands of books—including two of mine—were shredded by companies trying to avoid paying inventory taxes. I discovered very soon afterwards that some people were using materials from my books in Xerox form and not always asking me. And I got some requests to reprint them. So I decided to start my own small press, Hermagoras Press, which is named after a second-century rhetorician whose works have not survived but who very much influenced Cicero and Quintilian. The press started out entirely concerned with the history of rhetoric. There are now eight books in print, two under contract, and the new Landmark Essay series.

WOE: What are the Landmark Essays?

MURPHY: In every field there are some key book chapters or essays that define the field, that define the issues in the field or are seminal in the sense that everybody has to react yea or nay to them. At the same time, they are sometimes difficult to get hold of—especially if you're in a smaller school without a huge library. You may not even have access to all of the major journals, and getting all these pieces is a problem. So I started asking people to put these landmark pieces together. There's been an enthusiastic response, and the series covers a variety of subjects: Sondra Perl is doing one on the writing process; Charles Bazerman and David Russell are doing one on writing across the curriculum; Peter Elbow is doing one on orality and writing; Richard E. Young and Yameng Liu are doing one on invention in writing; Randy Harris is doing one on the rhetoric of science. There are twenty books under contract.

The purpose of these collections is to set minds in motion—teachers' minds. Publishing is an opportunity to make things available that will get people thinking. And again we get back to the principle that it almost doesn't matter where you start. Take the collection Sondra Perl is doing on the writing process. You know instinctively there are some things that will be in that collection because they are true landmarks, but a lot of teachers won't have read them. Publishing this series allows me to do the same thing I like to do in the classroom: to lay something out that will get somebody to start thinking. That to me is the primary classroom objective as well as the objective of this series.

So far it has been great fun. Peter Elbow called the other day and said just that—"Hey, this is fun!" Being able to make the choices about what to include is the best part. I suppose there are those who will accuse us of trying to set up a canon here. I don't look at it that way. It's not a canon; it's a starting point—a topos, a huge topos to start a line of argument.

WOE: Is there a common thread that runs through your teaching, your writing, and your publishing?

MURPHY: An interest in the use of language. I have acquired a great interest in the history of grammar as a consequence. Grammar is much neglected by rhetoricians and by philosophers. When you take the trivium of grammar, rhetoric, and logic, grammar is the most neglected in modern times because of the way it was damaged by detail. The same thing has destroyed classical studies—excessive philological study of texts so they lose their meaning in the search for abstrusity.

WOE: Do you think the teaching of writing has improved in the last fifteen years or so?

MURPHY: Certainly it's true that twenty years ago we didn't have anything approaching a national dialogue. I think that's an improvement. If you think about what we've been talking about in relation to students, that getting them to start thinking is the first step, then, yes, getting professionals to start thinking is important, too. In 1989 I wrote a piece in the *Quarterly Journal of Speech*, "The Renaissance of Rhetoric in English Departments," where I argue that people in composition are doing exactly what people in speech communication did in the forties and fifties—self-definition, choice of methodologies, self-inquiry. If you compare what was happening in the speech/communication journals in the forties and fifties to what is happening in current composition journals, there are some remarkable parallels.

WOE: Do you see any hope that the two camps we've already talked about—people who teach reading and people who teach writing—can ever be reunited into a more integrated curriculum?

MURPHY: I just don't know. That's a matter of prophecy. If a Wayne Booth can't do it, who can? If a Richard Lanham can't do it, who can? Mike Rose is a special case. It's hard to predict because institutions perpetuate themselves. And enormous amounts of resources are tied up in the ways things are. This makes change very difficult.

WOE: Is there nothing we can do then?

MURPHY: I would encourage everybody to publish if they can—not just in the commercial sense, but to put out whatever will get other people to think about what they are doing. That seems most important—to set minds in motion for the future.

JAMES MOFFETT

James Moffett (1929–1996) never considered himself a traditional scholar and never adopted the title of professor, even when he taught in Harvard's Graduate School of Education. He was a teacher who always wrote practically, with students and fellow teachers in mind. He gained national recognition for his work as a consultant, workshop leader, and writer, theorizing about discourse and writing across the curriculum, and promoting school reform. He is best known for his 1968 book, Teaching the Universe of Discourse, *and its companion, which he wrote with Betty Jane Wagner,* Student-Centered Language Arts and Reading, K–12: A Handbook for Teachers (1976; 1992 4th ed.), *a collection of lessons and ideas for teaching writing. He envisioned whole-language classrooms that spanned all grade levels and included reading, writing, art, drama, and singing, to name only a few of the creative acts of mind and body that he felt were essential.*

His K–12 work gained considerable recognition. The California Association of Teachers of English granted him a Distinguished Author Award for two books published in 1981: Active Voice: A Writing Program Across the Curriculum, *and* Coming on Center: Essays in English Education. *In 1992 he received the NCTE David H. Russell Award for Distinguished Research in the Teaching of English for* Storm in the Mountains: A Case Study of Censorship, Conflict, and Consciousness. *Moffett's work often united the nontraditional and practical. To him, writing blurs the line between inner and outer speech, and he saw classrooms as a place to explore the "disorder" of language, to break apart and eventually put back together—to compose—discourse for new audiences and situations.*[1] *His other works include* Detecting Growth in Language *(1992) and* Harmonic Learning: Keynoting School Reform *(1992). His final book,* The Universal Schoolhouse: Spiritual Awakening Through Education *(1994), encompasses his nonconformist style, merging Eastern philosophy and meditation with practical suggestions for teaching.*

—Sarah Powers

---

1 Moffett, James. "Writing, Inner Speech, and Meditation." *Coming on Center: Essays in English Education*, 2nd ed. Portsmouth: Boynton/Cook, 1998: (96). Print.

"Individualize"

Eric Schroeder and John Boe

Fall 1994

WOE: What was your own education like?

MOFFETT: I went to grade school in Jackson, Mississippi, and a big high school in Toledo, Ohio. I had a conventional education, and I accepted it all; I never questioned anything. I just did whatever they told me. Partly because of growing up Southern, probably more just because of growing up in that time, we were a lot more compliant as kids. I did fine in school, mostly just did what they told me. I learned little in regard to writing in high school. I was encouraged to use a lot of big words and fancy sentences, to pull out all the stops, which got me in trouble when I got to college.

I didn't do anything challenging until college. I majored in English at Harvard, but I shifted to French for a master's. They were trying to get roughage into the diet at Harvard, I guess, by bringing in a lot of kids from the Midwest and the South. I had a scholarship that was good all the way through the Ph.D., but for some reason I decided not to go that way after a master's.

I took a year off in the middle of college, just to go to France on my own, not for credit or anything. I had had it with college for a while. As a public-school kid in competition with private-school kids, I felt I was ill-educated. I didn't know much about literature at all when I left high school. We can say it was a kind of inferiority complex, but at the time I just had the feeling that I would get more out of Harvard if I took some time off and did some more reading and got caught up a bit, because in lots of discussions the private-school kids were crowing about books I hadn't even heard of.

WOE: So you took a year off and read?

MOFFETT: After my sophomore year I thought, "I'll read over in France—that'll be more fun." During the summers I had been working out west on various kinds of construction jobs to make money for the winter, and I made enough one summer to live very cheaply for a year. This was in '49 or '50. So I went to France. No junior year abroad or anything like that, no credit. But once I got over there, I ended up taking these college courses in French civilization at the Sorbonne, which covered history, philosophy, literature, language—everything. A lot of American GIs were there studying. So I took courses for half the year and got fairly fluent. I read a lot, especially in French. When I came back, I finished two years as an English major, and then in graduate school shifted into the Romance Language department.

WOE: Although you're fluent in French, you don't very often quote the trendy French theorists.

MOFFETT: I really haven't kept up much with literary criticism. For some reason those writers just haven't interested me much—Derrida, a little bit, but not seriously. I worry about people being more familiar with what's said about literature than with literature itself.

I was really very literary throughout college and graduate school. A great influence on me there was Albert Guerard Jr. He was at Harvard when I was there and then shifted to Stanford, where his father had been. He was an influence because he was a novelist himself and really knew literature and technique. Guerard was supportive and read some of my writing outside of class. He got me thinking about imperceptive narrating, which he was looking at with Gide and other writers. His ideas influenced me later when I did the anthology *Points of View*.

WOE: You ended up teaching at Exeter, which is interesting since you went to a public school. Why did you decide to become a teacher at a prestigious preparatory school?

MOFFETT: I didn't see myself as a college professor, which is mainly why I didn't go for a Ph.D. I thought, "If I teach, I'll teach at a prep school where I can teach what *I* want, and I don't have to have a teacher's certificate." Exeter probably wouldn't have hired me if I had had a teaching certificate. They were suspicious of people who did.

Exeter had a sabbatical program just like colleges, so in the seventh year there (I was there ten years), I chose to go to California. I spent a year in an informal association with S.I. Hayakawa and developed an interest in levels of abstraction. Hayakawa and the general semantics people were doing things that are now attracting more notice, but at that time the universities were shunning Hayakawa. (I think this is one reason he went into politics.) The semanticists were interested in totalitarian propaganda that arose during the thirties all over Europe. Stuart Chase and Hayakawa really got interested in the misuse of the language. So Hayakawa always had political interests, but he was a literary person, too.

This happened about 1960, just before Esalen; all the various kinds of therapeutic groups were about to burst out. The general semantics people were into that movement before anybody else And because the university didn't have a category for general semantics, they looked down on the field. The semanticists were interdisciplinary and holistic long before anyone else. They were looking at the total human being, the mind-body as an integrative organism, which is what they meant by general semantics.

WOE: Because you have had this interdisciplinary and even theoretical focus from the start, are you bothered that some teachers might use your work primarily to get practical help and just ignore the theoretical framework?

MOFFETT: I'd like to see teachers use my conceptual framework to individualize more, which is hard for them to do. In other words, I started off (like everybody else) thinking of a sequence of assignments as a group activity, a developmental activity, as if everybody could be ready to move on to certain stages at certain ages. The more I taught, the more it seemed to me that the only thing that really made sense was to individualize. You can use the notion of abstractive growth stages, but you can't expect *groups* to form into these stages. Individualization has gotten lost because most teachers find it extremely difficult to implement.

WOE: From the point of view of college teachers, individualization has an added difficulty—although you have fewer classes, you see the students less often.

MOFFETT: You put your finger on one of the main problems. It's much easier to individualize with elementary students than secondary, and easier with secondary students than with college. It's hard even in secondary because you've just got those kids forty-five minutes a day, and you've got two hundred, two hundred and fifty kids. As with college students, you just don't get to know them very well.

WOE: What can the college teacher do?

MOFFETT: I try to encourage teachers to individualize more, solely on the grounds of necessity. You have such a short time to work—a semester or at the most the luxury of a whole year course—and, if you're talking developmentally, you have to telescope years of development into months. It's too inefficient to take a whole group through stages of development; you can't do it in the amount of time you've got. But individualizing is really efficient: give each student only what he or she needs. There's enough time to track some kind of meaningful development for an individual in the amount of time you have. But if there's the least bit of inefficiency—if at any given moment some of them are doing things they don't need or it's the wrong time for them to be doing those things—then you've lost the one advantage you had.

WOE: But aren't institutions structured to discourage individualization?

MOFFETT: It's part institutionalism, but it's also partly the concept that teaching is emceeing a group of students. Some people go into teaching to sit with a captive audience and cast themselves as the star. There are literature and writing teachers who don't want to give that up. But many teachers today have a different view, are not so egocentric. The institution is the problem for them. The institution still wants to tell college teachers how they have to go about teaching, how they must limit their classes to certain kinds of writing.

WOE: How do you feel about the influence of institutions like ETS?

MOFFETT: I'd call the College Board composition exam fraudulent. If you have what's supposed to be a composition exam and there's no writing, it's phony. ETS says, "Well it's predictive of how high school kids will do in a college class." But it's predictive because the courses are like the tests: there isn't real writing in the courses either!

WOE: You really make that point in *Detecting Growth in Language*. But institutions always want measures of performance. How can we do this humanely and effectively within the university?

MOFFETT: At Exeter there was a lot of writing and we teachers were terribly grade conscious, but we quit putting grades on papers. Most of the instructors started using what are now called portfolios (we just called them "folders" then). The students would put their collected writing in the folders, and the teachers would make a blanket judgment on the folders. We had to hand in grades six times a year: not only a letter grade but what was called a cumulative report, a paragraph that traced trends in the student's learning. So we were really using a portfolio system. It's much easier to make a blanket judgment for the whole six weeks' work because you have a profile to look at.

If students are really productive, there's a lot to see, and it's easy to make judgments. Reading courses are much more problematic: you don't know what's going through the students' heads and have to give them some sort of an emetic to make them throw up so you can see what's going on in them.

WOE: How should we assess writing teachers?

MOFFETT: I once spent a month doing nothing but evaluating writing programs at UC San Diego. UCSD has four colleges, and each one has its own writing program. (This was just before Charles Cooper took over.) I just camped there for a month: I read the student writing, I interviewed the students and the instructors. Talking with the students was really very good; an awful lot of information comes out of that. It taught me about what they felt they learned and about the instructors too. But you need to get enough views of the writing process and of the instructor; otherwise a teacher could be really damaged by an idiosyncratic or unfair view. Unfortunately, this process is very time consuming. San Diego was a special project; I was brought in and paid to do this.

But maybe there is a way to build this into the university's institutional structure. There are often false analogies made between education and business, but the one analogous practice I'd like to see developed is to give education the same research and development money that business has. Build R&D into the budget, so you don't have to have a bake sale to get a little extra money for it.

WOE: Some of your own R&D work has been very impressive. I'm thinking in particular of your collaborative work on the Interaction program.[2]

---

2 *Interaction: A Student-Centered Language Arts and Reading Program* (1973) is an extensive collection of pedagogical materials for classrooms K–13. Some of these materials have been republished in digital form by EDVantage Software, cofounded by Jim Moffett and Robert Romano.

MOFFETT: There were thirty collaborators from all over the country, including a couple I never met. From consulting and working with different school districts I'd identified most of the key co-authors, the ones who had major roles. Most of them were classroom teachers.

The real stalwarts of the *Interaction* program, the ones with major roles, were people I'd known before. I knew how they thought and they knew how I thought, so if we needed somebody else with a certain specialty, they would suggest somebody. Often the publisher wants to select your partners, but Houghton Mifflin, at least in the beginning, gave me an unusually free hand. So I was able to put together a team. And it was really very exciting to see the team growing, to see them become a well-knit group and kind of a family, with a lot of feeling. We would have regional meetings, back east, in the middle west, and out here, where certain teams would get together. So people who had worked primarily by mail kept meeting each other, got to know each other.

It required a fairly non-egoistic group of people. It was complex enough that I had to fool around with the assignments: there are 185 booklets, and most of those had more than one person working on them. There were 185 little teams that were overlapping in lots of different ways, so that one person would be on five or six books and might have three or four different collaborators altogether. And then the activity-card teams were very large. Some of the people who worked on the books were also working on activity cards, some were not. I had to keep modulating the assignments. So the collaborators had to take a lot from me, be willing to put in or cut things out of a book or have a role reduced or enlarged. Because things shifted constantly they just could not get irritated by it. I'm sure they were sometimes, but not so much that it interfered in our being a kind of family. It was a great lifetime experience.

We also made a couple dozen films to demonstrate activities that were new then, like improvisational small-group writing, writing workshops. Nobody knew anything about these activities, and we were trying to show what they look like, with real human beings. So we went to Denver to shoot Readers' Theater, and we went to Miles Myers' class. We filmed a small-group improvisation done with mostly black twelfth graders in Myers' class. We filmed different activities all around the country. We'd hear that somebody was doing a certain activity, like choral reading or chamber theater, so we'd try to capture it so that other teachers and kids could see what the activity looked like.

Now I tell teachers just do this in their own school system: teach teams of kids or teachers to run camcorders and recording equipment, and they can record demonstration projects in their own district programs. Back then you had to have a very expensive film crew—it cost a fortune to send them all around the country.

Interaction was tremendously complex. Houghton Mifflin said it was the largest program ever put out. I don't think there was anyone besides myself who knew all of what was in there and all the ways they related to each other. The complexity was the result of flexibility. You had 185 paperback booklets, and several hundred activity cards, all modular, not in any particular sequence.

WOE: You could put it on Hypertext!

MOFFETT: Younger people have brought up the idea of doing all of this on computers. For example, the program did a lot of cross-referring; each activity card suggests several different activities. You could build in different media with CD-ROMs, so you could have awesome amounts of reference material and archives. With desktop publishing, you could easily make all the activity cards you wanted to, so students could go off in a corner and work on them or take them out in a field. Students could make their own activity cards, both electronic and paper ones. Kids could be a big part of the process. They could write up the activity cards, design activities, and help shape their own education.

And you could keep track of what everybody was doing—this was one of the biggest headaches we had in *Interaction*: we could never get a very good solution to how you keep track of what different kids have done. They were all going very different ways, often overlapping, but in order to chart their future paths, you had to keep track of individuals (a lot of that record keeping was real drudgery). Record keeping could be done on a computer and passed on year to year. So the whole problem of mobility could be solved, which would be a great boon for individualizing.

WOE: Wasn't doing something on that scale with so many people a radical idea?

MOFFETT: Houghton Mifflin was a conservative company, but they did this really far-out thing with *Interaction*. My professional books, *Teaching the Universe of Discourse* and *Student-Centered Language Arts*, had been doing fairly well, which is why they asked me to do *Interaction* in the first place. Also it was partly just the spirit of that shift from the sixties to the seventies, a real progressive spirit calling to a company like Houghton Mifflin to "get with it." A few years later, "back to basics" and the censorship battle hit all at once.

WOE: Did your experience with the censorship battle over *Interaction* discourage you about education in this country?

MOFFETT: No, I don't think so. I wasn't that surprised. It was a hard blow, but it didn't do in the *Interaction* program. There were a lot of canceled orders and then the salesmen deserted the ship. People don't think about that so much, but salesmen have alternatives within the same company. They don't have to sell your book or program; they can sell others. Most of them didn't like *Interaction* anyway because the Houghton Mifflin readers had been the cornerstone of the company, and the publisher made a fortune off of them.

Aside from censorship issues, the whole *Interaction* program was a calculated risk from the beginning, for every aspect of it was totally non-graded, totally individualized.

WOE: Your work often emphasizes the idea that we can practice and improve through concentration and meditation, a belief that seems drawn from Eastern religions. Was this part of the controversy? Did fundamentalists object to your bringing in Eastern religions?

MOFFETT: At the time this happened, 1974, the big perceived threat was communism. But the fundamentalists hated *anything* foreign, anything international, including books with international literature, like folklore or parables. We had one article on yoga, which was not religious, but of course they picked on that. They protested that we had yoga in the schools but they couldn't have Christianity. If that article appeared in a textbook today, they would call it "Satanic." And it would happen partly because they are suffering from a good old enemy—communism—being gone. They, like the Republicans, are looking for another enemy, and "Satanism" fits the bill. But in 1974 "Satanism" hadn't yet become a word on the circuits, although there were hints of it. (The censorship circuits have become standardized since then.) Still there were occasional feelings that came out in individual comments that something in the Eastern religions was somehow satanic.

WOE: But as part of the growth of the Western consciousness, Eastern religions have a lot to offer. That's a hard issue to give in on.

MOFFETT: They don't want alternatives. They want one thing, and they hate any kind of alternative interpretation, alternative books, alternative culture, alternative social actions. And English teachers and social studies teachers offer alternatives, talk about different possibilities—that was one of the things that bothered them the most. All the things they hated—role playing, values clarification—had this common denominator: offering alternatives. The book protestors said, "Look, we've settled all those things; you're just ruining our kids' minds."

WOE: I'm occasionally surprised by who you do and don't cite.

MOFFETT: I don't have the scholar's instinct about citing. I don't see much of what I say as occurring in an ongoing academic forum in which you're obliged to cite, to situate what you're saying in a university colloquy. I just don't think that way. Some people criticize me for not citing more, to show what others say about a topic. I'm not a great scholar, but I am instinctive.

I think Descartes, whom I've been recently reading, was very intuitive. He was an extraordinary meditator, in the tradition of the Jesuits, who of course have a great meditation tradition. I read that because he was such a powerful meditator at his Jesuit school he was given special dispensation to spend his mornings meditating instead of going to classes. Some of

Descartes' essays are called "Meditations." He was a mathematician and not a good observational scientist—he finessed that part. Sometimes it's hard to tell where he's deducing and where he's meditating. The pineal gland plays a major role in his "Treatise on Man" and "Passions of the Soul"; he attributed to the pineal gland a lot of the things that are true of other places in the brain. He had the wrong center for the sensorimotor switchboards, but his description of the afferent–efferent nervous system is astonishingly accurate. A lot of what he said about the pineal gland is being borne out today. Instead of observing, he was deducing, and sometimes instead of deducing, he was intuiting.

WOE: How did you come to so strongly emphasize the role of the arts in education?

MOFFETT: Well, my natural orientation is to the arts. I really became acquainted with them when I took the year off and went to France. I received a great art education in Europe that year I played hooky from college—going to ballets, concerts, and art museums. I feel there's a spiritual connection to the arts. I've tried to write about this connection here and there, but I don't feel I can express it exactly. I think the connection between the arts and spiritual disciplines is much more profound than generally realized. As their evolution from the ancient mysteries shows, the original purpose of the arts was literally to entrance. Esthetic notions of art represent a later degeneration. Thus literature is a secularization of holy writ.

WOE: Doing art can have a meditative quality.

MOFFETT: Doing art, like doing meditation, demands practice. I think all the arts were originally one, and the original purpose was to alter consciousness. We'll finally go back to that. Modern art is going back to that, with multimedia and performance art.

WOE: Do you see yourself as having clear connections with other composition teachers or theorists, particularly people in the composition movement today?

MOFFETT: Probably with most of them. They don't always put things the way I do, but when you get down to the activities, there's not too much disagreement between us. For example, maybe I can't tie into some of Jimmy Britton's terms very well, but on the praxis level there's never any problem.

There is only one big difference. It's not a difference in philosophy or attitude or anything, but most people in composition are college people. (Jimmy Britton has actually been an exception; he's more school oriented.) After all, college is just part of the whole school spectrum. But Ken Macrorie, Peter Elbow, Janet Emig, and most of the others are college teachers. I'm not saying they haven't thought about the schools or they haven't influenced school practice—they have. But they're more specialized. So I think college teachers rightly feel that these people have more directly contributed to them than I have because I've been spreading myself all over the curriculum. It's possible that if I could get schoolteachers to do what I'm advocating; it would make college teachers' lives much better. By the time the kids came up to college, they would be much easier to deal with than they are now.

WOE: This seems to tie into what you said earlier about the need to be in an educational environment that allows you to see different alternatives, rather than just having one way to view reality and live your life.

MOFFETT: But having all those alternatives is also anxiety producing. People get paralyzed sometimes from the decision making; however, part of an education has to do with teaching people to deal with alternatives, to be able to see them and choose among them, rather than wishing they couldn't see them because they don't know how to cope with them. This is one reason that people (not just fundamentalists) close their minds—because they don't feel capable of choosing safely among all these alternatives. One of the problems with fundamentalists is they don't want all those alternatives because they don't have the self-esteem and confidence to feel that they can deal with them. That's why I think self-esteem really is a big issue. It's mind-spinning and dizzying and very difficult to know how to act when there are many alternative perceptions. It makes you sympathize a little with people who want to close their minds. It makes you realize that you're often tempted to do the same.

America is in a crisis now about pluralism, about multicultural options. But "multicultural" is a prime metaphor for the whole smorgasbord of alternatives that goes with a culture granting freedom and personal liberty but not yet educating for them.

CHARLES BAZERMAN

Few scholars in the last 20 years have answered Richard Haswell's call to support RAD research (replicable, agreeable, and data supported) in the field of writing studies more than Charles Bazerman.[1] *Since this interview was conducted in 1995, he has continued to research and write prolifically, producing 13 books and more than 40 articles, editing 11 books, and serving as the series editor for many seminal texts in his areas of expertise: genre theory, writing in the disciplines, and the rhetoric of science.*

In Shaping Written Knowledge: The Genre and Activity of the Experimental Article in Science *(1988), Bazerman argued for textual analysis as a research method to investigate corpora produced by scientists. In* The Languages of Edison's Light *(1999), he traced Edison's development of the light bulb as a communicative act both within the scientific community and beyond. His companion sets,* A Rhetoric of Literate Action *(2013) and* A Theory of Literate Action *(2013), are testaments to Bazerman's continued work to situate writing studies as a social science. In* Theory, *he develops a model of rhetoric as a social construction based on communicative needs "rather than around rhetoric's founding concerns of high stakes, agonistic, oral public persuasion" (3). In* Action, *Bazerman outlines the means by which his readers can enact this theoretical stance, by providing "a way of understanding our writing situation and what we might do with it—not just how writing is generally done in these circumstances but how we might transform the circumstances through our participation" (4).*

In addition to serving as a chair of CCCC, Bazerman has worked to cultivate a culture of research within the writing studies community by co-founding the Research Network Forum and the Consortium of Gradaute Programs in Rhetoric and Composition. He has also collaborated with scholars worldwide to examine the social impact of writing, which led to the Writing Across Borders conference and the International Society of the Advancement of Writing Research. He founded Rhetoricians for Peace, which saw a period of robust activity during the Bush administration, and which he is currently trying to revive. He is the former chair of the Department of Education at the University of California, Santa Barbara.

—*Alison Bright*

---

1 Haswell, Richard H. "NCTE/CCCC's Recent War on Scholarship." *Written Communication* 22.2 (2005): (198–223).

"Writing Is Motivated Participation"

Margaret Eldred

Spring 1995

WOE: What is the distinction between writing in the disciplines and writing across the curriculum? Can you clarify what you mean by the two terms and define writing in the disciplines?

BAZERMAN: When I first started teaching at City University, I got interested in writing within disciplines through thinking about undergraduate writing and the way undergraduate writing was related to reading. In the mid-'70s I started working on *The Informed Writer*. It was based on a research paper course that got me thinking about what we now call intertextuality. As I was finishing that book, I started to see how intertextuality was organized within disciplines—the practices were different, the kinds of literature were different. So I began studying disciplinary reading and writing. I particularly got interested in the sciences because as an undergraduate I thought I was going into physics. Also there was a fair amount known about the sociology of science, and I was already thinking about writing as socially organized.

Writing across the curriculum at that time was pretty much driven by the process movement and writing to learn—these terms were just emerging as buzzwords. Interesting things came out of that early period; however, the writing-across-the-curriculum model still worked largely within an English Department concept of what writing should be. It was driven by literary models of the self, of expressiveness, of essays, of evaluation and value.

As a result of my interest in disciplinary writing in the second edition of *The Informed Writer*, I added a writing-across-the-curriculum section. I tried not to be too taxonomic, reifying disciplinary differences in ways that didn't make sense. I didn't want to oversimplify distinctions among social science, sciences, humanities. I thought a lot about how to indicate the approach in the title of the next edition, and I came up with the phrase writing in the disciplines (WID), as opposed to across the curriculum (WAC). That's the origin of the term. I think WID tends to distinguish the attempt to have more writing everywhere in college (the WAC project, which continues to be a good project) from an attempt to understand what the disciplinary organization of writing is all about. WID tends to have more of a research orientation, although it obviously has its applied end.

WAC–WID is still a useful distinction to make. Even though the university is organized by discipline, undergraduate writing is not simply a translation of professional disciplinary practices. Undergraduate education has its own dynamics. And that needs to be understood. As the writing across the curriculum movement has recognized the importance of writing in the disciplines, there has been a tendency to simply take writing across the curriculum into disciplinary training and say that we have no particular need for freshman composition, that we should go into professional practice in writing as early as possible. That does not make sense to me because every undergraduate is not headed towards a career in the academy.

WOE: And many freshmen don't know what they're going to major in.

BAZERMAN: There's a lot of development they have to do; there's a lot of personal, social, economic work that happens in the undergraduate years. Kids have moved out of the house, they've moved away from the kind of high school curriculum (and I do not mean this pejoratively) that is directed towards providing people the knowledge they need to get around in society. It's not the high school's task to give them an intellectual way of looking at life that makes them question everything. College does that, and, insofar as students take that aspect of college seriously, they start to explore a whole lot of things.

So there's a kind of college discourse which is really important. Some of that discourse is across the curriculum. It bears interesting relationships to writing in the disciplines, but it shouldn't just simply march headlong into very narrow professionalized discourses. Insofar as the critics of writing in the disciplines and writing across the curriculum sense a headlong rush toward narrow professionalization, they do have a point. But I think they miss the boat in dismissing the importance of disciplinary discourses, both the social importance and importance as sites for individual and group development. Disciplines have grown up as communal projects among people trying to do things, and individuals can find these remarkable fields in which to develop themselves and their own understanding. In certain disciplines and professions, you really don't gain by thinking about your own discipline in nondisciplinary ways. Critics also miss the ways in which those specialized knowledges and specialized discourses can be very interesting challenges and resources for somebody who is not even in those fields.

I just completed the manuscript of a new freshman textbook that addresses some of these issues.

WOE: Doesn't it address both the role of the freshman writing course in terms of learning about a particular discipline and learning about academic discourse generally?

BAZERMAN: It is a welcome to college directed toward first-term freshmen. Whatever passed for competence in your high school, whatever fulfilled the demands, the communicative tasks, you did it. Now there's a different kind of discursive realm you're entering which is largely organized by discipline. But this realm has a lot of rote reproduction. So you shouldn't look down on summary tasks; in fact, a lot of what you're doing is taking discourses and getting them at your fingertips, for your own needs. It's important to locate why you're memorizing this stuff, and it's also very useful to find the most efficient and effective ways of articulating the knowledge that you get. But over the long run, it's much more important for you to understand the meaning this stuff has for *you*, what you think about it, what you would want to use it for, and then to acquire critical abilities of your own.

A couple of opening chapters set the stance of the book and talk about rhetoric, but the first regular chapter is about journals. Then come two chapters: on writing to learn things and writing to reproduce what you learn. From there, the book starts making connections between illustrations and general principles, analytic writing, writing about complex situations, problem-solving writing. It ends with argumentation. Rather than having a full-scale research orientation, the book just introduces those discourses as part of the continuum of how you deal with and talk about knowledge.

WOE: So it sounds like you're trying to get students to look at knowledge not just as a collection of facts but as the way it's all put together.

BAZERMAN: That's right—I want to orient students towards a college experience. I want them to see education as something that they have a stake in and that they're full participants in.

WOE: Which is something that freshmen don't always feel.

BAZERMAN: That's why it's important for them—even with the rote learning they often experience—to see that learning is their decision; they won't do very well unless they discover their stakes. The key trope is involvement. The book is called *Involved: Writing for College, Writing for Yourself*. There's a lot of talk about why students choose particular majors—not just the differences between majors but the kind of engagements that students may have with them—and how these majors have to always sit behind your writing. Writing is motivated participation.

WOE: You mentioned a couple of reasons why it's worth studying the writings of specific disciplines in your essay "From Cultural Criticism to Disciplinary Participation." Can you expand on these reasons a little bit?

BAZERMAN: Communicating is one of the essential things that people do, and it's the stuff out of which disciplines are made. There's a material practice, of course—doctors dispense medicine and so on—but an awful lot of what surrounds those material practices is communication, particularly written communication, because that's what endures. It's a basic tool of what we do. It helps to understand what your basic tools are, how you're using them, which ones are available—not only so you can use them more efficiently but also to reflect on what your practice is. You can't see what the profession is doing until you uncover its great hidden understructure.

WOE: So your approach would make accountants a little bit more reflective about their own language use and would make teachers more reflective about how to teach those accountants and about the way they use language?

BAZERMAN: Let's take the case of accountants because there's all kinds of communicative practices accountants engage in. Most of them learn on the job, and they learn by looking at models, responding to situations with the tools at hand. But they don't necessarily learn to think whether they want to respond to a particular situation in an alternative way, or what the consequences are when making this or that choice, or how different alternative choices all coordinate, or how a decision can be made more efficient or effective. Those are the kinds of considerations that lead to the ability to make practical decisions about what your field does. If you're the teacher and guiding students down those pathways to those sets of practices, you need to be aware of what those practices are, how they work, what it takes to participate well within them, and what the range of options is—I think that's probably the biggest thing. Most people will find some way of surviving within the discourse. But they won't see the range of choices, and they won't have the tools for reflecting on the range of choices; they'll just do what seems to make sense at the moment. And of course if you have more choices, you open up the possibilities of what you can accomplish.

WOE: Can you say something about the Landmark Essays collection, *Writing Across the Curriculum*, that you did with David Russell? What does classical rhetoric teach us about what we're doing now?

BAZERMAN: Well, one of these things we argued in that introductory essay was that classical rhetoric has had a hard time with specialized languages because for various historical reasons it developed as a general *techne* in the agora. It wants, in a sense, to make every place be like the agora. Classical rhetoric has only made very sporadic attempts to discuss specialized languages. In the eighteenth century there was a movement towards rewriting rhetoric, both to encompass the new thinking about being human and to notice that discourse was now being organized into spheres, some of which were professional spheres.

There hasn't been any *organized* thinking about writing in the disciplines until recently. There was no reason for the eighteenth century to do it. As

David has documented in several places, technical writing and business writing arose in the early part of this century. Also the cooperative movement, before World War I, was a precursor to writing across the curriculum, encouraging a lot of writing, but without any special awareness of distinctions among discourses.

I think the study of specialized discourses is extremely important. It is something that we have not done at all seriously until recently; classical rhetoric has been one of the resistances to this. However, given what sociologists call the differentiation of society, with the rise of multiple institutions (even though we're maybe remixing them right now) and the specialized practices and the flow of communications in specialized channels to do ever more complex and specialized tasks, we need to understand specialized discourses to understand how our society works. Assuming that we are moving into the information age and that this information is going to be complexly organized and accessible to different people within different networks, we've got to understand how our society is going to work. Unfortunately, the history of rhetoric has not been all that helpful in this endeavor until recently. So I'm very proud to be part of getting this initiative going. And I think it's getting an enormous amount of momentum.

When I started working on this topic, a variety of things, like the rhetoric of science, had been studied on a philosophical basis, but without much substantive examination. In the field of communications there were large studies of who reads what articles, but without any detailed attention to language and what goes on in discursive workings. Nobody really studied what this skilled behavior is all about. Some linguists were very interested in scientific writing; I linked up with them early. There's been a lot of research on spoken language in sociology and linguistics in the last twenty years. In fact, when you're among the applied linguists, discourse in the professions largely means the spoken word, but there were a couple of people interested in writing, like John Swales. Now there seem to be increasing numbers of people interested in this topic, and they are bringing more and more tools to bear on it. Whatever ideas ultimately may emerge as most useful, just gathering the information, trying to find ways of describing it, and having a lot of interaction with students and professionals who are doing this writing have been valuable. But I do believe that in the long run something big is going to emerge out of this work.

WOE: Your first major academic success was *Shaping Written Knowledge*, and from my point of view it seems very innovative. You were looking at certain issues in a way other people hadn't. Did this innovation cause you problems?

BAZERMAN: I didn't know what a rhetoric of science would look like. So I was very self-consciously trying to discover how to talk about scientific writing.

Every day I'd read a short article and then start describing it and come up with different things to say about it in a notebook I kept. The first extended piece I did was a review of the literature, "Scientific Writing as a Social Act." It preceded my writing of "What Written Knowledge Does." That was my first attempt to really do a piece about the rhetoric of science. I was very aware that I was making it up, so I went through a fair amount of revision; there were aspects of it that I just got wrong—false starts. But that set me upon a certain kind of path (at least for a while) of using both exegesis and a sociological framework to talk about social action.

WOE: So the sociology of science was one of the things that helped point you in a good direction.

BAZERMAN: Yes. That and thinking about speech acts, although I didn't have the concrete way of translating these ideas to written texts that I have recently found. Speech acts was a very strong metaphor anyway, to try to get away from simply meaning and into social action. Along that line, Vygotsky and activity theory were very important to me.

WOE: Right now you're continuing to work on scientists. You're working on Edison and you've done work on von Guericke and Priestley. How do you choose who to write about?

BAZERMAN: When I finished *Shaping Written Knowledge*, I was aware that I didn't know enough of the detail and the context of science. I was trying to look for certain macrostructural things, using genre as an attempt to see how these framing devices developed over time. Nonetheless, I thought there'd be a lot gained by studying an area where I could reasonably know something. So I picked electricity and just started reading. I thought originally I might do a book on the emergence of electricity as a discursive phenomenon. I was very interested in the whole question of the material basis of scientific discourse. People were still arguing very crudely for a radical relativism and I was arguing for a more pragmatist orientation. In the same way that I started out looking at physics partly as a challenge to showing that science is rhetorical, I wanted to look at a phenomenon that would make my point. If you could talk about something which is as clearly generated—made up—as modern electricity is and still talk about its material basis, it would be a challenge that would make the point. So the idea was to learn something about electricity. In 1600, electricity was nothing. The term existed but referred only to a static charge. If you rubbed amber, chaff would adhere to it. That was electricity.

It was by accident that I studied Priestley first. Looking at a rare-book library one day when I had a couple hours free, I came across this real oddball book, an enormous compilation of his. Why would he write that book in what looks to us like such an idiosyncratic way? That experience got me into the project.

Then as I read more about electricity I wanted to focus on something earlier, something that was outside the mainline scientific development. Von

Guericke was a very odd-looking character in that respect. In fact, he was thematic for what I was writing about—what scientific results look like outside the life of science.

It was also by accident that I wrote about Edison. While working on von Guericke I used the Burndy Library in Connecticut. It had some Edison papers that I looked at one day; then I started to realize how massive the Edison materials were, especially with the Edison microfilms coming out. At that time I was living in New York near the South Orange National Site where the Edison papers reside. I started looking at some of the Edison material and said, "Oh, there's a book here!" The point at which electricity emerged was a moment when technical discourse was escaping from the small community out into the world. And it wasn't just electricity coming through the walls. Electricity started pervading every other discourse.

WOE: Edison certainly didn't seem in the mainstream of science; in one way, he was an outsider.

BAZERMAN: He was outside, but he was working in the world. He had visions of social reformation, not in social terms but in technical terms—in changing the technology of society. The Edison papers go from lab notebooks to patents to newspaper articles—they cover a large part of the discourses of the world. I wanted to think about the interaction between scientific and technical discourses and larger ways of life; that interaction has become the theme of that book. I'm exploring the multiple discourses in which the electric light gets played out, going a bit into the histories and social dynamics of these discourses. Getting houses wired up is a very large discursive activity—to convince people that they ought to be financing electric lights and making them and patenting them and wiring houses with them. All the discourses of the world enter in.

WOE: You assert someplace that scientists are beginning to examine their writing more.

BAZERMAN: I say this about social scientists. Experimental psychology still continues much in the way it has. But anthropology has been examining itself for a long time. In sociology, there's been a number of books written on this subject, and now there's a newsletter called *Writing Sociology*. It's a fairly straightforward, plain-writing newsletter that comes out four times a year and exhorts everybody to write plainly. It publishes funny passages from other people's writing.

WOE: So it's directed towards professionals and not students?

BAZERMAN: That's right, for sociologists. A number of psychologists have also been looking at their field, people like Kenneth Gergen, who espouse constructivist positions. In economics, Donald McCloskey has done much the same thing and has had an enormous impact within the field. At a recent conference on economics and literature, the economists all approached the topic through an examination of discourse. Reflectivity is a major endeavor in the social sciences.

In the other sciences I would say that what is happening is simply a recognition that writing is important. I'm not sure that there is a lot of reflective examination of the practices of writing. There's nothing comparable to the fundamental questioning you've been getting in economics and anthropology, rethinking the basis of the discourse entirely on epistemological or political grounds.

WOE: Did you use some of your theoretical ideas in the classroom when you were teaching technical writing at Georgia Tech?

BAZERMAN: Most of the students had a lot of experience within organizations. Georgia Tech had a very strong internship program, and I saw students in their junior or senior year, which is also when they were doing field projects and design courses. A lot of them had work experience, so they were ready to start thinking about the social situation of writing because they were thinking about organizational writing and the importance of getting their technical reports accepted by the right people, of understanding the path by which their documents would flow within the organization, understanding the tastes of the people to whom they're writing and the function of their documents. They were very receptive to talking about their own role in creating organizational realities.

WOE: Because they had had that outside experience.

BAZERMAN: Yes. The kind of resistance I would mostly encounter is the response, "I just want to do my engineering! And I don't want to be bothered by these people who are ignorant of my specialty." But others in the class would say, "No, no, you'd better pay attention to this." If you talk about the necessity of argument and the function of various kinds of articles, most students are not at all resistant to thinking about these issues. They all think strategically about publication.

In the rhetoric-of-science movement, just as in the social-studies-of-science movement, some people came in with a real chip on their shoulder—"it's just words." For a variety of reasons, they felt that in order to make their sociological rhetorical arguments, they somehow had to dethrone the authority of science and in fact establish the authority of their field in place of it. And that if you allowed anything like a scientific account of what science does, then there wouldn't be any place for their kind of work. That never was my view. There were plausible ways of thinking about all those issues without taking simplistic stances on any of them. But people wanted to pick those fights, so that's what they did.

WOE: I want to know a little bit about your own influences and practices as a writer. How did you learn to write?

BAZERMAN: There are a lot of moments in learning to write. I used to say to my classes when I was younger—this struck me as funny—that learning to write was a race against senility. Now that I am almost fifty, I no longer find that quite so funny! I was remembering one of those moments this morning, in fact. When I was an undergraduate at Cornell, I had one of my most boring and uninspiring teachers for a course in classic literature in translation. He didn't do any teaching except that every week he would assign us a five hundred-word paper to write. And I just had to pound it out. When we came into class everybody would read his paper, but the teacher wouldn't have any comments. Doing the papers was wonderful, however, because I realized that I could just sit down and write a paper. Up until then, paper writing was accompanied by a lot of moaning and groaning, deep angst, staying up all night, and three weeks of turmoil and headaches.

I remember something else. When I was in junior high school I was doing a lot of experimentation and imitation, so that I'd rarely hand in the regular assignments. I hated the five-paragraph essay; I was rebelling against it. But in seventh or eighth grade, I saw the movie *The River* [with poetry by Vachel Lindsay], which had these long, rolling, Whitmanesque lines. On the social studies exams we were asked to talk about a flood, so I wrote my exam in these long, flowing, Whitmanesque lines.

WOE: What did the teacher think?

BAZERMAN: Well, fortunately, I was rewarded for this. All through my school years and in undergraduate years, I used to do weird things with writing. And I think doing this helped a lot—to experiment and try things in different ways.

WOE: Was there any one teacher who influenced you, besides the one who just made you write?

BAZERMAN: In graduate school my dissertation advisor was James V. Cunningham. He talked very directly to me; he wrote very sparely and he really reined me in. He taught me to get a sense of what it was to talk sense and to the point. He was a very strong influence on me, as he was on many of his students. He was a terrifying figure in many people's lives!

WOE: Right now you're in a research position and have more time to write. What did you do earlier in your career? You taught composition early on, didn't you?

BAZERMAN: I taught composition for twenty years at CUNY. I was hired on something called the SEEK program, which meant I was given this specific charge to pay attention to open admission students and to basic skills. At that time teaching in a literature program didn't make an awful lot of sense to me. For twenty years my main task was to teach developmental and freshman comp. I took that seriously because I taught elementary school for two years during the Vietnam era—I was in the class that lost its graduate deferment. Teaching elementary school seemed like a useful way to spend my time. It got me really thinking about literacy. I still think of myself as a writing teacher. I prefer teaching composition to teaching literature courses.

WOE: What attracted you to composition?

BAZERMAN: After my first year in graduate school, I was unsure what the profession of literature was all about. Like most people, I had been drawn to literature because it spoke to certain personal issues. It gave me the chance to read books and to talk about things I wanted to talk about. Then I went to grad school, and I wasn't quite sure what it was all about. I guess I was starting to have premonitions about what we might call now a cultural studies orientation towards literature. Then, deferment removed, I found myself teaching inner-city elementary school, first grade and third grade, and literacy made a great deal of sense to me. It was something that an adult could do with his life and feel he was doing something useful. I wound up going back to graduate school because the life of an inner-city schoolteacher wasn't very good, and I wasn't going to become a victim. I saw that there were limits to what you could accomplish in that situation at that time. But I went back to graduate school with very much of an interest in literacy. My dissertation was not literacy oriented but it was trying to place practices of the literary within time and place; now I think we'd call it a new historicist dissertation. I wrote about occasional verse, which nobody then took seriously because it wasn't good literature. But I was learning how literary acts were socially situated; I was trying to understand literature as a communicative system among certain classes and certain times and places.

Then I was hired into the SEEK position, where I was very happy to teach writing. It was very compelling work—dealing with freshmen coming into college. I don't know why people have this distaste for it; it's real teaching! Freshmen are at a major transition point in their lives; they're about to discover (if one's institution lives up to its promises) all kinds of exciting things and head into interesting lives. They're having new thoughts, they're ready, they want to be inspired. And you're providing tools that can help them deal with all of this. I can't think of a better teaching situation, so I love it.

WOE: It sounds like you miss it.

BAZERMAN: Oh yes. It's fortunate for the Writing Program here at UC Santa Barbara that it is now independent of the English Department. But my being in the English Department means I can't teach in the Writing Program, and I find that personally unfortunate. I'm working with graduate students who are doing some TAing, but I'm working with them as graduate students, not as TAs within the Writing Program; they have their own training within the Writing Program. I'm trying to help orient them to the teaching of writing as part of their professional opportunity. But this is not anything like a full training in rhetoric. As you know, nowhere in the University of California is there anything like training in rhetoric and the teaching of writing.

There's an enormous need in California to have somebody training the teachers of writing, not just for the UC campuses but the Cal State and the community college system as well as all the other colleges here. It's an enormous opportunity to improve higher education, which is being missed. I think there are some very fine teachers of writing, many of whom have educated or are educating themselves. As I understand it, there are some M.A.

programs in rhetoric and composition at a couple of the Cal State campuses, but for the most part the teaching of writing is learned almost entirely on the job at all levels of California higher education. There's nothing like a core space, a research component; there's little formal training.

WOE: Since we're talking about the lack of training, do you have any advice for someone trained in literature who's assigned to teach writing in the disciplines, or writing across the curriculum?

BAZERMAN: My advice would be to take seriously the discourses, whether they're professional or undergraduate. The students engaged in them may not be very reflective about their language use, but they certainly have their reasons for wanting to do what they do. People in the English Department make certain choices for certain things and often against others. You may find yourself in situations where you're in contact with a field that you earlier chose not to engage with. But these discourses are what intelligent people interested in certain things have developed for themselves. They're very interesting if you take seriously what these people are trying to figure out. Then, using your knowledge of language and writing, you can say useful things that support the development of that kind of writing.

But you've got to take it seriously, and take seriously the students' desires to enter into those discourses. Over the years I've found that some people in English keep trying to save the souls of students who are in other fields. They're not recognizing those virtues that students have within their fields. When I taught at Baruch College, there were many very hardworking, decent students who wanted to be accountants. They had an *awful* time in their writing courses and their English Department courses, where their instructors were looking to save them from their fates. The students had made a perfectly reasonable choice: they wanted to be accountants! There's nothing immoral about it; it's a useful function. And they had a certain way of thinking—they were learning to think like accountants. There are certain kinds of writing that they will be very good at if you allow them to think like accountants and not try to make them think like English majors.

Once you get to know them, you may want to help students gain a critical distance so they can make choices about their discipline. But that's very different from having a distaste from the top for what the students are doing and for those discourses. When you get into professional discourses, they're as fascinating as any other complex discursive activity. Certainly in the literature department we've learned to love the weirdest stuff from the farthest corners; in fact, we pride ourselves on being able to recover these strange artifacts that nobody knows the meaning of or appreciates. It shouldn't be so hard, then, to come to appreciate what the sociologists or economists or accountants are doing. They're not so different in time or place; they are part of our world. And we should be able to recover what it is that those discourses are trying to accomplish.

WOE: What changes have you seen in the composition classroom?

BAZERMAN: In the last couple of years I've been amazed at the changes that have occurred in the teaching of writing since I entered the field. I'm just so proud of the field—even those people who I might have been at odds with or not been so interested in what they were doing. The changes have had an enormous impact on teaching everywhere, right down to elementary school.

During my first term in Georgia, I asked the students in one of my classes (as I always ask my freshman students) about their writing histories: whether they did drafts and how many papers they wrote last year. After class a young woman from a very rural part of Georgia came up to me and said in this very, very thick accent, "I was very confused by what you said about drafts; isn't it a natural part of the writing process?" This is now a naturalized fact in rural Georgia! I remember that I used to write everything one off as an undergraduate, and certainly when I first began asking students these questions nobody had ever heard of a draft. This has been an enormous change, and there's lots of other things like this. We have changed; whether we get respect as a profession or not, it's a much better situation now than it was. I'm just so proud of the many ways in which we have intervened in this culture and moved it along in very positive ways. I have had complaints—and there are obviously approaches I think are misguided—but as a whole the field has just been doing great stuff.

WOE: After you finish your work on Edison, do you know what direction you want to pursue next?

BAZERMAN: I'm turning lots of things over in my mind; I'm not quite sure. One possibility—I have several partial manuscripts pushing in this direction—is some kind of larger theoretical work that tries to tie together some of the genre theory that I've been working on with some social theory. But I also want to do something which talks about the organization of society today from a discursive standpoint; I don't know the right vehicle to get into that. And I also keep saying that I'm not going to do any more historical work. But I was reading microfilms this morning, and I was enjoying looking over this old stuff....

JOSEPH HARRIS

In A Teaching Subject: Composition since 1966 *(1996), Joseph Harris examines debates in composition theory and pedagogy in order to explain changing attitudes toward college writing. Harris recognizes a progression from seeing the composition classroom as an academic discourse community, in which members share values, assumptions, and purposes and use communication to achieve their goals, to seeing it as a conflicted "contact zone" (Pratt), in which students do not share values and assumptions but use communication to express difference. Harris prefers to view the classroom as a negotiated "common ground" (Spellmeyer), in which shared purposes are discovered and communicated effectively despite differences. His own hope is that college writers will be prepared to contribute to public spheres through "multiliteracies," including digital media genres, in which content is dependent on form in new ways. Harris argues that in the context of globalization, contemporary writers must know how to use multimedia resources to interact effectively with others—in formal, informal, dialectical, and abbreviated forms of English. In* Rewriting: How to Do Things with Texts *(2006), Harris fills a gap in rhetoric and composition scholarship by providing specific strategies for students rewriting argumentative papers that fall short of a high academic standard. With John Miles and Gary Paine, Harris is also co-editor of* Teaching with Student Texts: Essays toward an Informed Practice *(2010) and with Jay Rosen and Gary Calpas, co-editor of Media Journal:* Reading and Writing about Popular Culture *(1995, 2nd ed. 1998). He is a past editor of* SWR: Studies in Writing and Rhetoric *(2007–12) and of the journal* College Composition and Communication *(1994–1999).*

Harris was the founding and long-time director of Duke University's Thompson Writing Program (TWP), an independent, multidisciplinary writing program, where he continues to teach. In addition to overseeing the FYC and Writing Studio, he pioneered a WID program that received a total of $3.8 million in grants from the Mellon Foundation, focusing on the professional development of postdoctoral scholars. The TWP was awarded the CCCC Writing Program Certificate of Excellence in 2006.

—Jane Beal and Lisa Sperber

"Changing Habits of Thinking"

Thomas West

Spring 1996

WOE: In your first editorial at *CCC*, you say that you had "never looked forward very much to a career as a scholar writing to a small clique of other specialists, and so [were] pleased to find a field where so many people seem[ed] to try to speak to the concerns of experts and students alike." How has this emphasis on students' writing in composition influenced the ways in which you think of yourself as a writer?

HARRIS: It hasn't influenced the way I think of myself as a writer, but it certainly has influenced the ways I think of myself as an intellectual and a teacher: the kinds of projects that seem important to me, the kinds of questions that seem crucial. Let me illustrate with a story: I grew up in a world that was literally parochial, bound by parish neighborhoods and schools in Philadelphia, and from there I went to Haverford College. And though the geographical distance between my home and Haverford was quite short, it seemed as though I had changed worlds, from a working-class city neighborhood to an affluent suburb, from a Catholic school to an elite private college. That shift was daunting in many ways, but what I began to realize once I got to Haverford was that the other students were not necessarily as smart as they (and others) thought they were. Then, a few years later, when I started teaching basic writers in New York City, I quickly saw that those students were actually a lot smarter than they (and others) often thought they were. Those two counter-realizations have been very important to me. They suggested that the problem was not with intelligence per se but with what sorts of intelligence were made visible. And thus one of my ongoing projects as a teacher has been to try to gain access to the intelligence, to the insights, of students who are often dismissed as not being very smart, or as underprepared, to imagine that they have something to say to us that others don't, and to try to help them become more articulate and confident in saying it. That desire has strongly influenced whom I've chosen to teach and where, as well as the kinds of writing projects I set for myself.

In terms of how I actually go about writing, I would say that my influences there have been rather traditional and literary critical. That is, the important move in my work has been to treat student texts in much the same way as in a slightly different sort of career I might have been reading literary texts.

WOE: Would you talk a little about your writing habits?

HARRIS: I don't think I'm a very good model of the writing process as it is now commonly depicted. Even though I often find myself advising students not to worry about details of phrasing, not to get stuck on particular words and sentences, to begin at various points in an essay, and so on, I'm actually the kind of writer who very much needs to start at the beginning and to work out all the details as he moves through a piece. I need to have the illusion that I'm writing a piece from start to finish and that what I'm writing is something close to a final draft. Of course it doesn't always work that way, and I have to go back and revise.

But it's hard for me to write a new sentence or a new paragraph unless, at least for that moment, I feel confident of what I'm saying, that I've got the words right. This means I do an awful lot of revising, both stylistic and conceptual, as I move along. I also do a lot of what they used to call prewriting or percolating. I need to mull over pieces for a long time before I begin to write. But once I do begin, I then usually produce something close to a final draft. Sometimes the comments of readers require me to rethink what I've written, but I'm not the kind of person who can first block out a rough approximation of an essay and then go back and fine-tune the details. By the time I let anybody read my work, it's usually pretty close to what I want to say.

WOE: You have said that as a graduate student you were frustrated by what seemed to you the "planned irrelevance" of much scholarship. What are the differences between this scholarship of "planned irrelevance" and the problem-posing scholarship you advocate?

HARRIS: That's a good question, since I worry sometimes that much of the kind of revisionary work that I do could be dismissed as a kind of professional navel-gazing, an absorption with our professional discourse rather than a moving outward. But I don't think that's the case. In trying to figure out better ways of talking about what it is that we want to do, we can in fact learn to do it better.

For example, in a piece I wrote called "After Dartmouth," I looked at a set of educators and critics whom I was very fond of—growth theorists like John Dixon, James Britton, and James Moffett. I was attracted to their emphasis on getting students to use writing to reflect on their own experiences and concerns. However, I was also troubled by how these theorists imagined experience as almost always something felt or done—as actions in the world. I felt that such a view left out the role of ideas, of intellectual experiences, in ordinary life—that students were being viewed as people who came to class with stories to tell and deeds to recount but not with positions to argue. This seemed to me both unintentionally condescending and also simply wrong since it's clear that in our current media culture we are all immersed in texts—ads, movies, videos, songs—and that we all spend much of our time literally reading and interpreting the world around us. And so, if we are going to begin with student experience, it seems important we recognize that many of those experiences have a strong intellectual or critical aspect.

One result of this stance is that it helps break down some of the barriers between the classroom and the world outside since intellectual work is seen as something that goes on in both spaces. And so revisiting the work of the growth theorists and mulling over its limits helped me begin to form a different sort of pedagogy, one that would ask students to think and write about other aspects of their lives, that would ask them to be critics as well as narrators of their experiences.

But this is really less a matter of choice than temperament. I have always formulated a project as a response to other people's ideas; for me scholarship always seems to grow out of an engagement with other people's work. But of course so does my teaching.

WOE: What about the phrase "planned irrelevance"?

HARRIS: [*Laughs.*] That's what it seemed to me. I first attended graduate school in film studies. I've always thought that the aim of a liberal education should be to help students become critics of their lived culture as it actually exists around them and not simply some version of their cultural heritage. I enjoyed being an English major at Haverford, but in the classes I took we didn't get to the present very often, and I very much felt that we should have. So when I went to graduate school I thought that one way of getting to the present would be to study not books but film and television. I was disappointed to find out that the profession of film studies was doing to movies exactly what the profession of English had previously done to books: mystifying the subject so they could then re-explain it to students. The lesson I took from this was that you couldn't guarantee relevance simply through topic, that you had to always find ways of connecting your interests and concerns with the lived experiences of students.

WOE: You have mentioned an indebtedness to the work of James Britton and Raymond Williams. In what ways has their scholarship been an influence on yours?

HARRIS: Both Williams and Britton helped me rethink English studies as centering on a set of practices rather than on a set of texts, to see how the acts of reading and writing, producing and interpreting texts, are central to our work. If composition and cultural studies are to have any real impact on university study, I believe it will be through such a shift in emphasis. That is, the important move is not from *Moby Dick* to Madonna but from the study of texts to the study of how people make use of texts. And so, for instance, I still feel I share more in common with an English teacher who may seem to be teaching quite canonical or conventional texts but who does so in ways that engage with the views and experiences of students than I do with a cultural studies person who simply lectures at students about postmodernity or resistance or whatever.

WOE: What concepts do you see that require particular critical attention at this time?

HARRIS: In the last few years we've spent a lot of energy elaborating rhetorics of difference. That's been needed, and I don't in any way want to speak against the goal of diversity, particularly in a time when access to higher education is decreasing and racial tensions are worsening. At the same time, though, I think that, in addition to rhetorics of difference, we need to construct rhetorics of affiliation or identity, to find ways of talking about how we can negotiate as well as express our differences.

Similarly, the last decade has seen an explosion of interest in issues of power and resistance. Again, this has been useful. But I think that this interest needs to be flanked by an attention to terms like "pleasure." I find it disconcerting that the only pleasure that critics sometimes seem to allow themselves (or us) is an ironic rewriting of the text.

WOE: Or a guilty pleasure.

HARRIS: Exactly, a guilty pleasure. We might instead think about ways in which we can re-identify with and take some real joy or hope from the positions and projects of some artists, writers, and critics. We should be able to feel that the texts we read do not always have to be subverted, resisted, or ironized, that intellectual work is not simply an exercise in power but also an opportunity for pleasure and craft.

WOE: In "The Other Reader," you write, "Before we can have effective criticism of advertising, or any other part of popular culture, we need to admit that all of us respond to it in ways that are often at once both pleased and skeptical, open and resisting." How might effective criticism in other areas, say race and gender, be based on the recognitions you talk about in "The Other Reader"—for example, that we respond to these issues in mixed and complex ways?

HARRIS: There's an imputed purity in some kinds of criticism that is off-putting and that also blocks the writer from making certain kinds of realizations. A problem with a lot of talk about race and gender in our field is that it tends to locate sexist or racist attitudes in students and the culture but not in ourselves. This creates a kind of us-versus-them relationship that can get in the way of effective teaching and criticism. To really combat racism and sexism, we need to begin with self-criticism, with examining the ways that, as products of our culture, we all share in attitudes that we want to resist and transform.

In "The Other Reader," I tried to argue that we need to deal not only with our own conflicted responses to texts but also with the often ambivalent situations in which we find ourselves in the culture and in the profession, that we need to begin by admitting to certain contradictions rather than by trying to speak from some position outside of them.

WOE: You discuss the importance of distinguishing between writing which is strongly situated and writing which is merely confessional. Would you elaborate a bit on the distinction that you're making between these personal forms of writing?

HARRIS: I don't think this is an area where you can draw up rules in advance—to say that this is too personal or that this should be more personal or that this is just personal enough. I am suspicious, however, about claims for personal writing as being in itself radical or liberating. The claim of those writing autobiographical criticism is almost always for some sort of originality or authenticity—a breaking with convention and tradition. And yet the text produced is often highly conventional.

WOE: In "After Dartmouth," you say that "identity rises out of identification," that "we define who we are through whom we choose to stand with and against." You continually emphasize that identity involves provisional negotiations of affiliations within, and sometimes against, larger social forces in which we already find ourselves embedded and embattled. What does viewing identity in this way have to do with writing generally and composition studies specifically?

HARRIS: One advantage to a view of identity as constructed rather than simply given is that this makes the self much more open to change and revision. It's a self that we form, at least in part, from various voices and influences around us, a self that we can thus also reform. This strikes me as a more fluid and hopeful, a more educable, view of the self.

How does this relate to writing? Writing is useful because it gives us a way of stepping back from the positions we've taken and allows us to examine who it is, in a given text, that we say we are: whom we've chosen to stand with, whom we've chosen to stand against. Writing, that is, offers us an opportunity for critical self-reflection that ordinary speech doesn't usually allow. It makes language visible. Thus a more fluid sense of identity and an interest in writing together enable, it seems to me, a kind of teaching that can give students the chance to reflect critically on who they are, on how they compose and interpret experience, and on what ways they might want to change their languages and themselves.

WOE: You argue for making "aggressive use" of the insights into teaching and theory gained from students' writing. Obviously, you see pedagogy and theory as integrated. What might be the advantages for students of bringing theory into the classroom?

HARRIS: What you want to do is not so much to bring theory into the classroom as to set up situations where students are asked to become theorists. You can do this not only by asking them to read a certain kind of text but also by engaging in the sort of activity that I was just talking about, the practice of standing back from your own work and reflecting not only on what you said but on how you went about saying it, on what your language says about you, the stances or attitudes it implicates you in. The kind of teaching I'm after is one in which students are asked to take their own writings as seriously as the work of the people they're reading. This implies too that they should be doing some serious reading as well as writing. Such teaching seems to me to have a radical impulse and maybe even, sometimes, effect.

WOE: Some theorists see cultural studies as academic work that can influence social and political formations. Recently, however, Stanley Fish has argued that cultural studies only serves to replace the kinds of texts we study. He argues that cultural studies holds out promises about social change that it can't keep because it's embedded in the academy. How might we negotiate this kind of double-bind of wanting to work toward social change from within the academy?

HARRIS: I want both to agree and disagree with Fish. I agree wholly that our expertise and thus power lies with a particular sort of intellectual work and focus and that we move away from that focus at our peril. But I think that our work can be imagined, as I've said before, as centering not on certain texts but on certain activities or practices. I agree with Fish that if cultural studies is to make a difference, it will have to do something more than simply shift the texts we study. But I think that we can do something more, that we can aim to change how students deal with texts, to make them more articulate and confident as writers and more reflective as readers. And I suppose I disagree with Fish in feeling that such teaching can be more than simple training in the latest mode of textual criticism, that its effects can be broader and more interesting.

Having said that, though, it does seem to me that it's useful to distinguish between teaching and political activism, to suggest that while the aims of the two can be related, they are not identical. My wife runs a soup kitchen and free health clinic in what used to be the steel town of Homestead. She is an activist in ways I will never be, and I admire her work intensely. But my guess is that with my skills and temperament, I have a better chance of effecting change as a teacher. What I can hope to do is to put people in a situation where they see things a little differently, where they can form new and perhaps more critical habits of thinking. That can sometimes feel like a pretty limited and frustrating form of influence, though sometimes it can be exhilarating, too. But either way, it's what teachers and intellectuals do. I don't think we need to feel guilty that we're not out there on the streets. That isn't our job. Our job is to change habits of thinking.

WOE: When you became editor of *CCC*, you instituted an "Interchanges" section in which readers were invited to respond to articles which had appeared in the journal. What other discursive forms do you think we might use to challenge traditional scholarly forms in effective and productive ways?

HARRIS: The intent of the Interchanges section is to feature short pieces that are in some clear tension with or relation to one another. That sort of responsiveness is, in fact, a characteristic of much academic work. But most of the written dialogues we engage in occur over an extended period of time and literally appear in different spaces—in different journals or in different issues of the same journal. I'm trying to make that critical dialogue more dramatic and immediate, to showcase it within the space of a single issue.

Are there other kinds of writing that we could be doing in composition? I'm not sure that the way to encourage new forms or genres is to ask for them explicitly, to specify a certain kind of writing that a journal is looking for. Instead, I think the important thing for people to do is to think of their writing as writing, to view what they do as writers as not simply putting together research reports or commentaries on other people's texts but as crafting artifacts for certain kinds of effects. These effects can involve something more than the construction of a sense of authority or scholarly thoroughness; they can also include a sense of style, surprise, eloquence, play.

For instance, in his recent essay, "The Nervous System," Richard Miller not only offers incisive readings of theorists such as Foucault and Bourdieu but also supplements those readings with an intensely personal series of reflections on his family and his work, at one point even reproducing a poem of his own composition and then, most importantly, subjecting all these moves—critical, narrative, poetic—to an ongoing critique. The lesson to be learned from such a piece, then, is not to try to jam anything and everything into the space of a single essay but to look at how Miller is working against various conventions of the academic essay at the same time he is exploiting them.

Another example. In the May 1996 issue of *CCC*, there is a very interesting piece by Michael Spooner and Kathleen Yancey called "postings on a Genre of E-mail" that is set up as a kind of dialogue between two voices about whether electronic discourse is really a new use of language or simply a more familiar set of uses in a new medium. But what's really interesting is that neither of the voices in the piece is tagged specifically to Spooner and Yancey, so there's no way of reducing the text to two competing positions. And then their text is still further complicated by the introduction of even more voices, postings from the Internet, that interrupt and comment on their exchange. On top of that, the essay is formatted so that all these voices overlap and intersect with each other so that the boundaries between them are blurred visually too. All this seems to me more than just a stylistic or typographical fancy but rather an attempt to create collaborative text that is neither simply univocal (two or three people composing together, writing in the same voice) nor an old-fashioned point/counterpoint sort of dialogue.

My point is not that these pieces should represent a new genre of academic writing, that we should all write like Miller or like Spooner and Yancey, but rather that we should look for writing that, in one way or the other, pushes against the edges of the form it is working in.

WOE: So it's not so much about instituting new forms as much as it is about being open to stylistic alternatives necessitated perhaps by new technologies and different ways of thinking?

HARRIS: Right. David Bartholomae and Tony Petrosky talk about trying to get students to take on a hesitant and tenuous stance toward academic discourse. I think that goes for us too, that there are dangers in becoming settled in particular genres, even supposedly innovative ones. I like pieces that aren't quite one thing or the other.

WOE: Do you think that online publishing affords possible ways to work against elitist limits of conventional scholarship in English studies?

HARRIS: I think it can. I'm not sure it necessarily will, but I think it has the potential. For me, the most interesting aspect of online communication has to do with its ability to bring a number of people into the room at the same time, to get people talking not only over great expanses of space but also to get them talking across lines of age and profession and the like. Its most worrisome aspect is that so far most of these people still seem to form a fairly predictable group, that the users of the Internet are sharply defined by class and even gender. So if one of our desires really is to hear more from minority or dissident voices, the Internet doesn't seem to be the place to go right now.

The Net does seem to offer different stylistic opportunities to its users, though; it encourages a prose that is not exactly conversational but is clearly not formal. I also imagine that eventually—though I don't know much about this—we will see texts that really are structured differently, texts that are not merely distributed on the Net but are composed for it, articles and books that are hyper-textual rather than linear-textual. I'll be interested to see what those new forms are; I don't think I've seen any compelling instances yet.

WOE: What about prejudices against online scholarship when it comes to decisions about hiring and promotion?

HARRIS: There are already similar prejudices against entire fields—as is still often the case with composition—or against supposedly lesser journals or presses within a field. Academics is a status-obsessed and hierarchy-ridden profession. I don't see that changing much very soon, although I do think it's our responsibility to try to change the game as we play it. For the time being, I would simply point out that publication online can be refereed and can be as formal and rigorous as scholarship in other media.

WOE: As editor of *CCC*, you are not only exposed to the most recent scholarship in the field, but you help shape the field as well. What trends do you see or would you like to see in composition?

HARRIS: To begin with, there are several ongoing issues that have long been part of work in composition and that are likely to remain so: assessment and evaluation, identity within writing, classroom authority and politics. And since composition has long been closely identified with a reformist movement in higher education, pieces dealing with writing across the curriculum are still very important. I get a lot of submissions dealing with these issues, and I think appropriately so. They're not new, but they're a central part of much work in the field.

There is also clearly a very strong current interest in histories of rhetoric and composition, much stronger than I recall just ten or twelve years ago when I was entering the field. I feel a little ambivalent about this. Some historical work is quite interesting, but I guess I worry about it as something of a retreat back into the purely academic. This shift toward history springs, at least in part, from a very powerful theoretical argument about the historical situatedness of all discourse and thus the need to pay close mind to the material and institutional contexts of writing and teaching. I'm convinced by that argument. At the same point, though, when I read histories I find myself impatient to learn what use they might be put to, to find out how they connect up with current issues in theory and teaching, to make sure that they hold more than simply a professional or antiquarian interest.

As for writing I would like to encourage: we need to find convincing responses to questions about access to higher education that are being raised in both professional and public forums. Sometimes the code word for these issues is "basic writing," sometimes it's "placement," sometimes it's "standards," but talking about who is going to be allowed in our classrooms in the coming years and what sort of support they will need to succeed in school strikes me as absolutely crucial.

We will also need to study the workings of electronic discourse. Things are now happening very fast which could profoundly shape the ways people go about writing and the work we do as writing teachers. We need to be proactive here, to hazard some speculations and hypotheses and guesses, to try to shape our intellectual environment as much as we can.

IRA SHOR

Ira Shor is one of the major advocates for critical pedagogy within composition studies. His early work helped introduce Paulo Freire to North American writing studies. Shor's approach in Critical Teaching and Everyday Life *(1980) stresses the development of teaching practices in conjunction with political analyses of schooling. In 1987, he co-authored* A Pedagogy for Liberation *with Paulo Freire and published* Freire for the Classroom: A Sourcebook for Liberatory Teaching. *These works helped translate Freirian approaches from their original adult literacy contexts in Brazil to North American elementary, secondary, and postsecondary contexts. In these three works, Shor encourages students—and teachers—to discuss, write about, and intervene in local issues. Politics, economics, and social justice are major themes in all of his published writing.*

Central to Shor's theory and pedagogy is the technique of problem posing. Drawn from Freire's efforts to break down the hierarchies of teacher–student relationship, problem posing is a dialogic approach to teaching and learning. For Freire, problem posing is opposed to teaching promoted in the traditional "banking" model of education.[1] *In* Empowering Education *(1992), Shor describes how "problem-posing goes deeply into any issue of knowledge to indicate its social and personal dimensions."*[2] *For instance, he charts out how an ESL lesson can start with a picture of three women at work and a male supervisor. From this picture, Shor traces a lesson that asks for descriptions of the scene, students' feelings about the scene, questions about how the situation relates to their own lives, and then about whether the rules that apply at work are fair or not. The move is to start with specifics in a lesson, relate those specifics to students' lives, and then pose problems that generalize knowledge. Shor advocates for allowing students to create "empowering knowledge [that] is sought by questioning rules, work relations, and daily episodes often taken for granted."*[3] *His approach to teaching is "posing problems rather than [. . .] giving answers."*[4]

1 Freire, Paulo. "The Banking Concept of Education." *Pedagogy of the Oppressed*. New York: Continuum, 2000: (43). [First English publication: Freire, P. (1970). "The Banking Concept of Education." *Pedagogy of the Oppressed*. New York: Herder and Herder.]
2 Shor, I. (1992). *Empowering Education: Critical Teaching for Social Change*. Chicago: University of Chicago Press.
3 Ibid (44).
4 Ibid (43).

In addition to his work in critical pedagogy, Shor has contributed to the scholarship in cultural studies and education. His books Culture Wars: School and Society in the Conservative Restoration *(1986)* and Education Is Politics *(1999)* critique conservative efforts to undo educational reforms begun in the 1960s. He argues that during the 1970s and 1980s, conservative political forces in the United States reestablished control over the curriculum and reduced the autonomy of teachers for political reasons. Much of his work in the 1990s was devoted to providing teachers with strategies to counter this "conservative restoration." Empowering Education *(1992)*, When Students Have Power: Negotiating Authority in a Critical Pedagogy *(1996)*, and the edited collection Critical Literacy in Action *(1999)* connect the theories of John Dewey, Paulo Freire, and Lev Vygotsky with composition studies research. These works encourage composition teachers and researchers to consider the political contexts and impacts of how they teach writing.

—*Carl Whithaus*

"Every Difference Will Be Used against Us"

Andrea Greenbaum

Spring 1997

WOE: You have written that your parents felt "betrayed" when you became a Ph.D. rather than an M.D. This is surprising since in most circles there is a certain amount of prestige associated with being a professor.

SHOR: A Ph.D. certainly has prestige (though perhaps less so now than 30 years ago), but there's nothing like being an M.D. or corporate lawyer in terms of pulling down a heavy income, and that's what obsessed my parents, who were anxious about their retirement. As many working-class parents do, they thought of their children as their pension plan. They saw that I was very good in schoolwork and thought I was a good bet to go all the way to an M.D., so they pushed me relentlessly to become a doctor and get rich. On Sunday drives, they showed me the nice houses in the Westchester County suburbs which they wanted me to buy them. I was seduced by their plans for me and couldn't wait to live in one of those swell homes, so different from the treeless, congested streets of the South Bronx where I grew up. There's no question that they felt betrayed when I dropped out of pre-med.

WOE: They supported your education?

SHOR: They ran out of money in my sophomore year of college. I worked all the time and paid about half the bill for the first two years at the upper-deck University of Michigan. When they went broke, I was on my own for the rest of the ride. Of course, up until high school I lived with them, shared a room with my older brother Jerry, wore his clothes when he grew out of them. Then, at seventeen, I graduated from the Bronx High School of Science and went away to Michigan. I worked summers in New York (on Wall Street and in hospitals) and during the school year (as a dishwasher and busboy) and saved every penny. The night before I left the Bronx for my freshman year at Michigan, I emptied my piggy banks and accounts and handed my dad $600 to pay my first semester's tuition and the first payment of my dorm fees. Tuition was $450 a semester at Michigan in 1962. I took with me $108 for books and spending money. I remember all these amounts because of the anxiety connected to paying for college. When my pocket money ran out, I took various jobs for 90 cents an hour, the minimum wage then, believe it or not.

My folks didn't send me any money, they didn't have any to send really, but they did send me a salami or two from Katz's famous delicatessen and paid my tuition and dormitory fees. Then, in my second year, Dad was out of work for a while, Grandma got very sick, and they weren't able to pay anything more. So I started taking big loans, working more hours, and scrambling for grants and scholarships. From that time on until I finished my Ph.D., I took care of myself. Along the way, I dropped out of pre-med, faced a family showdown at home on this, and broke my parents' hearts and hopes, I'm sure, which left a lot of family tension for years and still hurts today when I recall the scenes. I remember coming home Christmas in my sophomore year when I was eighteen and telling them I wasn't going to become a doctor. My mother started crying, my father sank into the sofa, depressed. They tried to change my mind. Dad said some nasty things about me being too soft to take it. They suddenly faced old age without a rich son to retire them in grace.

WOE: Do you see this as a common experience for working-class kids who enter the academy?

SHOR: Working-class stories like mine probably vary from family to family, from ethnic group to ethnic group, from period to period. There's something historical in every story, though, because when my folks were kids, they were badly battered by the Depression of the 1930s. That era left them hungry for security and dignity, which made them long to have an M.D. for a son whose professional achievement they could wear like a medal on their sleeve and whose income they could relax into. As a humorous folkway among working-class urban Jews, "my son the doctor" is a typical parental desire. In my family, for me the smart one in school, there seemed to be no choice—everyone expected me to get an M.D. My working-class parents and relatives couldn't imagine how a kid with the brains to become rich would want to do anything else with his life. So when I dropped out of pre-med, I knew

I was making a terrible decision for my parents, but I was so bored with science in college that I couldn't imagine going on, no matter what they eventually would pay me. I had a good imagination and wanted to study philosophy, history, anthropology, and literature. I wanted to dig up ancient ruins and find out what happened to the Neanderthals. I loved language, writing, storytelling, and conversation, though few classes connected to these loves. My imagination and idealism woke up with the activist politics of the 1960s, when I got involved in the Civil Rights Movement. Like many kids in the expanding economy of the sixties, I didn't worry about earning a living or getting a job. I wanted to read, debate, travel, march, go to rallies, stop the war in Vietnam, end poverty and racism, and make the world better. It was a great time to be young.

WOE: You also seem fascinated by working-class markers—those traits most closely associated with people from lower-income communities, such as differences in communication (they speak louder, gesture more frequently), appearance (they have worse skin, bad teeth, and, for obvious reasons, dress poorly), and in their environment (they are subject to greater noise and environmental hazards). For those of us who emerged from the working class into the academy, do you believe that there is a distinct institutional pressure on students to erase those working-class markers, to become more homogenized, genteel?

SHOR: The pressures are institutional experiences. In doctoral programs, for example, there's a social incentive to become genteel, to fit in. People talk lower, slower, don't gesture as much with their hands, and put a premium on wittiness, literary allusions, and references to fashionable things. In addition, upper-deck places collect folks who learned to chew with their mouths closed. Folks in these places dress fashionably, whether they are dressing down or dressing up, pierced and balded or tweeded and beaded. Accents are okay as long as they are not working-class ones. Elite discourse manners teach you what it means to be an appropriate conversational partner. For example, I don't hear bawdy humor much in the academy, but I grew up in a male working-class site with ample bawdiness—not necessarily sex, just jokes about bodily functions and parts, about weird situations that people got into, and about making fun of each other.

There's no question that there's institutional pressure on working-class people to change—to speak lower and slower, to abandon their accents and their expressions, to edit out bawdiness, to smother guffawing laughter—all signs of lack of refinement. I'm more refined now than when I entered college 35 years ago, but from what I hear on videotapes made of me, I think I still have a Bronx accent. And I still have my bad working-class teeth, though I have learned to chew with my mouth closed.

I'd have to add that working-class men do have a certain privilege here, because men are allowed to take on the character of the slovenly eccentric professor, so we can look disheveled or unkempt and still be admired as a "brilliant mind." Women are not accepted as brilliant disheveled eccentrics. If a male professor wants to look awful, as long as he publishes a lot, it's okay. For example, I just gave a talk to the Brooklyn Library Literacy Program at its formal awards reception. Though I had on a tie and nice shirt, I discovered that I was the only speaker wearing running shoes and the only one not wearing a jacket. Because I was a white male professor, I was just fine, though I doubt that women or people of color would feel as free to underdress. In general, the more elite the institution, the more research-based, the bigger the endowment, the more pressure there is to conform to genteel styles of speaking, writing, dressing, and office decoration. On the whole, community colleges have more relaxed standards of dress and speech than do graduate schools. These are underfunded, low-tuition institutions without endowments that are set up especially for working-class students, so dressing down and speaking down are more allowed. Working-class academics will likely feel more at home in the community colleges than in the research universities.

WOE: You dedicated your recent book, *When Students Have Power*, to James Berlin, calling him a "scholar, mentor, friend." What is it about Berlin's work that inspires you?

SHOR: Jim was a brilliant guy whose histories and taxonomies of rhetoric taught me a great deal. In his final years, he made strenuous efforts to connect cultural studies, composition, and critical pedagogy into a framework he called "social epistemic rhetoric." Social epistemic rhetoric offers a cross-disciplinary theory and practice for oppositional writing teachers. According to Berlin, social epistemic rhetoric accepts that all discourse is constructive, a process through which we use language to discover knowledge, to develop ourselves, to build relationships with others, and to make or remake the social relations we are part of. By critically studying themes and texts from our lives and our society (cultural studies and critical pedagogy), we make writing and writing instruction into a knowledge-making (epistemic) activity, a developmental and investigative action located in a specific historical context (the social setting).

Jim Berlin not only taught me useful knowledge about rhetoric, but he also helped bring me back toward professional activity in composition. In the 1970s, when I was first developing critical pedagogy for remedial writing and freshman composition at Staten Island Community College, Richard Ohmann, then editor of *College English* and a brilliant rhetorician in his own right, would call me up and ask me to write articles. In my twenties then, I was pulled forward into this work by Ohmann's interest in my experiments. By the time Ohmann left the editorship of *College English* in 1978, we had become friends, but I was never again called by *College English* and never asked to review a book. (In fact, my first book, *Critical Teaching and Everyday Life*, was sarcastically reviewed in *College English*.)

The political climate was decisively shifting in the nation and in the field of composition studies. At that time I felt pushed out of the field of English and began a long association with Paulo Freire, producing a book with him and then a teacher's guide about his methods. (I also wrote a Freirean study of this era which I called "the conservative restoration," when oppositional politics emerging from the 1960s were marginalized.) So that's what I was doing from the late seventies to the late eighties, when I felt there wasn't an opening in the field of English for critical pedagogy.

Then in 1988 Jim Berlin published an article in *College English* called "Rhetoric and Ideology in the Writing Class," which offers a profound critique of expressivism and cognitivism and identifies the critical pedagogy I'd been working on as the best option for English studies and composition. I was astonished. I couldn't imagine how someone I never met or knew would designate my work as the best option for composition studies, so I owe it more or less to Jim Berlin for bringing me back into the field of English studies. He gave depth and purpose, theory and practice, to the famous "social turn" of English studies in the late eighties. Eventually, I wrote a letter to Jim; we began corresponding and speaking on the phone, met at CCCC, and began planning work together; we became friends, we ate, had beer, told stories. He was a wonderful guy who inspired me to study rhetoric more carefully. My personal tragedy is that Jim Berlin died in 1994 just as we were planning sessions at NCTE and CCCC. I miss him terribly, and this is why I honored him with the dedication to my new book.

WOE: You have a long-standing attraction to the theme of Utopia that surfaces in your writings and classes. I am particularly intrigued by the use of "Protest Rights," which you encouraged students to use in your "Utopias" class. Can you explain how this works and what you've gained from this pedagogical approach?

SHOR: "Protest rights" is a risky approach for me and for the students, so I have to keep encouraging them to do it in class and keep encouraging myself to tolerate it. Students exercise protest rights when they stand out from the rest of the class, identify themselves as critics of the learning process under way, and exercise their authority to propose alternatives to our immediate and long-term syllabus. They intervene in the syllabus or the class hour if they object to the way things are going. While students are used to sabotaging teachers and classes furtively or negatively through all kinds of tricks, it's not easy or familiar for them to take constructive responsibility for critiquing the class and proposing a better way to do the work. In the beginning of class, I say to the students, "Are there any questions, objections, proposals, or suggestions? Does anyone have any comments left over from the last class?" I look around the room and make eye contact with students to let them know that I'm not hostile or impatient or in a hurry, but that I'm dead serious. Then I might call on one or two students to ask if they'd like to make any suggestions for changes.

When a student does complain, I don't know what I'm going to hear—who knows what they'll say? But whatever they say, my response is to avoid defensiveness, to ask questions to draw out further the meaning of their protest. I think it's risky, but it's important for democratic pedagogy. I don't think power sharing or negotiating the curriculum will be comfortable or easy; how can they be? We have a mass school system that's undemocratic from kindergarten through graduate school. Year after year, we are trained to be authority dependent, to accept the teacher's unilateral right to make the rules. Becoming critical and democratic involves growing pains. There's an unavoidable period of adjustment to democratic habits and critical thinking about the status quo, which will not be easy or comfortable.

WOE: You often talk about your status as a "tall, veteran, white, male professor" and about the authority these characteristics bring to the classroom. Further, in your writings you concern yourself with ways to "give" power to the students. Would you agree that a true disruption of the status quo, a genuine form of resistance, cannot be granted by the one who holds the authority but must be forcibly made?

SHOR: I have to say yes and no. My answer is contradictory because I try to be a critical-democratic teacher in an undemocratic, anti-critical school system and society. Top-down authority is the only form of power allowed to exist in this culture's institutions. I'm attempting an oppositional, democratic practice: to negotiate the curriculum with students, to use my institutional authority to transform unilateral governance into mutual authority. In trying this, I draw on the authority of being white, male, tall, thin, and a veteran professor, using those power identities to legitimize the project, to encourage students to take authority, share authority, use authority they never exercised before to control their education. Now, these social relations of learning are news to the students. Most of them have not experienced power sharing before.

Critical practices open the chance to develop alternative habits of thought, feeling, speech, action, and imagination. The classroom is a site where the social self is socially produced. Students spend 12,000 hours in classrooms by age eighteen, developing their social selves under the discipline of teachers, texts, tests, syllabi, tracking systems, bells, and routines like lining up for lunch or recess. So if I pursue a critical-democratic pedagogy that shares authority with students, I'm creating a local disruption in the development of students into the status quo.

WOE: One of the disruptive strategies you use in *When Students Have Power* is sitting next to the "Siberians"—those students who sit in the back of the room and refuse to participate. Your presence is intentionally intrusive to them, but their only power, their only form of resistance, is that they *can* sit away from you.

SHOR: That's true. Bourdieu and Passeron talk about symbolic violence, the violence of unilaterally imposed routines, rules, and institutional discourse. Even if I don't sit near the students, the learning process and my voice could still impose on them from the front of the room. If I place my body near them, it creates a kind of physical discomfort, but if I stood at the front of the room and taught traditionally, they'd still be under the discipline of my authority and voice, so it's not like I remove intrusion by moving away from them. One student put it this way in her first-day advice to me on how she wanted the course to be run: "Don't kill us with your voice."

By getting close I create a local disturbance that has some possibilities. I'm trying to create an opening for change. Now, some students are uncomfortable and would rather not have me sit near them. But keep in mind it's also uncomfortable for me because I have to surrender that symbolic proscenium arch at the front of the room separating teacher space from the students'. I'm taking risks by leaving the space of authority to go into the student space. I'm trying to cope with my discomforts and hope they can cope with theirs.

WOE: Many of your works address the importance of aesthetics and its influence on the ability of students to learn. Further, you claim that mass colleges were intentionally designed without aesthetic considerations but rather as functional institutions designed to create workers rather than thinkers. How might teachers transcend the bleakness of urban colleges?

SHOR: I suppose you might say, "What you see is what you are." Handsome environs send a message to the people there that they count. Aesthetic surroundings as the routines of your life allow people to grow up thinking they are the best, they deserve the best, they should expect the best. This is the developmental impact of aesthetics, to pull people into differing expectations given the place they start out in life. In this regard, I have always taught in the low-rent district of the academy. I can't possibly rebuild the ugly functionalist surroundings, but I can use them as texts to teach about class inequality. Why do some students go to handsome schools while most attend drab institutions? In terms of aestheticizing the environment, as a teacher, I can aim for attractive social relations in class—friendliness, humor, concern. There are pleasures from human conversation I can aim for, but these exist within the limits of various unavoidable conflicts in the classroom—teacher–student, student–student, etc. And why not decorate our classrooms? One class took this on as a special project following a critical discussion of garbage.

WOE: You are an advocate of the use of peer groups as a "safe house," to use Mary Louise Pratt's term, a space away from teacher talk and idiom. But writers like David Smit have pointed out that peer groups are often oppressive, with the dominant, often white male voices dominating those who already feel marginalized and who naturally retreat into silence. Given this, might you reconsider whether a "safe house" is possible, given the hegemony of patriarchy and heterosexism?

SHOR: We need a critical attitude toward the notion of "safe house." Safe houses, as one form of collaborative learning, can function as places where peers develop a discourse at some distance from the agendas of authority and from the impositions of such things as male domination, or white supremacy, or homophobia. But for a safe house to function in ways that empower rather than oppress students, they have to be organized with ground rules and with assessment of the process during and after their convocation in class. If male students silence female students in a student peer group, this is not a safe house. If upper-class women silence working-class women in an all-female group, then the supposed safe house is functioning in a class-oppressive way. Perhaps Pratt didn't adequately theorize the politics of the safe house, but that doesn't kill the value of the idea.

Identity groups organized for and by people who feel disempowered in class or in society are needed because we have behind us thousands of years of patriarchy, racism, homophobia, and class inequality. We are also divided by age, occupation, region, religion, ethnicity, and physical abilities. My dream is for solidarity across differences so that we can build a democratic society. But I can't imagine this project will be simple when every difference is used against us to divide and conquer.

Our other responsibility besides guaranteeing the integrity of safe houses is to guarantee the building of solidarity across differences, which means an equal focus on what we have in common, what most people have to gain by a common cause against the unequal society around us. The questions, then, are these: What do we have in common? How do we achieve solidarity across differences without denying differences? How can different constituencies be protected in their own safe houses without exposing themselves to sectarian isolation?

WOE: In *Critical Teaching and Everyday Life*, you address the distinction between elite students—who expect and receive a broad liberal education—and worker-students, whose colleges often offer certifications which emphasize skills training. Do you see the same emergence in the field of rhetoric and composition, with degrees in literature emphasizing the life of the intellectual, while rhetoric and composition is institutionally viewed as a service industry, with its emphasis on technical and professional writing programs?

SHOR: We have several divisions to think about. On the one hand, there is the history of "English" that is widely known by now thanks to the scholarship of Sharon Crowley, Bob Connors, Jim Berlin, Susan Miller, Donald Stewart, Dick Ohmann, and others. In a nutshell, their work has shown that literature counts, comp doesn't. The study of literature has historically subordinated composition/rhetoric, setting reading over writing, research over teaching, lecturing over workshops. More than a century ago, English departments based their professional identity in literature and relegated writing instruction to the infamously cranky freshman comp course. This labor-intensive, highly profitable course has been staffed by notoriously overworked and underpaid instructors (mainly women). The field of comp/rhet is still struggling with the super-exploitation of writing instructors as cheap labor and with the use of comp classes as work which supports literature majors en route to literary doctorates.

A second conflict is within the field of comp/rhet itself. On the one hand, comp/rhet has emerged as a serious professional research community in the past thirty years, with many good journals, conferences, professional organizations, and graduate degree programs. The problem is that the high-status research layer of comp/rhet exists in a protected, elite corner separate from the vast enterprise of writing instruction carried out by exploited cheap labor.

Then there is another division in the field between those comp/rhet teachers/scholars who assert that all teaching methods are always already political and those who insist that they are only teaching good writing and are not political in their various approaches to this apparently neutral goal. Of course, I stand with those who understand all pedagogy and all discourse as situated in a social context which makes it political. As to the exploitation of cheap labor, I propose that all teaching positions be full time with full benefits. If any teachers want to work less than full time, they can do so at their choice, dividing full-time positions among themselves, with full-time benefits remaining for each writing instructor.

WOE: You don't think that will bankrupt universities?

SHOR: Bankruptcy is a bogus issue. Comp is a money-making operation. For example, when I visited Minnesota last year, where much-respected Comp Director Chris Anson was summarily replaced as the literature-based English Department forcibly took over comp, I was told that the comp program produced a million-dollar surplus for the university budget. How far might class size be reduced with that surplus? How many cheap part-time comp jobs might be converted into full-time ones with that million? Where is that million going now? It's produced by the underpaid labor of the graduate instructors and by the overcharged tuition billed to students. The money is there. The subordinate status of comp and the unorganized condition of comp instructors allow English departments and universities to take the money away, in colonial fashion.

Lack of money is a mythology imposed upon us. Corporations are recording handsome profits. Wall Street is at an all-time high. This is boom time for corporate America. During the 1980s when Reaganism was in high tide, the military budget was doubled from $150 billion to $300 billion a year. At the same time, we were told that money did not exist to finance smaller classes in public schools and to hire more teachers. Education, social services, the public sector, are all being starved out in a vast transfer of wealth from the bottom to the top.

I refuse to accept that there's not enough money in our fantastically wealthy society to finance high-quality education for all people, not just for the elite. I do not accept this myth of no money. We are fantastically wealthy. Enormous fortunes have been made in the last twenty years by all the wrong people. One percent of the population in the U.S. now controls 42 percent of the nation's wealth, twice what they controlled twenty years ago.

WOE: Gerald Graff claims that student mimicry is perhaps the first step toward acquiring intellectual power. You suggest that as teachers we need to look for a new critical language, a third idiom. Can't mimicry be a stepping stone for students? If they see that academic discourse is powerful, why then should they not seek to co-opt it and make it their own?

SHOR: What exactly does mimicry mean? Trying on a discourse for size? Experimenting with some phrases and sentence forms? I remember when I was nineteen and saw a Broadway production of James Baldwin's *Blues for Mr. Charlie*. Back home for the summer from college, back in the working-class South Bronx, I took out a pad and began writing a review of the play. I wrote for an hour or so in my room, crossed things out, changed phrases, tried to sound like a college person, etc., then went to sleep and left the pages on my dresser. My nosey Mom found them and read the lines. She was startled by my effort. She wondered how her son was able to produce a foreign discourse like that. I was trying to take a position on the Baldwin play, about racism in America, in an idiom I didn't really control. What came first was my project, that is, my relationship to racism and the play, which set the context for my exploration of an academic idiom. This situated project involving my connection to racism is not exactly an episode in mimicry.

I'd say that mimicry is closer to memorization, which is technical and not situated in a theme or project. Because the theme or project inspiring a language act must be considered first, I don't agree with Graff about mimicry or with David Bartholomae about students having to invent the university by mimicking the academic discourse of their teachers. What matters is not that the students mimic phrases but rather that they have a purpose embedded in their action. Do they sustain critical reflection about some material in language that is authentic to their moment of development? Technical writing skills should not be taught in isolation from a thematic context that gives them meaning. Writing should not be mystified as a set of specific skills.

Students have been taught wrongly that you can study techniques separate from purpose, from thematic interests, from ideas, from a goal, from a social objective. Human learning, thinking, and communication work best in specific contexts with specific projects or purposes in mind. General writing or thinking skills can't be deployed to make students better writers. Literacy develops through performance in contexts that are meaningful to people. Disembodied language arts—writing instruction based in grammar or paragraph practice—are not effective ways to develop technical skill.

WOE: You and Freire often talk about the notion of "rigor" in critical pedagogy, and you define rigor as "the power to know": an active search for making knowledge. I'm sure the irony does not escape you that liberatory classrooms are often characterized by the media as intellectually lax and nebulous. To what do you attribute this characterization?

SHOR: Progressive education has always been condemned as softheaded, not skills oriented and not based on the transfer of core knowledge. In the literature on critical pedagogy, there is ample documentation of the rigor in these classrooms. Critical pedagogy is not permissive. Students and teachers are not free to do what they want whenever they want. It's a negotiated relationship in the critical study of subject matters.

WOE: One pedagogical strategy you advise is "keeping your plans small and loose," adapting your curriculum to meet the needs of your audience. While keeping yourself open to students' needs obviously makes for a more vigorous dialogue, it also has to be somewhat disconcerting when you need to continually adjust the curriculum.

SHOR: Absolutely. That's one of the hardest practices for a teacher using dialogic pedagogy: conceptualizing for yourself the meaning of what you're seeing, observing, hearing, and reading so that you can organize it and pose problems to the students and then pull the inquiry to the next level of investigation. In the beginning, trying to speak to the students' learning unfolding in class, I felt like I was swimming in madness, trying to figure out what was going on. I still feel as if I'm trying to catch up to a conversation one step ahead of me. I keep trying to speed up my conceptualization so that I get a feel for what's happening and can pull out a problem to pose. I wouldn't presume to say that this is easy, but I always find it very exciting.

WOE: Ideally, how would you suggest graduate students be mentored?

SHOR: First, it's very important that graduate students follow their interests. My graduate students should not study critical democratic pedagogy because that's what I write books about. I would feel that it's inauthentic and undemocratic for me to impose my career interests, political interests, and orientations on them. They know who I am and what I do. If they want to go into this work, they'll let me know. It's important that graduate professors do not produce clones of themselves. We often send them out into the field as salespeople for our projects. That's not really mentoring: it's like being dragooned into a sales staff. That's not democratic. That's a corporate model of careerism—staking out territory and advancing a professor's career.

Instead, to be a mentor, I have to see what really interests them; they're adults, they're smart people, they've been through a lot of school, they've had a lot of experience. Mentoring should not be based on my dominating the students' career development. They should make their own choices.

Graduate students should attend professional conferences when they can afford it. They should also put on conferences locally, to begin practicing their own presentations. We should talk to them about institutional politics, about being a faculty member and how you can become an agent for change in the department and the institution, about what it means to get an article or book published. And we have to work hard at developing graduate students as rhetors who speak and write powerfully, who present their work to each other as often as possible for feedback. Graduate school is a long, authority-dependent experience where it's hard to assert your own development while working with a powerful doctoral faculty that has so much power over your fate. For this reason, graduate students should have their own organizations inside the program and sit on all committees making policy. I urge my graduate students to finish their Ph.D.s as soon as possible because graduate school is an infantilizing experience.

WOE: What projects are you currently developing?

SHOR: I've been collecting examples of how teachers in diverse settings practice critical pedagogy, so I plan to publish a follow-up volume or two to my book *Freire for the Classroom*. The field of critical pedagogy has expanded remarkably since then, and I'm really excited about the varieties of critical teaching I've been able to gather. In addition, I'm getting more interested in working-class studies. I want to write about working-class culture and pedagogy, perhaps experimenting with the discourse, doing a photo-ethnography as well as a study of working-class culture connected to my autobiography as an academic who comes from working-class roots. I'd like to draw some lessons for a working-class pedagogy from these explorations. My starting question is whether it is possible to recover a useful notion of class that can be integrated with the notions of gender, multiculturalism, sexuality, and ethnicity that have emerged in the last twenty years.

WOE: You have a distinct interest in what you've termed "comic styles of pedagogy," which you say is essential for a liberatory classroom. What strategies do you employ to encourage humor?

SHOR: I like comedy, and I try to take a humorous attitude toward the work that I'm doing and my role in the classroom. I'm doing an ethnography project now with my freshman comp class where I ask them to notice what anthropologists call entry and exit rituals. To focus their attention, I used the entry and exit rituals of our own class. One day, arriving to class, I opened the door part way, poked my head in, and yelled out, "The teacher is here! I'm about to join the entry ritual! I'm going to close the door and join the entry ritual, so please notice what we do and yell out loud 'Over!' when you think the entry ritual ends and the class proper begins." This seemed hilarious to me and to them too, provoking self-awareness about routinely invisible behavior, making implicit experience boldly explicit. This is humorous, I think. I feel kind of clownish when I disrupt routines and expectations. I'm so dead serious in class that without humor I'd find it unbearable to be there myself. Critical pedagogy and sharing authority are anxiety-producing, risk-taking adventures requiring deep concentration by the teacher and unusual responsibilities for the students. Doing this should not be one-dimensionally serious, so humor is a texture of relief. Overall, though, there is a hilarious quality to these changes, which I don't know quite how to put in words. I find something comic in questioning the status quo. It seems funny to me, in a Utopian mouse-that-roared way. Yet I feel drawn to it, even responsible for asking, saying, and doing critical things.

WALTER NASH

With a writer's love of language, Walter Nash's work has bridged the fields of rhetoric, language study, and literature, from translations of Horace to appreciations of graffiti. In his interdisciplinary writing, Nash has analyzed all manner of texts, connecting linguistic and rhetorical patterns to their social functions and the process of writing. In his important 1985 study of comic discourse, The Language of Humour, *he notes "in humour, the diversities of our living and thinking tumble together in patterns adventitious and freakish and elegant, like the elaborate conformations of a kaleidoscope."*[1] Rhetoric: The Wit of Persuasion *(1989) defines rhetoric as an "ordinary human competence"*[2] *and emphasizes that it is an act of "witting" because "it seeks assiduously to involve an accomplice in its designs."*[3]

In 1990, Nash co-wrote with Ronald Carter Seeing Through Language: Styles of English Writing, *in which he discusses "the cline" (a favorite word of his own devising) of literariness—that literary and nonliterary writing exist on a continuum. Just before this interview appeared in 1992, he had published* An Uncommon Tongue: The Uses and Resources of English, *a collection of essays and lectures that examine language usage as a question of creativity rather than following rules, as well as* Language and Creative Illusion, *which explores the imaginative as well as editorial processes that go into composing a text. In 2014, he and David Stacey, his WOE interviewer, released* Creating Texts: An Introduction to the Study of Composition, *an updated edition of Nash's 1980* Designs in Prose. *In* Creating Texts, *Nash illustrates his integration of close textual analysis, writing, reading, and teaching, when he writes, "Our progress in composition is a consequence of noticing . . . What remains beyond that is the effort to confirm intuition, to elevate noticing into knowledge."*[4] *Nash is a co-founder of PALA (the Poetics and Linguistics Association) and Emeritus Professor of Modern English Language at the University of Nottingham.*

—Sophia Bamert

1 Nash, Walter. *The Language of Humour*. New York: Routledge, 2013: (xi). Print.
2 Nash, Walter. *Rhetoric: The Wit of Persuasion*. Oxford: Blackwell, 1989: (ix). Print.
3 Ibid. (1).
4 Nash, Walter and David Stacey. *Creating Texts: An Introduction to the Study of Composition*. New York: Routledge, 2014: (17–18). EPUB.

"Incertitude's Her Element"

David Stacey

Spring 1998

WOE: Let's start biographically. You were born in the north of England?

NASH: I was born and brought up in a place called Barrow in Furness (which the inhabitants pronounce to rhyme with "furnace," though the BBC affects a more sophisticated style, with the accent on the second syllable, FurNESS). Furness is a little peninsula up in the northwest of the country, the area that's now called Cumbria. Originally, going back say 150 years, this was purely pastoral country, known for little more perhaps than being a stronghold of Quaker religion. It was the back of nowhere, but in the 19th century, somebody discovered a process for converting the heavy iron content of the soil into steel.

This is the way the Barrow Hematite Steel Company started, which was then the first of the big industries in the town, and that was followed presently by the shipbuilding industry. So throughout all my youth, there were only three things a boy could do: he could go into the steelworks; he could go into the shipyard, where my father worked all his life; or he could get a clerical job in the town hall. And the whole point of an education was to get that job in the town hall, because the other two weren't to be thought of. The other two were for boys who "didn't make it." They became apprenticed as carpenters, as shipwrights, as marine engineers, as fitters, like my father. Although in a way my father had made it. He was quite a clever boy at school. And he left school when he was twelve years old. It was a circumstance of the family. They needed to put him to some kind of work. Believe it or not, he'd been very good at school in Latin, and still had, when I was a boy, a whole bound set of Dickens, which he'd been given as a Latin prize at 12 years old. Then he left, and he had to go into the shipyard, and that, over 50 years, just ground him into ghostliness.

My mother left school when she was eight. To go into farm service. After a year or two in farm service, she got a superior job as a maid in a doctor's house in a place called Clitheroe. Really she had no childhood. She was already a bound servant from the age of eight onwards. My parents were of different and complementary temperaments. My father was in many ways a grave, sometimes sententious man, with language to match. But he could sometimes burst out into almost rebellious fits of humor—kind of Pythonesque, in their inversions of their own solemnity. So he could be like

Mr. Micawber, who suddenly realizes that he's being Mr. Micawber, and starts to laugh at himself.

My mother was a totally merry sort of temperament. Merry and deeply sentimental. She felt other people's troubles, particularly for children. She would often weep but she also loved to laugh. Goethe, talking about his own parents, says his father was a very grave sort of man but his mother had a deep *lust zu fabulieren.* My mother was magic at telling stories. She was ashamed of what she thought of as her own illiteracy, but she wasn't illiterate at all. It was just that she didn't know where to put the commas sometimes. Set her to tell a story and you would have ten minutes of magic because she instinctively knew how to tell a story. The two people together were wonderful parents to have.

Also the town itself was an influence upon me in this way: because of its industrial growth, it became a rather grubby and depressing town. It was always depressed because it was so far away from anything else. There was a communication problem, which meant that businesses didn't settle in the town and so on. Then I have these pictures in my mind of five and six o'clock in the afternoon with troops of clothcapped men coming home from the yard or the steelworks; ditto at six o'clock in the morning, the same troops of cloth-capped men going to the yard or the steelworks. It wasn't a very inspiring town in that way. Everybody really longed to get out of it. It had a good library, to which my father introduced me, early on.

WOE: You imply there was no escape from this town, and yet you did escape. You went to Cambridge.

NASH: I went to a grammar school in Barrow—like an American high school except that in those days, not everyone went to the grammar school. There were competitive examinations at the age of eleven; those who passed them went to the grammar school. The rest, the unfortunate, went to a local college, a day college, called a technical college. That was in preparation for a life in the shipyard, mostly, or in the steelworks. I was one of the lucky ones. I went to the grammar school, and in due course went all the way through the school to the sixth form, which brings you up to the age of sixteen or seventeen. In those days the only way of going to a university was by more competitive examinations. They had so-called "scholarship" examinations, particularly in the Oxford and Cambridge colleges, and you went up to Oxford or Cambridge and sat for these. It wasn't simply one paper, you were there for several days. If you were lucky you might get some kind of scholarship.

I went several times to Oxford and Cambridge on this kind of hunt, before eventually I won a scholarship. That in itself wasn't enough at that time to fund a poor boy through the university. So I had to go to other places where they offered scholarships, and there were all sorts of places that offered scholarships at that time. Monetary awards to sons of poor clergymen, for example. Finally I got enough money together to go to Cambridge, but I didn't get a chance to take that up for more than two terms, when I was conscripted, drafted into the Navy. Going to Cambridge in the first place, that was an escape.

WOE: What year did you start there?

NASH: That would be in 1944. Shortly thereafter, though, as I said, I spent two and a half years in the Navy, part of which took me out to the far East, to Ceylon, now Sri Lanka. I don't know that this was a terrifically formative experience because frankly, being in the armed forces is if anything a degenerative experience, but it made me realize actually that I was being present at the beginning of the decline of the British Empire. The whole of that show was beginning to go downhill. That was of importance for my later career because I spent a lot of my time teaching foreign students, "selling" the English language abroad. The old imperial attitudes were already going at that time, but out there, in Ceylon, I had glimpses of this. Of what that was like, and also of the kind of casual arrogance of the military. I don't want to get into that because it sounds as if you're running your own country down, but I was aware of these things.

There's a typical episode from being out there in Ceylon: I still have a book, in the flyleaf of which there's a stamp, which says something like this: "East Indies Station, Fleet Library, Return or Renew within Two Months." It's now fifty years late—a bit late I suppose to renew it, but the book is *The Sacred Wood* by T.S. Eliot. Finding it on my shelf the other day reminds me that at that time I had begun to take an interest in what were then very modern trends in criticism.

That was the escape. When I came back after the Service, I never really returned to Barrow in Furness, except on visits. Something had been broken. I had been cut off from that, and it had been left to float around, as it were.

WOE: When you returned from the Service you came back to Cambridge, in 1946. Were you able to take up where you left off or was everything different there, too?

NASH: It was different in that there was a new social mix in Cambridge after the war. It was no longer as it had been when I was trotting around looking for scholarships. It was no longer the natural home of the public-school boy, to which occasionally a few scholarship boys like myself were admitted. When I returned, it turned out that all that effort to amass scholarship awards which would just about get me through the system was unnecessary because a grateful government was handing out grants like Caesar to his veterans. So people who wanted to go to Cambridge and could satisfy the basic admission requirements could go. There were a lot of new arrivals, new men, like me.

WOE: Like the G.I. Bill in the States?

NASH: Exactly. But it wasn't yet time for the "new woman." That came later—it was still very much a male society.

WOE: This puts you squarely in the generation of Larkin and Amis. You mention Larkin often in your writing, but never Amis. Did you feel more for Larkin?

NASH: Certainly I feel more for Larkin as a poet than for Amis. Curiously, I didn't start to read Amis until I had come down from Cambridge and had done a stint at the University of London as an assistant lecturer, and then went abroad. It was then that I read his first novel, *Lucky Jim*, the hero of which is, of course, an assistant lecturer. This book made me howl with laughter because so many of Jim Dixon's experiences as an assistant lecturer were mine in exaggerated form. But I recognized this and felt an affinity, felt the same sort of rebelliousness about the pomposities of the academic community. And I enjoyed Dixon's or Amis's honesty, which some people found outrageous.

WOE: My students always respond to the juvenile strain in both Larkin and Amis. I think of it as a quasi-universal feeling for revolt or rebellion, but you could feel it more directly on your own pulse, I imagine. There was a lot of change going on.

NASH: That juvenile strain is often there, but it is often the exasperated response of some person who can't find a way of making a dint on the pomposity and stupidity of the opposition. And the only way finally is to somehow blow a raspberry, or to fart, or to cock a snook [*puts his thumb on his nose, and waves his fingers*]. It's to do that, you know. It's the last resort of an exasperated sensibility.

WOE: In your book on comic discourse you demonstrate an acute feeling for the form and format of verbal jokes and humorous narrative. In both the influence of your parents and in your appreciation of an Amis-like anti-academic ethos, you can perhaps see a source for your interest in humor and comedy.

NASH: A lot of it comes from my parents, from my father's way of telling a joke and my mother's way of telling a story. If I have humor, quite a lot of it comes from the defensive position of the underdog. I have noticed often in my life that superior people, or "top dogs," don't have humor. They may have a kind of quasi-humorous condescension, but they don't have humor. We boys from Barrow in Furness, of which there are millions and millions in the world, need this humor to defend, to make the opposition back off, to comfort ourselves in our own plight.

WOE: That feeling attaches itself to a political awareness in your writing, perhaps not as explicit there as in a good deal of contemporary teaching and writing, but there nonetheless. A reader knows in a book like *Seeing through Language* that you are liberal by inclination, probably a Labour voter: you attach the humor to politics in a way that a reader can detect.

NASH: With my academic or scholarly books, as I got older I found myself getting more explicit about political stance because I felt that I had less and less to lose. When you're an academic of say fifty-five (which strikes me today as enormously young), you have got to watch your tongue. When you're an old geezer of seventy—what the hell? If you want to make a lefty statement you can make a lefty statement, you know? What's going to happen to you? Very often what I was writing about didn't necessarily involve politics directly, so the political hint came in through some crevice in the argument or wording.

WOE: Just as often, a reader detects that political hint coming up through some stated or hinted dissatisfaction with academic politics, the politics of English departments. You have experiences that many young English professors across the world can identify with. Especially American academics interested in rhetoric and composition can, I think, identify with some of the battles you have fought over the years in developing the institution as it went along lines of literature, rhetoric, language teaching, linguistics.

NASH: What happened in these developments is that you get people, rather like in a gold rush, staking claims, establishing patches. "This is my patch!" comes from policeman slang, you know? "You don't come onto my patch!" This leads to all sorts of absurdities of infighting and all sorts of silly acts of injustice in academic departments. Academics will not consider the importance of that theological principle, "Ye are all members one of another."

WOE: In your personal life, you solved a lot of problems by writing your way through them, the way humor helps people surmount obstacles. Is there a way in which writing solved problems for you?

NASH: Yes. When I got back one of the first essays that I submitted to a tutor at Cambridge (I forget now what the essay was on, but it was a very long one) the first seven pages were crossed through! There was a line across the top of page eight and my tutor's comment: "Your essay begins here." That is an experience I've had often since then, except that now I am my own red ink. I am my own tutor. I have enough maturity, enough knowledge of myself to be able to say, "This chapter begins here. You have simply been clearing the ground, finding your way through the woods."

WOE: Would you say that it takes a lifetime to learn to write? It was obviously painful to get this kind of feedback from a tutor. As you mature, do you learn more about yourself as a writer?

NASH: [*Pause*] That's the important thing, I think. Sometimes I look at things I wrote thirty years ago and I think, "Well, I'm no better a writer now than I was then." But then I think, "On the other hand, I know myself better now then I did then. I know myself as a writing personality better." So that I'm aware of the validity or nonvalidity of certain choices or options that arise in the process of writing. It's like a manybranched tree or a many-forked river: you keep coming to the junctions where you have to choose one way or the other. I'm better at doing that now than I was then. To that extent I've learned something about writing—in learning something about myself, in learning to theorize without theorizing. You form a kind of personal theory stored in your intellect, about how it should go. Not really a theory but a set of maps that you have in your head, the experience of past journeys.

WOE: As an American coming to your books, I sense this learningabout-writing-from-experience. It seems that perhaps the most important thing you've learned is that writing is a process. That through writing you do discover things. "Seeing takes time," as Georgia O'Keefe once said.

NASH: Yes that's right. An extreme instance of this experience is the feeling that you are certainly going to have one day, that *having written* a book, you then say to yourself, "*Now* I am in a position to write that book!"

WOE: In *Designs in Prose* and also in your book on usage, you make reference to your own travails with writing, and in other books you describe writing more objectively—the structure of a classical speech or patterns in new rhetorical forms such as the singles ad. It seems to me that you enjoy describing discernible steps, structures, patterns and forms in new rhetorics—in many different kinds of texts. Does this interest in structure come from your own experiences writing, as well as from your reading of Quintilian and Cicero, Aristotle and Plato?

NASH: I have a tendency to look for a pattern in everything. That may be something kind of deep rooted in my personality. I've got to know how things work. I feel secure when I do that. I feel that I *know*, in the best sense of the word "knowledge," when I know what the pattern is. I cheerfully assign pattern to everything, when it may well be that there is no real pattern to discern, or the pattern is something in my own mind that I'm imposing on whatever it is I'm observing or writing about.

This urge to look for a pattern derives more immediately from my earlier studies in linguistics and language and from my readings in the writings of linguists who are not solely concerned with morphology, the actual structure of language, but with relating language to certain functions in society or even in aesthetics. That often involves them in devising a patterned approach. And so I suppose I was tacitly trained by reading these people into asking the first question: What is the pattern?

Show me the pattern and I'll show you the principle. Show me the principle and I'll explain the work. That kind of thing in all sorts of ways got educated into me.

WOE: I often find in your work on linguistics an appreciative sense for the social experience of patterns. What's being explored in your type of language study is a discovery process that's attached to function in social contexts. And that is what resonates in your work with people like me, trying to discover teaching processes for writing.

NASH: What you are describing here is Firthian linguistics. As you say, it "resonates" through the writings of lots of people who may never have read the writings of J.R. Firth. It's just something that's in the air or in the blood, something you breathe in if you happen to be studying language matters in England. Firth was our first Professor of General Linguistics at University College London. He got his chair in 1946, the year I came out of the Navy. He held it for ten years or so and was a very influential figure. The next generation of English linguists were practically all Firthians.

Firth's position as a linguist was that the business of the linguist was to describe meaning. How to mean. How things mean. He had a little mantra or tag—"Meaning is function in context." *Meaning* is how what you were saying or writing *worked* in the particular context, usually a societal context. He was associated with the anthropologist Bronislav Malinowski, who gives us the phrase "context of situation." You can see how this is coming on to aesthetics and writing and so on. This is the Firthian position. One of Firth's most distinguished pupils, M.A.K. Halliday, highlighted a Firthian interest in the functions of language in interpersonal dealings. The context must always be there; together with the structure, it makes meaning.

This thinking had a great influence on me when I came to write about stylistics and writing.

WOE: This may be why I sense in you and other British writers a feel for language rather than a fear of language. In the U.S. there's been a real dissociation of language study from rhetoric and the study and teaching of writing because of a tradition of prescriptive usage and a study of language divorced from context.

NASH: Chomskyan linguistics and generative grammars have tended to do this. I don't want to decry Chomskyan linguistics, there is no doubt that it is an enormous cleaning out of tradition in linguistics. Chomsky opened our eyes again. He gave importance to *thought*, which linguists like Bloomfield tended to dismiss, because of a behaviorist approach to language. But what happens with transformational linguistics is that all the time you're dealing not so much with language itself as with potential or invented examples. You're not dealing with real or natural language, or whatever you'd like to call it, but systemic or Hallidayan or Firthian linguistics is always dealing with it.

Here's a little story about my early days as a lecturer, in about 1949. Firth had been in place for about three years. He was giving some lectures on Modern English at University College. A colleague of mine at King's College, where I worked, got a couple of tickets to one of his lectures. As we were going there, my colleague, who was very much a traditionalist, a medievalist, an old-style philologist, said, "He's a funny fellow, this Firth, you know. He gets all his examples out of the morning paper!" Nowadays that would not be considered at all unusual. We all get our examples out of the morning paper because people like Firth have conditioned us to look at a society and individual relationships in society, at the validity of different types of discourse. My colleague felt you could only get a valid example out of, say, Jane Austen. Or a literary classic, a work of the canon.

Firth said, "Oh no! All language is interesting in its varying contexts." There are rules of engagement in different contexts. You can break these rules of engagement for satirical or humorous purposes, as Monty Python does, for example. Firthian linguistics opened the eyes of subsequent generations of academics interested in language who now take these things pretty much for granted.

WOE: I'm thinking about your colleague who takes his examples from classic or canonical texts, and the difference he encounters in Firth. At the most recent PALA Conference, Ron Carter talked about finding form in our everyday talk. The thought occurred to me that at a certain level of college teaching in the U.S.—about halfway between remedial and first-year composition—trying to teach academic writing to people who come to college from "non-traditional" backgrounds, we do this all the time. We often use the students' own experience to get a student writer to be fluent with language, and *there* take our example. *There* is where we start to discover shape and form and shaping and forming. Shaping at the point of utterance, as James Britton calls it.

NASH: I referred earlier to my mother and her ability as a storyteller. She left school at eight and so had no formal academic training at all. Yet she had an intuitive way with a story. I regret that I have no record of one of her stories. If you had one of her stories, it would have its own rhetoric. It would be like classical rhetoric in some ways because there are, I believe, universals in the way the human mind works in confrontation with its experience. But also there would be inventive things, discoveries of her own.

In a similar comparison, we were all interested in the language of conversation back in my early days. We were disabusing ourselves of notions of conversation found in books in order to know it better. We were using tape recorders to collect genuine examples of conversation, with all the switches, the loopbacks, the pauses, and hesitations of naturally occurring conversation.

Now doing that a lot taught me, inversely, a lot about literary dialogue, about what happens when talk is put on the page. And I concluded that actually we're talking about two rather different things here. Conversation is of this moment. Our conversation here and now is affected by you, by your responses to me; those factors affect the length of sentences, the shape which utterances take, and so on. But literary dialogue is an artifice, the purpose of which is often to supply an episode in a story. The author, instead of writing a description, of say an action, writes a dialogue. This supplies both the action and a commentary on the action.

WOE: You have described the process of an interview as "talking myself into talking the way I write myself into writing." I think you've produced what has to be about the most enlightened book on English usage ever written, precisely because of this sense that writing is a discovery process. Americans, in my opinion, are not used to books on usage that are built atop this assumption. They are used to books on usage that prescribe usage. In your book on usage you call that the usage trap.

NASH: This reminds me of a time when a publisher I won't name wrote to me to say that they were looking for a small book on usage that would be helpful to a student. Randolph Quirk directed them to me. They sent me a copy of Strunk and White, the little American book called what, *Elements of Style*? Whatever it's called, it's simply a makeup of Strunk's classroom notes with a bit at the end by E.B. White (which I happen to think is the most valuable part of the book).

Well, they wanted something like this. Something which would lay down concrete rules about usage. "Don't use this word, use that word." "Be careful how you use the word 'why.'" I had a hard time with this because every time I drafted something that I hoped would please them, I would get a sarcastic letter back, saying "You're talking nonsense! We don't want this talky nonsense. *This* is what we want. We want a British Strunk and White. It sells so well in America, it will sell as well here!" In the end we had to kiss and part. I couldn't write that kind of book, and they didn't want the kind of book I consider myself capable of writing.

English Usage followed on after that. It was the experience of finding myself at odds this way that led me to write down the sort of book I could do.

WOE: Throughout your books you often return to the subject of the teaching of writing. From literature to language to writing, in and out, back and around, on and on again. How do you see these different fields within a discipline? Rob Pope says that in a few years we'll all call it English Studies. We've always been an interdiscipline, according to Pope, and yet we're now moving into a period of interest in creative and critical things to do with many different kinds of texts. How have you worked out relationships between the different parts of the field?

NASH: What I have done has arisen, in part, out of professional necessity, both in my early studies and in the early part of my career when I was teaching abroad. I studied Old English and Germanic Philology. One of the values of *Beowulf* was realizing that I could not understand this poet simply by referring to the glossary or even simply referring to the very best available grammar of Old English.

I had to start to know something about the society and the culture in which this poem existed and grew up. And also I had to start to form a notion of the aesthetics of that particular kind of literature or poetry. It feels very strange for an English student going back to *Beowulf* because the aesthetic presuppositions of that poem are very different from those of say Romantic poetry, which is the staple food for people at school. If you are interested in the neoclassical period, Dryden and Pope, the Augustans, and then going back to the Medieval literature and Old English, you have to become more and more interested in the relationship between writing and culture. My own interest in this kind of thing was subsequently strengthened by the kind of linguists I chose to read. I began looking for a pattern again.

It began to seem to me, particularly when I was teaching in Sweden, that I had to perform that task on behalf of my own language: demonstrate the language *and also* how the language worked in certain ways and situations. There were three inter-related things to work with. There was the structure of the language—the grammar and lexicon. There was function, which I learned about from Firth and Co. And of course the third point, the aesthetic principles.

After Sweden (where I did a lot of reading), these three things seemed indispensable to any meaningful study of the English language. This was very unlike the position language had occupied in the curriculum when I was at university. There it occupied a very minor corner of the curriculum. The Medievalists were told it's okay when you teach *Beowulf* and Chaucer; otherwise keep out of it! The rest is the Great Kingdom of Literature.

WOE: And despite political squabbles and skirmishes you may have had with literary chauvinists, you still come across, to me at least, as a voice for unity. Some people in the U.S. want to break off from English, to start up departments of rhetoric and composition, or composition studies, or cultural studies.

NASH: There is always this kind of pressure and it is to be resisted. It is damaging, damaging to all concerned, even to those people who think they're getting rid of a nuisance. I learned a great deal in the sense of sympathies being affected and touched from the man I regard as the greatest of American classical linguists, Edward Sapir. If you read Sapir, you're not only reading about language. You find yourself reading about literature, about music, about anthropology. The anthropological interest has always been very strong in the writings of authors to whom I've been drawn. You find all this in Sapir, which makes him very inspiring. You *don't* get a direct lesson—"*This* is how you should teach composition"—or anything like that, but the ideas! His selected writings, edited by Mandelbaum in Berkeley about 1956, show the breadth of his interests. Here's a man whose central interest is in language, whose own language work, like that of many American linguists, is based on data from Amerindian tribes. He used his research and insights to think about language generally, about its social and aesthetic functions.

That's what I want to happen in an English department! It tends not to happen because people guard their patches, or because there is a kind of fear of disciplined language study.

WOE: That's especially so in certain quarters in composition studies in the States. Language study as so many people have experienced it is a rap on the knuckles from an angry schoolmarm.

NASH: That's right. And the word that always comes up is "arid" or "dry." Now the best linguists (like Sapir) would of course deplore an arid or dry language study.

There has been in the past here, a sort of assumption, a silly assumption in universities, that "if people haven't learned to write when they're at school, they ought not to be coming to the university at all" and maybe in very enlightened departments, "We'll give a few writing classes in the first year but not the second or third year or thereafter."

WOE: Rob Pope has quoted you at the very start of his book, *Textual Intervention*, taking a passage from your *An Uncommon Tongue* and using it to build "upon this rock," as it were. He builds the church of intervention upon your question "What if the text were different?" When you say, "What if?" or "As if," what comes to mind is one of the most successful recent parodies, loving parodies, of a literary classic, *Clueless*, which is a California-Speak version of *Emma*. And the tag line throughout is the girl saying in Valley-Talk, "As if!" "As if!" To a boy who asks her "Can I go out with you on Friday night?," she'll say, "As if!" It's a way of saying, "In your dreams!"

It's also, I think, the imaginative principle you worked out for Pope. There's something out there that you've tapped into with that passage in *An Uncommon Tongue*. Pope has picked it up as the principle of intervening of rewriting, of taking that text and changing it.

NASH: To me, of course, the question "What if the text were different?" is a major preoccupation. What is it that drives us to write? Why am I obsessed with writing? Why am I obsessed with the techniques of writing, even while I write, so that I reach the stage when I can say to myself as I write, "I'm writing this, I'm interested in it, and I am aware that I am writing this in this particular way."

WOE: And I think there's something here close to what we were talking about earlier: Your awareness of an oppositional stance to the normal expectations of academia. And an appreciation for the disruptions and inversions of humor. I heard you once say about something you'd been writing, "I can't get this published anymore because I keep making jokes and they won't let me do that!"

NASH: That's true [*laughing*]. I am haunted as an academic writer by my mother's love of laughter. My impulse is to make jokes and to talk about a serious subject through the medium of the joke, which is often the most insightful way of tackling it. A joke is often a door that will open up a whole new, serious track of discourse. How does my *Rhetoric* begin? (Quoting your own books is a terribly conceited thing to do!) "'I have designs on you,' as the tattooist said to his girlfriend." This propounds the scope of rhetoric so adroitly as to make further definition almost unnecessary. A colleague of mine, my oldest friend, commented on this when he said, "Only the old master from Barrow in Furness would dream of beginning a book on a serious academic topic with a joke."

I do this often and it's helpful to me because the joke lets me in. The joke is my heuristic device for my own purpose. But publishers look a bit cross-eyed at you, you know? *Language in Popular Fiction* almost couldn't get printed because of the rather elaborate joke of the aircraft, the flight from Britain to the United States, which to me was simply a framing device.

WOE: What are you working on currently?

NASH: A lot of the work I've been doing recently suggests the possibility of a reversion in studies of language and style to the study of the word, to a new kind of philology. (The original philology being lexicography, the tabling of word meanings, word derivatives, and so on.)

And the old philology was necessarily static. Even when a dictionary gives you not only a central meaning of a word but a number of derived meanings, then a number of technical meanings, that is still a kind of stasis. The very fact that you can give a central meaning suggests that stasis. Now the work I've been doing of recent months, over the last two years, indeed, particularly with newspaper discourse, suggests a more dynamic kind of philology, in which the word is not static but is rather like a particle in physics.

Physicists will tell you that you cannot define the position of a particle because it's in a sort of dance all the time, and you can only define it at any particular moment in relationship to the position of other particles. Now this kind of particle analogy suggests itself when you look at the way words are being used nowadays. I wrote an essay concerning current usages of the word "accept." And in fact you can trace it through the examples I collect; it moves from meaning "to receive" all the way through meaning "to reject." That particular particle is changing its position all the time, so you have to collect examples of the particular, of the context of the text, if you like, because there's a certain relationship within the text of one word to another and also to the context of the social function of this text. Every speech act is exactly as much reconstructive as it is deconstructive.

WOE: Would you describe yourself as a critical linguist?

NASH: I find it hard to find a label for myself. I don't really know what I am. I'd have to start writing and then I could tell you what I think I am. I think I'm a kind of born-again philologist. But in many ways in my writing and my work, I'm very traditional. Things I write about and think about, the ways I write and think, presuppose an adherence to the past, a feeling that the past remains important in the present and that we must keep the tradition there. But one can be, as it were, originally traditional, if you permit that oxymoron.

When I first published *Designs in Prose*, there were two reviewers who both made this point. And one of them said, if I remember correctly, "This is something, at one and the same time, highly original and completely traditional." And that pleased me not because I thought of it in that way, but because I realized that the reviewer had said something about my own temperament.

If you cut yourself loose from the past, you have no understanding of the present. This is the kind of point that's been made since Aristotle's time—that you understand the present in the light of the past and that if you cut yourself off from the past, you're in the state of bafflement. You don't know answers to the questions, "Where are we and how did we get here?"

WOE: When I read *Seeing through Language* I thought of Kenneth Burke's notion of literature as equipment for living, and also of a phrase I often hear nowadays, "doing things in and with language." This book has a practical and teachable content to it but it offers a disciplinary vocabulary, some very specific terminology. Roger Fowler in *Linguistic Criticism* suggests that the kind of language study that you've described as Firthian and Hallidayan is particularly useful because its terms have wide use, consensual validation.

NASH: A lot of things were already there to draw on, yes. When Ron Carter and I wrote *Seeing through Language*, to some extent we were devising ad hoc terminologies, but we always owned up to that. I think we did produce an ad hoc terminology. I don't know whether Firth is even mentioned in the book, but he and Halliday are there all the time, in intent and tendency, if you like.

WOE: As an American writing teacher interested in Burke, I was drawn to the book, but also as one working and hoping to find a practical, teachable method.

NASH: "Doing things with language." If I were to trace the history of that now common phrase, I would say that it went back to the title of a little book by the philosopher J.L. Austin, *How to Do Things with Words*. A lot of things in present-day language study have drawn on other disciplines, on sociology, on anthropology, on certain strands in philosophy of which Austin's speech act theory is one. And I think we began to talk about doing things with words and then, beyond that, doing things with language.

The notion of language as a tool is, I suppose, not a particularly new one. The classical rhetoricians would have recognized it. After all, they would've seen themselves as suggesting procedures for doing particular jobs. Western rhetoric began in fifth-century-B.C. Greece as a kind of aid for appellants in law court to present their cases. So that's doing things with language.

I don't always like the idea of doing things with language as the whole point of the thing or language as merely a tool because it seems to be saying, "Well, this is the justification for the study. You can do things with language." You know, otherwise there'd be no point in it! I'm not always doing things with language. I'm not always using language as a tool and I don't want other people to be forever doing things with language. Language is important to me, and this goes back to a much earlier point in the discussion: language is important to me heuristically as a mode of discovery. That's not so much doing things with language as using language to open yourself to insights, to open your mind to new connections and thought processes.

WOE: When you and Carter did that book, for whom did you write it?

NASH: We rather hoped that it would attract an audience in British universities and colleges of students in their second or third year of study. I don't think we would have ever thought of presenting it to first year, although there are things in it, themes in it, which might well be taken up in the senior years at school, at the high school or the ground school or whatever you call it. But as you know, publishers always ask this good question, "What is your audience? Who are you addressing?" I find this always a very awkward question. I never write anything with the intention of instructing anybody other than myself. But you can't tell a publisher, "Oh, I'm writing this to enlighten myself."

And, of course, it becomes a practical necessity, a stylistic necessity when you are writing, because the whole pitch, as teachers say, is determined by your envisaging some kind of audience. We would say perhaps the final year of A-level studies. I don't know whether it would have the same pitch in the United States.

WOE: Yes, and it's a whole different game too, a scientific rationalization of readership, which publishers are interested in, while you're more interested in discovering something important to you as a writer.

NASH: One thing I discovered very early is that publishers are not interested or convinced if you say, "I'm hoping for a general readership." One publisher, years ago, told me in so many words, "There is no such thing as a general reader."

WOE: In *Seeing through Language*, you and Ron were interested in literariness?

NASH: We got in quite a lot of trouble with the literary people about this because I don't think they could accept the notion of a tendency, a cline. There is a cline from the obviously literary all the way down to the obviously nonliterary. So there is such thing as literariness. And I think that the literature people dislike that, and we took some flak, I believe, on that.

WOE: Can I take a copy of a poem too, to go with this interview?

NASH: Of course, yes. You can have this one, "A Moment by the Acantilado." Let me do the explaining first and then read it.

I suppose that, for most of my life at the back of my mind always, there has been the question of certainty, degrees of certainty about our experience of thinking, about anything in life, prospects in life . . . life in general. Because it has always struck me that all the time we want to walk on a firm floor, you see. We want to have firm ground underneath us.

That kind of image of progress, both material and spiritual progress, runs throughout one's automatic idiom, so to speak. How again and again in life it has seemed to me that there is not firm ground, that we are always on a kind of fluent, ever-changing surface, that the only certainty is uncertainty, and that you must learn to live in uncertainty because the only true freedom is the ability to accept uncertainty. The image that keeps coming back to me is the image of a gull on the sea, a gull which has been flying and comes down to rest on the sea, because I've seen this so often. The bird just rests easily on the wave. And it's remarkable, really, when you consider how fragile the gull is. It's just a little bundle of feathers.

But it's not asking that it should be a master of this medium or that its certainties should be there for it all the time, like the firm ground. It rides easily on the current and on the wave. And this image comes into a poem I wrote some time ago called "A Moment by the Acantilado." The Acantilado is a great curtain wall of cliffs in Tenerife. They're about 1,000 feet high. They drop sheer into the sea. They go on for about ten miles, and in this poem I'm looking at the Acantilado, which is a sort of image of the most stubborn kind of certainty in poems. And also looking at the sea which is an image of, so to speak, permanent impermanence.

And on the sea, on the day when I conceived this poem, I could see a fisherman in his boat and also a single, solitary seagull out in the bay. Some of the poem is about the fisherman and some about the gull, and some about me asking, "What is life all about? Can I live with this uncertainty?" And this is the stanza about the gull:

But the gull that floats alone in the lee of the huge rock,
A fragile pinnace of feathers, is more at home in her dwelling,
Tenanted unconcernedly on the multiforming swell
That gathers and folds like a press, stretches and tugs like a rack;
Incertitude's her element; she keeps no account of what
The tale of moment by moment will bring; hope and despair
Are foreigners from the dry domain of human feeling; her airy
Trust in the tides of sky and sea shifts not a whit.

DAVID BARTHOLOMAE

David Bartholomae's work articulates a clear pedagogical role for the composition classroom: to prepare students to do academic work—a stance that contrasts with the expressivists' idea of a hands-off teacher allowing students to find their voice through writing groups. Bartholomae's response to the expressivist pedagogy is best articulated in "Writing With Teachers: A Conversation with Peter Elbow" (1995), where he argues that to ignore the academic power structure is dangerously idealistic and that teachers must take an active role assisting students as they struggle in the process of acquiring the authoritative voice of academic discourse. By taking such a role in the classroom, teachers make visible the power structure in and outside of the university, which students can then critically analyze through their reading of academic texts and their writing assignments about those readings.

Bartholomae's pedagogical stance is illustrated in his unique and widely used anthology Ways of Reading: An Anthology for Writers *(1987), written with Anthony R. Petrosky, which contains difficult and challenging readings that train students to accept difficulty as part of the academic reading process. Also written with Petrosky, the book* Facts, Artifacts and Counterfacts: Theory and Method for a Reading and Writing Course *(1986) describes their teaching method and provides their assignment sequence for first year composition. Bartholomae also expands on Mina Shaughnessy's work on error analysis in his seminal essay "The Study of Error" (1980), arguing that teachers should analyze students' error patterns not as failures but as attempts to imitate the language of academic discourse—and thus as part of the process of acquiring fluency in the language of academic discourse.*

Bartholomae is currently Charles Crow Chair of the English Department at the University of Pittsburgh. He has received numerous awards, including the 2006 CCCC Exemplar Award for outstanding contributions to the profession. His selected essays, Writing on the Margins: Essays on Composition and Teaching *(2005), includes this interview with WOE; it won the MLA's 2005 Mina Shaughnessy Prize for Outstanding Scholarly Book.*

—*Sarah Faye*

"Stop Being so Coherent"

John Boe and Eric Schroeder

Fall 1998

WOE: I'd like to start with my favorite question for a writer: How did you learn to write and care about writing, and what teachers influenced you along the way?

BARTHOLOMAE: When I was an undergraduate, no one would have ever accused me of being a good writer. I was not adept at it. I wasn't somebody who wrote a lot or wrote for pleasure. I was, however, going to become an English teacher because I was playing small-college football and my favorite football coach was an English teacher.

I think I probably learned the most about writing from the man who was the head of my graduate program at Rutgers, Richard Poirier. I was so enamored with the way he wrote that I wanted to write like that. He was formed out of the tradition of teaching at Amherst with Reuben Brower and a group of influential teachers, including Theodore Baird, Bill Coles, Tom Edwards, and Roger Sale. When Brower left Amherst for Harvard, Poirier went there to become part of the group teaching the Humanities 6 course. For this group, writing was fundamental to the teaching of literature, especially writing the short paper where you try to articulate a position in relation to a text. You would perform a short reading, and then your little short essay was itself close read. Usually the attempt was not to make you stylish, but to get all the crap out, to make your thinking sharper and more focused, to make you think about the consequences of the positions you had taken. I took an introduction to graduate studies with Poirier and wrote a lot. In graduate school, I experienced both the discipline and the routine of having to write a lot. I remember the kinds of comments I would get on my papers. But what I remember most is just really wanting to write the way he did.

The other great writing lesson I had was that I wrote my dissertation in England. I had one of the last of the NDEA fellowships, and so my wife and I went to Oxford. I was still a student at Rutgers, but we just wanted to be there—they had all the research facilities, and I thought, "Well, if I can write my dissertation in Oxford, why write in New Brunswick, New Jersey?" It meant that I wrote my whole dissertation without any interaction with my committee, and when I brought it back my chair just read about halfway through it and said, "You're going to have to revise this." And so I did; I really massively rewrote it, and I learned a lot.

I learned a certain level of humility, but I also learned about the grace of revision from that experience, that things do get better if you go back to work on them.

WOE: You seem to have had an unusual experience in graduate school, focusing so much on writing. For a lot of people in graduate school, there seems to be little attention paid to writing. I felt my writing atrophied in graduate school, compared with what I'd gotten out of my undergraduate experience at Amherst.

BARTHOLOMAE: You do hear that story a good bit, but it certainly wasn't my experience. When I was an undergraduate, I didn't take a composition course because I was exempted from it. And I don't remember really laboring over my writing. As far as academic prose is concerned, I did it painfully at the last minute and was always told that I had good ideas somewhere in there but the writing was awfully messy.

WOE: What you say about the comments you would get on the papers reminds me of how you have described getting your own students to revise their papers, telling them, "We've marked your papers where we were interested, puzzled, or bored." I was really struck by the word "bored" because I think a lot of pedagogy these days discourages us from being that frank with students and telling them, "This is really boring." Were those the kinds of comments you were getting on your own writing?

BARTHOLOMAE: Those were exactly the kinds of comments. One feature I remember that is still a part of the way I mark papers is to be very frank, to let that frankness determine the kind of editorial conversation that you have with students, where you really treat them as adults and you say, "This is boring," or "This is uninteresting," or "This is a dead end, don't do it." In the first course I took with Poirier, he would cross whole sections of a paper out—which I also will do. He would just draw a line through those three paragraphs you wrote trying to warm yourself up. I remember once I was trying to be profound and waxing poetic—the comment in the margin was, "Don't do that again." And, of course, I knew exactly what he meant. I knew what I was doing, and I was trying to figure out whether that was going to be currency or not, and he said "Nope." So then I went back to the drawing board.

WOE: Today we seem to coddle students so much that often they aren't ready for that kind of criticism.

BARTHOLOMAE: I do think that we coddle, but I also think they're ready for the criticism. Sometimes if I describe my teaching, people—both my graduate students at my own university or other teachers at the 4Cs—will think my class is a kind of in-your-face boot camp, a sort of Robin Varnum version of what Amherst must have been like.

And what I have to tell them is that I think my classes are actually very friendly places. My students laugh a lot, I've won awards for my teaching, and I think my classrooms are popular places. But I think students like to be treated as adults. And they are trying to develop some scale of value to get a feeling for what it means to be an adult intellectual. I don't think it coddles them when you do that. One of the Amherst legacies for me is that I think part of what we have to do as educators (and particularly as people who work with language) is help students escape the crap of contemporary culture. There's so much nonsense and so much easy generalization and so much bogus authority that I think the only way you can deal with it is to say, "Don't do that."

My sense is that one of the great holes, one of the great silences in the profession right now, particularly in 4Cs, is around the whole question of value. You don't ever find sessions where people are arguing about whether this particular piece of student writing is good writing or not. And you can construe good any way you want; it can be good in aesthetic terms, or good in terms of its social use, or good in terms of its intellectual value. But those are real questions, and they're questions about which we really shouldn't even agree, but we don't even know the terms of the disagreement. The 4Cs promotion of writing has been to confer the status of the writer on everybody, which is a wonderful thing to do. It's to enable writing as much as possible and to be promoters of writing. But as a profession this has kept us from not only giving students a way of writing, some procedures that they can use to get started in writing, but also from raising questions of value. I think different programs promote very different kinds of writing, and I don't think we argue these questions of value.

My generation comes out of the tradition of training (actually an elitist one) where we were expected to argue whether this poem was better than this poem, or this novel was better than this novel, and why. And I felt and I feel that to be an important and productive exercise. Today we don't carry that practice into the classroom where we engage students with it. One of the things I like to do is to engage students in productive discussions as opposed to mean-spirited ones. In most of my classes I'll hand out copies of two student papers and ask the questions, "Given what these papers are setting out to do, which does it better? Where does the other fall short? How would you work on it to make it a better piece of writing?"

WOE: Isn't that classroom activity very much out of the Amherst English 1 tradition? But a lot of people don't make student texts a central or almost any part of the writing course. Can you really teach writing doing that?

BARTHOLOMAE: I would say no. I would say that the person who really taught me to be a writing teacher was Bill Coles, who also came from Amherst. Although, over time, I learned to teach quite differently from Bill. One of the things that Bill said that remains a kind of watchword in our program is that the student's writing is the primary text in the course and that it must be; that must be where you begin and what you learn. You have to learn as a professional to read student writing, and students have to learn to read their own writing so that they can learn what work it represents, so they can learn how to work on it.

The corollary for me has been that teaching really begins once you have a draft, and then you begin the process of learning how to read it and revise it. Revision isn't something you do on the side or for extra credit; revision is the mode of instruction. It's "Here's this text; let's think about what this piece of writing does and what it doesn't do. And let's think about where it can go." I can engage the students in that process, and then I can say, "OK, now, go to work." And when I evaluate students, I will evaluate them, then, not on what they did on the first crack at it, but what happened in successive revisions. That's where I see them at work, and that's measurable. We can see what's different, and we can talk about it. And if it's the same paper all over again, I don't care how slick it is, they haven't done any work in the course. Or they're not yet learning how to do the work in the course as I imagine it.

WOE: You argue in your introduction to *The Teaching of Writing* that "Writing and writing itself, not some substitute or stand-in, should be at the center of the curriculum." Is there any chance of this actually happening, or is this rather like hoping it would rain beer?

BARTHOLOMAE: I think if I lower the horizon a bit I can ask, "Can English departments at this point in our history make this commitment and make it legitimately?" I think it's possible. Will they? I doubt it, but I think it's possible. And I think there is something to struggle for and to work for.

WOE: Another thing you acknowledge getting from Amherst is the use of sequences. One of the things I love about *Ways of Reading* are the carefully constructed sequences of assignments. Can you talk a little bit about sequences? They don't seem hugely popular in our profession, but it seems to me they ought to be.

BARTHOLOMAE: I agree they ought to be. I'll tell you an interesting application of sequences. I've had a long involvement now with the John S. Knight Writing Program at Cornell, which is a very interesting undergraduate program staffed largely by graduate students from all over the campus, but also with significant faculty involvement, and faculty from all across the curriculum. The faculty who run the program with Jim Slevin, who has played a central role as a consultant, were trying to figure out how to engage these graduate students with a writing course in productive ways. And their solution to this pedagogical problem was to have them write sequences. Not to ask them how to do one writing assignment, but to ask them to organize a sequence of writing assignments. Let's say there were going to be two books at the center of the course; then the problem is how you organize the engagement with those books in such a way that you're not only covering the material but students are learning to write. Where do you begin, then what comes next, then what comes in response? And you watch these graduate students suddenly think through the reading of these two books of anthropology not as learning the field or covering the field, but as taking you into a way of reading, a way of writing, that marks somebody's young professional entree into a community (a community of scholars I would say, not a community of anthropologists). The Cornell program gives out an award for the best assignment sequence. The sequences are brilliant, really wonderful!

I don't impose sequenced assignments on the world, but I can't imagine being a responsible teacher without, in advance, charting out the work of the course as a progressive engagement with X, Y, and Z. And that's whether I'm doing a graduate seminar or a freshman course or a class for majors.

WOE: You also write about the need to write impossible assignments, assignments that interfere with the students' writing.

BARTHOLOMAE: You need to give students a productive place to begin. That's very difficult. Say you've asked them to read *Middlemarch*, and you want them to write something; it's the first writing assignment and you don't even know where to begin. My shorthand for the course is that I want to point them toward something that they don't know how to do: that's what makes the course a course, pointing them toward some way of working with that text that they cannot imagine. To do that you really do two things: You help them to imagine what they can't imagine, and you interfere with the habits that they already have. My students think in writing about *Middlemarch* they can talk about Dorothea and Casaubon as if they were real people. So if I'm going to write a sequence, I'm going to ask them to think about where and how the book seems to invite identification. I want them at some later point to get to thinking about strategies of representation in a novel like that in particular, the way in which the narrator teaches you how and why to distance yourself rather than to simply identify with the people who are in front of you.

To get from the one place to the other, they have to do a lot of work. Some of it's just regular: They've got to learn how to work with a block quotation, they've got to learn how to write about a novel by both working with small pieces and doing some kind of summary. But there's also the interference part. I have to keep saying, "Remember, you're writing about an author, a reader, and a text. Some of your sentences have to be not about Dorothea, but about a reader, or about George Eliot, a writer, or about the novel and how it's working." You can set the task that specifically; that is, in the subject position of your sentence, there must be some reference to either the writer or the reader. Students learn to do a certain kind of reading that then puts them in a position to imagine—which in my rhythm of teaching is usually two drafts later—that they're no longer saying that they hate Casaubon and they also hate Will Ladislaw, but they're thinking about how and why a novel or an author is orchestrating a set of expectations and identifications and then thwarting them or satisfying them.

That's a long way of saying that I do think that you have to figure out in advance what you want students to do, and it should be something that they can't imagine. It's your job to help organize the work so it could be imaginable. That to me is organizing their work rather than telling them what to say. And one of the things you need to do along the way is interfere. It's not that students have been badly taught; it's just that they're moving now to this college-level literature class and a different way of thinking about reading—or in a composition class you're trying to get students to feel the flexibility of let's say the essay as a genre, rather than just rely on what they take to be its fixed structure. So you've got to say, "Stop being so coherent, stop proving every point; search for the example that doesn't fit, stop searching for the example that fits." I like to teach students to write parenthetically so they get a feel for what it means to say something and to say something else simultaneously.

WOE: Along with difficult or impossible assignments, you're known for giving students impossible readings, things that the teacher doesn't fully understand. I love the recent piece in *College English* where Lynn Bloom reviews all the textbooks and says, "The one exception to all my explanations again is *Ways of Reading*." Is it good news or bad news that you're the one exception?

BARTHOLOMAE: It was good news for me! But it wasn't a surprise. *Ways of Reading* actually came out of a tradition of teaching. One of the things that I brought early in my career to my own table as a teacher was a sense that the fundamental purpose of the freshman course should be to allow students to be engaged with those works that were generally valued inside the academy. And usually the freshman composition course and its readers didn't do that. Instead, the standard anthology took pieces that students could work on with ease, and so the course, the students, and everything associated with it was thought of with contempt because its materials were not of the value of the work that you were writing about as a graduate student or that you were arguing about with your colleagues. They would read E.B. White, and we would read Emerson! I felt all along that it was our job to give students works of value and teach them how they could use them. That assumed that you have to allow students to do things they couldn't do well in order to prepare them to do them well later.

A classic example is the course that Tony Petrosky and I did, the basic reading and writing course at Pitt. This course was for the small percentage who tested below Basic Writing, kids who were identified as being unable to succeed in school. We had them reading Margaret Mead and organized the course so they'd come up with a theory of development. The course was being evaluated by the college; someone from the Psych Department and someone from the History Department concluded, "God, this course is great! It really does give students an engagement with primary texts, gives them a feel for the excitement of intellectual life." And then they both had this moment of horror and said, "But then they can get it all wrong! They won't get the right theory of adolescent development until they know so and so, they won't get the history right until they read so and so." And we said, "Yes, but that's not what this course is about. It is not about covering the canonical texts and theories. It is about reading and writing, about using primary texts and articulating theories."

So *Ways of Reading* has proven to be a powerful pedagogical tool. Tony and I are also quite proud of it as an anthology of contemporary nonfiction, showing the range and the variety and the ambition of the genre. It's not a cross-curricular reader; it really is trying to represent what to us are not only really interesting but also teachable examples of nonfiction, nonfiction that's trying to do a kind of work that is adventuresome, in many cases unconventional, often compelling and memorable.

On my campus we have a group of people who do what's called creative nonfiction, the nonfiction in the Phillip Lopate anthology or published in the journal *Creative Nonfiction*. It's a writing that I know how to admire, but it's not a writing that I'd be interested in teaching. And then you have the writers in the composition texts, the canon Lynn Bloom identifies. The argument Tony and I make to the creative nonfiction crowd is that as you think about creative nonfiction, you want to also think about Roland Barthes or Stanley Fish or Paul Auster or John Wideman or Adrienne Rich, people who have done remarkable things with the genre of the essay—in other words nonfiction—but not in that more belletristic tradition. And yet their work has been left out of the educational anthologies, which have tended to go for more tightly organized and conventionally formed works.

WOE: You make it harder not just on the student but also on the teacher. You don't get to teach the old E.B. White chestnuts, the stuff you can talk about in your sleep. Instead you have to deal with something you really don't understand.

BARTHOLOMAE: I think it allows you to say to a class, "Well, let's figure out what this is, what is the meaning of this?" That's a real project, one you can do with some pleasure.

WOE: In that basic course, one of the metaphors you use is trying to get students to invent a discipline—so that they wouldn't have to borrow one of ours. But isn't there a problem when they get into disciplines because often nobody in those disciplines explains to the student how the discipline works? They assume that the students come in with the methodology. Elsewhere you say the problem with us as English teachers is we make them invent our discipline. Why don't we or how should we teach disciplinarity?

BARTHOLOMAE: Or should we teach disciplinarity? That's a hard question, and I can answer it on behalf of English (I don't think I have an answer on behalf of the undergraduate curriculum), which is that, traditionally we teach disciplinarity in the junior and senior years when you declare a major and you do a kind of focused work. I actually believe that. What I don't believe is that the first step is the foundational course as represented by Psych 101: 250 kids in a room memorizing terms that they don't sense the application for. On our campus, the foundational course is a small English course where you have material to work on, and in working on it you learn that there are tools that you need, tools like an ability to imagine the essay form, or having a vocabulary with terms like "narrator" or "sonnet" or "audience."

Should we teach students disciplinarity? I have actually quite mixed feelings. I think my primary commitments have always been to general education and to the introductory course. As a department chair, however, I have become more and more concerned about our failure as an English department to know very much about our majors, about their ambitions, desires, and career trajectories. We have about 450 English majors, but the numbers who go on to graduate school, who move toward an M.A. and Ph.D., are miniscule—maybe six a year. One of the things that we as a faculty have been trying to do is to come to a better sense of how to construct our required senior seminars, to make them capstones that allow students to move out into the world with some sense of their own orientation to what they have been trained to do or what they might be expected to do, to have a seminar, for example, that might actually point toward that much larger percentage of students who want to be certified to be English teachers. Their senior seminar probably should be constructed differently than it would be for those who need to be able to do the critical and theoretical work to write the kind of paper that they could use to get into our graduate school, as opposed to the senior seminar that would prepare somebody to think about how or why to teach *Huckleberry Finn* to 14-year-olds, or *The Scarlet Letter*; or what the language issues are; or to learn about Ebonics while preparing to go into the city and try to teach standard English in a world where English is not standard, where English is quite varied and its varieties are compelling.

One of the things that I sense in my own department is that we don't prepare students very well to go into the world of work. The community and we say that the English major is important because you learn to solve problems, to work with texts, to communicate. But the forms of that communication now are far beyond what we're prepared to teach students. We don't have the facilities or the expertise as a department to allow those of our majors for whom PowerPoint presentations and document design could be crucial to be prepared when they go to work for Westinghouse. I think we should do that. As a department, one of the problems we're working with right now is how you find the space and the money to be able to provide the equipment you would need to do this, and where you find the faculty expertise. Then there's the traditional set of arguments among the faculty about whether that's worth doing or not, about to what degree we are in the service of the culture, preparing students for particular vocational careers, and to what degree we are simply standing as the icebreaker, where we, the world be damned, are gonna teach them film studies or whatever.

WOE: At the 4Cs you often hear the argument that preparing for the real world means collaborative writing. As a person who's collaborated so much with Anthony Petrosky, do you encourage and teach your students to write and work collaboratively?

BARTHOLOMAE: No, never once.

WOE: Isn't there a contradiction since you do it so much and the real world does it so much?

BARTHOLOMAE: I have had students work collaboratively to prepare presentations. I'm teaching a course with *Middlemarch* in it, so I'll get a team of students and send them off to, let's say, find out something about nineteenth-century medical practices, and they'll come back and report. But collaborative writing as it's talked about in 4Cs, I don't do it. It could be that I'm just lazy, that I have patterns and habits to my teaching, but I think I probably would also be willing to say that I choose not to teach collaborative writing. I have fifteen weeks. Among the things that I want to work with, I can't do everything. And I think you can learn to collaborate with somebody as the need arises. The things I know I need to teach take priority over that.

WOE: You say we need to admit that we train people for Westinghouse and such, which makes a lot of sense. But in a review of Susan Miller's *Textual Carnivals*, you say that composition is irrefutably counterhegemonic. You say a composition course should be part of the general critique of traditional humanism, which seems to contradict sending people out to work for the corporation. How should we go about being counterhegemonic and subverting traditional humanists as composition teachers: to the ramparts! The sixties! [*Laughter*]

BARTHOLOMAE: There's nothing worse than having your own sentences come back! [*Laughter*] I don't know that I would say that as strongly any more. One of the things is, if you have children between the ages of 16 and 23—and I have three of them—you get a very different attitude toward resistance. [*Laughter*]

One of the reasons I love composition is it teaches you how and why to resist the forces of the country as you feel them in your sentences, like that easy generalization the kid writes that says that corporations like Westinghouse are the enemy of the people and are corrupt because capitalism is corrupt. Whether that's a political position that I want to promote or not is irrelevant to my teaching. But as a sentence, it doesn't begin to take its own terms seriously, or to examine its assumptions, or to imagine a rhythm of the syntax that would allow some moment of reflection on its own terms. I always say to kids who write these sentences, "How do you know that?" Or,

"How do you get to speak for the United States of America?" That's what I think of as appropriately counterhegemonic.

I do think that the person who goes to Westinghouse and rises will probably rise because of her writing. Yet she's going to write in very conventional forms. The history of writing shows us how to value work within conventions. And, in the workplace, we all know that somebody can do something inside of a memo that leads you to say, "There's a live person in there. There's a mind at work." "Who is that person?" your manager says. And that comes not because you're completely redefining nuclear energy but because inside the immediate project people are working on, you have a way of participating. You can participate as a writer in such a way that you not only get the work done well, but you get it done thoughtfully, with some sense of style and presence.

Somebody asked me once what the relationship was between *Ways of Reading* and *Paris 1968*. I said, "There is absolutely none." I know I was a great disappointment because it was at a time when some of the critiques of the book were that it seemed to promote or call for some kind of social activism. And yet because of its attention to reading and writing it was finally quietist. I have been involved with campus activism in one way or another so that I know there is no more cynical gesture than to imagine that in a required fourteen-week course you can teach somebody to have a political consciousness. I just don't believe that can happen. But I do think we can teach somebody to work on sentences. And I think that practice can be political. So that's how I've slipped my way out of the sentence about counterhegemonic. [*Laughter*] Susan Miller made me do that. [*Laughter*]

WOE: Early on in one of your pieces, you talk about the tyranny of the thesis. It seems to me that in freshman writing, we're often putting students in the box, teaching them that if they do these steps, have a thesis statement, they'll write well.

BARTHOLOMAE: To be a writer means to be aware of the box as a box. As a teacher, I know that I can produce the effect of the thesis-driven paragraph. And the culture has been determined to produce that effect over time. I wish actually that there were more flexibilities built in at earlier stages. I think it's not only a matter of giving young writers a kind of form that they can inhabit in order to get work done, but in turn it's the kind of work that they do. And the tyranny of the thesis is that you're stuck proving the commonplace. You begin with whatever comes in your head, and if you're smart enough you find everything you need to prove it. And you leave out everything that's interesting because it doesn't quite fit. Then you say it again. So one of the things that I like to do is to surprise my students early on by asking them to please not be so coherent. The rhythm of the course is such that for the course to work, there has to be a point where students really are writing much worse than they were, with less control and facility and ease than they were when they came in. And it happens even at the level of the sentence. They start to try to put together sentences, and they can't pull them off because they now have complexity. And in some ways, that's the point during the course when you teach students semicolons, and dashes, and parentheses, and how in fact to marshal together all these things that they want to do.

I teach the parenthesis. If we taught the parenthesis with the same vigor as a nation that we teach the topic sentence, we'd have a whole different world; our children would be different. They'd be able to say something in their funny voice as well as their serious voice, or think of a qualification while they were thinking of the assertion. So I like to teach the parenthesis. And I like students to feel that part of the way they should imagine themselves as writers is in a somewhat difficult and at times prickly and always potentially experimental relationship to the forms that they're given to do their work in.

WOE: The lesson of how students need to move backwards to move forward seems a particularly difficult one for new writing teachers to learn because it's so ingrained into teacher training now that what you're doing is trying to measure progress in student writing. What advice do you give to a new teacher about that?

BARTHOLOMAE: I would never say it's moving backwards to move forward. I would say that moving forward is always going to have to involve putting students in positions where they become less adept and sometimes less comfortable and less happy with you and the class. I think one of the really hard things about a writing class which is small and fairly intense and where you're responsible for organizing this work over time is that if you do your job well, there is a point that's sort of scary, where students aren't writing very well and they feel very much at sea and you have to be able to know how to pull that together by week fourteen. Sometimes it feels as though the bottom is falling out. But that's progress.

WOE: In your basic reading and writing course, you are co-teaching with one of your colleagues. How do you get an institution to support two faculty members teaching the lowest of the low at the university, when most universities will dump that on graduate students? Most universities would see that as an incredible squandering of resources. Doesn't that course make up half the students' semester load?

BARTHOLOMAE: If they had a 15-course load, it was 6 credits out of the 15. Well, how did we do it is actually in the introduction and the dedication to *Facts, Artifacts, and Counterfacts*. There was a dean, Robert Marshall, who remains a dear friend, who essentially said to the faculty, "It is wrong for us to bring students here and to not prepare them and then to fail them, when we know in advance they need additional help." So he was willing to invest the energy and the resources of the institution. That was quite a long time ago now. But the tradition of teaching and the success of the teaching on campus has been such that it's never been questioned. As a matter of fact, I can't imagine that it ever will be questioned. That course and its missions and its commitment of resources has defined part of the culture of writing and teaching on our campus, and it's something everybody's proud of. It's true that only our very best teachers get to teach the basic writing course. We do have graduate students teach it, but they tend to be the ones who have done a lot of teaching and who feel a real commitment to the program. And we still have tenure-stream faculty teaching the course.

WOE: It seems to me like this is a success story that none of the rest of us wants to hear! Because it runs counter to practice nearly everywhere else. Is there any hope for the rest of us? Can we get your dean?

BARTHOLOMAE: Or is it something that could be done now in this climate? I don't know that it was an accident of history; I think there are places where it could be done. But no individual should feel that he or she failed for being unable to pull it off, because it does require that amazing moment of a coming together of a sort of larger institutional commitment: The guards are asleep at the gates, and you sneak in and get something started, and then nobody can stop it!

WOE: I want to switch to a couple of questions about your famous debate with Peter Elbow. Among the many sparkling things you said was the following, which seems true to me: "The argument that produces archetypal criticism produces cognitive psychology, free writing, and new journalism. I've got Bruner, Linda Flower, Peter, Tom Wolfe and John McPhee all lined up in this genealogy, this account of the modern curricular production of the independent author, the celebration of the point of view as individual artifact, the promotion of sentimental realism, the true story of what I think, feel, know, and see." I thought this was a very perceptive, Leavis-like line you put these people in, but I wondered, you know . . .

BARTHOLOMAE: [*Laughs*] It got me in a heap of trouble!

WOE: I couldn't imagine trouble with the line so much as with the tone with which the line was treated.

BARTHOLOMAE: The tone was partly a product of the ritual of the debate, and of the moment. My department has a very old, very large, very active creative writing program. We offer an MFA, and we are in some ways now the center of creative nonfiction—which I called sentimental realism. My colleague Lee Gutkind, who edits the journal *Creative Nonfiction*, asked me to come to his seminar and to speak to students about sentimental realism and to account for the tone of that sentence. So that passage did get me in a heap of trouble!

I was in front of people for whom Tom Wolfe or his current equivalents are heroes. I mean that is exactly who they're trying to write themselves to be. And so I had to explain what I meant. I'm not against what they do, which I'll stick with calling sentimental realism. But I stick with the desire to not take for granted the cultural value that's given to the celebration of point of view.

WOE: Of what view?

BARTHOLOMAE: Of point of view. Of my point, here I am, front and center, I'm experiencing this and I'm going to tell you about it. I understand the cultural value of that work, I understand why that dominates the best seller list right now, I understand the pedagogical advantage. I think Peter's strongest argument is in the pedagogical advantage of inviting young people into that moment and anointing them as writers, to allow them to feel the authority of their own immediate experience and point of view. I understand all of that. I just don't take it to be the mission of the required first-year course. And that was what I said to the seminar, that I was speaking for a course that's required at schools all across the country. Anybody who is a program director or in some way administratively responsible must think about the rationale behind that requirement. You are beholden in some way to rationalize what you are doing in the required course to those who are requiring it.

My sense of that introductory course is that it is, in fact, to introduce students to doing a certain kind of intellectual work in the four years they're in college that in a way has to do not with their priority but with their secondarity, that is, the way in which they are in relation to somebody else. Let's say it's Adrienne Rich or something else they've read, let's say Robert Coles. I think it's then absolutely central that you ask students, "Where do you speak in relation to Adrienne Rich or Robert Coles?" I think Adrienne Rich in speaking does not want students to be silent. But she does want to be heard. And she wants to say something that they need to listen to. And it may very well run counter to their expectations and challenge the very sense of authority that allows them to imagine the world being constructed in a certain way. Here is a common situation in my class. A student is reading Adrienne Rich, she's talking about patriarchy, and the student, a guy, wants to write about how much he loves fishing with his dad. He loves fishing with his Dad, you know! And it's important that he loves fishing with his dad! But if he's going to read Adrienne Rich, he's got to think about fishing with his dad as part of a set of patriarchal rituals that serves the culture in certain ways. That's what I think the course is.

I think we teach students to do that so that they can have a four-year education and it will be a good one. So I said to the creative nonfiction seminar, "You know, the required composition course is one course in a four-year curriculum. If you want to go on and be creative writers, we offer a creative writing major as well as a literature major." They can spend the next three years as journalists doing journalism or in the nonfiction track writing nonfiction and learning to love Tom Wolfe or Barry Lopez or whomever. I don't have to do it all. So I argue in the name of the required course.

WOE: Peter Elbow got the last word in the debate, saying to you, "You assume discourse means argument and that difference means opposition." Is this a fair attribution?

BARTHOLOMAE: Yes, I think it is, in the spirit that I think Peter offers it. I've been trying to imagine opposition not as it's represented by resistance or as it's enshrined in sort of a new-left cultural politics, but opposition as in the questioning of common sense, not doing what comes naturally, calling attention to the terms that underlie what you do—argument not as polemic, not as stridency, but argument as in questioning the relationship to other people's texts but also to your own. I do think that writing instruction does require struggle, where you do put yourself in a questioning relationship to the culture that's given you its forms and its assumptions. You learn as a writer how to be present inside of all of that. But there's a part of Peter that wants to make me quibble—to say, opposition as I understand it is not the same thing it meant to Jim Berlin, or those who feel that writing courses are going to bring down postmodern capitalism—that's not part of my vocabulary, not my goal.

WOE: Can you talk a little about reading and how we teach students to do the kind of reading that you're advocating, because it does seem that we have to reshape the way they think about texts. It seems that rereading plays an enormous role in this. And it's one of those things we rarely ask students to do.

BARTHOLOMAE: Rereading is a form of revision. The course that I teach—whether it's a composition course or a literature course or something else—not only says to a student go back and revise this paper, but in order to go back and revise this paper, go back and reread what you've been working on.

I'll give students something hard to read like *The Pedagogy of the Oppressed*. They'll write a paper, their first paper, and the good students will just sum it all up. And you say to a student, "How did you do that? What allowed you to do that?" Inevitably they'll say, "Well, you know, I just ignored all the stuff I didn't understand in chapter 4." And of course they did! Because they're trained in the rhetoric of mastery you don't show your weak hand, you show your strong suit. So I think that the pedagogical rule is, "Go read chapter 4 and do a paper now. Bring those things that you don't understand to the front. And you're allowed to write a sentence that says, 'Well I don't completely understand what Paulo Freire means by problematization. I think he might mean the following.'" A moment of translation can then take place: "When Freire says X, Y and Z, I think what he's saying is the following." That's a very productive moment, when a student begins to speak for the parts of the text that can't be quickly summarized, or that don't fit with what the student has been prepared to know or understand. I think you have to give people things that are worth reading and that are teachable and where there's some work to be done.

One of my rules of thumb is that I tend to not want to talk about something in class until students have written about it. That is, you need to prepare students to take the plunge, take the responsibility for the first attempt to say what something means or say why it's interesting before you begin to organize it for them. It makes the teaching more fun. If I go in and tell everybody what I think is going on in Paulo Freire, I'll get twenty-two papers all saying the same thing, and that's not my goal. I'm really interested in getting students to feel that they can be the readers of something that they don't feel prepared to read. I think students need to understand that it isn't about memory—that books are themselves mnemonic devices, that that's why we love them. You can make marks in them, and then you open them up again; you don't have to remember, you can go back and look at it. Students need the ability to write the sentence that acknowledges the text as a problem.

I remember learning this from Mariolina Salvatori, who's one of the best teachers I've ever seen, who assigns what she calls the difficulty paper. She was a part of the group that did *Facts, Artifacts, and Counterfacts*. She learned early on that one of the things you have to have students do is articulate their sense of difficulty so that it's not shameful, but it's strategic and productive. Difficulty becomes not, "I can't do it." Instead, students explain what it is that makes it difficult. And in doing that, they're in a position to begin to imagine difficulty as part of the text's strategy, and its fundamental existence in relation to them, what their next move is going to be. Difficulty becomes part of the intellectual landscape you're negotiating, rather than something shameful that you have to hide. So that's another way to allow students to experience reading.

Many of us still enjoy reading things that we're not prepared to read. As you get older, certain things you can read very quickly, like dissertations. I've served on a lot of dissertation committees in our Spanish Department. My wife is a Spanish teacher and is fluent in Spanish, so I'll bring a dissertation home. And her Spanish is great, and I can read Spanish, but it is stumbling. I can read the dissertations in two hours, because, you know, they're dissertations.

WOE: Since dissertations are easy, what do you like to read that's hard, that challenges you? Confuses but attracts you?

BARTHOLOMAE: I find that I take much of my own reading pleasure now from reading contemporary fiction and poetry. Tony and I are doing a book that will be a literature anthology and textbook. It does not try to cover the genres or to cover a period or a national literature. But its argument is that one of the ways of imagining the one required literature course students take is that it should situate them in relation to their own contemporary literary culture. So they should know who Sonia Sanchez is and be able to think of that work in relation to their own reading and writing; they should participate in that particular cultural moment. I don't think that English departments generally define the responsibility of the required literature course in that way. What we're asking is that if students across the country are going to take one required literature class, what should be in it? I'm more and more convinced that what should be in it should be primarily serious literature written in the last ten years. And from that, students can come to an understanding of literary culture and literary value. Then if they want to do historical work or additional work, they can. So

I find myself reading a lot more literature with enormous pleasure. I'm more and more interested in the writers we bring to campus, not as display but as part of my own academic calendar. Before somebody comes to town, I want to read their work, I want to go to the reading, I want to have some sense of what's going on, who that person is, what's happening. That's what I like to read. And, of course, Tony and I are always reading new nonfiction as we work toward a new edition of *Ways of Reading*.

WOE: Going back to our earlier discussion of students and their reading and rereading, it seems that one of the problems we run into is that of coverage. In one quarter or semester we have to do so much work, and if we're asking students to reread and we're asking them to rewrite, then it seems to me the university could look at that course and say that you hadn't covered a lot of material.

BARTHOLOMAE: That's right. They would. I think that part of an English department's commitment should be to coverage. I couldn't imagine an English major who hadn't also done the *Norton Anthology* course, to get the sweep of British literature from Chaucer to Woolf. But I think of the general education course as having a different responsibility. One of the courses that I like to teach is a course called American Literary Traditions that fulfills the general education requirements, and most of the students are not English majors. My understanding of my responsibility in that course is not to cover all of American literature, but to give them some sense of the terms of the title. Why American? What is literature? And how do you understand tradition? So I'd rather do eight books that would allow me to put things in interesting pairs, where I would teach Robert Frost and Philip Levine. Or I would teach *Walden* and teach Gretel Ehrlich's *The Solace of Open Spaces* in order to think about how this literature functions in the service of something that you call America, and if you read *Walden* and *The Solace of Open Spaces*, what do you know about a tradition? Or read Emily Dickinson, and a woman whose poetry I admire very much, Lynn Emanuel. It's fun to get figures who work as a conversation with each other. I don't see coverage as the role of a general education course.

WOE: What happens when you get students who are juniors and seniors and haven't done general education and they have to do general education?

BARTHOLOMAE: In the real world, not everybody does things in order. I think that's the fundamental dilemma of teaching, that you can't get everybody to start on the same page, and you can't get everybody to end on the same page, and you can't get everybody to move at the same speed all the way through. I would say the skills of close reading are part of the general education imperative: Students who are juniors and seniors who haven't learned that, must.

I actually have a kid in my class this semester who's a senior engineering major, who is a pretty good student and pretty smart kid. He's really struggling in the course because he has to work closely with the material that he's writing about, and he's not prepared to do that. It scares him. What he can do is write a very glib paper about man's inhumanity to man, and I'm not buying it, and I haven't been buying it, and I keep saying, "You have to take me to one of the poems from Philip Levine's *The Simple Truth* to show me the way in which Levine is engaging this question that you want to write about: man's inhumanity to man." It's hard for him to want to do that. Because he thinks his education is over, he thinks that all he needs to do in this course is fulfill his goddamn requirement, and he wants me to get off his goddamn back. "I'm an engineer, I've already got a job, and you're telling me . . ."

WOE: "You're gonna keep me from graduating?!"

BARTHOLOMAE: "I like you, I admire your career, but this is what I'm teaching, and goddamnit you're gonna do it!"

WOE: This phrase just leapt out at me when you wrote about how much work the basic reading and writing course can be; you said underlying the teaching of such a course are "patience and violence." Violence?

BARTHOLOMAE: Oh, absolutely. I mean, that's what makes it such hard work. In the basic reading and writing course, I'd say the majority of students are working-class and minority kids for whom a variety of behaviors—and by that I don't just mean reading and writing, but ways of sitting, ways of being in class—have developed over time, in very hostile relations to white guys my age who wield authority. In that teaching I have to be a very enabling presence. But I also have to be the white guy who's in the position of authority.

Even pedagogically and linguistically, I have to be. So it's not only a matter of getting into the political sense of what it means to standardize the English of these kids who come in, whose English isn't standard, but also just the violence of scenes that I will never forget. For instance, we ask students to speak in sentences in class. And I think it's my job to engage everybody. So let's say we've got a young man whom I want to speak, and he'll say something like, "Yeah." I say, "I want you to not just say that you think something, but I want to hear it; I want you to try it out on us. We all want to hear it." And I'll wait. That silence is very scary. My feeling is that I must will him into a conversation that he both wants to have and doesn't want to have. So it's a very violent course to teach. And you're putting conditions on people's work, work has to come in on time, things have to be corrected, certain subjects aren't allowed, and all of that is hard.

I know it's sort of chic now to talk about violence in relation to the middle-class kid in your class, or violence in relation to those in minority positions generally, but I do a lot of teaching where I'll have minority kids in classes. I understand how I'm in a position of power that engages acts of violence. There's a very different feel in the basic reading and writing class. It's very volatile. Kids do stomp out. And women who teach the class have been sometimes treated in ways that are frightening for them. At an urban university, one of your commitments is to bring kids in who just aren't prepared to sit in "polite conversation." And we are absolutely committed to that. To pretend that it's not sometimes weird and violent is just a lie.

WALKER GIBSON

Walker Gibson developed one of the early graduate programs in rhetoric at the University of Massachusetts—Amherst, where as director of Freshman English, he was also an early advocate for student-centered pedagogies. He contributed to the change in focus from formalistic, grammatical approaches in composition to consideration of style and voice, both the authentic voice of the student writer and the constructed voices that define writing personae.

While James Berlin categorizes Gibson as an expressivist, his teaching practices demonstrate an early awareness of writing as socially constructed and discipline specific. In assignments from his textbook Seeing and Writing *(1959), students describe a church façade after reading Henry James's inspirational description of the Chartres Cathedral; then, after reading Henry Adams's* The Tower of Chartres, *they write a second description in the language of a historian. He encourages students to reflect on how experience and education affect meaning: "An engineer could see the façade in terms of stresses and construction materials; an atheist could call it a pablum for the masses; an artist could admire the 'glow in the late afternoon light.' " Such assignments encourage students to consider the influence of genre and discipline on knowledge. Gibson also edited* The Limits of Language *(1962), a collection of essays addressing the new horizons of science and philosophy and their effect on language and literature.*

Additional publications include Tough, Sweet and Stuffy: An Essay on Modern American prose styles *(1966) and* Persona: A Style Study for Readers and Writers *(1969); Gibson also published two books of poetry,* The Reckless Spenders *(1954) and* Come as You Are *(1958), and his poems appeared in the* New Yorker *and* Harper's.

Gibson's theoretical perspectives on voice apply not only to written discourse; they are also playfully manifest in his oral interview. In the text that follows, readers can recognize a speaker whose voice intones spirited whimsy and critical reflection—whether he is recounting the awkwardness of getting 20 English professors to agree on a writing syllabus or the effects of combining a section of first-year writing students and first-year teaching assistants.

—Matthew Oliver

"A Nest of Singing Rhetorical Birds"

Margaret M. Strain

Spring 2000

WOE: I'd like to begin with a general question concerning your experience as director of one of the Summer Institutes for Secondary Teachers of English held at New York University. You remarked in one of your letters to me that it was at that time you realized "The teaching of teachers could be a worthy enterprise." Could you talk a little more about the kind of work that the Commission on English did or what it was set up to do? Was it a high school project?

GIBSON: Absolutely, it was a high school project. As I understand it, the College Entrance Examination Board found itself with a million dollars to do something noble with, and they therefore set up a subsidiary organization which they called the Commission on English. Harold Martin of Harvard was the chief. They thought that their dough could best be spent in trying to help high school teachers, and, of course, I suppose most people will say high schools have been going downhill ever since. But, in any case, even back then that was considered to be a place where an effort should be spent. The Commission named twenty very different universities. St. Louis University was one and so was Tulane. Quite a large variety—some state universities, some private such as Harvard. They named twenty universities who would, in the summer of 1962, offer six weeks or so of training from a college teacher's point of view to fifty high school teachers at each place. One thousand high school teachers had this experience with sixty university instructors.

A few carefully chosen high school teachers joined us profs in tackling all of this. Even with their presence, there was an awful lot of innocence, as you could imagine, on the part of us guys about what goes on in high schools. Nevertheless, this program was pushed forward, and it meant that the sixty of us needed training to get going. We all met for three weeks during the summer of 1961 in Ann Arbor, Michigan, where I found myself at battle as one of the composition folk. There were twenty instructors in composition, twenty in literature, and twenty in language. The people in language, where we expected wild young Turks, were calm as could be, and the people in literature, who were in Harold Martin's charge, were also fairly serene, but we had a civil war among the twenty composition teachers in our group. Al Kitzhaber was in charge of the composition section, and

I think he was a little embarrassed and upset by the fact that we couldn't very well agree.

As time goes on, the issues get muddier, but I think even then I was trying to push for a program based on things like voice and tone and style. There were a number of elderly characters in the group who really wanted to talk about the four types of discourse—the traditional modes—that seemed to some of us old hat and dreary, so actually we split: We had to come up with two programs, two ways of going at the teaching of composition. At ten universities, the high school teachers were fed one line, and at ten other universities, they were fed another. I heard long later that some sort of analysis had been done as to the results and it came out even. [*Gibson laughs*] So it didn't make any difference, but it made a lot of difference then, at least to me, and I found myself in the position of carrying a banner for one of the few times in my life, I guess, and trying to make friends and influence people.

WOE: Was the emphasis on style and voice considered more student centered or was there a connection to classical rhetoric?

GIBSON: It was certainly student centered, and I think another issue was the question of basing the writing on student experience: "Tell us what you know."

WOE: There were people who objected to this focus?

GIBSON: Yes, now what they wanted to talk about I can't possibly remember. There must be records of this event beyond my autobiographical memories.

WOE: John Gerber did publish an analysis of the Summer Institutes entitled "The 1962 Summer Institutes of the Commission on English: Their Achievement and Promise" in *PMLA*. His coverage of the composition course describes one syllabus as "subjective and experiential" while the other was "basically diagnostic, stressing the art of writing." The participants who focused on the writer experimented with the Socratic method, integrating composition and literature instruction, and classroom conferences. The other section investigated class analysis and grading of themes, timed writings, and issues of structure. Members of both groups reported a conscious attempt to create shorter, more focused writing assignments, and they tended to be more discerning in their evaluation of student compositions as a result of their own writing experience in the Institutes. Overall, the feedback from the teachers who participated was positive.

GIBSON: For both groups?

WOE: Yes. Many thought the sessions on composition were especially beneficial to them.

GIBSON: Of course they were, and making composition at least one of the triumvirate was a breakthrough because the emphasis had been so much on literature in the past. Having a whole unit on language was also rather remarkable in those days. The linguistics people were reading Martin Joos's *The Five Clocks*, which was not yet published. The students had a mimeographed version of it. It's a fun book and was the bible of the linguistics side of the conference; it infected the rest of us too. That was a big experience for us all.

WOE: In your correspondence, you also remarked that while serving as Director of Freshman English at NYU, you proposed a graduate-level course in rhetoric and pedagogy. Was this decision influenced by your experienced with the high school teachers in the Summer Institute?

GIBSON: Absolutely, and I'm quite sure that it was my experience with the CEEB project and a following NDEA project that convinced me that graduate students at the university needed this material whether they were going to teach in high school or college. This was crucial stuff, yet I was frustrated at that time not being able to get that course through an extremely hidebound graduate committee.

WOE: Why do you think people were opposed to something that would be so beneficial to the graduate teaching assistants?

GIBSON: This is an old story. They felt that this was a "letting down of the barriers." One of the faculty, a medievalist, was heard to say, "I am not going to have freshman English taught to my graduate students." And there was a concern that rhetoric simply didn't rate with Wordsworth. I wonder if NYU has ever come around. I've never asked, but, in any case, I was also interested in getting back to the orchards and maple trees in western Massachusetts.

WOE: Was UMass–Amherst open to rhetoric?

GIBSON: Well, yes. UMass–Amherst didn't know what it was doing, so it was a perfect place for me because I could tell them what to do. But yes, they were open to anything. They hadn't been a university very long. It was a cow college and then it was a state university for a while. It really had a very low profile, but then the state began to spend some money, and the university began to get some very good people. By the middle sixties, they were getting quite respectable. They were open to new ideas so that I was able in the second year I was here to start that graduate course in which Joe Comprone was one of the first students.

Just to footnote that, one of the things that I did early on was to dragoon those students in the graduate course to sit in the back rows of a classroom while I taught my freshman section and the freshmen were very nice about that. They were very aware of the big audience back there. For a while I thought that worked extremely well. I can remember Joe Comprone in the back asking questions, sort of over the heads of the kids, "Why did you do that then?" and things like that. For me, as the Director of Freshman English, it was a question of "put up or shut up": "How do you do this? Show it, don't tell it. Show it." We had some quite dramatic learning experiences that way. Whether students would put up with that now I don't know. It takes nerve. You have to have an awful lot of confidence.

WOE: Was the graduate course part of the Rhetoric Program you helped create?

GIBSON: The two were almost simultaneous. The Rhetoric Program was a bureaucratic hassle. When I arrived, there was a three-credit requirement each of the first two semesters of freshman year, two of which were under the wing of the English Department and one other under the wing of the Speech Department. I felt that the first thing we had to do was to put it all together in some way, but this meant that I had to make all kinds of compromises with the Speech Department, who were not always terribly cooperative. The result was that we found a new name—rhetoric—that included it all. I suppose, in a way, we were on the ground floor in choosing that word, which became fashionable very soon. Karl Wallace was here at that time, and he and I got along fine, but it's really been better in recent years since the whole program has returned to the capable hands of the English Department.

WOE: The Rhetoric Program then was jointly run by Speech and English?

GIBSON: That's right. That is to say, I was director and Karl Wallace was my associate, my deputy. Speech people were very much involved, but, with all respect, this made for a messy program.

WOE: Was the graduate TA training jointly taught by members of both departments under the new Rhetoric Program?

GIBSON: The English Department did that entirely. The graduate course we called English 712 was in my hands during those years. We've now got a lot of people here and there's much more than that one course. The course has now proliferated into lots of graduate rhetorical training programs for the TAs. The department is a nest of singing rhetorical birds.

WOE: The *Rhetoric Review* (1994) special issue devoted to Ph.D. programs identifies the UMass–Amherst's program as a "Ph.D. in English with an Emphasis in Writing and the Teaching of Writing" and lists 1970 as the year the English Department granted its first Ph.D. in rhetoric and composition. How did this come about?

GIBSON: That was only three years after I got here, and I was able to persuade the local folks that it would be legitimate to have people writing dissertations in rhetoric and composition. They bought this without rancor that I can recall. It went through very smoothly, though during my time there was no great flood of people to join this great new revolution. Students saw their futures, probably rightly, as specialists in Shakespeare and Jonathan Swift. Well, they were wrong. The jobs that opened up in the next ten years in rhetoric and composition were many. Whereas, as you know, the traditional literature openings simply dried up. It was very hard to persuade graduate students that this was going to happen. I remember very well trying to do this, but nobody believed us. The kids didn't believe us, and some of the faculty didn't either. It was terrible. These poor kids would write all these letters. It was painful I gather things are a little better now, but my sense is that those trained in rhetoric and composition still have a better chance of finding positions.

WOE: How would you describe the theoretical focus of English 712? What background did you feel TAs lacked that they would need to teach writing effectively?

GIBSON: Linguistics, certainly. An interest in the way sentences go together, an interest that certainly carries over from literature in the way a voice is created by language and how to keep such a voice consistent. We used an anthology that I helped put together called *The Play of Language* that was really aimed at undergraduates, but it was all new stuff to our graduate students. It isn't exactly "pop" linguistics, but it certainly isn't technical either.

WOE: How had composition been taught at UMass–Amherst prior to this course?

GIBSON: It was done in fairly traditional ways with a strong literary component. I remember that they had chosen before I came here a rather highbrow textbook by Harold C. Martin and Richard Ohmann.

WOE: To this point, your description of your professional life illustrates strong support for teacher training as Director of the CEEB and NDEA Summer Institutes and Director of Freshman English at NYU and UMass–Amherst. Historical treatments of composition studies' professionalization, particularly accounts of the 1960s, often cite the publication of such texts as Richard Braddock, Richard Lloyd-Jones, and Lowell Schoer's *Research in Written Composition* (1963) as significant markers of the field's disciplinary development. For Ed Corbett, who I've also interviewed on this period, the 1963 CCCC convention was pivotal. Francis Christensen, for example, gave a presentation on generative grammar; Wayne Booth spoke as well. What is your sense of that time?

GIBSON: Well, all those things certainly influenced me, but none of them profoundly. Really, I got my education back there at Amherst College under my colleague, Theodore Baird. Not because he had any interest in teaching teachers—none whatever. That was entirely an undergraduate college. We were interested in getting students to say how they know what they know. All of that stayed with me in such a way that I translated a lot of it into terms that might help graduate students. More than Christensen and all those guys, it was that early experience of mine that made the difference for me.

WOE: James Berlin identifies classical rhetoric as an example of transactional rhetoric and places Ed Corbett, Albert Duhamel, and Dudley Bailey in that group. People such as yourself and Peter Elbow are identified as expressivists, proponents of subject rhetoric who advocate more student-centered approaches to writing. When one looks at the treatment of pedagogy in the field's journals during this decade, one notes that Corbett makes a strong call for classical rhetoric's place in the composition classroom. In your experience, had the field of composition expanded to the extent that it had identifiable pedagogical affiliations?

GIBSON: I suppose that in effect there was competition, but I don't think that graduate students were ever aware of it. For one thing, you wouldn't have competing approaches like this available on one campus, so I don't think this was very publicly known. It may be Berlin's hindsight that makes clearer what may have been going on.

WOE: I have asked Professor Corbett about the theoretical focus of his TA training course, a question similar to the one I posed to you regarding English 712. He remarked, "I basically just used my book" (i.e., *Classical Rhetoric for the Modern Student*) and admitted he surprised a few people who wondered about his decision to teach beginning writing instructors classical rhetoric. Perhaps it's fair to say that teachers drew from their own strengths.

GIBSON: Ed Corbett was always a good friend of mine. He used to tell marvelous jokes. He was one of the best raconteurs I ever knew, but I can see that if we were ever colleagues, we really would be batting different balls around. That's the way it goes. My uses of classical rhetoric are few and far between.

WOE: The status of composition throughout the 1960s could be described as both transformative and turbulent. For all those who were proposing pedagogical remedies for revising the course, there were others who called for its abolishment. One of the strongest rationales given for its removal was the lack of a research base to underpin classroom practice. How did writing teachers resolve tensions between publishing and doing research in a field which may not have been perceived as viable for purposes of promotion and tenure?

GIBSON: I would feel very sad to construct an introduction to writing that was firmly based on research. I'm kind of allergic to research in this field. It always seems to me a little bit inhuman, and there's really not much of a way to research my interests. I mean, how do you research voice? Maybe it's possible. Obviously, Janet Emig did a wonderful job with those high school kids, but that was very special and they were awfully bright kids. And that seems to me one place where you can say, "OK, something really useful was done there." But I have seen some studies that are really very dreary things, so I'm a little suspicious of the statement, "We've got to be research oriented." I don't see why we have to be research oriented. One doesn't want to fault research altogether. Economists would be lost without these techniques, but they can be misused in the humanities in an effort to sound scientific.

WOE: How did you negotiate tenure and promotion for the kind of administrative duties and the program development you achieved?

GIBSON: In my time, you had to be flashy to get away with the kind of pedagogical interests that I had. If I were not a published poet and a compulsive writer of all kinds of things, I never would have made it. You know, I never got a doctorate. I'm one in a million. I wouldn't recommend it to anybody. But when you don't have a doctorate, what you've got to be is not just as smart as your friends who are doctors but smarter and busier in lots of ways. A place like NYU would never, I don't think, have appreciated me if all I did was conduct work in freshman English. In fact, NYU really didn't know what I was doing in freshman English and didn't care. What they cared about was that I was publishing.

WOE: So the particular areas did not matter?

GIBSON: Well, if I published an article in the *New York Times*, they loved it. If I had some poems in *The New Yorker*, they loved it. That's right, it didn't matter. It wasn't even a rivalry; it was a unanimity in favor of literary scholarship. They were in their frenzy trying to catch up, to be as good as Columbia. As result, they were very conservative. Now as I say, that may have changed, but I bet it hasn't. Other schools could afford to take risks then, and Massachusetts could too at that time.

WOE: What changes have you observed in the profession of English studies during your career?

GIBSON: A couple of things have happened since I began teaching. One is obviously feminist criticism and another is concern about ethnicity. If you read the journals or look at the convention programs, the thing everybody is worried about is non–English-speaking kids and black English. In that sense, the teaching of English has become extremely diversified.

WOE: Is the awareness of diversity another version of the concerns raised about nontraditional students who streamed into college classrooms in the late 1960s with the creation of open admissions policies? Then as now, educators were acutely aware of a student population whose literacy skills are keenly different from the standards of academic discourse.

GIBSON: Back there in 1961 and 1962, we were absolutely innocent of this as a problem. We were teaching high school kids to go to college, and they were mostly white middle-class kids. Nobody would buy this anymore, the little triumvirate we had of language, literature, and composition. They would say it all depends on so many other things such as the population you are dealing with. I guess I'm glad I'm not your age because I think that's going to be awfully tough to handle.

And what happens to elite education? Is it doomed? I hope not, but I'm sure a lot of people would say, "Yes." I saw an article recently about Swarthmore College which raised the question, "Can a place like Swarthmore survive?" It costs so much, and it is so much effort per student I think it would be, from my old-fashioned value system, a great tragedy if Swarthmore College did not survive. And it survives because it has a lot of rich alumni. The same is true of many colleges and universities. And their survival is only possible because of money and, of course, a certain amount of willpower. In a capitalist system, such institutions depend on rich alumni, but this is not politically correct talk.

WOE: Do you think the concern for diversification has been seen not only in reference to shifts in student populations but also in other forums? Your effort to build an interdisciplinary rhetoric program that embraced the English and Speech departments strikes me as one example of institutional diversification. What do you think of institutions in which rhetoric and writing programs have separated from the English departments to become independent programs?

GIBSON: For myself, I think that would be a mistake. I would be unhappy in a situation like that. I was as independent as I would want to be at Massachusetts but still a member of the English Department. And here's another old-fashioned prejudice: It seems to me that good composition teachers are lovers of Shakespeare.

CHARLES MORAN

Throughout his varied career, Charles Moran (1936–2015) demonstrated that his university citizenship was never constrained by departmental and institutional boundaries but extended across disciplinary divides. This explorative and collaborative spirit was reflected in the diversity of his work. He published widely on issues related to teacher training, the National Writing Project, and Writing in the Disciplines, co-editing (with Anne Herrington) Writing, Teaching, and Learning in the Disciplines (1992) *and* Genres across the Curriculum (2005). *Yet he also retained ties to the field of literature, co-editing the NCTE volume* Conversations: Contemporary Critical Theory and the Teaching of Literature *(1990) with Elizabeth Penfield.*

His work with computers and writing included the historical account of computers and composition: Computers and the Teaching of Writing in American Higher Education 1979–1994 *with Gail Hawisher, Cynthia Selfe, and Paul Le Blanc. After retiring from the University of Massachusetts–Amherst, Moran continued to turn his attention to emerging literacies in the digital world. This resulted in a collection of publications, including* Teaching the New Writing: Technology, Change, and Assessment in the 21st-Century Classroom *(2009), co-edited with Anne Herrington and Kevin Hodgson. He served on the editorial board of the journal* Computers and Composition, *and in 2004 helped draft the CCCC Position Statement on Teaching, Learning, and Assessing Writing in Digital Environments, which provides a national framework for faculty, administrators, and programs to support their students' development of digital literacies.*

—*Aaron Lanser*

"A Sense of Professional Well Being"

Margaret M. Strain

Spring 2000

WOE: James Berlin and Stephen North have recorded the developments that marked the professionalization of composition studies. I wish to explore narratives of our disciplinary origins from another vantage—local histories—to consider how individual institutions, departments, and faculty contributed to our growth. Walker Gibson has described his involvement in teacher training not only as a Director of Composition here at Amherst and at NYU but also through special programs such as Summer Institutes and College Entrance Examination Board (CEEB) workshops. Could you comment on your own involvement with the kinds of experiences that shaped your entry into the field?

MORAN: Walker Gibson did a National Endowment for the Humanities (NEH) summer seminar for two-year college teachers here. It must have been 1971 or 1972. It was out of that seminar that the journal *Teaching English in the Two-Year College* began. The first issue was written by his seminar people. That's something I felt was significant. I also wrote an essay for Tom Newkirk about how writing-as-process theories came to UMass–Amherst. Gibson was a major piece of that, but what really worked for me was connecting with the two-year colleges. A guy named Roger Garrison did the two-year college circuit and ran teacher training workshops at the University of New Hampshire every summer with Tom Newkirk and Les Fisher. He also went out to California and did "New Hampshire–West" kinds of workshops. Garrison's model was the single teacher as a circulating editor with a bunch of writers in the classroom. He propagated this through the two-year college network, and we wouldn't have gotten hold of it at all except that in the 1960s and mid-1970s we were encouraged by our then-new department head, Joe Frank, to go out and do things. One of the things we did was to hook up with community colleges and have our graduate students do internships because it seemed likely they would be teaching there. The difference between our Ph.D. program and the places where our graduate students were likely to teach was extraordinary. We were putting out people who hated the idea of heavy teaching loads—and we still do at research universities. If you graduate from here, for instance, you hope for a 1/1 teaching load.

WOE: Those jobs are becoming harder and harder to find.

MORAN: Well, yes; thank heaven, in my view. Anyway, Walker was connected to that two-year college loop, and we connected to it, not through Walker, but through Roger Garrison. It's my feeling that an awful lot of teaching talk goes on in the two-year college loop and that that kind of teaching talk is sort of forbidden in four-year research English departments.

WOE: Why do you think that is?

MORAN: Well, this last semester we finally offered a course in the Teaching of Literature here at UMass–Amherst. Until recently, we have seldom even *thought* about teaching literature as a pedagogy. Pedagogy is not really part of English studies. If you take a look at the MLA program, you don't see pedagogy, but if you take a look at CCCC—

WOE: —It's central. It's all over the program.

MORAN: Yes. Composition studies is really unique; or it's different from English studies. If it isn't humanities, it was located in the humanities and unique in having a pedagogical component. You don't find teaching at the American Philosophical Association because there's not a lot of teaching going on.

WOE: Why do you think that pedagogy is not considered a critical aspect of teaching literature?

MORAN: I'd say that in the postwar university, English modeled itself on physics and to some degree on hard sciences. These were high prestige, and you can see a link, I think, between New Criticism and a kind of empirical science. If you buy that kind of link, then there's the answer. That's why we're not thinking a lot about teaching because we're *studying*, we're not teaching. We are studying despite the fact that a huge percentage (something like 70%) of the courses that are called "English" are writing courses, courses in which people *write*. The non-English world sees our function as literacy, basically. What we ought to be doing is improving literacy levels. The study of literature is a reaction to that: "No, we're *not* doing that."

WOE: Thus, English studies sees its *raison d'être* as preserving and conveying cultural values?

MORAN: Or we are teaching the great works of Western literature or the Great Tradition.

WOE: And cultural values are embodied in those texts. We transfer them to students who leave the academy as cultivated individuals.

MORAN: You read Cervantes long enough and you will become a good person. Yes, I think there are reasons that the structure of the academy after World War II, in a time when it was increasing at a remarkable rate, permitted English to say, "OK, we're not about teaching. We are about something else."

WOE: The great debate at many colleges and universities during the 1960s to abolish freshman composition is related to this issue. One of the arguments for its removal came from those who believed that "this is not the real business of English departments. Its business is literature. Writing should be the high schools' responsibility."

MORAN: Exactly. And that's coming back now. There have been panels on it at the last two CCCCs. Bob Connors talked about the history of what he termed the "Abolitionist Movement" within composition, and he gave a real nice paper on it.

WOE: Were you part of the early Rhetoric Program at UMass–Amherst?

MORAN: No, I was on the outside working with Walker on some other projects. I taught twice, maybe three times in the Rhetoric Program. The Rhetoric of Film course was great fun. I learned a lot but never felt that we had the equipment really to deal with the rhetoric of film. That is to say, you couldn't bring in a video and stop at a particular moment and read that image. We couldn't do that; we had to talk about it, and so it wasn't terribly satisfying. But just to back up a little bit, the rhetoric requirement was a fusion of the preexisting writing requirement and speech requirement. The two-semester, two-credit freshman course was given by the English Department; the two-semester, one-credit speech course was given by the Speech Department, which has since become Communications.

So this was a fusion of English and Speech—a kind of putting back together again of the pieces that had broken off when the Speech Association split away in 1914. After this had been accomplished—maybe even as it was being accomplished—Walker met with the English Department and asked, "How many of you know the texts that we are using in freshman writing?" Nobody put his hands up. And he said, "It seems as if we have a *de facto* tradition here. Would any of you all mind if we just took this off and set it up as an independent, nondepartmental entity outside of English?" People said, "Hot dog! Good thing. Great." The department voted for it practically unanimously. A couple people—Howard Brogan, who is now retired, for example—said that he thought this was a disaster. And it proved to be a disaster.

WOE: Why did Brogan think this move was unwise?

MORAN: Well, as a long-time department head, I think he knew that English departments depend for the strength of their major on the recruitment that takes place in freshman writing. When it's taught by English people, you would say to someone who is really skilled, "I think you should be an English major." A lot of overt recruitment goes on. And what Brogan predicted turned out to be the case. That is, when we lost Rhetoric, the number of majors dropped catastrophically. This was part of a national scene as well. One of the reasons Joe Frank was happy to send some of us down to Mina Shaughnessy's lab to work in the basic writing operations to see what was going on there or to send us off to community colleges to set up internships was that we didn't have enrollment in courses here. If Moran said, "I want to teach the eighteenth-century-novel course," he would be competing with two other people who wanted to teach the same course. If I showed some signs of wanting to do something else, the feeling was, "Maybe we should encourage Moran to teach in a Hampshire County jail or to work with the community colleges or travel to Mina Shaughnessy's lab or to work with the Springfield public school system—and I did all those things.

WOE: What type of work did you do with Mina Shaughnessy?

MORAN: For a semester, four graduate students and I would leave here at four in the morning, drive down there and be at the CCNY Bedford Stuyvesant Campus about eight o'clock. We'd tutor for a couple of hours, talk with some people, check stuff out, and debrief on the way back. It was kind of fun.

WOE: You mentioned earlier that you spent time working with Gibson on collateral projects. Was Shaughnessy's lab one of those?

MORAN: No, Walker was not a piece of that. He was a piece of something called the COPS Program where we got in airplanes here and flew down to Bedford Stuyvesant to work with those who were becoming certified to teach in the New York City public school system. Our School of Education won a grant and somehow convinced the granting agency that we were better able to do this than anybody who was in place in New York. We did this for one afternoon a week and Walker set that up.

WOE: What brought the Rhetoric Program back to the English Department?

MORAN: I guess a couple of things happened. Walker brought Jim Leheny, Joe Skerrett, and C. K. Smith and myself together, and we applied for an NEH teacher training grant. We were funded, thanks largely to Walker, and we brought sixty teachers here for eight weeks during the summer. They lived here and worked on their own writing. This was 1978, I think.

In applying for that, we realized we knew some stuff about the teaching of writing. As we worked our way through that project, we did a lot more writing and a lot more reading, and we got a lot more experience. We brought in people like Peter Elbow and Lee Odell and Nancy Martin and Don Murray. It was really quite wonderful. We got into the composition community through the NEH grant. Having done that, as time went on we began to feel that we kind of knew our stuff, at least about the teaching of writing We didn't know everything—God knows—but we were grounded in a way that we had not been by our literature Ph.Ds. So in some degree, we four English Department people brought composition studies into our own world and domesticated it.

WOE: The NEH participants were high school teachers, weren't they?

MORAN: Entirely. The point I'm blundering toward is that we became comfortable in the field ourselves, so there were four people in the English Department who felt attached to composition studies. We'd worked in it, we'd begun to publish in it, and we felt we knew the field. By this time, we'd gone to a couple of CCCCs, and so we were home.

It became thinkable to us to say, "Yes, the English Department can do a writing program. It would be responsible if we did it here. There's a critical mass of people who know enough about the teaching of writing so that we could take this thing on."

We were at a political moment when English *could* again take on the work of the Rhetoric Program. Walker had stopped working with the Rhetoric Program for a number years. It was run by people in the Communications Department and had begun to get bad press. English didn't like what it was doing. English didn't know what the Rhetoric Program was doing, but English didn't like it because it wasn't English [*Moran laughs*]. It got bad press in the Faculty Senate; the Rhetoric Program got bad press with the kids. As an activist campus, as we were then, our required courses came under siege, and the rhetoric requirement was a whole-university requirement. By this time it splintered: you could satisfy the requirement by taking a course in the Rhetoric of Film, or you could satisfy it by taking the Rhetoric of Social Science, etc., etc., etc. It had become its own microcollege, which makes perfect sense for a rhetoric program given what rhetoric is and does: it takes language and persuasion as its field, and media be damned. Any medium will work, and any discourse community will work just fine.

But to the outsider, it looked fragmented. The question, "What are you requiring everyone to take?" was hard to answer. It was unstable and doomed for the reason that, though a required course, it didn't have a clear shape. The dean was also playing the usual kinds of games that deans play with these kinds of programs. The Rhetoric Program was located within Fine Arts and Humanities, and the dean kept cutting its budget and saying, "We can't offer enough rhetoric courses." The university would eventually put more money into the dean's budget, and then next year it would be the same thing, "We haven't enough money." In its last couple years the Rhetoric Program was hiring teachers about the first week of September, and you can't run a program like that. The viability of the Rhetoric Program was eroding. There had been rumors that the rhetoric requirements were going to be dropped, and, as a result, people stopped taking rhetoric courses.

At one point there were something like six thousand students who had not taken the rhetoric requirement—an immense backlog. How was this going to be handled? Well, you could pour more money into the Rhetoric Program or you could try to change something. New administrators need new ideas, or at least they would like to create their own programs. This is one of the reasons the half-life of a writing program is about seven years: new administrators need a new program so they can claim credit for it and go on and be an administrator somewhere else with a portfolio.

All of this stuff came together, and C.K. Smith, Joe Skerrett, Jim Leheny, and I had resisted the English Department's growing feeling that it should take over the Rhetoric Program to save it, because if English took it over, it would get guaranteed enrollment. We resisted because we felt that people in the Rhetoric Program were doing good things. We knew pretty much why it had fallen into disrepair and general disrepute, and it had nothing to do with Rhetoric Program personnel. Hence, we fought it. There came a time when either something else was going to happen to it or it was going to come back to English. There wasn't any way it could continue the way it was. If English had not said, "We'll do it," it was going to get divided up. The School of Education would get a piece and someone else would get a piece of it. We thought, "At this moment, we know enough. We can do a pretty good program. English needs the program. English wants the program. Let's step forward." There was a Rhetoric Study Committee that had been studying this for some time. When we put our proposal through, they said, "Sure, do it. That's great." And that's how it happened.

WOE: What did the first courses in writing instruction for graduate students at UMass–Amherst look like?

MORAN: Good question. In the 1970s, it was an English Ph.D. and Walker Gibson was on the faculty, so you could do the English Ph.D. and write your dissertation with Walker and do independent studies with him. In 1980 or so, I proposed a course called Writing and the Teaching of Writing (English 712), which Walker and I taught the first couple of years. When I became Writing Program Director, I felt it was not appropriate for me to be hiring people and also recommending that they take English 712, which I teach. It was too tight a loop. I also didn't feel I could teach the course claiming, "I don't have any particular pedagogy I'm pushing; here, let's look at a whole range of pedagogies," and then say, "This is what you're going to do" when someone came to work for me in the Writing Program. It was hard, so Walker agreed to teach it until we hired Anne Herrington and Peter Elbow. The first time I taught the course, Richard Braddock, Richard Lloyd-Jones, and Lowell Schoer's *Research in Written Composition* (1963) was a text and so was E.D. Hirsch's *The Philosophy of Composition* (1977), Janet Emig's *The Composing Processes of Twelfth Graders* (1971), Peter Elbow's *Writing Without Teachers* (1973), and Donald Murray's *A Writer Teaches Writing* (1968). There wasn't much out there at the time. You could teach those things and a few articles from CCC, and whatever else you could find, and say, "We just did the field."

WOE: When I've asked others to identify what he or she sees as historical moments in the field, Walker Gibson talked about the Summer Institutes sponsored by the CEEB and the NDEA during the 1960s. Ed Corbett mentioned the 1963 CCCC convention. What is your moment?

MORAN: That's hard. Personally, I'd say it all began to come together in the summer of 1978 when we held an NEH Summer Institute. With the grant, I was able to meet Nancy Martin and thereby get connected with the London Schools Project. I met Peter Elbow and Anne Herrington, who was a grad student then, and Lee Odell, who had just finished his *Research on Composing* (1978), and Charles R. Cooper, author of *Evaluating Writing: Describing, Measuring, Judging* (1977). We were right in the middle of everything. It felt wonderful.

Aside from that, working with Jim Leheny and Jim Collins of Springfield Technical High School. We did a seminar on the Teaching of Writing (this must have been the summer of 1974). Leheny brought Garrison's monograph to us. Once we read it, we decided we'd go to Springfield and use Jim's high school class as a lab class and try out some of Garrison's techniques. Each of the people in the seminar would take five or six of Jim's students and would be in charge of their writing. We'd meet after Jim's class in his school in a one-hour debriefing seminar, photocopy a piece of student writing, and say, "OK, this is what Bill wrote today. What should Bill's teacher say to Bill tomorrow? What's the next step?" Jim Leheny would read the students' writing aloud so that it would feel like literature. Jim Collins went on from that experience to get his Ph.D. and now is a professor at SUNY–Buffalo and has published a half a dozen books. We are most proud of him. He got his M.A. in English and Ph.D. in the School of Education.

So for me, beginning to work individually with writers rather than working with writers in sets of twenty-five was a real turnaround. I had been teaching the advanced expository writing course as a conventional course. After the Garrison experience, I taught it entirely as a tutorial. I wouldn't do it again because you lose a lot; there's a power relationship that I don't much like in the tutorial. But having someone show up at the door every half-hour with writing once a week, looking at it with them, listening, saying a few things, having them go out and come back in a week with another piece—I really learned about how writers work and how my interventions didn't work.

If I suggested something and someone came back and couldn't do it, or it blew up or we'd have this terribly messy draft, we couldn't avoid the fact that it hadn't worked. Or you couldn't avoid the fact that what you said had an effect, and the effect was not one that, in your judgment, had improved the writing. It was a learning experience. That, for me, was a turning point: beginning to teach writing in a tutorial setting.

WOE: Can you speak to the kinds of accommodations that your department made for faculty who, as a result of this experience, were headed in a new professional direction?

MORAN: I don't think that there was a lot of resistance to what we did. I was permitted to redefine myself. That, in a sense, was a loss of a literature person. At the time, however, the department had excess resources, and it had too little to do. It didn't have a reason to complain. Now as to hiring new people such as Anne Herrington or Peter Elbow or Jean Nienkamp instead of an American Studies person, that's a choice the department has had to make. We've been able to make the argument that the people we are training are getting jobs and there's demand for what we're doing. Then we might say "Here's Charlie Moran running a writing program that annually teaches six thousand people. Charlie is doing all this by himself, and we should really hire one more person to work with him." And so you get one more person. In a couple years you say, "Look, we're still teaching six thousand people and we're developing a junior-year writing program that teaches another six thousand people." You continue to make those arguments.

We hired Jean Nienkamp on the grounds that the territory was larger and larger and we were harder and harder pressed. You've got to keep making arguments. There are times when I do feel like a marginal person, which is awkward for a white male of my generation and background, but I feel like I have to argue harder and work harder and be cleaner than someone else because we are composition people. The case is still there, but without feeling sorry for ourselves and whining too much, we have been able to make the case and we'll likely have another person.

When you phrased your question earlier you said, "You've got all this administration to do. Doesn't the English Department have to pay attention to that?" I guess we're doing "both/and," which is to say, working harder than anybody else, including the people who don't have to do both (i.e., administration and scholarship), but we've been running the writing program and publishing a lot of stuff.

We are so fortunate here to have the existing rhetorical structure, that is to say, Sarah Stelzner, Marcia Curtis, and Pat Sirkowski. They are three staff positions within the Rhetoric Program whose work is in teacher training and running the program. (We have two secretaries who are also part of the staff, which means that we, the faculty, don't have to schedule the courses or set up meetings.) All three have published. Each of them works with a group of teaching assistants every semester and we absolutely trust them. They talk to us about composition theory, so this is a kind of program extension. Really we have a class system here with faculty and staff, and that is sort of uncomfortable because we're doing some of the same work. It's collaborative, but some of us are better paid than others. That is (and should be) a source of friction. Peter, Anne, Jean, and I can spend some time writing books and articles because a lot of the program administration is done by this wonderful staff.

WOE: Since you've been here at UMass–Amherst, you've seen the creation of an independent Rhetoric Program and its return to the English Department. Where do you think the field of composition studies is headed?

MORAN: I'm scared. Part of it is because my wife and I have two children who are about to come out of graduate school.

WOE: In composition?

MORAN: No. I guess I'm glad they aren't. They reacted against the family in sort of a nice way—physics and marine biology. They are first class and have done everything right. They've gotten grants and so forth, but the academy is imploding so fast that I don't know if they are going to get jobs. Something that is happening and has been happening over the past ten years is that we in English are translating full-time positions into multiple part-time positions. In doing so, we are following the same lead or working in the same envelope as business and industry, where full-time benefit positions become temporary positions.

WOE: How is the field implicated in this pattern?

MORAN: As long as composition is in English and as long as English is turning full-time positions into multiple part-time positions (which it is) and is following the rest of the academy in doing that, then the MLA job list is going to look worse and worse and worse. Because when somebody retires not only is he not replaced, but should he be, he is replaced by five TAs or five part-timers. Half the English faculty in the California State System is part time. That scares me. Composition has been worse than English studies in using part-time help. We sort of inherited that, but it has always been low-status work done by part-timers and TAs. We've got a real class division in the field of composition. We have a few people who were lucky in the time of their birth or who they knew—they were fortunate to get jobs. I'm on a sabbatical this year, and, my God, it's wonderful. Full-time faculty members get sabbaticals. Part-time faculty do not. I don't mean to express guilt but a concern. I worry, "Where are we headed?" If you go to a conference, you meet graduate students trying like crazy to get their vitas full so that they can get jobs when they get out.

WOE: These are people who are presenting papers at conferences, publishing articles—what John Guillory has termed "preprofessional activity"—but which ten years ago would have been expectations for an assistant professor. That ante keeps going up.

MORAN: Yes. And you do this so that you do not fall back into the mire of the part-time instructor. You want to go first class. You want to get up into the top echelon, and if you can get up there and stay there, you're in business. If you fall back or should not get tenure, then, my God, it's multiple part-time jobs again. I just see us infected by that as a discipline. I can see the research we're doing, the journals that are proliferating—but they've got nothing to do with the positions that people will actually have. They are connected in the sense that the reason we have the journals is so that people can get credentials so that they can stay on top. As the fear level increases, the pressure to publish increases and the journals will proliferate. I don't like it. It is not a good future.

WOE: Should the field then become more selective and contain our growth, privileging quality over quantity?

MORAN: If I were a tenured associate professor, I'd say, "OK, I've got it. Now my obligation as a graduate faculty person is to work with, during the next twenty-five years, one person—not two—but one, and help that person become established in the field." That would be appropriate, but we're not doing that. So it scares me unless we adopt the Wyoming Resolution, which would mean, in effect, going to the provost and saying, "Now, all these courses that are taught by TAs, you can have 10% of them, but for the 90%, we need full-time faculty. And that means you've got to lop off Polymer Science or the School of Nursing and maybe a couple of others because this Wyoming Resolution is really important. We should abide by it." [*He laughs*] It's just not going to happen.

We have a two-tiered system now. The way you get into the tiered system is as a researcher, and as a researcher, you need to request release time. Release from what? Release from teaching. And as long as that is around, then we'll want our graduate students (for better and worse) to be able to teach as they choose. Not to teach 5/5 but to be able to teach 3/3 or 3/2 or something like that and have some time to reflect on their teaching. That's a good situation. Teaching 5/5—all composition—is not a good situation. I don't want our graduate students teaching a 5/5 load of composition, not because composition is bad work. It is good work, but the working conditions are terrible.

And what you really believe, you say to people you love. I've been saying to our children, "You've got to be fast-track kids. You've got to be researchers and publish." They say, "But I want to teach." I say, "God, kid, if you write on your application that you want to teach, you'll get killed. You want grants and so on and so forth. As you are getting established, then you can do some teaching." I believe that to be true in their fields, and I believe it to be true in our field or else I wouldn't say it. Here I am telling the kids to do this thing that I despise, and I'm sure we're in a similar kind of quasi-parental relationship with our graduate students: We wish the best for them, saying, "God, I hope you go first class" and "Yes, I value teaching" and "Yes, I do it myself sometimes."

WOE: These issues affect the quality of relationships among graduate students, at times cultivating an unhealthy atmosphere.

MORAN: Yes, and that is driven by the institution's need for cheap help. You don't need a rhetoric program that has a thousand graduate students in it. You don't need an English program with seventy-five graduate students. I'm thinking of a counter-model. Our son is working in geophysics. Geophysics grad students don't teach at all and so there isn't any pressure to staff classes. My son is his dissertation director's advisee and graduate student. Period. His advisor has funding for him and they write grants together, but that's it. This is a five-year relationship and it's one to one. The advisor doesn't feel the need for any more graduate students unless he gets another grant and gets some more funding. That's a model that we can't replicate here because freshman English is required to be staffed. Or rather, we could, but if we did, instead of having TAs we'd have part-timers. We tell ourselves, "Well, hiring TAs is more defensible because maybe TAs will eventually get full-time positions, whereas part-timers will end up piecing together a full-time load at three different institutions."

Again, my feeling is that we can talk about publication, we can talk about where the discipline is going, we can talk about specialization, or we can talk about a lot of stuff. But all of that, I think, is based upon a sense of professional well-being—or ethical well-being—that we're not walking toward right now. We're walking away from it. And if we do not think about it, we are not whole.

NANCY WELCH

Nancy Welch's first book, Getting Restless: Rethinking Revision in Writing Instruction *(1997), grew out of her doctoral work in composition and rhetoric and her own experiences as a writer of fiction. Drawing on narrative case studies,* Getting Restless *was originally part of a dissertation that included a series of short stories focused on working class families in the industrial Midwest, later published as* The Road from Prosperity: Stories *(2005).*

Welch contrasts her earlier work on individual composing practices with a more recent focus on public rhetorics: "Most of my writing and teacherly concerns through the 1990s focused on how to cultivate individual practices of revision—of restless questioning and creative textual improvisations—against social and disciplinary constraint. In recent years, however, I've faced a pileup of rhetorical situations that test the power of individual acts of revision."[1] *In* Living Room: Teaching Public Writing in a Privatized World *(2008) Welch makes an important contribution to the field's revitalized interest in public writing and rhetorical history.* Living Room *critiques our privatized era "of shopping malls and Clear Channel; of state-sanctioned ethnic profiling and militarized responses to public protest; of private economic interests colluding to shape public policy on everything from energy and interest rates to health care and access to the airwaves."*[2] *Welch argues that if we're to explore with our students when, where, and how they can deliver arguments that matter, we need to look to the lessons of earlier generations, and especially to the 20th century's struggles for labor and civil rights. This approach is evident in* "We're Here and We're Not Going Anywhere: Why Working-Class Rhetorical Traditions Still Matter," *which received the 2011 Richard Ohmann Award for Outstanding Article in* College English.

Most recently, she co-edited Composition in the Age of Austerity *with Tony Scott (2016), which chronicles how neoliberal political economy shapes the daily realities of composition programs, including writing assessments, curricula, teacher agency, program administration, and funding distribution. Other publications include* The Dissertation and the Discipline: Reinventing Composition Studies, *co-edited with Catherine G. Latterell, Cindy Moore, and Sheila Carter-Tod (2002) and articles on writing center pedagogy. Welch teaches at the University of Vermont, where she has directed the First-Year Writing Program and works with faculty across campus who teach in UVM's multidisciplinary first-year writing seminars.*

—Lisa Sperber

---

1 Welch, Nancy. *Living Room: Teaching Public Writing in a Privatized World*. Portsmouth, NH: Boynton/Cook: Heinemann, 2008: (4).
2 Ibid (5).

"Imagining Stories"

Fred Santiago Arroyo and Alice Gillam

Fall 2000

WOE: What and who inspired you to make the switch from creative writing to rhetoric and composition?

WELCH: I thought rhet and comp *was* English studies until I got to graduate school and then learned about literature. Everything started when I took basic writing classes at Northeastern University's night school in the early eighties, while I was working full time as a secretary. The company I was working for—I was working as a medical secretary—wanted me to take a medical terminology course, but before I could take the medical terminology course I needed to have passed English 1 or English 101. So I told them I would have to take this composition course. Then I went and took their little writing test and got placed in basic writing. I took two quarters of basic writing and then three quarters of first-year comp. At that point, I of course didn't even know what basic writing meant—I didn't know it was stigmatized, I didn't know it meant remedial. I just knew that three times a week I would go to the Huntington Avenue Y and have these writing classes. I was getting to write and I loved it. So I kept saying to the company I was working for, "No, now I have to take intermediate comp, now I have to take advanced comp," and so I just kept doing composition.

By the time I started college full time at UMass Boston, I thought that writing and composition was the center of the curriculum, and UMass Boston had such a cafeteria-style curriculum that I could keep up that idea because I took courses with Hephzibah Roskelly, Louise Smith, and Jack Brereton, writing courses and courses in literary theory and linguistics—to me all of it was about writing and working on writing. To me as a student, UMass Boston seemed like the place where everything was happening and composition seemed like something that was valued; being there led me to define myself as a compositionist long before I defined myself as a fiction writer. And from there particular teachers, like Kate Ronald and Joy Ritchie at Nebraska, modeled for me a way of being in the world and living through theory, living out their philosophies.

WOE: It's interesting listening to what you say because basic writing is so often seen as reproducing the status quo. But for you it was something different.

WELCH: For a long time I took the tack that ignorance is bliss. I thought I was in a real college classroom with a real college professor. I had no notion that this was night school, that this was basic writing, that all of these things were provisional. But I also question now the idea that this was liberatory because I didn't know it wasn't.

At one point I was having an argument with Steve North because he was talking in the most blanket terms that we should get rid of the whole enterprise of first-year comp. I said if you do that students like me wouldn't have self-selected into a writing course, selected into a writing track. I never imagined myself as an English major; I thought that if I ever went to college it would be for finance, for business; it would be for something to get a job. So I was telling North about this basic writing class, and I was probably very much romanticizing it until he asked who the instructors were, what their lives were like, and I couldn't answer that question. I have no idea who they were, but I don't doubt that they were graduate students, underemployed people who had finished their degrees, or freeway flyers. I think it's incredible that they taught the courses the way they did. One of the instructors had us reading Frantz Fanon and Herbert Marcuse in basic writing. I do have to wonder about their lives, about saying that they should sacrifice for me or for students like me.

But I definitely feel that when I say things about the enterprise of first-year composition, I do so knowing that's also how I came to be here.

WOE: We had a big argument in our graduate seminar this past semester because, except for myself and one other fellow student, there are really no people of color in the program and the majority of the class was persuaded by Sharon Crowley's argument for getting rid of first-year comp, especially her argument that we shouldn't teach first-year writing because it is a racist enterprise. One of the reasons the class was persuaded is that if you are a person of color and come through a comp program connected to an English department, you will learn only humanistic (Western, male, white) values that are oppressive. But, as you said, some people need this opportunity to get into the system, and the opportunity happens through language, through English. Do you hear from other people this narrative, that within systems we understand as oppressive there can be possibility?

WELCH: I do. There is a woman who is actually trying to put together a collection of essays of theorized literacy narratives from a range of people, coming from the perspective that often characterizes how we tell stories in composition—that everyone in composition is white, middle class and guilty of the whiteness and middle classness of this enterprise. There's almost become a kind of routine gesture of saying, well, of course, we are middle class. Or falling out of Lynn Bloom's essay "Teaching My Class," it's become routine to assume that this is a story of all composition teachers.

But what this woman realized in talking to more and more people is that there is great variety and difference in people's narratives of how they came to composition and how they came to teaching, and these differences are erased by the "story" that we were all good students, we were all good writers, we were all middle class, we were all people very comfortable within this system—when (I think) she dropped out of high school and has a GED. There is another woman who spent years following the Grateful Dead and got into school via discovering that there is such a thing as lesbian literature. There are different ways to find ways into the university and to find possibility there, and not just through a kind of assimilation narrative.

I think how well nontraditional students succeed also depends on the people who are currently making up a university and who in their daily practice and philosophy are committed to the belief that there can be many paths into a university, that there's not a stone wall between "us" who belong and "them" who either don't belong or need to be "invited" to join in just one way. At the same time, I see decreasing, rather than increasing, possibilities for these multiple entries. I mean, as I hear people speak of our being in a "post-open-admissions" era and as I talk with friends teaching in the CUNY system and in California, I realize that, at bottom, a late 1960s and 1970s experiment made it possible for me to go to college as I did, to even believe that I could go to college. As open-admissions universities start closing the doors and as schools like mine, like UVM, start back-pedaling away from any kind of affirmative action commitment, I think alternative narratives of entering higher education will be harder to compose. Maybe now more than ever we need imaginative, committed academics—and radical administrators—who are figuring out where the cracks are, the fissures, the alternatives.

WOE: It's been widely noted that the field of rhetoric and composition, especially the teaching of composition, often consists primarily of women. Terms like "nurturing" and "mothering," however, are often used pejoratively. What is your sense of this?

WELCH: First in terms of my own teaching, one thing students say again and again to me, and also in course evaluations, is the phrase "I felt encouraged rather than discouraged about writing in this class," which suggests a long history of writing instruction as finding lack, finding defect, and discouraging students. I want my teaching to focus on what is good and helping students learn to see as writers what is good, what is exciting, what is happening in this piece of writing and learning to push it or extend it or question it. People usually assume that if you are nurturing you are not challenging, and I don't think that's true at all. It is a *huge* challenge to ask somebody to read through a draft and find three moments that they just want to say "wow" about, or to think about one particular strength of the draft and how they would want to carry it on, or to think about the argument that the draft is making and consider where and how to extend it and where and how to question it. Those are things that nurture that writing, that believe in the writing, that say this is writing that's worthwhile—that you should keep working with it, that you should keep wrestling with it—and these are things that are very challenging, too. So I don't think that nurture has to be the opposite of challenge as the distinction usually gets set up.

But I'm also constantly worrying about what I am nurturing and what I am not. Where are the places in the draft where I say "wow" or "yeah" or "I'd love to hear more about that"—because sometimes then I'm choosing not to say "wow" or "yeah" or "I want to hear more about that" in other places. Also, those comments can tell me what my assumptions are, what my values are. When you are nurturing some things in a writer, that is also valuing and political. So I want to nurture and challenge, and I also want to find ways to keep being watchful of what I'm nurturing, who I'm nurturing, why and what the problems are.

One of the things I really respond to in my students' writing are moments of a kind of smart irony, especially in younger students, because when I see it, it reminds me of the contemporary fiction that I often read or certain kinds of very polished essays, like the way I think of David Sedaris's commentaries on NPR. And it's an idea of smartness that I find myself responding positively to, but I also think it's a problem to promote a kind of hip irony at the expense of other kinds of tones and other kinds of voices. So I am trying to be aware of this, and I'm actually introducing readings about the problems of tone and irony to make it a class discussion. I feel it is a problem in my writing as well—in my fiction, that it can tend to be too ironic—and so I try to watch for my tendency to respond to and note only that kind of moment or that kind of tone and not seeing and valuing other kinds of tones.

WOE: You seem to always find ways to challenge and disrupt how students become comfortable in how they see things, but you also seem to find ways to look at and question how comfortable you are. Don't we composition teachers need to question how comfortable we are in the things we are doing?

WELCH: Right, how to disrupt what I am doing and not necessarily to disrupt what the students are doing. People have questioned me on this idea of encouraging students to disrupt or get restless with or complicate what they are doing because of that power position I have as a teacher. Part of the way I address that is to try to create as much choice in the classroom as possible for students to decide what they are going to revise, what they are going to question and so forth, rather than my making that choice for them. But also I try to disrupt my position as a teacher by saying that in any classroom's narrative it's not just the students who need to be questioning and revising but also the teacher.

WOE: To really contribute to the field in the next century, a composition scholar will have to seriously learn from the many exceptional feminist scholars in the field. How do you understand the political and institutional challenges we face, and in what ways do you see feminist scholars addressing them?

WELCH: When I look at the generation of women scholars and teachers who have educated and inspired me, especially as a compositionist, I see women who have not only gained equality and positions of power but who have struggled—and with a lot of opposition, difficulty, and pain—to change the terms of engagement, to change the positions they and others after them would occupy. They've changed, I think, what it means to do work as a compositionist. I remember one of my advisors talking about article after article of hers being rejected some years ago and always the same reason given: too "soft," too "chatty," too "anecdotal." That's a kind of rejection I haven't had to face because of the persistence of women, like this advisor, before me. The stories I compose get critically examined and questioned and argued with by reviewers, but no one says, "You can't write this way at all."

Maybe I'm pointing to something fairly surfacey—a change in what's allowed in terms of our writing voices and forms, the relationship to students and ideas that these tones allow—though actually I don't think this is just superficial. But I always knew each time I sat down to write that I wasn't the first and only one to write this way, and I greatly appreciate those who were. I worry, though, about how much of a backlash there is against acknowledging and celebrating the presence of feminism in our field or how easy it is to erase feminism from composition. I mean, there's Joe Harris's book, *A Teaching Subject*, that doesn't make any mention of feminism's huge contributions to the field. The same is true for *Composition in the Twenty-First Century*. The essays collected there suggest by omission that feminism won't be a part of composition in the twenty-first century. And I wonder, then, what would happen, how we'd use words like "collaboration," "nurture," and "contest" without feminist examinations, histories, applications, and critiques of all these terms.

WOE: One of the areas I find most persuasive is the feminist use of noncombative rhetorics. What might noncombative rhetorics tell us about the teaching of writing, and about the truths and communities we create in classrooms?

WELCH: I think the term I try to use is "relational rhetoric." I tend to think of this as wanting to resist the Oedipal narrative of academic socialization—a narrative that says you must repudiate the mother, repudiate all attachments, and place yourself in the position of the father, then throw off all authoritative voices around you and emerge from that a post-Oedipal, distinct, separate, differentiated speaking subject—who then feels some guilt and some nostalgia for that pre-Oedipal world of attachment and community and so forth, but who is also rewarded in the end by achieving the father's position, by achieving a singular, authoritative voice. I'm reacting to that narrative of academic socialization and how one comes to voice. I see it everywhere, from Bartholomae's "Inventing the University" to Jane Tompkin's essay "Fighting Words: Unlearning to Write the Critical Essay" about critical writing as a kind of western gunfight or David-and-Goliath narrative. It's also found in any dissertation that says you start with the literature review and then by the end of that chapter you come to your statement or thesis and then proceed out alone into the territory or wilderness of your dissertation, having left all the literature behind. That model is an Oedipal one as well. It's a narrative I have difficulty with. First of all, Freud was never able to theorize how women come through the Oedipal triangle; they are kind of in that triangle forever, they just kind of languish there. They marry a man who reminds them of their father and then they have a baby or a penis substitute, and that's the end of the story for women.

So given that I never really liked Freud's story anyway, I don't like seeing it replayed in ideas of academic authority. For me, that's the appeal of object relations theory and people like Jessica Benjamin and Daniel Stern who say that differentiation and individuation are not the ultimate achievement of human identity and that, in fact, in terms of human development we should be reaching for learning to recognize that others can share your reality and you can share connections with them. This is what babies seem to already know when they delight in games of peekaboo (an example that comes from Jessica Benjamin): the delight that Mommy or Daddy is going away now they are back, they're going away, coming back, they share in my reality but they are also separate—that is the delight.

This is all a very abstract way of saying that what I would like to do in terms of my own critical writing is to start showing a sense of relationship, and then, yes, there are moments of differentiating my position from someone else's or saying that I do argue with this or I do disagree with that. But I'm trying to find a way from the first page of an article to the last to show my relationship with others, rather than having this idea that on page five I should have refuted all others and left them behind. And part of that, too, is trying to bring into relationship people who wouldn't normally appear together in the same essay. I think I have one where in the same paragraph I theorize through a student and through something from Jane Gallop, and I think that is important to do; they are both on equal footing in this paragraph, they both speak to the issue. Or putting Lacan and Minnie Bruce

Pratt in the same essay as important theorists to think through, instead of saying Lacan, male, Continental, dead therefore more important than Minnie Bruce Pratt, living, American, white, lesbian. And likewise Freud and Bakhtin because Bakhtin couldn't stand Freud, and because each opens up something that is latent and hushed up in the other.

I think along the lines of relational rhetorics because it helps me think about connection and separation happening in a dance—Jessica Benjamin's metaphor—that needs to continue.

WOE: Tropes for thinking about issues—tropes like "entering the conversation," "thick description," "carnivalization," "inventing the university," "the contact zones"—have become master tropes in rhetoric and composition, tropes, I will add, that have often been imported from outside rhetoric and composition to help us invent new ways of seeing ourselves. When do these metaphors or tropes become unproductive? And how do we avoid speaking through dead metaphors?

WELCH: My suspicion is that some terms, like "contact zone," will have currency for a while and then drop away. I definitely do think that that one was latched onto so intensely for a short period of time that probably it's not going to show up that much more. The problem it was trying to address will not drop away, however. Probably what we need to be aware of are the common, familiar, everyday terms that we don't recognize as professional jargon but that we constantly use; for instance, I think of Raymond Williams's *Keywords*, and Joe Harris's essay about "community." "Community" is definitely one of those keywords. Until Harris wrote that essay, most people did not stop to think about what it means to constantly use this word as a trope, as a dead metaphor. That makes me wonder what other words we constantly use; I mean, I'll be really curious to see what comes up at next year's 4Cs, given the call for "educating the imagination" and "re-imagining education," because "imagination" is another one of those words that probably needs a deep investigation.

WOE: Your work shows that it's not the terms themselves that do the intellectual work but the act of writing another essay, the act of going back and revising your ideas.

WELCH: I tend to end my essays with complications or references to what the essay cannot answer or to what I need to do next, and I'm starting to feel that that ending itself is starting to look ritualized. I really feel in this current chapter I am writing for a writing center book that I do need to have the questions I end with, but it's really beginning to feel like, "And at the end of all essays, Nancy ends by complicating what she has just written."

WOE: And doing this for you becomes in a way comfortable and resolves the problem of how to end?

WELCH: Exactly.

WOE: Do you think we can arrive at a point when we will understand what is intrinsic to rhetoric and composition? And will we ever be unified as a field or will we always continue to reinvent ourselves?

WELCH: I don't know the answer to that, but I do hope that the field will always be interdisciplinary and in conversation and interaction with other fields. I think that those departments that have removed themselves from departments of English, for example, have tried to assert a certain idea of what intrinsic means—we are self-sufficient; we are a department of writing and rhetoric separate from reading, separate from literary theory, separate from linguistics, separate from everything else. That kind of thing, I think, is impoverishing, just as I think it is impoverishing for writing centers to declare an identity that's totally separate from composition. I don't even understand the desire because I also teach in women's studies on a campus where there are a lot of cross-disciplinary conversations. For instance, I'm interested in finding out what social geographers are doing these days—geography is the coolest field out there, and at first I thought, "Oh, you poor geographers, you only deal with maps." Of course, geography is not just about my problems of dealing with Triple A maps—it's about maps, boundaries, spaces that are entirely political and fascinating and vexed. There are conversations I have been able to have with geography and sociology—really all across the arts and sciences curriculum.

WOE: I sometimes get impatient with people who seem to want to get rid of the composition part of the field, who see it as practice and messy compared to the more theoretical part, rhetoric; who claim, "After all, rhetoric's the first form of literary criticism, so we really deserve respect and we have just as much right as anyone to be in English studies, and we can do what they do better." Again, it's a way to eschew the messy, practical elements evoked by composition. It seems to me that we learn from these problems that rub together. A field that has these parts that don't easily fit together can be a productive thing. I remember years ago Diane Wakoski came to the campus where I was teaching, and when I was showing her around, she said it was always her advice to writers to major in something other than English because another major gives you a whole set of metaphors. As you were saying about your contacts in women's studies and geography, these contacts all of a sudden allow you to see things in unexpected and very productive ways.

WELCH: Right. And that's what I admire in the work of fiction writer Andrea Barrett. She did an M.A. and then started a Ph.D. in the sciences, biology I believe. Her fiction really presents a whole new metaphorical world, and her historical fiction of these scientific discoveries and the people behind the scenes is fascinating. It makes me mindful that no matter how educated I may think I am, I am completely ignorant about so many things. It is difficult to be a composition person in an English department, but it's important because it's also a point of contact. In my department, some of my colleagues try to build me up, boost me up, by erasing the composition part. The thing lately is, "Well, Nancy, you're really our department theorist. This is Nancy, she's our department theorist."

And I say, "Composition theorist."

"No, no, you're the *theorist*—not just 'composition' theorist."

Or they'll say "rhetorician." But "compositionist" is the word I use. And I theorize teaching and students' writing, which says that I'm not flattered or seduced by the term theorist but that I'm interested in composition and composing.

WOE: It's like in the old days, in the seventies, when there was a pride in being called a feminist and not being flattered by "Well, you know, you don't remind me of a feminist, you're not angry" or, "You like men . . ."

WELCH: It's definitely that kind of gesture.

WOE: Given your insistence on identifying yourself as a composition theorist, what do you make of those within our field who try to distance themselves from this identity, who speak in terms of "post-composition"?

WELCH: This is actually the first I've heard the term, but my first reaction is the same as my reaction to "post-feminism"—why are you setting yourself apart from, not in relation to, our histories? Composing suggests embodiedness, materiality—not something to distance ourselves from.

WOE: As the American philosopher Hillary Putnam points out: "there are two sorts of tools in the world: there are tools like a hammer or a screwdriver which can be used by one person; and there are tools like a steamship which require the cooperative activity of a number of persons to use. Words have been thought of too much on the model of the first sort of tool." Clearly your work and teaching seems deeply committed to teaching students how to use language as a form of cooperation, as a steamship. How do you see this "division of linguistic labor"? And in what specific ways do you try to use language in the classroom as a form of cooperation?

WELCH: First of all, it's in always trying to complicate the notion that some people have the language or the language of power or the keywords or the discourse or whatever, while others have to be invited through cooperation or community or scaffolding or whatever to acquire that language. That sets up a one-way bridge: there are those who have and those who need to be helped along. One of the things I try to think about in my teaching is how to make myself and my students aware of what, first of all, we are all bringing to the enterprise, so it's not a question of I have it and now I'm going to share it with them, or that certain students have the cultural capital that counts here. I also try to introduce the idea that it's more than language, or that language is a very small part. The whole argument of the English Only movement, for instance, is we need to have a shared language if we're going to be efficient, productive, get along, and so forth. But, in fact, one of the things my students talk about around this issue—and it usually comes up if we're reading Gloria

Anzaldúa's "How to Tame a Wild Tongue" or an essay by Anna Castillo or some student writings in our course packet—is those situations where they have actually communicated with another person, where neither of them shared the same language. Out of a sense that we want to talk, that we want to figure out what each other is saying, we find a way.

It is more than language. It's also hierarchies of language and of accents and of ideas about prestige. I can only think of these two examples: in my class people were talking about the difference of putting a French phrase in your writing and putting a Spanish phrase in your writing; or I talked about my husband going into a bank in Burlington, Vermont, after he had just arrived from France and barely spoke any English, and walking out with a ten thousand-dollar loan, and he says, very clearly, French is cultural capital. So I guess what I'm saying is that I try in my teaching to create an environment that focuses on the belief that we are all contributing to the classroom, rather than this idea of some kind of divide as Linda Brodkey talks about between the "literate us" and "the illiterate them." But I also try to bring that whole question of communication—understanding and literacy—into any class I teach. In first-year composition I would bring that in when we are talking about editing and what that means, so that we can question that idea that language is the only thing on which communication and understanding depends, that there's more to it than that: the willingness of an audience, for instance, to listen and respond and struggle against prejudices and assumptions that might prevent real listening.

WOE: These divisions do exist and sometimes they surely cause great harm, but isn't it important in our classrooms to also tell stories that don't erase the differences we have in writing, in communication, in understanding?

WELCH: I think of it this way. Sociolinguists like James Paul Gee emphasize that in a particular social situation, there is a Discourse—capital D—that includes not only a way of speaking but a way of doing, knowing, valuing, and not doing, not knowing, not valuing. And from Gee, one might conclude—as some have concluded, rightly or wrongly, from Heath or Bartholomae or others before Gee—that our task is to teach students how to get inside particular Discourses. But what I think is really important is to highlight how writers struggle with and struggle against the exclusions, silences, and violences of particular Discourses. I should add that this is something I've learned from Bartholomae and Petrosky's *Ways of Reading*. Though I don't use that or any textbook in my classes because I don't like all the apparatus, I admire and learn from how almost every selection in that textbook highlights a writer facing and grappling with—or maybe not quite facing up to and really grappling with—a particular, difficult rhetorical situation. These are the kinds of readings, I think, that help students articulate and examine their own particular difficulties and recognize them as social and shared, not just personal struggles and failures.

In my first-year composition class, for instance, we read a short essay by Patricia Williams, "The Death of the Profane," about her struggle with a law review that invited her, as an "excluded" voice in legal studies, to submit an essay—and that then tried to make race, including her racialized position, a "phantom word" that couldn't be mentioned in a law review article. This idea of phantom words that are present but taboo is one that students, in a variety of ways, can really think with as they talk about Williams's essay and as they write in the margins of their own essays. So there's a cooperative relationship that can form here between Williams's struggle to make visible the phantom word of race and students' struggles with phantom words in their own texts. But in any moment of cooperation, there's also the danger of co-opting Williams's text and reducing it to "she's making an argument against political correctness," or reading another student's text about struggling to articulate a gay identity in a very hetero college environment and saying (this is what one student wrote back to another recently), "You just haven't made the right friends yet." But maybe this danger is part of the initial problem, this constant attempt to diffuse and hush up any kind of dissent and struggle and insist on one unified, happy or inevitable story.

WOE: It seemed in discussing "cooperation" you were also pointing out how it can turn into a form of "co-opting"—that is, again, believing in only one version of the story or in one possibility. Is this partially why you focus on potential spaces, "worlds-in-the-making," and the possible worlds the members of a class can create?

WELCH: Yes. I don't want to take the words of Winnicott, Bakhtin, and post-Freudian feminist theorists like Jane Flax and Joan Copjec—people who focus on what can multiply our visions of the future—and turn them into just liberal platitudes about possibility. But because it's been so important for me to recognize how much I tend to write, think, and live in ways that shut down the future, and then to have learned strategies as a writer and a feminist to work against this, I want my students to consider such strategies too. And this consideration doesn't have to take place through overtly theoretical language. Just asking someone to consider the argument that is emerging in a draft and then how the opposite might be true, or to consider a moment that doesn't fit the argument or shows why it's a very hard argument to make—these are ways of enacting in practice this idea of worlds-in-the-making, not already finished and done.

WOE: In composition's desire to achieve disciplinary respect and legitimacy, there is a dismissal of practice as a scholarly subject. But what I really admire about your work is the intersection of theory and practice it represents, the sometimes indistinguishability between your using theory to interpret practice and practice to create or complicate theory. What do you see as the future of scholarly work that works at the nexus of theory and practice?

WELCH: I know this work will continue—I can think of so many recent examples. The challenge will be to value this work and not reward only scholarship that appears "purely" theoretical as higher, better, more authoritative. At the same time, I think we have to guard against the opposite, celebrating untheorized, unreflective narratives as somehow "purer" or more "true" as well.

WOE: It seems to me that reading for you is not consumption but creation; likewise, writing is not just production but creating and invention for your audience to use for their own creation. What is your sense of the importance of the poetics I'm reading/creating from your work? And how do you approach this relation to reading and writing in your teaching?

WELCH: Yes, I think that's true—creation, not consumption—but something else you just said—"for your audience to use for their own creation"—reminds me too of the need to always maintain a difficult, ongoing relationship and dialogue with those you're creating from, not leave them behind and not think you've really represented these sources, these points of contact, in all their complexity. Or to put it another way: in my classes, students are working on their writing and they're also reading from a course packet made up of both "published" writers and previous semesters' students. And since all the readings in the course packet highlight in some way some struggle with a rhetorical situation—like Patricia Williams with the law review editor in "The Death of the Profane" or Nancy Mairs arguing with her own "cocktail party" rhetoric in "On Not Liking Sex" or a student writing about caring for his child when he knows that stories from the domestic realm aren't considered "important" and "worldly" enough as essay topics—students very quickly form relationships with these readings, find articulation for some of their own writing struggles. But any relationship (this is what I learn from Jessica Benjamin) depends on recognizing, simultaneously, both sameness and difference. I would not want—though it's happened—a white, male, heterosexual, upper-middle-class student to form a relationship to June Jordan's articulation of anger (in her essay "Civil Wars") and the need to make anger heard without also considering how his anger, however real it and its sources may be, is different from hers and comes out of a much different history. Context, history, how meanings and arguments change as we pull them into different contexts and different histories, the difficulty and work of saying, "I identify" and "I can relate"—this thinking has got to be a part of our inspiration and responsibility as we create from others.

WOE: Could you talk about why the history of writing, specifically the history of the essay, is important, and the contributions that history might make in breaking down the divide between rhetoric and poetics?

WELCH: Wow, it's such a big topic and I can't claim to be a historian of writing or of the essay, just an extremely interested reader of what has been appearing more and more in books and articles in our field. But to give just one example: recently, in a writing class primarily for women's studies majors and minors, students were reading essays by both well-known contemporary women essayists and former students from the class about the politics of invention—the idea that each woman in this class isn't just in a personal dilemma about what to write about, what she's authorized to write about, but that these questions of invention and authorization are very much shared, social, and political. As we were talking about this in class, I was reading JoAnn Campbell's amazing essay in *College English* about women students at Mount Holyoke in the mid-nineteenth century and their struggles with the question of what to write their weekly themes about, given that, as women, they weren't socially authorized to write about much of anything. So I told students about Campbell's article, the historical context and questions it laid out, and I brought excerpts from the article for the students in class to examine and discuss. Just that kind of seemingly small moment—reading and discussing the writing of American college women from the 1840s and '50s—does so much to place our own writing and struggles in history. Since I've learned so much from composition's historians and especially feminist historians, I want to keep making these moments happen in my classrooms.

WOE: Earlier you discussed your own understanding that you tend to be too ironic, which you learned or appreciate from the kinds of fiction you like to read. I wonder how important imaginative or fictional writing is to your life and your work as a compositionist?

WELCH: My fiction writing is very important to my work as a compositionist because it's there that I can discover and grapple with both the possibilities of stories and the problems of narrative—how stories can feel so open to the future at any given moment, yet how narrative structure, traditional narrative structures anyway, demand an ending, closure, the narrowing down of possible futures to just one. That paradox is what Gary Saul Morson's *Narrative and Freedom* is about, and it's through my theoretical readings—of Morson and Bakhtin, for instance—that I've been able to return to my short stories with a desire, with a language, for intervening in this kind of narrowing down of possibility, and it's through my fiction that I've also learned new questions to ask about my theoretical work. For instance, a lot of my stories focus on relationships between girls and between women, especially on instances of betrayal and abandonment. What are the social forms, the economic conditions, the class structures, the internalized ideas about gender that lead to betrayal and abandonment? That's what I have to explore, in particular detail and particular settings, as I work on these stories. Through this work with particularity in my fiction, I also learn that the kinds of re-vision I want to call for in my composition work likewise must contend with the particulars, with the social forms, economic conditions, internalized ideas that make revision really hard to enact. So as I go back and forth between essay and short story or as I go back and forth within an essay between particulars and speculation, each seems to be opening up something hidden in the other.

WOE: What do you see as the most compelling current challenges to our work as teachers of writing and composition theorists?

WELCH: Maybe one challenge is a familiar one intensified by the "information age"—how to resist functionalist, reductive conceptions of composing and schooling in favor of what is more rich, critical, and complex—education for participation and agitation in a democracy, not education in service of the prevailing economic system alone.

WOE: What part does technology play in your classroom?

WELCH: Until I listened to Cynthia Selfe's chair's address at 4Cs, I would have said that technology played a hidden, unacknowledged role in my classrooms. Word-processing programs make it possible for us to put out our end-of-semester class books, for instance, but we don't talk about these programs or how each student gains access to a computer or how, socially, historically, a woman seated before a word-processing program is understood to be occupying a much different position than that of author, creator, programmer. For the most part I haven't wanted to think about technology at all because the story of "assimilate students to the technological world so they'll be good information processors, good knowledge workers, good e-commerce shoppers" seems so strong and because our current rhetoric divides participants in almost any casual discussion about information technologies into "techno-fans" and "technophobes." I haven't had a way to talk, question, theorize—and I should say I haven't, until very recently, gone looking for a way to talk and theorize—and so in my classrooms, I haven't said much of anything about technology.

After Selfe's address, though, I felt I had to consider that playing ostrich wasn't going to make my inchoate worries go away and that ignoring how much I and my students work through technology wasn't going to make it somehow neutral. So with others on my campus, I'm putting together a symposium for Women's Studies faculty and students on the theme of feminism and information technologies, and this will be followed by a pedagogy workshop that considers classroom technologies through feminist pedagogical perspectives and aims. My thinking in suggesting the theme of information technologies for this year's Women's Studies programming on my campus was, "I'm not sure what I think about this. I'm not sure how to articulate my questions and problems. I know I'm not alone. Who can help?" In addition to finding articles and books from composition theorists and from women involved in or wary of technological relationships, I'm finding a lot of people on my campus, in sociology, geography, mechanical engineering, who have been thinking about this too.

WOE: I have been thinking over the past year that maybe I have an ethical duty to introduce students to technology, especially since I teach "basic writers," writers who are—rightly or wrongly—already marked as different and disadvantaged. Perhaps I have a greater duty to introduce them to technology. And yet after talking to you, I realize that maybe this "inevitability of technology" is another retelling of only one kind of narrative, which, in fact, tries to deny the difference I might bring (and my basic writing students might bring) to composition. Do you think we have a duty to introduce students to technology, or is there still the importance of introducing them to the humane, the poetic, our multiple stories and histories?

WELCH: That idea of "it's inevitable" bothers me so much because it's just a way of dismissing the problems, uncomplicating our teaching situations: "Oh, well, what can we do?" It's a way of not acknowledging the power we might actually have. At the same time, I think it's likely to be inevitable that students coming into our classes have already been introduced to technology—or to the culture of technology—even if just through Microsoft ads on TV. My introduction came when I was fourteen and I walked into the clerk steno lab at the Lorain County Joint Vocational Center in Oberlin, Ohio. It was so beautiful to me, so neat and orderly, all those blue and red IBM Selectrics, a Dictaphone and ten-key on every desk. It was seductive, really sexy, appealing; I felt on some level that this neat vast, carpeted schoolroom that really looked just like a business office, a real steno pool, would get my messed-up life in order, and so I spent the rest of high school plugged into a Dictaphone and hunched over an electric typewriter.

As I think about this, I think that whether someone is introduced to technology through imagining themselves the master of it or an end user or, as in my case, imagining how it might help one master other chaotic areas of one's life—I am thinking not about the technologies themselves but about the broader stories, the wider cultures these technologies are embedded within. So, though I haven't given enough thought to this yet, I know I don't want to choose between "introduce students to technology" or "introduce them to the human and humane." I would rather create a classroom in which we research technological culture and research our own human stories of involvement or distance. What economic conditions, social forms, gendered assumptions, common tropes about the technological and the natural are writing our stories? I really would like to do this. I'm sure there are others already doing this. There's a lot to be learned.

WOE: Earlier you said that you'll be really curious to see what comes up at next year's 4Cs, given the call for "educating the imagination" and "reimagining education," because (as you said) imagination is another one of those words that probably needs a deep investigation. Obviously, you have already done some investigation into the "imagination" and what the "education" and the "reimagining" of writing might be. What importance do you hope these terms will have as a reality within composition's future?

WELCH: Since we're on the topic of technology, I hope that the idea of educating the imagination can be used to place discussions about the "inevitability of technology" in contact, dialogue, and tension with other articulated goals for composition and with composition's prior ideas of what was inevitable. Of course I hope we continue to work at telling stories and articulating goals that open up rather than close down the futures our students might live and write. But maybe I especially hope that reimagining education includes looking not just forward but back, to the radical, profound ways in which teachers have tried to reimagine education, what resisted and suppressed their imaginings (what has resisted and suppressed the open-admissions experiment, for instance), how these imaginings of others can be reclaimed.

There's such a strong notion that imagination works from a void, that a new story is made up from thin air, yet I know that everything I compose, everything I can imagine comes out of reading, whether it's reading Andrea Barrett or "reading" my first encounter with an IBM Selectric or rereading, after talking with Steve North about first-year composition, the stories I'd been telling about night school, or reading again, differently, after talking with you and Alice, the guilty stories compositionists tell of oppressed teachers. There needs to be this constant back and forth, looking to the past and looking to others in the here and now in order to imagine, critique, and multiply visions of the future. Yet this relationship between past and future, self and others, can't even begin to form unless we learn that "derivative"—deriving from other sources, not original and not brand new—isn't a pejorative and that saying, "Who out there can help me think about this?" is not a sign of weakness, a failure to stand out all alone.

LYNN Z. BLOOM

Lynn Z. Bloom's extensive body of scholarship investigates the values articulated in composition classrooms, the impact of the readings associated with teaching writing, and the history of advanced composition. She is the author of more than 80 articles and book chapters and more than 300 book reviews, poems, and works of creative nonfiction. In her exploration of the values of composition studies, Bloom consistently places the student at the center of the discipline's mandate to create, critique, and inspire. In Fact and Artifact: Writing Nonfiction *(1985)* she engages students as aspiring writers learning the craft of the essay. To demonstrate that craft, Bloom edited The Essay Connection: Readings for Writers *(2012)*. The comprehensive selection of essays from professional and student writers displays the range of rhetorical goals writers undertake, from interpreting images to fashioning reasoned arguments to setting an agenda for world peace. In The Essay Canon *(1999)*, Bloom historicizes and contextualizes the teaching of composition through a rigorous examination of the essays that have appeared in composition readers since World War II. Bloom further hones the discipline's definition with Composition Studies as a Creative Art: Teaching, Writing, Scholarship, Administration *(1998)*, a collection of essays examining the interplay of writing, teaching writing, and ways of reading. The collection asserts that these activities develop a creative space for students and instructors that is unique to the study of composition.

    Bloom taught and directed writing programs at Butler University, the University of New Mexico, the College of William and Mary, and Virginia Commonwealth University. From 1988 until her retirement in 2015 she held the endowed AETNA Chair of Writing at the University of Connecticut. In 2000 she was named a Board of Trustees Distinguished Professor.

—Hogan Hayes

"Once More to the Essay"

Jenny Spinner

Spring 2001

WOE: I'm interested in how you found yourself in the field that had no name? What appealed to you about—to name it now—the field of composition studies?

BLOOM: It was a deliberate decision made at the age of six when I learned to read and decided that to read and write were the best things anyone could do in this life. I still feel this way. In composition studies I can combine my interests in literature, creative writing, and composition studies research. I see these as reinforcing one another. Indeed "Freshman Composition as a Middle Class Enterprise" draws heavily on autobiography and *The Essay Canon* could be construed as heavily literary in orientation.

WOE: Looking back on your early years of teaching—perhaps not those earliest years but the ones in which you began teaching full time—how has your teaching grown and changed with you?

BLOOM: The most economical answer is that as I know more I also trust my students more and teach in a much more dialogic, collegial, interactive way than I used to. When process orientation came in in the late seventies, I was early and eager to embrace it, and still am, although there are a lot of variations in the process, depending on the level of the students, the type of writing they do, the audience, etc. I have always been very focused on *how* to do it, on the importance of a clear, economical, engaging style; a conspicuous and identifiable voice; and the benefit of many, many revisions.

What I probably allow more in recent years since I've been doing creative nonfiction writing myself is the importance of play, wit, and surprise. Some advice on good writing says that the writer should always surprise herself in the act of discovery. I believe this, and also that writers should surprise and delight their readers. I think Spenser in *The Defense of Poesy* said the aim of poesy, by which I mean all writing, is to teach and delight, to bring children in from their play and old men from the chimney corner. The call of stories, the power of a narrative so compelling that it makes readers want to respond by telling stories of their own right back, is what I aim for now as both a teacher and a writer. These are the qualities that I push for in advanced composition and the grad autobiography courses that I teach.

WOE: And the biggest change in your teaching?

BLOOM: My own willingness to take big risks as a writer, in style and in substance, and to encourage, even push, my students to do the same. This is true of the past fifteen years. You don't grow as a human or as a writer if you don't take risks. I don't want to encourage safe writing, or safe thinking, but I try to encourage an atmosphere in class (by not putting grades on papers and/or via a grading contract) that allows students to pay attention to their writing and doesn't penalize them for taking risks or for experimenting. I also push my students, even undergrads, to publish. Many do, and this is a great stimulus to their peers to write early, write often, and write better. I expect a lot and I get a lot. In my classes there's no place to hide. The students urge each other on, as a rule, and become a community of readers and writers with a common goal.

The grad rhetoric class I just taught this spring was extremely bright and very collegial in their class presentations and commentary on each other's work. They found that breaking up was so hard to do that we had a collaborative lunch on the day they turned in their take-home finals. I provided the lettuce and the ice cream. They brought salad ingredients and sundae toppings. Perhaps the nature of this menu epitomizes the class!

I realize this may sound too optimistic and idealistic to be credible, but samples of my students' writing are in *The Essay Connection* and in *Fact and Artifact*. I don't edit these essays. The major criticism of these books is that I've made up student writing. I haven't.

Finally, I suppose, I've become more comfortable not knowing. I realized just this semester that if students ask me questions about teaching, as they do in the grad class, I am willing to acknowledge that I don't have all the answers. But I also acknowledge the love and the passion for this perplexing profession. To do so in this most recent class moved the students a great deal. I'm not sure why.

I regard every writing class as a place to experiment with teaching writing. How can I create a climate where students can write with elegance, ease, and enjoyment? I want them to get over being scared to write and to free themselves of bad advice: Don't use contractions or the first person; get it right the first time or you're doomed. I want them to engage in serious play. Every day of every class is therefore an experiment in process, guerilla theater trying to find what works for particular students to solve particular technical issues about writing (and human issues, too, although I try hard not to play psychologist). I try to write about what happens in these classes, as many of my publications reveal.

WOE: Moving from innovation in the classroom to innovation in the field of composition studies, how do you see the pioneering work of yourself and others in the field?

BLOOM: I don't think anyone starts out thinking "I'm going to be a pioneer." And now there's so much going on in the field that it's hard to sort out who and what came first, with the exception of a few blockbusting foundational works like Mina Shaughnessy's *Errors and Expectations* and Peter Elbow's *Writing Without Teachers*. Every time I find a new question to ask and then figure out how to find the answer, it seems like a brave and beautiful new world (*a la* Shakespeare's Miranda) all over again, as indeed it is. I have been fortunate to have a steady supply of exciting questions to find exciting answers to. This has been more pronounced since I've been at UConn and have had the time and research support to pursue simple questions which turn out to have complicated answers. To digress, sort of, one of the appealing features of composition studies is its newness. The possibility to find new, important topics with potentially big implications never ceases.

WOE: Have some of those implications been the motivation behind your revision of the WPA summer workshops?

BLOOM: When I started on that, the WPA summer workshops were run as a two-week summer workshop, which was unwieldy for participants. We streamlined the workshop to five days, then the next summer it was cut down to two and a half days, a concentrated format that people could take time to come to. When we did the first one, I thought, well, if you were going somewhere for two and a half days in a small group, why not invite others to the Burkean parlor for another two and a half days? Rick Gebhardt organized it. The combination has proved irresistible and both have been very popular since 1985, 1986.

I guess in one concrete sense I have been something of a pioneer, though with mixed results. I was the first professional hired in composition studies everywhere I've ever taught—University of New Mexico, College of William and Mary, and UConn. Nearly everywhere, I should say. At Virginia Commonwealth University, I was the second—Jim Kinney was there before me.

WOE: So your career has paralleled the growth of the discipline in all those places.

BLOOM: But as I say, the results were mixed. When you're the only compositionist in an English department, or one of two, it's hard enough to make changes in writing curriculum and harder still to make campus-wide changes when the curriculum and culture are set. Such things change glacially, and are determined by economic forces and internal politics.

WOE: In that sense, what do you see as the most significant issues facing composition and those three million students?

BLOOM: The biggest and worst is Bush's proposal to test all schoolchildren in grades 3–8 every year on their ability to read and write. This will cost billions. It will end up as a multiple-choice test—they always do—which won't test writing but will test coaching and test-taking skills. You know the arguments. Teachers will be forced to teach to the tests. This proposal has enormous political, pedagogical, and economic repercussions. It will not improve students' abilities to write and will siphon off money and focus away from the real issues in composition instruction from kindergarten through college.

Writing folks aren't as a rule used to talking to politicians or legislators or other funders of programs. We don't do a good job of representing the discipline or our interests. Anne Gere (a very good personal and professional friend) is president of NCTE and an excellent spokesperson, but teachers' organizations tend to be overlooked when policy is set, even when the teachers have to enforce it. Compared to this issue, all the others are less important. However, those related to the discipline include such questions as: Where will composition be taught and who will teach it? What theories, what philosophies, will undergird our research paradigms? And what will those paradigms be? What do we mean by composition studies—past, present, future? What do/should we teach when we teach composition? How will new technologies change composition studies? In what language will our students read and write, and what will they write about? What political and social issues have shaped composition studies in the past and will shape this field in the future?

Another problem I see in the field is armed camps that attack one another, put each other down, and don't want to engage in meaningful dialogue. It's a truism that CCCC is becoming too much like the MLA as a context for internecine warfare. That is true, and it's very regrettable.

WOE: I can't help but wonder, as I look around your office, filled as it is with books, stacks of papers, and projects, with your husband Martin coming and going upstairs, and the gingerbread cathedral and lunch cooking on the stove, how do you manage to juggle so many things at once?

BLOOM: I've always liked to juggle lots of things, though I eschew the term multitasking. This has enabled me to be a wife, mother (of small and of course then older children), household organizer, cook, chauffeur, teacher, writer, editor, community (both academic and local) citizen and more. I swim every day, teach, am active in professional associations, cook, hang out with my family, especially the grandchildren (we're taking the caboodle to England this summer), and I lead book discussion series in local libraries as my community service.

On a pragmatic level, I get bored easily, so if I get tired of working on one project I can turn to another. I see these activities/works in progress as mutually reinforcing, not incompatible. I like to have at least one good idea a day. The more I have to think about, the more good ideas I get. Fortunately I have the energy, the support, the human happiness, and the background of knowledge to write most of these up.

WOE: Let's talk more specifically about some of your projects. What are you working on right now?

BLOOM: I have essentially finished "Textual Power, Textual Guilt: Telling (Other People's) True Stories." I gave it at CCCC this year and it will be published in *Writing on the Edge*. This deals with issues in writing about people who don't want to be written about, the case in point being my ninety-three-year-old mother. I have sketched out next year's creative nonfiction panel proposal topic: "Birth Certificate: Trusting Readers to Fill in the Blanks." It will be about my concealed twinhood and is intended for a creative nonfiction panel on what is omitted from any given creative nonfiction piece and why. I am also giving a plenary talk at CCCC 2002 on "What We Talk About When We Talk About Essays," and you know what that will be about.

I am also working on what will be the lead article in an issue of the *Journal of Information Ethics*, "How to Talk About Heartbreaking Works of Staggering Genius—and Those That Are Not: An Ethical Guide to Book Reviewing." This is in the research stage. I sent out a query on a couple of e-listservs and am getting some interesting material from a variety of disciplines, including medicine, where the ethical issues are particularly high stakes. As usual, what began with the simple question "What are/should be the ethical principles undergirding a review?" is getting much more complicated, more interesting, and more demanding than was the article I could have written off the top of my head on the basis of my extensive experience as a reviewer

I am gearing up to write "Shifting Paradigms," which will be my plenary speech at Composition Studies in the 21st Century in October 2001. I am going to examine the past twenty-five years of CCCC programs and calls for papers to see what research has looked like in five-year intervals over the past quarter century, and maybe supplement that with a look at the Braddock essays and MLA prize books in composition at the same intervals, as indicative of what's hot, trendy and/or passé and try to figure out why. Having been invited to submit a teaching idea for a book of ideas by award-winning teachers, I have submitted a proposal for "Renegotiating the Grading Contract: How and Why I Stole Peter Elbow's Excellent Idea."

But the biggest project of all is the essay canon book, which I'm taking a sabbatical year to finish.

WOE: Tell me more about your interest in the essay, why you decided to tackle the essay in this enormous project, a survey of the essay canon.

BLOOM: Who can explain why one loves what one loves? Because I love it. Because it's there. I have been interested in the essay as a genre for all the years I've tried to teach students how to write them, and to write them well—a complex set of issues that I tackled with great pleasure when I wrote *Fact and Artifact*. It's illustrated with examples of wonderful writing by my own students and by the usual, and some unusual, belletristic suspects. I had a lot of fun reading a realm of nonfiction in preparation for this book: McPhee, Didion, James and Jan Morris, Agee, Lillian Ross. And many, many more!

WOE: Did you catch the bug for writing creative nonfiction yourself from these authors?

BLOOM: I started writing creative nonfiction at the same time I wrote the first edition of *Fact and Artifact*, in 1985. I had many good role models in my head, lots of engaging voices and points of view, and a panoply of styles. They weren't in the forefront of my mind as I wrote, but in some ways I had already figured out how to handle some of the technical aspects of creative nonfiction by explaining them in my book. Then I could use them in my own writing.

I initially became interested in the essay because I was teaching, or trying to teach, students to write them. Then I got interested, really interested, in the technical aspects of what constitutes both good essays and other forms of creative nonfiction, from the perspectives of a critic, a teacher, and an author of a book about how to write this way. I decided to try practicing what I preached. Once more to the essay! Essays are very hard to write because they have no predetermined form or structure or organization (or anything else except the premise/promise to tell the truth). In the difficulty is also the fun. What a pleasure to get it right—at least some of the time.

WOE: You addressed this issue in "Why Don't We Write What We Teach? And Publish It?" Why don't more teachers of essays write essays?

BLOOM: Essays are largely ignored critically and even pedagogically. Despite the fact that everybody teaches essays, there's little understanding of what exactly they're teaching, beyond the usual generic boilerplate pieces of advice that lead to expansions of the five-paragraph essay (I overstate the case, but you get the point). If I can discover an entire canon—which I have done—then maybe I can find out more about essays from the corpus of essays of the top 175 canonical essayists. To me it's all a big, brave new world of potentially wonderful writing. Since the discoveries are still in progress, in fact have barely begun, I can't tell you what I'll end up with. But the lure of good reading and the actual thrill, as well as the hard work, of writing creative nonfiction is worth the effort. The pleasure is partly in the process, partly in the product.

The more I learn about the genre as a writer in it, the more appreciative I become of people who write wonderfully and well. And the more critical I become of people who write sloppily and thoughtlessly. This leads me to want to find more wonderful writers, partly to put them into the anthologies

I am editing and revising and partly because the really good writers are so illuminating.

WOE: Who are you reading right now?

BLOOM: My current favorite book *du jour* is Georgina Kleege's *Sight Unseen*. She has macular degeneration and about ten percent sight, around the periphery. She analyzes various prejudices people have against blind people and the stereotyping of the blind in fiction and in film, and it's a commentary on what it's like to be blind and to function fully, as fully as possible. Close reading takes on a new meaning as she holds the book literally right up to her eye. She'd have been taught Braille at eleven (when she went blind) had not her parents and teachers considered the use of Braille a mark of blindness. If she didn't use Braille, she wasn't blind, was she? And she learned to pass as sighted! A book full of amazing vision and amazing grace. As you yourself know as an essayist, every new author, every new perspective that's engaging is exciting to find. Because essays are a genre of (usually) short works, they don't generate a lot of hype, just elegance and engagement.

WOE: A genre of short works, but a second-class genre?

BLOOM: I never thought of the genre as second class—and I don't think E.B. White does, either, though he used the term. He is a first-class writer and full of so much integrity that I don't think he'd waste his time on a second-class endeavor. Nor would I. Of all essayists, he's my favorite. The integrity of his character as well as his style blows me away. The fact that we share the same birthday is a lagniappe. I just emailed a friend today that I would like on my tombstone Wilbur's tribute to Charlotte at the end of *Charlotte's Web*: "It is not often that someone comes along who is a true friend and a good writer. Charlotte was both."

WILLIAM E. COLES, JR.

William E. Coles Jr. (1932–2005) was a renowned, iconoclastic, and highly readable author of books on composition, among the first in the field to approach the subject through creative nonfiction. His The Plural I: The Teaching of Writing *(1978) is a fictionalized narrative of one writing class from the 1960s; his* Seeing Through Writing *(1988) incorporates a fictional teacher-persona, the Gorgon, who creates the book's writing assignments. Coles's other books on writing include* Composing: A Guide to Teaching Writing as a Self-Creating Process *(1974),* Composing II: Writing as a Self-Creating Process *(1981),* What Makes Writing Good *(1985), and* The Plural I—and After *(1998). Sometimes described as an expressivist, he rejected the label. The self he hoped to help his students express was not preexisting and autonomous but rather one that was composed as well as plural, as the titles of his books suggest. As John Warnock puts it, Coles's work aims to help writers develop a kind of literary, textual self "that may be inferred from the language that has been used."*[1]

Coles's success as a composition scholar grew directly out of his distinguished teaching career. Earning his PhD from the University of Minnesota in 1967, he taught at Amherst College, Case Western Reserve University, Drexel University, and, ultimately, the University of Pittsburgh, where he was a long-time professor and, from 1974 to 1980, the Director of Composition.

The young-adult novels that Coles wrote late in his life, Funnybone *(1992),* Another Kind of Monday *(1996), and* Compass in the Blood *(2001), seem a natural literary extension of the fictions of his books on composition. Innovative, charismatic, impatient with convention, he was, in the words of University of Pittsburgh English Department chair David Bartholomae, "one of the most brilliant and influential teachers of writing of his generation."*[2] *His refusal of formulaic approaches to writing in favor of intense, imaginative engagement with student minds continues to influence the teaching of composition today.*

—Greg Glazner

---

1 Warnock, John. "Coles, William E. Jr." *Encyclopedia of Rhetoric and Composition from Ancient Times to the Information Age.* Ed. Theresa Enos. Google Books.
2 Thomas, Mary Ann. "Obituary: William E. Coles Jr." *University Times.* The University of Pittsburgh. Web. April 14, 2005.

"Failure Is the Way We Learn"

John Boe and Eric Schroeder

Fall 2002

WOE: How were you taught writing?

COLES: Oh, pretty much the way my students tell me they are still being taught: with what I absorbed as a set of rules and regulations. You began with a kind of throat-clearing first paragraph called the introduction in which you announced what you were going to talk about. Then in three or four follow-up paragraphs (called the body) you made points or gave examples or listed reasons. And finally you concluded (with a paragraph called the conclusion) in which you said again what you imagined you'd already said. It was all very bloodless stuff. If the form was followed; if you had clear topic sentences, good grammar and correct spelling; if the paper, or theme as we called it, was clear, unified, and coherent; then you were certifiably literate. If the English was good, then the writing was good. Questions like why anyone would care to write the sort of stuff I went on about in my papers, or why anyone would want to read it, were never given a hearing, really—and to be absolutely honest, as an undergraduate I'm not certain I'd have wanted the boat rocked anyway.

In graduate school, the only teacher from whom I learned anything about writing—this was at the University of Minnesota—was Samuel Holt Monk, who spoke of "twitches" in my prose, by which he meant my fondness for meaningless doublets and triplets: "we must be cautious, careful, and circumspect"—that sort of thing. "You know," Monk said, "who will do this same thing sometimes and sounds very empty when he does? Samuel Johnson." "Well," I thought. "Dr. Samuel Johnson. That's not bad company." So when Monk added that from then on he was simply going to write "Johnson" in the margins of my prose whenever he thought it was called for, I accepted his right to do so. Without my being aware of it, that was one of my first lessons in the kind of marginalia that could help a writer—and in how my appearance as a writer could be evaluated and adjusted.

I got my first full-time teaching job at Amherst College, and it was Theodore Baird there who absolutely revolutionized the way I thought about writing. Ted may not have made my mind, but he certainly made it run, and more through his observations than through explanations. He explained very little really, but what he observed had a way of forcing listeners into explanations that in my case exploded into whole galaxies of meaning. He once said that Jane Austin writes "teachers' books"—a wonderful observation, it seems to me. And maybe not so wonderful, but equally important to me were his calling Kafka "boring" and saying that Scott Fitzgerald writes "for suckers." And I'll never forget the way he dismissed an article once by saying that it was simply journalism: "He writes one sentence that writes his next ten for him." My whole notion of Themewriting spun off that.

Bill Pritchard characterizes Ted as saying to people's faces what most of us would say only behind their backs, which he did—and to tremendous effect sometimes. Roger Sale was burbling on about something one day, and Ted began to look out the window. When Roger stopped, Ted turned to him and asked very pleasantly, "Why do you go on in that boring way?" Roger never forgot that, and in *On Writing* says that even though the remark wasn't about his writing, it was the only remark that taught him something real about writing. All of us who worked with Ted wanted his intellectual approval—the more because we knew he would never give it unless he believed it were warranted. He was very discouraging with anyone who tried to turn him into a God or a Daddy—which was very good for all of us. Just his presence forced us to take responsibility for what we said and wrote, for who we were. I was told a story recently about a young girl's hearing Bob Dylan for the first time. "Mommy, is that God singing?" she asked. "Why would you think that?" the mother wanted to know. "Because his voice is funny, but it doesn't make me laugh." Ted was that way.

WOE: What was it like going from teaching with Baird at Amherst to other schools, to a technological institute and then to a state-related university?

COLES: Well, it certainly was a learning experience. What I tried to do at first was become Ted, using his mannerisms and locutions, figuring no one outside Amherst would catch me in my mimicry, which no one ever did, but I never won over any of my colleagues at Case Institute of Technology either.

But at Case I did develop a composition course for students highly professionalized in science. Based on my experiences as an undergraduate engineering student at Lehigh, I figured there could be tremendous possibilities if I offered writing as a form of language using, an idea as germane to the study of the sciences as it is to the study of the arts. For me to invite those science students at Case, for whom English courses didn't have much more priority than they'd had for me when I was in engineering, to understand that language is the primary, if not the only way we have—as scientists or as anything else—of running order through chaos, thereby giving ourselves from moment to moment whatever identities we have, was to have a chance of persuading them that writing really could have something to do with them. I spun some wonderful things out of that idea. I think Ted was pleased, by and large pleased—nothing pleased him completely—with what I did. He was always generous about the books I wrote, even though the first couple were very dependent on him But with *Composing II* and *What Makes Writing Good*, I began to find my own ways of connecting assignments with one another, of building something into, say, assignment three or four that comes floating back as a concern in assignments seven, thirteen, and twenty. And I found my own ways of being playful in the midst of serious inquiry—which is more important than I think is generally understood. How oppressively serious-solemn-pretentious so much academic work is. But there's no question that the way in which a good sequence of assignments mimes a mind in the act of finding a direction for itself, searching for equilibrium in its acknowledgement of all contradictions, there's no question that I got that from Ted.

WOE: You mentioned the way you put the notion of writing as a form of language using at the center of the course. But it seems to me that there's another kind of theme or motif or essential guiding principle that runs through the courses you create in your books, and that's "know thyself."

COLES: Oh, yes, and that, by the way, is more my way of going at things than it was Ted's. Like Wittgenstein (whom he claimed never to have read, a claim I've always doubted—what the hell; he read everything else), Ted was tremendously interested in exposing balderdashy ways of talking about and locating the self and in exposing jargons of all sorts. But I don't think he was explicitly interested in writing as a way of growing or realizing one's own potential. Writing as a way of knowing, as a way of coming to know, yes, this interested him a great deal, as did assignments that revealed how much of life is mysterious and inexpressible. But self-realization was not what I'd call a characteristic concern of his assignments. Maybe it would be fairer to say that that was the sort of line he did not want either to crowd or to cross.

WOE: How did you pick up on the notion of getting kids to explore their selves?

COLES: It was through my study of twelve-step programs that I came to understand that addicted people break dependence on alcohol or drugs or whatever by renaming the world and by becoming somebody else through that renaming. It was that that helped me understand why so many Amherst students at the end of Ted's course—I was one; every term I was one—would be able to demonstrate, not just say how, but demonstrate, that they understood things about the world and themselves that made everything new. They were no longer dependent upon, that is addicted to, their old formulaic ways of seeing the world. They had in fact become different people. The putting together of what I'd learned from English 1–2 at Amherst with the healing principles of the twelve-step programs led me to experiment with constructing assignments that would enable students to develop as people, as their own people. My belief that literature could do that—it had done it with me—was why I'd majored in English to begin with.

WOE: One of the things you often do in your courses is to have the last assignment look back at the first in order to sum up the course. Is this your own idea rather than Baird's?

COLES: Oh no. Ted did it too, but in a different way. He always asked students in the course's next-to-last assignment to look back over the term and make their own sense of the order of the assignments: How would they explain why eleven followed ten and came before twelve? In addition, though, he would always construct assignments for a final paper and a final exam that would have none of the course's language in them, but would always turn out, after you got inside them, to involve problems that had been central to the course all term. I remember the final exam for a course in which the subject had been logic, I think, asking students to explain to a man from Mars where people were able to see reality as it Really Was, what really happened in a disputed play of a football game. People kicked that problem around the campus for over a year—to Ted's great delight, of course.

WOE: In several of your sequences you ask the students to explain the trick of Themewriting. Clearly, this is intended to be a fun interlude in the course, but it also seems to be a moment when teacher and student can recognize each other.

COLES: Can celebrate together, yes, by demonstrating that though writing can indeed be reduced to just a trick performed mechanically, routinely, meaninglessly, it is possible to describe this trick in such a way as to show how it can also be something else. It's kind of like Pope's being other than dull in talking about dullness in the *Dunciad*.

Of course, this is harder to do than most students initially realize. In *Composing*, I have an assignment that asks the students to represent how Themewriting is done with drawings and color. What usually happens with the assignment, however, is that the students, without realizing it, draw Themes about Themewriting—by rendering it as a huge bog, for example, or by drawing three squares labeled "Introduction," "Body," and "Conclusion"—which don't represent how Themewriting is done at all. Still it's a wonderful assignment with which to show students how deeply Themewriting—oversimplifying, skating over the surface of things, being imprecise—is engrained in all of us as a way of doing the world. I'm not being extravagant when I say I believe that Themewriting is an addiction.

WOE: Is it accurate to say about a writing course that a certain amount of initial failure is not only inevitable but also desirable?

COLES: I think it is, yes, in several ways, and for that reason ought to be considered as something other than failure. It ought to be named and planned for, built into a course and then capitalized on.

    Let me be clear though that by renaming failure I don't mean I think we ought to lie to students: to tell them something is a "nice try" when it isn't, or "possessed of certain strengths" when it doesn't have any. We do a great disservice to our subject, our students, and ourselves when we lie about what ought to be taken seriously in a writing course and what shouldn't, because we lie about a good deal more than writing. We lie about what creativity requires. We lie about how sloppiness and stupidity are recognized and judged by thinking people. We lie about what's smart or insightful and what's just run of the mill. We lie about the learning process, how far it is reasonable to imagine that a beginner in anything—let alone with a subject as complicated as writing—is going to be able to get in ten or fourteen weeks. We lie about what it means to grow up. And to say, "I don't want to hurt anyone's feelings" is a cop-out. There are all kinds of ways of telling students that a given piece of writing isn't good enough without mortally wounding anyone.

WOE: One of the things writing teachers love about reading *The Plural I* is the directness with which you confronted students when they turned in lousy papers. Are we free today still to have that kind of directness you had in 1965?

COLES: "That kind of directness"? Well, probably not. I was working with a very particular group of students, remember, all of them male, at a very particular school, an institute of technology, at a very particular time in history. Also, I'm not sure I was quite as direct in the flesh as my narrator is. You have to remember that that guy isn't me. The narrator of *The Plural I* is a fictional creation. I don't mean that I think he has no connection with how I go about things, but I do know I'm not as good as he is in a classroom. My timing and tone aren't as infallible, day by day. I don't always know the right question for a given student, the way he seems able to. Sometimes I just lose patience with their smugness, or stupidity, or boredom. Has anybody got any business working with the young who doesn't realize how really awful they can be?

    I still try to be direct with students, you understand. I'll intimidate if I think there's something to be gained that way. I tease a lot. But I have a better sense than I once did of how I can fool around with people and make it count for something. I don't make fun of students, though. I don't think I ever did that.

WOE: Is this why some of the time you yourself write the "bad" student sentences or paragraphs to use as examples in class?

COLES: Exactly—and I make more and more use of the technique the longer I teach. "This is a piece of writing," I say, "done by a member of this course [which I consider myself to be] who was a student in a different term [which I certainly was]. And I use this paper with his permission [which I'm happy to give]." It's an ideal way, without hurting anyone's feelings, to show students what certain kinds of bombast look and sound like in order to help them avoid it. It's also a wonderful way of giving students techniques for determining the hollowness or phoniness or tedium of certain kinds of writing. "In that first paragraph there, with which other sentence of the six comprising it might you begin? With any one of them! Really! What kind of writing would you say that paragraph is made up of then?" Too often I've heard beginning teachers tell students something like "this line is forced" or "this is just B.S." The real problem always is how you help the students to recognize when a line is forced or when something is just B.S.

I did once have someone in composition research say angrily to me: "But you're passing off your efforts as students' efforts." "Yep," I said. "In certain cases that's exactly what I do." I don't know why it should be so hard for some people to understand that our subject is writing rather than students in composition courses.

WOE: I love the way in your courses, as dramatized in your books, that students' texts become the center of the course—and how those texts become a kind of single text that all members of a class can make reference to. When that happens it seems to be one of these moments where people start to take themselves and each other seriously as writers.

COLES: Yes. It's an electric moment in a class when a student makes reference to something that has happened in the course—anything that's happened in the course—outside the hour we're meeting. I say it's electric. I make sure that I celebrate the moment so as to try to make it electric. I also seed such happenings by myself making the kinds of connections I want students to make: "Well, let's feed the problem to Jim here, who said last Friday that he found the final paragraph of the second paper addressing Assignment Eight 'offensive.' Is this final paragraph in this paper 'offensive,' would you say, Jim?" Communities have to be built, in other words. They don't just appear—and of course sometimes the students' engagement with me and with each other is better than others. I had very good students the term I did the assignments in *The Plural I*. I was very lucky.

WOE: You talk sometimes of a sequence of your assignments having an effect like the effect of nonsense. What exactly do you mean?

COLES: I'm using "nonsense" there not in the generic sense of the term, as a synonym for gobbledygook or gibberish, but in the sense that describes what Lewis Carroll, say, is doing in *Alice in Wonderland*. Plainly, or it becomes plain after a time, the narrative presence in *Alice* is constantly inviting readers to put together what will not go together the way we expect it is going to and should. Once this is understood, the reader takes a place alongside the narrative presence of Carroll, someone in on the joke that things in Alice are constructed precisely to frustrate ordinary (and pedestrian) ways of understanding them. I'd say my sequences of writing assignments create a relationship between assignment maker and students like Carroll's relation to readers of *Alice in Wonderland*. Which is to say that the students who most benefit from working with me—like the ideal audience for a writer of nonsense—are those whose heightened consciousness of language has moved them to a special kind of community: "I can now show you how I know that I am not being led to some cheap predetermined conclusion—such as thinking that to see all ideals, aspirations, and hopes as socially constructed is to be made free. Rather, I am being invited to use my skills as a language user to create a place for myself beyond such formulae and here goes."

WOE: When you designed a course in which you had each of, say, twenty-two students write thirty papers, how did you mark their work responsibly and have time for anything else—particularly if you had two sections of such a course?

COLES: I used to read between three and four thousand papers a year when I was teaching at Amherst—we all did, and I think did responsibly—mainly because there wasn't anybody around to tell us that it couldn't be done. We never put grades on the papers (I still don't) so we were freed from having to write a lot of self-vindicating stuff: "Here is why this paper didn't get an A." Also, our texts for composition courses at Amherst (and everywhere else I've taught writing ever since) were always student papers (reproduced anonymously, of course). That pushed us all to develop a highly metaphoric way of commenting on student work that was finally, I think, a lot more effective than mumbling on about organization and focus and the like. Once, for example, I spent a good half hour in class trying to get hold of an opening paragraph on some thumping platitude or other—on how good it was for all people to have choices or some such. "This is just bulletproof," one student cried finally in exasperation. And from that moment on that metaphor was the only written comment needed for that kind of writing from that group. The metaphors have been different in different terms, of course. "Skywriting" was one we got some mileage out of one term, I remember, and "cocoamarsh." I got more and more into the habit of using terminology from our classroom conversations in my comments. "You called this kind of writing 'mayonnaise' in class not two periods ago." For an attentive student that's all one needs.

Of course you have to adapt your style and manner to where you are, but for me that's meant mostly quantitative change. A set of English 1 assignments for Ted always consisted of thirty papers, thirty-two if you count the assignment for a long paper and the final exam. A new assignment for every class period. A paper due every period. A fresh set of assignments every year. Never repeat. I tried doing things that way when I was working by myself at Case and at Drexel with small groups of colleagues, but if you're working with other teachers, each of whom is teaching two or sometimes three courses in composition of twenty-two students per course, and you ask them to assign, read, and mark thirty-two papers from each student—you ask for more trouble than the enterprise is worth. By the time I got to Pitt I was still designing assignments in sets of thirty, but only twelve to fourteen were writing assignments; the rest were class exercises.

WOE: You've written that your course doesn't study "examples of what is called academic discourse, whatever that phrase may mean." Are you making fun of the phrase "academic discourse"?

COLES: Oh, yes. I guess I was. I get irritated with the phoniness in our profession sometimes, with the use of a term like "academic discourse" to suggest that a group of essays some English teacher has decided students in a composition course ought to read represent the way historians or social scientists or philosophers talk to one another, or are examples of how students taking courses in those departments will be expected to talk. I've done enough work in writing across the curriculum to know that that's more than a little arrogant.

Secondly, what are essays of "academic discourse" like those of Walker Percy, say, or John Berger, or Clifford Geertz doing in a composition course? I mean what are they really doing there, not how do their popularizers defend their use of them ("Here's Geertz looking at a cockfight: now you look at something in your life as though you were Geertz, etc. etc."), From what I've seen at the University of Pittsburgh, where TAs and part-timers teach most of the composition courses, all too often such essays become excuses for turning the focus away from the students' writing. The essays are so hard for students to figure out, but raise issues so trendily interesting to teachers, that the majority of class time goes to articulating the issues rather than looking at writing. Exactly the same thing happened with me when I was supposedly teaching composition in a writing and literature course as a graduate student, by the way. All I knew as a TA about teaching writing was what I'd experienced, so I had little to draw on. In consequence, I did what our TAs do. I taught where my head was which happened to be literature in those days, in that that was what graduate study in a Department of English focused on. So I taught the *Henriad* and the *Orestia*, and I gave my students the word according to E.M.W. Tillyard and C.S. Lewis and E.E. Stoll, and Green and Lattimore, and for the writing part of the course, I assigned sections of the *Harbrace Handbook*—without ever checking on whether the students had actually read or learned anything from them. The "academic discourse" mantra, so far as I'm concerned, most of the time anyway, is just another way of keeping the racket of composition as a requirement alive at the same time it sells students in composition courses down the river.

WOE: You don't sound much more optimistic than you did way back in "The Circle of Unbelief" when you talked about composition texts as barriers.

Are there any composition textbooks today you would say aren't barriers to a student's learning about writing?

COLES: Well, as Lincoln Steffens said, "It is possible to get an education at a university. It has been done." I guess there must be some good textbooks out there somewhere, but I'm not read up enough on what gets galloped into print by the major publishers these days to be able to name one. To tell you the truth though, I think a good teacher can make something out of even a very bad textbook, by quarreling with its assumptions, taking issue with its pronouncements, talking about why the study questions and sample sequences really aren't much good. Any teacher of writing who feels victimized by a bad textbook probably deserves to be. What the hell: I once had to work under a Director of Composition who referred to writing assignments as "prompts."

WOE: I was interested to see you defending writing across the curriculum, because this is not the thing that someone who has been labeled an "expressivist" is supposed to do.

COLES: Which is the trouble with labeling, isn't it? The problem with dividing people in the profession on the basis of some kind of taxonomic tag is that you invite a sketchy or superficial reading of what it is they really do and stand for. It's what Procrustes did with his famous bed. All you need do to make someone seem to fit a category is to lop off what you don't want to acknowledge or stretch out something to make it mean what it never meant in context. An expressivist is it I am these days? I was once an epistemist—and for a while a neo-Platonist. I can't decide whether I'm going down or coming up in the world.

Why wouldn't I be interested in writing across the curriculum? In the early eighties, when the big push for it was being felt throughout the country, you may remember the Four Cs and the NCTE declaring, "The teaching of writing is not just an English Department responsibility!" and people marching up and down with their banners saying writing had to play a substantive part in every course on campus. A number of administrations, bowing to pressure as always, simply required that their faculty comply. The panic, of course, was indescribable and was a golden opportunity for me—in every sense of that phrase.

All those years I'd spent developing sequences of assignments of different kinds, finding new ways of working with student writing, training TAs, all these things suddenly were things that other teachers wanted to learn—teachers who for the most part were not English teachers and had little experience using writing with their students. I went to a lot of colleges and universities around the country to run workshops, and it was wonderful work to be involved with. Those attending were very receptive to suggestions and quick to pick up on the implications of my main writing-across-the-curriculum idea: that the writing the students produce may be the least important benefit of having them do it.

I had a wonderful example of how this is true at a workshop I ran—it was one of my first—at St. Olaf College in Minnesota. I met with about thirty-five members of the faculty at 8:00 in the morning in January, which seemed the middle of arctic night to me, I can tell you. In response to my question about how their efforts were going, one guy, leaning up against the wall at the back of the room, said, "I can tell you about the time I worked out that this whole writing across the curriculum thing was a scam." Of course I had to let him tell his story. He was a sociologist who for his quizzes and exams and the like had half his class use writing while the other half he gave Scantron forms. When he examined his class on their understanding of some sociological principle or other, he found that the papers graded by machine showed everybody doing fine. Then he looked at the writing the other half of the class had submitted on the same principle. It was execrable, filled with mistakes and irrelevancies, and it was then, he said, that he made up his mind about the scam of writing across the curriculum. But when his class had a conversation about the principle, he saw that the students who had written about it, even though they hadn't written well, were much better able to engage in a conversation than those who had done only the Scantron test. They could better explain how the principle was important in relation to other principles, see how it was more useful in certain situations than in others, and so on. That's certainly far from the whole argument about how and why writing can be an important aid to learning, but I told that story at every workshop I ran after that.

In working with various faculties around the country, I did pretty much what I'd done for years with graduate students learning to become writing teachers. I worked a lot with pairings, putting assignments that had worked well for the teachers who used them against assignments that had been a bust. After a while I got quite a collection of such good and bad examples. I also used examples of effective and ineffective explanations of how writing was going to be used and evaluated in political science courses, philosophy courses, even math classes. I did a lot of work on different ways of using writing, on how and why to use ten-minute writing assignments, for example. And of course I distributed many samples of student writing and explained various ways of handling it in class. After a while, I trusted myself enough to reserve time for teachers to refine, or sometimes redraft entirely, some of their own material on the basis of small-group discussions so that everyone could leave the workshop with ideas for improving something having to do with writing in at least one of their courses.

The notion of writing I push—maybe this is why I'm supposed to be an expressivist—is that all writing can be seen as the expression of a sensibility. Actually, a sensibility is being created in and with a piece of writing. That holds, I think, as much for writing in mathematics as it does for writing in literary studies. The question is always one of whether or not readers think a particular sensibility is knowing, or trustworthy, or interesting, or has authority—whatever terms a teacher is comfortable with.

WOE: When did you start using writing groups?

COLES: Not until I started doing the writing-across-the-curriculum workshops, really—which was when I discovered that the best way to make them effective was to give participants a problem to work together on that each member of the group then reported on individually. The discreet application of pressure is necessary for anything of much moment to go on in small-group work, I found. Apply pressure. Create tension. They're wonderful aids to promote the kind of effort that can result in learning. I tried to dramatize this with the fictional dialogues and sketches I wrote in *Seeing Through Writing*. I wanted them to be metaphors for the both best and worst I can imagine going on in small-group work.

WOE: That's what I love about that book. All of the optimism it generates for a teacher, that students can and do actually learn from each other.

COLES: That's something I hoped the book would be seen as doing, but despite its positive reviews, it never sold and went out of print after just one printing. Maybe I made it too difficult a book for teachers to use. Certainly the notion that informed it—that story can be a mode for teaching and learning about writing—I continue to believe has profound possibilities.

WOE: The hottest topic at the CCCC these days is creative nonfiction, and *The Plural I* is probably the earliest example of creative nonfiction in composition studies.

COLES: Maybe, but as the failure of *Seeing Through Writing* to catch on suggests, just because you're the first to do something doesn't necessarily make you an influence. What will we do with the first fellow to swallow four alligators?

WOE: In the last few years you have moved to writing novels about young people.

COLES: About and for. I write novels for young adults, and I count myself very lucky to be in the field. Like my work in writing across the curriculum, the novels I've done—three have been published so far, *Funnybone, Another Kind of Monday*, and *Compass in the Blood*, all by Athenaeum/Simon and Schuster—draw heavily on things I've spent a lot of time learning about: like how to survive childhood and adolescence for starters. Whoever said that youth was wasted on the young I think was dead wrong. Young people need to draw on every bit of energy they have to find their ways in a world like the one we're living in. Can you imagine what it would be like to be eighteen again faced with the question of how to be a good man these days?

So generally, I guess you could say that my novels are about growing up—something I'm still at work on, just as I'm still at work on the question of how to become a good man these days.

WOE: Becoming an individual. Becoming one's self. Jung's term for this is individuation, and I can see the process at work in your novels.

COLES: I hope so. Because to find a way of living decently in one's own skin is surely the most heroic enterprise anyone can engage in. Vicky Hearne, who in her book on training animals, *Adam's Task*, writes better about teaching and learning than anyone I know, claims that human beings are born to the demands of the heroic, that we need to see ourselves as heroes in whatever work we do to avoid the death of the soul. I believe that. I've always written out of that assumption in both textbooks and novels I've done.

WOE: I think I can see in your work what you mean. In your essay "Looking Back on *The Plural I*," you mention that you see yourself as the hero/writer of the book but acknowledge that the students become heroic too—a feeling that seems to carry over to your young adult novels. The kids in your novels are not perfect kids, but there's something heroic about them too.

COLES: Yes. *The Plural I* became a book other teachers could learn from (rather than simply an exercise in self-celebration) when I began to imagine the classroom as a place that demanded not a hero, but heroes; not a place that pitted anyone against anyone else, no matter how much it might feel that way at times, but a place in which all of us were communally aligned against the same things: lazy imprecision, fear-inspired vagueness, self-reducing reliance on cheap clichés. And all of my novels involve choices and triumphs related to these things as well.

WOE: Are the novels more fun to write than your books on composition were?

COLES: I think both for me involve the same kind of imagining. It can be just as rewarding to work out why assignment twelve in a given sequence ought to be twelve and not eight, and not eighteen, as it is to plot a novel, or decide to give a particular character particular characteristics. And with both sequences and novels, I spend a lot of time wondering if I'm being solemn or preachy or pretentious, and thinking about how I can complicate easy assumptions people might be settling for about where things are going at this point in this story or in this course. I'm also delighted in exactly the same way when someone enjoys a move in a sequence or a detail in one of my novels. I did a workshop for a group of eighth graders a couple of weeks ago, all of whom had read my Pittsburgh-based novel, *Another Kind of Monday*. Eighth grade seemed to me maybe a bit young for the concerns I raise in the book, but at the end of the session, a young man sauntered up to me, hands in his pockets, smiling slyly. He had braces on his teeth and was maybe four and a half feet tall. Did I remember, he asked me, the scene in the novel where the heroine, after jogging around the reservoir, takes off her sweatband and squeezes the moisture from it onto the pavement—to the barely contained excitement of my hero? I did. Well, the boy said, he just wanted me to know that he thought sweaty women were sexy too. There we were, just a couple of fellas talking it over. That was a wonderful moment for me.

WOE: There's a very real way in which Pittsburgh, the city, becomes a place of wonder for the characters in your young adult novels. Is this deliberate?

COLES: It's quite deliberate. One of the things that's so wonderful about the city for me is its incredible variousness, how you don't have to travel for more than five minutes in any direction to find yourself in a different community, each with a different relation to the past and living life in a different rhythm. It's as though gigantic forces are at work in and under the city, forces of decay as well as of generation, of creation and destruction both, sometimes harmonizing with one another, other times tearing one another to pieces. In its history, its social structures, its architecture, even its geography, Pittsburgh contains all the greatness of America, its feisty adaptability, its smashing strength, its unkillable energy. It contains all the shame of America as well, its brutal grinding down of options and potential, its intolerance of difference, its waste and destructiveness. Of course any place looked at hard has similar contradictions implicit in it—and similar possibilities that may be made of them. That's what I want my novels to offer young people finally: a sense of possibility. I'm less interested in seeing Pittsburgh as a place of wonder than in having my readers see what's possible when wonder becomes a way of looking at the world. In this sense I'd like to be thought of as writing patriotic books.

WOE: Are there people teaching writing in the profession now who use sequences of writing assignments?

COLES: Oh, sure. I taught a number of graduate students who continue to use them. I did five NEH summer seminars for college teachers in which each of the twelve participants developed an ur-sequence; some of these I know for a fact were refined and are still being used. Carl Klaus at the University of Iowa ran several year-long NEH seminars in the teaching of writing—this was for about fifty participants or so altogether—and each participant developed a full sequence that the universities they came from then supported as regular college courses. These sets of assignments were later published as a book by Boynton/Cook called *Courses for Change in Writing*. I'd be surprised if a number of those courses, with modifications of course, weren't still being offered.

I need to add, though, that some courses offered as sequenced writing courses can be the very opposite of courses promoting free and open inquiry. Instead of miming the activity of a mind seriously engaged in serious inquiry—and encouraging students to develop their own views and voices—these courses seek to indoctrinate by marching students syllogistically to some predetermined, usually politically correct, conclusion. Students in such courses learn the latest phrasing of why things like civil rights are Very Important. They learn how to write elaborate slogans. But I don't think they learn very much about writing.

WOE: What do you see as the signs of a good composition course?

COLES: Everything begins with what the teacher's energy, courage, and literary imagination can make possible for a community of writers—which is to say that I think a composition course is valuable in direct proportion to the kind of centrality that *writing*, more particularly the writing of the students, has to its assignments, procedures, and conversation. Generally, teachers of such courses have found a way of getting rid of most of the apparatus that composition teachers have become so accustomed to peering at the students' writing from behind, or through, or under—the style manual, the anthology, the standard plays and novels, the various collections of short stories and essays—in order to focus on all those choices in writing that can so easily be dismissed as picky or irrelevant. What the members of such classes find good enough—as well as something to become good enough for—are the writing assignments and class exercises, the students' papers, and each other.

KEITH GILYARD

Keith Gilyard's scholarship intersects all areas of writing studies—rhetoric, composition, linguistics, literature, and creative writing—and his work has frequently been devoted to making connections between personal and professional realms. Gilyard's first book, Voices of the Self: A Study in Language Competence *(1991), won the American Book Award for its engaging blend of literacy narrative with critical analysis of language and literacy development in the public educational system. Much of his work contextualizes areas where race and rhetoric overlap. His 1999 CCC essay, "African American Contributions to Composition Studies" seeks "to trace a line of thought from early rhetors and scholars to contemporary researchers . . . that both emphasizes critical pedagogy and values Black culture, especially its vernacular,"[1] while his introduction to* African American Rhetoric(s): Interdisciplinary Perspectives *(2004) summarizes historical trends in the study of African American rhetoric. In* True to the Language Game: African American Discourse, Cultural Politics, and Pedagogy *(2011), he combines personal narratives about his early days in the field of rhetoric and language with later speeches on pedagogy and history. His work includes 7 monographs, 9 edited volumes, 5 books of poetry and fiction, and 27 articles. His analyses of major African American rhetoricians include* Composition and Cornel West: Notes Toward a Deep Democracy *(2008) and two books on writer John Oliver Killens,* Liberation Memories: The Rhetoric and Poetics of John Oliver Killens *(2003) and* John Oliver Killens: A Life of Black Literary Activism *(2010).* Louise Thompson Patterson: A Life of Struggle for Justice *is forthcoming this year from Duke University Press (2017). His other monographs include books on basic writing and critical approaches to composition and literacy. Gilyard is Distinguished Professor of English at Penn State, a former Chair of CCCC, and a former President of the NCTE/CCCC Black Caucus. In 2013, he received the CCCC Exemplar Award for outstanding contributions to the profession.*

—*Nathanial Williams*

---

1 Gilyard, Keith. "African American Contributions to Composition Studies." *CCC* 50.4 (June 1999): (626).

"I Have Fun Playing with Language"

Sharon James McGee

Spring 2004

WOE: Keith, you hold an MFA and have a background in literature and linguistics, so why do you make composition teaching and scholarship your disciplinary home?

GILYARD: That's a good question. I think that it made me inhabit it as much as I made it my home. In terms of pedagogy, I was always sort of a teacher; even as a child I was organizing readings and teaching my younger sister to read. So that's always been part of my personality. I just had a love of language, and I have a unified perspective about the possibilities of language. At one time I obviously spent more time on creative writing, but even my creative writing I always construed as political work. I was never writing just because I wanted to craft a poem about a tree or something like that. To me, years ago, interest in poetry or attempts at fiction were always part of the Black Arts Movement. We saw creative writing as being part of a political agenda, as being a sister, as Larry Neal said, to a political movement. So the move from that into composition really came about in terms of employment opportunities and is really just another point on the continuum. For me, it was always about language, the possibilities of language, whether it be the formal study of linguistics or the teaching of composition, which, to me, was always political in the sense of students becoming and growing through language and being able to have more life possibilities for themselves. It was all connected by a perspective. I guess I would say that I have pursued several things across disciplinary boundaries, but they are unified by a certain perspective about language and power and possibility.

It was always like that in a sense. I remember—I almost forgot this story—back when I was an undergraduate I was working with some people on a prison project at Trenton State Prison in New Jersey. Even then as an undergraduate, I was talking about ways to teach the inmate population things about writing—both composition as well as creative writing. So I've always been doing composition in a sense even though I was interested in trying to pursue an MFA, which was part of a dream.

So after my BA, I stayed in New York and went through Columbia's MFA program. Again, because I had an idea about developing as a creative writer with the notion that maybe—I was so naïve about the immediate worth of an MFA from Columbia—some school would hire me right away to teach creative writing. I found out it didn't really work that simply, so given the landscape in New York at the time with the changes that were happening in the City University system—demographic shifts, the increasing diversity—I turned my attention to that and said, "That's work to be done, too." I always did some of it anyway, tutoring and whatnot, so it wasn't that much of a leap from the MFA to composition because the composition was always there—maybe dormant or less dominant in certain phases—but it was always there.

WOE: As I've read your work, one of the themes or maybe influences that is prevalent is that you operate at the edges of all those parts of English studies—literature, linguistics, creative writing, composition. How have those multiple influences shaped your work, your scholarship, and your thinking?

GILYARD: They've helped me with perspective and clarity. A lot of times when you're locked inside any particular discourse, it's hard to think outside of that. It's the overused phrase, "It's hard to think outside the box." What's happened for me coming from all those tributaries, in a sense, into one common reservoir of awareness is that I've been able to use each of those sub-fields to shed a certain light, or have a certain angle, to look onto another part of what I was doing in a way that was fresh. Literature, for example, was important to me as a compositionist because, being interested in literature, I thought about what it is that I value about literature, which is the idea, as John Rouse says, that "Life will never be a substitute for literature because it's not long enough." The idea that you travel and get exposed to worlds through literature and see things in the text that you don't get a chance to see physically enables you to clarify values and gain understandings about this whole human drama. One of the things that motivated me and I suspected would motivate other people to really want to develop literacy skills was the chance to participate in those worlds. You know, you don't practice reading because you're trying to strengthen your eye muscles; you read because you want to know things. Understanding literature that way and having it have that kind of value for me allowed me to say that this would be something that I could incorporate into a composition pedagogy. Sometimes in the academy there are these fractious debates, literature as opposed to composition—I never saw it that way. I could never be on a composition side of the debate that would exclude the literary because the literary was so much a part of what I've always done. So that's one way.

Another way is the linguistics. For example, linguistics would influence composition pedagogy because linguistics would give you the concrete examples that you can apply to your thinking about pedagogy. If you say, "Okay, I understand that I'm dealing with a linguistically diverse student population," and you understand that situation intuitively, having some knowledge of linguistics or sociolinguistics allows you to go beyond that, to understand the systematic nature of their language. That knowledge of linguistics obviously can inform you as a composition teacher.

Coming to formal composition teaching from the field of creative writing, I had a certain understanding, I think, about the composing process that I may not have had if I had just basically been trained as a teacher and said or been told, "Now you've been taught, go teach composition." Having always been involved with the process of writing as a creative writer, as a poet, as an aspiring fiction writer at one point, I understood about process and understood what motivates writers. I had to get language for it so I could participate in the professional conversation, like with the CCCC crowd. But I really had an understanding of how important it was to struggle to be fluent and that the struggle to be fluent was the most important challenge facing a writer. And that when and as you were achieving fluency, you strived to be clear because you were trying to make the most sense with your message. Again, growing up in New York and knowing a lot of writers, I understood that getting the stuff correct in terms of presentation was the last phase. I saw professional writers working with editors. So I never would even come to composition from what they would call the current-traditional paradigm because I would have been outside of that already as a creative writer. To me, those are some examples of how each strand of what I do has informed the other strand.

WOE: In *Voices of the Self*, you talk about "Space Poem," a poem you wrote in elementary school, as your first poem. How did you learn to write poetry?

GILYARD: I think that was my first poem. It's strange because it's almost like asking someone how they learned to talk, or speak, or read; they don't know because it happened so long ago. The most sense that I can make of it is that obviously I was attuned to the rhythm of the language because poetry was being read to us. Prior to composing something like that we were obviously reading Dr. Seuss and the like. You're getting your ear, and you're developing an affinity for the rhythm of the language, how it sounds, and I guess when you start reading, you may have seen some models and that sort of thing. As I was learning how to write, I just sort of gravitated toward that. That's probably how it happened.

When I was working on *Voices*, I looked at my accumulated school record and noticed that my second grade teacher recognized I had this interest in poetry. I don't know how many second graders have that written on their school record, but it was first noted then: "He has a particular interest in poetry." It happened a long time ago, so it's not as though I can say, "Okay, when I was 21 I started doing this and that's how I started becoming a poet." It really started so much earlier than that. My work with poetry began at least by seven—a flirtation—there were different degrees of seriousness about it. I think probably around 19 when I was in college, I started getting more serious about it, taking volumes and volumes and volumes out of the library, studying form and getting really serious about writing poetry. I was going to school, but I was also always carving out time, making certain times sacrosanct in fact, to work on poetry.

WOE: So how did you make the move to being an academic writer?

GILYARD: Again, part of it comes out of the creative writing end. Part of it is a motivation thing—you won't want to practice for something if you're never going to get a chance to participate. Really, it comes from the participation. All right, if I've entered this world and I'm going to be in this world, and I already have some confidence about language because of early positive experiences with language, then I expect to do pretty well. Then other people might come to expect you to be able to do certain things with language, and with each new situation that you enter involving language use, you get better and better at adapting to situations. That's why I think it's so important to give students early successful experiences in writing, so that they can take that experience and translate it to novel situations. They can say, "Okay, this is how it works here, so let me see if I can produce some of that if I want to." And always we keep a little edge because for me to come into the academic world it's not like I ever wanted to sound totally like the academics I was reading. I'm going to bring some flavor to it, if I can. All of those moves are built on a base in which there was early encouragement. I imagine that if I'd been suppressed early and successfully the way that so many other people are suppressed by school, then I wouldn't have found my way into academe in the first place, and certainly would have no taste for academic writing.

WOE: For many people graduate school is a struggle to find one's professional voice. A lot of people will say that graduate school made their writing atrophy in some ways. Did you have that struggle, and how did you negotiate it if you did?

GILYARD: I got lucky since my first graduate school experience was in an MFA program. So when I went into an education program, I came to that with a sense of confidence as a writer. You look at some PhD programs and people are fretting about getting a long document done, about getting a dissertation done. Fifty percent of the people who are ABD never finish. I didn't have that kind of trepidation because to me it was just some more writing to do.

I remember when Toni Morrison was asked a similar question, she said she writes the kinds of books she'd want to read. I was guided by that philosophy no matter what I was attempting to do, whether it was to write a poem or story or write an academic essay. I always keep in mind the same thing that she kept in mind: if I had to read an essay about composition teaching or whatever, what kind of essay would I like to read? Then I have fun playing with language. You open some journals, and the essays—I guess there's nothing wrong with them—but some of them are a little too stiff for me. The writers need to loosen up a bit.

WOE: Your voice in your writing is clear, dialogic, motivating, and assertive. You have a message that you want to get through to the audience. It seems sometimes like you're trying to push the envelope to get people to explore some ideas in new ways.

GILYARD: I like to have fun with language, so sometimes, even if the stakes aren't that high, I just like fooling around with the form sometimes. But I want to get back to the notion of having a unified perspective. Not that I'm absolutely clear at all times and certainly not when an idea is evolving, but the clearer you are about why you're doing what you're doing and the clearer you are about what's at stake, that helps you find the voice that you want to find or push things in the way you want to push them. I don't want to talk about any kind of language teaching or what we call composition totally divorced from a social justice agenda, you see. As I said earlier, all of this work inside educational institutions I construe to be political work. And so, to me, what's at stake is the preparation of a new generation, the next generation of a critical citizenry, which I see as connected to our best chance for the nation to function in an enlightened way. It's going back to the best aspects of a Jeffersonian ideal: the notion of an informed citizenry making informed and critical decisions about the issues of the day. To me, all of my teaching is connected to that ideal. So I construe it all to be political, and the politics I'm most interested in is the politics of trying to push us toward greater social justice as a culture. When you know that's what you're about, it helps to clarify everything you're trying to do because all your investigations are linked to that central idea.

WOE: In your Chair's address at the 2000 CCCC, you stated that composition teachers and composition classes are key in working toward a more perfect democracy. Are you talking about first-year composition courses in specific or the whole composition curriculum?

GILYARD: The whole thing. First-year composition courses are one site, probably our most captive site because it's the most taught course in universities nationwide, and so certainly that site is important with respect to the kind of work that we're talking about. But I think that in all the courses writing is a key technology in this critical reflection that I'm talking about. So, yeah, writing everywhere—whether it be basic writing, first-year composition, or whatever. I was really talking about composition at all levels. Anywhere we can get students to be thoughtful and anywhere that we can get students to make a commitment beyond the self-centered pursuit of material goods, I'm for that. To get them to question it. Again, as I always say, it's never that we can guarantee any form of behavior, but we can certainly make habitual questioning a part of a liberal arts education. If we can't do this in a university, where is it going to be done? People debate nowadays the role of higher education, especially public higher education; to me, it's clear that the role of public higher education should be in the service of the public good. When you're clear about what you're about, you can take up these issues and you don't get blown all over the place by different questions that come up. A lot of times you have faculty walking around who haven't even thought about these questions. Ask them, "What's the role of the university? What's the role of liberal arts education in today's world? They will reply, "I hadn't really thought about that." But see, I do think about that [*laughs*].

So when someone asks me, I have an answer. It goes back to having a reason for what you're doing. Right or wrong. My answer is not the final answer, but if you think that the role of the liberal arts is that they protect the public good in some way and you can articulate that well, as a Henry Giroux can do brilliantly, then there's a decent rationale for what you do. It's better than not having a good rationale for what you do. Then you see everything you do with your syllabus, and the way that you engage students, and the model you represent, as political.

WOE: Let's talk about first-year composition and what role first-year composition instructors and courses should play in promoting social justice. What is at stake for composition?

GILYARD: I think what's at stake is this notion of critical language awareness, this deepening of awareness about language, this deepening of perspective, this idea of the liberal arts as contributing to the public good, this notion of us serving as more than agents of corporate expediency. To me, the role of the first-year composition course is really to try to promote this notion of critical language awareness more than anything else. When students are invested in the process in certain ways, the other things will fall into place, the technical concerns and so forth. I talk about this larger idea of being critical language consumers—how do you consume language? Let's interrogate language: What does it mean? How does it operate? Let's put it on the consumer model like we do other things. You consume things and you make decisions about them. Well, you're going to be bombarded with all kinds of language every day all the time. How are you going to consume that language? How are you going to make decisions about what makes sense to you, about what moves you, what should persuade you, what you should be dismissive of, or what you should interrogate more or ask more questions about? That's the stuff of education. Everybody's got to learn it at some level. Malcolm X talked about this idea years ago in his "Speech to Mississippi Youth" or some title close to that. He gave them the same advice: Even as I'm here talking to you, just don't take everything that I say at face value. Question me. Interrogate what I'm telling you. Go read for yourself. Don't wait until somebody else interprets it for you and tells you how to think and what to think. To me, that's really what's at stake: Whether we're going to create a bunch of automatons or whether we're going to create people who actually think and consume language in a critical way so that the people who manipulate language for perverse ends, as we know that there are many people whose job is to do just that, don't just win. That's the sort of outcome where they get the masses sleeping, so to speak, and just uncritically consuming their messages. So if nothing else, that's what's at play, and it's not a matter of whether you're coming from the left or the right or you're liberal or conservative. Everybody needs to do that. If someone goes through all of this, and says, "Okay, I make a carefully considered judgment that I support X." Well, that's how it shakes out.

WOE: How do we get students motivated in these kinds of issues?

GILYARD: Their goal is career oriented, and they have a pretty clear sense that composition is one of the requirements. We have to get through the gates, and what I need to know is where to put the commas, so I can pass the course, get the three credits, and move on with my major, and go ahead and get paid. I know that, but the reality of it is that you have to engage them in a conversation about what kind of language user do you want to be. Do you want to be really good at it? I'm presuming that since you're so career focused and so motivated, that you want to be really good at this thing. To be really good at this thing, you're not going to do it by rote assignments or uninspired rehearsal of some skill. This is sort of like what Macrorie talked about with his notion of Engfish: You've demonstrated some technical competence but you have nothing very interesting to say and you haven't said it in any way that's likely to be compelling or convincing to anybody else, though it happens to be technically correct. So, in my mind, you have to have some engagement beyond the standard "I want this technical expertise," and if you can get students invested in that process, then I think that's how their writing will develop beyond just a minimal competence into something more complex and sophisticated. You have to get them to buy into that process at some level and say okay, you can't just disengage yourself from these issues or what's happening in the world. I mean, what's going to be the subject of your prose?

I remember having a student years ago—it was very sad. This was after Khadafy's compound was bombed, and this event was red letter in some papers in New York. You couldn't get away from it. It was on every radio station, every television station, in every paper. I waited three or four days then went into class—this was in what was called a basic writing class—and

I asked them to comment or give their opinion about what had been on the news. This one woman asked me, "What happened?" I said, "You can't be in the world here in America and not know what happened." I was kind of joking, but she was really serious about it, and I had to explain to her what had occurred. I remember asking if she listened to the radio. She said no. I asked her if she watched television. She didn't have time. She was raising kids, a single parent. I said, "You had to pass three or four newsstands when you left the subway station on your way to campus." She didn't have time to stop and look at any newspapers. Yet, she was sitting in class and said she couldn't do all of that other stuff because she had to focus on getting her education. And she was serious. She was in a basic writing class, which means that she's already been categorized by the university in a certain way, and she did not see any connection between an engagement with the world around her and all that linguistic bombardment and her particular station inside the university or how that was connected to her goal of "I'm here to finish college because I got to get my education." She was not understanding that the person who can walk through life oblivious to radio, television, and print media, and be categorized as she was by the university, is not the kind of person who's going to go through four years of college successfully, you see.

So that's a true example but a really extreme one of what can go wrong when there's this disconnect between their understanding of what the linguistic task is before them and what they think they want. You won't develop much writing power writing in a virtual vacuum. Sometimes, then, you have to have conversations, and it varies according to classes, but you have to have conversations that sort of merge those two—I'm always trying to merge those two. "Okay, I'm really glad that you really want to get through this class and that you're not going to drop it [*laughs*] two weeks into the semester. I'm happy that you're here and that you have all this enthusiasm bubbling over to do well, but let's talk a little bit about what 'well' means. All right, so we've got to do some definitional work. Then, let me tell you what I think—you know, I've been doing this for a while—so I have some ideas about maybe the best way of going about doing it as well as you want to do it. Now, I'm not even doing it as well as I want to or plan to; I'm still working on my writing. But I've got some ideas about how you can do it as well as possible." So we start having that conversation. Then I try to get them off just the utilitarian model to a broader engagement model. It's an artful thing; teaching is artful. Dewey talked about teaching being more art than science, so it's not a formula you hand anybody and say go into the class and do this. It's who you are and reading the students, and that's where the art of teaching comes in.

WOE: In the Chair's address you said, "for any progressive pedagogy to achieve respectable results, students, among whose ranks are some of the important outsiders we need, have to feel invested in the roles they play in the process."

First, what are the respectable results we can use to measure our success? Second, how can students feel invested?

GILYARD: I think they have to feel that they have something at stake in the whole process. To get them thinking, what are we doing this for? I put it on them. Why are you getting a college education? "I'm getting a college education because I want this job." A lot of these students are classified as remedial students and in my mind I already know that getting through college for them could be a six- or seven-year trip, which is cool if they indeed finish. But I used to ask them about their five-year plan: What do you see yourself doing in five years? And you'd be surprised. I would have them do an essay and they would write: In five years, I plan to be working for this Fortune 500 company and maybe at the executive level. They would write that kind of thing. And, I'm like, five years? You won't even be finished here. [*Laughs*] It's so unrealistic.

Sometimes, just as we want them to be critical, we have to engage them in that sort of dialogic manner. So, okay, I have some ideas about what I think the role of a liberal arts education is in addition to the vocational aspects. What do you think you're doing? What are your goals, aspirations?

"Well," they say, "I'm going to open my own business."

I counter with, "Do you know that 80% of small businesses fail within the first two years? Is that anything that you ever thought about when you put this plan together?" Or you're going to play in the NBA? Did you ever think that you didn't even make your high school team—or college team? Did you ever think about that when you formulated this goal that you'd be in the NBA in four years? A group did a study in a high school in Brooklyn, I think. They asked over 300 male students what they were going to be doing, and something like over 250 students said they planned to play in the NBA. This is all out of one high school. And I'm thinking, they're going to be lucky if you get one player in that high school who gets to play in the NBA anytime within the next decade. So a lot of times, when students make these statements about what they want to do, it's not all that deeply formulated. Many times it's what they think they should be doing or should be saying about the fact they came to college. You have to try to get them thinking about different things, and thinking about their education and their setting in broader terms. When you see that happening, that is one positive result, one measurement.

If you saw more people being more critically literate in a certain way, that's another result. I don't know how you measure that in the short term; that's obviously a long-term thing—we probably need longitudinal studies about this kind of thing. We talk about these kinds of pedagogies all the time and there's always someone who will write an essay or design a study to show that his or her particular mode of instruction was successful. Obviously, for ethical reasons—you can't clone people or can't clone students or teachers or control environments in a vacuum—so you can't have these rigidly controlled experiments. So everything is always about testimony and lore and what I've done. You know, you go to CCCC, and these people give these fifteen-minute talks about some methods they used in class, and this worked. Everything works. [*Laughs*] So what we need assessment-wise is that we probably need to figure out some ways to do longitudinal work that gets us to see our successes because I don't think we really document our successes that well, especially in composition or basic writing. I think we get hit with too much criticism and we're told that we are responsible for everything that goes wrong in the students' whole education. No other department is blamed like the writing department. You could have had a student nine years ago and if they don't do something right in a psychology class or they leave a comma out or leave an affix off a verb form, then "You didn't learn how to write in your freshman writing class."

We're blamed for everything. Because we're so busy fending off attack all the time, I think we haven't really documented our successes as well as we might. Having some more longitudinal work—some testimony and some research studies that indicate the worth of a certain kind of pedagogy— would be useful. As you debate these things, it's useful to have that kind of testimony on your side.

But there are other things. We could talk about how well is the university functioning in respect to access, how well programs are functioning with respect to inclusion. How are students demonstrating commitment outside of the academy? Or what pedagogical models exist outside of the academy? I was reading recently about the literacy campaigns, for example, that Martin Luther King, Jr. ran under the Southern Christian Leadership Conference. I think they called it the Citizens' Education Program, and the central figure in that was a woman by the name of Septima Clark. As part of their citizenship campaign, they were going to areas and their aim was to get people to be literate, but literate toward a specific task, in this case to get ready to vote or get ready to pass voting tests. They had a particular agenda, and they had a particular methodology. I think we could look to some of those programs and learn what were some of the outcomes of them. It became in vogue in the '70s, '80s, and '90s to talk about Freire and emancipatory literacy, but you know, Septima Clark had developed this citizenship campaign, this model, fifty years before anybody in the U.S. was talking up Paulo Freire. Around the end of World War I, she was already developing this citizenship campaign. They had a whole curriculum that would get sent to different towns and areas. Again, it was very much like what I'm talking about. Something political was at stake, and so the question of literacy was tied directly to some kind of political empowerment. What were the results of that? I'd like to see an analysis or assessment of that kind of activity, that campaign, let's say, in the context of the Civil Rights Movement, and think about what that could suggest to us about curricular goals or the possibility of a certain kind of success in our particular political moment. So these are the kinds of things that we can do to begin to talk about assessing the results we'd like to see or assessing the impact of our particular work.

WOE: Many universities are beginning to relegate the work of basic writing and basic skills courses to community colleges, partly as a cost-saving measure. How do you see basic writing fitting into the mission of the university? Does it fit into the mission of the university?

GILYARD: I think it clearly fits into the mission of the university. If you make a commitment to admit students, at the same time you ought to be making a commitment to provide the resources necessary to give them a thorough education in the liberal arts or general education. In systems like the City University of New York, it's obvious that those moves to eliminate basic writing courses on some campuses have to do with who the student body is now as opposed to who the student body was say forty or fifty years ago. So I see basic writing as being certainly within the mission of the university, and I don't condone at all the activity that suggests, "You should have gotten this in high school, but you didn't get it, so you can't come to a four-year college until you get it." College is supposed to stand for something. To me, it's supposed to stand for education and improvement at some level, so colleges should be willing to take on that task. I can see why universities have relegated it to community colleges. Most universities haven't done so-called remediation well. But the reason they haven't ever done it well is because they never fully committed to it. You're not serious about a basic writing program, let's say, when you cram thirty-five students into a class, place an impossible work load on an instructor, and then get mad because the students haven't changed their surface errors dramatically in fifteen weeks through drills (probably the preferred mode in large classes). You have to find more creative ways to do it. One obvious way is decreasing class size to give a pedagogy that hinges upon the production of lots of student writing a reasonable chance. Another obvious way is to increase the status and stature of the people who do this work. But, as you know, in most departments that's the punitive work. If you're doing well, then you're trying to get as far away from basic writing as you can. But if universities were really serious about this problem, then they'd put the people they considered the best (even though we can talk about what best and better means) instructors on that problem. Obviously, that's not what happens. That's not what most colleges and universities are interested in. That's one of the problems to me, and the solution to me is not relegating those courses to the community colleges.

    Basic writing is part of the university's mission, but "basic writing" itself has become such an attenuated term; it has so many meanings and means different things in different places. I think Lynn Troyka talked about this once

"Walk on the Beach" is reprinted with the permission of Dawn Sunchild.

in an article; she talked about different conceptions of basic writing and who basic writing students are. One person would say, "These are the characteristics of my basic writing students." And another would say, "Not my basic writing students." So the basic writing students were all different. I've visited at some places where someone would show me essays from students in a basic writing class, and I'd think that those students would be in a first-semester or even second-semester class where I was teaching. It varies, so to make specific academic or structural recommendations about those programs, to me again, you have to study the institutional context.

 I've been on both sides of this issue; I think I talked about it in a *JBW* article. There was a time when I was all for mainstreaming. Then I went to a conference and I heard a presentation from students who were in a basic writing program and they were saying, "We hear you, but please don't argue successfully and outlaw us because we need this program to do the kind of work and make the achievement that we've been able to make in that class." And the students' testimony was very compelling to me. You have to really study the institutional context and see how basic writing functions as a mechanism in a particular context. What does it mean with respect to access to resources? If you remove this in this institution, what happens to the students who would be classified and put into these courses? So you have to move carefully. I don't want to do anything by administrative fiat that proves more disabling to students that I'm purporting to serve. Now, in another context maybe being in that basic writing program may be such a stigma that the student is hard pressed to overcome that in the context of the institution, so in that situation I may look at that and say let's get rid of it, it's not working, it's not doing any good work for anybody. Let's do something else. But, again, you have to look at how it's done at different institutions because the programs are not set up the same at every institution. You'll see wide variance as you travel the nation. We have to be cautious about totalizing claims, those sweeping reform statements that people want to make about any academic program, including basic writing programs. There's an old saying I recall from my old study groups, probably something from the *Red Book*, "No investigation, no right to speak." And so many people claim the right to speak without the investigation. That goes back, I think, even to what I'm talking about with pedagogy in a course. If I'm doing anything, I'm trying to get students to investigate. Of course you have an absolute right to speak, but the quality of the speech you make is directly related to the degree to which you investigate issues, topics, and so on.

WOE: Often, when we get together at conferences as a collective body, we talk about the things that are going wrong. What are some of the positive things you see happening?

GILYARD: There are a lot of positive things. I always try to tell teachers about the agency they have. Sometimes they want to paint this picture of their own helplessness. I say there is such a thing as subversion. Even if you're caught in a dilemma about what to do, there is such a thing as closing your door and doing the kind of thing you believe in. How did we lose all craftiness? I know I've been crafty about a lot of things. When we gather as a group I like to promote this notion that we have agency.

There are other things: that people feel that they have a conundrum when faced with the demands of the institution and their own personal inclinations. To me, that's a positive. Probably for a lot of years people weren't even conflicted like that. So the fact that you have people experiencing that kind of conflict means that they're at least listening to some of the things that are in the air.

If you go around to visit different places you sometimes get to see that the effort of first-year composition instructors is taken seriously. I've met with deans and administrators who took seriously the role of composition. In some ways it's a "politics makes strange bedfellows" story. Even though we argue against corporate encroachment in higher education, at the same time, we sometimes advocate for the same thing that business is advocating for: critical thinkers and people who have good writing ability. Because of that we get administrators beginning to listen because they're hearing that on the business side, and, of course, administrators are often trying to justify their existences to businesses. You've got to take advantage of a moment like that. The main problem, though, is that what you can do at an institution varies a lot according to the leadership. You can have a WPA who's doing a good job and making certain inroads and getting certain things done, then she leaves or her term is up, and someone else comes in and everything she did for four or five years can go back to the way it was.

Graduate students learning the field think there's this sequence to it: things used to be that way, now they're this way. I tell them, "No, it's like music. All the styles are always around. Dixieland might not be the dominant music, but I can send you to a Dixieland club to listen to it. It's not dead." Graduate students say, "Nobody does it like this anymore," and I say, "In some places, they do. They probably aren't the people who will come to CCCC and give presentations, but you must understand that the people who come to CCCC are probably a minority." You see movement; because of organizations like the 4Cs, you have people who leave a convention and have more confidence in the kind of arguments that they can make on their own campuses. I know that's how it's worked for me. In my early years in the profession, I used on my campus statements and resolutions from CCCC to some positive, at times, effect in terms of my interaction with administrators. As I said earlier, I would have fairly intuitive ideas about language and writing and how to do things. So when I walked into a classroom and someone would hand me a workbook and say, "These are basic writers; therefore, they need to fill in these blanks to learn how to write." That was just the most ridiculous thing I ever heard of without ever going to a conference. But I wasn't able to articulate this in the best way or even successfully resist dominant practice. Someone could outmaneuver me rhetorically. So going to conferences, becoming more professional, and getting tuned into the language helped me to strengthen the arguments I could make about certain issues. So to the extent that we can strengthen those forums, to give support to folks who already have some good impulses, that's good. Of course, we'd love to persuade others as well. There are a lot of places where there's a plantation mentality about writing programs, and there's a lot of work to be done.

Even to talk about language diversity, it's in a different place than it was twenty years ago, say. The practices aren't as far along as the articles, but there's some movement and some understanding. We just did a language survey, for example, at CCCC that indicated some different attitudes. If teachers had taken or been exposed to sociolinguistics, it made a difference in their attitude toward language and language diversity. This is very important given the prediction that we are going to have a large influx of college students over the next six to eight years that will be the most diverse college population ever in the United States.

Twenty years ago, could I do the things that I'm doing in the place where I work? Could I have had status and have a program around African American language and literacy? Where could that have been a concentration in a mainline English Department? Where would that initiative have gotten? Would we have ever made someone like me a full professor in composition or rhetoric? That there can be positive answers now, in today's world, to such questions—better answers than we would have received in the past—gives me hope.

KEN MACRORIE

Ken Macrorie (1918–2009) taught and wrote amid the sweeping changes in composition studies during the mid-20th century, exerting important influence over early critiques of current-traditional pedagogy. He published his first book in 1959, The Perceptive Writer, Speaker, and Reader, a traditional textbook that he later criticized as being "written by an author blind to what he was doing."[1] Long a champion of authentic student writing, Macrorie taught for 17 years before discovering an approach that would elicit this type of writing. One day in 1964, fed up with affected student writing— lifeless academic prose that he termed "Engfish"—he told his advanced writing students to go home and write for ten minutes or until they had filled a page. While the results were uneven, the prose was "often alive."[2]

Considered by many the birth of freewriting, this experience encouraged Macrorie to develop a new approach to teaching. Uptaught (1970) recounts these early experiences, while subsequent publications push his techniques still further. In A Vulnerable Teacher (1974), he argues that by opening themselves up to students, teachers can encourage a similar vulnerability in students, enabling them to write viscerally and authentically. The widely adopted I-Search Paper (1984), a revision of Searching Writing: A Contextbook (1980), leads students to choose a topic of great personal interest and then conduct research to satisfy their curiosity. In Telling Writing (1985), Macrorie argues for a classroom atmosphere that encourages students to connect their own ideas to the world beyond themselves, focusing on their inner life to foster personal growth and full engagement in the world.

Macrorie received a BA at Oberlin College in 1940 and served in the U.S. Army during World War II, after which he earned his MA at the University of North Carolina and a PhD at Columbia in 1955. He served as editor of College Composition and Communication (1962–64), and taught at Michigan State and San Francisco State before settling at Western Michigan University, where he taught until he retired in 1978. In later years, he taught summer courses at the Breadloaf Graduate School of English, living in New Mexico until his death at the age of 90.

—William Sewell

1 Macrorie, Ken. *Uptaught*. New York: Hayden, 1970: (14). Print.
2 Ibid. (20).

"Arrangements for Truthtelling"

Eric Schroeder and John Boe

Fall 2004

WOE: What led you to become a writing teacher?

MACRORIE: My father died when I was twelve and Mother and I moved to Toledo, Ohio, where her brother had been a newspaper reporter and advertising man. He had his own single-person radio news broadcast. He knew the city. He went out and got the stories. He came back and wrote the script. He didn't even have a secretary. He let me accompany him on his daily trips to check the police blotter and other sources of news. I didn't know I was learning anything I could use, but here was this uncle of mine having to fill the half-hour slot of airtime with all the stuff he collected during the day. What an incredible organizing job! He had to cut words, and that's how I learned to cherish cutting words and where I began to make some associations between speaking and writing because he was writing to speak. I thought about going into advertising. As a kid I played with the design and typography of the printed page, but I decided I couldn't stand working in advertising because so many advertisements were deceptive or outright untruthful.

One day much later, in 1964, as an associate professor of English sitting with a small class on the campus lawn, I found myself saying, "I'm sick of reading phony writing, including some of yours. It's not your fault. I believe you write that way because in composition classes like this one the aim is usually to get you writing without a lot of mistakes in spelling, punctuation, and grammar. You can't write well until you know those basics. I apologize. I'm a writer myself and I know there is something much more basic in writing than those basics. It's meaning. I'd like you to try an experiment. Go back to your rooms and try harder than ever before in your life to write truths—not the truth—whatever that is, but your truthful memory of an event in your life you can't forget. Try to get it right, your perception of it." A few students did that, and their writing began to influence other members.

WOE: How was publishing student work a piece of this process?

MACRORIE: In 1968, the Vietnam War was going on. The basic goal there was killing people, for both sides. John Bennett, my high school teacher friend who worked at Central High School in Kalamazoo, and I had begun to publish together our students' best writings in a little stapled magazine we called *Unduressed* (meaning out from under the duress of trying not to make mistakes in spelling, punctuation, and grammar). Patti Shirley in my college composition class said she couldn't write anything at that time. I said, "Don't worry about it. Just go into another room and write what comes to you." Patti came back with this writing:

> A friend alive last month is today, I'm told, a dead box of rocks en route from Saigon. Outside the smoke filmed window a boy balances on the edge of the fountain, dirty blue paint & empty. Only last spring it was my ocean.

Patti was so moved by the death of her friend in war that she couldn't jabber on and on about it with a bunch of clichés. Her feelings chose her words for her.

At the beginning of the experiment, which I eventually named Arrangements for Truthtelling, a few members broke into highly truthful writing. Others were quickly energized by the good models. I remembered that when I was a kid my mother said to me, "Don't lie, Kenny. One lie leads to another, and then you're in real trouble." One of the reasons I set up the experiment was to see if one truthtelling would lead to another. It did. A war was in the face of college students, so many of our experimenters let it choose itself as a subject to write about it. Another sample, by Jean Corey:

VIET NAM

That small country's image is so powerful for its size. When usually quiet Greg tells me about fighting there his manner gets aggressive and the conversation becomes one-sided. He still breathes the effects. From his unit, about half were killed and two-thirds were injured. He told of this composite picture taken after their initial training and he hated to look at it—a bunch of smiling faces and close friends that are no more. Imagine looking at your high-school yearbook and thinking that every other person on a page was no longer alive. You would wonder why you were one of the blessed—yet living a year in Vietnam may not be a blessing.

    Another incident remains in my mind. I can't comprehend it as I sit all folded up in my living room chair. One of the duties these guys had was to go over a field where they had battled and pick up the bodies of their friends and put them in bags to be shipped home. Some lost their sanity, understandably. One soldier had been fighting from a foxhole for two or three days and suddenly the head of his buddy rolled in beside him. He went into shock and was taken to a psychiatric ward. They had to feed him intravenously because he would do nothing but sit in a chair staring, with no response to voices, movement, pain, etc. Finally they made a papier-mâché head, painted it, and rolled it in front of him. He went into a screaming fit, but when he stopped, they were able to begin helping him. With all the years of schooling a psychiatrist needs, I doubt instructions for this case were in any of his texts. I don't think we can imagine what life and death are in that little country. My cousin has told his family that he prays he will be hit, so he can pull some of his time in the hospital instead of in the field. The hope for a precisely aimed bullet is common around here.

WOE: Publishing *Undressed* in the late '60s sounds like a revolutionary move. Did you have institutional problems with what you were doing?

MACRORIE: Both the president of the university and the vice president who was the faculty dean read *Undressed*. So once I got a note from the vice president saying, "You know I read every issue of *Undressed*? I just want you to know I missed the last one because I was on so many plane trips around the country that I didn't get it, so I want a copy of it because it's so good." And the president, he let the students write freely. He didn't like it sometimes when they protested in an ugly way. The students had a private non-school paper that they put out every couple of months called *The Western Review*. They said some mean things and put on the cover a big picture of shit raining down on President Johnson. The president of the university didn't like that and he picked up the copies that were left out with that on it. He said, "I believe in freedom but I can't believe in that, coming out with the name of our university underneath." I didn't want him to do that, but I didn't complain because I thought, "You and the Dean have been really wonderful to support these students." 'Cause they were writing about the war, their parents' divorces, and all kinds of stuff.

I thought that was wonderful of him to let them publish controversial stuff. He also donated some money to me to get this magazine published because I was paying for some of the printing costs.

WOE: Your own storytelling is very shaped by your students' voices.

MACRORIE: Nowadays I can't talk about learning unless I have student writings with me. They are my texts. Other people can't learn what I've learned except through them. Once students began to write powerfully, I began to see how powerful writing could emerge from people of many ages. I then became a learner along with them. The human habit of telling stories exists within all of us. Composing those texts is a more unconscious process than I and other members of the experiment had realized. At the beginning, some of the writers who had broken through the plastic wall of academic style admitted that when writings were read aloud in our experiment it was usually stories that evoked the strongest responses from listeners—in body language or laughs or gasps of surprise.

WOE: I'm interested in story, but as a writing teacher, if I emphasize narrative, the university tends to say that I'm not preparing students for writing in the academic disciplines or for their professions.

MACRORIE: I've been reacting to that thinking for many years. And learning more about what stories can do. Here's a writing by Esther Rosbuck, a college student in the Experiment:

122

> While we were driving back from Thrifty Acres tonight they started reading the first 122 birthdates of the draft lottery—'the certain to be called' group. When I heard February 14th in the number four spot I physically melted against the door in the back seat. How come you never know how things will affect you until they happen? I haven't shaken so hard in a long time—it was more than shivering from the cold. February 14th belongs to Dave. I wanted to be with him to see how he felt; scared, accepting, nonchalant, bitter, how? It seems like he'd want someone to talk to, but maybe not. He doesn't know how I feel or that I care and I'm not sure if it matters to him. That's the hardest part.

Like many good writings, this one is not an essay and not a story. Both forms appear in it and I sense that while writing, Esther is learning what is happening to her and to Dave. She's placing where and how feelings arose. This hybrid way of communicating is stronger than a pure essay marching along with characterizing adjectives that in themselves are usually abstract. They don't act out things as if on a stage.

WOE: How did your experiment operate?

MACRORIE: In my classes I try to have five groups of three students each. Then three members of the experiment every week become the editors of a weekly magazine. So everybody experiences the whole publication process. Each member is a writer, reader, and editor. They all get to know each other. They develop a common desire to put out a magazine of powerful writing. The editors' names for each week appear on the masthead. But every once in a while someone says, "That's one of the best pieces of writing I've heard in a long time," and somebody else over in the corner replies, "I found it weak in several places." Then the three editors for that week have to choose from the writings each group has turned in. As a team of three editors, they make the decisions about the writings accepted during their week. They begin to think in real terms what it means to perceive a piece of writing with their peers who have had many of the same experiences but come up with different reactions.

WOE: How did your early interest in perception shape your later work in writing?

MACRORIE: In the late 1940s I was knocked out by the demonstrations Adelbert Ames, Jr. designed in Hanover, New Hampshire, of how we all perceive ideas and events. I mean whatever we open our eyes to, or turn our ears to, bang! What happens? And why? We perceive whatever is here on the basis of our expectations, the situation, thought, or objects before us, our purposes at the moment, our value system. We make a bet on what we are seeing or hearing and that bet is based on our past experiences. It's not simply what we bring to it ("the eye of the beholder"). In one darkened room Del Ames Jr. presents twin faraway lights enlarging as they come toward us. Watch out! A car is going to crash into us! No, they were just balloons lighted from inside, being pumped up to become larger and larger. They were stationary, not moving toward us. Yet we would have been crazy not to jump out of the way.

That's perception. It's looking through eyes that have been focusing and focusing under the influence of our past experiences. And it's the same with our ears and those familiar and unfamiliar sounds we may hear. It's such a basic process. Automatic, yet as difficult to forecast as splitting an atom and killing several hundred thousand human beings by dropping the bomb in the center of a big city.

We perceive everything through that process. Del Ames, Jr. and some helpers figured out the process by setting up distorted rooms, playing upon that necessity of placing bets on what we perceive. Ames's discovery amazed John Dewey, who in 1922 had written a book titled *Human Nature and Conduct*. It outlined the developing behavior patterns of human beings and prognosticated accurately just what has been happening on Planet Earth in the last ten years. But few people paid attention. The emergence of the television screen as supreme authority with its news bytes and web networks, gigantic, and also small and personal, has largely supplanted the reading of books and oiled up the brains of humans for fast, fast travel. Goodbye to thoughtfulness and understanding. Hello to larger and larger cartels of control and conquest. Perception and nuclear fission have hastened the evolution of mankind from small gangs to global financial empires that eat each other up.

Recently I exchanged letters with the third Del Ames Jr. He feels his father the perception man didn't get much notice for his world-shaking discoveries, and I agree. He sent me on the track of a book called *The Morning Notes of Adelbert Ames, Jr*. Hadley Cantril of Princeton University worked with Ames and in that book published sixty pages of letters between Ames and Dewey. Those two worked to compose a description of the process of perception. They were ever refining the meanings of the words they were using, hoping to improve their understanding of the consequences of their discoveries in the changing world. They had intended to share their understandings with the populations of the world rather than bomb, rape, and force others to give up their power.

Schools could help students master storytelling. A story can describe how persons live and work in contexts of families, businesses, courts of law, governments, and military structures. Maybe stories are weapons of living that are superior to suicide bombs and military conquests. Stories can easily be shaped by identified, named writers, although real names may put us right back into the concentration camps of people's minds and spirit by corporate, political, and even religious forces. Detention, excommunication, or low wages can produce human beings who don't use all their powers. Looking at what is on the great screen in quick blips predominates over the reading of whole books that help human beings understand their lives.

WOE: What are the risks when you try to get students to tell the truth?

MACRORIE: One of my teachers at Bread Loaf was having problems trying to publish student writing. I went out west and met some of the Indians he was working with. Here's a little piece that a high school girl wrote; it's called "Walk on the Beach" and was published in a collection that the students produced:

> There was a fat, pale man and this beautiful, sexy woman, his wife. They walked along the beach hand in hand. Then suddenly this muscular man came over and grabbed the woman and carried her off in the water. She screamed and punched him. He got mad, then threw her in the water. She went under, and her fat husband grabbed her hand and lifted her up. She smiled and said, "Why didn't you do anything?"
>
> He said, "If I did he would have nailed me into the ground." Then they laughed. He turned and kissed her.
>
> She said, "I love you," and he replied, "And I love you." So they grabbed each other's hands firmly and walked down the beach into the sunset.

Now there's a story. I read it as a humorous comment on the notion of machismo. The husband wasn't going to try and show what a strong guy he was by getting himself drowned. The teacher had been in one of my Arrangements for Truthtelling at the Bread Loaf School of English at Middlebury College in Vermont. He wrote this in his introduction to their publication:

> The world of teenagers is a pretty lively place wherever you go. This collection of student stories from the reservation—bits of dialogues, descriptions, memories, fantasies, slices of life, poems, essays, scripts—proves it. It is as lively as a fresh hooked trout in a beaver pond. The selections printed here

were chosen because they reveal something of the personalities, perceptions, moods, and imaginations of the students. Their writing is interesting and full of life. Teenagers aren't perfect, neither are schools, teachers, communities, almost anything human. Neither is this book. The writers themselves will be among the first to spot any flaws and will wish they had taken the time to rewrite.

WOE: Can you talk about Bread Loaf School of English and your involvement with it?

MACRORIE: It's complex. At Middlebury, there's a school for learning Spanish and a whole lot of foreign languages, but the School of English was for English teachers. In 1981 I was invited to teach there by Dixie Goswami, director of the writing program, who was from South Carolina. The moment I met her I felt comfortable and confident. And I saw other teachers and students respond to her likewise. So I stayed there for thirteen years, every summer. It was the most wonderful experience I ever had in teaching, by far.

WOE: What was a typical session there like?

MACRORIE: Six weeks for the degree courses. You could get a Master's Degree in English. The faculty was so good and there was a lot of freewheeling going on. Then there was this theater program going on, which didn't cost anybody any money—all the students and teachers could go to the plays for free. You could go to any rehearsal you wanted. For example, the first meeting when the actors were reading the play together for the first time.

Carol Elliott was the acting teacher and Alan Mokler, her husband, was the director of the theater department. (Now they are also in those positions during the regular school term at the University of Iowa.) I taught one class in what we called improvisation in writing and theater. Carol and I had people writing about their experience in theater and also doing little improv acting scenes and exercises and seeing if they could transfer any of that to their writing. The students from my writing class had to do improv theater and students from Carol's acting class had to do freewriting. The students really learned a lot.

WOE: It sounds like part of the appeal of Bread Loaf was that it was a program where you used language in different ways. There was writing, there was theater, there was literature, there was improvisation.

MACRORIE: Nobody I knew ever did a class like that before, but Carol and I thought, "Well, that would be a good idea." When I went to her things, and then when she read my students' writing, we would say, "Hey, this story is like that thing we've been doing in acting." And I find myself more and more thinking that good writing has a lot to do with the way words are sounded. And if you read aloud your own writing you always can spot passages where sound enhances meanings and where it doesn't add meaning. You wonder how you did them—well, you did them unconsciously. When we talk, we don't know when the sentence is going to end, we never do.

In my own classes I finally got down a capsule way of asking people to write and I haven't departed from it in a long time. I say, "Think of an event that you find yourself remembering all the time, that you can't forget." That is what Samuel Butler, who is one of my gods, meant when he said, "Let your subject choose you." If you can't forget it, it shows it has chosen you. I don't say anything about being specific or anything like that; I just say, "Whatever it is, that event, try to get it down so it comes alive." Students come up with all sorts of stuff they put in their stories. They remember back and find new things and experiences in their past.

WOE: Are there other lessons that you learned from your "Arrangements for Truthtelling"?

MACRORIE: In our experiment, more women than men wrote powerfully. In the past on Planet Earth women generally haven't been expected or allowed to write for publication as men have. But the twentieth century saw a tremendous increase in publication for women. Offhand I think of Barbara Ehrenreich's *Nickel and Dimed*, Barbara Kingsolver's *The Poisonwood Bible*, Irini Spanidou's *Fear*, Amy Chua's *World on Fire*, M.M.B. Walsh's *Grass Heart*, Barbara Beasley Murphy's *Life! How I Love You!*, Arundhati Roy's *The God of Small Things* and *The Cost of Living*. Ms. Roy's fiction and nonfiction speak truths to each other. That's a funny-sounding sentence—"Her fiction and nonfiction speak truths to each other." But it's good to hear someone talking about truthtelling instead of lying.

Even in the Dewey/Ames letters I find a storytelling flow. It's a scientific story of two guys working together instead of doing verbal battle. What they did first, what they did second, and so on. Many scientists have recently moved in the direction of reporting their researches in story form, even people making DNA discoveries.

WOE: You seem to suggest that narrative has a transformative power.

MACRORIE: That's true. John Bennett's and my Arrangements for Truthtelling could be carried out by adults of all kinds, retirees and people of all ages dissatisfied with mass communication and weakened by the now common obeisance to money power. I want to show how narrative is life. Here's a story from a fourth grader at East Cooper Elementary School in Parchment, Michigan, which I visited for several months and where I was allowed to set up for a few hours a week a modified form of an Arrangement for Truthtelling. The story is called "Power" and was written by Joe Wooden, a ten-year-old boy, as I remember:

> We had a walnut tree in our yard which was about 45 feet high and its branches were sort of an oval circle. It was a nice tree with grassy green

leaves. One day my father and I went to pick walnuts. We got about 50 or 60 and took them inside. We put them on a board and let them dry. One day my father and mother went downstairs to crack walnuts. First they hit them with a hammer, then picked out the insides and stored them in bags in the pantry. Now when my mother bakes she uses walnuts.

One day last week some men came from the electric company to cut down some trees that were in the way of power lines. When I got home they were still working. They had only cut down part of the spruce tree. Then I asked him, "When are you going to do the pine?"

"In a couple of days," he said.

Then the day before yesterday I came home from school. I found out that they had cut down the walnut tree.

In this fourth-grade arrangement, I acted as editor because there wasn't time to set up a publishing structure. The students helped each other one on one by exchanging writings to copyread them and make suggestions on revision. At the blackboard I gave them demonstrations of how professional writers cut out wasted words.

As usual I demonstrated how to end a story without explaining everything to readers. Joe found a perfect place in his manuscript to end it. He stopped in a dramatic way, leaving readers surprised and with a shock and understanding of what that tree cutting had done to him. I never told him to be specific. He knew he had to convince his readers of why this was an unforgettable experience in his life, so he did what was necessary.

The story approach doesn't seem to come naturally to most power people. They want force and action right now. We'll proceed to carry out our mission, with whatever means are necessary. We know. We are always inventing new technology for killing. Or for increasing your portfolio of stocks and bonds.

If you're driven crazy by automatic telephone marketing, you could join a group of storytellers. Likewise if you're exasperated when you hear, "If you want to take advantage of an amazing new drug cure for halitosis, press 3. If you want to learn what you can do with the stunning new tin credit card, press 4. For a big surprise in buying a house, press 5." And free, free, free—all those plans and household magic tools.

Telling stories in an Arrangement for Truthtelling can be a change from all those money offers. That's a common happening in all kinds of fields, a form of professional witchcraft with language. I'm purposely making fun of this habit also practiced by doctors, insurance agencies, drug companies, priests (who speak in Latin to the unschooled people), and gangsters—whatever. For a moment here I want to make fun of this insane language that can be used to destroy your nerves and clot your brain. To develop family values you can put down your children as incompetent and ridiculous, and maybe evil.

In a similar vein, I think it's unfortunate that in the last twenty to thirty years the Deconstructionists, who were interested in perception too and were saying wise things about it, did so in a way that was difficult to follow. I could hardly wade through anything they were saying. I think they did that in large part because it became the English teacher's way of getting a promotion: "We got this new language and this new thing, and you young people coming up, if you start learning this then we'll make you part of our department. And if you write articles about it that are equally astounding and indecipherable, that shows you're very brilliant and very philosophical." I like to be philosophical too but I don't want to be philosophical like that. I like to have a language that gets its power by reaching a lot of people.

WOE: You seem to appreciate journalistic writing more than academic writing. Is that a fair assessment?

MACRORIE: I certainly don't like some journalistic writing, but, yeah, I guess that's fair. I got interested in the process of perception in graduate school partly because my uncle had been in advertising and journalism. I got so interested that I wrote a doctoral degree on objectivity and subjectivity at Columbia University. As part of my research I traveled with newsmen around the New England East and in New York City. The editor of a small weekly paper in New Jersey also sometimes acted as reporter. He showed me a published story he had written, and said, "How much was I conscious of being partial or biased? I really felt bad about that one. The woman I talked to was wearing shorts. She had a lot of hair on her legs, and that really offended me." He was unrolling the story of how some kids had gotten in trouble throwing a fake bomb in the street, and this woman was pissed off at the kids though he wasn't pissed off at them. He didn't think they had done anything wrong. He said, "I just couldn't forget the hair on her legs," as if it was the most traumatic thing he had ever encountered.

I enjoyed following those reporters around in my thesis work. An editor at *The Hartford Courant* was a great teacher of beginning reporters. I once went out with a novice on assignment and he praised and praised the old veteran. I asked, "What did he first say to you?" "Remember you're telling your readers a yarn," he said. At that point in my life I began to understand how much a place and a situation help a reader or listener pick up breath and life in any piece of writing. A word doesn't mean much standing alone by itself.

WOE: In your books, when you talk about using common language and own voice, it reminded me of the preface to the *Lyrical Ballads*. You sound like Wordsworth and Coleridge. Is it fair to say you're in the Romantic tradition?

MACRORIE: I took a course on Wordsworth from one of the greatest teachers I've ever had, at Oberlin. But I didn't think Wordsworth was himself very strong that way. He wrote that wonderful preface about coming down to earth in poetry. But at times he didn't do that. He should have let himself move more in that direction, like William Carlos Williams did.

WOE: One of the things you do so well is create terms and metaphors that help us think in different ways about teaching. Two of the terms associated with you are "I-Search" and "freewriting." Did you coin these terms?

MACRORIE: I coined "I-Search," specifically because that term tells you what I believe about perception, that you can't look at something with no preconception. You can't kill your life off and look at something. You will always be in there and you cannot block yourself out. So I wanted to emphasize that any search also has got you in it, and you've got to check and see what you can do to make sure you aren't biased when you don't want to be biased. And correct for it if you can. But you'll never get yourself entirely out.

"Freewriting," no. I just made that term out of the two words from Dorothea Brande's book *Becoming a Writer* in which she talked about the need to "write freely." So I just called it freewriting and a lot of other people did too. Peter Elbow edited with Pat Belanoff and Sheryl Fontaine a whole book about freewriting.

WOE: Your other famous term is "Engfish," which you got from the student who had wanted to be a teacher but was discouraged by a professor who said she couldn't write. In another class she had been reading James Joyce, and she wrote a comment on her discouraging instructor in Joyce's style: "the students in his class lisdyke him immersely. Day each that we tumble into the glass he sez to mee, 'Eets too badly that you someday fright preach Engfish.'"

MACRORIE: Isn't that a great passage?

WOE: It gets better the more you read it. Another word that you use in an interesting way is "vulnerable." In *The Vulnerable Teacher* you describe your process of getting kids engaged in their work—to begin by having them write freely and recognize truth. But then you go on and say the final step is to make them vulnerable to the material of the course. What do you mean by this?

MACRORIE: I mean make themselves open up to truth and go after it in ways where they take risks. And sometimes, just like I've done, take a risk and make up a word. It's not a phony operation, it's not a cover-up thing, it's just the opposite. Using Shakespeare I had so much success by simply letting them be affected by the work. When I first started teaching, I used to ask teacher questions. But then I decided to let the students look at one or two actions in the play and let them write about anything that gets to them in some way, that touches them (though not necessarily the other people in the room), and then say why. I stopped choosing for them. I used to do so much choosing for them that I was poisoning their confidence.

WOE: I love the playfulness in your writing. For instance, you quote Lu Po Hua at the beginning of some of the chapters in *The I-Search Paper*. As I read these,

I thought, "This is some Chinese writer I don't know." Then later you confessed that you were Lu Po Hua. You made up the quotes.

MACRORIE: I never would have had the nerve to do it if I hadn't studied the life of James Murray, the guy who put together the O.E.D. He put a couple things in the dictionary that he wanted to put in but that he wasn't supposed to and nobody else thought he should be putting in there—he did this in honor of his niece, or something like that. With all the rigor and discipline that it took to put that sixteen-volume dictionary together, he must have thought, "Well, I'll do something crazy." I think he made up a word, too—one that didn't exist.

WOE: In your *I-Search* book and in your other books, you'll talk about how you just wrote a bad sentence or look back on a sentence you wrote eight pages ago and say, "Oh. I made this mistake there."

MACRORIE: I think it's essential for students, who get hammered for making mistakes, to know that professional writers can admit they're not perfect.

WOE: You have talked about having had metaphor paralysis for the first thirty years of your life, and claim to have cured it. Now metaphor seems to be one of your strengths as a writer. How do you teach students to use metaphors?

MACRORIE: When I was editor of the CCCC journal, a woman from Boston, Clara Siggins, sent in a letter about metaphor and included with it these wonderful metaphors that these really young kids—grade schoolers—wrote: "the trees outside our window look like they was nitted with brown yarn." She had a very down-to-earth belief that everybody uses metaphors and similes. When we're young, we hear people in our family use them, and of course we invent words in our families. But when we get to school, metaphors get scared out of us.

So we tell students don't try for metaphors. Don't try. That's fatal I think. Maybe you know you want a metaphor here, but don't try to make one. Wait until it comes to you or forget it. Because I think you can do terrible things to metaphors and get students going back to clichés, which they monkey around with. Writing good metaphors comes from freeing them up. The thing is to be open and when your metaphor machine starts working, write them down. Then you can judge them later. Metaphor is such a wonderful instrument.

WAYNE BOOTH

One of the most widely read and admired rhetoricians of the twentieth century, Wayne Booth (1921–2005) continues to influence the study of rhetoric, composition, creative writing, and literature. As a devoted teacher, he mentored thousands of students, including many eminent teachers and scholars. "Booth's work," writes protégé James Phelan, "has a remarkable coherence—remarkable given its wide range of subject matters: fictional technique, irony, metaphor, modernist philosophy, critical pluralism, teaching, the ethics of fiction."[1]

Booth is often associated with the Neo-Aristotelian methodology of the "Chicago School," as developed by Booth's teacher R. S. Crane and by Richard McKeon. His first book, the highly influential The Rhetoric of Fiction *(1961), examined rhetorical aspects of fictive works and introduced concepts such as "implied author" and "unreliable narrator," now standard concepts in literature and creative writing pedagogy. His accounts of narrative "sympathy" and "distance" have further helped shape the study of both fiction and creative nonfiction. Booth followed with a host of works, including* A Rhetoric of Irony *(1974)—in which he developed the concepts of "stable" and "unstable" irony—*Modern Dogma and the Rhetoric of Assent (1974), Critical Understanding: The Powers and Limits of Pluralism (1982), The Company We Keep: An Ethics of Fiction *(1988),* The Rhetoric of RHETORIC: The Quest for Effective Communication *(2004), and the popular handbook* The Craft of Research (1995, 2012), *co-authored with University of Chicago colleagues Joseph Williams and Gregory Colomb. Booth's approach to the teaching of writing informs* The Harper & Row Rhetoric *(1984) and* The Harper & Row Reader *(1984), which he produced with Marshall Gregory. He also founded and co-edited the influential journal* Critical Inquiry. *Booth continued to publish throughout his life; his autobiography,* My Many Selves: The Quest for Plausible Harmony *(2006), was published posthumously. A leading figure of ethical criticism, Booth often expressed concern for the effects of rhetoric and literature. He states that* A Rhetoric of Irony *"is unabashedly in a tradition of evangelical attempts to save the world, or at least a piece of it, through critical attention to language."*[2] *In* The Company We Keep, *he aims "to restore the full intellectual legitimacy of our commonsense inclination to talk about stories in ethical terms."*[3]

—William Sewell and Glen McClish

1 "Wayne Booth," *Encyclopedia of Rhetoric and Composition*, ed. Theresa Enos [New York: Garland, 1996], 81–82.
2 Booth, Wayne C. *A Rhetoric of Irony*. London and Chicago: U Chicago P, 1974: (xii). Print.
3 Booth, Wayne C. *The Company We Keep: An Ethics of Fiction*. Berkeley, CA: U California P, 1981: (x). Print.

"Covering Almost All of Life"

John Boe

Spring 2005

WOE: You've coined a number of useful terms in your career, and I wanted to start by asking you about what is probably your most famous, the "implied author."

BOOTH: The idea developed slowly over the time I was working on *The Rhetoric of Fiction*. I felt strongly that the contrast between the author implied by the text and the manifestations in the text was terribly important. It was a kind of revelation for me: the discovery of a sharp contrast between the author implied by every narrative choice and the various narrators and all of the various manifestations of them in the text.

WOE: The idea of the implied author suggests one of the metaphors you use in several books, the writer as a friend and reading as conversation. Many of us do view certain implied authors, Jane Austen comes to my mind, as friends. Or even an implied author in a nonfiction work.

BOOTH: Yes, that's my basic point in the invention of that term. The life you live with the implied author is what makes the thing real for you. The implied friendship with the author is so deep and so revealing if it works. Sometimes, of course, it doesn't.

   I don't think I've dealt adequately with the topic of nonfiction, but I think it's absolutely real. When you encounter an author like Aristotle or Plato, you develop a friendship there.

WOE: One of the books that opened my eyes was *Rhetoric of Irony* and especially the concept of "stable irony." I had the experience, having been taught the New Criticism, of thinking all ambiguity is irony.

BOOTH: Your experience relates to what happened after 9/11 with the word "irony" and the claim that irony was dead. What they meant by irony was simply nonrationality. They thought we finally found solid proof that really bad things can happen and irony is thus dead. But this has no relationship to my definition of irony as stable irony. It's a small branch of the whole term. I've been really amused by how broadly it's been defined.

   The idea of stable irony came to me partly because I had so many students who didn't understand irony, particularly in *The Catcher in the Rye*. Students were identifying with the young character and not catching Salinger's ironies about how many flaws that young character exhibited. They were just missing the ironies, what I call stable ironies. That experience primarily led me to dwell on stable irony.

WOE: Many of your ideas, like listening rhetoric and the rhetoric of assent, apply equally well to the teaching and the reading experiences.

BOOTH: These ideas also relate to why I do extensive commentary on student papers. If you can demonstrate in what you've said that the student has really been heard, then the student has some reason for responding. If you just do silly comments, marginal comments, the student has no reason to think that you've heard what the student has really said.

What I try to do when a debate arises is address John and say, "John, can you repeat what Mary has just said in such a way that she would accept it if you were her attorney." I get them ready to try to reconstruct what each other has said. That sometimes works, but it sometimes bores other students.

It only works with people who are really listening to each other. If you get students trained to listen then they can do it. It always thrilled me when students left the classroom still debating and invited me to come to another session.

WOE: An interesting term of yours which hasn't caught on as much as some others, but which I quite like, is "coduction." Can you tell me what led you to need that term?

BOOTH: I saw a conflict between induction and deduction and suddenly realized I needed a central term, coduction. Induction and deduction are my enemies in a sense because if you do merely induction or merely deduction, you're trapped. But coduction produces some kind of communion. It seems to me terribly important if in a debate people come out at a higher level, having understood each other and produced a new truth. That's more important than if they actually win this or that subject. Sometimes coduction works.

I was taught pluralism by Richard McKeon, where pluralism means there are many rival truths. You can't reduce truth to this philosophical tradition or that philosophical tradition. If you go to Plato and he's reasoning from the top down, that's one version of truth. If you go to Hume and he's reasoning from the bottom up, that's another version of truth, and both of them are revealing real truths. There is a multiplicity of truths, and McKeon actually sometimes develops about 16 different varieties of truth. You find that this author is fully persuasive and that author is fully persuasive. Many of them, including Bertrand Russell, think they can just refute everybody who doesn't take his or her side. In fact, they can't refute the others because they don't really listen to the other side.

McKeon often attacks people for being naïve or not doing things right. When I first encountered McKeon he was teaching Plato and I had the amusing experience of meeting the chairman of the department who'd recommended the course. He asked me, "How's the course going?" And I said, "Well, it's fine but I don't like taking a course from a dogmatic Platonist." He said, "He's not a dogmatic Platonist, he's a dogmatic Aristotelian" (which was also not true. He's a dogmatic Humian). He was, in a way, my hero. I've got an essay coming out in an introduction to a second volume of his essays. There I celebrate his pluralism.

WOE: Recently you introduced a new term, "rhetorology." Why wasn't "rhetoric" good enough? Why do we need "rhetorology"?

BOOTH: I think a lot of people are going to be offended by the term. It came to me because of all the other "ologies." Where did "meteorology" come from, etc.? I felt that we needed a term for the deeper probing of rhetorical studies. It may be a mistake; I'll never know.

   I felt very strongly that the word "rhetoric" had so many bad connotations in most popular views that we needed a new term. "Rhetoricians" for the deeper study and "rhetorology" for the deepest study.

WOE: In talking about rhetoric or rhetorology, I'm struck how often for you rhetoric leads to ethics. In one place you say you want to save the world through critical attention to language. Not everyone is willing to admit to such lofty concerns or that the study of rhetoric and language really has anything to do with ethics.

BOOTH: I think part of my motive comes from my upbringing as a Mormon where everything was ethics. It seems to be totally impossible to separate ethical judgments from technical judgments. You can do technical judgments on one side and in one sense separate them out, but basically every judgment about whether a speech is successful will depend basically on the bias of the person who makes an ethical judgment.

   For me the difference between the author I love and the author I don't is whether they make me think. Even Shakespeare makes me think. Jane Austen makes me think and produces a bonding as we think through the issues.

WOE: Don't you also like writers who make you feel?

BOOTH: Sure.

WOE: It seems to me Shakespeare makes me feel as much as think, or more so. I just feel this human sympathy with all these characters.

BOOTH: Yes, but he makes you think about how you feel. That would be my key answer.

WOE: In a lot of your books the last chapter talks about religion in some way. Can you talk about why your study of rhetoric leads not just to ethics but also to religion?

BOOTH: Well again that's probably my Mormon background. Do you consider yourself nonreligious?

WOE: I wasn't raised with any religion, but I consider myself religious. For me the crucial thing is whether you use the word "God" seriously.

BOOTH: Absolutely. My God, at this point, is the totality of possibilities and impossibilities that makes life possible, makes this conversation possible. It's very different from the Mormon God, who's very personal and who has "body parts and passions," and so on. For me what leads to the religious bias is that I was brought up that way. I keep trying to find this or that bonding with some God up there.

As the last chapter in the new book dramatizes, it seems like the quarrels between science and religion are just absolutely nonsense. There's an absolute bonding at the center if you probe deeply enough. Scientists are religious, even if they don't acknowledge it.

WOE: Your methods seem to be empirical and developed out of the practical criticism side of things. Can you talk about your methodology?

BOOTH: It seems to me that you have to have some kind of evidence for what you say, but not hard scientific data for what you say. You should at least be persuasive in the sense of appealing to genuine reasons. It relates back to *Modern Dogma*: the whole question of reducing things to mere motives is reductive. It doesn't really show that you've paid attention to people's presentations of evidence.

WOE: Almost every chapter you write starts with four or five quotes from an astonishing range of writers. How many journals or commonplace books do you keep?

BOOTH: My journals are obviously full of quotations from this or that author. I've kept journals almost all my life. These days it is somewhat more rarely than formerly. But the journals are full of this or that quotation, which then get embodied in my work. But I should confess that I also sometimes refer to *Bartlett's Familiar Quotations* or other quotation books—which is not to say I don't consult the real philosophers.

WOE: Your writing style is so inviting, with your willingness to acknowledge your own limitations and your erudition, your ability to quote Aristotle and also use the word "fuck."

BOOTH: I felt a strong motive both in *The Rhetoric of Fiction* and throughout my work to present a persona that is friendly. I deliberately sought to be accessible. Gerald Graph, in his recent book *Clueless in Academe*, quotes me as having introduced him to an author who has an accessible style instead of the formal, highfalutin' style. I was pleased about that.

WOE: Isn't there a conflict between being accessible and getting credit as a serious intellectual in academia?

BOOTH: Absolutely. I have to tell you a story. A colleague invited me to come to his house for lunch. When I got there he said, "You know why I've invited you, don't you? Because I hate you! Because your accessible style is just bullshit." We sat down and I ate his soup, and my wife Phyllis said later, "Why did you eat his soup? It could have been poisoned!" But I argued that if he intended to poison me, he wouldn't have done it at his house.

I asked him, "Why did you invite me?" and he said, "Because my psychologist told me I should." He just went on and on about why my style lacks substance and why his book, which was a good book, just got ignored and my book got all the attention.

WOE: What writers influence you in your own writing? Stylists along with others?

BOOTH: Certainly not McKeon. McKeon is just absolutely dense. One of his articles begins, "Consequently."

WOE: That's hilarious.

BOOTH: I think he intended it as a joke.

WOE: But what writers *did* influence your style?

BOOTH: How would you feel if I answered, "None of them influenced me at all; I invented my own style"? Let me tell you an anecdote about the composition of *The Rhetoric of Fiction*. It had been accepted by the UC Press, but then we went to Italy. I worked on it and worked on it, adding an introductory chapter. Then Phyllis and I sat down and read aloud every part of it and she modified line after line after line, making it more accessible. Perhaps I should have suggested that she was co-author. But I can't answer your question about who influenced my style. I think I felt I was inventing a new style.

WOE: I want you to talk about your philosophy of teaching and especially the suggestion that I loved, that a teacher with a vocation will "burn all his previously useful syllabi, class notes, assignment sheets, and exams to teach to each class and will also resist planning too far in advance." I thought these were wonderfully radical suggestions. How often did you follow them?

BOOTH: I'm afraid I have to answer very rarely. I tried to and sometimes succeeded. But it's hard to do. You just go in with your dogmas and you come out with your dogmas, and students accept your dogmas, sometimes. But it's hard to do, hard to practice. There's been lots of modern, recent articles about how hard it is to avoid one's bias in the classroom. It's very hard not to impose your preconceptions.

But allow me to impose another anecdote. In a freshman class I taught I was pursued after the class by a woman freshman who came to my office and said, "Mr. Booth, you changed your mind about that poem! My father is paying ten thousand a year for you to be an authority and you violated that principle."

WOE: Well I assume you told her that's what real education is.

BOOTH: I tried to but she went on being that dogmatist right through the whole course. She just infuriated me, of course, because I had changed my mind because of something a student had said about the poem.

WOE: Can you say something about this gap or the relationship of rhetoric to those people actually teaching comp?

BOOTH: I can say flatly, there's no difference. Everybody who is teaching composition should know about the history of rhetoric but they don't. When you're teaching composition you're teaching rhetoric.

WOE: I know you've taught writing in various courses and basically have said to teach English is to teach writing. How did you teach writing?

BOOTH: First I have to boast that throughout my time here at the university, I always taught freshmen. Even though my contract said you don't have to; you can teach only graduate students. But I always taught a freshman course and that always entailed teaching a lot of composition.

My favorite story about how to do it was breaking up my students into groups of three and meeting with them, even though it took a lot more time, and having them criticize each other's papers as they attempted to grapple with what the other person was saying. That worked extraordinarily well. It just felt to me that the students were really learning about how to grapple with what the other person was saying and not simply backing away. But it took a lot of extra time.

The downgrading of the teaching of composition is really scandalous, it seems to me. It's the most important single thing we can do. That's why I committed myself to always doing it.

WOE: You have said that the weekly staff meetings you had while teaching the composition core course were much more important to your education than the graduate courses you took. Can you talk about the staff meetings and what you learned from them?

BOOTH: Weekly meetings were required here. When I first began teaching in 1947, I was working on my M.A. and got honors on it, so they hired me. I started joining these groups. It was simply wonderful because each of us was assigned to do the briefing for the staff. There would be about fifteen people in the room. Then you'd have an attack from this or that guy: "You missed what was said on page 27."

You just were learning constantly in a way that I didn't feel my professors were quite managing. Some of the professors were very good, Ronald Crane especially. But I did feel that I was learning more from these required weekly meetings when I would present my briefing and my colleagues would slap it down.

WOE: Can you talk about *The Craft of Research* and getting undergraduates to do research?

BOOTH: I can't resist mentioning that *The Craft of Research* is selling so well that nobody is selling their used copies. The students are just keeping it on their desks. The essential center of the book is summed up by one of my colleagues, Joe Williams: you have to learn to ask the questions of the reader before they're asked. If you really think hard about what the reader will say in answer to the question, "So what?" then you have a center to your whole project. If you can predict what the reader will ask then you can really move on.

WOE: You wrote that you converted to the religion of arts in the 1930s. What is religious about your relationship to the arts?

BOOTH: When art works, you get that ecstatic feeling that transcends the world of time, and that's what religion does. If religion works, you transcend time. If art works, you also transcend time.

WOE: Can you talk a little bit about how your Mormon upbringing, specifically your mission experience, influenced you to become a rhetorologist?

BOOTH: Becoming a Mormon missionary was a difficult choice for me because I was already having lots of questions about Mormonism. But then I talked with one of my favorite professors, a professor of psychology, who said, why not go out and do good in the world, if you can, for two years? You don't have to get them under the water. He talked me into accepting it.

But then I faced really difficult questions every day of how do I relate this vocabulary to that vocabulary. How do I talk to this group in such a way as not to offend them but at the same time really show that I'm listening to them and their convictions. That really was what got me into rhetorology: To try and think hard about trying to reach an audience without deep offense and get them to join you.

I found myself respecting the true believers much more when I labored throughout the mission. The true believers have a point and there's no real reason to combat that point unless you can find a real reason to.

WOE: You've talked about how fiction can change you, and I think that's true. I was curious about what fictions you think changed you the most in your life, how did they change you, and at what age were you touched by what books?

BOOTH: That the hero in *Les Miserables* gets a transformation into doing the right kind of charity in the world really had a strong influence on me. Also Trollope's *The Way We Live Now*, which I thought was just fabulous. *The Way We Live Now* is a kind of indictment of the way we live now. A lot of novels had strong influence. I would say Tolstoy really influenced me wonderfully. Dostoyevsky's *Crime and Punishment* was a major influence.

WOE: I've often heard the phrase "the Chicago School" and I was wondering how you fit in.

BOOTH: About the relationship of me to the Chicago School, I have to confess that when *The Rhetoric of Fiction* came out, Crane was not pleased. He was basically a bit favorable, but he was very critical because I had violated a principle of the Chicago School: that the point of all inquiry was to find the unity of this work. Instead of that I had extended it out to the rhetoric of all kinds of things. He wasn't hypercritical, he was just a little dubious.

But the Chicago School was deeply committed to finding the unity of a particular work. What I had done in my dissertation was investigate the unity of *Tristram Shandy*. A very difficult one. But I found it—maybe. Anyway, that project provided the drive and when I did *The Rhetoric of Fiction* it was a violation, to some degree, of the unity principle.

WOE: I really loved your book on music, *For the Love of It*. I was struck thinking about listening to rhetoric and how one becomes a musician to hear this music.

BOOTH: In one chapter I do pursue the relationship of the rhetorical drive to the musical drive and listening rhetoric to listening to others. The deep commitment to really hearing what other people are playing is the center of that.

WOE: I love the optimism of the refrain that comes into *For the Love of It*: playing better than ever before. How do you encourage that attitude in others? How do you learn to think that way?

BOOTH: I think that gets back to the Mormon upbringing, which insisted that you've got to improve, day by day. As a consequence in the long run, as a male, I'd get to be God of another universe, of another planet, if I kept improving and improving. Of course I don't think that explains it completely, because I think there are rational reasons for wanting to get better. Right now I've suddenly just recently decided I'm going to practice one hour every day, and I've been doing it after a long time of not doing it. It's having an effect.

One thing that keeps me sort of half active as a Mormon is this teaching that there are genuine values in the world. This is part of what leads me to all my effort: to establish that there are genuine values in the world. Even though Mormonism has a lot of fake values, in my current view, there are still real values.

I have a colleague who is absolutely convinced that if we could get rid of religion the world would be immeasurably improved. I disagree with that strongly.

WOE: I was hoping I could get you to talk a little about your work on metaphor.

BOOTH: One of my articles on the subject is basically about how we appraise metaphors and how we evaluate metaphors, what are good ones and what are bad ones. It seems to me that's a crucial question about metaphor: how do you decide which are good ones and which are bad ones. It's not an easy question to answer but on the whole it's essential. Some metaphors are just lousy and some are really brilliant.

WOE: Can you teach people how to *write* metaphors?

BOOTH: I've never put much effort in that direction. But I do have to tell you an anecdote about what Norman Maclean did. When his book, *A River Runs Through It*, was almost finished, he sent a copy to a former student at Yale. She wrote back and said, "Unfortunately, you just don't have enough metaphors." So he went back and added a bunch of metaphors. It's just a brilliant story. If you look carefully you might be able to see what metaphors he added.

WOE: I also love your idea that stories themselves are metaphors for our lives. They're replacement lives. I just think that's a central important idea.

BOOTH: That's absolutely true. So that inflates the term "metaphor" to covering almost all of life.

PAT HOY

Pat Hoy spent 16 of his 28 years in the Army teaching English at his alma mater, West Point. During that time, he created an innovative program in essay writing that focused on teaching freshman how to write the modern essay—not the five-paragraph, thesis-driven, academic argument paper professors were used to—but the kind Orwell, Dillard, E.B. White, and Woolf wrote. At the time, very few programs in the country were teaching this form to students.

Hoy's own essays have appeared in numerous journals, including the Virginia Quarterly Review, Twentieth Century Literature, Agni, South Atlantic Review, *and especially* The Sewanee Review, *where he became a regular contributor. In 1992, his selected essays were published in a volume called* Instinct for Survival, *arguably Hoy's most influential text. In these essays, Hoy defines the modern essay as one that affects people and makes them think. For Hoy, the familiar, personal essay should shape related stories so that they become compelling forces acting on the reader rather than loosely related events that attempt to communicate a moral. Hoy argues that while essays have some agreed-upon boundaries (a beginning, middle, and end, for example), their success is dependent upon the writer's ability to start with a question/problem and, in the course of investigating this question, develop an overarching idea. Whatever Hoy's topic—soldiering, Vietnam, his home of origin in Hamburg, Arkansas, the father who went missing early in his life—it haunts first him and then the reader.*

Hoy has published several textbooks and anthologies, which are highly regarded for their methodology of teaching the essay form. Five of his essays have been named "Notable Essays" in Robert Atwan's annual Best American Essays. *Hoy is a professor of English at New York University, where he has also served as director of the Expository Writing Program.*

—Katie Arosteguy

"I Want to Rip Your Heart Out"

Mel Livatino

Fall 2006

WOE: Your book *Instinct for Survival* seems to be eight attempts to answer the question "Who am I?" In "The Spirit Was Willing" you write, "Marlow's problem is our own: How to read our lives in the clearest light, a light that may very well shine out of our own dark interior." What did you learn about yourself from writing the book?

HOY: I wrote the book to learn something, so every one of those little essays involves a personal problem. I had my own name for each of those essays: the mother essay, the father essay, the dirty-old-man essay. And so each one is a personal psychological problem that locates me in the space of an investigation.

Let me translate that into another language. James Hillman talks about images, and he advises us not to think about them only as something that can be optical and intellectualized, but to think about them as context, content, mood, etc. I could articulate how each one of those essays involved some image that had me in its grip, so that my job is to read the image. For example, in the father essay, "Mosaics of Southern Masculinity," I've got myself in a bear contest with my father who left me and my mother when I was five, six years old. I don't have any bitterness about that, but I'm deeply curious about what would send a man off on that kind of journey and what kind of legacy he left me. So when I sit down to write that essay, I'm trying to resolve something for myself in a way that lets me go on living fully and richly without being burdened by the abandonment. The mother piece is the same way. The dirty-old-man essay was occasioned by the fact of women at West Point for the first time. And I was there.

Women come into your classroom for the first time, you gotta deal with it. They're sitting there, and you're working in an institution that has public pronouncements against their being there. The superintendent stood in front of the nation in 1976. He sounded like George Wallace: "The world will come to an end before a woman steps inside this place." And the next year he's saluting as a good soldier and saying we gotta go down to New York and work on this uniform so they really look good when they get here. So there they are in my class, and they are live, living sexual beings, and the institution is in an uproar about their being there. Right now cadets are still talking about the damage that women did to the Corps. So how could you not go to work against that kind of idiotic response?

And so I get myself into this image. It turns out to be psychosexual, so it's fun. I've gotta figure *something* out. What am I supposed to be doing? In the piece, there's this encounter between me and this young woman who comes in my office like a seraph. It's late afternoon and the sun is coming in through the window, she's bathed in light, she's got on this perfume, and she's in a total funk. She's amazingly mad at the superintendent (who's the equivalent of the president of a college) because he wanted to have a required picture taken of only the women at West Point. She was highly offended by that, and had to come somewhere to complain.

WOE: That was the most erotic image in all of your writing, that image of her in your office bathed in sunlight.

HOY: That's interesting because it was literally and honestly an asexual experience for me. But that room was so charged with her anger and her body and her presence, and the whole thing she's worried about is a fascinating problem: How am I going to be able to put this uniform on my body—fatigues, boots—and still be a woman? That's the question. And after these women graduated I visited a group of them at Fort Sill, Oklahoma, as a follow-up. As I sat with them, they were singing songs about mommies wearing combat boots. They had gotten into the place in their lives just weeks, months after they graduated where they could start thinking about being mothers. Then the conflict is not just about the body, what you're going to do with it, but what you're going to do with the kids.

WOE: What do you want readers to do with your book? How do you want them to receive the book?

HOY: I met a woman photographer out in Texas at an autobiography conference. She said something that astounded me and affected everything that I do with my writing. She said to us in the audience, "I edit my photographs to rip your heart out." I didn't know you could edit photographs, I hadn't thought about that, but I liked a whole bunch that phrase "rip your heart out." So I want to rip your heart out. That's what I want to do. I want to create a piece of writing that is so compelling that you can't come away from it without having been affected. And I don't mean affected in your mind. I want to blow a hole in your psyche if I can. So that's what I'm trying to do and that shapes every scene I write. I'm not a reporter; it's not my job to tell you what happened to me. It's my job to put you in the piece moment after moment after moment, and that work, if I get it right, will spin you around. You're going to have to rethink something.

WOE: Do you not want the reader to find intersections with his or her own life reading it?

HOY: I think about that hard and often. I think the best thing I ever thought about it occurred at a Southern Autobiography Conference where I was not speaking. I was invited down to be a guest and teach classes in the college, but not to give a talk. So I found myself in a listening position over three or four days. Because of what was happening in my mind as I listened to these familiar essayists tell their stories, it occurred to me that what writers do is repair memory. When you read something from one of your essays and I hear it, my way of understanding that is to tell myself a story out of memory, a corresponding story; it's not going to be the same, but it's the way I align what's inside me with what's coming at me from the outside. So I really want that to happen.

I left that conference and went down to south Arkansas, where I came from, and gave a reading. I had never given a reading in that part of the world. It was in a choir room in a Baptist church. The room was absolutely full of people. I had been gone from there thirty years plus. I didn't know a single soul in the room except the person who was introducing me, and that was someone who had known me in high school. So I told this very nonliterary group of people essentially what I just told you, that I had come from this conference and that I had discovered something that interested me—that writers are in the business of repairing memory. I just said that because I needed to say it to get started, and then I read the scene out of "The Spirit Was Willing and So Was the Flesh" where my aged aunt is washing her husband's feet I read that love scene to this group of people. That was the only thing I read. At the end everybody in that auditorium, almost without exception, walked up to me and told me a story in response to that story. Some of the stories were two sentences long. Some of the people in that room knew my aunt and uncle. so they had something to say to me about them.

So that's what I'm trying to do. If I could have my wish of wishes, it would be that I would set up conversations that I could hear. I want that correspondence between the reader's soul and my soul. I want readers to recognize themselves and their life patterns, but I want them to be making something new too. I think that's really important. I want to have said something that makes them question the story they say back to me in their head.

WOE: In several of your essays you've written about a certain moment when you were writing your dissertation. You were thirty-eight years old, a military officer, and out of nowhere came a sentence you could not have anticipated, a beautiful sentence you had little to do with in any deliberate, conscious way. You write, "All of a sudden there was before me fully formed a fairly long, complex sentence, lazy and graceful and full, a Newmanesque sentence unlike anything I had ever written before, and it made perfectly good sense, something about a world intoxicated by growth and expansion, the staggering of empire, I called it, an English culture gone berserk, drunk on the chilled white wine of rationality." Your advisor wrote a single word in the margin: "Nice." No teacher had ever said that to you before, so at thirty-eight, with only this one sentence as evidence, you write that you began to think of yourself as a writer. How did you think of yourself before that sentence?

HOY: I thought of myself as someone writing, and I thought of myself as someone who was doing a competent job of communicating fairly accurately what he was thinking, but that writing had no transforming power for me. It was just an act of competence. But there was something about that sentence that made David DeLaura, my advisor, say "nice," something about that rhythmic sentence that involved him. There's something about those enveloping rhythms that's transformative. I had probably written something like that before, but Miss Brophy said you straighten this thing out, too flowery, get this fixed, give me a simple declarative sentence, I don't want any of this.

WOE: Miss Brophy was your high school English teacher?

HOY: Right. Miss Brophy said, "Get thee behind me, Satan. I don't want to see any more of that in my classroom." Graduate teachers did the same thing, or they said nothing. You might, if you were lucky, get brief one-line comments that said, "lively," "well-written," "engaging" that you don't want to hear, but right by this sentence DeLaura said, "Nice." It was a huge moment, and I was confirmed.

WOE: I gather it was because you mention this sentence at least three times in your pieces, although you never give the whole sentence in any of those places.

HOY: Do you know why?

WOE: No, but I'm curious.

HOY: Because I don't have it. It got lost. I had only one copy of my dissertation; moving it from place to place to make use of it in workshops, I lost it, so I don't have that sentence. I can go to Dissertation Abstracts and get it, but when I sat down to write about it the first time, I had to make up a new sentence. So the sentence you have behaves exactly the same way that the sentence I'm describing behaved. That too is a Newmanesque sentence. I had fun writing that version of the sentence because I got to know what I was doing that time. Having enacted the form—any form—a writer can go back then and use it, but the first time, it's like Willie Nelson said: "The devil made me do it the first time; the second time I done it on my own." So you can do it on your own after that, but the great thing, the greatest thing, about writing is the way in which something like that generates itself, and you can't claim credit for it.

WOE: I asked you how you thought about yourself before that sentence, and you said not as a writer but as a man writing. But apart from the writing how did you think of yourself?

HOY: Let's get this thing in perspective. In 1967 I first went to graduate school at the University of Pennsylvania at the height of the Vietnam War, ignorant. I went on the coattails of the success of other Army officers who had also gone to Penn. Penn knew that we would make up for what we didn't know. It was part of the way we had been trained, not educated, that we would come into a place behind everybody else, and the least we would do would be to catch up. So I went to Penn with one semester of literature—one—behind me at West Point, and I was competing with four-year NDEA fellows, all of whom were concentrating and working their fannies off because they didn't want to go to Vietnam. I didn't know it, but I was going to go to Vietnam anyway. So these are the people I'm trying to survive against, and I don't know anything. But I survived.

Less than a year later I had an MA, and I had a good enough record to go back to Penn eight years later. But I had to go to Vietnam first. After Penn, I was supposed to go to West Point to teach. But a general in the Pentagon, looking after my welfare, said this boy and several others haven't been to Vietnam. They're not going to West Point now. They're going to Vietnam before this war is over. So I went to Vietnam, 1968–69. And I came back to West Point for three years, 1969–72. I taught and loved it. I thought the moment I left that I had reached a level of intellectual achievement that I was never going to be able to get back to, that I was going to go back out there in the Army and do my good soldier thing that I had been doing with the best of them, and that I'd never see academia again. But then I get this chance to go back to graduate school. I was only half as ignorant this time, but still half filled up.

So it takes all that to tell you what it was like when I wrote that sentence. I still knew only half my ass from a hole in the ground. So there in 1967, I was literally writing for my life. It was writing for competence. I was trying to be good enough to get certified. That's what I was doing. It never occurred to me that there was any kind of joy or transformation or ultimate fulfillment in the act of writing. That's where I was before I wrote that sentence.

WOE: Why did you decide to get a Master's and later a Ph.D. in literature? You surely knew that that wasn't the way to the top in the Army?

HOY: You have to understand that West Point has an incestuous faculty. We choose our own and get in bed with one another. You get pinned or tabbed or flagged, as the Army would say, about the time you graduate.

I was flagged in math, thermodynamics, and literature. That means I did well in all those subjects. So then I had a choice. I leave knowing that if I go out and be a good soldier, there's going to be a time when one of those three departments, or all of them, somewhere around year five to seven in a typical career pattern, are going to ask me if I want to come back to West Point and teach, and if I say yes, then they'll send me to the best graduate school I can get into for only an M.A. (because that's all they want me to get). My orders were "You've got sixteen months, go to the University of Pennsylvania and get an M.A. You had better not show up without one."

WOE: But you could also have said, I don't think so; I want to become a regimental commander, a division commander. Instead, you said you'd like to go back to West Point and teach. Was there some kind of excitement in that one course you took, or earlier in your life, or were you just out on a wing?

HOY: I was not out on a wing at all. I knew exactly what I was doing. It is only right to say that the movement of the mind and the spirit toward the literary text came out of the Southern Methodist Biblical background. The church hymns and the rhythms of the Bible and the stories were extremely important to me in ways that I had no idea about. But when it came time for me to decide what I wanted to do at the three-year mark, when I could have gotten out of the Army and had no Vietnam, had none of this stuff, the only thing that interested me was the intellectual exploration of theology. I knew I had no business being a minister, didn't want to be one, but I wanted to study theology. I was reading that wave of Protestant theologians like Tillich, Bultmann, and all those guys who were at Union in New York City. I was trying to figure out some way I could get the Army to send me to Union to study theology.

Because the Army had sent people to Columbia to get degrees in literature, I thought maybe I could bend the whole thing. So it all came out of that deep desire to understand mystery, and out of the rhythms—there's that word again—of that Biblical, hymn-singing culture that was the focal point of the social order in that small Southern town where I was raised. There were Methodists and there were Baptists and there were others. There was one Catholic married to the druggist. There was not a Jew within a hundred and fifty miles. Whatever the other sects were, nobody knew about 'em. The struggle was between the Methodists and the Baptists. That was the social order. So everything we did for fun, we did through the church.

WOE: So here you are doing your dissertation, a man writing, doing a workmanlike job, and then you write this sentence. What happens after that?

HOY: Before that sentence where DeLaura wrote *Nice*, I was going to go back to West Point and teach, and I didn't have to write a word if I didn't want to because in that strange, incestuous system, when you get tapped to be a permanent professor at West Point, you get tapped before you have a Ph.D., and you get tenure. As soon as you come back with your degree, you're tenured. So I could have done anything I wanted to do. What most people do at West Point is either become a lifelong administrator with a modicum of teaching, or they go fanatical with the teaching. But they don't write. I knew that I was going to go back to West Point and be a different kind of tenured faculty member. It so happened that I went back there with five or so other people who had reached the same resolve through very different routes. So there we were, mavericks, which is just what we wanted to be.

WOE: All in the English department?

HOY: All over the place. So we start writing, and we start talking about that, and we start talking about changing the selection procedure so that, of course, we bring in more people like ourselves. I said, I'm gonna publish one thing a year. I hadn't typed a word on a computer up to this point, including dissertation work. I paid somebody to do that. I had this elaborate drafting system. Now I type backwards as fast as I type forward, and I start revising after the first sentence is complete. I did the same thing with a fountain pen. My drafts were so complex and so messed up that I had to go back over them with different colored pencils so that the typist could type them.

This was sometime around 1980. I had sent this editor on *The Wall Street Journal* a short essay that I had written about my mother that later became the long essay that's in *Instinct for Survival* called "Goings and Comings." He wrote back and wanted me to turn that into journalese. He was essentially telling me I didn't know how to write. That act of resistance against my writing caused me to sit down one day, turn on my computer, and start writing on the computer. I did it that way because I had to do it fast, and I had no typewriter, so it became my typewriter. I responded to him at length, and it was a fiery rebuttal. It made me crystallize my thinking about the difference between the kind of writing I was trying to do and the kind of writing he would want someone to do for *The Wall Street Journal*. I discovered that afternoon how absolutely fast I could be with that computer, so literally what happened was that I went from trying to publish one article a year to a book a year, and that went on for three or four years.

When I went to Harvard, I was working on the third book, and I had all these essays either written or working inside my head at the time. Sam Pickering wrote me a letter and said, "I think you ought to tell Malcolm Call at the Georgia Press that you've got a book of essays." I picked up the phone and told Sam I didn't have a book of essays. I had three essays. Sam had read them, and he was telling me to call. It was a friendship gesture. Well then, he said, tell him you've got three essays written and tell him what all the rest are gonna be about. So I sat down one afternoon and told him what this book was going to look like. And *Instinct* was the book. All I'm saying is that I got really fast, and I got really productive, and I got really good. There was no doubt after that about what I was going to be doing with the rest of my life.

WOE: When you look back on that piece you had sent to that editor at *The Wall Street Journal*, was it any good or was he right?

HOY: It was a nine-page preliminary draft of "Goings and Comings," and I hadn't written one of those pieces before. It was written close to the bone. I started it in the room where I was seeing my mother for the last time, and I read it to her. I wrote enough of it so that the second day when I went to see her, I asked her if she wanted me to read it. She asked me what I was doing, and I said, "I'm trying to make you famous. I'm writing a story about you. Do you want to hear it?" And she said, "Yeah, take me out of bed." So I had to pick her up and put her in a chair, and she said read, and I started reading. She closed her eyes, and when I stopped reading, she opened her eyes, and I laughed. I said you're not paying attention, and she said back the last sentence I had read. Then she said keep reading.

So I was that close to this material. Was it good? It was a hell of a lot better than he gave me credit for, and I knew that. It was good enough in that form that the editor of *The New York Times Magazine*'s "His and Her" column asked to see it again revised. He didn't take it, but it was good enough to get back what I call a good rejection and a second look, but it still wasn't right. But the argument between me and *The Wall Street Journal* editor had been about form. He believed that the familiar essay was not legitimate. He wanted me to write measured, in column form with short paragraphs, to make my point up front. Everything would reinforce that point. He was applying journalistic criteria to a form that had nothing to do with his chosen genre. It pissed me off, and I got fired up and began to look into the essay. That got me into the familiar essay.

The second thing that made me go to the familiar essay was Joan Didion. The first semester I was back at West Point, 1979 or '80, my second tour there, I was told I had to teach a course in American literature covering 1945 to the present. I had spent the last two and a half years thinking of nothing except modern British literature at the turn of the century. So I say, okay, I like Salinger, I like Roth, this will be fun. I'll have this crazy course, and I don't have any obligation to make it meet anybody's standards except my own. And somehow I had read *Slouching towards Bethlehem*, and I said, well, I'll put this on the syllabus. Of all the sex-filled, crazy books I put on the syllabus, the one they liked best was *Slouching towards Bethlehem*. So I said to myself, if they like this so much, why don't we change our whole writing course, which I'm now in charge of, and get rid of argument? Let's see if we can get cadets to write personal essays. And that's exactly what we did.

I'd read *all* of Forster. I'd read a lot of Woolf. I'd especially been blown away by *Moments of Being*. Forster and Woolf provided the impetus for this move into more modern essays. I had read Addison and Steele. I'd had a good 18th-century course. I had some background without knowing really that I had it. It had not yet coalesced in my mind. And I'd read Johnson, I'd read a lot of Johnson.

So it didn't take me long to get my energy focused on that mother essay, "Goings and Comings." I got close enough with this first piece I had written, so I said, "What more could a boy want?" I went after it. I had published two academic pieces that I still love, and I've never published another purely academic piece in my life.

I know precisely the moment where I got good. I had written a couple of short reviews in *The Sewanee Review*. George Core liked them. A guy named Bill Berry at a small college in Arkansas decided he wanted to put together a first-rate Southern Autobiography conference. He basically had in mind inviting mainline Southern critics, writers, poets, etc., people like George Garrett. George Core said to Bill Berry, "You ought to ask Pat Hoy to give a paper at this conference." Of course he said, "Who the hell's Pat Hoy?" George said, "Well, just trust me. Call this guy up and talk to him." This was around '88 or '89, and I was absolutely still in the Army. So Berry calls me, and he says, "How would you like to give a paper on Male Myth-Making in Southern Autobiography?"

And I said, "Well, to tell you the truth, I know a lot about male myth-making, but I don't know the first thing about Southern Autobiography." And he said, "Well, that's not a problem. I'll tell you what to read." So I said, "Okay, that's fine." He put me on to William Humphries, Sam Pickering, and some others, and I read these books and really loved them.

WOE: Is that how you got to know Sam Pickering?

HOY: Yeah, and I also reviewed Sam for *The Sewanee Review* before I knew him. So all of the heritage started to come together. I'd published the first two academic essays, so I was competent. So I get invited to this good '01 Southern boy conference, and everybody knows everybody coming to that conference, except me.

WOE: But you got the right accent.

HOY: I said to myself, "Look here, boy, you go down there with an academic essay and they're gonna laugh you out of that place. You gotta do something radically different." I knew enough about the familiar essay by that time to be dangerous, so I said, "Okay, that's what I'll do." But I also knew that there had to be some legitimate intellectual activity, there had to be some rigorous examination of the texts I had been asked to read. So I wrote this essay, and when I got through with that essay, I knew, I *knew* that I had done something good. There was also something about the way I went about writing that essay that made my wife say to me, "Can I read it?"

And I said, "What? You've never read my essays. Why do you want to read this one?" "I just want to read it," she said. So she read it and was blown away. It eventually became "Mosaics of Southern Masculinity." After I delivered that piece at the conference, George Core walked to the base of the podium, looked up at me, and said, "I want to publish that essay. And besides that I want to ride to Memphis with you. Have you got room in your car for me and my wife? I want to talk to you about this essay." So that was the coming-out for me. When that essay was published in the *Sewanee*, my judgment is that it was a bifurcated essay, that it was half familiar and half academic. I knew what the problem was, so I fixed it before it appeared in my book. What I managed to do was eliminate the seam that was right down the middle of the essay. Virginia Woolf's in that essay. Erich Neumann. Sam Pickering. Bill Berry. Allen Tate. Humphries. Roy Reed. And they're in there in pretty big chunks. But they're integrated.

WOE: I think of it as an essay about you, not about them.

HOY: It's not about me; it's about an idea. And I'm using myself to get you to entertain this idea. You don't have to be conscious of the fact that this idea is working on you if you don't want to, but as a writer I have to be conscious of that idea to hold this essay together.

WOE: You say *idea* holds an essay together. How do you define idea?

HOY: For me and for my teaching of young writers to write this kind of essay, I can't do without idea. Let me tell you why. The answer to this question of why we can't do without idea in an essay we see most clearly in young writers who are seduced by the power of story. A story can have all those things in it that you're talking about, and you can line fifteen related stories up together and still have a continuation of all those things you're talking about, and you still won't have an essay. Those stories that are being told and lined up and reprinted just because they have the power of story—we can celebrate that, but we don't have an essay. We begin to have an essay when we have some compelling force working on the writer to shape those stories so that they are in a tighter relationship with one another about this thing that the writer wants you to think about. That's why the idea is important. It's not important that you, the reader, get it. It's not important that you say to me, "Okay, I know exactly what the binding force of that essay is." I don't care whether you say that to me or not. But I guarantee you that I can go to any one of those essays, and I can show you what that idea is, and I can show you how it binds that essay together, and I can show you how it makes me tell those stories in a particular way, and they wouldn't be told that way without that shaping idea, which is both shaping and binding.

And, *and*, as you're writing it, it's got to be moving. The idea cannot be a thing that's sitting still. In the mother essay, for example, I'm having an argument. I'm arguing against a psychological truism, which is that to go back to your mother repeatedly is to be regressive. I'm saying to you at the end, standing over her grave, I'm the one coming back here forever, and I'm trying to demonstrate to you at the same time how that's healthy. I'm resolving a problem. I don't want to have to think about my movement back and forth, inside and outside of the mother, as some kind of regressive, retarding activity because I know damned well it's not. So my idea is to run against that current. Now, do you have to see me doing that running? No. Over the life of this essay? No. But it's there. And for me, for this writer, I couldn't have made that essay without knowing that's what I'm doing.

WOE: Do you actually state that idea in that essay?

HOY: You don't announce ideas in familiar essays. That's why you can have it both ways. I guarantee you, now that I've told you that—it may spoil your reading of the essay—but if you read that essay again, you will see all the way through that that's what I'm doing. That's why it's titled what it's titled. It's not "Comings and Goings." You have to go first, and then you come back. It's "Goings and Comings," that's the rhythm of life. The healthy male rhythm of life is to keep going back and keep leaving the mother. On a higher or more comprehensive psychological level, it is to embrace your own femininity. So then we're into Jung, and we're into *syzygy*, and we're into *animus* and *anima* and all this other stuff. That's why a woman can say to me, "I would have thought a woman wrote this book," because there's so much woman-consciousness in it. In a way that's a central piece necessary for understanding the psyche that's represented in my collection of essays.

WOE: Do you start out writing an essay with a problem or with an idea?

HOY: I usually start out with a problem. I usually start out with a question I'm trying to answer. I seldom start out knowing what my idea is. I discover *that* in the process of assembling the stories, or they allow me to discover it because they've already assembled themselves.

The images have already coalesced in my imagination and built up enough energy that they do what the Jungians call breaking the threshold of consciousness. And I have to pay attention to the images. They are presenting me with the thing I need to figure out. So I have to start with the image that's bugging me the most.

The first essay I wrote, the one we were just talking about, started with an image of my mother ironing, and my brother comes in and watches me do my arithmetic. He says, "Hey, make a five again." So I make this five. And he says, "Pat Hoy. Nobody but Pat Hoy makes a five like that." I wrote that image thinking I was going to start the essay with it. It was so powerful to me, I said to myself, this is how I'm going to get the attention of fifteen well-known literary scholars assembled in Blytheville, Arkansas. And as soon as I wrote that image I knew that I couldn't start with it because there's no way for you to know enough about what my brother meant without your knowing that my father had left. So I had to have another image precede that image. I put myself in a car with my mother crying with these three other women, crying over the fact that my father's leaving. That becomes the generating image of the essay, the moment of abandonment. So here I am within the next image, without a father, behaving genetically like my father. That piece begins, ' He simply wasn't there." The whole essay proves that he was there. So that's the idea. It's not a complex thing. It's a deep-structure notion.

The last paragraph begins this way: "There is mystery. My father, I used to think, simply was not there. I had discovered over time that he was still is; he's there like the plague. He's in my bones. I know it by the fives I make." So that's what I'm doing. I'm developing an idea about the ethereal and genetic presence of the father figure. That's the idea.

WOE: I can see why you would suspect the merely personal narrative. It's too easily manipulated. It's like a bad democracy: too easy for the strong man to come in, too easy to slip over into sentimentality.

HOY: But that's not why I won't go there. I'm absolutely courageous about getting into that tricky place. The problem is the pedagogical methodology that I'm trying to sell: a frame of mind with which one approaches a certain kind of writing. I understand fully what it is you want and expect and like the most in these kinds of essays. The problem is I can't tell students how to give me that, and what I have found is that they'll give it to me inevitably if I have some kind of shaping mechanism in front of them that I can get them to think hard about. An idea turns out to be very convenient. It also turns out to be the thing that allows me to move the qualities from the familiar essay to the academic. It's a very short move from idea to thesis, but you can't go from idea to thesis without altering the way people think about thesis, and that's what I'm trying to do. I'm trying to alter the way they think about thesis. They've forgotten about the roundedness of that term. They've forgotten about antithesis. They've forgotten about question.

As kids come to our classes from high school, thesis is all about certainty; it's all about proving something. On the first day of class I give my kids a one-page essay, either Virginia Woolf's "Old Mrs. Gray" or Gretel Ehrlich's "Looking for a Lost Dog" or Andre Dubus's essay "Grace." Those are one- or two-page pieces that students don't have to have read before they come to class. On that first day I say read it, and tell me whether this is an essay, a short story, or something else. When it is an essay for them, it is something that is trying to prove a point. That's the universal language, whether the kid comes from an East Coast prep school, low mediocre high school, or home study. It is so much a part of their inheritance that that's what they bring to my classroom.

I'm trying to break that down. I don't want an essay to prove anything. I don't believe that's what essays do. Essays look into, I'm going to say, idea: they look into something that the writer is trying to figure out. In the best of essays you get to see a writer thinking about that idea, that thing being investigated: through stories in familiar essays, and through text and stories in academic essays. Idea moves right across that whole spectrum. It morphs with thesis, which they know about, but by the time they get to the end of the course, they can't ever think about it the same way again. I call it a "shaping cone." I think it's a thing through which you put material that's larger than the cone itself, and you press it through there under pressure, and you get something out the other side that's different. Or you put it in there *just* to press it; it may not have a hole on the other end. You put it in there to press it, compress it, and bring it together. I think that's what idea itself, as a concept, can do for you, if you learn to play with it.

Every teacher trying to teach a student to write well has got to have some kind of boundary. There's a bounded playground in which students have to do their playing. They can't write an essay without a beginning, middle, and an end. That's one set of boundaries. And then over the term we start identifying other things together that are characteristic of good essays. A few years ago I called them "writerly moves." Women objected to that. Sounds like male jargon. So I said okay, we'll call them something else. We'll call them "rhetorical moves." We'll call them "techniques that writers use to get their jobs done." And that's all this is about: closing it up a little bit and establishing the guidelines against which a mind can be reflective or reflexive.

WOE: Reflective or reflexive?

HOY: Both. So in my writing program we work under a concept I call progressions. It's an old math term, having to do with a certain kind of movement, with a certain kind of concentrated accumulation that's associated with that movement. A progression is a series of reading, writing, thinking, and imagining exercises that I design to lead students in the direction of a particular kind of essay that I want them to write.

Then there's the second thing with that essay that I want to do. I want to teach them the hardest thing in the world that they have to do—and it's related to my passionate response rather than my angry response—I want them to learn the difference between the various Is that appear in the stories within the essay. I want them to know the difference between those Is, and I want them particularly to know the difference between that set of Is and the discerning writing "I" who's making the essay. The writer is not the same person as the "I" in those stories even though they have the same name. And the writer is in the position of having to decide what she's trying to do with them and how she's going to do it. And what she's going to do is related to the concept of idea. She's got to be making those stories come together in such a way that she's trying to tell us something that she's figuring out.

The joy and the value of the familiar essay is that it operates under the requirement that we deliberately see the writer's mind in motion. It is an illusion of the highest artistic order that we are actually seeing in the final form of that essay all of the writer's mind in motion. There are lots of things that get subtracted. There's a lot of shaping that goes on, but the requirement is that we retain the mind's movement, the reflection of it, so that we create the illusion that the listener, the reader is actually getting to see the mind figuring out whatever it's figuring out. And the mind's got to be trying to figure out something other than itself.

I say to my students in their drafting stage, "Okay, you have been writing inside this space that you have been constructing for yourself for a week. What is it that you're trying to figure out? And if you can't tell me by that time that you're trying to figure out something, you better go home and get focused because we don't have but two more weeks to get on with this project, and it's not okay to just be swimming around." So we use time as a forcing cone.

    The next time I read something by that student I'll have a different question, and the question is going to be: What is it you think you have started to figure out? Not: What are you trying to figure out? But: What is it you are figuring out? That is the idea. Why are you marshaling all this evidence? Why are you marshaling all these pieces together? What are these pieces together saying to you? What is it they are trying to tell you? What is it you are hearing? As soon as you start hearing something, you'll have a reaction to that. You're either going to believe what you're hearing or you'll have some movement against it or around it. That movement against it is the initial formation of your idea. And now you have to look at the information or the images that you have marshaled in a different light. Some of them will drop out; some of them are gonna stay and have to be modified. They need slight modification in order to work for you.

WOE: How does this reshaping manifest itself?

HOY: That's an interesting question to ask at this point. The beginning student's first reaction is to take an image of experience (or story) and add a moral to it and then another image of experience and add another moral to it and then a third image of experience and another moral. And then when you tell them to write a first draft, they go to the computer and put all three together one after the other just the way they created them, and there'll be image/moral, image/moral, image/moral.

    Then we have a conference. They bring their draft, and I read it on the spot. They walk in the door. My routine is: nice office, lots of books, telephone, mail all over the place, you can read my mail, read my books, use my telephone, the bathroom's down the hallway, and I'm turning my back on you for seven minutes while I read your essay, and then I'll turn around, and you and I will talk about it. And what I talk about is what they've made me talk about. It depends on what they've done.

WOE: Do you ever get writing that's just flat, dull, dead, the typical freshman stuff?

HOY: Not very often. You have to remember that I've got them reading writing that does the same kind of work that I'm asking them to do. So they always read an essay or two by a professional and an essay or two by a student who has been through this before them and has figured out how to do it. Students can see how to do the work.

WOE: And in the conference, what are the possible things that are happening in their pieces?

HOY: Most often the parts aren't working together; it will not be apparent to me what the relationship is among the parts. The student hasn't worked out the relationship. So the questions are usually about what does this part have to do with this other part. And they'll say, "Well, that's a problem. I'm trying to figure that out." If they say that, I'll say, "Let's read these two images together. Let's see what these two things are saying and see if there's any overlap, see if noticing what you've done somehow makes you ask the question whose answer will put you on a better path." It's very interactive.

WOE: How far are we into the course when this first conference takes place?

HOY: Three weeks. And the course is 27 lessons, two a week. Each session is an hour and fifteen minutes.

WOE: You started off at West Point teaching the traditional five-paragraph theme, outlines, and so forth. How did that come to change?

HOY: It came to change with that book of Didion essays. I taught the American lit class 1945 to the present, in which students were so astounded by Didion's essays that I changed the nature of the course. I went from that lit course to the writing course, and I said, "We're gonna learn to write this way." And 35 teachers said, "I don't know how to write that way, I don't know how to teach that." And so I said, "Okay, first thing ... I want a 6-page essay from you. And Didion's going to teach you how to write it. And when you give it to me, I don't want your name on it. But I'll come back before the term's over, and I'll tell you which one you wrote."

I did that. And so then the requirement to write became central to our developmental methodology for the teaching faculty.

WOE: You had this experience with Didion in the classroom. They loved it, so you decided we're gonna learn to write like that. But at that point *you* didn't write like that.

HOY: I was beginning to. I learned by reading. I selected an anthology that Bob DiYanni had done with John Clifford, called *Modern American Prose*. It had multiple selections by about ten essayists, and I knew it all. I just read it and reread it and reread it, and then I read it with students. I began to be able to explain the difference between one writer's way of doing things and another's. I got more and more interested in what were the common generic characteristics of all these essays.

So I wouldn't say to you what one of the panelists tonight said, that there are a thousand definitions of essay. There are editors selecting essays based on certain features they like, but they're not trying to tell you that this is all an essay is. As I see and practice and read and love this form, the essays I select manifest the things that are important to me. That's not a definition of an essay. The simplest generic definition of an essay is—this will get to you—a composition with a beginning, a middle, and an ending, which develops an idea in an interesting way.

The two devil terms are *idea* and *interesting*. But the more you look into it, *beginning* becomes a devil term, *middle* becomes a devil term, and *ending* becomes a devil term. What I mean by devil term—I'm borrowing this from Richard Weaver—is a term that's so rich that it's troubling, and we need to trouble over it. It's something that's so basic that it's inexhaustible; you cannot read and know all you need to know about it, so you can't know everything there is to know about beginnings in familiar essays, but you can talk about the characteristics that beginnings share. You can't ever tell a student what the hell one ought to look like. That's the difference between having a guideline and trying to prescribe something like all the old rhetorics that had a SEER paragraph: statement, explanation, evidence, restatement. Never ever get into that kind of place with a student because that's not guidance, that's a box.

So you're saying, okay, you're learning together by reading a variety of essays. These are the characteristics of all the beginnings I've ever known. It's like a Willie Nelson or Julio Iglesias song: all the women I've ever known. That's what it amounts to. I tell teachers, "You have got a CD-ROM spinning in the back of your head called essay, and that sucker better be changing all the time. And it is against what you know on that CD-ROM that you are able to make judgments about what students are doing. The less you know and the less you are able to see, the less you'll be able to see the potential in any work that students do. So our primary job together is to get smarter and smarter and smarter about this thing we're asking them to write. It keeps us from getting uptight about it; it keeps us from getting rigid about it. It allows us to allow them to have flexibility.

WOE: You learned how to write an essay based on reading essays. It seems like it was entirely inductive.

HOY: It was entirely inductive. The only guy at that time in the universe who was writing about the familiar essay was Phillip Lopate. And Phillip had a piece years and years and years ago in the strangest of places—in *The New York Times Book Review*. It started on the bottom third of the front page. It was on the personal essay. And I read that, and I was off and running because here was a writer, an essayist, a good one, making a case for the essay. And then in of all places where you would never expect it, there was a first-rate piece in *College English* about the exploratory essay.

WOE: The first familiar essay that you finished was "Mosaics of Southern Masculinity." Is there some moment in there where you connected and you knew it?

HOY: It happened as quickly and immediately as it did with the sentence. It was when I sat down in my study at West Point and wrote the scene about making upside-down fives. As soon as I wrote that scene—I'd never done one before, I didn't know it was a scene, I didn't know what it was, it was just a moment—I did exactly what I say my students learning to write do. I wrote the story, and then tacked on a moral at the bottom of it. It's a smart rhetorical move because the moral sets up the next three things I'm about to do. But it's a move I would never make now. I try to make everything come together now in a way that's so seamless you can't tell when I'm moving from one section to another section. But later, if you ask me how the essay works, I can tell you exactly how it works. But when I'm *writing* it, I can't tell you because I don't try to figure it out. I really do let the images guide me.

What's so lovely about it is that as a writer, I don't know what the hell I'm supposed to know about these images. So I have to investigate what I've been told to write down. I like to tell my students that in high school, in graduate school, for God's sake, my advisor thought her primary business was to reorder my thinking. It was always about reordering my essay so that it would answer the logic of *her* imagination. She was not willing to follow the logic of *my* imagination. It was uncomfortable for her. It didn't fit the format. I don't mean this in a negative way. I mean that the help I got, in terms of writing, was always about reorganizing. It was never about my writing. I couldn't tell whether they liked my writing or not, except that I got good grades.

WOE: I'd like to ask about your absent father and his influence on your writing.

HOY: I never heard my father put three sentences in a row, ever. I saw him, but there was never a single meaningful conversation about anything. I only remember one sentence he ever said. I was sitting in his lap in the hardware store that he owned, and he was talking to a bunch of other people, and we ended up by ourselves, and he looked down at my knee and he said, "You've scunt yourself, haven't you?" He meant skinned. "You've scunt yourself, haven't you" are the only words I ever heard him say to me in isolation, directly to me. So I need a notion of fathering. I've got to make it out of something, so I make it out of the residual. I get to a place where I'm doing something, and I can't figure out why I'm doing it, and I can't attribute my motives to anything that I know. Then I have to say, "Well, it must have something to do with him." And usually it does.

There's no other way to explain this aspect of me, no way—my yearning, for example. No way, no way to explain the yearnings of my heart except to say that my father gave them to me.

WOE: What's the yearning for?

HOY: For connection and understanding. I'd pay money for it, but how often do you have it? And I really think, strangely, that this is the core of the writing, and it's the core of what you end up caring most about in my writing. I am actively seeking powerful correspondence with the reader—that goes back to rippin' their hearts out.

WOE: There are people who do write short things that do, I won't say rip your heart out, but move you. I'm thinking of some very short Kafka pieces, for example, a section of *In the Penal Colony* called "Meditations." Some of the pieces are no more than a paragraph.

HOY: My problem is that my own methodology is more or less in place. I know when I do it, and I do it under the influence of Newman. In one of the Discourses from the *Idea of a University*, Newman says, "We know, not by a direct and simple vision, not at a glance, but, as it were, by piecemeal and accumulation, by a mental process, by going round an object."

That's how I know to do it, by going round the object. It's the circuitous route, so that when you get to the ending, if the ending is constructed properly, and if you've built up the proper sentiment and the proper understanding along the way, when you unload that ending, it will rip your heart out.

CLAUDE HURLBERT

Claude Hurlbert is best known as a gifted teacher: he has won numerous teaching awards and is ranked among the 300 best professors in the U.S. by Princeton Review (RateMyProfessors.com lists him as number 8). A distinguishing assignment Hurlbert uses in composition classes is described in his book Letters for the Living: Teaching Writing in a Violent Age *(1998). He asks students in his undergraduate composition classes to write an entire book in a single semester about something they are burning to tell the world. In these books, students often recount scenes of violence and social injustice that they themselves are still working to grapple with.*

In addition to his impressive teaching record, Hurlbert has repeatedly called for reform and resistance to the corporate influences found in the composition industry. In his co-edited volume Beyond English Inc.: Curricular Reform in a Global Economy *(2002), Hurlbert recognizes the reality that corporate interests influence English teaching curricula, advocating for curricular approaches that serve students and provide academic and interdisciplinary freedom to teachers within (and beyond) such corporatizing of composition instruction. Hurlbert has further emphasized and re-envisioned how to tackle difficult social issues in composition classes through three other books:* Composition and Resistance *(1991),* Social Issues in the English Classroom *(1992), and* National Healing: Race, State, and the Teaching of Composition *(2012).*

Currently a professor of English at Indiana University of Pennsylvania, Hurlbert has taught composition and writing classes there since the mid-1980s. He received his MA from the Bread Loaf School of English, Middlebury College. Working on his PhD at the State University of New York at Albany, he focused on the history of rhetoric and composition theory, 19th-century American nonfiction, and poststructuralist literary theory. His dissertation, Writing and Reading Subjects: The Dialogics of the Teaching of Writing, *directed by C.H. Knoblauch, won a State University of New York at Albany Distinguished Doctoral Dissertation Award in 1986.*

—Grant Eckstein

"Where Meaning and Being Gathers"

Krystia Nora, Roseanne Gatto, Dawn Fels, and Elizabeth Campbell

Fall 2007

WOE: Your scholarship has been influenced by a mélange of sources: classical rhetoric, feminist rhetoric, poststructuralism, and all of the modern compositionists. We notice references to Bakhtin, Marx, Freire, Heidegger, Socrates, Nietzsche, Barthes, Foucault, Eagleton, Berthoff, and more recently, Tove Skutnabb-Kangas. Which scholars have been most influential on your work in the last twenty years?

HURLBERT: Without a doubt, Cy Knoblauch, my dissertation director, because studying with Cy was like studying how to think. He encouraged his graduate students to question everything and understand the philosophy behind the theories we invoked. In Cy's classes it wasn't enough to say something like, "Oh, I'm a process person." You'd have to know what you were talking about. You'd have to understand what process. How has it been articulated over time? Are you speaking of process in Kantian, Hegelian, or Marxist terms? And if you were tempted to start slicing and dicing the writing process into component parts, Cy would simply ask if you had read Whitehead. In my interactions with Cy Knoblauch I always felt encouraged to go find out what I needed to know.

Ann Berthoff certainly also influenced me because she told us compositionists that we need to understand the role of the imagination in meaning making, and, therefore, in our composition classrooms. We in composition have still not realized the revolutionary importance of that insight. The model Ann Berthoff set for us as compositionists requires that we unflinchingly explore all questions in our quest to reclaim the imagination, that we be, as she put it, "philosophers in our own classrooms." Whether we can live up to that model is another matter.

And, of course, Jim Berlin was an influence. Anyone working in political concerns in our discipline learned from him about the nature of thought and commitment and ethics, as well as the more gracious ways one can go about one's work. I don't know of anyone who did more to support younger scholars—much of what he did without anyone's knowledge. He was a generous man—a true model.

I can go on to various things I've read that I keep returning to, but really, as I think any good compositionist should, I read in any and all fields where writing is an issue: poetics, rhetoric, philosophy, etc. The list you began with is as solid as any that I could think of, except that I would add some poets who continue to make me rethink what a text is and what a text can do, like Ezra Pound and the people who have continued to work in and beyond that tradition: Don Byrd, Juliana Spahr, Robert Creeley, Susan Howe, and Robert Duncan, who showed, among other things, the way that a text articulates interbeing connections. Duncan's poems, besides being about the articulation of self, are also about how articulate silences can be. In his long lines of poetry, there are spaces, stops between words. The beat of the line continues in the reader's head, going on without interruption in the split second it takes to get to the next word. Somehow, these spaces are incredibly elegant and articulate for the rests they inspire, the manner in which they invite readers to fill the lines with associations, to live within the lines.

WOE: We've noticed a Marxist thread in your work. In "Toward Collectivist Composition: Transforming Social Relations through Classroom Practices," you wrote about how we might take a closer look at the "inseparability of social relations and relations of production" in the courses that we develop. What relationship do you think students have with their composition classrooms today?

HURLBERT: You know, when we talk about composition instruction, we talk about it as if it were a monolith: there's this course called Composition, which is taught in a certain way. But, of course, we all know that behind that monolith is this great diffuse country, and composition is taught in so many ways in so many different places, it's almost impossible to talk about it. Yet we continue to talk about it because it's our discipline. I fear that, too often, composition is a course enacted in the service of those who would commodify the imagination, rather than a course in how to articulate the most important meanings of one's lives. That's what worries me, and that's why I critique the textbooking of composition and the corporate influences on composition. Often, compositionists serve imperatives to create workers when they should follow the humanistic and ethical impulse to encourage students to be thinkers and interpreters of their own lives and to take up activist roles in the shaping of their lives.

WOE: Your writing often foregrounds thinkers who believe in the importance of individual subjectivity in written communication. You show that even deconstructionists, whom we often associate with the death of the author, were preoccupied with subjectivity. In fact, there is a moment in your dissertation where you write:

> [C]ommunication and thought "implies a transition from one subject to another." In fact, Derrida reminds us "I have never said that there is not a

subject of writing." He claims that "not only am I conscious of being present for what I think but I am conscious of keeping as close as possible to my own thought."

HURLBERT: Yeah. And look at Foucault. In the early part of his career, he was known for the "death of the author," right? And he spent the last years of his career writing about the self and a reconstruction of theories of the self. When we try to say deconstruction eliminated the authorial subject, it's only our way, in our field, of grabbing onto a thinker and encapsulating what they do into a slogan. It's only our way of using the schools of composition, the names of the schools to stand for a rigid set of dictums that do not encapsulate the entire wisdom of the school. Ultimately, the problem is that we turn movements into monoliths, and they're not monoliths. We try to associate other compositionists with one school or another, and we try to be examples of one school or another. But composing and teaching are never that simple or easy, of course. There's little of that sort of purity in the historical schools of composition. I think that's what's so enticing about post-process theory: the old pieties about writing fall away and the insights behind the slogans remain.

WOE: That brings to mind something that Freire talked about. After writing *Pedagogy of the Oppressed* in the 1970s, he spent the rest of his intellectual career honing those ideas as he evolved as a scholar. And yet one of his complaints later in life was that no one seemed to have read anything other than that and they didn't understand that he had different ideas at different points in his life.

HURLBERT: I've changed in how I view history. Borrowing from Michel Foucault, in *Rhetorical Traditions and the Teaching of Writing*, Cy Knoblauch and Lil Brannon wrote that the history of epistemology is a history of radical disruptions, and, therefore, classical rhetoric has little or no relevance in a classroom of the contemporary episteme. They later revised their position in interesting ways, but my take is this: classical rhetoric has a questionable relevance (in a positive sense) for the writing classroom at this point in history. In other words, one's position in relation to classical rhetoric will be influenced by the model of history one adopts, and I see our relation to history in a hermeneutic sense, that history is a matter of interpretation and subsequent action.

I think of Paul Ricoeur's work in this regard. When I am faced with a text of the past, I enter into a process of appropriation and distanciation. I try to appropriate the meaning of the text through my interpretation of it, even as the pull of the historical past distances the text from me, making my interpretation incomplete and my applications problematical. I may try to appropriate, through conscious action, the meaning of a passage by

Quintilian and apply it to my classroom, for instance, but if I am to be honest about it, the interpretation I make and the subsequent application I enact can be errant and inappropriate or meaningful and useful. There are no easy, one-to-one correspondences between classical rhetoric and our classrooms, not even for the work of rhetoricians or philosophers closer to our own time. You have to work out the meanings and the applications, where they can be made at all, through continuing critical thought and dialogue.

After poststructuralism, our profession took a hard political turn, and I certainly took it, too, as you can see in my "Collectivist" articles in David Downing's two NCTE collections. When I wrote them, I was taking Marx, interpreting him, and finding ways to apply him in teaching. I thought that by my doing so the profession might make an important gesture toward better lives for ourselves and a better world for each other. In a sense, I think my idea to have students in my introduction to literature class write class books together and to share the grade for the books was an appropriate action in that it did encourage some of the students to think about the reality of individualism and competition in the United States. But from a Marxist point of view, I also see that my pedagogy was wildly divorced from any significant contextualizing in historical process and progress, which is, of course, crucial to Marxist philosophy. These books of creative writing and critical analysis served an educational purpose those semesters in my literature classes, but I needed to do more to help the students see the historical process within which the books were created.

WOE: Speaking of student books, we'd like to talk to you about the evolution of the book project you have your students do in your composition classes. In this project, you have students take an entire semester to individually write short books about what they are burning to tell the world. You and Michael Blitz write about this in *Letters for the Living*, discussing how such an assignment gives students the chance to grow as powerful, thoughtful writers who can make a difference in not only their own lives but also in the world. This project has traveled across institutions and is used by people who may not know your book or you. How do you feel about the project living beyond your classroom?

HURLBERT: This might sound corny, but as you just described the book project moving beyond me, I have found myself thinking that Michael Blitz and I, in some odd sense, wrote a poem. It was a poem about teaching, and it was a poem about students, and it was a poem about living, and it was *Letters for the Living*. Poems, after all, do outlive the poet. Poems move on with the meanings they contain and the meanings people add to them. But it's not like it's the only poem, you know? It's just one among many. It's amazing to think about people reading what you write and maybe using it in places and ways you never imagined. That's humbling. But writing gathers us together in ways we can barely articulate, if we can imagine them at all. How do I see the idea of having students write their books affecting the field? I can't see that. Look, having students write a book in our comp classes is not so very original. It's been done in elementary education, and it's been done in high schools. Telling the issues of one's life has been a part of feminist practice and theory for over thirty years. So, there's nothing new in the poem that Michael and I wrote. We simply put together our love of writing, our care for students, and our love of books and made a project based in what we said was the one thing most worth doing in our classrooms. What's the one thing we love about writing that we can offer to our students so that they might learn to love writing, too? And it was the book-writing project.

WOE: If it's nothing new, if it's something that's been used by so many theorists, then why does it become something controversial at the college level?

HURLBERT: Well, part of the problem is that compositionists still look to classical rhetoric with its pedagogy of exercises and practice sessions rather than to more contemporary views about studios and the making of art. I mean, Cy and Lil did have some serious points to make that lots of people listened to and immediately dismissed for various reasons. Roland Barthes argued in "The Old Rhetoric: an aide-memoire," in *The Semiotic Challenge* that classical rhetoric will always be defended because some of us have our power and identity invested in it. That's the academy and that's human nature.

WOE: There's a lot of tradition behind it, too.

HURLBERT: And there's a lot of tradition, with all of its weights, burdens, graces and inheritances. And compositionists want a history, and so we claim classical rhetoric. I think that's a fine choice for others to make if they execute it well and fully, but sadly, that's not how it often goes. I also want to argue that other traditions of thought offer just as much insight into the nature of writing. That's the reason why I have been teaching a doctoral course, Rhetorical Traditions, for the past twenty years. There are many traditions from which to learn: the rhetorics of cultures around the world, philosophy and poetics. Discursiveness is, after all, a large topic. So it amazes me that there would be resistance to book writing in place of modal practice or argumentation or whatever. Part of it is, you know, the English department's half love, half disdain for creative writing. I can see people saying, "This is just a little too much, too creative-writing, having students write books. Students are not writers. Writing books won't train students to do the work of the academy." All of that is nonsense. Book writing is exactly what many of us do What better way to train students to write well, to be fluent, to be invested in their work, their scholarship. to care about their product, and to care about getting it right than to have them write books about what they are burning to tell the world?

Sometimes you'll hear these critiques of student-centered writing projects because some people don't know what to do to fill the time in their composition classrooms, so they try and turn the composition class into a junior literature, sociology, political science or whatever class. They have the students read essays in some reader and discuss the meaning of the essays or answer those silly questions-for-discussion sections. I say that writing teachers need to develop their own visions and commitments to students and teaching writing in order to do their best teaching. That only comes through serious and copious reading, thinking and writing. There are no shortcuts, least of all the corporate textbooks. When we adopt textbooks, we also adopt an educational agenda set by transnational corporations. Sure, some gifted teachers can find degrees of success by relying on the strength of their personalities, classroom presence, and some good lesson plans. But when these qualities are combined with a vision for the subject matter and the pedagogy, whatever shape that vision takes, truly great things can happen. But again, we have to earn our visions. I don't think that they come automatically or by gift or divine selection. Of course, universities don't want to pay people to take the time necessary to create their visions, but that's another part of the material dimension that needs addressing.

WOE: While many students feel empowered as writers by completing the book project, this project also scares some students away. Do you remember last year when a girl in one of your classes literally came from another English class across the hall where she was going to be asked to write a book, and she ended up in your class? And when she found out that she was writing a book in your class, too, she said, "But that's what the person across the hall was going to get me to do."

HURLBERT: [*laughs*] And she dropped my class, too! Some people don't want to write books. And that's why students should have choices. Not everyone should write a book about what they're burning to tell the world. Some students would prefer not to have something that they're burning to tell the world. Or not have to burn. Or not have to tell. We all have our ways of getting through and negotiating the complications of our lives. There are always other sorts of good work to do, too.

WOE: One of the criticisms that we've encountered is that the book project is dismissed off the cuff as being too expressivist and charged with not being as rhetorically effective as traditional argument or the research paper. One of our colleagues even asserted that it was "too nice." After bringing student bound texts to departmental meetings and defending the critical inquiry involved in the creating of books, our department eventually acknowledged the importance of the project, but why is student self-expression, in particular, met with such opposition? What is so threatening?

HURLBERT: What a great question! I suspect a number of things. For one thing, certain aspects of the Harvardization of rhetoric are still at work in the academy. We're still convinced that we need to teach short, separate essays or papers in response to literature or essays or scholarly writings that can be easily collected and graded in an evening. The idea is that students do a variety of short papers during the course of a semester because they will learn more about writing by completing a variety of writings. I'm not convinced that's true. I think that having students write longer works offers the opportunity to teach a lot more about coherence, structure, and form: issues that are hard to maintain over a long text. They're hard to maintain for any writer. And teaching some of those skills is crucial. Also, it's funny, expressivism, well, just the word has become such a shibboleth in composition, you know.

WOE: Even Peter Elbow, who is often identified as an expressivist, doesn't like being labeled that way because he feels the term is too limiting.

HURLBERT: There you go. Some people deny they're expressivist even as others say they are. Well, I'll wear that term. Don't get me wrong. It is always tremendously gratifying to read when someone has interpreted my work and located it within one school or another because it tells me that my work has a place and a role to play in the profession. It also sometimes helps me to reconceive my teaching in order to develop it, and I am grateful for that. But, ultimately, I don't particularly care what term I'm called by. I'm a teacher and a writer who uses whatever coherent insights he can glean or construct to create a meaningful classroom.

It does seem to me, though, that expressivism has gotten a bad rap because it's supposedly about touchy-feely stuff and only about valorizing the individual subject. Well, the fact is that people do write about what they feel and because they seek contact with others; it is touchy and it is feely. Beyond that, when a student writes about what they're burning to tell the world, they're not just writing about themselves. They're articulating important aspects of their cultures. I think it's crucial that we encourage students to think about what those cultures are and how their politics and economics operate. So I have students write forewords to someone else's book, exploring the cultural insights of others as they do. Actually, I'm revising that idea. Maybe students need to write critical introductions to their own books as well as having a foreword from someone else. Getting perspective on culture, through their texts, and from many angles, is just as essential as individual expression.

What is wrong with the individual? Social constructionism wasn't about giving up individuality. You do not need to give up the individual to understand the influences of the social on composing or to explore the political ramifications of writing, not to mention the construction of political projects. Personally, I maintain my individuality the best that I can in this modern world where it is under pressures and stresses every day. Maintaining that precious individuality is a problematic enterprise at best, but I'm not about to throw in the towel on my individuality without a fight. I've spent a great deal of time and effort trying to construct a semi-unified, coherent, healthy subjectivity. I'm not about to offer that up to the social guillotine for the sake of some misguided or under-theorized political theory. I mean, we're talking about 1984 here, for crying out loud. The expressivists gave us student centeredness. That was an incredible gift to our profession. Thank heaven that people such as Lad Tobin continue to argue that we cannot afford to lose the best of what the expressivists taught us. I fear we are in danger of losing track all the time.

Nevertheless, if I have anything at all wise to say about my writing it is that my work moves from school to school to school and back because I just don't think any one of the schools had the whole story of composing. Now don't get me wrong. I also recognize the problem inherent in carelessly drawing from the various schools and rhetorics. It is all too easy to create pedagogies that confuse students with contradictory statements about writing, meaning and human being. We have choices to make and difficult, critical work to do when we construct our pedagogies. The goal, it seems to me, is humanistic, ethical education devoted to the development of each student in the context of who they are, where they are, and the work they need to do. Remember, Marx knew that each of us finds fulfillment in our creativity and in healthy relations with others.

WOE: As a follow-up, let us go back to something that you wrote in "Collective Pain," thirteen years ago, imagine that?

HURLBERT: [*laughs*] No.

WOE: You wrote, "I hope, of course, that my pedagogy promotes democracy, collaboration, dialogue, and even collectivism, but none of these principles means that I should leave my subjectivity outside the doors of my classroom."

HURLBERT: Wow! I'm glad I wrote that. I'm glad I said that thirteen years ago.

WOE: And what you just said shows that after thirteen years, you're still committed to that. So it's not only a pedagogy, but it's who you are as an instructor, as a teacher. We're wondering what young professionals in composition should do when faced with mockery of our work, like the book projects, that asks students to bring their subjectivities to the center of the writing table?

HURLBERT: One of the great values of post-process, and you can see it so clearly in Peter Vandenberg, Sue Hum and Jennifer Clary-Lemon's *Relations, Locations, Positions*, is that it has taught us to remember context. There's no one way of teaching for all places. The book project, I suspect, would be adapted to where you are. But that's an easy answer. There are places where there is no such thing as discursive freedom. And there are places where if you don't teach according to the textbook-commodified practices of composition in one of its most mechanical and weak sophistic sorts, you will, yes, run into trouble. I have no answer for that.

The university, the college, is a curious place. Each one is different. Each one is full of graces and dangerous in its own ways. I think each person, each teacher, wherever they are, has to negotiate the politics and the freedoms and the constraints. There are no answers except to connect with people in the field who think and teach as you do or who are wise enough to respect diversity and dissensus. You keep emailing and writing and staying in touch and going to conferences and then looking for a teaching position in a respectful environment if you have the luxury to move. You try to find a place where you can do your work. I'm lucky to have found such a place, and I can do my work because it's a union shop. I have academic freedom as guaranteed by my collectively bargained contract. I have luxuries that a lot of people don't have. And, yes, I'm a tenured, full professor. I have freedom to teach as I see fit as long as I can articulate the reasons why I do what I do. I live in academic luxury in that regard.

WOE: But that hasn't been an easy road. A lot of what you've written has suggested that you've really had to fight, with the help of colleagues, the tendency of the department or the state to come in and say, "No, you really need to do it this way."

HURLBERT: Yeah, that's true. Back in 1993, my colleague Don McAndrew and I wrote a small piece for the *English Leadership Quarterly* on teaching students to make intentional grammar errors. Although the article won the Article of the Year award for the journal, Don and I ended up being listed on a conservative website in California which named educators to despise, or some such thing. We were then referenced, disparagingly, though not by name, in an editorial in . . . I forget whether it was *Time* or *Newsweek*. The next thing we knew some conservative member of the Pennsylvania state legislature wrote a letter of complaint to the president of our university, and the letter made its way down the chain of command to us. Grammar, of course, is a hot-button issue with conservatives, and we had really hit it. So, yes, the state can come in at any unexpected time. When you write what you believe, you have to be prepared for repercussions.

WOE: How do you effectively resist that?

HURLBERT: I just keep doing what I'm doing, and I just keep . . .

WOE: Flying under the radar?

HURLBERT: Yes, flying under the radar. We some or many times do that in order to teach as we should. I don't know how you withstand the pressures of institutions alone. I've found a place where I'm not standing alone.

This is not a very good answer. It's not very hopeful for people. But I don't have a better one right now. You can't do your students any good if you get fired. You don't do your family any good if you don't feed them. You don't do yourself any good if you don't do the things in life you love to do, which is perhaps teaching writing if you're reading this interview. So you have to find a way to negotiate these needs with the reality of the situation. I'm lucky I'm protected. So maybe that helps me protect my students. The union helps me protect my students so that my composition classroom is going to be about, as Bill Readings said, the meaning of thought and our obligation to others. I think that's what those books my students write are about. They're about the students thinking their lives out on paper, telling their stories, examining them with others, researching them and learning about their obligation to others, and themselves. But how can other teachers effectively resist without a union to protect them? I'm not sure.

WOE: We don't simply struggle in our classrooms with conformity, but in our academic writing. For example, we have to write dissertations one way for the institution and another way for distribution in the field. You wrote with Michael Blitz in "The Institution('s) Lives!" that what we are in the business of trying to do is "producing model students whose performances in the classrooms, theatres, playing fields of higher education, will receive favorable review from the critics," i.e., the committee. So we're wondering if it is too much to say that we're still caught in this institutional web that you described fifteen years ago?

HURLBERT: Yeah, and sometimes I think that the web is tightening.

WOE: Well what do you think grad programs are doing, then, to perpetuate and/or fight that?

HURLBERT: In some composition programs there's still a desire to have students write the traditional dissertation which is scholarly in the way that dissertations in literature or education typically are: they follow that five-chapter format, and they do make certain discursive gestures and some of us in comp seem to think that our students need to perform these moves as well. Why? Maybe it comes out of a felt need for legitimacy.

But of course composition—composing—is about writing, and writing is about sharing writing with others, about publishing, and there's so much room for innovation. A writing teacher or a dissertation director ought to help a student learn how to produce what they and others want and need to read. There's certainly room for the traditional five-chapter dissertation in the world. If it meets the needs of the study and if it's what people want to write and read, then they should. But there are also other things to do, and maybe encouraging someone to do work that doesn't fit the traditional format is one's way of trying to open up the discursive space of a dissertation to new innovations. I mean, every dissertation has not been written. There are more to do, and there are more ways to do them. And so how to keep that space open is the question.

WOE: It's funny you say that because in that same article that we referred to, you encouraged students, department members, etc., to "turn their institutionally sponsored expertise against the institution itself."

HURLBERT: As we've pointed out this morning, people change over time. At that point, I encouraged subversive action. Now, I would like that gesture to be a generous action that we offer the institution. We should be generous to offer what we've learned and know about writing. Back then, I'm sure I didn't mean it so generously, but that's how I mean it today. If generosity doesn't lead to positive change, then people may need to explore other options.

WOE: You've written and you've stated that you keep your politics out of the classroom. How?

HURLBERT: The writing class should be about composing. Heaven knows that writing is always already infused with politics. But the composition class shouldn't be about how a teacher reads a particular situation or figure or text, unless the class is a topics class and advertised as such in advance. On the other hand, composition scholars such as Nancy Welch are writing about teaching for civic responsibility and engaged living in important ways. I remember that in one piece, Nancy Welch writes about a class session where she brings a soapbox in and stands on it to speak about political issues. The important thing is that she invites her students to take their turn up there as well. Now I wouldn't characterize Nancy Welch's whole pedagogy by this one example, especially since I don't know her pedagogy with any depth, but in it I see both the invoking of tradition and the sparking, perhaps, of student-centered activism, and I admire that. It is true that I tend to speak my politics softly in the classroom, but my point is that there are many ways to be both student-centered and politically responsible in our teaching.

WOE: This reminds us of the importance of silence in your classrooms. You'd only know this about your classes by observing you. We've been impressed by your restraint in the class, noticing that some of the undergraduate students sometimes offer invention or revising advice to each other that you might disagree with, but you would let them take their turn in whole-class workshops without correcting them, without even making a face. Our question for you is: how do you envision the role of silence in teaching?

HURLBERT: Again, I take the spaces in Robert Duncan's poetic lines as my starting point. I remember that as a grad student I met Duncan, and I wasn't nearly as bright as I thought I was, and I said something like, "It always seemed to me that in those spaces, that's where meaning and being gathers. You just have to listen in those spaces and you hear it happening." He said that he liked the idea. Of course, he'd no doubt already thought it because he had planned it from the beginning, and he'd maybe heard it a million times before from other people, but he was kind enough not to point that out to me. After all the intervening years, though, it seems to me that this idea really does inform my pedagogy. In the classroom, when the teacher is silent, meaning gathers. Remember that article, "Wait Time" by Mary Budd Rowe? Meaning and being take time to gather themselves and come forward in simultaneous appearance and process. You just have to be silent for the invitation to be made and the process to happen. And that's being student centered. But listen, all this talk about being and gathering might suggest that I endorse the philosophy of Martin Heidegger. Because of his Nazi ties, who could? But his personal ugliness does not negate the insights one can glean, with care and healthy suspicion, from his work. When he writes about poetry, he writes about how a poem gathers meaning from elsewhere. Meaning comes forward, and we are changed by it if we open ourselves to change. We just have to be careful about the sources and effects.

WOE: To be student centered, you need to listen. This idea seems to be at the root of your pedagogy.

HURLBERT: Yes. You've all been in the room with me, and you've all looked at the students when they're talking. Have you ever noticed how many times when someone speaks, especially in the beginning of the year, their hands are trembling? Their hands are trembling and so you have to give them space to work out the meaning of their presence in the environment we call the college or university. As a teacher, our subjectivity comes endorsed with our prestige, our position, our time on earth, our writing. We need to step back if the other subjectivities are to come forth—that's the only way. That's what Freire said, though in other words.

WOE: What do you do, though, for those students who take your silence as, "Oh my God, he thinks I'm a blithering idiot" or "He doesn't like what I'm doing"? Our students have often been conditioned to believe that validation must come from the teacher, and silence can suggest a lack of approval.

HURLBERT: I hear you. We can't control the hermeneutic processes of each subjectivity. People will always interpret us; all we can do is try to make the most articulate discourse we can in the classroom and hope that it's received. I mean, it's not like I never speak in the classroom. I assent to the meaning of a comment or dissent by articulating my own, differing opinion when it is my turn in the circle to speak. The point is that everyone has a turn and time and some obligation to the other students to speak. I just try to be silent so students feel the weight and value of that obligation, each to the extent that they can; each in the way that they can at the moment in which they find themselves.

WOE: You do things, though, to make students feel more comfortable and to articulate your approval of various student ideas. You sometimes play off your graduate assistants, leaning over and nodding approvingly at a student comment. You also smile, and you sometimes even say, "How good it is for the author to get a variety of feedback, even conflicting feedback, because the workshops reveal the variety of choices the author could make."

HURLBERT: Yeah, there are ways to offer help, but I can see how some people can misinterpret silence. The silence is certainly a space, so people will fill that space with all sorts of meaning.

WOE: Would you talk about how you developed the class workshop technique where the whole class sits in a circle and everyone has to respect the space of allowing a person to speak, whether teacher or student?

HURLBERT: I asked myself at some point, "Do you trust dialogue or don't you?" And I decided I did. And then I said, "Well, if you trust dialogue, if you trust the people in the room to make a dialogue, how best to enact the trust?" After some thought, I said, "Well, just try it. Sit and listen for awhile when they go around the room and don't say something after every student." It's funny; I realized something that Michael Blitz and Jim Zebroski and Nancy Mack and I have talked about at 4Cs when we get together. Nancy, Jim, Michael, and I all come from the working class. We grew up hearing critical talk at home, or in the bars, or on the streets about class structure and the economic situation in the United States that was sharp, pointed, and realistic. Then, much later, when we became academics, we read scholarly, critical work about class structure and analysis of the economic situation in the United States, and we realized that even though we were four people from four different places, we were hearing the same points we heard growing up, but now these points were being made by academics.

So I started to put that together with my trust in dialogue, and I said, "Okay. Listen to the students. Put them in a whole-class circle, as in a creative writing class, and see if what they say about the writing is smart. Is it as smart as you, as an academic, would think you are?" And I started to hear them talk about each other's writing in ways that was astoundingly sharp and insightful and critical and helpful and collaborative. But before I got to hear the students, I had to make the pedagogy match the theory. If the pedagogy informs the theory and the theory informs the pedagogy, if that process is a sound one, it'll happen. The students come forward to claim their places in the circle. And as they do so, they become more capable writers, more fluent both in their writing and in how they talk about writing. Every class? No. But most classes.

WOE: What do you do with the small percentage of students who try to destabilize this very student-centered environment by trying to take all the power to themselves, like a class clown who needs everything to be about him or her?

HURLBERT: Lad Tobin says that when students bring their subjectivities to the classroom, they also bring their neuroses. So you know you're going to have those problems. And as a teacher, your subjectivity counts. You have to intervene.

We're talking about dialogue in its most ideal sense here. The fact is that it's a human process, as complicated as all human processes. I mean, look: the hermeneutic process is rife with failure. We can interpret incorrectly. A literary theorist with whom I studied at SUNY Albany, Helen Elam, once said in a class, "If I read a recipe for baking a cake as a poem and start interpreting it in creative ways, I could get into trouble"—or some such thing. So, yeah, the teaching process can go wrong and we have to intervene. But that's our expertise. We have a responsibility to use that power and to use it judiciously.

WOE: In your dissertation you quoted Heidegger saying, "The real teacher, in fact, lets nothing else be learned than learning." And, in "Making CCCCs Matter" in 2005, you said, "Our task as teachers it to help students begin this lifelong study for themselves." We talked before about being student centered and communication/dialogue oriented. To come down to a practical matter, how does that influence how you grade?

HURLBERT: I make this assignment, "What are you burning to tell the world?" I know that that assignment will foster the creation of texts that I will have trouble grading. That challenge is true for every single book, every single student, every single semester. I think it's important that I feel discomfort when I grade; I've written about that, too. But we are working in institutions and there are constraints. Despite all my freedoms I am still required to assign a grade, and I do. I realize that it is a part of what I'm paid to do, and so I do it with as much integrity as I can. That means creating situations where I can't be mechanical about grading, or embracing those situations when I unintentionally create them. Being uncomfortable is not the problem. The problem is mechanical exercises, mechanical discourse, mechanical grading, nonrenewing consumption.

WOE: One thing that we've observed from your classes is how students are so actively involved in their own assessment. You have them look at the manuscripts of their books and find the strong parts and weak parts and then tell you why they are strong or weak. Can you comment on involving students in the process of assessment?

HURLBERT: When I ask them what are you burning to tell the world, in some respects they're saying, "I'm here." Then, I use a self-evaluation process that I adapted from various people like Mary H. Beaven, whose essay on self- and peer evaluation appeared in Cooper and Odell's *Evaluating Writing* years ago. In the evaluation process, I want the student not just to say "I'm here," but to say "I'm here and I'm writing."

That's the metacritical level of the composition class. And yes, I do try to get them involved so that the dialogue continues even through the grading process. They're not all approaching the book writing in the same way, through the same experiences, from the same level of expertise. They need to be heard on that level, too, the metacritical level we're teaching for.

WOE: Claude, we were talking a minute ago about discussions you've had with colleagues about your working-class background and how it influences what you do in the classroom. You talked about this briefly, too, in a 1992 conference paper, "White Trash: *Out of the Rain* and into the Professoriate." How has your working-class background steered you in this direction and sustained you?

HURLBERT: My working-class background certainly informs my politics. I grew up seeing the injustices of a small town dominated by mills and mill owners and I saw the violence and poverty of the particular neighborhood I called home. I learned to rail at the economic injustices in our country, and I chose to turn these experiences to my work with students. I really did pick my audience well. I picked a school where I'm teaching first-generation college students, many of them from the working class or the lower or middle class. I picked a school that is unionized. Like any of us, I am trying to work through my personal and political issues, many of which, of course, stem from childhood.

WOE: In *Letters from the Living*, you say what students "need to know is that there is still someone living out there to respond," which connects to something you said twenty years ago, where you talked about endnotes written in response to student papers: "Endnotes might let the student know that he or she is not alone in the process of meaning making, of thinking critically about the world." We notice that you seem acutely aware that students often feel alone. Why?

HURLBERT: Because, like any of us can, I feel alone. And like any of us, perhaps, I always have. You asked me about my sources earlier in this interview, and one of the key texts that has stayed with me over the years since I read it in grad school was Elizabeth Cady Stanton's "The Solitude of Self." We can say composition is a social act, and it is, but you know what? Elizabeth Cady Stanton said that we come into the world alone, and we find we have to live life, largely, alone, fight for our own rights, and, finally, we leave the world alone. That has always stayed with me. I remember something Michael Blitz wrote in the Jim Berlin memorial issue of *Works and Days*. He said that if the Internet is supposed to bring us all together, why tonight when I sit at the computer do I feel so alone? Solitude. We're not taught to understand and make the most of solitude in this culture, are we? We're told to shut down in the face of it. Watch TV. Buy something. At times you realize just how alone you are and how maybe ill equipped you are. And, you know, composing is an intimate act, so who are you composing with and for is always a key question. I hope students discover the meaning of some of that in my classes.

WOE: You talk about writing for peace, teaching for peace, and writing for healing. At one point in the article "Equaling Sorrow" you talk about writing for life, writing as "an act of living." How do all these ideas, combined with the need to feel less alone, tie together?

HURLBERT: What are we trying to find answers to? We're trying to find answers to our needs including our need to heal and to address the largest questions of our lives. Why do we make meaning? It's to be whole. When we sit down at the computer isn't it because at times we're seeking connection to our self, other selves, higher selves, spirituality, health, life? I think we write to clarify the connections that get foggy in the day to day and the pain of hearing again and again about war. That's why the teaching of writing seems to me as much a calling as a vocation. When we write and the words come freely, our being seems to open, and at times you suddenly know, really know, why you're alive. That's a lot to have to teach for, but that's the call.

WOE: Recently you've been writing and presenting with Anestine Hector Mason about your concerns about the role the World Bank is playing in the teaching of English around the world. How did you become interested in studying the relationship between literacy, the World Bank, and the International Monetary Fund?

HURLBERT: As we've discussed, I've always been interested in Marxism, and the concept of an oppressive world bank certainly runs counter to Marxist principles! But I think the students standing up across the country and demonstrating against world debt and the oppressive economic practices of the United States, with all of their political implications, taught me most dramatically. Watching them, I realized that I had to begin to understand the workings of the World Bank, and as I explored, I discovered, to my horror, that one of the Bank's objectives is to control literacy through the crushing of indigenous presses, the privatization of education, the unbridled proliferation of distance education, and the breaking of teachers' unions. For these reasons, Anestine Hector Mason and I wrote our article "Exporting the 'Violence of Literacy'" for *Composition Forum*. We were trying to say to literacy educators that, as literacy educators, we have to pay attention. It's not enough to say, "Oh, I can read about the World Bank in *The New York Times* and understand." No, it's important to know how the World Bank is attempting to commodify the human imagination on a global scale. We need to join the students and literacy educators around the world who are raising their voices in resistance. And we need to understand how the Bank's neoliberal project plays out in our own classrooms through the workings of ideology. Healing will never happen if we don't do this necessary work. Isn't that the enemy: commodification of who we are?

WOE: But some literacy educators know nothing about the relationship between the World Bank, the IMF, and literacy around the world. What do you think they need to know?

HURLBERT: To begin, that textbooks aren't simply teachers' aides. They are merchandise produced by corporations to make money, and they surely do. Some of these textbook companies have been adopted by the World Bank so that their textbooks are being used in classrooms in other countries around the world to the exclusion of indigenous presses. There is a reason why Longman was recently reported to have become the largest publisher in Nigeria. We need to know that as Americans we participate in global processes when we adopt textbooks from major corporations. We need to consider the extent we participate in the commodification of the imagination and the exportation of oppressive literacy policies. Longman is owned by Pearson Education, the largest producer of standardized testing in the world. Do we complain about the stupidity, not to mention the inherent racism, in standardized testing as it is currently enacted even as we adopt Longman texts? If so, what does that mean? And do we think about the oppression of students and teachers around the world, or do we say that has nothing to do with us? I think it's our obligation to understand. It's one thing to live economic contradictions in our private lives, but it's quite another to script our students into the economic and political contradictions that textbooks represent. We're supposed to be professionals. We are responsible, to greater or lesser degrees, depending on the context in which we teach, for the spaces we call our classrooms.

WOE: How have commercial interests and accrediting agencies' standards affected composition curricula? What factors are the linchpins?

HURLBERT: You know what? Some compositionists have tremendous freedom to decide what's going to happen in a writing program. When they choose to take a truncated, commodified view of discourse, when they acquiesce to accrediting agencies that champion mechanistic, positivist (in the worst sense of the word) outcomes assessment initiatives, they force that manner of thinking and acting on everyone in the program.

WOE: We can't talk about your work and thoughts without talking about your collaborations because most of your work is a collaboration. When asked about collaborative writing, Jim Strickland once said that he and Kathleen "give each other writerly support rather than constructive criticism." He compared themselves to a dance team, asserting that they "try to make their partner look good." You have a long successful collaboration with Michael Blitz. How have the two of you sustained such a successful collaborative relationship? What makes a good writing relationship? And what advice would you give other writers looking to work collaboratively?

HURLBERT: You know what? It doesn't always work. Finding the right collaborator is like finding the right best friend. I found Michael. As he and I said in Michele Eodice and Kami Day's book, *First Person*[2], we are family now. That level of intimacy was hard earned by collaborating over years. It still is a surprise to me. Every time we write together, it's still a discovery. Advice? Be very careful who you sign up to collaborate with. To work in its deepest channels, collaboration has to be with someone you love or respect in some way. Otherwise, you may not be willing to give up control of the words, and that is essential.

WOE: How did that begin?

HURLBERT: We went to grad school together. We were acquaintances though we ran in different circles. And then, after graduating, we bumped into each other at a CCCC in a hallway. We tell different versions of this story, but I say he was looking disgusted and sad. He says I was looking disgusted and sad. But somehow we connected and talked about all the things we wished people were talking about that we didn't seem to hear. And that turned into a CCCC presentation, thanks to the encouragement at a meet-and-greet session by the following year's conference chair, Andrea Lunsford. And that turned into a book, *Composition and Resistance*, thanks to the encouragement of countless people, especially Bob Boynton and Peter Stillman. So, we just met in a hallway and started talking and connected with tremendously generous people in the profession who encouraged our efforts.

WOE: To get back to the question we asked you earlier about institutional expectations, have you ever encountered any feedback about the consistency with which you collaborate with Michael? Has it ever been a troublesome issue in terms of tenure, promotions, etc.?

HURLBERT: No, not for me. But I know it has been difficult for a lot of people who collaborate. For instance, when Michael went up for—I forget if it was his tenure or promotion—I wrote a letter for his file asserting that he did half the work. Once I was a reader for two students who wanted to write a collaborative dissertation, but the graduate school said "no." And so we had to split their dissertation idea into two. At any rate they produced two fine dissertations. Still, it's a shame. My university missed an opportunity to directly foster something unique. The work turned into a wonderful collaborative book, though.

WOE: After looking back at your career, what if we look forward? We're wondering how you see composition now as opposed to twenty-five years ago when you were in school.

HURLBERT: Well, remember in the eighties we in composition were already looking to other fields: literary theory, cognitive psychology, education, political and economic theory, philosophy, etc. Still, the field is opening up even wider today, so that it includes, for instance, ecological research. There is hope in that. There's something in the imagination that continues to escape the corporations' attempts to commodify it. The desire to compose is alive. The desire to do necessary, relevant work is alive. These desires are genuine and valid, and I hope we hold them close as we continue the search to understand our art.

SONDRA PERL

Sondra Perl's "The Composing Processes of Unskilled College Writers" *(1979) has deeply influenced composition pedagogy. From her meticulous coding of the writing processes of unskilled writers, Perl showed that writers have recursive, internalized processes that both help and hinder them. She demonstrated that revising for grammar during the composing stages disrupts discovery, which led to the now-universal view that editing should take place in the final stages of the writing process.*

Over the years, Perl's many contributions to writing pedagogy have exemplified the human element of writing, as Perl writes honestly and vividly about teaching and learning, not afraid to share her struggles, questions, and knowledge with others. For Perl, even academic writing can be a place where humans interact profoundly with themselves, others, history, life. In Felt Sense: Writing With the Body *(2004), Perl describes writing as deeply embodied: "The process of creating new sense, of saying something fresh from all that came before and from all that lives within us, is a bodily one. [. . .] It is from within this interconnectedness of bodies, language, and situations that a theory of embodied knowing is derived."[1] With felt sense, we heed our physical sensations as we work to articulate what our bodies know.*

In Through Teachers' Eyes: Portraits of Writing Teachers at Work *(1998), Perl and Nancy Wilson show ethnography at its most powerful, presenting over two years of in-depth observation, documentation and interpretation of six writing teachers trained in the process approach to writing instruction. This book reflects Perl's deep commitment to the power of writing and ethnography to document human experience—in this case the intricate experience of teaching writing.*

Perl's humanism is epitomized in On Austrian Soil: Teaching Those I Was Taught to Hate *(2005). She writes of her transformative experience as an American Jew teaching Austrian educators whose families were complicit in the Holocaust. Perl brings an anthropological perspective to personal questions of identity, religion, legacy, and the role education and friendship play in healing. She went on to direct an instructional video,* Reading, Writing, and Teaching the Holocaust *(2008). Perl is a professor of English at Lehman College in the City University of New York (CUNY). In 2016, she received the CCCC Exemplar Award for outstanding contributions to the profession.*

—*Agnes Stark*

---

1 Perl, Sondra. *Felt Sense: Writing with the Body.* Portsmouth: Heinemann, 2004: (52). Print.

"There's Humor and There's Tears"

John Boe

Spring 2010

WOE: To what degree is your work feminist? I associate your process approach, the de-emphasis on performance, and the acceptance of feeling in the body with feminism and a female point of view.

PERL: Last Friday I attended a conference at the CUNY Graduate Center on Feminist Pedagogy. I went, in part, because the keynote address was delivered by my colleague Michelle Fine. I also went, in part, because I'm not sure I ever fully understood what it means to call pedagogy "feminist."

I always resisted this label. In my view, there's pedagogy plain and simple, and when it's done well, it is done by men and women. Certainly the field of teaching writing is populated with many wonderful men who are accessible, warm, student centered, learner centered, inquiry based, and who care about voice—all attributes I associate with people who take a feminist stance. But the label "feminist pedagogy" strikes me as exclusionary. I don't understand why the teaching of writing that values voice, individual experience, and often puts the learner in the center is necessarily feminist. I think of it as humanist.

While I don't characterize my pedagogy as feminist, I do think of myself as a feminist. If it weren't for feminism, I don't think we'd be having this talk today. Betty Friedan's *The Feminine Mystique* was published the year I entered college. By the time I graduated, the idea that white women with higher education could join the professions was beginning to influence American culture. Prior to that time, I had no career in mind and had imagined no life for myself after college other than marriage and motherhood. The feminist movement—and supportive professors—enabled me to think beyond such circumscribed roles. I learned that I could take the first step and after that I've never stopped walking.

WOE: There are certainly lots of process-oriented men, but I think that without feminism, the process movement wouldn't have been what it is.

PERL: In my view, feminism and writing process grew up in parallel universes. I often felt that what we were doing in the teaching of writing was similar to what feminists were talking about. But we did not appropriate that label. I think of my own classes as nonhierarchical. My students and I often sit together and work collaboratively. I value the individual voices of my students and aim to engage them in dialogue about the subjects we are studying, the texts we are reading and their own writing in progress. I think I share these nonhierarchical values with feminists who may (or may not) teach in similar ways. To my mind, there are affinities between the teaching of writing and feminism, but one doesn't necessarily imply or subsume the other.

WOE: Since as a teacher you're teaching the whole person and you want to change the person, you're dealing with their inner life. How do you stay on the teacher side and not cross over to therapy?

PERL: It's extremely important to distinguish between psychotherapy and writing. During composing, if writers are invited to go to a deep or heartfelt place, a place inside themselves where they recognize a felt need to write, there may be a psychotherapeutic component. Writing that leads to self-discovery often touches on personal issues or evokes important memories. This comes with the territory of opening up a space where writers are invited to write about what matters to them. But this doesn't mean that the teacher who opens that space is a therapist or is trained to help the person solve his or her problems. If a writer becomes enmeshed in something painful, the teacher needs to acknowledge it, needs to have a human response, needs to be able to reach out to the person in pain. It is certainly crucial to check whether the writer is okay or needs to seek help. But this does not mean that the writing teacher is a therapist or that the writing teacher can engage in psychotherapy.

WOE: Isn't it easier for women teachers to put an arm around someone than it is for men teachers, legally or otherwise?

PERL: In today's climate, probably. But, you know, over the years, I've discovered that most writers know when it is safe to write revealing and painful things. In a writing classroom, most writers don't go where they're not ready to go. And often just writing about difficult content will be sufficient for a writer to feel some relief, to take a deep breath, to decide whether or not he or she wants to pursue this particular issue in therapy or to pursue it as a piece of writing. But if a writer pursues a hard topic as a piece of writing, that's where the teacher's role is crucial. Our job is not to solve the dilemma or heal the pain. It's not to make the person whole as a human being. Our job is to work with the text, to help the writer see what in this piece of writing is going to speak to other people. So the goal of the writing I engage people in is not therapeutic as a psychotherapist would see it but to create a piece of writing that is strong, vibrant, thoughtful, revealing and aesthetically pleasing.

WOE: Who influenced you to write when you were young?

PERL: Actually, no one. Although I went to good public schools, I don't think I ever had a teacher in elementary, middle, or high school who understood me or responded to me. I was shy and held back in the style of first-born, dutiful, conscientious children. I did my homework and received good grades, but I left high school perplexed about the whole school game. I could do it, but it didn't mean much to me. When I went to college, I found my way to art history. The department was small. And it was in this department, through the study of art history, that I learned how to write. Instead of requiring us to memorize the names of famous artists, the titles of famous paintings, and the dates they were created, my professors took us to museums. They asked us to stand in front of paintings and to write what we saw.

Most of my peers were perplexed. They seemed not to grasp what we were doing. "Write what?" they would say. But somehow, writing about what was in front of me made sense to me. We would stand in front of a painting and write for about an hour. I didn't know it then, but I now realize that I was training my attention. I was learning how to look. I slowly began to understand that there was a transaction that occurred between the canvas and me. Between the universe of the canvas and my perceptions of it. Between what I was seeing and writing. I later understood that the process I engaged in echoed Louise Rosenblatt's description of the transaction that occurs between readers and texts. It was invaluable training for a writing teacher and researcher of writing.

WOE: You were at the vanguard of people who were trained in rhetoric and composition, rather than getting a literature or an art history PhD. How did you end up on this path?

PERL: My PhD is in English education. In the early '70s, I entered the department at New York University that had been created and was forever influenced by the work of Louise Rosenblatt. In just about every seminar, we spent time reading and writing and studying how we read and wrote. The focus was almost always on how people learn and on designing curriculum that would be based on sound theories of learning. At the time, no one knew much about composing processes, Janet Emig's work was just being published, and this question, especially since I was also teaching in a basic writing program at CUNY, began to intrigue me.

WOE: So you started looking at five writers' composing process.

PERL: Yes. I was hired at CUNY at a time when there were so many unanswered questions in the air. Mina Shaughnessy was beginning her study of basic writers and the main question on everyone's mind was "How do you teach writing to people who can't write?" I knew that at NYU I could design a dissertation that would help me answer this question.

WOE: In your first article in *RTE*, which had an objective scientific tone, you showed how unskilled writers edit too early. There is a shift in tone between that and the second article in *CCC*, when you're writing in the first person. Why did you move away from the quasi-scientific approach?

PERL: When I was in graduate school, the field was under the sway of Braddock, Lloyd-Jones, and Schor's *Research in Written Composition* published in 1963. In order for research in our field to gain respectability and move out of what was referred to as 'the age of alchemy,' researchers were instructed to control variables and to be as objective as possible. We were told that we had to control the writer variable, the topic variable, the time variable and so on.

When I designed the dissertation, I followed these proscriptions. And when reporting results, it was also assumed that the researcher would be faceless and voiceless. The dissertation and the *RTE* article reflect this tradition. When I wrote the article "Understanding Composing" for the December 1980 issue of *CCC*, I felt I could begin to write in a less detached manner.

But I do want to add that there was real value in careful coding of the data I collected for the dissertation. I had so many tapes of students composing aloud and I needed a way to systematize what I had in front of me. I still believe in doing very fine-grained analysis of data because it's in the immersion in data that the findings begin to emerge. But I don't think we need to report results in a voiceless, detached manner

WOE: And you ended up documenting, in what became a famous phrase, the recursive nature of writing.

PERL: Yes. I devised a coding system that allowed me to follow or chart the directionality and duration of composing for each student. The composing style sheets I developed showed how often and for how long students paused, moved back, reread, moved forward or edited during a composing session.

The style sheets were purely descriptive. But once I had four charts for each of five students, I could look at twenty sessions and determine what, if anything, was common to all of them. It turned out that students almost always moved back before they could move forward. They might return to the topic, or to the last sentence, or even to an important word. They also turned inward to what I later referred to as turning toward their bodies, to felt sense. In other words, by doing careful coding, I was able to document the recursive nature of composing.

These students also shared another feature of composing. Almost all of them, almost all of the time, engaged in what I called premature editing. They tended to short-circuit their own processes of composing, spending so much time on unproductive editing that they lost focus and could barely remember what they were trying to write. Both of these findings have important implications for teaching.

WOE: Let's move to *Through Teachers' Eyes* and the influence of the Writing Project. Your involvement in the writing project preceded this book, which was a study of teachers who had been through summer Writing Project institutes.

PERL: In 1977, I was giving a talk at CCCC on my dissertation. Jim Grey, the founder of the National Writing Project, happened to be in the room. Following my talk, he asked me if I would be interested in running a Writing Project. I said yes, introduced him to Richard Sterling and John Brereton, two CUNY colleagues I was working with, and within a few months, we launched the New York City Writing Project. It was about that simple.

Before we began, though, Jim traveled to New York to give us a few guidelines about how writing projects work. We were seated around a table at Lehman College and were totally in agreement with the first principle: "In a Writing Project, everybody writes."

But Jim's second point did not go over so well with us: "In a Writing Project, everybody shares his or her drafts with everybody else." Remember, this was 1977. We were taken aback.

Rolling our eyes at one another, we smugly replied, "People in California might sit around and share their writing, but not in New York. New Yorkers don't share."

Jim, never one to mince words, said, "To do this Writing Project, you will." And of course, he was right. That summer institute changed everything I ever thought about the teaching of writing. Never before had I sat with a group of peers in a small writing group and shared my work or listened to their work as it evolved. I was so deeply impressed and touched by what people wrote; I saw so much promise in the practice of simply listening to another's words and of participating in the process of helping to shape another's text. After that summer I felt as if I had a new understanding of what is possible in writing classrooms and I have used writing groups ever since.

WOE: How long did the project last that turned into *Through Teachers' Eyes*?

PERL: Following our first summer institute in New York, Richard Sterling and I were invited to bring the NYC Writing Project model to a school district at the end of eastern Long Island. We taught summer institutes to 25 wonderful teachers in July 1979 and 1980 and agreed to do follow-up visits during the school year. The book or rather idea for the research project that led to the book grew out of one of those visits.

One afternoon, after school had ended for the day and the halls were quiet, I was walking past a classroom in the middle school and noticed one of our teachers conferencing with a student. I stood at her door and watched. It was one of those moments that just struck me: her body posture and visible interest in him, his curiosity and what seemed like his delight in sharing his draft with her. It was intimate and real, and I felt that I had just glimpsed a true moment of what happens when teaching and learning take place. I had the sense that this kind of learning does go on in all sorts of classrooms in all sorts of schools but that it is rarely visible. My desire to document the ways teaching and learning of writing were unfolding in the Shoreham-Wading River school district was born at that moment.

To secure funding, I wrote a grant to the National Institute of Education, but this time around, I knew I wasn't going to impose a scientific model meant for laboratory experiments on a school setting. I was not going to control the variables as I had been instructed to do in my dissertation. I was, instead, going to use the methods anthropologists use for studying cultures which include becoming a participant-observer, taking fieldnotes, and working collaboratively with the participants in the culture to construct a view of their universe that resonates with them.

I also knew that this time around, I would not be a distant researcher. My coresearcher on the project, Nancy Wilson, and I knew from the beginning that everything we would write would be funneled through our own sensibilities, our own points of view, and our own values. Our goal was not to write an objective report but rather to bring stories of the classroom to life in a way that would reflect our voices.

WOE: You're not taking the personality of the observer out of the equation. You're not disguising the fact that you are Sondra Perl in the room, not "the researcher."

PERL: Yes, that's right. I could not pretend that I was a valueless and faceless recorder of classroom events or that I did not have particular preferences and predilections in the way I see the world. I could not pretend that who I am as a person would not influence what I saw and what I wrote down. I thought it was far wiser and far more honest to show myself as part of the equation. If readers can get a sense of who I am and begin to trust my voice, then they can decide for themselves if the stories I am telling ring true. Given the same setting, another researcher with other values and views might certainly have told different stories.

WOE: You write, "Writing only develops through the development of the writer." And these young people you worked with were obviously developing. I think college writers develop, too, but you might not see it so dramatically. Again, you're on the edge of psychotherapy, teaching them writing but helping them become different people through writing.

PERL: I can't ignore the human element when teaching writing. To me, there's not a lot of difference among different groups of writers, those in high school, college, graduate school, or adults out of school. Whenever writers gather together to read their work aloud and to listen attentively to one another, something special can happen. There is a unique kind of fellowship in writing groups; they encourage a kind of dialogue that is rare in educational settings. When they are working well, writing groups allow for the development of individual voices and at the same time for the improvement of writing. People learn from and with one another. They come to appreciate one another. It's both human and academic. There's humor and there's tears. And I don't think it is dependent upon age or grade level.

WOE: Different people bring out their commitment and passion in different ways.

PERL: Yes, that appears to be as true for writers as it is for teachers. The problem for Ross, the teacher in *Through Teachers' Eyes* who had a dismal year, was that he was trying to teach like his wife, Diane. He was working against his own grain. He is a natural performer and when he tried to squelch that part of himself based on the erroneous assumption that the writing process approach required a more laid-back kind of teaching, he failed in his efforts.

WOE: So performers are still allowed to be performers and use that as their strength as a teacher?

PERL: That's what Ross taught us. We came to understand that it's not the approach or style a teacher has that matters as much as what is being communicated to students through that style. If teachers can see the writer in the student, believe that the writer will emerge, and communicate this faith to the student, the actual pedagogical style may not matter all that much. James Herndon once called it believing in secret fly-fish and continuing to cast our lines even when we can't see them. This is why I say it's our stance as teachers as much as anything we do that makes the difference in our classrooms.

WOE: What did Ross think of the book when it came out?

PERL: Ross repeatedly told me that I was too kind, that I made him look better than he was. But what's interesting is that Ross received more letters from teachers around the country than anyone else in the book. So many teachers thanked him for allowing a story of a bad year to be told. They felt reassured and heartened that a bad year did not mean one was a permanent failure. And it is clear in the book that Ross learned from his mistakes and went on to have more productive and powerful years of teaching.

WOE: I was struck that the writing in all six teachers' classes crossed genres. The students wrote poetry, essays, memoirs—whatever. That seemed so unlike college writing courses, where we limit the genre. Should we be offering more genre inclusiveness in college writing?

PERL: If it were up to me, the answer would be a resounding yes. I don't know why including other genres goes against the grain of what is traditionally thought of as academic discourse. I've always thought that one learns how to write a strong expository essay by comparing it to other genres. Once one understands how the essay differs from a poem or a narrative or a letter, one can exploit its strengths for certain kinds of writing. Classrooms in which students are encouraged to take a theme and explore it in four or five different genres enable them to see the range of possibilities as well as the strengths and weaknesses of different genres. It is working from the richness of genres rather than limiting instruction to only one that makes most sense to me.

WOE: Recently I had lunch with Jerry Murphy, the general editor of the Landmark Essay series, and he mentioned that *On Writing Process* was the bestselling volume in the series. Why do you think this is?

PERL: I don't know, but I am willing to speculate: I think the book is unique in that it presents a mini-history of the process movement. Many of the articles I selected are known individually, but there is no other single volume that details the diverse places the process movement came from or lays them out chronologically.

WOE: In 2004 you published *Felt Sense*, with a CD. I assume there was some sort of shock at the idea of this book that asserts we write with our bodies and not just our minds.

PERL: This question harkens back to your question about feminist pedagogy because another thing Michelle Fine talked about was how important it is to recognize that we are embodied, that knowing and feeling are rooted in the body. Isn't it obvious that the writing we do emerges not only from our minds but also from our bodies? My book *Felt Sense* explains how this happens and what it takes to access the wisdom of the body.

I learned about felt sense by studying and working with Gene Gendlin, who is both a philosopher and a psychotherapist. Gene points out that when you're struggling with something and you don't quite have the words, you can slow down, breathe, and tune into your body. You can become very quiet, and if you're patient, the words to describe what you're struggling with will come. Gene developed a set of guidelines to help people access this realm, what he sometimes refers to as 'the unsaid' or 'the not yet said.' When I was working on my dissertation, I realized that my inexperienced writers were also struggling to find words. They would pause and they would get quiet. It seemed to me they were also engaging in this process Gene described. So I began to experiment in my classrooms and find ways to adapt what Gene had done in his field to help writers find what they wanted to say in writing. I created what I call the Guidelines for Composing, which I have used in undergraduate and graduate classes and in Writing Project institutes for many years.

WOE: And they're in the appendix of *Through Teachers' Eyes*.

PERL: Yes, they are in the back of that book and they also comprise the second chapter of *Felt Sense*. But the most useful thing about the book, I think, is that the Guidelines are also available on the CD so that teachers can use them in classrooms with their students and writers can use them at home on their own.

WOE: Peter Elbow once said he doesn't freewrite that much himself anymore because he has internalized the process. Do you use your own guidelines for composing or is that more for other people, less expert writers?

PERL: That's an interesting question. I think the Guidelines can be put to wonderful use in classrooms. I've adapted them to help graduate students find research topics. I've used them in creative writing classes to help students write poems. But with my own writing, like Peter, I have internalized the process.

WOE: *On Austrian Soil* is a teaching book that turns into a creative nonfiction book. It's a conversion experience book, a friendship book, a Holocaust book. Were you conscious of the strain of doing different genres?

PERL: I was very conscious of it. Austria represented a real crossing of borders for me. So my goal in writing was to have the book's style mirror this crossing. The problem came with marketing. "Where does this fit?" was the question most frequently asked. "Where does it belong on the bookshelf—in Holocaust studies or in education?" In memoir or research? Somehow it couldn't be all of the above.

WOE: When it turned into a friendship book, I wondered about the role of love in teaching, about how you seem to teach out of love. I had a teacher of mine who said there are two kinds of teachers, those who teach out of love and those who teach out of fear.

PERL: For me, love is the underpinning of teaching. But the meaning of love probably differs for different teachers. There are those who teach out of love of subject matter, those who teach out of love of interaction and connection, those who teach out of love of the students whose voices and personalities light up the classroom. Sadly, there are also those who don't teach out of love at all, for whom teaching is merely a job. For me, I think, it's a mix of all three loves, but I can't not admit that in just about every course I teach, it's the students who touch my heart.

WOE: So *On Austrian Soil* is really as much about how this experience changes you as it is about how this experience changes the students.

PERL: Yes it is. I went on a journey I could not have predicted before it began, and I think the teachers did too. Raising the question of the meaning of their history to teachers whose parents were implicated in Hitler's Third Reich was risky. I knew that I was, as I said earlier, crossing borders, trespassing on certain well-defined boundaries. But I couldn't pretend with these teachers, especially in a writing classroom where the professor writes and also invites others to write from the heart.

WOE: When did you decide that your experience in Austria was going to be a book? And how did the decision that it was going to be a book affect what you did?

PERL: After my first trip, I couldn't stop talking about what happened. It haunted me. When the opportunity to work with the same group of teachers arose, I knew I had to return. At that point, I realized the story was larger than I had at first recognized and that it would make sense to keep a journal. That was the beginning of the book.

WOE: How have the people in the class responded to the book now that it's published?

PERL: In general, they have been very supportive. Most came to the book talks I gave both in Vienna and Innsbruck. Many stay in touch with me. Whatever hard parts they had to go through and whatever they initially felt about the questions I asked, by now, I think, they consider me a colleague and a friend, which is certainly how I see them as well. And many of them now choose to teach about the Holocaust in ways they would not have considered prior to my work with them. Many of them now feel a sense of social responsibility not only about the past but also more importantly about the future.

WOE: Can you talk about the Holocaust Educators Network that this book has led to?

PERL: When I wrote this book, I couldn't have known where it would lead. I didn't expect myself to be doing Holocaust work. But the book came to the attention of a small nonprofit organization in New York that was looking to create an educational project for teachers. When the leaders of the foundation found me, I couldn't have been more delighted. After I left Austria, I had become a student of the Holocaust. I had started to teach interdisciplinary seminars to undergraduates, and what they proposed to me was exactly what I had been hoping to do for the next decade of my academic career.

They wanted to fund a Holocaust education project for teachers. I wanted to combine my commitment to teaching about the Holocaust with my long-standing interest in and experience with teacher training. Out of our initial conversations in 2005, I founded the Holocaust Educators Network. I enlisted the National Writing Project as a partner, and for the past four years, I have been able to invite 24 NWP teachers from all over rural America to New York for a two-week summer seminar on Reading, Writing and Teaching the Holocaust. We are now branching out. We will be running a Leadership Institute this summer and funding five teams of teachers to begin their own satellite seminars for teachers in their states. Our agenda has also become larger. We now include a focus on other genocides, we are looking to help teachers put action projects related to issues of social justice in place in their classrooms and communities, and we welcome applications from teachers committed to this work who may not be members of the National Writing Project.

WOE: I wanted to end by talking just about your work with Mimi Schwartz on *Writing True: The Art and Craft of Creative Nonfiction*. Can you talk about why you decided to do this book and what it tries to do?

PERL: Sure. Mimi had written a textbook once before, but I never had. I always thought textbooks were too formulaic. And I still tend not to use them. So the challenge for us was to write a textbook that would speak in a conversational tone and that would avoid formulas. We wanted to write as writers to other writers about creative nonfiction: what it is, how to do it, why it matters, what the issues are and so on. We wanted students to feel respected and we wanted teachers to feel as if they are also our audience, that we are putting something in their hands that they can learn from and use well. So that's what we tried to do. We're pretty happy with the result and in general the feedback has been good.

WOE: What's your new project?

PERL: I just finished, with Charles Schuster, *Stepping on My Brother's Head and Other Secrets Your English Professor Never Told You: A College Reader*. Charles and I invited 10 well-known professors of college writing to write something that they had never before revealed to anyone who knows them. Our goal was to create a reader for freshman comp classes or for upper-level seminars on the essay or on creative nonfiction that would engage students with surprising stories—stories that are personal, funny, poignant, and revealing—and by being so engaged also encourage them to write.

We took the title from Charles's essay since he is the one who stepped on his brother's head. His humorous story is followed by another humorous tale told by Lad Tobin, who details an escapade where, as an adult, he challenges himself to break the law by sneaking into a multiplex theater and viewing five first-run films for the price of one. The book moves from there into increasingly serious stories about people wanting to understand their pasts. Mary Pinard writes about learning to fly on a trapeze. Mike Rose writes about revisiting his hometown of Altoona, Pennsylvania, and also revisiting family secrets. Rebecca Fairy writes about a mysterious great-grandmother, and I reveal a range of family secrets through poems I have secretly written over the years.

DEIRDRE MCCLOSKEY

Deirdre McCloskey is Distinguished Professor of Economics, History, English, and Communication at the University of Illinois at Chicago. She has written 16 books, edited 7 more, and published some 400 articles large and small (her Joyce Carol Oatsean level of productivity makes it hard to be sure of the current number). McCloskey has received six honorary doctorates and is well known for arguing that the field of economics should be focused more on historical, naturalistic, and narrative analyses than on mathematical proofs. In the 1980s and early 1990s, when she was Donald McCloskey, she wrote If You're So Smart: The Narrative of Economic Expertise *(1990),* Knowledge and Persuasion in Economics *(1994), and* The Rhetoric of Economics *(1998). The books reveal the unacknowledged rhetorical side of economics. Superbly written ("slashing and witty" according to* The New York Review of Books*), the books are full of humor, stories, and wisdom. In 1999 she published* Crossing: A Memoir, *an account of her transition, at the age of 53, from male to female. With typical precision and self-deprecating humor, she has described herself as a "literary, quantitative, postmodern, free-market, progressive Episcopalian Midwestern woman from Boston who was once a man." Her latest books include* How to be Human Though an Economist *(2000),* The Secret Sins of Economics *(2002),* The Cult of Statistical Significance: How the Standard Error Costs Us Jobs, Justice, and Lives *(2008),* The Bourgeois Virtues: Ethics for an Age of Capitalism *(2006), and, in 2010,* Bourgeois Dignity: Why Economics Can't Explain the Modern World. *She has two additional volumes drafted in the* Bourgeois *series; these will further her argument that economic progress and modernity during the industrial revolution were less a product of new markets, trade, and innovation, but more a function of rhetoric: words and persuasive devices used to communicate about and ultimately approbate markets, free enterprise, and the bourgeoisie itself.*[1]

—Grant Eckstein

---

1 McCloskey, Deirdre N. "Bio." *Provcentia*. McDonald Magazine, 16 Dec. 2015. Web. 16 Dec. 2015.

"Humanomics"

John Boe and Ed Kahn

Spring 2012

WOE: Can you define the rhetorical approach to economics?

MCCLOSKEY: It's the study of how people in a strange and word-hostile field actually persuade each other. Any field of study or of practice has an official rhetoric, declaring that you must persuade your audience with statistical significance or Lacanian readings or whatever. Then there's the *actual* rhetoric and hermeneutics, the writer's tricks and the reader's habits of understanding. A study of rhetoric in economics is not merely an exercise in stripping away foolishness—though Lord knows there's plenty. It's a matter chiefly of becoming serious about the conversation. During the 1980s we started the "rhetoric of science," the scrutiny of the very words and persuasive devices, whether or not officially admitted.

In the past couple of years, though, what has hit me is that rhetoric also applies to the economy. I think it is a more important discovery than the older one that economists, like everyone else, depend on metaphors and stories. Economists are trained to believe that language in markets and businesses doesn't matter. But every noneconomist knows that language does matter. Game theory says that the language out in the economic world is mere "cheap talk," *mere* rhetoric in the newspaper sense of the word. Say the economists, "It doesn't matter what people say." Such an antihumanistic attitude is, I increasingly think, grossly scientifically mistaken.

WOE: How do you do a rhetorical analysis of the *economy*?

MCCLOSKEY: The same way you do a rhetorical analysis of *Paradise Lost* or of the latest article in the *Journal of Economic Behavior and Organization*: you watch how people write, how they use their language to achieve their persuasive ends—or how sometimes they forget their ends, or in the enthusiasm of speaking come to serve transcendent ends. Amazingly, it took me a quarter of a century after beginning my studies of the rhetoric of economics as an academic field to realize—as my more-wise friends like Arjo Klamer and Jack Amariglio kept telling me—that *the economy* is rhetorical. I am a very slow learner.

Examples of the importance of language in the economy abound. An employee of Japan Air realized that the company could make a great deal of money by shipping blue fin tuna for sushi from Nova Scotia to Japan. So much was the silent, cost-benefit, unspeaking, narrowly economic calculation. But then he commenced talking, and talking, and talking. To close the deal he spent months, for example, playing cards with the fishermen in Nova Scotia. *Of course* businesspeople talk. The talk is not merely sales or advertising—though commercial free speech is not to be scorned. Most of the talk is management, which in a free society must be a matter largely of persuasion instead of violence; and in a progressing society the talk is, as the rhetoricians say, invention.

About a third of the books in the business section of the airport bookstall are rhetorics: how to persuade your customers, your bankers, your employees, yourself that what you're trying to do is golden. A wider indicator is that one quarter of national income is earned from sweet talk—not orders or information or physical action but mere persuasive talk. Yet we as teachers are supposedly just "conveying" information. That's the rhetorical theory espoused by journalists and boards of regents. It's silly. On the contrary: we are trying to *persuade* our college kids to have an intellectual life. So too is a boss or a foreman or a banker *persuading* free people to get on the program.

WOE: Can you talk a little bit about what you took from—what you "stole" from (to employ a metaphor you have used)—Lanham and Booth and other people in rhetoric? It's so rare that someone in another field actually reads the people in my field.

MCCLOSKEY: The feeling of neglect is widespread in composition and rhetoric, and as you say the feeling is not paranoid. In most colleges the philosophy department is on the top floor and composition is in the basement. It was that way at Iowa. In the so-called English-Philosophy Building, the Philosophy department was at the top, then English, then way down at the bottom, Rhetoric. The philosopher pursued a critique of pure reason, the English professors (when not taking political poses about an economics they know nothing about) a critique of judgment. The critique of rhetoric that Kant should have written was scorned. The English-Philosophy Building was close to the Iowa River, and often in the spring the Rhetoric offices in the basement would flood. That's how much the university cared about such an excellent and useful department!

The blessed Wayne Booth made it all happen for me. In the 1970s I had a reputation among the economists at the University of Chicago of being slightly less barbarous than the rest of them. A low standard. Booth ran an undergraduate program called Philosophy, Rhetoric and Law, and in the fall of 1979 he asked me, "Will you give a talk in January on the rhetoric of economics?" "Sure," I replied amiably. "Glad to. Great idea. Uh . . . but what's 'the rhetoric of economics'?" I can remember his look of alarm. He told me to read his own *Modern Dogma and the Rhetoric of Assent,* Toulmin's *The Uses of Argument,* Perelman's and Olbrechts-Tyteca's *The New Rhetoric.* I somehow also got into the list Polanyi's *Personal Knowledge,* and over Christmas I read all four in my father-in-law's house in Vermont. They came as a revelation, and this former positivistic materialist was truly launched on the sea of rhetoric. I even became an Alta-Conference-goer, and would like now to do it again, for old time's sake. Much later I hitched up with people like Dick Lanham and Stan Fish and Jim White.

Before rhetoric, in those late 1970s, though tenured there, I was getting more and more uneasy with the Chicago School of Economics. I was not against its conclusions. Nor am I now. I'm a free-market lady, the sole libertarian in our fine Department of English at UIC, and routinely if inaccurately lumped with the merely two other "conservatives" in my beloved Department of History. But the *arguments* for the Chicago-School conclusions struck me increasingly as phony. "Oh, we have run a statistical regression and the slope comes out this way, therefore . . . ." They always expressed their claims as if the world or the data was "consistent with the hypothesis" that everyone is perfectly rational. Funny thing: at Chicago the world *always* cooperated with the rationality hypothesis (the new field of behavioral economics has finally started to find otherwise, even there). I believe that people *are* pretty rational, and anyway evolutionary pressures will arrive at the best hotels or autos or barber shops winning out, usually. But—I knew from the inside that the scientific arguments in support—the "warrants" as Steve Toulmin of blessed memory put it—had little to do with how the conclusions were formed.

I had gotten all my degrees at Harvard, and Harvard economics in the 1960s was fiercely anti-Chicago (now the two schools have merged). From inside Harvard I knew that *its* arguments were phony too. Not always wrong; but always phony. Both Chicago and Harvard, I concluded, came to their conclusions from politics or from beauty or from authority. I wanted them to start realizing how they were actually arguing, in order, as Kenneth Burke put it, *ad bellum purificandum,* to lead us by rhetorical self-awareness out of mere warfare. Needless to say—disciplines are conservative—economists haven't paid much attention to such a humanistic point.

WOE: You don't specialize as much as many people. In my own field I see how narrowly people read—for example, the English professor who only writes about Faulkner for forty years. There is an economic advantage to specialization in the academy. How do we change it so people don't have to specialize quite so much?

MCCLOSKEY: We have deans who were once English and chemistry professors who talk in just such a hard-nosed, economistic way. They think, "We've got to specialize: the hard-nosed economics says so." They talk about centers of excellence—an excuse to fire people in important fields like linguistics or geography or education or rhetoric. Yet what the deans have wrong is precisely the economics. You have to specialize, sure. *But then you have to trade.* But the deans kill the trade, every time. They are protectionists, protecting the invisible college of specialists in econometrics and algebraic topology against having to compete with any other way of thinking. It's like specializing in making kelly-green golf shoes that no one wants to buy, then piling them up in the back yard. Lots of fields specialize without trading—for example, economics (the science of trading).

If we're going to do it right we've got to get people talking to each other so that you and I can learn from sociologists and physicists and medical doctors and so on, and they can learn from us. A field will have its special topics, sure. Got it. But it also draws on general topics (*koinoi topoi*), which we can help each other handle more honestly. We need to take rhetoric seriously, as my former colleagues still do at Iowa in the Project on Rhetoric of Inquiry, Poroi (it means "ways and means" in Greek, being the plural of "river fords": it's a coinage I am especially proud of). It gets you such mutual learning, and is a much better premise for an interdisciplinary conversation than the aggressive trading of expertise of most substantive seminars. You can analyze the rhetoric an engineer or a historian is using even if you know nothing of her field in substance.

WOE: Is there any hope in getting the academy to start doing that?

MCCLOSKEY: Not much, alas. Many people understand more or less uneasily the excessive specialization of kelly-green golf shoes, and want to do something about it. But then the deans start worrying about the rankings of their departments, rankings that force uniformity on intellectual life. A few years ago for example, Notre Dame destroyed its excellent Marxoid and institutionalist department of economics and replaced it with a drearily conventional one. We call it in economics the "median voter theorem": the mediocre *middle* sets the standard, because they live happily around the 50% that tips a majority. A recent provost at UIC was a chemist and was obsessed with seeing more of us in such confidence games as the American Academy of Arts and Sciences—I call it, in honor of its stunning geographical bias, and to the irritation of my friends who are members, the "Cambridge and Princeton Academy of Arts and Sciences." The median voters rule, and originality is crushed. Deans always begin their time in office talking about international studies and interdisciplinarity. Then they get worried about the plumbing diagram of the university, and how many credit hours this or that "unit" produces. And so they murder the *inters*.

John Nelson, a political philosopher, and I in the early 1980s formed Poroi, which at one point had a hundred faculty members involved from all fields, from medicine, engineering, English, communication, rhetoric, law, and so forth. We'd have a seminar every week. That's one tip, to have a seminar not once a month but every week. In the seminar you would present something in draft, in your own field, like in engineering. The paper would always be circulated beforehand. The subject of the seminar was not the engineering or the medicine but the style of argument in your paper. If an audience member didn't know any math, she could nonetheless follow what was happening rhetorically in a math paper. She could look at the words in between: "It is obvious that. . . ." or "This comes out of the following problem. . . ."

It was I say a good premise for truly interdisciplinary seminars. But getting support for it was hard. Very hard. We didn't need much, a little photocopying money and salary for an administrator. But, oh my God! We'd go to endless meetings with deans and provosts, and explain it over and over again to people who thought only of the plumbing diagram and the rankings. "It's like the Iowa Writer's Workshop," we'd say hopefully, "something that Iowa could be very strong in, something new, something no one has ever done. It involves a bunch of faculty. It's becoming quite well known." They would sit there and say, "Mm hmm. What *department* should it be in?"

WOE: One department has to get the credit. But there's also no way to measure the benefits. And administrators are typically obsessed with measurement.

MCCLOSKEY: You're telling me! That's why I, as a certified quantifier, like to torture the deans with books showing that their quantities are rubbish. My current book, just out, is called *Bourgeois Dignity: Why Economics Can't Explain the Modern World*. Yet I like numbers, and if they're decisive, I want to hear about them. But the book is arguing that a lot of the easy-to-measure things—foreign trade, slavery, imperialism and so on—have nothing to do with the explosion of innovations like reinforced concrete or the University of Berlin that made our world. (There isn't anything about high science in concrete, by the way. It had to do with ingenuity and the idea of an engineer.)

WOE: Often when I read you, even about topics I know little about—statistical significance and blackboard economics and social engineering—I keep thinking of *The Emperor's New Clothes*, and you're like the little boy who points out the obvious but neglected truth.

MCCLOSKEY: By the way in that story everyone says it's a little boy, but I've checked the Danish.

WOE: It's a girl?

MCCLOSKEY: It's a child, *et barn*, which as in German is neuter. It's not a boy (*en dreng*)—it's a child. And I'm sure it was a girl (*en pige*), because girls have more sense!

WOE: Ha! In spite of your devastating critique of these leaders in economics, you nonetheless say that they are good economists. I would like to hear from you how do you hold the two things in balance—that the methods of the economists are faulty but nonetheless they are good economists? Is it that they tell good economic stories?

MCCLOSKEY: They tell good economic stories; they use good, fruitful economic analogies. The most famous one is Gary Becker, who approached Al Harberger at a cocktail party where everyone else was drunk except for Gary. Gary came up to Al and said, "You know, Al, children are like durable goods." Al (now at UCLA) was and is a famous expert on durable goods, especially in his work in the '50s and '60s. He knew about automobiles and refrigerators, and here was this kid saying children are like refrigerators. It's sort of nuts, in the way metaphors like "the whale's road" (the sea) often are. But it was fruitful.

WOE: It was a successful metaphor.

MCCLOSKEY: Yes. Becker's poetic fancy—and all scientific theories are metaphorical or narrative fancies—was successful because it's so rich in implications: for example, that children if they are durable goods can be looked on as investments, and fertility behavior can be brought under the economics of investment. What the economists don't realize is that a metaphor can be rich even in its disanalogy, even in its failure. You say children are long lived, they're expensive to produce—kind of like a fridge. But unlike a fridge, they're objects of affection and concern. Often in the failure you can see more than in the success. It's one of the many uses of a literary-rhetorical sensibility in economic science.

Metaphor is one of the big problems with analytic philosophy. A linguistic philosophy that doesn't have an account of the force of metaphors and stories is never going to capture human language or logic. It's the deep problem with the project of reducing language to symbolic logic. The classic example that Stan Fish and a number of others have talked about is the proposition that France is hexagonical. Is it true or false? Well, true for some purposes, false for others. If you're designing (*hélas*) a Maginot line, then the hexagon idea is helpful, and it might even draw your attention to the other side of the hexagon, Belgium.

WOE: Can you talk a little bit about your writing process and how you're able to get so much done?

MCCLOSKEY: One thing: don't ever publish any item only once! Seriously, though, for a long time I wrote books by having a bunch of articles and making a book out of it.

But I've stopped doing that, partly because I have become so annoyed in my old age with the journal-and-referee system (which is deeply corrupt and stupid: more of the median-voter theorem). I've started doing throughwritten books. You write the whole book rather than collect the articles. It's the humanistic rather than the social scientific procedure. *The Bourgeois Virtues* (2006) was through written as was *Bourgeois Dignity* (2010). Maybe that's why they're so long. Once I knew how to write short books. Now all my books are 500 pages—it's getting out of hand! But again to be serious, I have learned a great deal from studying books on writing.

WOE: What books?

MCCLOSKEY: From Richard Lanham's books and from lots of others. I have a whole row of writing books upstairs, which I studied as though I were studying mathematics or French grammar. I realized, as many people don't, that there's a technique to writing that can be learned, just as there's a technique to regression or cost-benefit analysis. So I got obsessed with that about thirty years ago. One book that was extremely influential for me was Robert Graves and Alan Hodge's *The Reader Over Your Shoulder: A Handbook for Writers of English Prose* (1943: It is a testament to British civilization that such a book was published with rationed paper in the middle of a great war). Here is their technique: they would grab a book lying around and start to read. When they got to a place where they lost their way, they'd try to figure out what was wrong. By looking at good and bad writing they discerned the rules (as Joe Williams puts it) of clarity and grace. They watched writers failing to put the emphatic word or phrase at the end of the sentence, burying it in the middle. And on and on. I was also bred to Strunk and White, and use daily—nay, every minute—their command to Express Parallel Ideas in Parallel Form. I came from a literary family, and my training in economics was never quite able to persuade me that words don't matter.

WOE: I love what you say in your wonderful little book, *Economical Writing*, about the importance, for example, of repetition. I've been repeating that advice to my students. I'd seen that idea expressed before, but never so well.

MCCLOSKEY: You are very kind, but it is merely a theorem provable from Strunk and White on H.W. Fowler in 1908: Avoid Elegant Variation. The example I give in the book is "economic development," "economic growth," "economic change," "modernization," and "industrialization." In one paragraph people will use all of those expressions to mean the same thing. You come out of the paragraph thinking, "What the hell was all *that* about? As Fowler said, "Many writers of the present day abound in types of variation that are not justified by expediency, and have consequently the air of cheap ornament." I favor getting your words and ideas lined up once and for all, and not being terrified by some schoolteacher's rule against repetition.

WOE: Repetition is a way to make a paragraph coherent.

MCCLOSKEY: Right. The pattern is AB, BC, CD. If you do it too mechanically it looks crazy, but if you keep in mind that you're trying to link ideas—that once you use a word it's a good idea to use it again in the same meaning—it makes the writing cohere.

WOE: In *The Rhetoric of Economics*, you analyze other economists' writing, doing explications of economists' writing—like a close reading of Andrew Marvell poems, but with economics papers.

MCCLOSKEY: I learned it from you-all. I've learned over and over again from English professors, communications people, composition people that language is not a window. It's a gathering. It's a conversation.

WOE: I thought the introduction to the second edition of *Rhetoric and Economics* was probably the best introduction to a second edition I've ever read.

MCCLOSKEY: You are too kind.

WOE: It was so self-reflective. You decided that the deductive approach to the first edition was a failure and what it needed was an inductive approach, so you switched the book's organization around and started with the particulars and then the generalizations that followed would make sense to the reader. You were very frustrated with the response to the first edition because people never got to the meat.

MCCLOSKEY: They thought it was a philosophical point I was making. And I *was* making philosophical points, rather trivial ones. But the main point was practical, what the linguists call pragmatics—how the language actually works.

WOE: I love the attention you pay to metaphor. It seems to me that early on you criticized a lot of masculine metaphors—for instance, economics as war and as football.

MCCLOSKEY: That was before Deirdre.

WOE: Yes, before Deirdre, writing as Donald. You had a feminist point of view from the start. Maybe that's why you call your interest in composition intellectual cross-dressing. I love that phrase.

MCCLOSKEY: My women feminist friends often express the regret that I became a woman.

WOE: They think you could have helped them more as a man?

MCCLOSKEY: They said, "You were Donald, this macho kind of guy screaming at people about being unfair to women. That's much more helpful to us than another one of us whining about not getting promoted." Sorry, ladies: I can't help you!

WOE: You mention several times that love is part of economics. Could you talk about that?

MCCLOSKEY: Love is part of the economy, as I argue at length in *The Bourgeois Virtues*. You can't run a creative business on prudence only—on mere monetary incentives alone. But to go back to my earlier work on economics as an academic field: I slowly realized that the way a seminar works well and is really helpful is if the people *love* each other. So affection makes for real intellectual exchange. If you hate each other or if you're strangers, then you spend the seminar posturing and shouting. We've all had this experience. You remember how it is on the first day of an academic conference? Imagine a small fifteen-person or thirty-person intellectual get-together that lasts for several of days.

Early on, you guys will be displaying your peacocks' tails. But then you have a few drinks and you get to talking to each other about this, that, and the other. By the second day you're actually engaging with each other intellectually, saying, "Gee, you may be right, but how about this other point" and "I don't think so because here's how it goes"—which is impossible among strangers. I said the same to Hunter Rawlings when he was my president at Iowa, way back, again before Deirdre. He said, "That's good, that's good. We've got to make room for more love." But he didn't do anything about it.

WOE: I really enjoyed your trilogy—*If You're So Smart, The Rhetoric of Economics and Knowledge* and *Persuasion in Economics*. The books seem made for somebody in my field. You explicitly compare economics to poetry, fiction, and philosophy. Can you summarize what you got out of those comparisons?

MCCLOSKEY: I'm glad you like them: most humanists find it old news that even economists are poets and novelists! In economics, I said, models are metaphors. The notion is a commonplace in some branches of the philosophy of science. So you can say that the housing market in Chicago is just like these supply-and-demand curves I can draw for you. But what's that all about? We go outside and don't see a big demand curve in the sky. It's a comparison of one realm of talk to another, a mathematical analogy to the area of social interaction called the housing market.

Stories are at the other extreme. They're metonymies. They're about things being contiguous. They are not about things being compared to each other but things being close to each other. The White House is close to executive power, so we say "the White House did such and such." Roman Jakobson, the great Slavic linguist at Harvard in the 1940s, made the point that metaphor and metonymy are at the ends of a spectrum. Stories go like this: once upon a time, then after that, after that, after that. They're causally connected if the story coheres, but they don't have to be. They can just be one damn thing after another. So you can tell the story of the First World War and it doesn't have to be thematized; you can just tell one damn thing after another.

The furious reaction among economic methodologists to such simple ideas as that a science like physics depends on metaphors and one like evolutionary biology on stories prompted me to write the third book. The economists and their ersatz philosophers said "No, no, we're not poets! We're not novelists! Don't tell us this! We're scientists! What are you talking about?" The reaction came from all over the place—from the left, from the right, and massively from the middle.

WOE: In the second book, *If You're So Smart*, you show how so much of economics and other scientific work is storytelling. How do you train people in storytelling? Especially, how do you get economists to be good storytellers if that's important?

MCCLOSKEY: The important skills are precisely what we don't teach. I've often thought that what we teach in graduate school is always slightly off the point. We teach economic theory as though it were existence theorems in mathematics. The actual theories that most of us use to think about the economy are little supply-and-demand curves and consumer surplus, very simple stuff. But we don't teach them how to tell stories—economic history and the intellectual history of economics have long been banished from the programs. We don't teach them how to think up new metaphors. The places in economic theory that should be occupied by such talk are filled up with terminally boring mathematics taken straight from the Math Department (in preference to the much more interesting math taught in engineering or physics).

WOE: But the ones who succeed somehow figure it out.

MCCLOSKEY: Robert Solow of MIT, the great economist of my teachers' generation, is an example (alas, I was never directly his student). He was an undergraduate at Harvard, a veteran of the Italian campaign. He didn't resist his education or throw it away, as many economists do. And so he allowed his science to merge with a graceful literary sensibility. (He's sometimes scientifically wrong, by the way. But never stupid or ugly in his error.)

Graduate schools of course train specialists. I'm all for that. They should actually know what they're talking about in economics narrowly conceived. But I would have a course or two that introduced graduate students to the wider intellectual world, the metaphors and stories. If they had a bad education, or ignored a good one, if they only studied math and didn't learn anything about literature, or if they went to a liberal arts college but actually didn't take anything but economics, they should learn so that later on they can approach economics with an appreciation of the rest of the culture. I give such a course at UIC—though most of my courses touch anyway on more than economics.

I had the experience of general education for specialists myself, accidentally. After my first year of grad school I decided to become an economic historian instead of a transportation economist. The economist Alexander Gerschenkron, my supervisor, supervised in a very light fashion, but he was a model. (His grandson, the writer Nicholas Dawidoff, wrote a fine biography about him, *The Fly-Swatter: Portrait of an Exceptional Character*.) Gerschenkron knew thirteen languages, he knew mathematics, he knew everything—we thought. I was once in his office, told to wait for him to come in. His office was complete chaos, things piled high, one of the great messes in academic life (Ralph Cohen in English at the University of Virginia and Leo Goodman in sociology at the University of Chicago have competed in this league). On top of a pile of stuff was a textbook on topology, and below it was some sort of book in Russian—I couldn't even read the title—and then there was some Greek poetry, and then down at the bottom was a copy of *Mad* magazine. I said to myself, "This is the kind of person I want to be!" The only teaching I did as a graduate student was in Harvard's undergraduate program called "Social Studies," where I had to read great sociologists and Marx to teach the kids. It took away my right as an ignorant economist to sneer at sociologists and Marxists. A couple of such courses should be compulsory in grad school. Fat chance!

WOE: Another thing that might also stand a fat chance of happening is your recommendation to teach ethics and speech morality in graduate school. How might we go about doing that?

MCCLOSKEY: In the old days, our teachers told it to us or showed it in such an exemplary form in their life and work that we caught on. But another strain developed after the war. James Watson, for example, brought a ruthlessness to scientific scholarship that was new and impolite, not what you should do. For example, Watson stole the key evidence for the structure of DNA from Rosalind Franklin, and celebrated his theft in *The Double Helix*. Nice guys finish last. But that's not a rule for a sustainable scientific or scholarly community.

WOE: In your book with Stephen Ziliak, *The Cult of Statistical Significance* (2008), in regards to R.S. Fisher, but also in *The Bourgeois Virtues* in regards to Kant, I thought you use *ad hominem* very effectively, but what you did is nonstandard, to put it mildly.

MCCLOSKEY: People claim it's nonstandard, but it's not. They say, "Oh yeah, we'd never use *ad hominem* arguments," but in the Faculty Club they're saying, "That guy's a terrible jerk." Scholarly disagreements are almost always *ad hominem*, when there's real disagreement. In *The Cult of Statistical Significance*, Ziliak and I call it The Stupidity Hypothesis—"the other person doesn't agree with me because she's *stupid*." If we're polite, we say "misled." But really we mean that even though we're making a very simple and conclusive argument, she doesn't get it. "What's wrong with you? Aren't you an economist, or aren't you a historian? Don't you understand?" I think it's un–self-aware to say there's not *ad hominem* going on all the time. Life is politics.

WOE: I thought you demolished Kant in a charming way.

MCCLOSKEY: Kant, the son of a saddler, rises to revolutionize philosophy. I admire him extravagantly for that. But he had no rationale for his ethics, though fiercely asserting that he attended only to the claims of reason.

WOE: When you talk about the postmodern, you say "meta-modern." Can you talk about in what sense you consider yourself postmodern and what that means?

MCCLOSKEY: It's simply to be against the modernism in which all we progressive intellectuals of the 1950s were educated. My views against it have moderated a little in the past decade. I've lived since 2000 on Dearborn Street in Chicago, which is a virtual museum of modern skyscraper art. Modern architecture starts here in Chicago. I was quite sure when I first returned to Chicago that I was against modern architecture. (Architecture is, of course, where the term "modernism" comes from.)

I hated Mies van der Rohe. Now I belong to a club in which one fifth of the members are architects, and I've listened to them. So I started saying, "Whoops, I'm wrong about Mies." Philip Larkin, the English poet, railed against Pound, Picasso, and [Charlie "Bird"] Parker, who were in his opinion the murderers of modern arts, and the makers of modernism. But I've started to like modern jazz, and I even have returned to an early admiration for Pound too. As a poet. An editor. Early on.

But modernism has some nasty effects in the social sciences. I'm against modernism in its coercive form. It's a dogma. The dogma that there's such a thing as the Scientific Method—which we were all taught in high school—is, of course, to use a technical term, hooey. I started to learn so reading the four books at my father-in-law's house at the end of 1979. I suppose the problem is that I saw dogmatic modernism being used aggressively all the time. "We are modernist. We do it this way. Shut up."

WOE: I wanted to turn to your fascinating memoir *Crossing*. What made you bold enough to write it? It's so self-revelatory that I would think it took courage.

MCCLOSKEY: Courage isn't quite the word. I'm always looking out for books to write, and having such an unusual experience made it natural. I don't mean that sheer literary ambition was the main motivation, but it was a part. A bigger part was to write an open letter to my family—to my birth family, which after some exciting episodes came on my side; but to my marriage family, too, especially because it had already shown that it was alienated. (Nothing, though, has persuaded my former wife and my two grown children to forgive me. I have two grandchildren I've never seen.) A third motivation was professional: to explain myself to other academics.

It still sells, though it didn't make as much money as the University of Chicago Press hoped it would, and I'm embarrassingly behind in paying off the advance. The book got very good reviews, and then a few angry second-wave feminist excoriations. It seems to get assigned in college courses in gender studies and in American autobiography. I still get e-mails from women born women and from people transitioning. Not every day but about every fortnight or so. The women say, "Gosh, this is such an interesting reflection on what it means to be a woman." And the gender crossers have their own reasons to like the book.

WOE: How have your metaphors, speech, and thought changed since becoming a woman?

MCCLOSKEY: For one thing I got sharper on love. As economists we're told, in a manly way, "No use of the L word!" But organizations, departments, commercial relationships—they all depend to some degree on feelings of warmth. Recent theories of the origin of language stress that hominids went about in large groups requiring loving solidarity beyond the nuclear family, and therefore needed to talk about it. Prudence is an important virtue, as economists can teach us. But grass is prudent, in seeking light and water. Humans love.

The largest shock for me in changing gender was the quality of female friendship. Hundreds of women helped in my transition, and a few became deep friends. As a man I thought, "Oh jeez, that's kind of embarrassing. Women hugging and kissing each other, saying all the time how much they love each other." Most American men don't get deep friendship, though there are cultural variations. Dutch men, for example, are somewhat better at friendship than American men. I found that many people loved me and that love is very important to women.

WOE: Is it a coincidence that the *ad hominem* arguments came out more in your new gender role?

MCCLOSKEY: I don't know if they came out more. I think it was more merely getting older, and less willing to put up with nonsense: you know how old people are! I joke that I grew up . . . and became a woman. The older I get the more urgently I feel that I have to do what needs to be done—my insane project, chiefly, of defending capitalism for an audience who believes it needs a defense. Always at my back I hear / Time's chariot hurrying near. Who else will defend capitalism in a way that proposes a "humanomics"? Gotta do it.

WOE: Does Goldman and the financial crisis give you pause in the project?

MCCLOSKEY: I was acquainted with some of the people who caused the latest recession, the group that invented modern, mathematical financial theory. I ate with them, every lunchtime, in the bar of the faculty club at the University of Chicago. But as an economic historian I regard 2007–09 as just another, if rather severe, business cycle. Since 1800 there have been forty of them. And every time, even in the dreary 1930s, the poorest have come out of them better off.

So economics is not evil. It merely needs to realize that it is human. We need not more freakonomics or econometrics but humanomics. If true, a finding in humanomics—such as I claim in *Bourgeois Dignity*—that an ethical and rhetorical and ideological and conjective change made the modern world would be scientifically important. The Victorian travel writer and skeptic Alexander Kinglake suggested that every church should bear on its front door a large sign, "Important If True." So here. Economic history faces no more important question than why industrialization and the reduction of mass poverty first started, and especially why it continued. The continuation made us richer and freer and more capable of human achievement than our ancestors. The latest continuation—located most spectacularly in China and India, of all surprising places—shows that the whole world can be so.

If ideas and ethics and "rhetoric" contributed largely to such a happy result, then perhaps we should point our social telescopes also toward ideas and ethics and rhetoric. Looking fixedly at trade or imperialism or demography or unions or property law—very interesting though all of them are—will not do the whole of the scientific job. Ideas are the dark matter of history, ignored for a century or so, 1390–1980.

To be able to detect the dark matter, we will need a new, more idea-oriented economics, a "humanomics," which would admit that ethics permeates economic life and that language shapes an economy. For such a humanistic science of economics the methods of the human sciences would become as scientifically relevant as the methods of mathematics and statistics now properly are. Such a widened economic science would scrutinize literary texts *and* simulate on computers, analyze stories *and* model maxima, clarify with philosophy *and* measure with statistics, inquire into the meaning of the sacred *and* lay out the accounting of the profane.

It is not very difficult, as one can see in the education of graduate students. A bright humanist can learn enough mathematics and statistics in a couple of years to follow their uses in economics. A bright economist, with rather more difficulty, can in a couple of years learn enough about rhetoric and close reading to follow their uses in the English Department. What prevents such scientific cooperation is sneering ignorance, not the difficulty of the task.

DOUG HESSE

Like many in the field, Doug Hesse did not start out seeking a career in rhetoric and composition. His dissertation at the University of Iowa is titled The Story in the Essay *(1986) and combines rhetorical awareness with an emphasis on personal writing and literature. The writing program he went on to found at the University of Denver has garnered national recognition and serves as a model for building a faculty from across English studies of full-time non–tenure-track lecturers, of which the WOE interviewer was a member. Hesse has held leadership positions in many of the most important organizations within rhetoric and composition. He served as chair of CCCC, president of the Council of Writing Program Administrators, editor of* WPA: Writing Program Administration, *chair of the Executive Committee of the MLA Division of Teaching as a Profession, and as a member of the Executive Committee of NCTE, for which he served as president from 2013–2016. He continues to teach and direct the Writing Program at the University of Denver, where he is Professor of English.*

Hesse has written more than 50 essays and has coauthored four books, including the Simon & Schuster Handbook for Writers. *With his wife, nonfiction author Becky Bradway, he wrote the guide and anthology* Creating Nonfiction. *He edited a special issue of* College English *focused on creative nonfiction and has written about the relevance of creative writing pedagogies for composition. With personal anecdotes and a genuine sense of inquiry and commitment, Hesse's writing retains those essayistic qualities that first attracted his scholarly interest. His contribution to the essay* "Evocative Objects: Reflections on Teaching, Learning, and Living in Between," *cowritten with Nancy Sommers and Kathleen Yancey, has him thinking of how our students are somebody else's children, reflecting on the competing demands of work and relationships, and finally writing a letter to his then–six-year-old son who "mist" him while he was away at a conference.*[1]

—Eric Leake

---

1 Hesse, Doug, Nancy Sommers, and Kathleen Blake Yancey. "Evocative Objects: Reflections on Teaching, Learning, and Living in Between." *College English* 74.4 (2012): (325–50). Print.

"Cultivating Writerly Sensibilities"

Eric Leake

Spring 2013

WOE: How did you arrive at a career in rhetoric and composition? I don't imagine you started school with this in mind.

HESSE: I actually was a chemistry major at the University of Iowa. I was working really hard and I was getting Bs but had no framework for it and thought, "This is not good." I was looking through the catalog and saw that you could major in English, and I didn't know there was such a thing. I took expository writing and literature classes and was absolutely fascinated by all of this cool stuff that you could learn about writing—in particular, style. I especially loved the fact that we could spend 75 minutes talking about four sentences and still feel at the end of that hour that we didn't say everything that could be said—that was a great time.

I got into what was then a Master of Arts in Writing at the University of Iowa. That degree later became an MFA in nonfiction. They had a very catholic view of writing there—people were writing poetry, writing personal essays, doing whatever. It was all fine. So my view of writing was a very broad one. I was perplexed later when I was in the PhD program and reading about the literature/writing divide because I didn't experience that. It was probably there and I was probably naïve, but in my experience as a student you could of course do all these types of things.

WOE: At what point did you start identifying more with rhetoric and composition?

HESSE: When I went into the MA program I was very blue collar and pragmatic. I thought that there are probably jobs to be had teaching writing and especially first-year writing. If I'd had more guts I would have tried to be a writer. As a result, I was taking a lot of writing theory and pedagogy things at the same time. Before my PhD I started teaching at this tiny college, then Findlay College, in Ohio. At that time the English Department could have faculty meetings on the racquetball court; there were four of us. But I think it was finally when I became a writing director and all of a sudden I was not just worrying about my classes—where I thought I could indulge whatever I wanted to do—but I was responsible for a program, that I really started to identify with rhetoric and composition. It was pragmatism squared then.

WOE: I see that your dissertation is on the essay, which seems appropriate given your interests and writing style. How has that background and emphasis on nonfiction and craft influenced your view of rhetoric and composition?

HESSE: I'm just really interested in the usefulness of cultivating writerly sensibilities. I think of writing as a liberal art rather than as a service. This has caused all sorts of conflicts for me over the years because I sometimes feel duplicitous. On the one hand, shouldn't we just have students do interesting things with writing and go wherever that might take them? On the other hand, developing skills is important. Learning how to write for the academy doesn't seem like the most important kind of thing. And yet in programs that I've directed, it's been important, and I feel responsible to the larger university community that has instituted this requirement. I always find myself asking questions about our mission: Is it the identity of students as academic writers? Is it students as budding journalists? Is it students as belletristic essayists in all of the good senses of that term? I feel very split allegiances. Were I not directing a program and were I only teaching my own classes, I'm thinking my feelings would be quite a bit different.

WOE: When you speak of "the usefulness of cultivating writerly sensibilities," what exactly do you mean?

HESSE: It's both students as writers and readers. That writing takes a lot of work to do well, but it's worth the work. I think both of those notions are really important. I think they're important in terms of being a citizen in a democracy where issues are really complicated and yet the imperative seems to be to simplify them. But then also there are other corners of life as a citizen or as a worker or a reader where it's important to have some sense of what's going on with a text.

WOE: What kinds of relationship would you like to see among rhetoric and composition and the related fields of creative writing, literature, journalism, etc.?

HESSE: I think they're all really productively related. I understand why curricular turf has put these in separate camps. But one of the confusions and disservices we do to students is not inviting them to think about the relationships among these various kinds of writing. And the differences between them. There are differences between writing a short story and a news article. They're important and meaningful differences. Yet writing need not be so compartmentalized that students don't think of what techniques are common to both or what it means to write a short story about theme or plot X versus writing a personal essay about theme or plot X. For example, what does it mean for David Foster Wallace to go to the Illinois State Fair as a journalist but with a creative sensibility so that he goes both to take notes and also to make curiously strange and endlessly fascinating what he's seeing at the fair? Yeah, that's a sort of essay/memoir/piece of feature journalism/whatever, but it's informed by an interest in style and in how you plot the facts of life.

WOE: What are the most significant ways in which your views on writing have changed over the course of your career?

HESSE: Early on the personal essay was the filter through which everything else happened. I remember, though, showing up for my first teaching job. We had to exchange a set of papers. There were all of these notes: "your thesis is unclear" and "where are your topic sentences?" My sort of romantic view of writing—and I mean that in an honorific sense—was tempered by this vocabulary for talking about writing and the usefulness of rhetorical concepts. I've migrated from a fairly pure workshop notion of writing, a more "organic" sense of writing, to a more deliberative approach that includes teaching concepts and skills.

The next change for me came in the early '90s with the notions of discourse communities and genre theory. I thought these were important, too. I found genre theory pretty interesting because it could overlap with some literary theory, with the notion of writers working in traditions that they themselves didn't invent. There was the question of whether genre is determinative in some really profound sense or where creativity enters, even in the academic article. These became really fascinating ideas.

Most recently two things have captured my attention concerning writing. The first is obviously the interest in multimodal stuff if you're no longer writing for the page. The second has been almost a return of interest for me in creative nonfiction because I'm really fretting these days about what writing spaces are available to students. It's a concern about what our positions are as observers in the world and how those factor in writing. It's essayistic. Because finally, in a place where data and information are endless, it really is writerly consciousness that is, I think, the source of any originality. And so I've been really struck by assignments in which students are doing qualitative research and they're interviewing folks. But some of this, I think, is that you get to be a certain age and you start having remorse, like why didn't I thirty years ago have the gumption to become David Shields rather than Doug Hesse?

WOE: In an upcoming piece you describe your first-year writing course as a "service course for writers." That seems clear enough, although I can't recall having read such a description before. Can you say a little more about what you mean by that and how it relates to other views of first-year writing?

HESSE: It begins with how big of an identity you want to focus on. I would have to look and see the context of my exact phrasing, but historically and pragmatically, we could cast the first-year writing course as a course in academic writing. We've managed to complicate that in all sorts of reasonable ways.

It takes two forms. One is we posit some generic academic discourse: you know, thesis and support. We just figure that's the best common denominator we can come up with. Or, alternatively, we hypothesize about these genres within the academy. That's a very practical thing to do, but that's only one kind of way you could orient toward writing.

Another way is civic discourse and argument. We live in what one hopes to be a deliberative world, or at least a world in which opinions and ideas are shaped, so how do you transact in that area? Again I think we almost necessarily idealize that a little bit. Then obviously there remain those very romantic expressivists—and I'm somebody who has always worried about the ways we have reductively cast expressivism. It seems to me that something that was a service course for writers and writing would pay attention to the multifarious ways and roles that writing plays in our lives. Rather than trying to beef up people in producing certain forms of writing, we could be giving them lots of experiences, talking about what makes this a good example of writing X, and adding reflection about what that kind of writing experience has to do with other forms that they might produce or encounter.

WOE: Let's talk some about your teaching. First, how long have you been teaching?

HESSE: Oh, golly, thirty-three years.

WOE: Over those years, what are the most significant ways in which your views of teaching have changed?

HESSE: I don't know entirely if they've changed so much as certain features over time get foregrounded or backgrounded. Let me take four kinds of activities that are common in my teaching. One is workshop—the discussion in some fashion of student work in progress. The second is outright presentation—here is advice about writing. The third is discussion of other people's writing—model texts and such. And the fourth is in-class problems or challenges. I think I've always done some mixture of these things.

One of the things that has changed recently is that I do a lot more in class with setting up a problem or an issue, having students work on it for twenty minutes, and seeing what they come up with. For example, Tuesday in class students are doing some "primary research" that they're writing as an article for a popular magazine. I found an interesting article about child beauty pageants. It was a great combination of the writer observing some beauty pageants from the front, from backstage, and interviewing pageant participants, with lots of research. I went through that piece and extracted ten bits of information. Here are some quotations, here is a narrative description of a beauty pageant. I took that into class and I said, "Let's imagine that you're doing this thing and so far you've gleaned these notes. They're helter-skelter. Based on these, what will be the plot of your article and what other kinds of research do you have to do? You've got twenty minutes to sort these out." Then I put them in small groups. After that, I showed them the decisions this writer had made. It was an organic way of talking about the challenges that somebody working as a journalist and researcher faces in gathering and organizing notes without the consolation of the academic intro, review of literature, methods, but rather having to do something that's interesting to readers, who can choose to put down the piece or continue reading.

One of the challenges with this particular assignment is getting them to see research not as academic hoop jumping but as something somebody might do in other kinds of writing and to get them to think of journalists as researchers but in very different traditions. We still do all those other activities in class, but increasingly I find myself setting up scenarios, some of which they perform outside of class, and then using class time to do something that's a live problem and talk about it in the moment.

WOE: Part of what is appealing about that exercise is that it combines a rhetorical emphasis with an attention to craft.

HESSE: In a case like that people can say, "Well, let's use the *in medias res* approach." But there were three or four quotations or situations that could have started the piece. Once you're looking at the finished piece as it was published it just seems ordained or predestined. I'm trying to get to them to see that, no, he actually had two or three equally good options available, and he didn't use those; this one was great and it was published.

WOE: Why do you think it is that we're continually reading public accounts about the decline of student writing? What does that anxiety speak to?

HESSE: I think there are a lot of levels to this question. One is a misguided nostalgia, always imagining that things were better in the old days. I think a lot of people who are journalists and pundits see the old days through their personal experience and don't recognize that next to them in their high school class in the glory days were people who were struggling. It's a case of the victors writing history. I think another part of it is related to that. With the massive access to writing and publishing that people have these days, you see incredibly more varieties of writing than you ever did. It's public. Thirty years ago you had newspapers and magazines that could publish only so many letters to the editor. You didn't see then the hundreds of bizarre and frightening comments that you can see on a chat, not to mention the grammatical issues. The third thing—and this I think is more complicated—is the economics. In an era of globalization it's consoling in some ways to blame specific things for why people don't have jobs, and so I think there's a misguided idea that the schools are failing and somehow if the schools were doing a better job the economy would be in better shape. Maybe. But I guarantee you we could have the most perfect writers ever, and still economic forces are a lot bigger than that. I think it's that confluence of all those things.

We know that with the situation of writing and moving from the academy to workplaces, there is always going to be transfer gaps. You're always going to have that dissatisfaction. We need to better articulate for publics the complex ways that writing develops and how doing something like thinking about the way this beauty pageant article gets written actually has implications for writing memos at work, and we need to do that in a plausible and compelling way.

WOE: In what ways do you think writing can maintain its identity in a digital age when you have various forms of composing and remixing and content consumption on iPads and such?

HESSE: I do think that language as language, alphabetic literacy, can do things that other modes of writing can't do. It has ways of teasing out nuance, ways of making thinking explicit. The other thing, though—and I think this is probably more important—is to emphasize production. Not only do you see remixing now but also just shuttling. It's the difference between reposting something versus making "an original thing" or supplementing it through words or language. I don't denigrate at all when people say, "Thought you might find this interesting." But that's a different thing. You might just send people images that you think are cool, but are you making images yourself? Are you producing content? I find what we've seen happen fascinating. Back in the early '90s I was making websites, and you had to do all of this stuff. Then pretty soon you had templates and you could drop stuff in them. I think that's mostly good, but something is lost in the creative process. I think the way for writing to find its place in relation to these other things is to really emphasize the making of things and not only the analysis of things made. I find interesting the number of courses on visual rhetoric that are entirely analytic—and very smart and very compelling. But they really say, "Writing's relationship to this is to critique it or analyze it."

WOE: You've done a lot of work with contingent faculty issues. Can you point to anything that makes you optimistic that conditions for contingent faculty will improve?

HESSE: Yes and no. I think one of the things that's happening is there's a real increase in full-time positions. I recently did some consulting with an Ivy League university that has a lot of contingent faculty, and they were really interested in the model of things here at DU. This is happening enough, and people are realizing the value of having a more permanent faculty. That's some cause for optimism. The working conditions for contingent faculty are better. The downside of that—and this is what I worry about—is the difficulty in preserving a full sense of what it means to be a faculty member teaching writing. And that is, you need to be producing knowledge about writing at the same time that you're teaching writing. It doesn't have to be as a researcher necessarily; it could be as a writer. What I really worry about is the hyper-instrumentalizing of the teaching of writing, so that your role and identity are exclusively as writing teacher. I really think if you're teaching in a university, you've got to be producing either *about* or *of* what you're teaching. If you're teaching sculpting, you've better be a sculptor or working in the art history or theory of sculpting. I understand the dynamics here. Tenure-track faculty with reassigned time to do the scholarship have reduced teaching loads. Contingent faculty don't. It's a numbers problem. But I really worry that this constrains the roles.

The other solution is that if you get rid of first-year writing, you get rid of the contingent problem. And you align that with writing in the disciplines or writing across the curriculum or "every teacher is a writing teacher." It even gives you some very smart theoretical justification. But places that have done that soon find themselves reinventing a writing class simply because faculty can't or won't attend to writing in the same way that a dedicated writing class does.

WOE: You write about "writing" a lot as an idea, so I don't feel too vague in asking, what do you see that makes you more or less optimistic about the future of "writing"?

HESSE: I worry very broadly about attention and attentiveness. I live and perform this, too. We encounter so many things in life in fragmented fashion. And we're increasingly encountering texts in fragments and shards, whether as readers or as writers. When I write something, my browser's always open, my email's always open, and I vacillate. You can say as a writing species we're evolving, and multitasking—and this is the way it is, it's not good or bad—it's just the next evolutionary step. Historically though, producing sustained texts—either things that take a while to work out or that you immerse yourself in reading—has been really important. So I worry in an increasingly fragmented society that any sort of cultural memory or significance of that mode gets dissipated. Even novels and so on become thought of as some exotic thing that other people do. I'm not saying that novels will disappear, but they will seem increasingly exotic to daily experience.

My optimism, though, is that people will find an interest to counter that tendency. I've been really fascinated with some of the interest these days in material rhetoric and object rhetoric. For example, when people decide in retro-hipster fashion to send postcards rather than emails. It could just be my projecting desire, but there could be a backlash against the digitization of life and a sort of insistence on the materiality of life. That will create some interesting other options for writing.

I've mused about this, the difference between having my grandmother's cookbook and then digitizing it. I took pictures of all of the pages and, yeah, they're barely legible, but I can preserve them in this way. I can do this and I can then send these pictures to Amazon. It makes this nice little book. But I also have the physical cookbook, and there's something about having the object, too. I make an artifact of this and I write a little biography and memoir of my grandmother and so on. I think the same kind of thing has people knitting and scrapbooking. There is something about the materiality, and it participates with the digital, too. I think at some point—this is my romantic projection—from some place that people can't name, there will be a sort of yearning, a questioning, "Well, is this all there is?" To supplement or complement Twitter life (which I think is fascinating and fun), we'll wonder, "What other artifacts can we make that will stand against a shifting temporality?"

VICTOR VILLANUEVA

Throughout the course of his career, Victor Villanueva has critiqued the nuanced ways that rhetoric can reinforce cultural, linguistic, and racial hegemony. He has approached this task as a true rhetorician—using highly stylized rhetoric as a means to examine that hegemony. Villanueva's rhetorical virtuosity plays a prominent role in the nearly 50 articles and chapters he has written and is most evident in his award winning autobiography Bootstraps, From an American Academic of Color *(1993). In* Bootstraps, *Villanueva employs the digressive Spanish-Arab rhetorical style to frame his personal narrative and to confront the English language–based sociocultural hegemony that is embedded within the discipline of rhetoric and composition, a move which was a first for the field.*

In 1986, Villanueva transcended his humble beginnings as a high school dropout completing his PhD in English with an emphasis in rhetoric and writing at the University of Washington. Since then he has served as the chair of CCCC (1997–2000) and has received a bevy of awards including the Advancement of People of Color Leadership Award (2008), Rhetorician of the Year (1999), and the Richard A. Meade Award for Distinguished Research in English Education (1994). In 2009, he received the CCCC Exemplar Award for outstanding contributions to the profession. Students new to the field of Composition and Rhetoric may first encounter Villanueva through his widely-used anthology Cross-Talk in Comp Theory: A Graduate Reader *(1997) 3rd edition co-edited with Kristen Arola in 2011. His other publications include* Language Diversity in the Classroom: From Intention to Practice *(2003) co-edited with Geneva Smitherman,* Latino/a Discourses: On Language, Identity and Literacy Education *co-edited with Michelle Hall Kells and Valerie Balester and* Rhetoric of the Americas: 3114 BCE to 2012 CE *co-edited with Damian Baca (2010). His fourthcoming book with Wendy Olson and Siskanna Naynaha is* On Language and Value: Political Economies of Rhetoric and Composition.

In addition to his work as an author, editor, and scholar, Villanueva's teaching career spans the course of 30 years. He currently serves as the Regents Professor, Edward R. Meyer Distinguished Professor of Liberal Arts and Director of the Writing Program at Washington State University. During the course of his professorial work Villanueva has mentored more than 100 graduate students; WOE interviewer Donna Evans is one of his past mentees.

—Kenya Mitchell

"Some of It Is Serendipity"

Donna Evans

Fall 2013

WOE: You've written about your past in *Bootstraps*, but tell us again how it is that you began adulthood as a high school dropout and Vietnam veteran, and became a Regent's Professor at the top of your field nationally.

VILLANUEVA: I think some of it is serendipity and some of it is notions of a higher power that I can't understand. So much of it amazes me. The serendipity has to do with timing. I came into the community college in '76, and by a particular fluke, a particular teacher, and the way he taught—his name was Larry Lukens—I decided to drop out of chemistry and to stay in English, even though I knew one led to an income and the other one didn't. But I was having fun, and there's a lot to be said for having fun.

I moved into English literature at the University of Washington. I wasn't very good at it at first. There was a kind of knowledge that I didn't possess about how one writes about literature. But I enjoyed reading it. Somebody said to me a few days ago that one of the reasons she switched from literature to rhetoric and composition was the feeling that her love of literature was being ruined in literature classes. And I understand that. The idea in a literature class is to get a fuller idea of what's going on in the literature, but then having to produce something of your own without a thirty-year background and without having done all of the reading that's a part of being a literary scholar, it seems like you end up minimizing something that struck you as powerful. Be that as it may, I enjoyed my literature. I wrote a master's on Milton, and I still love Milton. I think the best science fiction novel I've ever read was *Paradise Lost*.

I stumbled into rhetoric; well, two stumbles, really. One, I stumbled into the University of Washington because it was available. I had gotten out of the army in Tacoma, so I was living nearby, moved to Seattle, and transferred to the University of Washington. I could afford it because of the G.I. Bill—and this will break people's hearts—I was paying $177 a quarter for tuition and getting $350 a month from the G.I. Bill. In 1977, $350 was not a living wage, but it wasn't abject poverty, either. It paid the rent, got me food, and I could cobble together enough to pay the $177 a quarter for the tuition. Anyhow, I stumbled into this rhetoric and comp program that at the time had one of the biggest names in the field, William Irmscher, who had been chair of 4Cs, had been editor of 3Cs, and had been president of NCTE. He knew the field, and his own specialty within all of that was the theories of Kenneth Burke. I liked him and he liked me. And then there was this young up and comer, ambitious assistant professor, Anne Ruggles Gere, who was phenomenally interesting, and this American literature professor who jumped ship and became a rhetoric and comp person (for which he was penalized at the time), Chuck Schuster, who was doing Bakhtin in those days.

I was in a wonderfully rich environment for rhetoric and composition. Not only that—I didn't realize it—but rhet and comp was new! As I was preparing for my dissertation, Anne Gere gave me everything that'd ever been published in rhetoric and comp for me to read and make 3 × 5 cards. And I did it. It took me about the length of a quarter, putting in the long hours that a graduate student does, but it was possible to know *all* of the field.

I didn't realize that was the ground floor. I just knew that rhetoric, especially, caught my fancy, and composition, the pragmatic offspring of rhetoric, which is how I thought of it, made sense to me. Historically, we now know from Susan Miller, it's really quite the reverse, that composition developed a genealogy back to rhetoric. But I did see it in that linear way [of decadence] that was constructed. It was phenomenally interesting for me.

Part of what ended up happening was because I was in on the ground floor. And because I was naïve, I wrote about the things that mattered to me, questions that were occurring at the time. When I wrote *Bootstraps*, one of the questions that Pat Bizzell asked me was why I didn't include more multilingual stuff like Gloria Anzaldúa did. Well, I'd never heard of her. Somebody else said it's so great that I am the counter to bell hooks; I had never heard of her. And somebody else put me together with Trinh T. Minh-Ha; I hadn't heard of her at the time. I've read all those folks since, and I see the overlaps. All I knew at the time was Richard Rodriquez and Mike Rose because those were being read and discussed in comp. And Richard Rodriquez was aggravating. My first *English Journal* article, "Whose Voice Is It Anyway?" was arguing the case that I don't disagree with Rodriquez. I thought he was being slotted by the majority, by white folks, as the same as someone like me, when in fact he was an immigrant with an immigrant's sensibility. We didn't know he was gay yet, that came out in the second book, which would also have affected his world view. So I had my differences with Richard Rodriquez that said I needed to tell a different story from the one that he was telling, and that of Mike Rose, even though I thought he was phenomenally sympathetic. He's actually been like an informal, in-the-background, hardly-know-it advocate of mine from the very beginning. And prior to *Bootstraps*, he was one who said that I should publish this story as a book. He and Anne Gere were the two who most promoted this idea that what I had written in the *English Journal* could be expanded into a book. I didn't see how at the time.

So I became a first who doesn't recognize being a first. I did intend to be experimental with how *Bootstraps* was written, and with a couple of articles that came before *Bootstraps*: the *English Journal* article, "Considerations for American Freireistas," and "'Rhetoric is Politics,' Said the Ancient. 'How Much So,' I Wonder."

John Trimbur is the one who provided some very telling feedback and helped me to clarify the things he didn't understand. The best kind of feedback you get for a revision is when somebody, rather than correcting you, questions you. And realizing that the questions themselves were in some sense inappropriate allowed me to reformulate this stuff. Conversations had to do with "how is what you're experiencing any different from what my grandfather had to experience when he first came to this country?" So those questions started me making distinctions between the immigrant and the person of color, which ended up in the *English Journal* article.

Bootstraps was intended as a swan song. I figured I was never going to make it in the academy, and I wanted to tell the story about how it is that I was still not being allowed in, despite what I had accomplished, and I wanted to do it in a way that was compelling. So it had to be theory, research, and autobiography. And it had to blur the lines between orality and literacy, the big discussion of the time, thanks to Walter Ong and Eric Havelock. *Bootstraps* allowed me to take part in a conversation that was right there. It was fortuitous, at a time when the cognitive model was being challenged by the social construction model, and here I was, presenting a particular social construct. But I didn't intend that—there's the serendipity. Now, a quarter century later, twenty years since the book, I come to realize that I was the first Latino compositionist. I didn't know I was a first, but there I was.

WOE: Where were you working and living when *Bootstraps* was published?

VILLANUEVA: It was written and published in Flagstaff, Arizona. I wrote *Bootstraps* in the course of one summer. In that same summer, we were collecting food stamps, I was working as a line cook for a restaurant called Miz Zip's, and teaching 101. After I finished at the restaurant, I would go back to my office and work on the damned book, get home around ten o'clock and talk with Carol, and then do it again the next day.

So, how did I do this? Well, I think luck, and then my own fixation with theory. Here's one body of theory, which is what does it mean to be a person of color in the academy, and first generation, and with a world view so radically different from the majority of the people. I've now been in this business, oh, thirty years. I started graduate school in '79, I got my first assistant professorship in '85 and the PhD in '86, and so, '85 to now is, what, almost twenty-eight years that I've been in this business. I have not yet met another Vietnam veteran in academia who was enlisted. I have now met a couple of people who were high school dropouts. But high school dropout, Vietnam veteran, Latino from the projects in Brooklyn—it's still one worldview, and that says a hell of a lot about how the filtering processes remain in this postracial era.

I realized many years later that I had a storehouse of knowledge. The scholarship was there, but I didn't come to think of myself as a writer until relatively recently. The "*Memoria*" essay was the first time I felt like "this is the work of a writer."

WOE: What kind of response did *Bootstraps* get in the beginning, and when did you start noticing that it was impacting your career?

VILLANUEVA: *Bootstraps* came out and I got the Richard A. Meade Award in 1994. Then maybe not even a year later, I got another letter that said I had gotten a national award for *Bootstraps*. I thought that the people had screwed up and had already given me the award. And then I realized that it was different, the David H. Russell Award.

Almost immediately interest in my work picked up. My first keynote speech (and I've done about a hundred of them) was over *Bootstraps*. I think I put people to sleep because I read so much from the book.

The problem with *Bootstraps*, which aggravated me a lot at first, was that most of the comments had to do with the writing—with the style, with the changing voices—rather than with the content. Most people think of it as having two voices, but my intention was three voices: the *I*, the *he*, but also the *non*, which is the academic voice. So, three voices, the dispassionate third person, second person, and first. I don't know when, but folks started to pick up what I was saying about Gramsci and intellectuals. Eventually the book started getting quoted a lot.

For all of that, I do think that I am best known in this business for *Cross-Talk*. By the early '90s, that whole history of comp, which was only twenty years old, seemed to be lost. I put together this phenomenal coursepack that took up two loose-leaf binders. And then—and this is what I mean about serendipity—Kinko's got sued for copyright infringement, and suddenly they were making sure that they got copyright permissions for every Xerox they put together in coursepacks. My coursepack became outrageously expensive. So, in order to save students money and get prettier copies, I went ahead and proposed that as *Cross-Talk*.

WOE: When you say "this business," do you consider it to be a melding of composition and rhetoric?

VILLANUEVA: It is becoming less so, maybe even decidedly less so. A part of me still wishes, and I might go to my grave wishing, that I were better known for rhetoric than for composition. But it is what it is, and my scholarship has really been talking to this community, which is principally a composition community where some of us do rhetoric. Even in doing rhetoric, it tends to be in the service of composition.

I'm much more concerned with the polemics of racism, but as I look back to answer your question, we want to talk race, class, gender, and sexuality. Class is a funny one because in America, we still want to associate it with income. But class can be cultural. And then there is political economy and the ways in which our economics and our abilities to assume any power over it is always compromised, and that compromise has to be by way of rhetoric. So even though I'm still thinking mainly about racism, I think that one can't know it without knowing more about political economy, rather than economics, because political economy is the relations of power to the economy. And how is power exerted? Only in two ways: one is by force, and that means you've already lost the fight, and the other is rhetorically. Does it manifest in the classroom? Of course it does.

Within the Latino community, I am still held up as something of a symbol of possibility, a possibility unseen. It's not quite true: I'm seen as an uncompromising possibility. But the compromise is still there. I'm writing in English, for crying out loud.

WOE: Do you consider yourself a speaker or rhetor?

VILLANUEVA: I see myself as a rhetor. It's one of those funny things that happened. My daughter—the one who's in rhetoric—she saw a documentary of Fidel Castro, and said, "Do you know that your style is a lot like Fidel Castro's?" And I had to tell her that that was very intentional.

WOE: Why?

VILLANUEVA: Because it struck me as phenomenally emotive—the hand gestures, the tempo, and the changes in tempo—phenomenally emotive, which is what I write about. I write about that in "*Memoria*," for that matter. Where's *pathos*? Where's the pathetic appeal? Do you rile the people up? I'm talking polemics after all. I'm trying to get people who I really like to think about racism a little bit more deliberately, beyond tokenism.

When Fidel Castro wrote, the revolution took place. And I'm not gonna talk about him as a leader, 'cause he did turn into a despot, finally. He should have allowed the democratic process to take over, but people in power don't let go easily. For all of the good that has happened in Cuba, there's a lot of bad that's happened, so I'm not doing all of that. I'm talking about one personality's ways with words.

WOE: We're not talking about his politics. We're talking about his style. . .

VILLANUEVA: Right. But here's a bit of magic—a white dove—you know what white dove means to Christians?

WOE: Peace.

VILLANUEVA: Yes, great peace, and the Holy Spirit. And so, Castro wins the revolution. It's his inaugural address to the people. In celebration of the revolution, they let these white doves go. And while he's talking, a white dove came and sat on his shoulder. So I said, "Man, that's an orator!" In my dissertation defense, that was one of the things that was said, "Boy you're a much better speaker than you are a writer.' I was encouraged as a speaker. When I got a fellowship for people of color—the Dorothy Danforth-Compton Fellowship—and I had to give a talk, those were the comments I got from there, was how powerful my speaking was. And I was quite unconscious of it; I was doing it. So, yeah, I think that I got that somewhere along the way, in my upbringing. My father was very political.

WOE: Do you think such a realization may have delayed your sense that you were a writer?

VILLANUEVA: Hell yeah. I wrote about it in *Bootstraps*. I failed phenomenally at my first piece of writing at the university, as opposed to the community college.

WOE: Which I think is something to bring up because that's a common thing to happen to people who transfer from a community college to a university. Just changing institutions, the requirements and the rigor are different.

VILLANUEVA: Oh yeah, the articulation is purely bureaucratic, and it gets misread by those of us who started at the community colleges as just an inexpensive way to do those first two years. Not so. There's a reason why it's less expensive. I knew something happened in writing *Bootstraps*. I knew that I tapped into something, and I figured that the reason I was able to do that was because I had decided, since I was going to write this book and then get out of academics, not to worry about academic discourse. I was just going to write it my way, and then to hell wit' y'all.

What was supposed to be my swan song ended up being the launch pad to my career, and it was because I didn't realize that everybody's stifled by this academic discourse.

WOE: In your teaching, and in chairing or serving on master's and dissertation committees, has your perspective on what should happen in the university changed?

VILLANUEVA: I could be dead wrong about this. I think that we carry on a lot in higher education about the cost of switching the model for universities to a business model because of the exploitation of contingent faculty, which is part of the business model. There're even agencies for temp employment. The university has latched onto that, especially in English studies, probably more than any other department. The university has a two-or-more-tiered income structure, in which administrators who are not intellectuals get the lion's share of salary, and they do so because they tend to bring in more money for the university. There's a lot of talk about the business model, but it's always from that administrative viewpoint. Like I said, I could be dead wrong, but I think that the same has happened all the way down to our teaching. Our teaching is somehow reduced to getting a good ranking with Rate My Professors.

I think that we kowtow to students and worry so much about entertaining them that we forget that people enjoy learning. Early on, I was like every other young teacher, and I worried about the gimmicks. Now I do less of the gimmick and talk more about how language is how we function, that language is epistemological, we're all language users, we're all language creatures, and writing is just a complex set of skills. Given that it's alphabetic literacy, it's a pretty easy set of skills to acquire if you just stop being so scared of it.

I walked back into undergraduate teaching just last semester. I have spent most of my time with graduate students, and I think it's because my attitude with graduate students has been "I don't have to teach; I have to supply things to read, and then have some real conversation about it." But that's also true for undergraduates. I will put up overheads and show YouTube videos that will demonstrate some of these principles in contemporary times. But that's not a gimmick; that is necessarily demonstrating the ways in which rhetoric continues to obtain and that written discourse is another rhetorical form. I think that's what has happened, mainly because of the influence of working with so many graduate students—nearly a hundred who've completed a thesis or dissertation since around '90. For half, I sat on committees and had some influence in that way; for the other half, I was principal advisor. What I learned from them is that graduate students overwhelmingly tend to be intellectually engaged. But if you just take a few extra minutes to explain some principles that we can assume that the graduate students already know, it will work with undergraduates as well.

I'll say things to my undergraduate class and see the wonder. I'll see them saying, "I didn't know that. Wow! That's interesting." Actually, I went off on Fido. Fido was the faithful companion of Socrates. Socrates drank the hemlock when he was executed, and Fido was right there by him. Then I talked about how in Greek it's "Phaedo," but for the Latin it's "Fido." It means "faithful one." And I go from there to the Marines, *Semper Fidelis.*

WOE: "Fido" is also a common name for dogs...

VILLANUEVA: Exactly! That's where my students went. I could see eyes and mouths getting big as they said, "Oh, I get it!" We can all be intellectually stimulated. I think I lost track of that in the very beginning because I was so worried about being entertaining. And the greatest entertainment the academy can provide is learning.

Another problem in teaching is the demonization of lecture. There is some advantage to having studied a particular body of knowledge for thirty years. I went into graduate school in '79, so that's getting pretty close to thirty-five years. How can I assume that these kids who were born in 1991, in talking to each other, can know some historical artifacts? They are all thinkers. Back when I was Director of Comp, which was a long time ago, I used to caution graduate students about teaching students how to think. They already know "how to think." But there is some factual knowledge that needs to be passed on, to the degree that anything can be factual at all. I'm thinking about the Sophists. That's Gorgias's thing, that nothing is knowable.

I think the fun of teaching is if you enjoy what you're doing and pass it on. I have students who write responses, and talk to each other, and they get animated about it. I have had students in a 101 class read Paulo Freire's *Pedagogy of the Oppressed*, know what he's talking about, basically, and can talk animatedly about it. I have said that the most successful 101 course that I have ever taught used Ed Corbett's edition of Aristotle's *Rhetoric* as textbook. The students were intimidated with the first chapter and flinging shit back to Aristotle by the time they were in the second book, when he's going on about the ages of man. By the third book, it's a handbook and stuff they've always heard. They walk away knowing they have not just read Aristotle but taken on Aristotle. That's what they want, as opposed to high school comp classes rehashed.

WOE: Where do you think the field of composition and rhetoric is headed?

VILLANUEVA: I don't know. I look at the WPA list and I can see that the overwhelming number of jobs available are for professional and technical writing. I understand the business reasons why that's the case; that is, this is where writing serves the capitalist political economy. Also, students tend to be pragmatic, and professional and technical writing is a knowable field, as opposed to a "what do you do with an English degree" question. What troubles me about that is the potential I see in the advertising—not so much in the people I've seen that we've hired—to separate out rhetoric from composition. We're talking about a subdiscipline of composition studies. If all of the jobs are in a subdiscipline of composition studies, and we as a service to our graduate students want to make sure they're ready for that job market, then we're going to spend more time with that subdiscipline. This means we're probably going to have to do some overview of the discipline, which tends to be composition studies. And that means less emphasis, potentially, in rhetoric. That troubles me. The people that we have hired over the last several years here at WSU have all had some background in rhetoric. But I don't take it for granted. I think

I wrote years ago that all rhetoric people, especially English-department-type rhetoric people, know composition. You can't be a rhetorician in an English department; it's always rhetoric and comp. But it is possible to be comp without rhetoric, and I don't think that ought to be the case. I think we need to do language study writ large. Am I favoring rhetoric over linguistics? It really annoys the linguists I know, but to me linguistics is rhetoric within a scientific paradigm. I worry that there are some, like me, who will want to claim rhetoric and not composition, and that probably isn't a good move either.

But I've been flooded with proposals and manuscripts for the Studies in Writing & Rhetoric series since I've taken over the editorship. I think it's because folks in general want to continue to connect rhetoric with composition studies. The job market is asking us to disconnect. Joe Harris—and this isn't the usual doff of the hat before insulting somebody—I see him as a really great editor. But his emphasis has always been the teaching of writing. I think one of the reasons why there's a sudden flood of manuscripts and proposals when I took over was that I'm not seen quite so narrowly. That suggests that there is a whole body of young academics (most of them have been young) and they're involved in rhetoric. There're even a couple who have done rhetoric with no clear implications for teaching writing. I think the predisposition of the students themselves, if they are introduced to rhetoric, is to keep rhetoric and composition together. But I worry about the heavy influence of the market.

Students come into the rhetoric and professional writing (RPW) track that we have here for the professional writing. When they enter my rhetoric course, they're lost; they have no idea what they're doing there. As it turns out, this semester my class is a capstone course for RPW students. Maybe half of the class is history or communication students, folks who want to know something about language as language. I think the interest is there if they can only be introduced to it. My hope is that rhetoric and composition continues to be rhetoric *and* composition, not rhetoric/composition that argues of synonymity that I don't think exists. They're not synonymous. After all, I'm teaching Classical Athenian Greek scholars, followed by Roman scholars, followed by a Spaniard scholar who taught in Rome. So this is not English studies. It's understanding that we have to know something about how language itself operates to understand how to use the power that is potentially there in the language in written discourse.

WOE: Fundamental roots in our current culture stem back to language. What is the importance of being aware of what's old and what's new?

VILLANUEVA: In my class, we were just reading the Sophists, and I asked them to respond. What's funny is that there are a few graduate students in the class. The graduate students say, "Wow, the Sophists are just like contemporary discourse, not contemporary academic discourse, with its relativism." The undergraduates said that it's really quite a shame that it looks like the kind of discourse that came out of the Sophists is no longer there in political debate, that there is no desire for relativism but just binary ideological points. The students see it, and that's good because they are the future.

WOE: What do you have left to do? Is there any culminating inquiry that you want to complete?

VILLANUEVA: Well, I'm not sure. I do think I still have one more thing to do. I'm not sure because I seem to volunteer. I've always thought that I need to join Volunteers Anonymous.

I'm interested in—and I just don't know how to do it—a particularly outrageous kind of set of intersections. That is, I have been looking at, as part of "*Memoria*," what I call the rhetoric of the first Indians, the Taíno, the folks that Columbus called Indians. We can't really know the rhetoric of the Taíno, who weren't American Indians in the way that we think about them, but the original inhabitants of the Caribbean, or at least the Greater Antilles. They evidently spread Taíno influences as far as Georgia and Alabama. This was interesting for me because my year in Alabama was the only sustained time in my life (I had a little spell in Costa Rica) when I was free of all allergies. You've got to watch out for biological explanations, but it is interesting to me that something within an American consciousness would be so foreign (the Deep South), but in a biological or long-historical term, consciousness might actually be home. And like I was telling you earlier, I miss the weather. I've been allergic my whole life—but there, not a thing, not a thing.

QUINTILIAN

Marcus Fabius Quintilianus is best known for his treatise on education, Institutio Oratoria, *or* The Education of the Orator, *published around A.D. 95. The treatise, which combines the theoretical and educational aspects of rhetoric, is divided into 12 books and includes four major works: a treatise on education, a manual of rhetoric, a reader's guide to the best authors, and a handbook on the moral duties of the orator. The book emphasizes moral purpose and rhetorical skill and is essentially a description of the complete rhetorical education from birth to adulthood—in short, an outline for the education of the perfect orator. Quintilian defines oratory as "the good man speaking well"—the good man being someone publicly active and courageous in pursuing his ideals.*[1] *Quintilian does not just describe specific guidelines but includes helpful explanations and examples from his experience for each point he makes.*

Quintilian was born around A.D. 35 in Calagurris in Spain. During his career he held a public position as a teacher of rhetoric and also practiced law. As a well-known teacher, he was specifically distinguished for emphasizing moral values in education. He wrote Institutio Oratoria *after he retired from his teaching position. The book has been described as "the most ambitious single treatise on Education which the ancient world produced."*[2]

—Michal Reznizki

---

1 Murphy, James J. and Richard A. Katula. *A Synoptic History of Classical Rhetoric.* Mahwah, NJ: Lawrence Erlbaum Associates, 2003: (205).
2 Murphy, James Jerome. *Quintilian on the Teaching of Speaking and Writing: Translations from Books One, Two, and Ten of the Institutio Oratoria.* Carbondale, IL: SIU Press, 1987: (xvii).

"Data Don't Breathe"

James J. Murphy

Fall 2013

QUINTILIAN: How did you find me?

WOE: Well, the other day I was in the library and ran across a copy of Walter Savage Landor's "Imaginary Conversations" that he published in the 1820s. And I thought to myself, if Landor could revive Dante and Princess Elizabeth and Louis XIV, maybe I could find you. On the Internet, of course. So here we are—but the problem is that it's for a sample time of only 20 minutes. After that there's an enormous fee to be paid to somebody called Microsoft, and I don't think the journal could possibly pay it.

QUINTILIAN: But why are you interested in me?

WOE: Because everybody knows—or should know—that you were the most famous educator and rhetorician of ancient Rome, author of one of the most influential books in Western culture.

QUINTILIAN: I never thought I was going to be famous!

WOE: But what led you to spend two years writing just this one book? How did you get into all this?

QUINTILIAN: As you know, I was a lawyer for a while before I began teaching. All those years working with ideas and words made me want to help others use language. The standard lore in those days for anyone interested in public life was rhetoric, and I do spend a lot of time on that subject in the book. But I also realized that I didn't want to just publish long lists of specific "rules" or precepts like the little handbooks that were on sale at every street corner. Precepts are advice for future activity, all right, but they are advice for human beings who must decide how to use them. So in this book my concern for language-using human beings is set in the context of how human learning begins and keeps developing right into retirement and old age. Maybe another title for the book could be "The Learning Context of Rhetoric."

WOE: Then let's talk about your book title. Your major work is called *Institutio Oratoria* in Latin. The latest English translation by Donald A. Russell calls it "The Education of the Orator."

QUINTILIAN: I think I may have made a mistake in my title; perhaps also it could be "Formation of the Perfect Orator," because it's about shaping the psyche of a young person into a new capability for language use. It's not only about the subject of rhetoric, it's about the person, the rhetoric user.

WOE: But why "perfect"? Isn't that impossible?

QUINTILIAN: All our experience tells us that you hardly ever accomplish everything you want to do. So, if you think you are going to fall short of your highest goals, why shouldn't you aim for the highest?

WOE: That's a pretty high standard!

QUINTILIAN: Well, what alternative do you suggest? Purposeful mediocrity? Or giving up before you start? You yourself gave an interview in this journal a few years ago about "Setting Minds in Motion." Isn't that what it's all about? And in another issue Howard Zinn laid it out nicely in his interview, "If You Don't Want to Take Risks, Then You Have to Be Silent." I think your journal's on my side.

WOE: All right, I can't argue with that. But you lay out what looks like a very complicated set of ways to get students into your way of learning. You want them to learn the precepts of rhetoric, you want them to practice Imitation of other works and speeches, you want them to go through that whole set of twelve learning-ladder exercises you call *progymnasmata*, you want them to engage in oral and written debates in case studies of problems (what you call Declamations), and, worst of all, you want all these things sequenced into what we today would call a curriculum. How could any modern teacher make this work?

QUINTILIAN: That's a pretty good summary. I have an outline of the teaching methods that I can download for you while we're talking.

WOE: Thanks—I'll make it an Appendix to this review—that should give our readers a better idea of how you think everything should fit together. Even so, how does the modern teacher with such limited time make all this work?

QUINTILIAN: My answer is that the whole really is greater than its parts. Or, to put it another way, why would a teacher do any one particular thing in a classroom? I take it as a principle that everything done should be done for more than one purpose. For example, to put one of my ideas into modern terms, why couldn't a student be asked to write or speak the way that Lincoln did in his Gettysburg Address? I call this "Imitation"—an idea which I find to be very much misunderstood these days. But look at the elements involved—the types of ideas, the sequence of ideas, the vocabulary, the features of style like tropes and figures, all embedded in a historical situation which has to be understood by the student to make the assignment work. There are thousands of writings and speeches today which could be used the same way. This is not a plagiarism, but an emulation which forces the student to look closely at the text—and to the mind of the writer—in order to do better in the future. Or "Declamation," which you have renamed "case studies." I used to pose very difficult situations, asking students to respond with a written or oral solution. For example, suppose your sister has been kidnapped, and the kidnappers say they will kill her if you call the police. The student must prepare an answer persuading you to call them, or not to call them. Imagine the factors involved in preparing the answer!

WOE: But you had students in your classroom for years. You could give them carefully sequenced assignments and watch them develop over a long time. Today's teachers have only short classroom periods, two or three times a week. They don't know the students for a long time. Even if you have some good ideas, where does the teacher start?

QUINTILIAN: I laid down in my book a principle which I think still holds true: "For what object do we have in teaching them, but that they may not always require to be taught?" (2.5.13). Today, I suppose, this would translate into a question of "classroom objectives." The basic goal, as I see it, is to enable the student to acquire a Facility (*facilitas*) of language use, a strategic sense of what language can do. Whatever arouses that strategic sense will be a help to the student over a lifetime. But teaching is an art, and art involves making choices based on circumstances. So the teacher needs to know all the possibilities before making a choice, and above all needs a strategic sense of what language can do. So my book is in a sense an exploration of teacher sensitivities.

WOE: But in your book you constantly talk about the value of Habit for the students—doing things over a long time so that they gradually become second nature. And you insist that everything in your program fits together. You make it to be a whole system. This doesn't sound like you intend the book to be merely a cafeteria of possibilities.

QUINTILIAN: You're right, but for two thousand years other teachers have been using these methods, in wildly differing circumstances, even if they didn't always know where the ideas came from. There must be some good reason for that. Perhaps knowing more about how others have done it over the years would be a good introduction to modern usage.

WOE: I'm getting nervous about the time. So far we've been talking about cosmic questions like goals and principles, but my students have encouraged me to ask you some very specific questions. Actually their focus group came up with nineteen questions if time permits. Is that all right with you?

QUINTILIAN: Of course. Go ahead.

WOE: Some of them say they could never tolerate an exercise like the transliteration of models, the rewriting or resaying of one thing into another form, like verse into prose or vice versa.

QUINTILIAN: Ask them why people do crossword puzzles. Or why game consoles are so popular. There seems to be an innate competitiveness in the human psyche that creates pleasure out of doing difficult things. As I point out in Book One, education should not be equated with torture in the student's mind, and as much as possible "let his instruction be an amusement to him" (1.2.20). In other words, whatever creates achievable goals in language use can be pleasurable if properly handled. Transliteration is by nature a double exercise, requiring comparative knowledges to be used in a puzzle-like situation, and can be treated as one.

WOE: Another point is that some of my students think you are sexist because you only teach boys.

QUINTILIAN: In my time that was the way of the world—not just the Romans but the Jews and the Greeks and the Phoenicians and everybody else. Even the Christians only had male Apostles, though many women were named as helpers. For us, there was no point in taking time to educate girls for whom there could be no public function as citizens, let alone lawyers or Senators. There were some girls in elementary grammar classes, but not in the rhetoric schools. For that matter, how many women did you have writing your American Constitution? But I have come to realize that language is language, not male or female, and therefore we should base our teaching on the person, the language learner, rather than some future job hope as we used to do in my day.

WOE: Another question—which is more important, writing or speaking?

QUINTILIAN: They cannot be separated. In fact, there are four equally important functions involved in language learning—that is, speaking, writing, reading, and listening. You can't just download lingual ability. In Book Ten of my work, which involves adult self-education, I explain this more carefully.

WOE: But isn't this an impractical idea in today's interactive postdigital world?

QUINTILIAN: You Americans are so hampered by your lack of a historical sense! Until the 1880s there was a common approach of teaching writing as part of a total communication apparatus. Then came the separation of literature from writing—i.e., the modern English Department. Then in 1914 came the separation of speech from both writing and literature. Then with radio and television, listening became associated with entertainment rather than learning, and now very little is interesting to an audience without a visual component. But I would argue that the interactive classroom is the antidote to all of this. If we are to form the person of lingual discretion, then carefully designed exercises can be used to begin the awareness that all four of these functions are critical. Today's (and tomorrow's) technologies can even help us, not get in our way.

WOE: Okay, then, which rules are most important in speaking and writing?

QUINTILIAN: What is needed is not rules but discretion, the ability to make lingual decisions based on circumstances. Let me quote my book: "Let no man require from me such a system of precepts as is laid down by most authors of

Quintilian: "Data Don't Breathe" **439**

books of rules, a system in which I should have to make certain laws, fixed by immutable necessity, for all students" (2.13.1–2).

WOE: Wait a minute! What do you mean by "lingual"?

QUINTILIAN: I mean the melding of thought with its expression, what the Greeks used to call logos. Can you have a thought without words? (I realize that some people today say that language creates experience, but I don't find their arguments very convincing.) When you have a thought, you can express it by choosing from among up to a million words in English. (In my time we didn't have that many words in Latin!) That word "lingual" is what I use to describe that word-choosing process.

WOE: That's an interesting concept. It would seem to have a bearing on the next question, which is whether it is better to write quickly or to write carefully.

QUINTILIAN: Again, let me quote me: "By writing quickly we are not brought to write well, but by writing well we are brought to write quickly" (10.3.10). There are two reasons for this: first, the careful use of language helps create a habit of discretion that carries over to later writing, and, second, it is hard for writers to abandon their own words once they're set down in a hasty first draft.

WOE: Do you think texting is a good invention?

QUINTILIAN: First of all, it is not a modern invention. My scribe used to use all sorts of abbreviations and even personal symbols to record my thoughts, and even merchants used a kind of shorthand to keep track of their merchandise. Moreover, secret societies have always used special phrases and symbols, even handshakes, to let each other know who were members of the society. And the invention of the telegraph created a special language set of linguistic shortcuts because each word was so expensive to transmit, creating terms like "update" for "bring up to date." I find it ironic that today's texters are mostly members of a certain self-selected social class—teenagers—it's too early to tell whether they will abandon the habit when they grow older. On the other hand Facebook lets everybody with a computer reveal to the world that everything is open to the world, as if to prove that the writer surely does not belong to any secret society. A knowledge of writing history is a good thing.

WOE: How do you know these things?

QUINTILIAN: I try to keep up.

WOE: Since we're now talking about the current world, is writer's block a modern problem?

QUINTILIAN: *Procul ignorantia*! I'm sorry, but you startled me so with such a silly question that I lapsed into Latin. I guess you could translate it as "What a dumb thing to say!" Every writer who has ever lived, it seems to me, has complained about "dryness" or "blankness." Even Virgil, the author of the great Roman epic the *Aeneid*, lamented that there were some days he could not write at all; Virgil, as Varro points out, wrote only a few verses a day. And writing this book took me two years, even when I was retired and had nothing else to do. In my Book Ten I recount the story of Florus's son who after three days still could not figure out how to begin a school assignment. In my view the more learned the writer—the more numerous the choices—the worse is the risk of blocking, like the fox in Aesop's fable who is torn to pieces by the hounds because he cannot choose between all his escape methods. This is an ancient version of the Heisenberg Uncertainty Principle. I talk about some remedies in Book Ten.

WOE: You talk about learning "developing" even into old age. But today even the youngest person can call up on a phone every text, every picture, every idea mankind has ever produced. Why even have schools, let alone tough programs like yours?

QUINTILIAN: To paraphrase your Christian Bible, "Can man live by bytes alone?" Information availability (I don't know the latest technical name for it) is surely a blessing we never had in my day. We didn't even have newspapers. But viewing human beings only as input mechanisms has some hazards, not the least of which is data overload (as in the case of Aesop's fox). In my day we had to fight for the concept of "school," the interactive idea exchange system where humans could help each other become more human. See my Book One. We won that fight, not just for Western culture, but for the whole world over the last couple of thousand years. The modern dreamers who envision someday putting an expandable life-long learning chip into the baby at birth simply don't understand the nature of humanity. Data don't breathe.

WOE: My students would call your ideas "old fashioned."

QUINTILIAN: So what? What is, is.

WOE: Even so, I want to ask you one more time how can you justify declaring that the improvement of language-use depends on the interrelation of the four elements of reading, writing, speaking, and listening? My students say that's so twentieth century!

QUINTILIAN: Ask your students to look at some of the recent research in cognitive science. All these lingual activities can be tracked to sections of the brain, mainly grouped around the corpus callosum. For example, look at the "cultural neuroscience" studies of Kitayama and Jiyoung, whose MRI research leads them to state that repeated participation in socially scripted forms of behavior can actually alter the neural structure of the brain. To me, that sounds a lot like my insistence on the value of habit properly understood.

WOE: Well, that should give them some homework to do! But I'm really getting worried about the time. You can't possibly answer all their other questions in the little time we have left. So, do you have any final remarks for us before the time runs out and you get cut off?

QUINTILIAN: That's like asking a father which of his children he likes the best! I was really beginning to enjoy this conversa—

Sources for Further Study

Agnew, Lois. "The Classical Period." In *The Present State of Scholarship in the History of Rhetoric: A Twenty-First Century Guide*, ed. Lynee Gaillet with Winifred Horner. Columbia: University of Missouri Press, 2010. 7–41.

Baldwin, Charles Sears. *Ancient Rhetoric and Poetic*. New York: Macmillan, 1924. Rpt. Gloucester, MA: Peter Smith, 1959.

Bonner, Stanley F. *Roman Declamation in the Late Republic and Early Empire*. Berkeley: University of California Press, 1949.

———. *Education in Ancient Rome from the Elder Cato to the Younger Pliny*. Berkeley: University of California Press, 1977.

Clark, Donald Leman. *Rhetoric in Greco-Roman Education* New York: Columbia University Press, 1957.

Clarke, Martin Lowther. *Rhetoric at Rome: A Historical Survey*. London: Cohen and West, 1953. Rpt. New York: Barnes and Noble, 1963.

Colson, F. H. "Introduction." In *M. Fabii Quintiliani institutionis oratoriae Liber I*. Cambridge: Cambridge University Press, 1924.

Corbett, Edward P. J. and Robert J. Connors. *Classical Rhetoric for the Modern Student*. 4th ed. New York: Oxford University Press, 1998.

Crowley, Sharon and Debra Hawhee. *Ancient Rhetorics for Contemporary Students*. 4th ed. White Plains, NY: Longmans, 2009.

Dominik, William and Jon Hall, eds. *A Companion to Roman Rhetoric*. Oxford: Blackwell, 2007.

Erickson, Keith V. "Quintilian's *Institutio oratoria* and *Pseudo-Declamationes*. [A bibliography]." *Rhetoric Society Quarterly* 11 (1981): 45–62.

Fritz, K. von. "Ancient Instruction in Grammar according to Quintilian." *American Journal of Philology* 70 (1949): 337–366.

Gwynn, Aubrey. *Roman Education from Cicero to Quintilian*. Oxford: Clarendon Press, 1926. Rpt. New York: Columbia University Teacher's College. Classics in Education No. 29. N.D.

Haarhoff, Theodore. *The Schools of Gaul*. Oxford: Clarendon Press, 1926.

Hubbell, Harry M. *The Influence of Isocrates on Cicero, Dionysius, and Aristides*. New Haven: Yale University Press, 1913.

Kaster, Robert A. *Guardians of Language: The Grammarian and Society in Late Antiquity*. Berkeley: University of California Press, 1988.

——— "Controlling Reason: Declamation in Rhetorical Education at Rome." In *Education in Greek and Roman Antiquity*, ed. L. Too. Boston: Brill, 2001. 317–339.

Kennedy, George A. *The Art of Rhetoric in the Roman World: 300 BC–AD 300*. Princeton, NJ: Princeton University Press, 1972.

——— *A New History of Classical Rhetoric*. Princeton, NJ: Princeton University Press, 1994.

——— *Quintilian*. New York: Twayne, 1969; 2nd ed. Sophos, 2013.

Lausberg, Heinrich. *Handbook of Literary Rhetoric: A Foundation for Literary Study*. Eds. David E. Norton and R. Dean Anderson; trans. Matthew T. Bliss, Annemick Jansen, and David E. Norton. Leiden: Brill, 1998.

Little, Charles, ed. *Quintilian the Schoolmaster*. Two vols. Nashville: George Peabody, 1951.

Lopez, Jorge Fernandez, "Quintilian as Teacher and Rhetorician." In *A Companion to Roman Rhetoric*, eds. William Dominik and Jon Hall. Oxford: Blackwell, 2007. 307–322.

Marrou, Henri-Irenee. *A History of Education in Antiquity.* Trans. George Lamb. New York: New American Library, 1964. Rpt. University of Wisconsin Press, 1982.

Murphy, James J. "The Modern Value of Ancient Roman Methods of Teaching Writing: With Answers to Twelve Modern Fallacies." *Writing on the Edge* 1 (1989): 28–37.

——— "Quintilian's Advice on the Continuing Education of the Adult Orator: Book X of the *Institutio oratoria*." In *Quintilian and the Law: The Art of Persuasion in Law and Politics*, ed. Olga Tellegen-Couperus. Leuven: Leuven University Press, 2003. 247–252.

——— "Roman Writing Instruction as Described by Quintilian." In *A Short History of Writing Instruction from Ancient Greece to Contemporary America*, ed. James J. Murphy. 3rd ed. New York: Routledge, 2012. 36–76.

Parks, Brother Edilbert P. *The Roman Rhetorical Schools as a Preparation for the Courts under the Early Empire.* Johns Hopkins University Studies in Historical and Political Science Series 63, no. 2. Baltimore: Johns Hopkins University Press, 1945.

Quintilian. *Quintilian: The Orator's Education.* Ed. and Trans. Donald A. Russell. Five vols. Loeb Classical Library. Cambridge: Harvard University Press, 2001.

——— *Quintilian Book 2.* Ed. Tobias Reinhardt and Michael Winterbottom. Oxford: Oxford University Press, 2006.

Rhetorica: A Journal of the History of Rhetoric. Two special issues on Quintilian: 13 (1995): Numbers 2 and 3.

Too, Yun Lee, ed. *Education in Greek and Roman Antiquity.* Leiden: Brill, 2001.

Welch, Kathleen E. *The Contemporary Reception of Classical Rhetoric: Appropriations of Ancient Discourse.* Mahwah, NJ: Lawrence Erlbaum Associates, 1990.

Wilkins, A.S. *Roman Education.* Cambridge: Cambridge University Press, 1914.

An Outline of Quintilian's Teaching Methods

Perhaps the most important aspect of these methods is their coordination into a single instructional program. Each is important for itself but takes greater importance from its place within the whole. The outline below may illustrate how these elements are fitted together in the first two books of the *Institutio*.

1   **Precept:** a set of rules that provide a definite method and system of speaking. Rhetoric as precept occupies eight of the twelve books of the *Institutio Oratoria:*

   a   Invention
   b   Arrangement
   c   Style
   d   Memory
   e   Delivery

2   **Imitation:** the use of models to learn how others have used language. Specific exercises include:

   a   Reading aloud (*lectio*)
   b   Master's detailed analysis of a text (*praelectio*)
   c   Memorization of models
   d   Paraphrase of models
   e   Transliteration (prose/verse and/or Latin/Greek)

  f Recitation of paraphrase or transliteration
  g Correction of paraphrase or transliteration

3 **Composition exercises** (*progymnasmata* or *praeexercitamenta*): A learning ladder of a graded series of exercises in writing and speaking themes. Each succeeding exercise is more difficult and incorporates what has been learned in preceding ones. The following twelve were common by Quintilian's time:

  a Retelling a fable
  b Retelling an episode from a poet or a historian
  c Chreia, or amplification of a moral theme
  d Amplification of an aphorism (*sententia*) or proverb
  e Refutation or confirmation of an allegation
  f Commonplace, or confirmation of a thing admitted
  g Encomium, or eulogy (or dispraise) of a person or thing
  h Comparison of things or persons
  i Impersonation (*ethologia, ethopoeia, prosopopeia*), or speaking or writing in the character of a given person
  j Description, or vivid presentation of details
  k Thesis, or argument for or against an answer to a general question (*quaestio infinita*) not involving individuals
  l Laws, or arguments for or against a law

4 **Declamation** (*declamatio*), or fictitious speeches, in two types:

  a *Suasoria* or deliberative (political) speech arguing that an action be taken or not taken
  b *Controversia* or forensic (legal) speech prosecuting or defending a fictitious or historical person in a law case

5 **Sequencing**, or the systematic ordering of classroom activities to accomplish two goals:

  a Movement, from the simple to the more complex
  b Reinforcement, by reiterating each element of preceding exercises as each new one appears

NANCY SOMMERS

Nancy Sommers has a reserved place in composition anthologies. In her award-winning essay "Revision Strategies of Student Writers and Experienced Adult Writers" (1980), she challenged linear models of the composition process with a recursive understanding of writing that brought revision to the forefront of the field. In "Responding to Student Writing" (1982), also an award winner, she warned against teachers appropriating student texts in their comments and instead offered strategies for response focused on revision and discovery. An attention to pedagogy and student writers, especially in revision and response, has been a hallmark of Sommers's career. She received her doctorate in education from Boston University and went on to direct Harvard's Expository Writing Program for 20 years. Sommers served as the principal investigator for the longitudinal Harvard Study of Undergraduate Writing, which tracked the writing experiences and development of 400 students. She has also produced three short films focused on amplifying student voices within composition pedagogy. In "Beyond the Red Ink," she spotlights student perceptions of teacher comments. Sommers currently teaches in Harvard's Graduate School of Education and is the lead author of the Hacker handbooks series published by Bedford/St. Martin's. Her later writing has tended to be more personal as she has explored family histories, personal narratives, and evocative photographs in order to better understand the work of writing, teaching, and living—which she also presents as a process. At the end of "I Stand Here Writing," Sommers notes, "With writing and with teaching, as well as with love, we don't know how the sentence will begin and, rarely ever, how it will end."[1]

—Eric Leake

---

1 Sommers, Nancy. "I Stand Here Writing." *College English* 55.4 (1993): (428). Print.

"Enter the Process in Uncertainty"

Eric Leake and David Masiel

Fall 2014

WOE: What was your path into rhetoric and composition?

SOMMERS: In graduate school I taught writing and loved it. At that time, in the late 1970s, it became clear that there were jobs in the expanding field of rhetoric and composition, unlike in literary studies. My first job was directing the writing program at the University of Oklahoma. Then I took some years off from teaching to have children—years I call, using a wonderful phrase from Simone de Beauvoir, "in service of the species." While my children were very young I found a way to continue teaching part time as an adjunct. Fortunately, a full-time job opened up at Rutgers. in 1985, and I taught graduate comp theory and practice in the English Department. Since 1987 I've been at Harvard. It's been a long run.

WOE: Who were some of your early mentors or people who really formed your early thinking about writing?

SOMMERS: I came into the field around the time Mina Shaughnessy published *Errors & Expectations*, and Shaughnessy's research and understanding of students' writing were an inspiring influence. I also came into the field around the time when Sondra Perl and Linda Flower first published their research on the composing process, and I found their work inspiring, too. I also look back to Donald Murray as one of the most important influences on my work. I love Murray's voice and his approach—a writer teaches writing. At one point when I couldn't figure out how to balance motherhood with a professional life, he said to me, "just forget the profession and do work you love. The rest will take care of itself." Murray's words became a sustaining mantra for me.

One of the most important things for me now is to be a mentor and advocate for young scholars coming into our field, because so many established people were generous and welcoming to me. I think of Ed Corbett, Win Horner, Wendy Bishop, and others who invited me to give talks at conferences and included my research in their anthologies. I felt as if the established people in our profession were saying, "you come, too." I want to say "you come, too" to all the young scholars entering our profession. This is a big tent of a profession; there is a place for you.

WOE: When you first began to write about revision, as a teacher and as a scholar, were you aware of your own revision process?

SOMMERS: No, not really. The reason I started studying revision is that my students were having so much trouble with it. I had a sense that there was something different about what they were doing and what I understood to be the revision processes of more experienced writers, but I didn't include myself in the category of an experienced writer. I didn't really focus on my own revision process until I wrote the essay "Between the Drafts." In writing this essay, I explored questions about what prompts revision, what makes it possible, and why the writing work "between the drafts" is so central to a writer's identity. Revision shapes both writing and the writer and I began, for the first time, to write as a writer and consider my own revision process.

Now, I love to revise and am much more aware of who I am as a reviser and how important revision is. I don't really understand a piece of writing until I get inside my own words and begin revising. I start revising from the first moment I write a sentence. I keep reading and rereading each word and each sentence with the hope that they'll reveal their secrets and will lead me in a surprising direction. It doesn't always work, but when it does, it is hugely satisfying.

I do have in mind another research project on revision. I've studied both revision and responding and am really excited about the wonderful, very smart scholars who've studied responding and pushed our understanding of this topic forward. But revision—why hasn't it been studied more intensely? I'm always surprised that the article I wrote about revision continues to be the piece people read and anthologize. I'm pleased that young scholars and practitioners, even students, find the article useful, but I hope a new generation of rhetoricians will begin asking questions about revision and provide a deeper understanding of this important topic.

WOE: You bring that up with the idea that we begin revising as soon as we consider a choice, discard it, and make a different decision, which could happen before we ever put a keystroke to a screen. In a way that's an extreme level of recursivity in writing, which you talked about from the very beginning.

SOMMERS: I just finished writing a teaching narrative. This is a piece that I revised and revised, probably thirty drafts to understand what I wanted to say. What interests me about revision is how the sense of the whole develops through the process of using language. I always say to my students, if you knew ahead of time exactly what you wanted to say, there's no reason to write. You would have no discovery because there would be nothing you're trying to understand. You have to enter the process in uncertainty, in that unknowing. I think that's difficult when you're a new writer, that unknowing and uncertainty. I didn't know if this narrative I was writing would be any good, but I never had any doubt that I could write an essay. But for students there is a lot of uncertainty, especially for basic writers. They work so hard on a paragraph and then a teacher comes along to say, "Well, that doesn't make any sense." The student has no idea where a new paragraph will come from.

I always tell my students that you've got to be in a trance when you write. You've got to be so absorbed in what you're writing that you're always thinking about it—thinking about it when you're driving although it's not so good for the other motorists, and in a trance when you're cooking, although it's not so good for the chicken, but you have to do that. There's something about that trance that allows ideas to just keep mixing and living inside you. It's almost like you're trying to attach something to yourself, even when you don't know what it is. Sometimes the process is a search for an idea or word to match an inchoate sense of what you're trying to say, sometimes it just takes living inside a sentence for a long, long time before you understand what it is trying to say. It takes language to produce language and this messy, exciting process only happens for me when I'm in the trance and filtering life through what I'm trying to write. I love that, that sense that everything in life is relevant, everything might fit into an essay I'm writing or it might just lead me to something I'm trying to figure out.

But then, of course, you write words down and what was so exciting in your head looks awful on the page. You have to tolerate a lot of that awfulness. You have to tolerate a lot of uncertainty and confusion. But as a more experienced writer, that's what's exciting about writing and revising. Revision is trying to figure out what you're trying to say as you're saying it and as you're trying to understand what you're trying to say. There are so many levels you're working on simultaneously. You write something that may not get you any closer. Maybe one sentence or one word stays, and the rest is deleted. The process continues.

WOE: Are there things that you have found to be successful in communicating the nature of that moment to students?

SOMMERS: I think so. Sometimes, especially when I teach creative nonfiction, I use one or two of my essays to model some element I want to illustrate, including drafts of published essays, to explain the process behind the printed page, especially those moments of being in the trance and discovering a surprising direction. For instance, I think it is important for students to learn how to think against themselves, to question their ideas and assumptions, to ask lots of "why" and "so what" questions. If students are writing arguments, I want them to learn how to pose counterarguments and to enter into the frame of mind of someone who might not agree with their interpretation. I often show early drafts and talk about the backstory of a particular revision decision—it could be one conversation with a friend or an interview in a newspaper that causes me, in the trance, to think against myself and rethink my argument—or it could be a phrase I hear on the radio that forces me to question my own assumptions.

WOE: So many people encounter your writing first through anthologies. Is there anything important that you think is left out in those encounters?

SOMMERS: I think the anthologies are wonderfully useful because they allow new teachers to gain a big picture of our profession. I would much rather have colleagues read a brief book I wrote for Bedford/St. Martin's, *Responding to Student Writers*, than the article on responding because the book is a much fuller treatment of the pleasures and challenges of responding. I also think the responding article, when I look at it now, is not generous towards teachers. The article reads as if I'm a researcher studying the subject, not as if I'm somebody who sits on weekends and reads stacks of papers. If the anthologized article speaks to new and experienced teachers, I'm pleased to know that the observations I made in the 1980s seem relevant today. If I had to imagine why it might seem relevant, I would think that it succinctly identifies some of the universal problems all teachers have in responding to their students' work. It's so easy to take over a student's piece, to edit it for them, or to rubberstamp vague comments. It is so easy to take a deficit approach to student writing by seeing what is wrong with it and by believing that our job, as responders, is to fix what is wrong. I hope that in my book on responding, more than in my article, I show myself as a teacher, someone who is inspired by her students' drafts, and who wants to respond to them as fellow writers.

WOE: Do you think there's anything built into the system that causes that deficit model to always be lurking, even with our best intentions? Sometimes it seems to lurk in the students also.

SOMMERS: One of the most important things writing teachers can do at the beginning of the semester is to talk about comments and open up a conversation about responding. In such conversations, students will say, "The purpose of comments is to tell me what I've done wrong." That's the place where you have to begin, because if students think that you're commenting to tell them what they've done wrong, and if you're actually commenting to say "good insight" and "develop this," there's a real mismatch. I learned a lot about how students interpret teachers' comments from interviewing students at Bunker Hill Community College and creating a film—*Beyond the Red Ink*—to showcase seven students in the project. In the film interview, I asked students, "If you could give feedback to your teachers about their comments, what would you tell them?" One student said, "teachers should say on the first day of class that comments are to help you learn: 'Here's how I comment, and here's why I comment. Welcome to the class.'" That was so profound to me. I realized I don't do that. I realized that I needed to show my students the type of comments they would receive, the purpose behind these comments, and how they might use the comments to revise.

WOE: Could you say more about what you personally find most challenging in responding to student writers?

SOMMERS: Restraint comes first: I can't comment on everything, so I need to figure out what kind of comments would most help a student at a particular point in the process. I need to be able to diagnose the draft and imagine both the kind of comment I might write and what I would hope the student could do with the comment. I need to ask: what are the two or three things that I could comment on that would make a big difference in the next draft? I'm less likely to rewrite a student's sentence because I comment electronically and hate to see that tracked change; it's so violent.

In responding, I try to take the big perspective on a student's draft and say, "Ah, this is an area to comment on because it will really open up a question or an insight for the student and provide a student with 'new eyes' to see his/her own words."

WOE: I run into that problem of feeling like I'm going to have to read a piece twice to know it well but that I'm so pressed for time.

SOMMERS: I feel this enormous responsibility every time that I read a student paper. Not so much that it cripples me and I can't do it, but that maybe I didn't get it right, maybe there's another way of seeing a student's ideas and responding to them. One of the things that helps me as a reader is to ask students to compose a writer's memo, which they attach to their draft. I call the memo a "Dear Reader letter," a way for students to reflect on what they've written and to provide their readers with answers to questions, such as What's the thesis in this paper? What's the argument? and Why does this argument need to be made? I also ask them to tell me about the challenges they had in writing the draft and, too, the successes. The answers to these questions help me read their drafts to understand their intentions and to respond directly to them. I often ask, too, what they might change about their draft if they had another day to spend writing. The answers to this question, in particular, always give me a place to start my response.

WOE: Some of your writing is more traditional and some is much more personal. How do you view the relationship between personal and academic writing?

SOMMERS: I write a lot of different things, but I love writing creative nonfiction because it gives me a chance to write about important subjects—my family or my teaching, for example, or about evocative objects—in a comfortable voice. I recently wrote two essays I loved writing—"Don't Tell the Aunts" and "Dated, Labeled, and Preserved"—both essays about evocative objects and the role objects play in our lives.

I'm also happy to write academic essays, such as "The Novice as Expert: Writing the Freshman Year" or "Across the Drafts," essays that came out of the longitudinal study I conducted. These academic essays are, I hope, written in a more comfortable, engaging, and generous voice than some of the first articles I published.

It is possible to be both personal and academic, and I hope students will have multiple opportunities to discover what matters to them through their writing assignments. Clearly, all students need to understand academic writing, its conventions and expectations, to write successfully in college. I would want students to write researched arguments in their first-year writing course, learn how to argue with and against sources, but always have a personal stake in the argument.

One thing that became clear in the longitudinal study I conducted was that students don't always make the most of their college writing experiences because they often see writing as an assignment, a hoop to jump through, a task they are doing for a teacher, not for themselves. One of the students in the study, when asked what advice he would give to future freshmen, said something to the effect of, "Every time you write, try to get something and give something." I think that's a great formulation, to get something and learn something from the process, but also to be able to give something back to your reader and to feel that you have an insight that will matter to your readers, too. That's something students can learn in their first-year writing class, how to choose topics that matter to them, to be both personal and academic.

WOE: Everybody is a little bit different as an instructor. How important is it to make room for those different strengths and personal qualities in teaching writing?

SOMMERS: It's so overwhelming when you first start teaching, overwhelming on every level. You don't know what's possible for yourself or for your students. You don't know what writing development looks like and don't know how to take a "less is more" approach. And, too, it is hard to find your voice as a teacher, a voice that is comfortable in the classroom. It's hard to say to a new teacher, "Be yourself. Tell stories. Let students know who you are and why you're teaching." I say to my students, "I'm a Jewish mother. I feed people, and so I'm going to bring food to class. That's who I am."

WOE: What allows for the variation within a program? Is it a matter of instructor preference?

SOMMERS: There has to be some commonality within a writing program or else there is no program, no coherence, just a collection of classes. I think themed writing courses work really well. One of the things I found in the longitudinal study was that the students who made the most progress as writers over four years were students who developed expertise in a content and a method. If they were studying philosophy, for example, and they had the opportunity to read Nietzsche in two or three different courses, maybe read the same Nietzsche text over again, they developed an expertise in the content that made it possible for them to argue with Nietzsche and his critics. They developed a kind of surefootedness and fluency with the arguments so that they could engage with them. Too often in writing courses we deprive students of building expertise in content because the course lacks thematic continuity. It's unlike any other experience they have elsewhere in the university. In sociology, for example, if they're taking a class in deviance, everything they read and write about has to do with deviance. But in most writing classes students are writing about topic one, then topic two, then topic three, and they can't build expertise in content across the assignments. When this happens, we put students at a disadvantage because they are writing without expertise.

WOE: To what extent do you think this huge body of research in composition has had an influence in the way that writing is taught in lower levels? Do you see changes in incoming undergraduates?

SOMMERS: Students definitely come in much more aware of writing as a process. You see the biggest difference with students who were taught by National Writing Project teachers. The influence of the National Writing Project is remarkable. These students understand the workshop method right away. Unfortunately, what has become increasingly more difficult for first-year composition is that our students have overlearned the five-paragraph theme because of all their testing. It's really hard for students to discard that five-paragraph theme; it is their default. We try to move students from their rigid five-paragraph structure, but one semester isn't enough for students who have practiced this structure since sixth grade. I would love to see a researcher study this problem to help us understand the developmental writing stages students go through to break away from the five-paragraph theme.

WOE: Are there counter expectations in other departments?

SOMMERS: First-year writing isn't meant to teach students everything they need to know about college writing or to prepare them to write across all disciplines. WAC/WID programs have had huge influences to encourage faculty to introduce their disciplinary methods and styles of writing. Students in history classes, for instance, need to understand historiography and need a method for understanding how to analyze the historical debates about a given topic. For students to think and write as historians, they need to receive this kind of training. When students don't receive training in their chosen field, they take more of a trial-and-error approach, a sink or swim, and can't understand that disciplines are defined by the questions they ask, the evidence they use. If students are really lucky, though, they'll have a thoughtful teacher who will say, "Come to my office and let's sit and work on this."

Teaching writing—no matter where it happens, in first-year writing or in courses across the discipline—is a sacred responsibility. As college teachers, we have a far-reaching mission to show students how to read critically, write effectively, and join ongoing research conversations as contributors (not just as consumers) of ideas. I hope all students will encounter thoughtful teachers across the disciplines, teachers who care deeply about their students learning to think and write. And I hope that all students will learn to read deeply and write clearly, that they will find in their reading ideas they care about, and that they will write about these ideas with care and depth. Learning to think and write is, after all, a goal of college—to be shaped by writing and to become a literate, thoughtful citizen with things to say.

KATHLEEN BLAKE YANCEY

Over the course of a distinguished career, Kathleen Blake Yancey's published writings have reflected her varied interests in the field of rhetoric and composition, including portfolio assessment, WAC assessment, multimodal writing, the role of prior knowledge in writing development, and an ambitious study of skill transfer across academic disciplines. In Reflection in the Writing Classroom *(1998), Yancey emphasizes reflection as a practice that encourages students to be responsible for their own learning: "while many of us advocate student-centered pedagogy, we are still struggling to see how to get the student into that center" (20). In* Teaching Literature as Reflective Practice *(2004), she explores, among other things, validating students' personal interpretation of literature as well as the knowledge they bring to class. In her most recent book,* Writing Across Contexts: Transfer, Composition, and Sites of Writing *(2014), Yancey and coauthors Liane Robertson and Kara Taczak evaluate current theories of transfer and establish their own research-based teaching for transfer model (TFT).* Writing Across Contexts *offers a model based on systematic reflection, key terms, and students' development of their own theory of writing.* Writing Across Contexts *won the 2015 CCCC Research Impact Award and the 2016 CWPA Best Book Award.*

In addition to her scholarly works, she has coauthored two textbooks with Elaine Maimon and Janice Peritz: A Writer's Resource, *3rd Edition (2005) and* The New McGraw Hill Handbook, *3rd Edition (2008). A prolific writer, Yancey frequently contributes work to scholarly publications while maintaining her work in object-based creative nonfiction (see WOE, Fall 2015). Her best-known articles are "Postmodernism, Palimpsest, and Portfolios: Theoretical Issues in the Representation of Student Work" (2004) and "Made Not Only in Words: Composition in a New Key" (2004). The latter is noteworthy both for its message (that the field of composition should embrace multimodality) and for its layout (a Four Quartets–inspired structure that uses marginalia and images to interact, compete with, and support the main text). Yancey is currently the Kellogg W. Hunt Professor of English at Florida State University. She has served as head of the Association of Writing Program Administrators, chair of CCCC (2004), president of NCTE (2008), and editor of* College Composition and Communication *(2010–2014).*

—Eric Leake, David Masiel and Lisa Sperber

"It's Their Story that Turns Your Head"

David Masiel, William Sewell, and Hogan Hayes

Spring 2015

WOE: So let me start with our first interest at *WOE*: What brought you to writing and the teaching of it?

YANCEY: When I was in high school I thought I wanted to be a lawyer, but my father and my guidance counselor told me I should consider marrying one instead. If I absolutely *had* to have a career, they both said, consider teaching, because the first assumption (as we have already established) was that I'd get married so I could fall back on teaching if my husband died. That would be good too because I'd have summers off to care for the children. So that gives you an idea of what things were like for a woman of my generation! [laughs]

WOE: What year was this, and what did you end up studying?

YANCEY: I went to college in 1968. I majored in history and then flipped to English. I did earn a credential to teach both English and history for grades 6–12, but English felt immediately natural, like breathing. I also found I identified with the faculty. Many of them were ABD or nontenured faculty, young, and they were smart, and interesting. And I could read myself into that position. It was really in that moment that I thought, well, K–12, maybe I'll give that a go, but what I really wanted was to be a college professor. Because I could see how your own intellectual interests could play into a curriculum. I could also see how you could manage your own time. I could see what it looked like to be a scholar. I had good high school English teachers—very good—but I didn't understand them as scholars.

WOE: So reading and writing and writing about writing—they were always bound?

YANCEY: Oh yes. I student taught, got my teaching credential, and then went to graduate school where I taught. The teaching part—and let me say, I do think teachers have to develop—but teaching did feel like a natural fit. I wasn't interested in the stage model of teaching; I was interested in what we called at the time the interactive classroom, and that seemed to be a very good fit with the teaching of writing. I had a wonderful mentor, someone who was very active in the National Writing Project, Marjorie Kaiser. She was extraordinarily influential in any number of ways. Even so, my master's thesis took Theodore Dreiser as its topic, and when I went to do graduate work, I thought I might specialize in the 19th-century novel, which I loved. Still do. The fly in the ointment through all of this was actually my own writing.

I didn't do it very well. I'm not saying I do it well now, but I think I do it better. In fact, going through some old materials earlier this term, I came across a paper I wrote on romantic poetry at Purdue University, where I did my doctorate. The faculty member I was working with, Michael Yetmen, gave me a lot of commentary, but one adjective stood out: *turgid*. It was a well-earned assessment, I must say!

So I really needed to learn to write, and I think that Doug Hesse makes the point about work in writing program administration: it's important not to lose the writing part. If you're teaching writing, it's important to think that you're at least a competent writer. And that took me a very long time.

WOE: I wonder if it isn't something of an advantage *not* to be one of those people for whom writing comes easily. Having to struggle to learn it yourself—has that informed your pedagogy?

YANCEY: There's no question about it. I also tell my students this: when I was in college I failed three courses. Now to be fair, on two of those, it turns out when you stop going to class, they fail you. [laughs] So I certainly did my part! But in the third course, I actually tried, and still failed. So I had any number of struggles. So yes, it has informed my pedagogy. You can imagine the impact, when you're talking to students. I stand up there, and I have some idea how they see me, and I ask, "Has anybody here failed a class?" and nobody says anything, and then I say, "Well, gosh, I have." I mean, this isn't just *I think I'm failing*, I actually have documentation to prove it! And they're just kind of astonished, but there I am as their instructor, and I've lived to tell about it, so failure in whatever form is part of the learning process, and we might want to talk about that. And speaking in terms of writing, I often bring in my own writing—as I did back in the days of dot-matrix printers, so I'd have a long sheet of tractor-feed paper and I'd bring in something like a chapter of a book I had written. In one case I remember, the editor genuinely liked the chapter, yet gave me *four pages* of notes on what I needed to do for the revision. It was very effective to hold it in front of them and just let the pages unfold to the floor, one by one by one by one. [laughs] I think there's a lot of value in living the life of a writer.

WOE: As a writer, you inhabit territory between several kinds of writing, certainly the creative and the scholarly. As a scholar with at least a foot in the creative writing camp, how do you see creative writing pedagogy, the state of it, and how it relates to composition studies? Have the two been artificially separated, or is there common ground that can bring them together?

YANCEY: In that I'm influenced by the work I did with a student who graduated from our program in Creative Writing. In our doctoral program, students have to take a minor, and she took her minor in rhetoric and comp, and I was her advisor for that. She took several courses from me, one of which was in comp theory. At her dissertation defense, I was struck by an entirely different vocabulary used in the creative writing setting. I wasn't completely unfamiliar with it, but it's not the vocabulary that I use. And that's really interesting to me. Terms like "rhythm," or "refrain"—those aren't terms I'd typically use. That's my way of saying that one way to think about how the two areas view writing might be to look at the vocabulary in each discipline, and what that vocabulary helps you see, and also what it prevents you from seeing.

In terms of pedagogy, the writing workshop in creative writing is canonical at this point, and subject to considerable critique, if I read accurately. It is interesting to me again, though, how that version of a workshop relates to the workshop as it's used in rhet-comp, which I think has a similar aim, but a very different set of activities moving toward that aim. And also a different set of assumptions. Lastly, I do think there are, and have always been, efforts to reach across the boundaries. I don't think there's any question about that. The editor of *Fourth Genre*, Laura Julier, and I met through rhetoric and composition, but have worked together on creative nonfiction projects. And it doesn't stop with creative writing, especially now. Genre conventions and genre exclusivity are being questioned and broadened. Ned Stuckey-French, the book editor at *Fourth Genre* and a good colleague of mine at FSU, is bringing in a group of people next month to think about the essay in the context of video. These kinds of explorations will change how we think about the languages of writing. Especially in creative writing, there is such affection for, respect for, and some anxiety about language, which is not fully shared on the rhetoric and comp side. People in rhet-comp are more concerned with, and perhaps more eager to embrace, multimodality. I don't mean only digital multimodality; I mean composing with all the means available to affect an audience. It's an interesting question. What do you gain? If I try to describe that chair, what do I gain by relying exclusively on language to do that? What do I gain by using other modes? I would not make the argument that one mode is better than the other. I would make an argument that they're different, and that it's worth exploring what those differences are.

WOE: Which is reflected in some of the things you were bringing up ten years ago with your essay "Composition in a New Key."

YANCEY: But in fact, in terms of multimodality, it's perhaps not all that ambitious. It might look that way to a traditional academic, but if I had published it in a place like *Kairos*, a more digital journal, I could have gone even further to include video and other digital media. In the end, "Comp in a New Key" is an interesting exercise in verbal and visual literacy, and I think it's also a very interesting exercise in assemblage. I like it, and people have responded positively to it, but I don't think it's that ambitious. Though the arrangement of it is more juxtapositional than linear, a lot of what I was doing there in terms of the verbal-visual interface is not unlike what students will be doing in junior-level classes in their majors. If you're doing geography, or social sciences, you'll be making a lot of the same moves that I make there. So another way to think about this is to ask the question—and I think this is important, and not well attended to—what's the interface between lower-division courses and what we think students will be doing in their majors? When you start looking at it, you realize that the only discipline working strictly with language is philosophy. All the others are doing some significant work in the visual presentation of information. So I don't believe that first-year comp is accountable to other majors, but I also do think it's situated relative to the other curricula. And if you pursued that question from that vantage point, then we would be obliged to teach those other literacies. And I think we are obliged because no matter how much students practice these on their own, they do so, ordinarily, from a tacit working knowledge rather than from an explicit working knowledge. So one of the things that we want to do is help them articulate exactly what that tacit knowledge is, and when it's congruent with what we want them to do, show them how it can support those efforts.

WOE: I'm curious what you think about some of the tensions that this creates in the composition classroom, when trying to address these other literacies yet running headlong into the challenges of trying to teach writing skills in a single semester or quarter. This is a major pedagogical challenge.

YANCEY: I'm with you on that. So one very big question in comp, especially first-year comp, is what precisely are the limits or boundaries, or *are* there limits or boundaries? For instance, those who want to teach sonic literacy, they will often argue that we've done a lot with visual literacy but not very much with sonic literacy. People will make the same argument about video, so it's not just what are the boundaries, or what are the outcomes, not just what we're hoping to do, but what do we expect students to get out of this? Whatever the "this" is. Institutionally it goes further—what certifies us to have expertise in those areas? I spent some time a while back with first-year comp faculty doing some very interesting things at their university, which also happened to have a very strong media studies department, and from that discipline's perspective, the comp folks were poachers on their domain, or worse—amateurs, or dilettantes.

WOE: Given that tendency of other disciplines to see us as interlopers, how would you argue writing contributes to these broader academic concerns?

YANCEY: It's essential. The work on prior knowledge is pretty clear. In the best-case scenario students come to us with an understanding that's very similar to ours, and in that instance you can build on it. But in other circumstances they come in with an understanding that's very much at odds with ours. For example, a student comes into a composition classroom with the attitude that they are very creative in their writing, but what they lack is grammar, and since grammar is the most important thing, they're glad to be here. Well, actually, that's not what I think. So we have to have a different kind of discussion.

A different situation exists when a student comes to a classroom with a prior knowledge that is at odds with the academy more generally. That doesn't happen as often in comp classes as it does in other fields, but the classic example would be, say, a student comes to the university from a community or a system of beliefs that asserts that Darwin's theory of evolution is merely a theory, and that it's no better or worse than intelligent design. Or a student believes that global warming is all politics—that's a different prior belief and a different set of problems. So I like to focus on prior knowledge, and given the lack of time we can't delve into all prior knowledge, but we do need to make judgments about where they are, what they know, and what they believe, and we can make those judgments based on the differences among students and folding that into what we do. Jeff Sommers had an interesting article about this in the *Journal of Basic Writing* that traces a set of student beliefs about writing, which isn't exactly the same thing as prior knowledge, but it's related. Students were asked to come in and identify three things they believed to be true about writing, and then asked to trace the evolution of those beliefs over the course of the term. Now, Jeff is not a miracle worker, and neither is any of the rest of us, so there were some students whose views didn't change very much. And I respect Jeff for helping us to see that. At the same time there were many—most—students who did see that their ideas were not capacious enough or were erroneous and they could see why. And that's an interesting kind of text to run alongside the basic content of the course.

WOE: So how would you characterize some of the challenges in this, from the perspective of program administration?

YANCEY: There are many, among them helping students develop a vocabulary for writing. As we're finding out in the second phase of our study—the first phase having led to the book *Writing Across Contexts*—the problem of how the vocabulary of transfer is established and retained is exacerbated by a number of factors, in particular when you shift from semester to quarter, because you lose a third of your time, so you have even less time to lay the groundwork for a deep understanding of what concepts mean across disciplinary applications. Now if you have a program with a two-term requirement—which could be two semesters, or two quarters—there may well be benefits to delaying the second course, which is another issue. For example, at FSU, we're moving the second course for first-year comp to the sophomore level. Our course has long been process based, and the second is focused more on research methods.

In that course, there has not been very much attention to genre, I might add, but as we move it into a sophomore class we're focusing on three things: context, genre, and inquiry. Context in part because research has shown that that term provides a revelation for students, as few have encountered it or worked with it before college. Genre comes next—though in fact I think it should come in the first course. Again, I think it's clear from lots of research that genre is a portal to writing, and that it's almost impossible to write as well without some understanding of genre. We use inquiry rather than argument because our research and other research shows—and this tends to be true whether students are coming to us from high school or as transfer students—that they've been so rewarded for argument, that when you say "you're going to write an argument," their prior knowledge is very clear: a) they know about argument, and b) it informs almost every facet of their lives. When they were in high school if they wanted to borrow the car, they needed to make an argument, and the one thing they understood was the need to pummel their opposition. That's very different than how we think about argument. And I've seen regional differences in comp classes, with some students saying they did not want to do argument because in the South, it's impolite to argue. All of this is to say that argument is underexplored as a practice in this regard. And I think inquiry is better, more expansive, more plastic. It gives you permission to make a claim if you're so inclined, but it doesn't oblige you to do so.

WOE: So it's fair to say you see argument working as a subset of inquiry. It's one kind of inquiry.

YANCEY: Yes. I'm struck here by Jim Kinneavy's work, "The Basic Aims of Discourse," which in its time exerted a fair amount of influence, though less so now, and a comp class informed by "Aims." I used that text, and one of the main reasons I chose it was that he had a chapter called "Writing as Inquiry," but I came away disappointed. And I have enormous respect for Kinneavy's work. But in the end he subordinated inquiry to argument—and that's not what I was looking for.

So I've shifted instead to asking fundamentally unanswerable questions, questions that people of reason and good will might disagree on. Such questions as, "Is there such a thing as a good war?" Depending on the class, I have students do small projects that are not worth very much, and/or case studies, and that works very well because I think there is an association in their minds of big projects that are worth a lot in which they have to make an argument. That's the history they bring with them, and that's the expectation. But if you give them a small project that feels low stakes, where it's very clear that their intent is to learn, then they actually tend to learn what it means to inquire.

WOE: How does this fit into the teaching for transfer, exactly? In my own experience, you can tell them how things transfer, you can even provide a project that helps in transfer, but in the end they have to do it on their own, and it can sometimes seem accidental.

YANCEY: One thing we can do is cultivate a habit of thinking and of seeing what might be similar across writing contexts. After all, that's what transfer is all about. If students come into the writing classroom thinking that what they are going to learn in English is not going to have any relationship to any context—to their own, to the future, to contexts that might be going on concurrently—then the table for transfer—and really, for learning—has not been set. The first thing they need to understand is that there is something going on in the class that is parallel to other things going on in their world. And the beauty of this is that *we* do not know what these connections might be: only *they* know. So there's agency in this approach. Only *they* can find the connections. I don't know what the relationship is between their prior knowledge and what I'm about to teach them, because I don't have their prior knowledge. So guess what, this is a collaborative enterprise. We're going to need to do this together. The thing we can do is help students develop a vocabulary to describe what's going on in these contexts, and it helps to begin developing a reflective habit of mind that is less concerned, I think, with justifying what they have done, and much more interested in inquiry, in trying to discern similarities and differences across these contexts so that you can transfer appropriately. Because there are cases clearly where people don't transfer appropriately. If we don't set this table, here's what I think can happen, and this will come out of my own experience. I had a student who took my class, in which I used the theme of "Voice, Genre, and Technology." She went off the next semester and took a technical writing course, after which she came back and said, "Everything you taught us in this class was wrong in tech writing. What's going on here?" And it's a fair question.

WOE: And probably one of the most common complaints among students, that the rules seem to change from class to class.

YANCEY: Exactly. So I told her, let me give you a question that I probably should have put to you earlier. What's your theory of writing? Maybe your theory of writing isn't capacious enough to describe these differences. Take genre: genre could be a lens that will help you understand. Genres are not free floating; they are located. What can we do to help students describe these differences across these contexts? And maybe there are similarities that you're not seeing because you're focused so much on the differences. That's what we are trying to do with students, help them develop a legitimate expertise that only they can do, but which we can help foster. That's our goal.

WOE: Can you talk a bit about your experience with the transfer of narrative to expository writing, or narrative to argument?

YANCEY: That's a great question, but a hard question. When I was in college, the approach given to us was the traditional modes: narrative, description, explanation, argument. And then things like Kinneavy's "The Basic Aims of Discourse" helped people begin to see that the aim and purpose made a difference. Then you see another flip and people begin to think of narrative and exposition as rhetorical strategies. I think that's right; however, I guess

I also think it's wrong. My concern is that you can so often win an argument in terms of the discourse, and yet in fact, lose the argument. So often it isn't about the argument, it's about something else. And narrative, in particular, can be a more welcoming invitation. If I'm at a curriculum meeting and say anything about "outcomes," I'll have a number of colleagues react.... They're all very good teachers, by the way, but when I say "outcomes" they hear "Satan." If I say, however, can you describe for me what you want your students to be able to do—paint me a picture, set me a scene? What does that scene show? If I put it that way, they're on board.

As a culture, argument tends to be our overarching rubric, and if I'm acting in that vein, whatever my other rhetorical methods are, their purpose is to serve argument. And I'm *not* on board with that. I'm much more interested in the way that narrative moves toward exposition, or nonfiction in general. You see it in the *New Yorker* or the *Times*—long-form journalism brings us a narrative that creates a personal angle on the story and is then juxtaposed against exposition. And it's interesting that we don't teach that typically. I think it's very effective when done well, since that approach can do more to persuade than pure argument. Especially when issues are seriously vexed.

WOE: We can humanize through narration in a way we can't through argument.

YANCEY: Absolutely, of course. I would point to gay rights. One of the reasons that issue has moved so fast, and I know it doesn't seem fast, but in historical terms the last three years have seen an astoundingly rapid change—is through narrative. Even in the courts. If you look at the decisions, for example, that the Supreme Court issues, narrative is very much a part of them. I realize that argument is still the main mode in the courts, but in the court of public opinion, issues often come down to someone you know. It's their story that turns your head. That, it seems to me, is what makes the difference. It's the narratives that will persuade people. I wish you could win on the argument for social justice alone, for example, but it's too abstract. What makes it seem less abstract is the human face. And when you see particular strategies that work across discourse communities whose behaviors, ideologies, and values are very different, then you have more reason to say this is an approach we really need to think about. I also think it's a good question of what students can get personally by taking an inquiry rather than an argument approach. I know in my own personal case, writing on the objects, part of which Doug Hesse and I published in *WOE*, I forced myself to write about an object without recourse to anything but words. And when I enforced that discipline—it started out as a discipline and then became a passion—it helped me see something I not only hadn't seen before, but because it's also associative, it took me some place that I hadn't fully explored. It was an inquiry. So I feel I end up more thoughtful, with a greater appreciation. It isn't always a sunny moment, but the juxtaposition of narration and exposition is engaging both intellectually and emotionally. And that, at the end of the day, matters.

CAROLYN MILLER

Carolyn Miller is widely considered the founder of North American rhetorical genre studies, a subfield of rhetoric and composition. Her groundbreaking essay, "Genre as Social Action," published in The Quarterly Journal of Speech in 1984, sparked a scholarly debate, still vibrant today, about the differences between genres and forms based on rhetorical situations. Though recognizing that genres have recurring patterns of textual conventions, Miller views genres as primarily human, social constructs with a pragmatic orientation. She has consistently argued that genres arise as a response to recurring rhetorical situations grounded in complex communities, where audience expectations shape how genres emerge and change. In order to clarify the idea that genres are "cultural artifacts," Miller revisited her essay and published "Rhetorical Community: The Cultural Basis of Genre" in 1994. Later, because of her growing interest in the rhetorical aspects of digital media, Miller analyzed the emerging genre of the digital blog in "Blogging as Social Action: A Genre Analysis of the Weblog" (2004). Her latest work, "Discourse Genres"(2016), published in The Handbook of Verbal Communication, highlights her interdisciplinary focus on communication science, linguistics, and the cognitive sciences.

Miller earned her PhD in communication and rhetoric from the Rensselaer Polytechnic Institute in 1980. She is currently SAS Institute Distinguished Professor of Rhetoric and Technical Communications at North Carolina State University. Though her dissertation and subsequent essay were primarily based in speech communication literature, Miller's work is decidedly interdisciplinary and, like the concept of genre itself, defies easy classification. She has focused on the environmental movement, scientific communication, technical communication, film and media studies, and psycholinguistics. Miller is currently interested in how scholars in film and media studies examine genre and how genres in digital media and gaming provide new research opportunities in that field and in writing studies. Along with her scholarship, Miller is known for supporting the career development of graduate students, and in 2016, she won the Rhetoric Society of America's Cheryl Geisler Award for outstanding mentor.

—Brenda Rinard

"A Set of Shared Expectations"

Brenda Rinard and David Masiel

Fall 2016

WOE: "Genre as Social Action" has become a foundational work in the area of genre studies. What got you thinking about genre at a time when it was typically defined as categories of literature, categories of music, etc.? What was it about your background and your personal interests that made you think about the subject rhetorically?

MILLER: It wasn't really personal interest at all. It was a suggestion from my dissertation director because I was floundering around trying to figure out "What's this dissertation going to be about?" My director was Michael Halloran, and he had recently attended a Speech Communication Association summer conference on "'Significant Form' in Rhetorical Criticism" put together by Karlyn Campbell and Kathleen Jamieson. And it was about both form and genre, which they tended not to distinguish in a particularly strong way. I think this was '76 and the essays from that conference came out in an undated collection a while later.

I knew I wanted to work on environmental impact statements because I was interested in the environmental movement, having come into the doctoral program [at Rensselaer Polytechnic Institute] after working with our local Sierra Club in Raleigh. I took some courses focusing in that direction. And Michael [Halloran] said, musing, "Well, maybe you should do a genre study," because he had just been at this conference. And I said, "Okay." And then I needed to figure out what that involved. So I began to study the literature, and mind you, this is the literature of communications studies.

Campbell and Jamieson had spun off from Edwin Black's book, *Rhetorical Criticism*, which was published in 1965, and had helped revolutionize rhetorical criticism and free it from the chains of neo-Aristotelianism. Black was part of that movement in the late '60s that said we really have to look at discourse in addition to political speeches—we needed to move beyond the "great white man" approach to political rhetoric. We have to broaden our scope and look at the rhetoric in the streets—and there was a lot of rhetoric in the streets at that time. So this conference was an exploration of what kinds of forms and genres are available to us beyond the presidential inaugural, for example.

WOE: You got interested in the noncategorization of it.

MILLER: Right. When I looked at the genre literature more closely, I realized that they weren't using the term consistently at all. Some of them had a very formalistic understanding of genre. But Campbell and Jamieson were really pushing a view of genre more as dynamic action, pragmatic action. So I saw it as my job, as a graduate student, to make some order out of all this. But it was very instructive for me to see these various perspectives and think, "Well, what is it that a rhetorical angle on genre can bring and how would that be different from a literary angle? And what is it that an action orientation brings to a formalistic orientation?" So that's where I was coming from and how I was trying to make sense of the stuff I was reading.

WOE: Which was clearly interdisciplinary.

MILLER: Yes, but it was really grounded in speech communication literature. I dipped a little bit into the composition literature. I had taken a seminar in which we read James Kinneavy's *A Theory of Discourse*, which no one seems to read anymore, but I found ways to reject his approach. And others too, but I mainly wasn't reading that literature at all. That wasn't part of my graduate education and wasn't what I was looking at (my degree is in communication and rhetoric, not English). There were the people in England—I associate them with James Britton—but they were working more from the pedagogical angle.

WOE: I'm curious how you think about that now—the pedagogical angle. What attracted me—and I think a lot of people in our field—to your approach is that we're thinking about genres from the standpoint of writers forming actions using genre sets or genre systems. There's the rhetorical aspect, the overlapping elements in genre, and not the categories or how to teach specific genres in specific ways. So as much as we might like that, it can be a struggle to get students beyond a more abstract notion of genre. Do you have thoughts on pedagogy in that sense?

MILLER: I think part of that struggle is that students, particularly when you're talking about workplace writing, find it hard to imagine themselves in the roles in which they would be undertaking those actions—having the knowledge and the authority that they would need to write a progress report, or do an accident analysis, or something like that. So one of the strategies that I like to use is a case study approach—or what we might now call simulations, or games. Getting students to play a role in a game so that they can begin to understand what motivates a manager to say, "I want this report on my desk by 5:00 today," or, "Tell us about your field trip to the substation." What questions does the manager need to have answered?

WOE: And what genre would be required to perform that action?

MILLER: Right. If I'm just being a student, I have no idea. But if you can engage them in this role-playing stuff, which I think this generation of students ought to be really good at, you can bridge that gap. So when someone says "trip report," that signals some actions, and questions, some answers, some expectations that are just going to be opaque to the student, but a role-play can allow students to get inside a situation.

WOE: Interesting. Because that is one of the biggest critiques—that you cannot really teach genres outside of their rhetorical situations.

MILLER: That's right. And I think one of the ways to address that is the very old emphasis on imitation from the rhetorical tradition. You do declamations about the Trojan War or Pericles—ancient Greek students did that, so role-playing has a very long tradition. "How does Zeus persuade one of his lovers?" or whatever. And the progymnasmata, the ancient teaching tool is full of role-playing games like that. So it's partly just a matter of finding a role that the student is willing to play with. Probably not Zeus, these days, but . . .

WOE: I can think of a few.

MILLER: I wouldn't know. World of Warcraft? I don't know, but it seems like the same kind of stuff. There used to be textbooks that had case examples—rather complex case examples—but it now strikes me that a lot of that could be done online with video interactions and all kinds of electronic simulations that could get students engaged in the game. I think there might be a market for that.

WOE: The question about video games and genre seems relevant here. I watched the talk you gave at Indiana University about the evolution of genre, and you discussed the video game genre in that. Given your thoughts on games and new media, do you still think that genres evolve?

MILLER: Well, that's a metaphor and it seems to be a very handy metaphor. I think it describes a lot about how genres change—how they come into being, how they change over time, how many of them become obsolete. I've looked at a lot of different models—literary models, for example: Alastair Fowler talks about genre in evolutionary terms. But one of the things I have learned from broadening my reading from rhetorical studies to film studies and TV and media studies—and they're all really interested in genre—is a better understanding of the many different influences on genre change, influences that people in rhetoric and composition often tend to overlook. When it comes to video game genres, users have a lot to do with it—there's this incredible feedback loop. But financial interests, producers, publishers also have a lot to do with it. It's not just the isolated writer or even the workplace writer—it's an industry in the way that films are. Richard Altman has talked about films in evolutionary terms and Jason Mittell talks about television genres in evolutionary terms. What we learn from them are the industrial components, and the economic pressures, and a different kind of relationship with the audience where you're producing a commercial product and seeking an audience in a different way from the classroom or the workplace, where there's more of a captive audience.

WOE: Then, too, there's the application to multimodal composing, which we are grappling with now with approaches to new media.

MILLER: Thinking in terms of genre there can be helpful. If you want to compose a multimodal text and think about the relationship between image and word, well, what's the context of the rhetorical situation? What's the genre? Are we doing an online instructional video? Are we creating a video game? Are we doing a university website? There's a huge number of genres there, and each one is going to have conventions for handling multimodality—or is going to be "evolving" in its own context.

WOE: All with very complex relationships between the writer, the audience, the organizational structure. But we also face this desire to go beyond teaching particular skills for a particular industrial application.

MILLER: Well, teaching some discrete technical skills is important but so is looking at the variety of contexts. I think it's necessary to impress on students that there isn't really one right way—different contexts, different industries are going to have different conventions. Some of the conventions are going to make absolutely zero sense at all, but you've got to do it that way. But if you're presented with a set of requirements and conventions that seem counterproductive, there are ways to tweak, and push, and try to adapt a genre without violating its conventions. Learning how far you can go is part of learning the genre.

WOE: And still fulfilling the audience's needs?

MILLER: That's right.

WOE: So does all of this lead to any redefinition of genre?

MILLER: More and more, I've come to think about the genre itself as being the repetition—how do I put this—of expectations. It's a set of shared expectations, social recognitions and expectations. And that locates the genre—and this has a lot to do with research strategy—it locates the genre not in a corpus of texts but in social understandings, in people's heads. There's a lot of work in linguistics and technical communication, taking social science approaches to collections of texts. I was just in a workshop yesterday with Scott Graham talking about his "big data" approach to genre that he calls "genre fingerprinting." He's been working with people in health communication to learn statistics and quantitative analysis. But that looks for typicality in texts to locate the repeated conventions, not for typicality in people's expectations.

WOE: It's like corpus linguistics. But it also seems that doing that kind of work would lead to statements like "This is the genre. This is how it must be performed"—or reformed in order to be effective or rhetorically successful.

MILLER: And that has its place. That can be useful, but I would want to continually insist that if you're analyzing text, you're not looking at the genre. To look at the genre, you basically need to do reception studies as a way to get at those shared expectations. How do people talk about it? How do they respond to it? What do they do with it? What do they do with violations? And this analysis requires indirect evidence rather than direct evidence. So that's where I've found myself in a tension with some of the work that's going on. I don't think it's wrong. I just think that it's looking at something a little differently. What Scott Graham has been looking at is the transcripts of advisory committee meetings that the FDA sponsors when a decision is made whether to approve a new drug, or to approve a new use for a drug, or to retract approval. During these meetings, there are all kinds of people involved—20 or 30 people in the room. There are patient representatives, and consumer representatives, and drug companies, and FDA scientists and positions, and so forth, and they ultimately reach a decision about the drug—an up or down vote. Graham is looking at how the presence or absence of certain representatives or certain kinds of arguments might be able to affect the outcome. If the patient representatives get more time, does that give you a decision that is different than if they have less time? So examining these features allows you to score those kinds of correlational or semicausal actions and effects—the relationships between features and outcomes—that I can't really do. I think that's a very interesting development and, since the FDA has put all this stuff digitized online, Graham has access to huge databases. So this work requires a new research strategy. Among other things, it requires armies of graduate students to do all the coding it takes.

WOE: I want to go back to something you wrote. Originally you wrote that genres were cultural artifacts and then you also discussed how difficult that can be to explain the definition of culture, what a cultural artifact is. And you often teach students that genres arise within these discourse communities. A discourse community, as Swales defines it, is where people have shared common goals. In that context, if you think about a genre as a cultural artifact, does that imply that culture is too unified? And therefore the explanation too simplistic?

MILLER: I think it's really complex, yeah, and I think it's possible to oversimplify that. But I certainly don't intend it as a simplifying definition. Again, discourse communities expand, and contract, and change their minds, and have internal disagreements and struggles. They have fuzzy edges and they overlap other communities, and I certainly don't see communities as homogenous happy places. And the fact that genres are continually evolving, and adapting, and being tweaked and pressured by users seems to me to suggest that it's not at all a simple picture. Again, when you bring it into the classroom—and this is the constant problem of the teacher—you have to simplify in order to teach it. You have to systematize something that is unsystemetizable in order to talk about it.

WOE: Yet students are often uncomfortable with anything else. It's difficult to get them to understand that variations exist within a genre, and that there isn't just one right way to engage with a genre. They say, "Tell me what I need to write."

MILLER: Yes: "What am I supposed to do?"

WOE: And, if you show them variations and say that it depends on this complex mix of audience, purpose, and other aspects of the rhetorical situation—including context—they are even more uncomfortable.

MILLER: It seems to me that, if you talk with undergraduates about the genres that they know without knowing that that's what they know, like video games, for instance—they know the difference between a first-person shooter and something else. How do they tell the difference? What is important to them? What changes? "If you did this, would it still be a first-person shooter? If you did that—?" Or different kinds of tweets or different kinds of Facebook postings. "How do you tell a tweet from a Facebook posting?" They know it, so elicit from them the cache of knowledge that they have about probably hundreds of genres. And help them see that they have certain tolerances for variation and some places where they're not tolerant of variation, or some places where people argue online about what is or isn't an appropriate thing to do in a forum because it violates genre conventions.

WOE: I recently noticed that there's now a Special Interest Group at CCCC on cognition. For so long now we've been focused on the social, yet it seems that maybe we're experiencing a cognitive turn. Do you have a sense of how cognitive elements might play into genre?

MILLER: Well, I think genre recognition is dependent on pattern recognition and that, certainly, is a cognitive phenomenon. I suspect that the cognitive work in schema theory—and there's a whole bunch of different terms for it—frame theory and others. I did a review of literature not too long ago with Ashley Kelly, to try to pull these together for a chapter of Rocci and de Saussure's *Verbal Communication*. We were given a model—we had to have an introduction, a section on social aspects, a section on cognitive aspects, methodologies, and applications. So I thought about the cognitive aspects in a way I hadn't before and I looked into some of the psycholinguistics work and text linguistics work that relies on pattern recognition. We had a severe word limit so I couldn't go deeply into that, but I made some gestures in that direction so I could go back to it. But I suspect that that's a direction to go—certainly not a direction I'm going to go, but the field could benefit from it. I think Chuck Bazerman's probably the person in our field who has thought most about the cognitive half of the socio-cognitive. Most other people gesture toward the cognitive and then run with the social. In part, I think it's because we often don't have the research skills to move much in that direction. If we're not doing brain scans, or neurological tests, or stuff like that, how do we get at the cognitive?

WOE: The closest we can get is think-aloud protocols.

MILLER: Yes. Right. And that's an old research strategy with real limitations.

WOE: Many of my colleagues want to teach students genre awareness without dipping into genre acquisition. Do you think genre awareness alone is productive, and would you consider it a threshold concept in composition?

MILLER: I am not qualified to speak on what the threshold concepts in composition are. I don't know. But I would guess—and this is just an intuitive hunch—that genre awareness is a very useful gateway to genre acquisition. Earlier I was talking about making students aware of the genres they already know in their own mediated environments and helping them learn to ask questions about the culture in which they're already immersed—this of course is the metacognition. First they need a concept of what a genre is and what it does for people, then you can talk to them about the genres that you're interested in having them acquire. If you want to immerse them in a different culture—a more academic or professional culture—you could get them to reflect on how they learned how to make a Facebook posting and then by analogy, you can ask, "How are you going to learn to write a job application letter? Or a sociology field report?"

WOE: Do you think that learning about genre might help people engage in advocacy and social change?

MILLER: I'm brought back to the historical moment when genre studies emerged in speech communication in the late '60s when it was the rhetoric of the streets that brought scholars out of their neo-Aristotelian cocoons to look at street protests and body rhetorics and other forms of expression, at advocacy and protest. This may be a similar moment. I don't know that genre studies, as such, would generate such an agenda, but it can certainly be applied that way. I can imagine a course designed around genres of social justice. Or genres of protest, or whatever. Wherever you can combine some genre theory with examination of citizen action—what forms do citizens use to express themselves and to create social change? Again, that's a theoretical answer. I'd like to see somebody do it.

WOE: What other future genre research would you like to see?

MILLER: Well, I certainly think that the new media—the digital media—have really opened up the area of genre study. That's what got me back into it. Somebody invited me to contribute to a collection on blogging and I thought, "Huh. I wonder if blogging is a genre," and that's when Dawn Shepherd and I did the piece "Blogging as Social Action." There are all kinds of possibilities there. Where else? The cognitive turn, I think, can add something that we haven't had. And then I'm particularly interested in the ways that different disciplines are using the notion of genre. What do they have in common? How are they incompatible—if they are? Can we learn something from the film studies approach? Can they learn something from us? Because a lot of film studies work—again, I'll go back to Rick Altman's work—is very compatible with what genre studies is doing in rhetoric, but he's never heard of it. Then there's musicology, and art history, and there's information sciences, and anthropology. I'm working with my former student Ashley Kelly on a website called Genre Across Borders that is intended to provide an interdisciplinary, international forum for genre studies and genre scholars. It's at <genreacrossborders.org>.

WOE: Obviously, the Internet not only presents evolving genres, but also a medium for exploring them internationally.

MILLER: Right. I was first invited to go to Brazil to talk about genre studies in 2007. Chuck Bazerman had been there the year before—he's become a real missionary to South America. I taught a four-week short course in Recife, which is a city I'd never heard of before. And I was astonished to discover there's this whole community of scholars who are deeply invested in genre studies because they'd had a national curriculum reform several years before, a reform for language arts instruction that was based on genre, both first- and second-language instruction. All of their teachers needed to be trained so the university curriculum was affected. So they're reading SFL [systemic functional linguistics] from Australia, they're reading Bazerman, they're reading Miller and Devitt from the US. They're also reading some Swiss scholars whose work derives from Vygotsky and Piaget, as well as others that I had never heard of, basically people working in education. And there's a bunch of people in Norway and other parts of Scandinavia who've been really interested in genre for some time. I thought, "We get together once maybe every ten years for an international genre conference, but in the meantime we've got this thing called the Internet— there ought to be a way we could be in better touch with each other."

This thinking resulted in genreacrossborders.org. It's been a much more complicated project than I ever envisioned, and it's the kind of thing that has to keep developing. I hope we've solved the technical problems this year and then we can begin to build the user base a little better and publicize it.

WOE: What has surprised you the most about how scholars have built on your work?

MILLER: Just the fact that they've done it at all has been astonishing to me. Of course, as I've said, I was just trying to get an article out of my dissertation. I thought I had something to say, but it's continually struck me that the people I thought I was talking to really didn't pay any attention to what I said. That piece in the *Quarterly Journal of Speech* is hardly ever cited in that journal—it's cited in a whole bunch of other places. And it was really the applied linguists who first picked it up and, again, this was a community of scholars I didn't know anything about. I was talking to people I didn't even know existed.

WOE: That certainly complicates the question of audience and discourse community.

MILLER: Yeah, it was very bizarre—a very bizarre feeling. Also very surprising, and I've been really pleased and interested to see what other people have been able to do with it. Things I just never thought of. I didn't continue my own work in that area because it seemed to me that nobody was picking up on it and I was thinking of myself more as someone in the rhetoric of science. So I went on to other things until I noticed that people were using what I said, and that got me thinking, "Maybe there *is* something there. Maybe I'll go back to thinking about that." But the work that Amy Devitt has done, the work that Anis Bawarshi has done, and Cathy Schryer and Aviva Freedman and Chuck Bazerman—who was really the first in rhetoric and composition to pick up the general idea and he did a lot of historical work that I think has been enormously useful—all that has taken my initial insights much farther than I could.

And then the whole pedagogical movement. What strikes me there is I think genre is a useful construct for thinking about what it is that novices need to learn as they move into a discourse community. I think that's why the people in speech communication aren't so interested in genre. They're not interested in novices. They're only interested in experts engaging in the consummate rhetorical performance—the exemplar. Genre seems to emphasize the typified, the average. Rhetoric and composition is interested because that's exactly what the novice needs to learn. So if we can find a way to help people understand what those social expectations are and how they can manifest them in a new situation, we can do something useful for people interested in the socialization of novices.

LINDA ADLER-KASSNER

Linda Adler-Kassner's work is motivated by the questions she addresses here: how "good writing" (and its inverse) is defined, assessed, and taught, by whom, and with what attendant values and ideologies. She has examined, for instance, how labeling students "basic writers" shapes public discourse, the historical roots of such conceptions, how to help writing program directors and instructors shape and change stories about writers and writing, and how instructors and program directors can contribute to public policy.

People new to the field of writing studies might first encounter Adler-Kassner's work through Naming What We Know: Threshold Concepts of Writing Studies (2015), *which she co-edited with Elizabeth Wardle, and which was awarded Outstanding Contribution to the Discipline by the Council of Writing Program Administrators (2016). Adler-Kassner has worked on threshold concepts as a framework for teaching and learning both inside and outside of writing studies.* Naming What We Know *articulates key concepts in writing studies in a series of entries written by leading scholars. While well poised for use in the undergraduate writing classroom,* Naming What We Know *was also intended to facilitate conversations about writing with broader audiences.*

Adler-Kassner's earlier work centered on basic writing and community literacy. In Basic Writing as a Political Act: Public Conversations about Writing and Literacies (2002), *co-written with Susanmarie Harrington, the authors work to reframe conversations around students labeled "basic writers" and courses labeled "basic writing." She also co-edited* The Bedford Bibliography for Teachers of Basic Writing (2002; 2nd ed., 2005) *with Gregory Glau, and* Writing the Community: Concepts and Models for Service-Learning in Composition (1997) *with Robert Crooks and Ann Watters. Reflecting her pragmatism and grassroots orientation,* The Activist WPA: Changing Stories about Writing and Writers (2008) *offers WPAs concrete strategies for collaborating with faculty to establish shared goals. Widely recognized,* The Activist WPA *won the Council of Writing Program Administrators' Best Book Award (2010).*

Adler-Kassner is the author, co-author, or co-editor of nine books and more than 45 articles and book chapters. She has directed writing programs for many years, first at Eastern Michigan University and then at University of California, Santa Barbara, where she is currently a professor of writing studies and interim dean of undergraduate education. She served as president of the Council of Writing Program Administrators from 2009–2011. She is currently the associate chair of CCCC.

—Lisa Sperber

"Everything Gets to Writing"

Lisa Sperber and Carl Whithaus

Spring 2017

WOE: Could you tell us a little about your graduate work and what led you toward composition studies and basic writing as areas of inquiry?

ADLER-KASSNER: I had been a history teacher, and then an arts administrator running the education programs for a nonprofit in Minneapolis, where I lived at the time, and then I went to get a Master's degree in communication history in the School of Journalism and Mass Communication at the University of Minnesota. The first class I took, Introduction to Qualitative Theories of Communication, focused on rethinking the ways that ideas and information travel across time and space, and how that is facilitated by communication, and communication writ large, like transportation and education. It had many of what I now think of as threshold concepts moments for me, but at the time I just thought, *this is blowing my mind!*

Then I got a job teaching at the University of Minnesota General College, which was a college for students who were labeled "unprepared" by the university. For our first-year composition (FYC) course, we had to teach an educational narrative by someone with a marginalized educational experience, and Mike Rose's *Lives on the Boundaries* had just been published in paperback, and it too blew my mind. I started to think about constructions of literacy—ideas of "good" and "not good" literacy.

At the time, in the early 1990s, cultural theory was a powerful lens that people were using to look at questions associated with communication. So I brought these different kinds of interests together, education and literacy practices, marginalization, historiography, and looked at these intersecting issues through the lenses of cultural studies.

I wound up asking questions about why students were labelled basic writers, what it was about their language practices—who controlled those practices and how, and whose values were reflected in them. In my dissertation, I looked at these questions historically, and that historical research informed and was informed by my teaching. How could the students and I work together, with the college, which itself had sort of an activist outlook, to change these frames around "appropriate" literacy practices?

WOE: Did your graduate studies inform your day-to-day work as a WPA?

ADLER-KASSNER: This idea of trying to reframe literacy practices has informed everything I've ever done. I see it in the work that I did at Eastern Michigan University and now at UCSB, in the work we did with the CWPA (Council of Writing Program Administrators), and *The Activist WPA*. It really informs the way I move through my life.

The idea that "appropriate" literacy practices reflect particular values and ideologies, and that our role as writing educators and writing program administrators is to make the broadest spaces possible, and have those spaces be informed by the literacy practices of everyone that comes to us—that's foundational to what I believe.

WOE: Can you point to a specific moment when you applied those beliefs?

ADLER-KASSNER: In our first year at Eastern, my colleague Heidi Estrem and I were meeting with the FYC TAs, who were talking about all the incredible work that their students were doing—and we were also thinking about complaints we heard about student writing. And we said, "It would be so great if we could just create a thing where students could show this work publicly as a way to try to change the conversation!" So we created the event called the Celebration of Student Writing. Our idea was, by showing this work in a large, very public venue, we would generate a very different kind of public conversation about students and writing, and what students *could do* rather than what students *couldn't do*.

When people talk about student writing in the abstract, it's easy to fall into stereotypes and generalizations and forget that the people we are talking about are *real people* who have *real* experiences and *real* prior knowledge, and we need to honor those, and work with them, and understand them more thoroughly. When we make them more visible, their remarkable qualities emerge.

I remember well standing in the ballroom of the student center for the first Celebration of Student Writing, waiting for people to come with their classes and put up whatever it was the students had created and thinking, *this is either going to be great, or it's going to be a really big, really public face-plant*. And the second the first class came in and started putting up their stuff, we were like, "It's going to be AWESOME!" And it *was* awesome, and it became more awesome over the years because it really *did* change the ways people talked about writing in that space at that time.

This kind of activity, making the work of writing more public and more visible and getting people—and by people I mean students, faculty, staff, administrators, people in the public—to talk more specifically about the actual work of actual writing, has, in my experience, contributed to shifts in conversations about writing.

WOE: Were you trying to show other people how to achieve what you're talking about with the Celebration of Student Writing in *The Activist*

WPA? As you were talking, I was wondering if *The Activist WPA* might be thought of as a kind of guidebook for changing conversations around writing.

ADLER-KASSNER: That's an interesting question. I see that book as trying to do a few things. One is to try to help writing program administrators think about what being a WPA is about. So, it's not just about getting bodies in motion in space and getting classes scheduled, but really to think in some systematic ways about big picture goals and about building those goals with the people we work with in writing programs. So, in that sense, I hope there are some practical ideas about how one could go about that. I spent a lot of time with community organizers, and some of the philosophies and strategies come from community organizing. I also thought it would be useful for people to consider the historical construction of literacy and literacy practices. Remember that I had been a history teacher, and I've always studied history, so I think that historical context is really important.

The other thing I was thinking about is how important it is for all of us to work from a foundational set of values and principles. I think we all do that, and that in and of itself is an ideologically loaded statement, but to me, that's a reality in my own thinking that's hard to escape. So, how do we figure out what those values and principles are, and how can we identify them among groups of people and move forward in some systematic ways? Instead of just critiquing, we need to think about what we want, what is going to be of most value, and how we can try, within the many competing forces and complexities that we all exist in, to make some kind of action.

WOE: Those of us new to the field of writing studies may be introduced to your work through *Naming What We Know*, which does not explicitly reflect your deep interests in literacy and activism. Could you talk about what led you to this project, and how it connects to your other interests?

ADLER-KASSNER: *Naming What We Know* came out of the thinking that's reflected in *The Activist WPA*, and that goes all the way back to General College, that is, thinking about definitions of "appropriate" and "inappropriate" literacy practices, and how those definitions get spun up into public policy. I spend a lot of time thinking about public policy, and I've had some opportunities to create policy documents that try to reshape things.

Right now, in the current policy climate, we're in a tough situation. The climate revolves around a desire for people—inside the university and outside the university—to "see" what's happening. We want to know, we want to see the outcomes, we want to see how you're working toward the outcomes, we want to see what students are achieving, what they're not achieving.

So there's this push toward quantification and accountability practices that I think is challenging in lots of ways.

In terms of education, writing is a central part of seeing. Writing is seen as a representation of what people have learned. Writing is also a way that we get to understandings of things, which is a different understanding of writing. So in this context of the desire to see, we thought, let's get a group of people together to name the things that we do know, and lay them out so that they are accessible and can be part of conversations moving forward.

The ideas synthesized in these threshold concepts aren't new; lots and lots of folks have said these things. We're just bringing them together and saying, "From our research, empirical, qualitative, grounded, this seems to be something that we know."

Another factor at play in *Naming What We Know* is the issue of perspectives in the current policy climate: what is the optimal or best perspective from which to understand what's happening in education? In our discipline, I think we default to a close perspective. We like to look at learners in context, writers in context; what is the writer doing, what is the context where writing is happening?

At the policy level, it's a very big perspective, and this is one of the reasons people are so drawn to big data. They say that big data can show the small in the context of the large. I think threshold concepts are a very valuable way to engage in this discussion, though, because they move us beyond outcomes toward embodiment and engagement.

WOE: As a potential classroom text, *Naming What We Know* might enter into the debate about the role of FYC as a service course. Do you think the main goal of FYC is to prepare students to succeed in their other courses, or should FYC be a gateway to writing studies? Some of us worry that in our efforts to establish writing studies as a discipline, our commitment to student writing could be compromised. As an activist, how do you reconcile these potentially conflicting goals?

ADLER-KASSNER: I don't think there's a conflict between thinking of ourselves as a discipline and first-year writing. In our discipline, in my opinion, we study composed knowledge, and we study knowledge composition. So we study who does it, what it looks like, what values are associated with it, who teaches it, how it's taught, how it happens, who does it in what ways, all those kinds of questions. If the purpose of a composition class is, in part, to help people learn to study writing and practice with writing, then in first-year composition we start introducing people to the process of studying writing—how is it that you study writing, and how do you practice with writing? To me, what we do and the unique perspective that we bring is a service, and it's a service to many people.

It's very useful to be able to have somebody who looks through particular lenses say, "gosh, when I see you talking about writing, or I see the ways you think about writing, or I see you writing, it looks like this to me," or composing, because it's not just writing, right? If we reflect this to people, then they can think about how they want to act, what practices they need to learn, what choices they want to make as informed human beings within particular contexts. That's a pretty valuable service. Now, I never refer to us as a service discipline; I refer to us as discipline that provides a pretty useful service across the university.

WOE: Where is the line in the spectrum between producing students who will write effectively in bio or chemistry, or whatever their discipline is, versus students who are very fluent in writing studies knowledge?

ADLER-KASSNER: Writing is a subject of study and an activity. To me, FYC is a remarkable opportunity to help people become critical practitioners as they move through space and time. If they do that in a writing major, that's great. But they need to do that everywhere—we all do that everywhere.

WOE: I really like that articulation, "writing is a subject of study and an activity," as foundational belief about what FYC should do—it's a subject of study and it's an activity.

ADLER-KASSNER: It's the foundational threshold concept. So, at UCSB, our writing program helps students study and practice with writing across a range of contexts. In Writing 2. our lower-division academic writing course, students learn to study writing as a subject of study, and as they move into upper-division courses, the context for the subject of study is narrowed because we have about 45 different upper-division courses in three different areas. Then in our professional writing minor we have five areas of focus, and then we have a PhD emphasis. I don't like to use this metaphor, but sometimes I do: it's a sort of narrowing, a more and more immersive opportunity to focus on studying writing in context.

But in FYC the goal is to help students learn to study and practice writing and to see writing as a subject of study because again, we want to help students make the most informed, conscious, conscientious choices as they move through the university, and as they move outside of the university! Right? I mean, that's what we want people to do, because we don't want writing to be a form of violence, and we don't want it to be a form of unconscious indoctrination and acculturation.

WOE: In *Naming What We Know*, many of the writers identify ways in which the threshold concepts are troublesome, counterintuitive, or alien (terms identified by Meyer and Land, and Perkins). They almost seem like Zen koans, which require intensive practice in order to realize. What genres did you look to when you were envisioning the entries?

ADLER-KASSNER: That is such an interesting question. So the writers refer to Meyer and Land and to Perkins because we sent them chapters by Meyer and Land and by Perkins. I came across threshold concepts research when I was doing a project with my colleague John Majewski, who is a historian at UCSB, and we were studying the ways that students thought about the subject matter in a writing class linked with a history class.[1] So the students in my section of FYC were among the 450 students in his History 17B class. We had surveyed and interviewed the students and done interviews and focus groups with the TAs; we had reams of data. And *then* I came across threshold concepts and I was like, "Oh my gosh! This is the thing we're trying to get at!"

It reminds me of something Etienne Wenger says: "Theory is just a way to give a name to something you already see." We couldn't quite articulate what we were talking about when we said "that thing underneath the thing" and it was this epistemological participation idea, which I know is an incredible mouthful, but it's a really useful idea.

When Elizabeth [Wardle] and I started talking about this project we emailed a bunch of people and said, "We want to try this," and we set up this wiki and sent out those book chapters and said, "Let's just see what happens." When we got to "What should the threshold concepts look like?" we said, "Here's kind of what we're thinking" and we made a little template, I mean very little, like a four-sentence template. We thought, "Let's see what this seems like." After a fair amount of discussion online, when we got to the point where people started drafting, we did some back and forth and we all said, "How does this seem?" And then we'd do some editing. That's how we kind of created this genre. But it's like other things: genres are typified forms that circulate in social contexts, and there are other things that look like this, like key words. It was all a thought experiment that we asked people to ride along with us on, and it came together incredibly well. It was a fascinating project.

WOE: What kind of reader engagement were you hoping to invite?

ADLER-KASSNER: We were hoping for this book to be useful—it's very much about trying to develop a vocabulary and then make that vocabulary useful for folks. At my core, I'm such a pragmatist. We thought about faculty, graduate students, undergraduate students, having conversations with administrators and with folks outside of the disciplines, external stakeholders, community members. We didn't imagine it as something that people outside the field would necessarily read (even students I consider as inside the field). We did intend, though, for it to be a resource for people inside the field as we talked with others outside. That's why there's an example of what the threshold concepts might look like in "everyday discussion" in the introduction that [Elizabeth] and I wrote.

What will be useful for people as they engage in conversations about writing across a whole range of contexts, and why do we want them to

---

1 See Adler-Kassner, John Majewski, and Damian Koshnick. "The Value of Troublesome Knowledge: Transfer and Threshold Concepts in Writing and History." *Composition Forum 26* (Fall 2012). http://compositionforum.com/issue/26/.

have those conversations about writing?—because so much is wrapped up in people's judgements about writers and writing. If I'm fundamentally about access and equity, then this is how I hope I can work with others to make some contribution to that.

Brian Street and Mary Lea have this great article where they're interviewing faculty colleagues about the issues they have with student writing, and their colleagues say, "Well, we don't like their grammar." So Street and Lea ask, "Well, what do you mean by grammar?" "Well, the focus and the structure and sometimes the language" [Laughter]. I call it the grammar-basket. I mean, some people just have such an impoverished vocabulary when it comes to talking about writing, so if we can help people develop language to name the things *they* know, then the whole conversation becomes broader.

WOE: I wanted to ask a question that might continue the idea of pragmatics and usefulness but with a bit of a contrastive approach. *Naming What We Know* came out a little over a year after Yancey, Robertson, and Taczak's *Writing Across Contexts*. I know both of these books are in part a response to, or come out of the work that folks did down at Elon [Transfer Institute].[2] Do you see a difference in approaches between the threshold concepts model in *Naming What We Know* and the TFT (teaching for transfer) model developed in *Writing Across Contexts*?

ADLER-KASSNER: I don't see them as in opposition to each other. If we understand that literate practices flow from knowledge and beliefs, then I think threshold concepts articulate some of those foundational concepts. The Yancey, Robertson, and Taczak book is very much related to what we're trying to do, making that curriculum, engaging in that study. TFT has a distinct curriculum associated with it; our work doesn't exactly. But *Naming What We Know* has foundational assumptions that underscore a teaching for transfer-based curriculum.

WOE: Maybe that's the difference I'm trying to get at. I don't want to imply an opposition between threshold concepts and TFT, and yet, there is a relationship I'm trying to tease out.

I agree that *Writing Across Contexts* is much more tightly associated with a particular curriculum, whereas *Naming What We Know* is more conceptual, though I can certainly see pragmatic stances coming out of it. *Naming What We Know* requires a reader to apply the important threshold concepts they see in their own contexts. So, a WPA or a writing teacher is still responsible for developing their own curriculum, whereas the particular model of TFT developed in *Writing Across Contexts* provides a little bit more of a structured curriculum, or ideas that are more closely tied to the classroom.

ADLER-KASSNER: I think that's exactly right. They have a model, and their book came out of an empirical study of that model. Through the study, they are

---

2 Elon University Research Seminar on Critical Transitions: Writing and the Question of Transfer. For a summary of their work from 2011–2013, see the Elon Statement on Writing Transfer.

finding that the model helps students transfer their knowledge. Our interest was in making explicit some of the foundational presumptions that underscore our discipline. And really, as a WPA, that has always been my approach. My approach working with writing programs and writing instructors has been to articulate principles, values, ideas, concepts, ways of thinking, and then to say to people, "What do you think are the best ways to operationalize this in a writing class?"

Now, there are some boundaries around that. I always say, "It has to be in the ballpark. The ballpark is big, like Yankee Stadium, and we're all going to make sure that everything is in the ballpark together." So I have certainly said to people, "That's outside the walls of the ballpark." But some of the best applications of these ideas have come from people who think about them way differently than I do. I look at what they've done, and I marvel.

Encountering things that are different, and doing things that are different, I think that's important, but within the boundaries of the big ballpark. And the boundaries of the big ballpark are what we are trying to outline in *Naming What We Know*, in some sense. So if I had a writing faculty member or a TA who said, "You know, I don't think revision is central to developing writing," I'd be like, "Well, actually, that's pretty important here."

WOE: We have been in a faculty reading group talking about transfer, and we've looked at *Writing Across Contexts*, *Naming What We Know*, and Elizabeth Wardle's and Doug Down's work on Writing about Writing,. I was imagining how to teach these approaches in graduate courses on teaching composition or on being a WPA. Would you think about asking graduate students to choose one of these three approaches to be loyal to as they go on to WPA work themselves, or would you say "You've got to draw on all three of them?"

Do you think it's important for graduate students to see these as different approaches to FYC and writing studies as a field, or do all three complement and engage with each other, where you don't have to decide, "Oh, one of these is my primary loyalty, and I might be informed a little by the others?"

ADLER-KASSNER: If you think about something spinning, one shoots an arc over to the left side, one shoots an arc over to the right side, but I think they're all spinning around the same kinds of questions. I think it would be a really interesting thing to say to people who are in a WPA class, "What to you seems like the best way of moving forward, or what do you want to do, what would you do? Do you engage other faculty in a program in a discussion about these things? Would you mandate one way to do this, and why would you do those things?"

I have my own opinions, obviously, about what the discipline is, what it should do, what it should be. But I am always about inclusion and access, so it would not be my way to say to people, "This is the one way you should do this." It would be my way to say, "Here's three texts that represent some ways of thinking about what the discipline is. . ."

I think one of the most important things in a WPA class is to help graduate students think about their foundational principles and values and how they're going to enact those as they work with people who bring a whole bunch of different interests, experiences, values, ideas to a writing program. But beyond the ballpark, I don't think that mandating is very productive. That's never been the kind of program I've worked in or that I've directed.

WOE: Would you answer differently if the course were a TA (teaching assistant) practicum?

ADLER-KASSNER: Another route to *Naming What We Know* actually came from a TA practicum course, which I've taught a lot over the years. And as I taught it, I thought, "Boy, it would be really interesting if we had a way to share some of the things we know about writing." In a class like that, the goal is to help students bring their knowledge and interests to the big ballpark that the program has collaboratively constructed.

At UCSB I work with the instructors in the program, and we think about questions associated with the values of the program and how to operationalize that in our curriculum across the program. So when graduate students come to the TA program, the big ballpark is already there, but I still want to try to make space for people to bring their ideas, principles, values. When I talk to graduate students who are interested in teaching in the writing program, the first thing I do, and this is before they even apply, I say, "There's some things that it's really important to understand about this program, and one is that it's about writing as a subject of study. It's not about your dissertation as a subject of study that people will write about." Because that is one way that people have taught writing in the past.

The first year I taught the TA practicum here at UCSB, we had just revised the curriculum for Writing 2, and we didn't have any models. So I said to the TAs that year, "Here's some of the ways this could look; now, let's work together and write some other ways this could look." I had this great group, and we just put together lots of models. Over the years, we've amassed more and more models. I'm also not a big user of textbooks, as you can tell.

WOE: It's more defined than in a course with students who are studying rhet-comp and likely to go on to do WPA work. Do you teach threshold concepts in these classes?

ADLER-KASSNER: I use them quite a bit in the TA practicum class. In the workshop part of the class, which meets for two weeks before the quarter starts, we talk about what are the outcomes, what are the strategies we're going to use to get there, what might the assignments look like. And I periodically introduce a threshold concept to discuss these things: "Wow, well, that has to do with that threshold concept of our discipline." And we talk about how they seem to go together or not. It works really nicely since the threshold concepts idea came out of that class.

When I taught Writing in Civic Engagement, which is one of the tracks in our professional writing minor, I would introduce them a little bit there just to provide a broader context—because that class was about studying both what civic engagement is and the ways in which communication plays roles in people's civic engagement. Some of the threshold concepts were really useful there, too, for helping people think about writing and the role that writing plays in civic engagement.

WOE: Do you think those TAs picked up threshold concepts and used terms from them in FYC, or in their other classes, or did the threshold concepts remain theoretical knowledge for them?

ADLER-KASSNER: This is an article that Heidi [Estrem] and I have to write; we have all the data for it. We did a study on this for two years, interviewing TAs about whether and how encountering threshold concepts of writing studies changed their approaches to teaching, both in composition and when they went back to their "home" disciplines. And the answer to that is, there's a range, as you might imagine.

Generally, they would bring threshold concepts into their teaching because our FYC is about how do you study writing. Some of the threshold concepts were quite applicable. So if an assignment was, for example, what are the literacy practices in another class you're taking, how do you analyze those and what do they mean in terms of the work that you're doing—there's some threshold concepts that are going to be pretty useful there. Or even threshold concepts like "revision is central to developing writing," since they all do portfolios.

To me, there's a range of most interesting responses to this, too. We have one person who never bought that writing was a subject of study, so what happens there is interesting. We also have a couple of folks who we've now written things and done conference presentations with for whom threshold concepts have changed ways of operating in writing courses and in their "home" disciplines.

Threshold concepts can transform students' approach to learning. They think about learning as "I've got to perform these steps, or I've got to jump through these hoops, or I've got to manifest these qualities" to "Oh, there are some ways of operating here, and they have to do with some bigger-picture things, and I need to start thinking about what that means in terms of my own practice."

We could also think about a threshold concepts framework for teaching across the disciplines, which is also really powerful and transformative. Not necessarily the threshold concepts of writing per se, but the idea that threshold concepts are critical for epistemological participation in a location, a community of practice. To faculty outside of writing, that idea can be very powerful and can transform their approach to teaching.

WOE: I like ending with the threshold concepts as a framework for teaching. It suggests ways that the other pedagogies we've discussed are focused within writing, but part of the utility of threshold concepts is as a framework for teaching. It's an approach to pedagogy that future higher education faculty could take back to other disciplines, and it might be as transformative there as it is for folks who are specializing in rhet/comp.

ADLER-KASSNER: Absolutely. And there's a very extensive body of research on just that question. I'm hardly the first person who has suggested that threshold concepts are an effective framework for teaching across disciplines. Ray Land has a great piece on it in the new threshold concepts book *Threshold Concepts in Practice* (ed. Land, Meyer, and Flanagan); there's a threshold concepts website maintained by Mick Flanagan, an engineer—it includes a bibliography of everything that's ever been published using threshold concepts, and there's a whole range of things about threshold concepts framework and threshold concepts faculty development. There's lots of people thinking about these things.

I don't want to say that threshold concepts are the hammer that will hit every nail, but I will say, it has been a very, very useful and productive way to talk with faculty about their thinking. Back in our discipline, we have moved far away from messianic approaches to WID (writing in the disciplines)—it's not like anybody is going, "I know about writing, let me tell you some things"—but it's such a useful meeting place where I can ask some questions of people. Because in our discipline we think so much about architectures and structures, we think about what are the conventions of a genre; that's an architecture, in a sense. What are the architectures of things like writing? What are the architectures of ways of thinking? Those are foundational interior spaces.

Threshold concepts are a great way to say to people, "What are those things that really shape the lenses you see with? What are the threshold concepts of your discipline?" and people will say, "I can't name them in my discipline because I'm in a subdiscipline," and it's like, "No. For somebody to be successful in your major, there are some ways that they have to think about things. And that's what we're going to get at, and then we're going to work on developing some teaching practices around making those more explicit."

WOE: That is fascinating as a way of thinking about threshold concepts for developing curriculum in a variety of disciplines. It's a utility. There are certain affordances that threshold concepts offer—they can include stuff in writing studies, but it's not limited to a focus on writing studies. It becomes about curriculum and pedagogy. The participants, faculty, or graduate students, name their own threshold concepts that apply to their daily, lived experiences.

ADLER-KASSNER: Two things that you said are just so smart there: one, threshold concepts have affordances, and like all affordances, there are, of course, limitations. But for now, it's an affordance that I find very productive. The second thing you've articulated, and that I think is so important, is that it gets to writing. It always gets to writing. It doesn't start with writing. Everything gets to writing. You can't help it because everybody has to represent the things they know, and that happens in writing or in speaking; it happens in representation. If you think about our field as being about composed knowledge, that process happens in lots of different ways.

APPENDIX
Composition Flow Chart

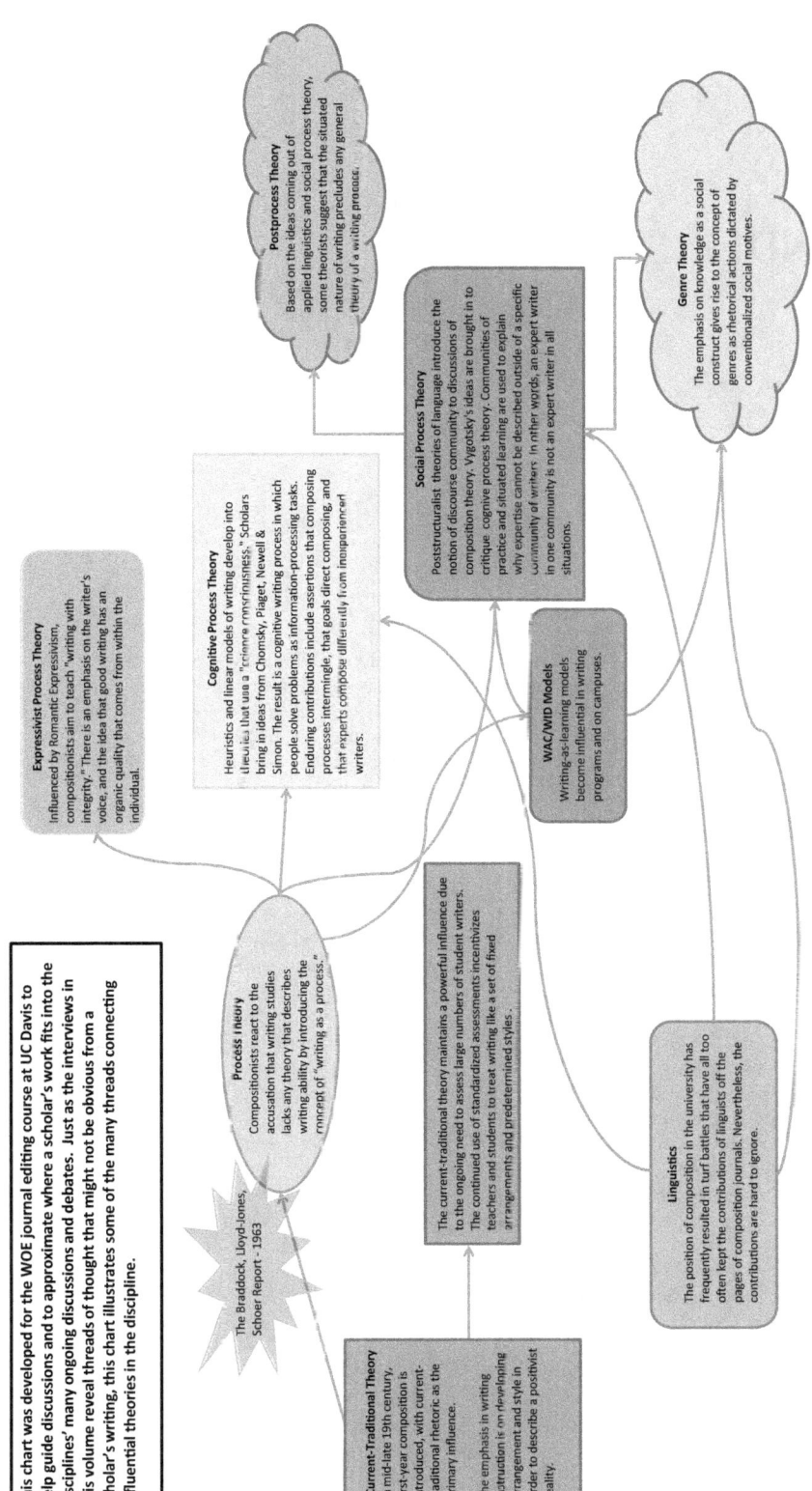

Created by Hogan Hayes

INDEX

academic discourse 94, 306, 429
Academic Discourse and Critical Consciousness (Bizzell) 148–9
academic genre studies 463–71
academic writing: benefit of 449–50; conformity and 378; fairy tale analogy 135; first-year writing course as 417; focus on 94, 202, 317, 477; journalistic writing *vs.* 338; personal writing and 146, 449–50; problems with 123, 126–7, 136–7; pursuit of 129; shaping/forming of 226; *see also* writing; writing pedagogy
The Activist WPA: Changing Stories about Writing and Writers (Adler-Kassner) 474–5
ad hominem arguments 410, 412
Adler-Kassner, Linda 472–83
aestheticizing the environment 211
African-American students 18–19
"After Dartmouth" (Harris) 196, 199
AIDS research collaborations 51
The Alchemy of Race and Rights (Williams) 146
Alice in Wonderland (Carroll) 304–5
all-Black school districts 103–4
alternative education 276
Altman, Richard 465, 469–70
Amariglio, Jack 400
American literature pedagogy 7
American Medical Association 130
Ames, Adelbert, Jr. 333

analytic philosophy 405
Anglo-American copyright law 41
Another Kind of Monday (Coles) 310
Anson, Chris 213–14
anthologies 120, 241, 296–7, 445, 448
Anzaldúa, Gloria 282–3, 425
applied linguistics 186, 470
Aquinas, Thomas 162
Aristotelian tradition 160, 431
"Arrangements for Truthtelling" (Schroeder, Boe) 329–40
Arroyo, Fred Santiago 274–89
arts and transcendence 348
assessment 273
attention/attentiveness in writing 421–2
Austen, Jane 300, 342, 344
Austin, J.L. 231
autobiographical criticism 199
autobiography 21–2, 38, 216, 291, 352, 411, 426

Baird, Theodore 257, 299–300
bankruptcy concerns for universities 213–14
Barrett, Andrea 281
Barrington, Dave 6
Barthes, Roland 76–7, 373
Bartholomae, David 94, 95, 147, 202, 214, 234–51
basic writing mission 324–5
Bay Area Writing Project 148
Bazerman, Charles 169, 181–93, 468, 470

Beaven, Mary H. 382
Becker, Gary 405
Becoming a Writer (Brande) 339
The Bedford Bibliography (Bizzell) 147
behaviorist perspective 13
Belanoff, Pat 93
Belsey, Catherine 108
Benjamin, Jessica 280
Bennett, John 329, 336
Berlin, James 66–80, 88, 208–9, 257, 262, 369, 383
Berry, Bill 359
Berthoff, Ann 70, 369
Bizzell, Patricia 145–56
Black, Edwin 463
Black Arts Movement 314
Blitz, Michael 372, 378, 381, 383, 385–6
blogging and social action 469
Bloom, Lynn 240, 275, 290–7
Boe, John 82–101, 172–80, 235–51, 299–312, 329–40, 342–9, 388–98, 400–13
Booth, Wayne 170, 257, 341–9, 401–2
Bootstraps (Villanueva) 425–7, 429
Bourgeois Dignity: Why Economics Can't Explain the Modern World (McCloskey) 404, 412
The Bourgeois Virtues (McCloskey) 407
Brande, Dorothea 339
Brannon, Lil 371
Brantlinger, Patrick 67
Bread Loaf School of English 334–5
Brereton, John 392
Britton, James 179, 197
Brodkey, Linda 283
Brogan, Howard 264
Brooklyn Library Literacy Program 208
Brower, Rueben 235
Bruner, Jerome 14
Burke, Kenneth 32, 402, 425
Butler, Samuel 336

Cage, John 34, 40
Campbell, Elizabeth 369–86
Campbell, JoAnn 286
Carnicelli, Tom 119
Carroll, Lewis 304–5
Carter, Ron 226, 231, 232
Case Institute of Technology 300
Cassidy, Fred 129
Castillo, Anna 283
Castro, Fidel 428–9
CCCC Research Network 60

Celebration of Student Writing event 474–5
Challenger disaster 52
"Changing Habits of Thinking" (West) 195–203
chaos theory 33
Chase, Stuart 173
Chicago School 348–9, 402
child development research 57
Chomsky, Noam 151
Chomskyan linguistics 225
Christensen, Francis 257
Christian Century magazine 89
civic discourse and argument 418
Civil Rights Movement 207, 323–4
Clark, Septima 323
Clary-Lemon, Jennifer 376
classical rhetoric 157–70, 186, 226, 258
Classical Rhetoric for the Modern Student (Corbett) 165
classroom as testing center 72–3
classroom inquiry 59, 62
Clifford, John 365
Clueless in Academe (Graph) 345
Coghill, Neville 84
"Cognition, Convention, and Certainty" (Bizzell) 152, 156
cognitive composition studies 153
cognitive dimension of writing 10–25
cognitive mapping 154–5
cognitive psychology 11–14, 55–6, 76, 246, 386
cognitivism 70, 209
Cohen, Ralph 131, 409
Coles, William E. Jr. 237–8, 298–312
"Collaboration as a Subversive Activity" (Calderonello, Nelson, Simmons) 43–53
collaborative planning 56
collaborative writing styles 45–53
College English magazine 72, 94, 107, 166
College Entrance Examination Board (CEEB) 253, 262, 267
Colomb, Gregory 128–44
comic styles of pedagogy 216
commercial free speech 401
communicative practices 184–5
community college teachers 71
Composing II (Coles) 301, 302
"The Composing Processes of Unskilled College Writers" (Perl) 387
Composition and Resistance (Blitz) 385
composition pedagogy: benefits of 291–7; career in 415–22; changes to 193,

194–203; coding data in 391; cognitive composition studies 153; consumption and 284–5; controversy over 258; cultural studies field 76, 197–200, 208, 228; first-year studies 473–7; flow chart 485; future of 431; importance of 379, 385; innovation in 292–3; linguistics and 315–16; research on 54–65; rhetoric of 67–80, 346–7, 415–22; social justice and 318; uniqueness of 263; writer's role in 122
Composition Research (Lauer, Asher) 62
Composition Studies as a Creative Art: Teaching, Writing, Scholarship, Administration (Bloom) 290
composition theory 2, 15, 29, 269
Comprone, Joe 255
Computer-Assisted Instruction in Composition: Create Your Own (Selfe) 107
Computers and Composition journal 114
computer-supported writing facility 105–9
computer use 95, 113–14, 177
conferencing 325, 327, 352, 359, 364–5, 377, 407
Connery, Brian A. 67–80
Connors, Bob 44
consumption and composition pedagogy 284–5
contract grading 292, 295
Cooper, Marilyn 107
Corbett, Ed 44, 50, 165, 257–8, 431
Core, George 359
Corporate Authorship: Its Role in Library Cataloging (Carpenter) 51
co-teaching of writing programs 245
Courses for Change in Writing (Boynton, Cook) 311
"Covering Almost All of Life" (Boe) 342–9
The Craft of Research (Booth) 347
craft of writing 124
creative nonfiction 241, 246–7, 291, 295–6, 298, 309, 396–8
creative writing 314–16, 455–6
Creek, Mardena 158–70
critical-democratic pedagogy 210, 215
critical pedagogy 208–9, 215–17
critical readers/writers 106
Critical Teaching and Everyday Life (Shor) 212–13
critical theory 107, 113
critical thinking 4, 9, 98, 111, 127, 210, 326

Cross-Talk (Villanueva) 427
Crowley, Sharon 70, 165, 275
Crusoe's Footprints (Brantlinger) 67
Cuban missile crisis 110
"Cultivating Writerly Sensibilities" (Leake) 415–22
cultural studies field: composition studies and 76, 197–200, 208, 228; impact of 75, 107, 473; literary texts and 67, 191
Cultural Studies in the English Classroom (Berlin) 75
current-traditional pedagogy 316

"Data Don't Breathe" (Murphy) 435–40
data impact on grammar 162
Dauterman, Jennie 73
Dawidoff, Nicholas 409
Day, Kami 385
The Debater's Guide (Murphy, Ericson) 158
deCerteau, Michel 109–10
The Defense of Poesy (Spenser) 291
DeLaura, David 354
De Magistro (Aquinas) 162
democratic pedagogy 210
Derrida, Jacques 370–1
Descartes, René 178–9
Designs in Prose (Nash) 224, 230–1
Detecting Growth in Language (Moffett) 175
devil term in essay writing 365–6
dialectical confrontation 164
"Dialectical Notions" (Connery, Hillard) 67–80
didactic teaching style 5
Didion, Joan 296, 358, 365
digital media 456, 469
digital multimodality 456
discourse communities 11–13, 55, 123, 417, 461, 467, 470–1
disruption in writing 135–6
dissertation writing 378
diversification concerns 260
Dixon, Jim 222
Dixon, John 196
DiYanni, Bob 365
Dobrin, Sidney I. 146–56
Down, Doug 480
Downing, David 372
drawing and writing 117–18
Dreiser, Theodore 454
Duncan, Robert 379

Eagleton, Terry 108
Eastern religions in teaching 178
Ebonics 242

Economical Writing (McCloskey) 406
economic approach to rhetoric 400–13
Ede, Lisa 43–53
educating the imagination 288–9
Ehrlich, Gretel 250
Elam, Helen 381
Elbow, Peter: academic debates with 246, 247; composition influence 72, 73, 81–101, 375; freewriting 395; ignoring audience 69; *Oppositions in Chaucer* 88; orality and writing 169; student-centered approach to writing 257; *Writing Without Teachers* 88, 89–90, 96–9, 293; *Writing With Power* 89–90, 97–8
Eldred, Margaret 182–93
Elements of Style (Strunk, White) 227
Eliot, George 239
elite education 259
Elliott, Carol 335
Emig, Janet 258
empirical research 62, 153, 164
"Engfish" 339
English Leadership Quarterly 377
English Only movement 282
English studies programs 73–5
English Usage (Nash) 227
"Enter the Process in Uncertainty" (Leake, Masiel) 445–52
Eodice, Michele 385
epistemological participation 482
Ericson, Jon 158
Errors and Expectations (Shaughnessy) 12, 293, 445
The Essay Connection (Bloom) 292
Estreem, Heidi 474, 482
Evans, Donna 424–33
"Every Difference Will Be Used against Us" (Greenbaum) 205–17
"Everything Gets to Writing" (Sperber, Whithaus) 473–83
exigence xi
expert/novice paradigm of writers 56–7
expressionism *see* expressivism
expressivism 209, 375–6, 418

Facility (*facilitas*) of language use 437
Fact and Artifact (Bloom) 292, 296
"Failure Is the Way We Learn" (Boe, Schroeder) 299–312
fairy tale analogy 135
Fanning, Ron 125
Fanon, Frantz 275
Farkas, Paul 130
Farrell, Ed 104

Farris, Christine 75
Fels, Dawn 369–86
Felt Sense (Perl) 395
The Feminine Mystique (Friedan) 388
feminist rhetoric in pedagogy 278–84, 388–9, 395, 407
fiction writing 286
Fine, Michelle 388
First Person (Eodice, Day) 385
first-year composition (FYC) courses 473–7
Firth, J.R. (Firthian linguistics) 225–6
Fish, Stanley 152, 200
Fisher, Bob 82
Fisher, Lester 119, 262
Fisher, R.S. 410
Fitzgerald, Scott 300
The Five Clocks (Joos) 255
five-paragraph theme 365
Flanagan, Mick 483
Flesher, Gretchen 26–42
Flower, Linda 54–65, 69, 72, 153, 164, 445
Flower-Hays model 164
formalist criticism 8
For the Love of It (Booth) 349
Foucault, Michel 51, 68–9, 371
Fourth Genre (Julier) 456
Fowler, Alastair 465
Fowler, Roger 231
Frank, Joe 262, 264
Franklin, Rosalind 410
Freeman, Ron 31
freewriting 90–1, 96, 339, 395
Freire, Paulo 97, 150, 209, 215, 248–9, 323, 371, 431
Freirean methods 79
Freire for the Classroom (Shor) 216
freshman writing courses, *see* FYC/first-year composition
Freud, Sigmund 70, 279–80
Friedan, Betty 388
"From Cultural Criticism to Disciplinary Participation" (Bazerman) 184
Fulwiler, Toby 1–9, 140–1
FYC/first-year composition 283, 318–19, 326, 450–1, 473

Gardner, John 51
Garrison, Roger 262–3
Gatto, Roseanne 369–86
gay rights narrative 461
Gee, James Paul 283
Gendlin, Gene 395
"Genre as Social Action" (Miller) 463

genre studies 463–71
geophysics graduate students 271
Gerber, John 253–4
Gere, Anne Ruggles 294, 425–6
Gergen, Kenneth 76
Gerschenkron, Alexander 409
Gibson, Walker 252–60, 262–7
Gillam, Alice 274–89
Gilyard, Keith 313–27
"Going in Two Directions at Once" (Boe, Schroeder) 82–101
Goodman, Leo 409
Gould, Stephen Jay 133
graduate school: geophysics graduate students 271; influence on pedagogy 473–4, 480–1; rhetoric pedagogy 255–8; teaching in 430–1; writing focus in 236, 317–18, 326
Graff, Gerald 78, 214, 345
Graham, Scott 466–7
Graves, Robert 406
Greenbaum, Andrea 205–17
Greenleaf, Cyndy 17
Greenway, Bob 88
Grey, Jim 392
Guerard, Albert, Jr. 173
Guillory, John 270
Gutkind, Lee 246

Ha, Gail 112
Hairston, Maxine 73
Hall, G. Stanley 71
Halliday, M.A.K. 225
Halloran, Michael 463
Handa, Carolyn 26–42, 103–15
Handbuch der Literarischen Rhetorik (Lausberg) 29
Handlist of Rhetorical Terms (Lanham) 29, 35, 36
Haraway, Dona 110, 111–12
Harbage, Alfred 85, 405
Harrienger, Myrna 73
Harris, Joseph 156, 194–203, 278, 432
Harris, Randy 169
Havelock, Eric 426
Hawisher, Gail 107, 114
Hayakawa, S.I. 173
Hayes, Dick 55
Hayes, Hogan 454–61, *485*
Hearne, Vicki 310
Heba, Gary 73
Hebdige, Dick 73
hegemonic discourse 79

Heidegger, Martin 380, 382
Heisenberg Uncertainty Principle 440
"Helping Writers Build Mansions with More Rooms" (Wilson) 54–65
Hermagoras Press 168
Hesse, Doug 414–22, 417, 455, 461
Hillard, Van E. 67–80
Hillman, James 351
Hirsch, E.D. 15, 151, 167
Hodge, Alan 406
Holocaust Educators Network 397
home language 81
Homer, Winifred 165
hooks, bell 425
Houghton Mifflin 177
How to Do Things with Words (Austin) 231
Hoy, Pat 350–67
Huddle, David 120
Hull, Glynda 12
Hum, Sue 376
humanizing teaching 100
"Humanomics" (Boe, Kahn) 400–13
humor in writing 207, 211, 216–19, 222–6, 229
Hunger of Memory (Roderiguez) 20
Hurlbert, Claude 368–86
Hypercard programs 34, 35
hypertextual environments 113

Idea of a University (Newman) 367
identity groups 212
ideology 69–70, 76, 108, 154, 209, 384
If You're So Smart (McCloskey) 408
"I Have Fun Playing with Language" (McGee) 314–27
"Imagine a Writing Program" (Palo) 10–25
"Imagining Stories" (Arroyo, Gillam) 274–89
implied author 342
"Incertitude's Her Element" (Stacey) 219–33
"Individualize" (Schroeder, Boe) 172–80
individual subjectivity in written communication 370–1
individuation process 309
information age impact 287
The Informed Writer (Bazerman) 182
Instinct for Survival (Hoy) 351
Institutio Oratoria (Quintilian) 164, 435–40
intellectual differences in students 141–2
Interaction program 175–8
Interchanges editorial section 200–1

interdisciplinary scholarship 86–9, 161, 173–4, 260, 281, 397, 403–4, 464
International Society for the History of Rhetoric 72
interview process 227
"Inventing the University" (Bartholomae) 279, 280
Involved: Writing for College, Writing for Yourself (Bazerman) 184
Iowa Writer's Workshop 404
Irmscher, William 424–5
The I-Search Paper (Macrorie) 339–40
Isocratean tradition 160
"It's Their Story that Turns Your Head" (Masiel, Sewell, Hayes) 454–61
"I Want to Rip Your Heart Out" (Livatino) 351–67

Jakobson, Roman 408
Jarratt, Susan 154
Jencks, Charles 38
Jerome, John 120
Johns, Donald 129–44
John S. Knight Writing Program 238
Johnson, Nan 165
Johnson, Samuel 299
Johnson-Eilola, Johndan 107, 110
Joos, Martin 255
Joseph, Miriam 29
journal-and-referee system 405
The Journal Book (Fulwiler) 1
journalistic writing 338
Journal of Basic Writing 458
Journal of Economic Behavior and Organization 400
Journal of Information Ethics 295
journals in literature class 7–8
Joyce, James 339
Julier, Laura 456

Kahn, Ed 400–13
Kaiser, Marjorie 454
Kant, Immanuel 410
Keifer, Kate 114
Kelly, Ashley 468, 470
Kinahan, Frank 131
Kinglake, Alexander 412
Kinneavy, Jim 104, 105, 459, 463
Kinney, Arthur 38
Kinney, Jim 293
Kitzhaber, Al 253–4
Klamer, Arjo 400
K–12 language studies 167–8, 454

Klaus, Carl 311
Kleege, Georgina 297
Knoblauch, Cy 369, 371
Kökeritz, Helge 32
Kuhn Thomas 75

Laclau, Ernesto 112–13
Ladislaw, Will 240
Land, Ray 483
Landmark Essay series 169, 185
Language in Popular Fiction (Nash) 230
language of conversation 226
"The Language of Exclusion" (Rose) 22
language study 229
Lanham, Richard 26–42, 170, 406
Latino writers 120
Lausberg, Heinrich 29
Lea, Mary 479
Leake, Eric 415–22, 445–52
"Learning by Going Along" (Handa, Flesher) 26–42
learning-ladder exercises 436
Leheny, Jim 268
Letters for the Living (Hurlbert, Blitz) 372, 383
Levine, Philip 251
Lewis, C.S. 100
liberal arts education 79, 319, 322
Linguistic Criticism (Fowler) 231
linguistics: applied linguistics 186, 470; Chomskyan linguistics 225; composition pedagogy and 315–16, 432; corruption of 144; Firthian linguistics 225–6; sociolinguistics 143, 283, 316, 327; systemic functional linguistics 470
listening rhetoric 343
literacy and critical consciousness 150
literacy narrative 473
literacy practices 474
literary-critical scholarship 160–1
Literature against Itself (Graff) 78
literature as pedagogy 263
Little Red Schoolhouse writing curriculum 131–2, 139
Livatino, Mel 351–67
Lives on the Boundary (Rose) 16–23, 104–5, 473
long-form journalism 461
Lopate, Phillip 241, 366
Lorain County Joint Vocational Center 288
Lucky Jim (Amis) 222
Lukens, Larry 424

Lunsford, Andrea 43–53, 166, 385
Lu Po Hua 339–40

McAndrew, Don 377
McCloskey, Deirdre (formally Donald McCloskey) 33, 76, 188, 399–413
MacFarland, Jack 19
McGee, Sharon James 314–27
Mack, Nancy 381
McKeon, Richard 343–4, 346
McKoski, Nancy 155
MacLeish, Archibald 117
Macrorie, Ken 89, 328–40
Maimon, Elaine 2–3
Mairs, Nancy 285
Majewski, John 478
Making Thinking Visible Project 60
Malcolm X 319–20
Malinowski, Bronislav 225
Marcuse, Herbert 275
marginalization 141, 212, 473
Marshall, Robert 245
Martin, Harold C. 253, 257
Martin, Nancy 268
Marvell, Andrew 406–7
Marxism 68–70, 370, 372, 410
masculine metaphors 407
Masiel, David 445–52, 454–61, 463–71
Mason, Anestine Hector 384
material rhetoric 421
"The Mechanism Is Writing" (Schroeder) 1–9
mentoring process 78, 216
metacognitive process in learning 57–8
metaphor 339, 349, 405, 407
Miller, Carolyn 462–71
Miller, Richard 201–2
Miller, Susan 243, 244, 425
mimicry 214
mind-body integration 173
Minh-Ha, Trinh T. 425
Mitchell, Ruth 11
Mittell, Jason 465
Moby Dick studies 8
Modern American Prose (DiYanni, Clifford) 365
Modern dogma and the rhetoric of Assent (Booth) 345
modernism in writing 410–11
Moffett, James 171–80
Mokler, Alan 335
Monk, Samuel Holt 299
Moran, Charles 261–72

Mormonism 348, 349
Morrison, Toni 317–18
Morson, Gary Saul 286
Mortimer Adler Great Books system 158–9
motherhood and writing 146
The Motives of Eloquence (Lanham) 27–8
Mouffe, Chantel 112–13
"Mucking about in Language I Save My Soul" (Zirinsky) 117–27
multimodality in writing 456
Murphy, James J. 157–70, 435–40
Murphy, Jerry 395
Murray, Donald 116–27, 445
Murray, James 340
Myers, Greg 76
Myers, Miles 176

Naming What We Know (Adler-Kassner) 475–6, 479–81
Narrative and Freedom (Morson) 286
narrative writing: educational narrative 473; gay rights narrative 461; Oedipal narrative of academic socialization 278–9; transfer of narrative 459–61
Nash, Walter 218–33
National Council of the Teachers of English (NCTE) 104, 107, 112
National Endowment for the Humanities (NEH) 262, 265–6
National Institute of Education 393
National Research and Education Network (NREN) 111
national writing assessment 273
National Writing Project 392, 397, 451, 454
Native American writers 120
"The Nature of Narrative" (Rosen) 22
Nazism 97
Neal, Larry 314
Nelson, John 403–4
neo-Aristotelianism 463, 469
"A Nest of Singing Rhetorical Birds" (Strain) 253–60
New Criticism 263
Newkirk, Tom 124–5, 262
New Literary History journal 34, 131
Newman, John Henry 367
Newmanesque sentence 353–4
The New Yorker 259
New York Times 259
New York Times Magazine 357–8
Nienkamp, Jean 269

Nilsen, Alleen Pace 77
"Nomadic Feminist Cyborg Guerilla" (Handa) 103–15
noncombative rhetorics 278
nontraditional students 276
Nora, Krystia 369–86
North, Stephen 262, 275

object rhetoric 421
Oedipal narrative of academic socialization 278–9
Ohmann, Richard 76, 208–9, 257
On Austrian Soil (Perl) 396–7
"Once More to the Essay" (Spinner) 291–7
Ong, Walter 426
open admission students 190, 259, 276, 279, 289
Oppositions in Chaucer (Elbow) 88
oral language 3
"The Other Reader" (Harris) 198–9

packet-switching technology 109
Palo, Susan 10–25
The Paris Review journal 120
pattern recognition in genre studies 468
Pearson Education 384
pedagogy: American literature pedagogy 7; comic styles of 216; critical-democratic pedagogy 210, 215; critical pedagogy 208–9, 215–17; current-traditional pedagogy 316; feminism in 278–84, 388–9, 395, 407; graduate school influence on 473–4, 480–1; liberal arts education 79, 319, 322; of liberation 150; literature as 263; poetry pedagogy 16; portfolio pedagogy 28, 93–4, 175, 267, 482; progressive pedagogy 321–2; radical pedagogy 8–9; Scientific Method pedagogy 411; student-centered learning 9, 374, 388; transfer pedagogy 420; virtual classrooms 112; women writers and 351–2; *see also* composition pedagogy; rhetoric pedagogy; teachers/ teaching; writing pedagogy
Pedagogy of the Oppressed (Freire) 371, 431
peer groups 212, 382
perception process in writing 333–4
Perl, Sondra 169, 387–98, 445
personal essay writing 146, 350–67, 449–50
Persuasion in Economics (McCloskey) 408
Petrosky, Anthony 202, 240, 243

phantom words 284
Pickering, Sam 357, 359
Pinard, Mary 398
"planned irrelevance" of writing pedagogy 196, 197
Platonic tradition 160
The Play of Language (Gibson) 257
The Plural I (Coles) 303, 304, 309–10
pluralism 21, 23, 343–4
poetry 16, 372–3, 379
Points of View (Moffett) 173
Poirier, Richard 235
political speeches 463
Pope, Rob 227, 229
portfolio pedagogy 28, 93–4, 175, 267, 482
positivism 70
Poster, Mark 108
post-process theory 371, 376
poststructuralism 68–70, 76, 369, 372
power sharing 210
pragmatism 187, 415, 478
Pratt, Mary Louise 212
prior knowledge 457–60, 458, 474
Pritchard, Bill 300
process of writing 58, 224, 316
process pedagogies 116–27
process-tracing studies 63
professionalization issues 71
professional writing 134–5, 316, 337, 340, 432, 477, 482
progressions concept 363–4
progressive pedagogy 321–2
progymnasmata exercises 436
Project on Rhetoric of Inquiry (Poroi) 403
"Protest rights" approach 209–10
psychological nature of writing 96–7
psychotherapeutic component to writing 389
Putnam, Hillary 282

Quark Express 37
Quarterly Journal of Speech 170
Quintilian (Marcus Fabius Quintilanus) 434–40, 442–3
Quintilian on the Teaching of Speaking and Writing (Murphy) 166
Quirk, Randolph 227

race and identity 76–7, 198, 284
racism concerns 18, 214, 428
radical democracy 112
radical pedagogy 8–9

"Radical Pedagogy" (Dobrin, Taylor) 146–56
Rawlings, Hunter 408
reader engagement 478
The Reader Over Your Shoulder: A Handbook for Writers of English Prose (Graves, Hodge) 406
reading-to-write study 63, 65
Reclaiming Rhetorica (Lunsford) 166
reform-minded educators 107
relational rhetoric 278–9
Relations, Locations, Positions (Vandenberg, Hum, Clary-Lemon) 376
Renaissance Nonfiction Prose seminar 28
requirement-driven writing programs 149
research: AIDS research collaborations 51; CCCC Research Network 60; child development research 57; composition pedagogy 54–65; empirical research 62, 153, 164; methods of 54–65; scientific research using historical documents 62
research and development (R&D) 175
Research in Written Composition (Lowell, Lloyd-Jones, Braddock) 391
Responding to Student Writers (Sommers) 448; comments by teachers 448–9
Revising Prose (Lanham) 30, 35
revision process 445–6
Rhetoric (Aristotle) 166, 431
Rhetorical Criticism (Black) 463
The Rhetorical Tradition (Bizzell) 147, 154
Rhetorical Traditions in the Teaching of Writing (Brannon, Knoblauch) 154, 371
rhetoric and professional writing (RPW) 432
Rhetoric and Reality (Berlin) 69
Rhetoric in the Classical Tradition (Homer) 165
rhetoric of assent 343
rhetoric of composition 67–80
rhetoric of difference 198
The Rhetoric of Economics and Knowledge (McCloskey) 406–7, 408
The Rhetoric of Fiction (Booth) 342, 345–6
The Rhetoric of Irony (Booth) 343
rhetoric of science 169, 186–9, 400, 471
The Rhetoric of the Human Sciences (McCloskey, et al) 33, 76
rhetoric pedagogy: classical rhetoric 157–70, 186, 226, 258; composition pedagogy 67–80, 274–81, 415–22; economic approach 400–13; future of 431; graduate studies 255–8; Harvardization of rhetoric 374–5; impact of 423–33; neo-Aristotelianism 463, 469; noncombative rhetorics 278; relational rhetoric 278–9; social epistemic rhetoric 208; theoretical and educational aspects of 435–40
Rhetoric Program 266–7, 269
Rhetoric Review journal 256
Rhetoric Study Committee 267
rhetorology, defined 344
Rich, Adrienne 246
Ricoeur, Paul 371
rigor notion 215
Rinard, Brenda 463–71
Rodriguez, Richard 20, 425
Root, Robert L., Jr. 120–1
Rose, Mike 10–25, 33, 104, 170, 398, 425, 473
Rosen, Harold 22
Rosenblatt, Louise 390
Rouse, John 315
Rowe, Mary Budd 379
Russell, David 169, 185

safe houses 212
Sale, Roger 300
Salvatori, Mariolina 24, 249
Sanchez, Sonia 249
Sapir, Edward 228, 229
scaffolding 14
Schilb, John 68
"scholarship" examinations 220
Schroeder, Eric 82–101, 172–80, 329–40
Schuster, Charles 398
Schwartz, Mimi 397–8
Scientific Method pedagogy 411
scientific research using historical documents 62
Scientism 153
Scully, John 38
Sedaris, David 277
Seeing through Language (Nash, Carter) 222–3, 231–2
Seeing Through Writing (Coles) 309
Selfe, Cynthia 102–15, 287
self-evaluation 382
semantics 173
The Semiotic Challenge (Barthes) 373
"A Sense of Professional Well Being" (Strain) 262–72
"A Set of Shared Expectations" (Rinard, Masiel) 463–71

"Setting Minds in Motion" (Creek) 158–70
Sewell, William 454–61
"Sexism in English: A Feminist View" (Nilsen) 77
Shakespeare's Use of the Arts of Language (Joseph) 29
Shaping Written Knowledge (Bazerman) 186–7
Shaughnessy, Mina 12, 265, 293, 445
Shepard, Dawn 469
Shields, David 417
Shirley, Patti 330
Shoptalk: Learning to Write with Writers (Murray) 122
Shor, Ira 204–17
Shroeder, Eric 235–51, 299–312
Shuster, Chuck 425
Siggins, Clara 340
Sight Unseen (Kleege) 297
silence in classroom 379–80
The Simple Truth (Levine) 251
Slack, Jennifer 107
Slatin, John 113
Slevin, Jim 238
small-group work 8
Smit, David 212
social contexts 16, 156, 213, 224, 478
social contstructivism 375–6
social differences in students 141–2
social epistemic rhetoric 208
social justice 155, 318–19, 397, 461, 467
social turn 209
social use of language 144
sociolinguistics 143, 283, 316, 327
Socratic method 254
Socratic powers 64
The Solace of Open Spaces (Ehrlich) 250
Solow, Robert 409
"Some of It Is Serendipity" (Evans) 424–33
Sommers, Jeff 458
Sommers, Nancy 444–52
Sophistic tradition 160, 432–3
South Atlantic Quarterly journal 34
Southern Autobiography Conference 352–3
speaking *vs.* writing 438
Speech Communication Association 161, 463
Speed and Politics: An Essay on Dromology (Virilio) 109, 110
Sperber, Lisa 473–83

Spinner, Jenny 291–7
Spooner, Michael 201–2
Stacey, David 219–33
standardized testing 384
Stanton, Elizabeth Cady 383
Stasis–Disruption–Resolution method of writing 135–6
Steffens, Lincoln 307
Stepping on My Brother's Head and Other Secrets Your English Professor Never Told You: A College Reader (Perl, Schuster) 398
Sterling, Richard 392
"Stop Being so Coherent" (Boe, Schroeder) 235–51
storytelling 334–6
Strain, Margaret M. 253–60
strategic knowledge concept 63
Street, Brian 479
Strickland, Jim 385
structuralism 70
Stuckey-French, Ned 456
student access to open admission 190, 259, 279, 289
Student-Centered Language Arts (Moffett) 177
student-centered learning 9, 374, 388
student conferencing 58
student learning outcomes 378
student writings 329–33
"The Study of Error" (Bartholomae) 234
Style: Basics (Lessons) in Clarity and Grace (Williams, Colomb) 134–5
Subculture: The Meaning of Style (Hebdige) 73
Sullivan, Pat 118–19
Summer Institutes for Secondary Teachers of English 253, 254, 255, 262
Swearingen, Jan 154
systemic functional linguistics (SFL) 470

tacit knowledge 457
"The Takeaway" (Johns) 129–44
Taylor, Mary 11
Taylor, Todd 146–56
teachers/teaching: built-in obstacles 6; comments by teachers 448–9; community college teachers 71; co-teaching of writing programs 245; didactic teaching style 5; Eastern religions in teaching 178; graduate school 430–1; guided teaching style 5; humanizing teaching 100; making

a difference 103–4; metaphors for teaching 339, 349; open admission students 190, 259, 279, 289; teaching to the test 293–4; technology in the classroom 34, 106, 109–12, 460; traditional models of writing instruction 19; writers, impact on 353–4; writers as 148; *see also* pedagogy
Teaching English in the Two-Year College journal 262
teaching for transfer (TFT) model 479
The Teaching of Writing (Bartholomae) 238
A Teaching Subject (Harris) 278
Teaching the Universe of Discourse (Moffett) 177
technology in the classroom 34, 106, 109–12, 460
Texte journal 39
Textual Carnivals (Miller) 243
Textual Intervention (Pope) 229
Themewriting technique 300, 302
A Theory of Discourse (Kinneavy) 463
"There's Humor and There's Tears" (Boe) 388–98
Thorndike, Edward 71
Threshold Concepts in Practice (Land) 483
Through Teachers' Eyes (Perl) 392–4
Tobin, Lad 381, 398
Tompkins, Jane 146, 279
top-down authority 210
Toulmin, Steve 402
"Toward a Phenomenology of Freewriting" (Elbow) 96
traditional models of writing instruction 19
trance state and writing 447
transfer of narrative 459–61
transfer pedagogy 420
truthtelling in writing 329–40
Twain, Mark 71
twelve-step programs 301

UCLA Writing Program 18
uncertainty in writing 445–52
An Uncommon Tongue (Nash) 229
Undressed Magazine 330, 331
Utopian theme 209

Vandenberg, Peter 376
Victorian literature 67
video game market 465
Vietnam War 329–31
Villanueva, Victor 423–33

Virilio, Paul 109, 110–11
virtual classrooms 112
Vitanza, Victor 68
Vivion, Michael 75
voice and writing 98–9
Voices of the Self (Gilyard) 316
voluntary writing program 148–9
The Vulnerable Teacher (Macrorie) 339

Wakoski, Diane 281
Wallace, David Foster 416
Wallace, Karl 256
Wall Street Journal 357–8
Wardle, Elizabeth 478, 480
Watson, James 410
Ways of Reading (Bartholomae, Petrosky) 238, 241, 244, 250, 283
Weaver, Richard 365
Welch, Nancy 273–89
Wenger, Etienne 478
West, Thomas 195–203
What Makes Writing Good (Coles) 301
When Students Have Power (Shor) 208, 211
"Where Meaning and Being Gathers" (Nora, Gatto, Fels, Campbell) 369–86
White, E.B. 240, 241, 297
Whithaus, Carl 473–83
whole-language event 69–70
Williams, Joseph 128–44
Williams, Patricia 146, 284, 285
Williams, Raymond 197
Wilson, Gordon 129
Wilson, Jill 54–65
Wilson, Nancy 393
Winter, Robert 34, 36
Winterowd, Ross 75
women writers 120, 278, 351–2
word-choosing process 439
Working at Writing: Columnists and Critics Composing (Root) 120–1
working-class culture 205–7, 216, 382–3
writers: critical readers/writers 106; expert/novice paradigm of 56–7; Latino writers 120; role in composition pedagogy 122; teacher impact on 353–4; teachers as 148; women writers 120, 278, 351–2
Writer's Block: The Cognitive Dimension (Rose) 17, 33
writing: academic writing 126–7; attention/attentiveness in 421–2; basic writing mission 324–5; computer use for 95; context in 458–60; craft of 124;

creative nonfiction 241, 246–7, 291, 295–6, 298, 309, 396–8; creative writing 314–16, 455–6; disruption in 135–5; dissertation writing 378; freewriting 339; habits of 196; history of 244, 276, 285; humor in 207, 211, 216–19, 222–6, 229; identity in digital age 420; influences 195; journalistic writing 338; multimodality in 456; organized thinking about 185–6; perception process in 333–4; personal essay writing 350–67; process of 58, 143–4, 146, 224, 316, 405–6; professional writing 134–5, 316, 337, 340, 432, 477, 482; psychological nature of 96–7; psychotherapeutic component to 389; revision process 445–6; speaking vs. 438; storytelling 334–6; truthtelling in 329–40; uncertainty in 445–52; Vietnam influence on 330–1; voice and 98–9; *see also* academic writing

Writing Across Contexts (Yancey) 453, 479, 480

Writing Across the Curriculum (Bazerman) 185

Writing Across the Curriculum (WAC) 1–9, 139–40, 182–3, 307–9, 451

writing consultations 131–2

Writing for High School Teachers course 29

The Writing Habit: Essays (Huddle) 120

writing in the disciplines (WID) 9–, 182–3, 451, 483

"Writing Is Motivated Participation" (Eldred) 182–93

Writing on the Edge journal 120, 121–2, 295

writing pedagogy: challenges to 232; changes in practice of 137–8, 329; computer use in 114–15; critical-democratic pedagogy 210, 215; democratic pedagogy 210; focus in graduate school 236, 317–18, 326; freewriting 90–1, 96; freshman writing courses 122–4, 127, 183, 263–4, 323, 473; genre studies 463–71; humanizing teaching 100; hyper-instrumentalizing of 420–1; individualization in 172–80; metaphors for teaching 339, 349; method of 299; "planned irrelevance" of 196, 197; poetry instruction 16; process pedagogies 116–27; progressive pedagogy 321–2; radical pedagogy 150; scaffolding 14; student writings 329–33; *see also* graduate school

Writing Program Administration (WPA) 414, 455

writing programs: co-teaching of 245; importance of 23–5; Iowa Writer's Workshop 404; John S. Knight Writing Program 238; Little Red Schoolhouse writing curriculum 131–2, 139; progressions concept in 363–4; requirement-driven writing programs 149; voluntary writing program 148–9; workshops 6–7

Writing Research Project (UCLA) 11

The Writing Trade: A Year in the Life (Jerome) 120

Writing True: The Art and Craft of Creative Nonfiction (Perl, Schwartz) 397–8

Writing Without Teachers (Elbow) 88, 89–90, 96–9, 293

Writing With Power (Elbow) 89–90, 97–8

Written Communication journal 46

Wyoming Resolution 271

Yancey, Kathleen Blake 201–2, 453–61
Yetmen, Michael 455
Young, Art 105
Young, Richard E 67, 169

Zebroski, Jim 381
Ziliak, Stephan 410
Zinn, Howard 436
Zirinsky, Driek 117–27
zone of proximal development 14

For Product Safety Concerns and Information please contact our EU
representative GPSR@taylorandfrancis.com
Taylor & Francis Verlag GmbH, Kaufingerstraße 24, 80331 München, Germany

www.ingramcontent.com/pod-product-compliance
Lightning Source LLC
Chambersburg PA
CBHW051533230426
43669CB00015B/2582